THE CIVIL WAR IN
NORTH CAROLINA

THE CIVIL WAR IN NORTH CAROLINA

By

JOHN G. BARRETT

Chapel Hill

THE UNIVERSITY OF NORTH CAROLINA PRESS

© 1963 The University of North Carolina Press
All rights reserved
Manufactured in the United States of America

The paper in this book meets the guidelines for
permanence and durability of the Committee on
Production Guidelines for Book Longevity of
the Council on Library Resources.

ISBN 0-8078-0874-1
ISBN 0-8078-4520-5 (pbk.)
Library of Congress Catalog Card Number 63-22810

99 98 97 96 95   12 11 10 9 8

For my daughters Becky and Meg

Preface

THE PRESENT STUDY is the extension of an earlier work, *Sherman's March Through the Carolinas*. It became apparent in doing research for the previous volume that little has been written concerning the war in North Carolina. Invaded from the east, the west, the north, and the south, the state was the scene, nevertheless, of much fighting. Although the numbers involved in many of these operations were comparatively small, the campaigns and battles themselves were not unimportant in the grand strategy of the war. Lee's operations in Virginia were controlled to a large extent by conditions in North Carolina. The historian's failure to record adequately the fighting in the Tar Heel state, therefore, has left incomplete not only the story of the conflict in North Carolina but also that of the war in the eastern theater. In an attempt to correct these omissions the author has undertaken this work.

I have been most fortunate in the help I have received in preparing this study. A generous grant from the John Simon Guggenheim Memorial Foundation made possible a year's leave of absence from my teaching duties, and summer grants from the American Philosophical Society, Southern Fellowship Fund, University Center of Virginia, the Virginia Military Institute, and the Society of Cincinnati of the State of Virginia enabled me to complete all necessary research.

Sincere thanks go to Professor Hugh T. Lefler of the University of North Carolina and Professor Bates McCluer Gilliam of the Virginia Military Institute. These two scholars read the manuscript in its entirety and made invaluable suggestions.

In addition I am indebted to Cadet William M. Kolb of V.M.I. for drawing the maps, to the University of North Carolina Press for allowing me to quote fully from *Sherman's March Through the Carolinas* and to Mrs. William O. Roberts of Lexington, Virginia, whose careful examination of the manuscript prevented many literary errors.

I am especially grateful to Miss Mattie Russell of Duke University, William D. Cotton of Pfeiffer College, and Charles L. Price of East Carolina College who very kindly allowed me to use their graduate theses. I also wish to thank Professor Robert H. Woody of Duke University for granting me permission to examine the work of several of his former students.

Special thanks go to Nat C. Hughes of Webb School, Colonel Paul Rockwell of Asheville, North Carolina, Tom Parramore of the University of North Carolina, and William T. Rutledge of the University of Virginia for making available to me valuable material on the Civil War in North Carolina.

The staffs of Southern Historical Collection of the University of North Carolina, the Manuscript Division of the Duke University Library, the North Carolina Department of Archives and History, the North Carolina Collection of the University of North Carolina, and the Preston Library of the Virginia Military Institute have all been extremely helpful.

My wife, Lute, had the unenviable task of typing the manuscript from a rough pencil draft. Without her endeavors, encouragement, and understanding this volume would not have been possible.

Lexington, Virginia   John G. Barrett
October, 1962

Contents

Maps

NORTH CAROLINA 1861 - 1865

Kirk's Raid on Morganton	⠿⠿⠿⠿⠿⠿⠿⠿
Stoneman's Raid	<<<<<<<<<
Sherman's March	●●●●●●●●●●
Wild's Raid	xxxxxxxxxxxxx
Foster's Raid on Tarboro	→→→→→→
Foster's Raid on Goldsboro	-------------

CHAPTER I

"Will There Be Civil War?"

NORTH CAROLINA, a state in the upper South, did not play a leading role in the great secession drama of 1860-61. While the "fire-eaters" in South Carolina and the states of the lower South were talking secession, North Carolinians, for the most part, still favored the national Union. Since the soil of the state was not well suited for the growing of cotton, there were relatively few wealthy planters with large slaveholdings to agitate for a break with the Federal government.[1] The non-slaveholders from the mountain districts of the west and the swamp regions of the east, and certain Quaker and small farm elements in the central region, saw no reason to become vitally concerned with the preservation of a slave system in which they had little part.[2] These non-slaveholding whites had considerable influence in the state, and their attitude toward slavery and secession had to be reckoned with. As a prominent citizen put it: "Seven-tenths of our people owned no slaves at all, and to say the least of it, felt no great and enduring enthusiasm for its [slavery's] preservation, especially when it seemed to them that it was in no danger."[3]

On November 5, 1860, the telegraph flashed the word that Abraham Lincoln had won the presidency of the United States.[4] This shocking news created dismay and concern among North Carolinians.[5] Expressions of alarm were heard on all sides. One of the state's leading newspapers questioned whether "too gloomy or too serious a view" could be taken of this development.[6] A husband wrote his wife: "I would not tell you my feelings if I could find words to express them. . . . May God avert the danger which threatens our country—guide and protect us."[7]

Lincoln's victory triggered the secession of the states of the lower South. Yet in North Carolina there was little talk of secession. The great majority of people did not regard the election of a "Black Republican," however distasteful, as sufficient grounds for withdrawing from the Union.[8] Elder statesmen like William A. Graham urged moderation. The general sentiment within the state seemed to be one of "watch and wait." Lincoln, it was thought, should be given a reasonable length of time to show his course of action.[9] One prescient observer noted, however, that the masses would not favor secession for the benefit of the slavocracy but would flock to the banner if coercion were resorted to.[10]

North Carolina's Governor, John W. Ellis, was not in the least surprised at his state's cautious approach to secession. Back in October, 1860, he had written Governor William H. Gist of South Carolina that the people of North Carolina were far from being unanimous in their views and feelings concerning the action the state would take if Lincoln were elected president. Ellis said that some would yield, some would oppose Lincoln's power, and others probably would adopt the "wait and see" attitude. Many of the people believed that the President "would be powerless for evil with a minority in the Senate and perhaps in the House of Representatives"; others said, however, that his election "would prove a fatal blow to the institution of negro slavery in this country." The Governor did not believe that a majority of his people would consider Lincoln's election "as sufficient ground for dissolving the Union of the States."[11]

With the people of North Carolina generally disposed to accept the results of the election and to await developments, the General Assembly met in Raleigh on November 19, 1860. The Governor's message to this body was anxiously awaited throughout the state, since it was expected to outline the policy that North Carolina was to follow in this time of crisis.

Governor Ellis' address was closely in accord with the thinking of the "secessionists or radicals, who favored immediate action by North Carolina. . . ." Those who opposed the Governor's program were generally classified as "Unionists or conservatives." They saw no necessity for a withdrawal from the Union.[12] In his message the Governor did not openly advocate secession, but he did recommend that North Carolina call a conference with "those States identified with us in interest and in the wrongs we have suffered; and especially those lying immediately adjacent to us." He also recommended that, following this conference, a convention of the people of the state be called and that the militia be thoroughly reorganized.[13]

In the General Assembly, the message received an enthusiastic approval by the radicals, but a severe condemnation by the conservatives. Yet on the matter of military preparedness, these factions seemed to be in agreement. Both the radical and the conservative felt that the state must prepare itself for any eventuality. A $300,000 appropriation for the purchase of arms and ammunition passed the Senate on December 18,[14] and the House on January 8, 1861.[15] A military commission was established to help the Governor administer the funds.

While the legislative halls resounded to heated debate, public opinion throughout North Carolina reached a fever pitch, primarily as a result of the growing strength of the secession movement. As early as November 12, 1860, a secession meeting had been held in Cleveland County.[16] A week later a similar gathering took place at Wilmington.[17] And by this time, radical speakers in all parts of the state were urging the call of a convention of "the people to determine upon a policy" for North Carolina.[18]

In the midst of this agitation for a convention, South Carolina, on December 20, withdrew from the Union. In strongly secessionist Wilmington, the news created great excitement. As one hundred guns fired a salute to South Carolina, the streets filled with an anxious citizenry. On every corner groups of men could be seen engaged "in serious converse upon the one topic of the day."[19] Wilmington, though, was not speaking for the entire state. It was only among the radicals that South Carolina's action was received with any true expression of joy. Conservative North Carolinians strongly condemned their neighbor for making this move* and thereby rendering it more difficult for the other Southern states to gain their rights.[20]

Although South Carolina's action was strongly denounced in many quarters of North Carolina, the people of the state stood united in opposing the use of force to bring the seceded state back into the Union.[21] A contemporary expressed the feeling of many when he wrote:

* The story is told of a "North Carolina mountaineer who attended a secession meeting where each speaker in turn laid emphasis upon the action or the opinion of South Carolina. Finally when a fresh orator began with a similar allusion, the mountaineer could restrain himself no longer, and rising to his full height, with arms upraised he shouted, 'For God's sake! Let South Carolina nullify, revolute, secess, and BE DAMNED!'" J. G. deR. Hamilton, "Secession in North Carolina," *North Carolina in the War Between the States— Bethel to Sharpsburg* (Raleigh: Edwards and Broughton, 1926), I, 33.

"I am a Union man but when they send men South it will change **my** notions. I can do nothing against my own people."[22]

Two days after South Carolina's momentous decision to withdraw from the Union, the General Assembly of North Carolina adjourned for the Christmas season, and the legislators were not to return to the capital until the first week of the new year. During this interval, the conservatives in North Carolina, noting the increase of disunion sentiment throughout the South, began to increase their activities.* As a result, many Union meetings were held, especially in the central and western parts of the state. The majority of those attending these meetings, although preferring to remain in the Union, expressed a willingness to follow the lead of the other Southern states if attempts at compromise failed.[23]

The members of the General Assembly returned to Raleigh on January 7 and had scarcely taken up their duties before news reached them that the citizens of Wilmington and vicinity had seized Forts Caswell and Johnston.[24] Fort Caswell, a bastioned masonry structure of great strength which was located some thirty miles south of Wilmington on the west bank of the Cape Fear, controlled the river's main entrance. Fort Johnston, though in reality not a fort but a barracks, at Smithville (present-day Southport) was also vital to the defenses of the lower Cape Fear. It was situated on the same side of the river as Caswell, between that place and Wilmington. The citizens of the port city, fearful that the caretaker ordnance sergeants at Caswell and Johnston would soon be replaced by large detachments of Federal troops, wired Governor Ellis on December 31 for permission to seize the forts.

Despite the urgency of the request, the Governor refused to sanction such an aggressive act. But the coastal residents were not easily dis-

---

* Adding to the tensions of the time was the location in the state of four United States army posts, Forts Caswell, Johnston, and Macon, and the Fayetteville arsenal. See below pp. 6-21. For many years the forts had been manned only by caretaker ordnance sergeants, but now an excited people feared all three would be fully garrisoned. Already there was a sizable complement of troops at the arsenal. In October, 1860, the mayor and citizens of Fayetteville, fearing a raid similar to that at Harper's Ferry, had requested that United States troops be sent to their town "for the protection of the arms and ammunition at the . . . arsenal." This turned out to be a most embarrassing request when by mid-November the fear of insurrection was replaced by deep concern over Lincoln's victory at the polls. Under these changed circumstances Governor Ellis was quick to point out to Secretary of War J. B. Floyd that the request for troops had been "notoriously unnecessary" and was productive of "no little irritation in the public mind." The Governor asked that the troops be withdrawn at once. *OR*, I, Ser. I, 475-77, 481; Hamilton. "Secession," p. 27. See page 393 for list of abbreviations used in the notes.

couraged. On the first day of the new year, a delegation from the port city, headed by William S. Ashe, arrived in Raleigh by special train. This group called on Ellis and once again requested permission to take the forts. Ashe made special note of the disturbed public response in the Cape Fear region to the rumor that the revenue cutter *Harriet Lane,* with troops aboard, was on her way to Carolina waters.[25] The delegation's persuasiveness fell short, however, and for the second time the Governor refused even to consider their proposal. He doubted not for a moment the patriotic motives behind the request, yet he thought such action, if carried out, would be without the warrant of law. North Carolina was still in the Union.[26]

Still undaunted, the delegation returned home to await further developments. Secession meetings became almost nightly occurrences in Wilmington. Young men sauntered about the streets wearing secession rosettes made out of small pine cones. A group of citizens, about twenty-five in number, organized a committee of safety and issued a call for volunteers to be enrolled for instant service. Commanded by Major John J. Hedrick, these recruits became known as the "Cape Fear Minute Men."[27] Amidst these exciting developments, a dispatch dated January 8 was received in Wilmington. It stated that a United States "Revenue Cutter with fifty men and . . . eight guns" was on its way to Fort Caswell.[28] Disturbed over this news, the "Minute Men" decided to risk no further delay in seizing the forts.[29]

With provisions for one week, and carrying such private arms as they possessed, Hedrick and his men embarked on a small schooner and started down the river. By 4:00 A.M. on the ninth, they were at Smithville. Ordnance Sergeant James Reilly, the only United States soldier at Fort Johnston, gives the following account of what happened that morning:

I have the honor to report herewith that this post has been taken possession of this morning at 4 o'clock a.m. by a party of the citizens of Smithville, N. C. They came to my door at the time above stated and demanded the keys of the magazine of me. I told them I would not give up the keys to any person with my life. They replied that it was no use to be obstinate, for they had the magazine already in their possession, and that they had a party of twenty men around it, and were determined to keep it; if not by fair means, they would break it open. I considered a while and seen it was no use to persevere, for they were determined to have what ordnance stores there was at the post. I then told them if they would sign receipts to me for the ordnance, and ordnance stores at the post, I would give it up to them. (There was no alternative left me but to act as I did.) They replied that they would do so. The receipt was signed, and [they] left fifteen men in charge of the post; the remainder proceeded to take Fort Caswell, which is in their possession by this time. I do not know what arrangement Ordnance Sergeant Dardingkiller made with them.[30]

Sergeant Frederick Dardingkiller did exactly what his friend Reilly had done. He turned over the fort to this citizen group, receiving in return "signed receipts . . . for all the ordnance stores at the post. . . ."

Major Hedrick assumed command at Caswell and immediately prepared to make his position as secure as possible. Armed primarily with shotguns, his men patrolled the beach and stood guard on the ramparts. No gun crews were needed as the two mounted guns in the fort were unusable. Their carriages were dangerously decayed.[31]

When the news of this action reached Governor Ellis in Raleigh, he immediately sent Colonel John L. Cantwell of the Thirtieth North Carolina Militia to Smithville, with orders for the immediate restoration of the forts to the federal government.[32] So, in the words of Sergeant Reilly: "They came back to both me and Sergeant Dardingkiller and asked us to take back the public property. I answered, yes; if there was none of it broken, or none of the ammunition expended. It was returned in good order."[33] At Fort Caswell, Hedrick informed Colonel Cantwell that "We as North Carolinians will obey this command. This Post will be evacuated tomorrow [January 14] at 9 o'clock a.m."[34]

Before the evacuation of the forts, the Governor had hastened to inform President James Buchanan of their seizure. Ellis wished to give the President the true account of the happenings and, at the same time, to secure information as to the Chief Executive's intentions with respect to garrisoning the North Carolina forts. The President's reply came on January 15 through Joseph Holt, his Secretary of War. Holt assured Ellis that the President did not contemplate garrisoning the forts of the state.[35]

The occupation and subsequent evacuation of Forts Johnston and Caswell aroused a great deal of excitement throughout North Carolina, as did the secession of four more states by January 19. Mississippi, Florida, Alabama, and Georgia had all joined South Carolina outside the Union by this date. These developments put tremendous pressure on the General Assembly of North Carolina to call a convention. Conservative opposition dwindled, and on January 29, the Assembly adopted a bill directing the people on February 28 to vote on the question of calling a convention and to elect 120 delegates.

During the short pre-convention campaign, both the radicals and the conservatives worked hard to gain control of the convention. The entire state debated the question. David Schenck, a Lincolnton lawyer, recorded in his journal: "We are in the midst of revolution! Every hour and day brings some startling news . . . men, women and children look anxiously for the mails and fireside conversation is confined to the great issue of the day—'Will there be Civil War?' "[36] At this time the sentiment in the state was still overwhelmingly Unionist, but the secessionist element was gaining strength.

At Ansonville, on February 1, four young bloods fashioned a flag out of calico "which they hoped would prove an incentive and aid in determining the State of North Carolina to secede from the Union." Nevertheless, when the flag was raised from the framework of an unfinished building in the village, the cautious people of Ansonville cut it down.[37] And such was the attitude toward secession of a majority of the North Carolina electorate, for on the twenty-eighth, the proposal for a convention went down to defeat by a clear majority.

Despite the returns, neither the conservative nor the radical elements accepted the issue as settled. With the Washington Peace Conference a failure and secession an accomplished fact in the "Cotton States,"[38] both factions knew that North Carolina must soon make a definite decision on whether to join her sister states in secession or to remain a part of the federal Union. While this momentous question dominated the thoughts of all, the state's economy came practically to a standstill. One observer noted: "The political troubles of our country and state are unabated. . . . I do not want Abe Lincoln to drive me from my native soil. I am for resistance to the death by means legal if possible but illegal if necessary." Then turning his thoughts to local matters, the writer commented: "Business stagnant on every line; merchants . . . all waiting for something to turn up—clients quarrel on politics instead of property and have no money for lawyers. Everyone is in a panic and ready for any change which may give them employment. The suspense is irksome and revolution will be the only safety valve of things. . . ."[39]

In April, the course of outside events dictated the stand North Carolina would make. On April 13, 1861, Fort Sumter surrendered, after heavy bombardment, to Confederate forces. Accounts of this victory at Charleston created wild excitement in North Carolina.[40] Radicals greeted the news joyously. Young William Calder, a cadet at Hillsboro Military Academy, exclaimed: "Fort Sumter is taken. Glorious news! A bloodless victory is ours. God be praised that right and justice have triumphed over treachery and deceit."[41]

Unionists, on the other hand, were deeply saddened to learn that war had commenced. B. F. Moore of Raleigh, upon learning of South Carolina's action, commented, "Civil War can be glorious news to none but demons or thoughtless fools, or maddened men."[42] William A. Graham shuddered to contemplate what the next sixty days held for the nation. "Truly indeed," he wrote, "may it be said that madness rules the hour."[43] Catherine Edmondston, at home in Halifax County, could not believe her eyes when she "opened the dispatch" and saw in "large capitals 'Bombardment of Fort Sumter.'" Bursting into tears, she threw herself into her husband's arms and "wept like a child."[44]

On April 15, President Lincoln issued a call for seventy-five thousand troops to suppress the Southern "insurrection," and the Secretary of War wired Governor Ellis to furnish two regiments of militia for immediate service. To this wire the Governor replied immediately: "Your dispatch is received, and if genuine, which its extraordinary character leads me to doubt, I have to say in reply, that I regard the levy of troops made by the administration for the purpose of subjugating the states of the South, as in violation of the Constitution, and as a gross usurpation of power. I can be no party to this wicked violation of the laws of the country and to this war upon the liberties of a free people. You can get no troops from North Carolina."[45]

On the same day, Governor Ellis ordered Captain M. D. Croton and his "Goldsboro Rifles" to occupy Fort Macon and Colonel John L. Cantwell to take possession of Forts Caswell and Johnston.[46] Unknown to the Governor, Fort Macon, which sat on Bogue Banks guarding Beaufort harbor, was already in state hands. On the afternoon of April 14, Captain Josiah Pender had moved a group of volunteers from the Beaufort area across the harbor to Fort Macon, a substantial casemated work completed in 1832. There, Ordnance Sergeant William Alexander quietly turned over the federal property to Pender. On his own initiative the Captain had seized the fort* in order that North Carolina should "oc-

* This was the first time that the local citizens had in any way interfered with Fort

cupy a true instead of false position, though it be done by revolution."[47]

Captain Pender found his prize in a sad state of repair. The wood-work of the quarters and barracks and one of the drawbridges "required renewing and painting"; much of the iron work was rusted, and the "masonry in many places required repainting. The embankment of the causeway needed repairing and the bridge across the canal to be rebuilt." Only four guns were mounted and they were on "decayed and weak" carriages. Thirteen others lay at the wharf.[48] The picture brightened considerably on the seventeenth when Captain H. T. Guion arrived with sixty-one slaves and free Negroes and a schooner full of supplies that had been donated to the fort by the citizens of New Bern. Lumber, railroad iron, tools, implements, bedding, and provisions were all un-loaded in the course of one afternoon.[49]

These early days saw not only the arrival of men and supplies at the fort but also several changes in command. Captain Pender remained in charge only until Captain Croton arrived. Croton himself served only a few days, being replaced on the twentieth by Colonel Charles Tew.[50]

While these changes in command were taking place at Fort Macon, Colonel Cantwell, at Wilmington, carried out his orders "to take forts Caswell and Johnston . . . and hold them till further orders against all comers. . . ."[51] On the afternoon of the fifteenth, the Colonel ordered Wilmington's volunteer companies to assemble, fully armed and equipped, ready for duty.[52] The next morning, at the sound of a signal gun, detachments from the Wilmington Light Infantry, the German Volunteers, the Wilmington Rifle Guards, and the Cape Fear Light Artillery formed at the corner of Market and Front Streets. "Amidst great excitement and hearty cheers of the populace," Cantwell marched his men to the bottom of Front Street where he embarked them on board the steamer, *W. W. Harlee*. With the transport schooner *Dolphin* in tow, the *Harlee* set course for Smithville. On the wharf, a large number of ladies stood waving handkerchiefs until the vessels disap-peared downstream.

At 4:00 P.M. the *Harlee* docked at Smithville. Fort Johnston for the second time was surrendered by Sergeant Reilly to a group of Wilming-tonians. At this post, Colonel Cantwell detached Lieutenant James M.

Macon. In fact relations were so good that some of the fort's cannons were used by the town of Beaufort to fire salutes on national holidays. R. S. Barry, "History of Fort Macon" (M.A. thesis, Duke Univ., 1950), p. 120.

United States Arsenal at Fayetteville. Captured by state troops on April 22, 1861.
(From Lossing's *Pictorial History of the Civil War*)

Stevenson's company of artillery. With the rest of the command the
Colonel proceeded to Fort Caswell, which was taken possession of at
6:20 P.M. Cantwell provided quarters for Sergeant Dardingkiller, fort-
keeper John Russell, and a Sergeant Walker of the United States army,
who were residing at the fort with their families. Sergeant Walker,
however, was soon under close confinement as the consequence of repeated attempts "to communicate with his Government. . . ."

Colonel Cantwell found Fort Caswell "in a dismantled and almost
totally defenseless condition." Two thousand sandbags sent down from
Wilmington on the seventeenth helped the situation somewhat. Still
he reported to the Governor on the same day: "Unless I am adequately
reinforced or am prohibited by orders from you, I shall cause the lights
at the mouth of this river to be extinguished tomorrow night, the present garrison being totally inadequate to the defense of this post."[53]

With all three coastal fortifications now in state hands, Governor
Ellis considered it was time to take over the United States arsenal at
Fayetteville, and the Branch Mint at Charlotte.[54] On April 20, a company of the Charlotte Grays seized the mint, and two days later, Captain J. A. J. Bradford, in charge at the arsenal,[55] surrendered that installation to the "State of North Carolina . . . backed by a force of
between one thousand and one thousand one hundred men, well armed
and equipped, having also several pieces of field artillery."[56]

The Federal troops remained at the arsenal until the twenty-seventh,
at which time they were allowed "to march out" with all of their personal property and depart for Wilmington to await transportation north.

They left behind in state hands not only buildings and valuable machinery but also thirty-seven thousand stand of arms, large quantities of powder, several cannons, and considerable military stores. For a state on the brink of war, these captures were of inestimable value.[57]

This seizure of Federal property, which followed the firing on Fort Sumter and Lincoln's call for troops, helped cause Union sentiment in North Carolina to disappear over night.[58] All were "unanimous" now.[59] Former Unionists and secessionists alike urged resistance. Lincoln became a symbol of despotism, and Northerners a "fanatical and bloodthirsty" lot.[60] One young girl in Stokes County would have been happy "to see and know that old Lincoln, his Congress and every other black Republican were dead."[61] Lawyer Edward Conigland was in court at Warrenton when he learned of Lincoln's call for troops. Since his immigration to this country from Ireland in 1844, Conigland had always supported the Union, but now, to his wife in Halifax County, he wrote: "I am bowed down that the best government the world ever saw, the happiest country the sun ever shown upon is to be torn by internal strife, that the hopes of our people are to be quenched in blood. . . . I feel for my family." He went on in the letter to ask himself where it all was to end and what was "to be the state and condition of the country, a little while ago so happy and prosperous. . . ." Although Conigland could see nothing to avert "a hand to hand war," he was ready "to take the sword, to throw away the scabbard and to die sustaining the resolve that a foot of their[s] shall never pollute the soil of North Carolina. . . ."[62]

At Hillsboro a Confederate flag was raised over the courthouse while a "Southern Rights" meeting was in session. Study was out of the question for the cadets at the military academy; so drills were substituted for recitations. Cadet Calder said he never saw so much excitement in all of his life—even "old gray haired men were ready to fight."[63] A western North Carolina politician "was addressing a large and excited crowd . . . and literally had . . . [his] arm extended upward in pleading for peace and the Union . . . when the telegraphic news was announced of the firing on Sumter and the President's call . . ." for troops. "When my hand came down from that impassioned gesticulation," he wrote, "it fell slowly and sadly by the side of a secessionist. I immediately with altered voice and manner, called upon the assembled multitude to volunteer, not to fight against but for South Carolina."[64]

Meanwhile, Governor Ellis had issued a proclamation notifying the General Assembly to meet in special session on May 1. Certain that withdrawal from the Union was only a matter of time and the drafting of proper documents, the Governor began the task of putting the state on a wartime footing. Before the General Assembly convened, W. H. C. Whiting was made inspector general in charge of the defenses of North Carolina.[65] Military companies were organized, and an encampment named after Governor Ellis was established near Raleigh. In a short while over five thousand troops assembled at this hastily established camp.[66] After the soldiers disembarked from their flag-draped trains, they marched to Camp Ellis through streets lined with cheering people, and at every train stop on the way to the capital city, ladies showered the men with "flowers and Godspeed."[67]

Troops arrived at Fort Macon in such large numbers during these early days that as many as forty men were compelled to bunk in each casemate. These new arrivals were tense, as an attack was expected at any time. But they were confident of success. "We do not know what day we may be attacked, but we are prepared for them no matter when they come," wrote young James A. Graham.[68]

The jittery troops at Fort Caswell were also expecting the enemy to appear at any moment.* On April 17, the Wilmington "Committee of Safety," in view of this expected attack, resolved that "the chairman accept a loan from Governor Pickens of the powder now here belonging to the State of South Carolina and that John C. McRae Esq. be appointed to visit Charleston and have an interview with the Governor and borrow such cannon and gun carriages our necessity requires and he may be able to spare us."[69]

The work of such groups as the Wilmington "Committee of Safety," coupled with the Governor's actions and the mad rush to the colors, put North Carolina well on the road to war before the General Assembly met in special session on May 1. Fully cognizant of this fact, Governor Ellis recommended a convention to the legislative body as the only legal means by which secession could be accomplished. After author-

---

* Two days after the fort was seized a large steamer was sighted rounding Frying Pan Shoals. Immediately the long roll sounded. The troops mustered under arms and prepared to challenge the passage of the steamer. Since the men had only small arms, a tremendous sigh of relief went up from these green recruits when the vessel was recognized as the steamer *North Carolina* on her regular run from New York. E. S. Martin, "Services During the Confederate War" (Unpublished reminiscence), NCC.

izing the Governor to tender military aid to Virginia, the Assembly passed a convention bill. The convention, which was to be unrestricted in powers and final in action, was to be composed of 120 delegates. The election was scheduled for May 13, with the convention to assemble on the twentieth.[70]

The General Assembly then turned its attention to preparations for war. After a vote of thanks to the Governor for his promptness in preparing for war, the legislators passed a law making it unlawful to administer the oath to support the Constitution of the United States. An act was passed providing for the manufacture of arms at the Fayetteville arsenal, and $200,000 was appropriated for this purpose. The Governor was authorized to appoint a commissioner to the Confederate government and to raise ten thousand state troops along with twenty thousand twelve-month volunteers. Provision was made to accept with equal rank all officers who resigned from the United States army and navy to enter state service. To provide for public defense, a $5,000,000 bond issue was authorized. Following the passage of this emergency legislation, the General Assembly adjourned.[71]

During the short period between the call for a convention and the election of delegates, "the martial spirit . . . [remained] unabated . . . ." North Carolina was an "aroused" state. Practically "all labor" ceased. Men thought only of "volunteering and mustering."

"Never I reckon in the history of the world has such patriotism evinced, never such an unconquerable resolution to maintain independence or die in its defence. It far exceeds the spirit of '76. . . ." The writer of these lines went on to say that the ladies were doing everything but mustering. He thought they would do that if necessary. Throughout North Carolina the only point of difference concerned the method by which the state should leave the Union and join the Confederacy.[72]

The convention met as scheduled in Raleigh on May 20. Many of North Carolina's ablest men were present. The gravity of the situation had caused the people to forget political differences and select only the best qualified as delegates.[73] After selecting the venerable Weldon N. Edwards of Warrenton as chairman of the convention, an ordinance of secession was passed. As the last delegate said "aye," the hall rang with cheers and cannon boomed in the streets. Within an hour the convention also passed an ordinance ratifying the Provisional Constitution of the Confederate States of America. A member of the convention described the gathering as resembling "a sea partly in storm, partly calm, the Secessionists shouting and throwing up their hats and rejoicing, the Conservatives sitting quietly, calm, depressed." On the following day in the crowded-to-overflowing hall of the House of Representatives, the engrossed ordinance of secession was signed. As each of the 120 members of the convention signed the document, he was given a loud round of applause. Outside, soldiers stood ready to fire a one-hundred-gun salute, while in front of the capitol a military band awaited the signal to strike up the "Old North State." On the capitol grounds the crowd overflowed in every direction, making it necessary for sentries to mark off sufficient space for working the artilley. When the last signature was affixed to the ordinance of secession, someone waved a white handkerchief from the capitol window. This was the signal for the artillery to commence firing, the bells of the city to start ringing, and the bands to begin playing martial airs. "Amidst the thunder of cannon, the ringing of bells and 'the inspiring music' the assembled multitude went wild. Old men rushed into each other's arms; young men, soldiers and civilians yelled themselves hoarse, and all sorts of extravagances were indulged in." For the secessionist, it was a day of victory. For the old Unionist, it was more a time of tragedy, marking certainly "the death knell of slavery and possibly eventual defeat."[74]

CHAPTER II

"We Are All One Now"

ALTHOUGH NORTH CAROLINA was reluctant to leave the Union, once the move was made, there was no indecision in support of the Confederate States of America. The staunch Unionist, John A. Gilmer of Guilford, was correct when he remarked to a friend, after Lincoln's call for troops: "We are all one now." As a member of the new family of states, North Carolina threw her entire strength behind the Southern cause.[1] Yet "no people were ever less prepared for an appeal to arms." North Carolinians were dependent upon Northern and English markets for practically all manufactured articles. Within the borders of the state there were only 3,689 manufacturing establishments, and these employed very few laborers. Out of a total population of 992,622, only 14,217 were employed in any sort of manufactures. In wrought iron, there were only 129 workers; in cast iron, 59; in making clothes, 12; in making boots and shoes, 176; in compounding medicines, 1. Not an ounce of lead was mined in the state, and hardly enough iron was smelted to shoe the horses. Revolvers and sabres "were above all price, for they could not be bought." And forty-four diminutive factories had the tremendous job of supplying both the army and civilian population with saddles and harness.[2]

This state of unpreparedness was of great concern to the General Assembly and to at least one resident of Brunswick County, who complained in a letter to the legislators about the "defenseless and unarmed condition of the State. . . ." Writing before North Carolina joined the Confederacy, this east Carolina citizen urged the legislative authorities to act wisely by preparing for war "in time of peace."[3] The General Assembly did act with foresight by inaugurating a preparedness program several weeks before the matter of secession was submitted to the voters of the state.[4] But once the break with the Union was made, the task of preparing for war took on an added and serious intensity.

In overwhelming numbers the youth of the state responded to the Governor's call for troops.[5*] A young North Carolinian wrote his mother: "We are busily engaged in getting up volernters all over the state. Gov. Ellis has called for 30,000 volernters he can get at least 50 thousand if he wants them I was among the first to volerntier my cevices in the company at Kinston which will march next week."[6] At Salisbury, the Reverend Adolphus Mangum noted that "Soldiers-soldiers is the sight and talk here—companies coming from the western counties on their way to war. Mr. Vance's company is here now."[7] Training camps were established at Raleigh, Garysburg, Weldon, Warrenton, Ridgeway, Kittrell, Halifax, Carolina Beach, Smithville (Southport), Fort Caswell, Company Shops (Burlington), High Point, and Asheville.[8] West Point graduates resigned their commissions in the United States army to accept commissions in North Carolina regiments. Also, local citizens were made commissioned officers so they might raise volunteer companies. Circulars such as the following were used for this purpose:

One Hundred Men Wanted
For the First Regiment
of State Troops

The undersigned are now raising a company of State troops to complete the first regiment of which Col. Stokes is in command. It is desirable that this company should be formed as speedily as practicable, that it may secure a position under so efficient and experienced an officer as Col. Stokes and the more speedily it is formed the more speedily will it be led to meet an enemy now ready to commence its long threatened attempt to invade our homes and subjugate a free people.

Recruits will be enlisted at Greenville, Pitt County, by the undersigned until the company is formed.

E. C. Yellowly, Capt.
Greenville, July 10, 1861 A. J. Hines, 1st Lieut.[9]

* In the rush to the colors, several Virginians living in North Carolina at the time decided to remain in the state and serve with North Carolina regiments. James Keith Marshall, a native of Fauquier County, Virginia, and an 1860 graduate of the Virginia Military Institute, is an example of one who cast his lot with North Carolina. Marshall eventually became colonel of the Fifty-second North Carolina Regiment. He lost his life at Gettysburg. James K. Marshall File, VMI.

It was usually a gala occasion when these newly organized companies departed for camp. The night before the Scotland Neck Mounted Riflemen left for duty, a "brilliant military ball" was given at the Vine Hill Male Academy. In attendance, along with all the young belles of the area, were the Enfield Blues, Halifax Light Infantry, and Scotland Neck Mounted Infantry. In the words of one present: "It was indeed a military ball."[10]

When the Washington Grays left for the coast, practically the entire town assembled to watch the departure. Since it was Superior Court week, Washington was full to overflowing. The local newspaper estimated that 2,500 people were present "to witness the pageant." The editor called "the occasion . . . one of unprecedented interest. . . ." A highlight of the day was the presentation of a flag to the Grays by Miss Clara B. Hoyt, who also used the occasion to make a patriotic speech. Present were several young ladies dressed in white and carrying insignia with the names of the seceded states. Captain Thomas Sparrow received the flag and "responded in his usual happy manner." Afterwards, a minister offered a prayer. As the "fully equipped Grays" boarded the steamer *Post Boy,* they gave a "very creditable appearance" and to the newspapermen reporting the embarkation, it seemed "that the expression of each countenance evinced a determination never to yield or show their back to the enemy, if assailed."[11]

For troops assigned to inland camps the trip was made either on foot or by train.* The Scotland Neck Mounted Riflemen had to march to their camp at Wilmington, but the hardships of the move were lessened considerably by the "ovations" they received at every stopping place along the way.[12] A Robeson County company, more fortunate, made the trip to Wilmington by rail. A young soldier in this outfit wrote his sister that the boys got "a big thrill out of riding the train from Robeson to Wilmington." Company A, he said, rode in an open car next to the engine, but the train was so long that the men could not hear the "hindmost ones cheer the Ladies . . . some of them . . . buteful" that they passed. "Several bunches of flowers were thrown to Company A but," added the youth regretfully, "I was not the lucky one and little strips of paper were on them telling us to 'Defend the soil they grew on' every one we would pass we hurra and

---

* The state's railroads could not handle all of the troops. D. H. Hill, *North Carolina in the War Between the States—Bethel to Sharpsburg* (Raleigh: Edwards and Broughton, 1926), I, 63.

wave our hats and they handkerchiefs all except some ugly ones that we pas in Bladn."[13]

The old militia organizations of the state up to this time were comprised of no more than "holiday soldiers." Their principal labors had consisted of an occasional target shoot, picnic, or Fourth of July jubilee, where "each private was encumbered with a gold-laced . . . epauleted uniform, and plumes that would have done credit to a field marshal of France in the days of the Napoleonic Empire, and where profuse perspiration was the certain torture inflicted on the warriors that wore them." At these military junkets, nearly every man was accompanied by a Negro servant, bearing hampers of refreshments. The liquid portion of these refreshments was, perhaps, responsible for the wretched marksmanship at the target shoots. When these units were mustered into regular state service, the gaudy uniforms were usually given to the Negroes and new gray ones were made by the ladies.[14]

For those too old to volunteer there was the home guard. This branch of the service was not officially organized until July, 1863, when the General Assembly passed a law abolishing the militia and substituting the Guard for Home Defense (home guard). However, in unofficial correspondence for the first two years of the war the term "home guard" frequently appears. In fact, in some areas notices were sent out for the organization of a home guard even before North Carolina left the Union.[15] A contemporary, in an article written after the war, described this venerable organization as being "composed of infantry and cavalry . . . the combined age of horses and men . . . [suggesting] not only the venerable but prehistoric." The writer's father was a lieutenant in the cavalry, and when attired for dress parade he carried "a sword so married by rust to its scabbard that divorce was impossible, and a pair of flint lock pistols whose calibre would have accommodated a broom stick. . . ." Nevertheless, the old gentleman looked "very impressive" to his son.[16]

The troops rushing to the colors were organized under two separate laws. Under the old law of the state, twelve-month volunteers were accepted. In accordance with usual routine, Adjutant General John F. Hoke's office placed these men in camps of instruction to be "armed equipped and drilled." Those men coming into the service under the act of the May convention were called "State Troops" and were in for three years or the duration of war. Major James G. Martin, a one-armed veteran of the Mexican War, was given the task of organizing the ten regiments of State Troops.

This dual system of organization resulted in two sets of regiments with the same numbers, which, of course, led to much confusion. To eliminate the overlapping, the volunteers were required to add ten to their original numbers. The First Volunteers, therefore, became the Eleventh Regiment, the Second Volunteers, the Twelfth Regiment, and so on. The State Troops, having enlisted for the longer length of time, were allowed to keep their original designations.

In the summer of 1861, Hoke resigned his position as State Adjutant General to become Colonel of the Thirteenth Regiment. Thereupon Martin became Adjutant General for all the troops of the state. The General Assembly, recognizing the efficiency of this officer, "conferred upon him all the military power of the State, subject to the orders of the governor. It consolidated under him the adjutant-general, quarter-master-general, ordnance and pay departments." Martin's service in the United States army on both line and staff duty had thoroughly prepared him for these duties. By January, 1862, this "highly efficient officer" had forty-one regiments armed and equipped and transferred to the Confederate government.[17]

The medical and hospital services of the state were organized by Dr. Charles E. Johnson, who was appointed by Governor Ellis on May 16, 1861, as surgeon general of the North Carolina troops. Within two months Dr. Johnson "had in operation a general hospital at Raleigh, three field hospitals in Virginia, and 'wayside hospitals' at Weldon, Tarboro, Goldsboro, Raleigh, Salisbury, and Charlotte." In May, 1862, the Confederate government took over all military hospitals and Johnson was replaced by Dr. Peter E. Hines. The following year the Governor appointed Dr. Edward Warren surgeon general for North Carolina.[18]

Although the women of North Carolina were never officially organized for war work, their contributions to the war effort were varied and tremendous. Not the least of the contributions came from the womenfolk of the common soldiers. The majority of soldiers' wives in North Carolina "were rural nonslaveholding women," who could expect little or no money from their husband's meager pay. It was up to these women, therefore, to find the means to support themselves and their dependents while their menfolk were away. The burdens these lowly people were called upon to bear were enormous. A North Carolinian described the women of his section as "heroically plowing, planting and hoeing while their babes lie on blankets or old coats in the corn rows."[19]

The first North Carolina troops to leave for the Virginia front were commanded by Colonel D. H. Hill, whom Governor Ellis had brought up from the Charlotte Military Institute to command at Camp Ellis. By May 11, Colonel Hill had organized the First North Carolina Regiment, and within ten days this command was on its way to Richmond. The departure of the First North Carolina from Raleigh was a colorful affair. Practically all the citizens of the capital city turned out to see the first North Carolina troops depart for the front. With colors flying, ladies waving handkerchiefs, and the band playing "The Girl I Left Behind Me" and "Dixie," the men marched down Fayetteville Street on their way to the railroad cars that would take them to Virginia.[20]

The soldiers found Richmond a beautiful city. Its paved streets "and many superb buildings" made quite an impression on the youths, many of whom were away from home for the first time. Lewis Warlick wrote his lady friend: "I have to laugh at part of our company when they get into a city. They look at everything and in every direction and their fingers pointed at every curiosity, which their eyes may behold; it shows at once they never traveled a great ways from their native place."[21]

Virginians overlooked this provincialism. They were happy, indeed, to see the First North Carolina Regiment. The state's newspapers were filled with testimonies to North Carolina's patriotism and the fine appearance of her troops. The Petersburg *Express* of Monday, May 20, 1861, contained the following:

Three companies of the First Regiment of North Carolina Volunteers . . . arrived in this city by a special train from Raleigh at 7:30 o'clock on Saturday evening. Each company had its full complement of one hundred and nine men, thoroughly armed and in the best spirits. If we may form an opinion of the whole regiment by the material and appearance of the above three companies, we should unhesitatingly prononuce it to be one of the finest in the world. North Carolina marshals her bravest and her best for the coming contest, and sends to Virginia men who will uphold and transmit without blemish to posterity the honorable and enviable glory and fame of their patriotic sires. Drilled to perfection and armed to the full—with brave hearts to lead and brave hearts to follow—they will do their duty, and that nobly.[22]*

* The Richmond *Examiner* of May 23, 1861, had this to say: "Without waiting for the form of a legal secession, the State of North Carolina commenced sending her gallant

During these early months patriotism was at its height, as very few North Carolinians realized the tragedy of war. Young men left home for camps of instruction in the spirit of a holiday outing. The Warren County Guards and their ornately uniformed officers arrived at camp near Raleigh with a wagon train big enough to transport the baggage of an entire army corps. The type of baggage was even more remarkable than the number of pieces. There were banjos, guitars, violins, huge camp chests, and even bedsteads. The young bloods of Warren County obviously intended to enjoy the luxuries of home while in training.[23]

A rude awakening was in store for these young men, as evidenced by the following letter:

When I first came here I expected, as this encampment had been so long under the supervision of the State Government, that we would have comfortable quarters while we remained, but I was mistaken.

Nothing has been built but miserable log huts with doors four feet high. (I've broken my head a dozen times.) Our beds consist of board plank laid upon poles about three feet high and extending along the whole side of the hut. We lay our blankets on these (no straw) and sleep happy as Larks, only a little sore and stiff in the morning when we first arise. We get plenty to eat such as it is but nothing to cook in or eat out of. Our whole stack of cooking utensils consist in three sheet iron concerns, in which we have to bake beans, cook meat, rice and several other things, make tea, etc. Our eating establishment consists of one tin pan. Our manner of procedure is as follows—In the morning we wash our faces in the tin pan. Then bread is made up in same vessel. After the meat and bread and sage tea are done we all drink tea out of the same tin pan. We *wash the dishes* in the same tin pan and then our feet at night. The same thing happens every day. We break off a piece of bread, use our pocket knives to the meat and eat with our fingers. All drinking sage tea out of the same tin pan. You can thus have a vague idea how we live in the eating and sleeping way. . . . We either have to stand up or lie down. No benches, chairs or

sons to join those who were already in the tented field. On Wednesday morning the rest of the regiment (of which the first installment arrived on Sunday), amounting to seven hundred, reached this city by the southern road at 1 o'clock. They were soon formed into line and marched through the city, in splendid style, to the airs of a fine band. Those who saw their close columns and steady march as they moved down Main street, in perfect order, their polished muskets glistening in the moonlight, with none of the usual attendants of loafers and negroes crowding upon the ranks, describe the scene as almost spectral in its appearance, so regular and orderly were its movements." E. J. Hale, "The Bethel Regiment," *Histories of the Several Regiments and Battalions from North Carolina in the Great War 1861-'65. Written by Members of the Respective Commands,* ed. W. Clark (Raleigh: E. M. Uzzell, 1901), I, 76.

stools being in the community. If we all stand around the fire it is too crowded and tiresome and if we lie down we will freeze, so we are upon the horns of a dilemma, either of them provoking. Besides this our tents or rather huts rather leak. You know the maxim "It never rains but it pours." Well that is as true as Gospel in our case. It never rains unless it pours through the roof wetting the bedding and everything else, and I have noticed the striking fact that it always rains harder inside of our house than out. You can judge from this our manner and style of living. Our mess does very well if it was possible to get along with out so much dirt.[24]

Despite crude living quarters and poor food, camp life during the early stages of the war was anything but rigorous. Discipline was lax, and furloughs, especially for married men, were easy to get.[25] Except for roll call at reveille, occasional guard duty and some drill, the men were free to do most anything they wished. Guard duty was seldom very strict and many a sentinel spent considerable time playing cards with anyone who came along. A soldier stationed at Fort Caswell commented that there had been several false alarms lately and that he "din't look for anything but false alarms as long as we have sentinels who cannot recollect anything of the counter sign (as they misunderstood it) except 'Halt' and 'who goes there!'" For the men on duty along the coast, fishing was a favorite pastime. They did not hesitate to fall in for reveille half dressed, carrying fishing lines, and as soon as ranks broke, they would make a mad dash across the sand dunes to the beach. Games of all sorts, as well as pranks, took up much of the day.[26] A banjo or fiddle could be heard at any hour,[27] but good brass bands were at a premium. Captain Robert B. MacRae, in camp near Carolina City, wrote his brother: "We are suffering here for music and if we do not soon have an improvement upon our fife and drum all sentiment will die out of the Regiment." He urged his brother to find one Frank Johnson in Wilmington and send him to Carolina City with his band.[28] One of the best musical groups in the state was a brass band from Fayetteville. When it played and the "soldiers in their humble caps" sang "the National air of the Confederate States (Dixie Land)," it was always a moving occasion.[29]

Profanity, as well as music, could be heard around the camps. The peripatetic David Schenck thought that the soldiers had forgotten God "literally." He remarked that it was impossible even to ride the trains without hearing "the foulest profanity and the most offensive and obscene language."[30] At Camp Carolina during the swelteringly hot days of June, 1861, a soldier, with hands tied, could be seen walking back and forth. Attached to his back was a board upon which was printed in large capitals "ungentlemanly conduct in grossly insulting a lady."[31]* In view of this type of conduct, it is little wonder that President Davis initiated the practice of setting aside certain days for "fasting, humiliation and prayer. . . ."[32]

Whether calloused and profane or responsive and God-fearing, these early volunteers were, for the most part, unprepared for military life; yet the great majority of them developed into excellent soldiers. Much of the credit for this success must go to Adjutant General James Green Martin, under whose "genius . . . recruiting, drilling, organizing, and purchasing all took 'form.'" North Carolina contributed bigger names to the Southern cause, but it is doubtful if anyone contributed more to his state and the Confederacy than did this unassuming officer.[33] Martin's job of raising and equipping an army, however, put a staggering burden on North Carolina. On May 27, 1861, Governor Henry T. Clark, who had succeeded to office upon the death of Governor Ellis, informed the convention that the $5,000,000 appropriated by the General Assembly had already been spent and that an additional $6,500,000 was urgently needed. Though dismayed at the mounting cost of war, the lawmakers set about to find the needed funds. Before the end of the summer they were able to shift part of the financial burden to other shoulders. On June 27, arrangements were made for the transfer of the state's military and naval forces† to the Confederacy.[34]

These early weeks of the war saw equipment more sorely needed than men. The youth of North Carolina had volunteered in such large numbers that it was extremely difficult to find arms for them. Colonel Josiah Gorgas (Chief of Confederate Ordnance), who had the apparently hopeless task of providing the necessary materials of war, commented on the situation he faced in April, 1861:

Within the limits of the Confederate States there were no arsenals at which any of the material of war was constructed. No arsenal except that at Fayetteville, North Carolina, had a single machine above a foot-lathe. Such arsenals as there were had been used only as depots. All the work of

* Captain Henry MacRae at Camp Macon complained that his company had some "awfully hard eggs in it" who required hard work and discipline to "lick them into shape." Henry MacRae to Brother, Sept. 3, 1861, Hugh MacRae Papers, DU.

† The North Carolina navy was small indeed in 1861, but it was destined to play a leading role in some of the early fighting. See below pp. 35-37, 50-55, 77-80.

preparation of material had been carried on at the North; not an arm, not a gun, not a gun-carriage, and except during the Mexican War, scarcely a round of ammunition had for fifty years been prepared in the Confederate States. There were consequently no workmen, or very few of them, skilled in these arts. No powder, save perhaps for blasting, had been made at the South; there was no saltpetre in store at any point; it was stored wholly at the North. There was no lead nor any mines of it except on the Northern limits of the Confederacy in Virginia and the situation of that made its product precarious. Only one cannon foundry existed: at Richmond. Copper, so necessary for field artillery and for percussion caps, was just being produced in East Tennessee. There was no rolling mill for bar iron south of Richmond; and but few blast furnaces and these small, and with trifling exceptions in the border states of Virginia and Tennessee.[35]

This shortage of ordnance supplies was somewhat lessened when the State of North Carolina took over the United States arsenal at Fayetteville and acquired the 37,000 stand of arms located there. Many of these muskets, however, were old flint-lock affairs dating back to the American Revolution. As soon as workmen could be found who knew how to operate the machinery at the arsenal, they were put to work altering these ancient firearms. William Bell, supervisor of the arsenal, reported in August, 1861, that he had "eighty-seven hands . . . engaged in changing flint and steel muskets to percussion, in rifling smooth bore muskets, and in putting up ammunition." In the meantime, agents scoured the Southern markets in search of firearms, while in the state ordnance officers scraped together rifles of all sizes, shapes, and descriptions.[36]

The Fayetteville arsenal did not begin the manufacture of rifles until the fall of 1861, and then with machinery moved down from Virginia. When the United States Armory at Harper's Ferry was set on fire by the evacuating Federal troops, the gun-making machinery was saved by the Virginia soldiers, "who entered on the heels of the retiring Unionists." All the machinery used for making the Mississippi rifle was sent to Fayetteville, but it took several months to put this equipment in working order. Parts were missing and there was some injury done in the hasty transfer from Harper's Ferry. But, above all else, skilled workmen were not to be had. After the installation of the rifle-making machinery, however, the arsenal was capable of manufacturing ten thousand rifles a year (a figure seldom reached).[37]

Supplementing the work at the Fayetteville arsenal was a "combination plant, consisting of foundry, shops and ordnance laboratory at Salisbury." But the "private arsenal" at Asheville, after being taken over by the Confederacy, was moved to Columbia, South Carolina, for greater security.[38] General Martin compensated for the loss of the Asheville arsenal by making arrangements with several small establishments in the state to make arms.* He also engaged two Frenchmen at Wilmington and establishments at Raleigh and Kenansville to make sabers, swords, and bayonets.[39]

In spite of these efforts, arms were so scarce that some companies reported to the Virginia front without any rifles, while others were equipped with state manufactured pikes, which were nothing more than wooden poles capped at one end with iron. A member of General Martin's staff was of the opinion that during the fall and winter of 1861, North Carolina could "have had ten thousand more men in the field had there been arms to put in their hands."[40]

The state was even worse off for artillery than for small arms. Besides several antiquated artillery pieces taken at the coastal forts and the Fayetteville arsenal, North Carolina entered the war with only four old smooth-bore cannons. These had been purchased from the military schools at Charlotte and Hillsboro. Recast church bells and scrap iron provided but little of the precious metal needed for making cannons; therefore, many artillery companies, like infantry units, left for the battle area without proper equipment.[41]

Scarce along with small arms and artillery was the supply of ammunition. In an effort to alleviate this shortage, the state advanced Messrs. Waterhouse and Bowes $10,000 toward the erection of a powder mill near Raleigh. The niter and sulphur were furnished by the Confederate Ordnance Bureau, which in turn bought the entire output of the plant. There were a few private mills in the South to help with the production of powder, and one of these was located in Charlotte.[42]†

---

* Some mechanics in Guilford County entered into a contract to make three hundred rifles per month. Rifles were also made at Jamestown, Asheville, and Laurel Hill; rifle stocks at High Point and pistols at New Bern. R. D. W. Connor, *North Carolina, Rebuilding an Ancient Commonwealth* (New York: American Historical Society, 1929), II, 194.

† At Charlotte state authorities established a sulphuric acid plant in connection with the Southern Chemical Works and in the spring of 1862, when it became apparent that the Confederacy stood a fair chance of losing the Norfolk area, Confederate officials decided to move the Gosport (Portsmouth) Navy Yard inland. Charlotte was selected as the sight for the installation. The city was well in the interior but still had rail connections with the seaboard cities. A number of machines were hurriedly shipped to North Caro-

To economize, leather accouterments such as the cartridge boxes and waistbelts were made of prepared cotton cloth, stitched in three or four thicknesses. Bridle reins and saddle skirts were made in this way also. In order to preserve "state supplies," a large portion of the provisions used in the early part of the war came from Kentucky, as did the mounts for the cavalry.[43]*

As the first winter of the war approached, North Carolina authorities were faced with scarcities other than arms, ammunition, and supplies. Forty regiments in the field had to be clothed.† To meet this emergency, General Martin established a clothing factory in Raleigh. He then ordered every yard of cloth from the state's thirty-nine cotton mills and nine woolen mills sent to the capital city for manufacture into uniforms. The output of these mills was supplemented by the spinning efforts of the women at home. These ladies furnished blankets, quilts, and whatever they could. According to one soldier, "the troops of North Carolina were clothed the first winter of the war, if not exactly according to military regulations, at least in such a manner as to prevent much suffering." Eventually, North Carolina undertook to clothe her own troops, and in so doing not only brought up the entire output of all the mills in the state, but sent agents into other Southern states to buy up cloth.[44]

North Carolina's efforts to sustain an army in the field were so tremendous that her resources were strained to the limit. It became necessary to complement the state's provisions with supplies brought in through the blockade. In April, 1861, President Lincoln had proclaimed a blockade of the South, but for quite some time it was not effective. During these early months, many vessels slipped through the blockaders with ease to unload valuable cargoes at North Carolina ports.[45]

While North Carolina's contributions to the Confederacy in materials of war were unquestionably great, her chief contribution was in man power—"the huge number of soldiers who bore the brunt of scores of battles." With only one-ninth of the population of the Confederacy, North Carolina furnished approximately "one-sixth or one-seventh of all Confederate soldiers." Of the 111,000 offensive troops supplied by

lina in May, 1862, and with their arrival the Charlotte Navy Yard began operations. R. W. Donnelly, "The Charlotte, North Carolina, Navy Yard, C.S.N.," *CWH,* V (March, 1959), 72-75; Connor, *N.C.,* II, 194.

* To get oil for mechanical purposes a fishery was established on the Cape Fear.

† North Carolina was the only Confederate state to clothe her own troops.

the state and organized into 72 regiments, all were volunteers except about 19,000 conscripts. Reserve and home guard units brought the grand total up to 125,000 men, a larger number than the state's voting population.

North Carolina furnished the Confederate states with two lieutenant generals, (T. H. Holmes and D. H. Hill—Hill's promotion, however, was not sent to the Senate); eight major generals (R. Ransom, M. W. Ransom, R. F. Hoke, W. D. Pender, W. H. C. Whiting, Bryan Grimes, S. D. Ramseur, and J. F. Gilmer); and twenty-six brigadier generals. Notable naval officers from North Carolina were Captain J. W. Cooke of the ram *Albemarle,* Captain J. N. Maffitt of the cruiser *Florida,* and Captain James I. Waddell of the *Shenandoah,* which cruised the Pacific and Arctic waters destroying more Union commerce than any other Confederate ship except the *Alabama.*

North Carolinians fought and died bravely on the sea, in the state, and in the West but chiefly on the great battlefields of Virginia. In the entire war 19,673 North Carolina soldiers were killed in battle. This was more than one-fourth of all the Confederate battle deaths and, moreover, 20,602 died of disease. This total loss of 40,275 was greater than any other Southern state.[46]

It has been truly stated that "North Carolina heroism hallowed and marked every important battlefield." And no state contributed more to the Southern cause in men, money, and supplies.[47]

CHAPTER III

"Oh! The Horrors of War"

GENERAL WINFIELD SCOTT, Lincoln's aged military advisor, warned that the war would be long and costly, but the "hot heads" in the South only "laughed at the absurdity of the old soldier's prediction,"[1] maintaining that all attempts "to subjugate a free people" would be in vain.[2] And their position was strengthened when the opening military events seemed to assure a quick Southern victory.

On June 10, 1861, at Big Bethel, near Yorktown, Virginia, a small Confederate force under Colonel John B. Magruder soundly defeated a much larger Federal army under Major General Benjamin F. Butler. Over half of Magruder's men belonged to D. H. Hill's First North Carolina Regiment. For raw recruits, Hill's men behaved most gallantly on this hot day.* "Not a man shrunk from his post or showed symptoms of fear," Hill reported to Governor Ellis.[3] After the battle a young soldier wrote his sweetheart back in North Carolina: "The balls, grape, canister, and shell sung around us during the engagement tremendously. The enemy numbered forty five hundred (4500) and our force fifteen hundred (1500). Although they had three to one, we came out victorious—gave them a genteel whiping and sent them off running for life. . . . Surely the Lord was on our side."[4] For their gallantry, the North Carolinians received public thanks from both the Confederate Congress and the North Carolina Convention, and Hill gained a promotion. After Bethel he filled "more of the military eye than anyone" in the state.[5]

---

* Henry L. Wyatt of Edgecomb County was the first Confederate soldier killed in action. One of the proudest boasts of North Carolinians is that the state was "First at Bethel, fartherest at Gettysburg and Chickamauga, and last at Appomattox." Hugh T. Lefler, *History of North Carolina* (New York: Lewis Historical Publishing Co., 1956), II, 497.

Bethel was little more than a skirmish, but in the South it aroused great enthusiasm. This victory was taken as proof that the Confederate soldier was the finest soldier in the world. In North Carolina the war spirit received such a boost that the convention moved ahead rapidly with a vigorous prosecution of the war.[6]

North Carolinians now confidently expected another Confederate victory once General Irvin McDowell moved his Federal army out of the protective confines of Washington for a push on Richmond. These expectations of victory were fulfilled on July 21 at Manassas Junction, Virginia. Here McDowell's army was routed and hurled back on the nation's capital by a Confederate force which included three North Carolina regiments.* This victory in the first major battle of the war brought "great rejoicing" through the state. People rushed for the newspapers to read "the last reports from the scene; and groups . . . gathered at every corner . . . [to discuss] the results—Business . . . [was] forgotten everywhere."[7] But for the sober minded it became clear that ultimate victory could be won only at great cost and sacrifice. "Oh! the horrors of war," wrote a contemporary. "To think so fair a country as ours to be almost laid waste by it, and this Civil War is worse than all."[8]

The Battle of First Manassas (Bull Run) ended the major fighting in Virginia for the year 1861. North Carolina, nevertheless, was not so fortunate for, during this lull after Manassas, the Federal authorities turned their attention to the eastern part of the state.

The coast of North Carolina is indented by Currituck, Albemarle, Pamlico, Core, and Bogue sounds. The waters of these sounds vary in width from one to forty miles, and into them empty most of the rivers of the coastal plain. "From Albemarle Sound, the Pasquotank River offered navigation to Elizabeth City; the Perquimans River to Hertford; the Chowan River to Winton; and the Roanoke River to Plymouth. From the Pamlico Sound the Pamlico River extended to Washington, whence the Tar River was navigable to Tarboro; the Neuse River opened wide and deep communication with New Bern, and further up to Kinston. Beaufort and Morehead City could be reached from Pamlico through Core Sound." Connecting these North Carolina sounds with Virginia waters were the Dismal Swamp and Albemarle and Chesa-

---

* North Carolina had fewer troops at First Manassas than in any of the other great battles in Virginia. D. H. Hill, Jr., *North Carolina*, ed., C. A. Evans, *Confederate Military History* (Atlanta: Confederate Publishing Co., 1899), IV, 21.

peake canals. Federal military commanders realized early that control of these sounds, along with the navigable rivers flowing into them, would mean command of more than one-third of the state and, at the same time, threaten the Wilmington and Weldon Railroad, one of the main lines connecting Richmond with the south.[9]

To command the sound region, Union troops first had to control the long sand bank which reached from near Cape Henry, Virginia, to Bogue Inlet below Beaufort, North Carolina. This long strip of sand, separating the sounds from the ocean and comprising two-thirds of North Carolina's coast line, was broken by narrow inlets at different intervals. Inlets at Oregon, Hatteras, Ocracoke, and Beaufort provided safe passage from the usually turbulent Atlantic to the smooth inland waters. As long as these entrances and the mouth of the Cape Fear River were in state or Conferderate hands, North Carolina was safe from invasion by sea. Hence, it was of paramount importance that these "gateways" be protected.[10]

Soon after North Carolina seceded from the Union, the Governor made preparations to defend the coast. To assist him during this critical period, the legislature created the Military and Naval Board which, under the chairmanship of Warren Winslow, took over most of the military affairs of the state, including the coastal defenses. Two departments of coastal defense were created by the board. The northern department, extending from Norfolk to New River in Onslow County, was put under Brigadier General Walter Gwynn; the southern, comprising the coast line from New River to South Carolina, was given to Brigadier General Theophilus H. Holmes.[11] These officers immediately began to strengthen existing fortifications (Macon,* Caswell, and Johnston), and to build new ones. Fort Fisher at the mouth of the Cape Fear was begun,[12] as were forts at each of the unguarded inlets along the Outer Banks.

Few officers ever had to erect defenses and organize departments in

---

* David Schenck, accompanying Colonel William Johnson on a tour of inspection of the coastal defenses, reported from Fort Macon: "The sound of the pick and the busy motion of spade and shovel indicate a speedy readiness to receive a visit from old Abe's Hessians." However, General Gwynn was disturbed that Fort Macon was more exposed than he had anticipated and had only one heavy gun mounted on the channel. He reported work in progress leveling the sand banks adjacent to the fort but he noted that this was being done by "hand barrows." The General, therefore, directed that a number of wheelbarrows be made and sent to the fort at once. Schenck Journal, June 28, 1861, SHC; W. Gwynn to J. W. Ellis, May 27, 1861, Rec. Gr. 109, NA.

the face of more obstacles than did Gwynn and Holmes. In the northern department, the sand banks on which the forts were being constructed were little more than barren wastes infested with mosquitoes in the summer and swept by biting winds in the winter. All supplies, including water, had to be brought in by boat and the nearest supply depot was New Bern, ninety miles distant. Heavy guns in an unmounted state had to be transported all the way from the Norfolk Navy Yard. Their carriages were constructed wherever workmen and material could be obtained. Ammunition was a very scarce item also.[13] To alleviate the labor shortage, General Gwynn urged the citizens of Currituck County "to send laborers, slaves or free negroes" to Major D. S. Walton at Roanoke Island. "Send them at once," he urged. "Delay is dangerous." Roanoke Island, between Albemarle and Pamlico sounds, occupied the commanding position in the upper sound region. Gwynn also asked for farm tools, promising that they would be returned once the work was complete.[14]

These obstacles, though monumental, were not insurmountable. Forts were constructed at Oregon,* Ocracoke† and Hatteras inlets.

Since Hatteras was one of the state's busiest ports in 1861, with an annual tonnage that surpassed Beaufort and almost equaled that of Wilmington, the fortifications at the inlet were of primary importance.[15] The principal installation, Fort Hatteras, was situated one-eighth of a mile from the inlet in a position to command the channel. This roughly square dirt fort was approximately 250 feet wide. Its outside was sand, sheathed by planks driven into the ground in slanting positions and covered with turfs of marsh grass. Twelve thirty-two pound smoothbore guns of short range comprised the fort's chief armament. A second but considerably smaller installation, Fort Clark, was situated east of Hatteras and nearer the ocean. Mounting five thirty-two pounders and two smaller guns, it provided a cross fire against the channel.[16]

Work on the forts‡ was briefly interrupted on July 10 when the

---

* Fort Oregon was built on the south side of Oregon Inlet.

† Fort Ocracoke (or Fort Morgan) sat on Beacon Island just inside Ocracoke Inlet, "The Fort is mud," wrote a member of an inspection party, "pentagonal, 8 barbette guns mounted with capacity for 50—magazines are bomb proofs. . . . Although of earth it is so protected as to not wash away." Schenck Journal, July 1, 1861, SHC. See also W. Gwynn to J. W. Ellis, May 30, 1861, Rec. Gr. 109, NA.

‡ Federal vessels ofttimes stood off shore at a distance of one and a half to five miles and closely watched the work. W. Gwynn to W. Winslow, July 9, 1861, Rec. Gr. 109, NA.

Federal side-wheel steamer, *Harriet Lane,* suddenly appeared on the horizon and let fly three salvos, "the first hostile shots fired by the U. S. Navy at Southern held territory." Other than creating pandemonium among the sweating soldiers and Negroes working on the forts, the shells did little damage.[17] Of far more concern to the men on the island were the mosquitoes who "held possession of it by day and night." A Confederate doctor, stationed at Hatteras Inlet at this time, wrote: "While one laborer worked upon the fortifications another had to stand by him with a handful of brush to keep him from being devoured by them. The poor mules looked as if they had been drawn through key-holes and then attacked with eruptions of small-pox."[18]

Notwithstanding these difficulties, the major work on Fort Hatteras was completed by the middle of June, 1861,[19] and the following month the Confederate flag was hoisted over Fort Clark. "These two redoubts," boasted Major W. B. Thompson, chief engineer for North Carolina's coastal defenses, "secure to us a cross fire upon the bar and the entrance to this inlet. I now consider this inlet secure against any attempt of the enemy to enter it." But the Major thought three or four additional companies were needed to make the inlet safe "in case the enemy should effect a landing in the bight of Hatteras."[20]

The first troops arrived at Hatteras in early May. Yet, by the end of the summer, there were no more than 350 men from the Seventh North Carolina Regiment, Colonel William F. Martin commanding, and some detachments of the Tenth North Carolina Artillery on the island. The commands at Oregon and Ocracoke inlets brought the total number of troops on the Outer Banks to only 580.[21]

For this small group, isolated from the mainland, the hot summer days dragged by. Since Negroes were used to construct the forts, the soldiers had little to do. They whiled away their days drinking whiskey, fishing, and writing letters.[22] Of the three pursuits, drinking seems to have been the most popular. It was called to the Governor's attention on one occasion "that intoxication to an alarming extent prevails among the officers and men . . . on the northern coast defense."[23] When possible, the soldiers visited the village nearest to their post. Captain Thomas Sparrow, stationed at Camp Washington near Portsmouth, complained that his men were "worse than school boys ten years old." They annoyed him "no end with applications to go into town," and Portsmouth, according to one visitor, was that "little ugly village . . .

on the point."[24] Occasionally there were "stirring times," such as the night a Federal steamer "came up to [the] bar" at Ocracoke and appeared to be "coming in." Immediately the call to arms was sounded and a company of "Islanders" was formed to act as scouts on the beach. Lights in the fort were extinguished and preparations were made to blow up the houses nearby. The excitement caused considerable panic among the Negroes, who "poured out of the windows three and four at a time." By morning, though, all had returned to normal at Ocracoke—the enemy had not attempted to land.[25]

"Stirring times" rolled around more often for the sailors on duty in the coastal waters. As a second line of defense, the state had bought and armed five small steamers and sent them to the sounds. This North Carolina navy, jokingly called the "mosquito fleet,"[26] was under instructions not only to act in defense of the sounds and rivers but also to seize enemy shipping moving along the coast.

The first of the steamers to be placed in commission was the *Winslow*, formerly the *J. E. Coffee*, plying between Norfolk and the eastern shore of Virginia. She carried a thirty-two pounder and one smaller rifled gun. Her commander was Lieutenant Thomas M. Crossan, previously of the United States navy.[27] The next vessel sent out was the *Beaufort*,* followed by the *Raleigh* and the *Ellis*, all three craft mounting a single gun each.[28]

This diminutive fleet of small river boats was manned not by sailors but by "soldiers, or farmers, hurriedly taught to fire a gun." Fuses were uncertain; guns were liable to burst after a few rounds; and when coal became scarce, green wood had to be cut for the boilers.[29] Still the *Winslow* was singularly successful in capturing Federal ships moving along the coast. Operating out of Hatteras in one six-weeks period, she captured at least sixteen prizes. Around the last of July, this small craft got assistance from privateers which began to rendezvous

---

* On July 21, when off Oregon Inlet, Lieutenant R. C. Duvall, commanding the *Beaufort*, reported "the first entirely naval engagement which has as yet taken place between our forces and the Lincoln forces." The Federal vessel, a large, three-masted propeller carrying a battery of eight guns took position, not exceeding 1¼ miles from the *Beaufort*, from where she opened fire across a narrow strip of land. The Federal shots were answered as long as the *Beaufort* could sufficiently elevate her gun to clear the intervening sand hill. The firing closed after forty-five minutes with Lieutenant Duvall claiming victory on the grounds that the "enemy finally, not fancying our shot, cowardly moved around . . . behind a higher sand bank. . . ." *NR*, VI, Ser. I, 21-23.

at Hatteras.[30]* When the lookout in the lighthouse signaled that the coast was clear and a merchantman in sight, the raiders, anchored in the inlet, would "dash out," bewailed a Federal naval officer, and be "back again in a day with a prize."[31] If the vessel happened to be loaded with food stuffs, the men ashore would have a feast but sometimes with ill effects. An officer, after eating his fill of captured bananas and coconuts, admitted he had overdone it: "They vomited me last night & purged me today."

The success of the Confederate raiders caused violent repercussions in Washington. Irate merchants and ship owners in the North denounced the feebleness of the blockade. The New York Board of Underwriters demanded protection against further captures.[32] The State Department reminded Secretary of the Navy Gideon Welles that "the rebels are doing a very active business through the various inlets and sounds of North Carolina, thereby meeting the wants of the army in Virginia directly through the railroads of those states."[33] Even junior naval officers were bold enough to write the Secretary suggesting that something be done about Hatteras.[34] Welles in turn admonished Commodore Silas H. Stringham, commanding the Atlantic Blockading Squadron: "There is no position off the coast which you are guarding that requires greater vigilance or where well-directed efforts and demonstrations would be more highly appreciated by the government and country than North Carolina, which has been the resort of pirates and their abettors."[35]

The necessity of an expedition against Hatteras by the Union forces is, therefore, clear; its origin, however, is vague.[36] As early as June, 1861, General B. F. Butler had suggested to the War Department "that something should be done to break . . . up" the "depot for rebel privateers" at Hatteras. He thought "a small expedition might achieve that purpose." The Federal army command, it seems, paid little attention to Butler's memorandum, but naval authorities saw the wisdom of such an expedition.[37] It was their intention to capture Forts Hatteras and Clark and then to seal the entrances to the sounds by sinking in the channels old vessels loaded with stone. Hatteras Island, however, was not to be permanently occupied.

On August 9, Commodore Stringham received a confidential dis-

* During the summer of 1861 the North Carolina navy was transferred to the Confederacy. See above p. 25.

patch advising that "the obstruction on the North Carolina coast" should be "thoroughly attended to. . . ."[38] Within a week's time, Major General John E. Wool, commanding at Fortress Monroe, was under orders to organize a detachment of troops to assist the navy in an operation against Hatteras. Wool pressed General Scott for 25,000 men, but got only 880.[39] This land force, commanded by General Butler, consisted primarily of the Ninth and Twentieth New York Volunteers, plus a company of the Second United States Artillery. Butler at the time was smarting under a sense of injustice, having only recently been removed as commanding officer at Fortress Monroe. Anxious to refute the judgment of his superiors by winning a military victory, the General felt the Hatteras expedition "was made to order" for him.[40]

The naval force assembled for this expedition was under the command of Commodore Stringham. It consisted of seven warships—the *Minnesota, Susquehanna, Pawnee, Monticello, Harriet Lane, Cumberland,* and *Wabash*—mounting a total of 143 guns. Two chartered vessels, the *Adelaide* and the *George Peabody,* were sent along to carry troops. Each had in tow "a stone-weighted hulk with surf boats lashed topside." A retinue of smaller vessels, including the tugboat *Fanny,* accompanied the fleet.[41]

While preparing for the Hatteras expedition, Stringham received an intelligence report that contained valuable information on the activities of the Confederate raiders at Hatteras and the location and condition of the island's defenses. It so happened that Daniel A. Campbell of Maine and Henry W. Penny of New York, after losing their vessels off Hatteras Inlet, had been detained there as prisoners for a short while. Immediately upon their release they reported to Federal authorities that they "saw as many as 50 vessels pass in through the inlet (9 of them prizes) and as many go out. . . ." Furthermore, they provided Commodore Stringham with a remarkably accurate description of Forts Hatteras and Clark, estimating that no more than three companies were stationed at these installations. They understood, also, that the supply of ammunition was very short at the forts and "with the wind offshore, troops could be landed anywhere along the beach without the use of surf boats or difficulty, if not opposed by a force on the land."[42]

With this valuable information at hand, Commodore Stringham departed from Hampton Roads on Monday, August 26. Early the next morning, a Confederate officer at Norfolk wired Governor Clark: "The enemy's fleet . . . left last evening; passed out of the capes and steered south, I think to coast of North Carolina."[43]*

The passage down the coast was rough enough to make the Federal troops seasick, but not so bad as to swamp the smaller vessels.[44] At 9:30 A.M. on August 27, Cape Hatteras Light was sighted and that afternoon the fleet anchored off Hatteras Inlet. Surf boats were hoisted out and preparations were made for landing the troops the next morning.[45] In the wardroom of the *Minnesota,* officers gathered to go over operational details. The plan of attack, worked out before leaving Fortress Monroe, was a simple one. "Our plan," General Butler wrote from aboard ship, "is to land the troops under cover of the guns of the 'Harriet Lane' and 'Monticello' while the 'Minnesota' and 'Wabash' try to shell them out of the forts. We are then to attack on the land side, and my intention is to carry them with the bayonet."[46]

Across the water at Hatteras, Colonel William F. Martin had been an interested observer of the fleet's arrival. With the aid of his glasses, the island commander had made out the formidable proportions of the expedition and had concluded that his small garrison could not withstand a Federal assault. Hoping the attack would not come before he could bring up reinforcements, Martin sent word to Lieutenant Colonel G. W. Johnston at Portsmouth to hurry forward with his command. On this day, as fate would have it, none of "the public—or private—armed vessels of the Confederacy were on station" at Hatteras, which

* The possibility of an expedition against Hatteras had not been overlooked by North Carolina authorities. A member of the state's Military Board wrote from Beaufort: "As we are taking prizes . . . the U.S. will certainly make some efforts to break up this nest; that is, if they have not been bereft of their sense." Back in early July, General Gwynn had warned that the capture of prizes would attract the Federals to the coast "more and more" and would lead eventually to assaults on "its present defenseless condition." He pointed out that the enemy, in getting control of the sounds, could cut off communications between the coast and the interior, as well as block water communications between Virginia and North Carolina. This, he feared, would open the way for pillaging and marauding. "None could yield him a richer harvest and at the same time occasion such disaster and distress. The occupancy of the Sounds by the enemy may indeed be regarded as the subjugation of the state." In concluding his letter to the chairman of the Military Board, General Gwynn urgently requested more men and more guns for the coastal defenses. Despite the urgency of this request, when the Federal fleet anchored off Hatteras Inlet on the afternoon of August 27, the island's defenses were still woefully inadequate. W. Gwynn to W. Winslow, July 9, 1861, Rec. Gr. 109, NA; D. H. Hill, *North Carolina in the War Between the States—Bethel to Sharpsburg* (Raleigh: Edwards and Broughton, 1926), I, 163. Outside of high-ranking civil and military officials, however, very few Southerners were aware of the peril of a coastal attack. R. B. Creecy to "Cousin Lizzy," Aug. 23, 1861, Creecy Papers, SHC; J. M. Merrill, "The Hatteras Expedition, August, 1861," *NCHR,* XXIX (Apr., 1952), 210-11.

made it necessary for the courier to make the trip by small boat. As a consequence, this dispatch, which Martin had hoped and expected would reach Colonel Johnston in a few hours, did not get to him until some time in the morning of the next day.[47]

In the meantime, the Federal assault had commenced. Long before dawn on the morning of August 28, the soldiers, sailors, and marines had been aroused from their bunks aboard the warships and transports, and by sunrise "there was a scene of almost frantic activity" throughout the Federal fleet. Gun crews rubbed down their pieces and gave them last minute inspections while the troops prepared to board the landing craft (wooden fishing boats and iron-hulled surf boats) drawn up beside the transports.[48]

Early in the morning the *Minnesota*, flying Commodore Stringham's flag, stood in toward the outer bar, followed by the *Wabash* and the *Cumberland*. At 10:00 A.M., the *Wabash* and the *Cumberland* opened fire on Fort Clark. The fort promptly returned the fire, but a shout of "derisive laughter" was heard from the gundeck of the *Minnesota* when the shells fell far short of their target.[49] At 10:10, the *Minnesota* passed inside her two sister ships (and a quarter of a mile nearer the shore), delivered a broadside at the fort, and then moved out to sea again.* From this time on, the bombardment continued steadily, each of the three vessels passing inside the others to deliver a round.[50] And when the *Susquehanna*, returning to Hampton Roads from the West Indies, appeared on the scene at 11:00 A.M., she was directed to join in the bombardment.[51] The air soon became "so filled with smoke" that the navy gunners could not see the shore batteries.[52]

Shortly before noon, the Federal troops began to land under the protective guns of the shallow drafted *Harriet Lane, Monticello,* and *Pawnee*. However, reported one eyewitness, "as fast as they neared the beach the breakers carried them aground. . . ." A strong southerly wind blowing in toward Hatteras on this morning had caused the surf to run high. One after another the landing craft were caught in the breakers and thrown on the beach. The wooden boats literally broke up

* This constant moving of the attacking vessels was a new maneuver in American naval warfare and a very effective one. Nevertheless, Admiral David Porter of the United States navy thought this maneuver, though having the advantage of bothering the enemy's gunners, "was not the best calculated way to bring an engagement to a speedy conclusion." In his opinion the larger vessels should have been "anchored in line abreast of the forts, with the small vessels on their flank. . . ." D. D. Porter, *Naval History of the Civil War* (New York: Sherman Publishing Co., 1886), pp. 45-46.

in the surf, while the iron-hulled ones filled with water and sank. Even so, 318 men made it ashore without the loss of a life or serious injury. More remarkable, two heavy field pieces were somehow put upon the beach. But, because of the continuing high winds, efforts to land more troops and equipment were stopped. Colonel Max Weber, whose Twentieth New York had been put ashore, pictured the condition of his men as "very bad. . . . All of us," he said, "were wet up to the shoulders, cut off entirely from the fleet, and without provisions. . . ."* The Colonel might have added that his ammunition was wet, fresh water was not to be had, and for support he had to rely solely upon the guns of the fleet.[53] Weber's troubles, however, were not as acute as he thought because Colonel J. C. Lamb, commanding at Fort Clark, had expended all of his ammunition by noon and was under orders to spike his guns, take off what could be carried and evacuate his position.[54]

During the afternoon the Confederates abandoned Clark and started making their way across the narrow marsh causeway to Fort Hatteras.[55] Among those racing across the sand to safety was John B. Fearing of Elizabeth City, who later wrote his wife: "We retreated under the heaviest shelling any man ever saw; we were compelled to run and fall at almost every step to escape the fragments. Some of our men were killed, some wounded, some cut off."[56]

From the *Minnesota* the shout rang out, "They're running!" At this moment it was also noticed that neither of the Confederate forts was flying its flag, and in the sound beyond the inlet "boats were seen laden with men, evidently intent upon getting away as fast as possible." General Butler, a witness to this spectacle, telegraphed a request from the *Harriet Lane* for the fleet to stop firing. On board the flagship a correspondent for the *Boston Journal* reported: "Of course the day was ours, and accordingly the gentlemen of the ward-room mess, who that morning had asked the surgeon all sorts of questions about wounds and

---

* On board the warships there was great concern for the safety of Weber's men when a "detachment of horse" was seen galloping up the shore toward the soldiers. Quickly the fleet opened fire, only to learn that the detachment of Confederate cavalry was a "herd of terrified Hatteras beach ponies seeking safety from the bombardment." David Stick, *The Outer Banks of North Carolina* (Chapel Hill: Univ. of N.C. Press, 1958), pp. 123-24. Colonel Weber's men, most of them German immigrants, provided the islanders with something new. For the first time the natives heard profanity in German. B. D. McNeill, *The Hatterasman* (Winston-Salem: J. F. Blair, 1958), p. 152.

the treatment thereof, met again to congratulate each other upon victory. . . ."[57]

Commodore Stringham, thinking he no longer needed the *Cumberland*, sent her out to sea, and then ordered the light-draft steamer *Monticello* to enter the channel and take possession of Fort Hatteras. When this little vessel got almost within hailing distance of the fort, she was hit with a broadside from the Confederate guns. The *Monticello*, although struck several times, managed within fifty minutes to wiggle back out of the channel and resume her station.[58]

To cover the *Monticello*, Stringham had resumed his fire against Fort Hatteras. In the confusion, a large number of shells fell on Fort Clark where Colonel Weber had raised the United States flag and had stationed a detachment of his men. So intense was this misguided fire that the fort had to be abandoned.[59] Darkness and threatening weather finally halted the bombardment. Stringham then ordered his ships out to sea with the exception of the *Monticello, Pawnee,* and *Harriet Lane,* which were "ordered to go in shore and protect the troops. . . ."[60] During the night these vessels were driven out to sea by the weather, leaving Colonel Weber's small force at the complete mercy of the Confederate garrison at Hatteras.

This critical situation prompted a war correspondent aboard the Commodore's flagship to write: "The feeling throughout the ship . . . was that we were beaten. . . . During the night the secessionists might make our soldiers prisoners, reinforce their own forts, repair damages, and be ready to show that they were not easily vanquished."[61]

On shore Colonel Weber made what preparations he could for the expected attack. He posted several pickets and deployed a small detachment on the beach near Hatteras. The remainder of his men discussed the possibility of capture and, at the same time, tried to make themselves comfortable in the foul weather. Suffering from thirst, they scraped holes in sand, only to find brackish water. Hunger pains were eased, however, for a number of them when some sheep and geese seized on the island were spitted on bayonets and roasted over campfires.[62]

A short distance away, Confederate spirits were high. About dusk, the *Winslow,* the *Ellis,* and other Confederate vessels had landed reinforcements, including most of the Portsmouth garrison and Commodore Samuel Barron, chief of coastal defenses in Virginia and North Carolina.[63] The new arrivals found the Hatteras garrison "fatigued and careworn." Crowds of men were sitting outside the fort.[64] Colonel Martin, "utterly prostrated" by the day's fighting, invited Commodore Barron to take over command and "direct the succeeding operations."[65] Barron consented to take on this "grave responsibility" but said later that he was unaware at the time that he "could be shelled out of the fort." Expecting reinforcements from New Bern at or before midnight, the Commodore made preparations for an attack on Fort Clark. Unfortunately for the State of North Carolina and the Confederate cause, the additional troops failed to arrive. Thus, during the night, Commodore Barron gave up the idea of recapturing the fort and turned his attention to strengthening the defenses of Hatteras. A council of war failed to appreciate the importance of an attack on Fort Hatteras. One of the officers present at the meeting commented afterwards: "Much of the disaster which occurred on Thursday may be attributed to the fact that we did not possess ourselves of Fort Clark by the bayonet that night. But wiser heads than mine thought otherwise."[66]

Pickets were stationed and patrols sent out. Candles were secured so the ordnance personnel could make up cartridges. Cooks stayed busy preparing food and coffee for the men, many of whom had had little to eat for twenty-four hours. Captain Thomas Sparrow spent most of his waking hours trying vainly to get a ten-inch gun into the fort without the use of block and tackle.* His efforts were halted only when it was pointed out that "there was neither 10-inch shot nor shell in the fort, and therefore the gun would be useless if mounted."[67]

When daylight finally came, Captain Sparrow and his weary comrades could see "off the bar to seaward" the heavy outlines of the Federal vessels. The storm had abated and, at 5:30 A.M., the fleet weighed anchor without incident and stood in toward shore.† Two hours later, the *Minnesota* gave the signal "attack batteries,"[68] and then for three hours and twenty minutes the "firing of shells became . . . literally tremendous. . . ."[69] Captain Sparrow, in describing the barrage, stated that

---

* Fort Hatteras was so small that only those men on duty were allowed to remain inside of the fort. All others were to seek protection outside of the parapet facing the sound.

† The sailing frigate *Cumberland* "stood into under 'all sail for the line of the engaged ships and buffing ahead of the leading one . . . executed a simultaneous evolution of shortening and furling, dropping anchor, and opening fire. It was a very smart and inspiring piece of seamanship. Old officers who saw the maneuver have spoken of the magnificence and beauty of the ship on the last occasion of an American frigate going into battle under sail." A. Gleaves, *Life and Letters of Rear Admiral Stephen B. Luce, U.S. Navy* (New York: G. P. Putnam's Sons, 1925), pp. 73-74.

"such a bombardment is not on record in the annals of war. Not less than three thousand shells were fired by the enemy during the three hours. As many as twenty-eight in one minute were known to fall within and about the fort. It was like a hailstorm. . . ."[70]* The Federal fleet, anchored in smooth water beyond the range of the fort's guns, had turned the engagement into a question of Confederate endurance.

By 11:00 A.M., the situation at Hatteras was so critical that Commodore Barron called a council of all staff officers and captains. It was decided to spike the guns and effect a retreat. Then, before a single gun could be put out of commission, a shell hit the ventilator of the bomb-proof, starting a fire in the room adjoining the principal magazine. Word immediately spread through the fort that the magazine was on fire. The council of officers now agreed unanimously that "holding out longer could only result in a greater loss of life, without the ability to damage . . . [their] adversaries." With this, Commodore Barron ordered "a white flag to be shown."[71]†

At the sight of the surrender colors, the sailors on board the *Minnesota* "flew to the rigging." From ship to ship shouts of victory rang out.[72] Once more the fleet moved in toward Hatteras Inlet, the tug *Fanny* out front. Aboard this small vessel was General Butler. After the *Fanny* anchored, Butler sent his aide ashore in a small boat "to demand the meaning of the white flag." The aide soon returned with a note from Commodore Barron offering "to surrender Fort Hatteras, with all arms and munitions of war" provided the officers would be "allowed to go out with side arms, and the men without arms to retire." Irate, Butler replied: "Cannot admit terms proposed. The terms offered are these: Full capitulation; the officers and men be treated as prisoners of war. No other terms admisable."[73]

Despite the demanding tone of this note, the moment was one of great anxiety for Butler. The *Adelaide,* loaded with troops, and the

* Governor Clark said, "Hatteras sustained the heaviest and most incessant firing that this country ever witnessed." H. T. Clark to S. L. Fremont, Sept. 2, 1861, NCDAH. Another witness to the bombardment described it as "terrific beyond description." L. D. Starke to Wife, Aug. 30, 1861, Starke-Marchant-Martin Papers, SHC. Joining in the bombardment were two field pieces operated by naval gunners on shore, and one of the guns from Fort Clark. Stick, *Outer Banks,* p. 126.

† At first a white sheet or piece of canvas was flown but the firing continued. So "someone . . . got a large Confederate Flag, tore all but the white bar from it, attached this to a pole and planted it on the bomb-proof." After two more shells the firing ceased. Sparrow Diary, Aug. 29, 1861, SHC.

Fort Hatteras just before its surrender to the Union forces under General B. F. Butler, August 29, 1861. (From *Harper's Weekly*)

Harriet Lane had both grounded upon the bar within range of the enemy's guns. But determined "not to abate a 'tittle,'" Butler waited forty-five minutes for the Confederate reply. His fears were eased when Commodore Barron, accompanied by Colonel Martin and Major W. S. G. Andrews, boarded the tug and informed him that his terms of surrender had been accepted.[74]

General Butler took the Confederate officers to the *Minnesota* where the final terms of capitulation were signed. Upon reaching the Union flagship, Commodore Barron and his party were amazed to learn that Butler had "complete information about their defenses." The General had gained this information from one of his aides, who had gone ashore that morning and returned with "the official documents, letters, and books of the commanding officers which he had found in Fort Clark." Barron also wanted to know who it was on shore that the fleet had signaled. He did not get an answer to his question, but one of his own men thought they "were betrayed by a local preacher who the Sunday before [had] preached and prayed for the success of our [Confederate] army."[75]

After the surrender negotiations General Butler went ashore to take formal possession of Fort Hatteras. Joined by Colonel Weber's men, who had moved up the beach when the firing ceased, Butler marched into the fort and raised the Stars and Stripes. Thirteen guns barked a salute as the Federal soldiers rent the air with cheers.[76] Although the Hatteras expedition was a joint army-navy operation, its success must be attributed primarily to the navy. The accurate fire of the Union fleet brought about the surrender of the forts.[77]

Casualties in the Battle of Hatteras were surprisingly light. No deaths were reported on the Federal side, while conflicting reports of Confederate losses in numbers killed ranged from four to fourteen.[78] A few Confederates escaped on the *Winslow* and *Ellis,* but the majority were taken prisoner. Approximately seven hundred of the defenders, including Commodore Barron, were herded on board the Federal ships and carried to New York.[79]

Throughout the North, the news of this victory was received with great rejoicing. Coming so close after the defeat at Manassas, it considerably bolstered morale. In New York a columnist declared that the victory "contributes to the cheerful feeling that prevails by encouraging hope that the tide of victory is now turned from the rebels to the Union arms." In Washington the Hatteras expedition greatly strengthened the position of the Navy Department, and Commodore Stringham was congratulated on all sides for his great victory.[80]

The scene was totally different in the South. The engineers who built the forts were censured for lack of skill. At the same time, the Ordnance Department was blamed for not furnishing better guns and shells. Allegations of drunkenness, inefficiency, and even cowardice on the part of the officers and men were made.[81] An angry Confederate Congress demanded the true story on Hatteras.[82]

In North Carolina, officials scrambled to lay the blame and a Raleigh newspaper asked the pertinent question: "Why did not our force of seven or eight hundred men kill, drive into the sea, or capture the enemy's force of 300 or 400 men who spent the night 600 yards of our troops?"[83] Private citizens and soldiers alike felt "most keenly the loss of reputation to . . . [their] state."[84] Writing from Virginia, a soldier lamented: "Must history record in after years that in our struggle for freedom the first repulse our cause received was on the soil of the Old North State. . . ."[85] An eighteen-year-old girl, of Everittsville, recorded in her diary: "This evening we heard the startling intelligence. That the Yankees have possession of 'Fort Hatteras' on the cape. . . . It makes every vein ready to burst with indignation. When I think of such *vile* feet treading the soil of the Proud old North State. Arise, Ye Men of N. Cr. Off with cowardly hordes."[86] William Pettigrew of "Magnolia" plantation went as far as to say that the surrender had shaken the confidence of many people in the ultimate success of the Southern army.[87]

With Hatteras secure in his possession, Butler wisely decided to take a second look at his orders, which were to abandon the place after blocking the inlet. The General, a far better politician than soldier, seldom grasped the military picture. Hatteras, though, proved an exception. It appeared to him that this island was "a very important situation" that should be held. He wrote: "It was the opening to a great inland sea running up 90 miles to Newbern, and so giving water communication up to Norfolk. It seemed to me that if we ever intended to operate in North Carolina and southern Virginia, we should operate by way of that inland sea." Accordingly, Butler met with Stringham in the Commodore's cabinet where it was "determined to leave the troops and hold the fort." Since this was a direct violation of his orders, Butler proceeded at once to Washington, so he said, "to be court-martialed or to make such representations as I could to have my actions and doings sanctioned."[88] This apprehension was unnecessary for, on September 5, Secretary of War Simon Cameron wired General Wool: "The position at Cape Hatteras must be held, and you will adopt such measures, in connection with the Navy Department, as may be necessary to effect the object."[89]

The force which General Butler left behind to hold the inlet consisted of detachments of the Ninth* and Twentieth New York under command of Colonel Rush C. Hawkins, and a naval force composed of the *Monticello, Pawnee, Susquehanna,* and the grounded *Harriet Lane.*[90]

Meanwhile, Forts Ocracoke and Oregon had been abandoned by the Confederates without a fight. The gunboat *Ellis,* after picking up "the sad and weeping wives" of the officers captured at Hatteras, took on board the garrison of Fort Ocracoke. Before boarding the *Ellis,* the

---

* Islanders who ventured out to see what was going on were amazed to see the men of the Ninth New York garbed in outlandish uniforms. This regiment was patterned after French Zouaves whom Colonel Rush C. Hawkins, commander of the Ninth New York, had observed in Europe. "Their garments were baggy-kneed as to pants and multicolored as to jackets and the whole was topped off by a piratical cap that could have served also as a stocking." McNeill, *Hatterasman,* p. 152.

men spiked the guns and set fire to their platforms.[91] At Fort Oregon a council of war resolved to evacuate the place and remove the "guns, etc. to Roanoke Island." At this meeting Colonel Elwood Morris, who had designed and built Fort Oregon, voted against this move. He argued that "the evacuation of a strong Fortress just finished, just mounted with its armament, and not even threatened by the enemy, *was not justified by any military necessity.*" He thought the evacuation of Fort Ocracoke even "more extraordinary, as that Post . . . [could not] be approached within 5 miles by the heavy ships of the enemy and . . . [could] only be attacked by vessels of light draft of water, and inferior power." The majority of the council in voting for evacuation justified the decision on the grounds that, with Hatteras and Ocracoke in Federal hands and enemy steamers in the sound, it would not be possible to hold out for any length of time. The departure from the fort was orderly. Upon four schooners and the steamer *Raleigh* were "transferred all the men and everything belonging to the companies, cannon balls and all public property that could be carried off." After several unsuccessful attempts to remove the cannons nine of them had to be spiked. Three were lost overboard and the rest left behind. All the barracks were burned.[92]

The loss of the defenses guarding the inlets to Albemarle and Pamlico sounds was a serious blow to the Confederacy. It provided the enemy with a base for operations against eastern North Carolina and, at the same time, eliminated the sounds as a rendezvous point for privateers. A leading military figure of the North, writing after the war, called the Hatteras expedition "our first naval victory indeed our first victory of any kind and [one that] should not be forgotten." This writer pointed out that "the Union cause was then in a depressed condition, owing to the reverses it had experienced." Therefore, he said, "the moral effect of this affair was very great, as it gave us a foothold on Southern soil and possession of the Sounds of North Carolina . . . and ultimately proved one of the most important events of the war."[93]

The capture of Hatteras was, indeed, a timely victory for the Union, but a lack of foresight on the part of those who planned the expedition kept it from being even more complete. Had Butler and Stringham been furnished with more troops and light-draft vessels, they could have easily pushed into the North Carolina mainland, as Federal troops were to do a year later.[94]

CHAPTER IV

The Outer Banks, 1861

COLONEL RUSH C. HAWKINS, whom Butler had left in command at Hatteras, was a young, energetic New Yorker whose duties, it seemed, would be relatively simple and uneventful.* Not a hostile soldier remained on the island. One half of the native population had fled, and those remaining were not a "gun toting" people.[1] Nevertheless, Colonel Hawkins had his troubles, and soon. Left with an inadequate food supply, he had to feed his men for ten days on black coffee, fresh fish, and "sheet-iron pancake[s]" made of flour and salt water. "This diet was neither luxurious nor nutritious," to say the least, "and it produced unpleasant scorbutic results."[2]

Within two weeks, however, fresh supplies arrived, along with six more companies of the Ninth New York, and by the end of the month the strength of the garrison had almost doubled.[3] The Colonel now had men available for work on the forts. The southwest face of Fort Hatteras was extended to a point where it would command both the bar and channel of the inlet. Preparations were also made for the installation of heavier guns, and from Hatteras village regular details were sent out "to explore and subdue."[4] One such expedition was ordered on September 16 to Ocracoke Inlet to destroy the abandoned Confederate fort located there.

This was a mixed command of land and sea forces under Lieutenant

---

*Hawkins served in the Mexican War while still a minor. He later organized the "Hawkins Zouaves" which became the Ninth New York. The morning after President Lincoln issued his call for troops, Hawkins was in Albany, New York, offering his troops to the state. His men were the first body in New York to volunteer. Margaret B. Stillwell, "Hawkins of the Hawkins' Zouaves," *Bookmen's Holiday Notes and Studies Written and Gathered in Tribute to Harry Miller Lydenberg*, ed. Margaret B. Stillwell (New York: New York Public Library, 1943), p. 86.

James G. Maxwell of the United States navy, Maxwell found Fort Ocracoke deserted,* but he decided that eighteen heavy caliber guns† with only their carriages burned had to be put out of commission. While a portion of his men were engaged in disabling the guns, the Lieutenant sent a launch across the inlet to Portsmouth. The men found a ghost town, as most of the villagers had left their homes during the Battle of Hatteras. By 6:30 A.M. on the eighteenth Maxwell was satisfied that all military property at Ocracoke and Portsmouth had been destroyed, so he ordered the expedition to return to Hatteras.[5]

Of more pressing concern to Hawkins than the abandoned installation at Ocracoke were the intentions of the Confederates on Roanoke Island. "Before the first week of our occupation had expired," he wrote, "I became convinced that the enemy was fortifying Roanoke Island, with the intention of making it a base for immediate operations, and that his first offensive work would be against the forces stationed at Hatteras Inlet . . . and that they would land a considerable force at the upper end of the island . . . and march down."[6] To meet this supposed attack, Hawkins dispatched Colonel W. L. Brown's Twentieth Indiana, approximately six hundred strong, to the north end of the Hatteras Island with instructions to establish a base at Chicamacomico. And two days later, October 1, the armed tug *Fanny* steamed north from Hatteras with supplies for the regiment.[7]

Contrary to Colonel Hawkins' intelligence reports, the Confederates on Roanoke Island were not preparing for a major offensive move. Instead, they had in mind no more than the seizure of a lone Union gunboat.

For some time before October 1, Colonel A. R. Wright, senior army officer on Roanoke Island, had been working on a plan "to intercept and capture" a Federal steamer reportedly seen in the waters off Chicamacomico. By capturing the vessel the Colonel hoped "to learn the intentions of the enemy, who were evidently meditating some hostile movement upon his position."[8] This plan, warmly seconded by Com-

---

* Lieutenant Maxwell had information before departing from Hatteras that Fort Ocracoke was deserted. Commander John P. Gillis of the *Monticello*, before leaving for Hampton Roads, had cruised southward several times and run in close to Ocracoke Island. He reported the fort abandoned, a white flag flying over one of the houses in Portsmouth, and only a few Negroes on the beach. *OR*, IV, Ser. I, 590.

† The Confederate steamer *Albemarle* was able to carry off two of the abandoned guns at Ocracoke before the Federals arrived. *NR*, VI, Ser. I, 223.

Capture by Confederate steamers of the Union tug *Fanny* in Pamlico Sound, October 1, 1861. (From *Harper's Weekly*)

modore W. F. Lynch* (who had succeeded Commodore Barron as Confederate naval commander in the sounds) set the stage for a convergence of the Union and Confederate forces on Chicamacomico, "each to thwart the offensive moves of the other." The "result was about as confused an engagement as can be imagined."[9]

Confederate strategy called for the use of the "Mosquito Fleet" even though the *Raleigh* alone of the vessels available had any sort of armament. On the *Junaluska,* a canal tug boat, Commodore Lynch had to mount a six-pound field gun, while on the *Curlew,* which had been in passenger service, he placed a thirty-two pounder (taken from one of the forts) and a smaller field piece. Since there were no naval gun crews available, the guns had to be manned by personnel drawn from Colonel Wright's Third Georgia Regiment whose previous naval experience consisted of the journey from Norfolk to Roanoke Island through the Dismal Swamp Canal. After drilling the gun crews for two days, the Commodore loaded three companies of Colonel Wright's infantry aboard the ships and set out to do battle.[10]

Late in the afternoon of October 1, the *Fanny* was sighted off Chicamacomico. When the *Curlew,* the Commodore's flagship, got within range she opened "a brisk fire . . . which was promptly responded to," but in less than thirty minutes the *Fanny* struck her colors.[11] This small vessel was seized along with its cargo valued at over $100,000.[12] Thirty-

---

* At the outbreak of war Lynch held the rank of captain in the United States navy, but he resigned his commission in April, 1861, to offer his services to his native State of Virginia.

five members of the Twentieth Indiana under Captain Simeon Hart and the ship's gun crew belonging to the New York Zouaves were also captured. Making their escape, however, were the ship's crew and captain, J. H. Morrison. Upon the approach of the Confederate steamers, Morrison refused to assume any authority on the premise that Hart "was the commander of the expedition, and responsible." Then bidding Hart adieu, the Captain, his son "who was lying sick in his berth," and the ship's crew pulled ashore in a small boat, leaving those still aboard the *Fanny* to care for themselves as best they could.[13]

From his camp at Chicamacomico, Colonel Brown witnessed this naval engagement with more than passing interest. He was well aware that the loss of the *Fanny* would put his command in "a destitute and suffering condition." Provisions were on hand for only one day, and there was little possibility of getting any from the local inhabitants.[14] In view of these circumstances the day's developments almost proved disastrous for the Colonel. He called the loss of the *Fanny* "a shame, a betrayal."[15] Nevertheless Brown himself was partly responsible for the loss of the tug. As commanding officer ashore, he should have seen to it that the vessel was unloaded as soon as she arrived off Chicamacomico. The *Fanny* anchored around 1:00 P.M., but two and a half hours passed before any attempt was made to take off her cargo and personnel. If Brown had acted promptly, "all of the soldiers and equipment and provisions could have been on shore" before the Confederate steamers arrived.

For the victors the story was different. The capture of this small vessel, the "first capture made by . . . [Confederate] arms of an armed war vessel of the enemy," dispelled some of the gloom of the Hatteras disaster. In addition, the supplies taken off the *Fanny* were badly needed and did much to make the soldiers' life on Roanoke Island more comfortable. But when it was learned from the prisoners that a large Federal force was encamped at Chicamacomico, some of the gloom returned.[16] This revelation, thought a Confederate officer, put the troops on Roanoke Island in an "alarming" situation. "It was evident," he said, "that the new position taken by the enemy was intended as a base of operations . . . from which to assail Roanoke Island and capture the small garrison thereon."[17]

Immediately rumors began to circulate around the Confederate camps that as many as two thousand "Yanks" had landed "30 miles below."

These exaggerated reports of the size of the Federal force at Chicama-comico caused Colonel Wright, commanding on Roanoke Island, to risk an offensive action.[18] "Seeing that a crisis was near at hand, and fully appreciating the danger of being isolated and attacked at a dis-advantage, [he] determined at once to move forward and strike the first blow."[19]

The Colonel and Commodore Lynch worked out a plan whereby the "mosquito fleet" would transport all of the available troops to Chica-macomico. Here the Third Georgia would land on the Banks above the Federals while Colonel H. M. Shaw's North Carolinians would land at a spot down the beach, thus catching the Twentieth Indiana in a trap. After disposing of the Indiana regiment, part of the land forces would proceed down the Banks to destroy the lighthouse at Cape Hat-teras. At the same time, the remainder of the troops, with the vessels of the fleet, would attempt to recapture Forts Hatteras and Clark.[20]

It took Colonel Wright and Commodore Lynch three days to get the *Fanny* unloaded and to prepare for the expedition to Chicamacomico. A visitor to Roanoke Island on October 3 found the officers and men

> . . . all very busy in making preparations and embarking troops. . . . I remained with them until just before they left. The scene was very animat-ing. The evening was calm and the Sound smooth as glass. Steamers and barges crowded with troops were anchored off from the shore. Cheers of welcome arose from the troops on board, as new companies marched down to embark. I went on board a schooner to return to N. H. [Nags Head] and remained near the steamer and barges until about 10 o'clock at night. Every-thing was animate with excitement. From my position and the favorable state of the atmosphere you could hear every word that was said. From one steamer the lively notes of Dixie filled the air; from another the notes of the violin floated on the air and from others the solemn service of praise and prayer to God, rendered more solemn by the circumstances, went up from the mingled voices of a large and apparently devout congregation of worshippers.[21]

Around 1:00 A.M. on the fifth, the expedition got underway. "Pass-ing through Croatan Sound into and down Pamlico Sound, the little fleet arrived off Chicamacomico, just after sunrise."[22] The lookouts at the camp of the Twentieth Indiana reported enemy ships on the horizon "and steering straight for the encampment." Colonel Brown imme-diately dispatched a courier to Fort Hatteras to inform Colonel Hawkins of the situation at the north end of the island.[23] The long roll sounded

The *U.S.S. Monticello* shelling Confederate troops during the "Chicamacomico Races," October 6, 1861. (From *Harper's Weekly*)

and the troops formed to await developments. With his glasses, Colonel Brown made out the steamers *Curlew, Raleigh, Junaluska, Fanny, Empire,* and *Cotton Plant.* He also noticed launches and barges loaded with troops. When, in response to several signal shots, the steamers moved out, it became evident to Colonel Brown that the Confederates planned to put troops ashore both above and below him. Learning from local citizens that it was possible to effect a landing with light-draft vessels at several places below Chicamacomico, and under instructions "to return to Hatteras under such circumstances," Brown gave the order to retreat.[24] His men left "everything behind them, except their arms and accoutrements" and started down the beach, soon to be hotly pursued by Colonel Wright's Georgians.[25] This was the beginning of what was aptly referred to later as the "Chicamacomico Races."[26]

The race down the beach was the Twentieth Indiana's "first march" and, bemoaned Colonel Brown, "under the circumstances a sad and a painful one to my men." The sun, "shining on the white sand of the beach," heated the air to furnace temperatures. The soldiers "unused to long marches," their feet sinking into the heavy sand "at every step," could hardly make "the first ten miles." Man after man staggered from the ranks and fell upon the hot sand. "Hunger was nothing compared with thirst. It was maddening. The sea rolling to . . . their feet but nothing to drink."[27]

Preceding the Federal soldiers down the beach were "the people of Chicamacomico" who left their homes "without shoes and hats and almost in rags. They could be seen in groups . . . mothers carrying their babes, fathers leading along the boys, grandfather and mother straggling along from homes they had left behind." It was a "mournful sight," said Colonel Brown, to see the aged and the young trudging "through the hot sun and sand."[28]

By late afternoon the Confederate fleet was in position to attempt a landing of the North Carolina regiment below the retreating Federals. But this operation turned into a fiasco when the vessels grounded far out in the sound. "We could not get nearer to the land where we were sent than two miles," said a North Carolina soldier. "We got out of our boats and tried to get ashore, but after wading about a mile, the water got too deep, and we had to go back. Our boys hated to go back. . . . Had we landed we would have taken them all prisoners and blown up Hatteras lighthouse. Bad generalship on the part of Colonel Wright prevented it. He had boats but would not let us have them to land in. He kept them to make good his retreat."[29] While the North Carolinians were attempting to get ashore, Colonel Brown's men moved over to the ocean side of the island and "silently stole along, the roar of the surf drowning the footsteps. . . ." Finally around midnight, the weary troops reached Hatteras lighthouse where, said one of the Indiana soldiers, "we found water, and using the lighthouse as a fort, we encamped for the night, and woke up next morning feeling like sandcrabs, and ready, like them to go into our holes, could we find them."[30]

Meanwhile, the pursuing Georgians, unaware of Colonel Shaw's failure to get ashore, went into camp for the night between Kinnakeet and the lighthouse. This day, too, had been a difficult one for them. At first they laughed at the fleeing "Yanks" for discarding extra clothing, but before the sun went down they were doing the same thing.[31] The next morning, when it was learned that the Eighth North Carolina had not effected a landing, the order was given to march back to Chicamacomico.

The Confederate soldiers had moved but a short distance on their return march when the Ninth New York, hurrying up from Hatteras,

reached the lighthouse and started in the pursuit of the now retreating
Confederates. The race back to Chicamacomico was rugged. An officer
of the Third Georgia, who had the misfortune of participating in the
race, had this to say:

After marching only a few miles upon our return, a Federal steamer
anchored off the coast and opened upon us with shell, shot, and grape shot.
They fired the first gun at 5 minutes after 1 o'clock, and continued the fire
till dark, throwing by Commodore Lynch's count 441 shot. It was a miracle
that numbers of us were not killed. One man of the "Burke Guards" and
Clay Moore of my Company were slightly wounded. We marched 18 miles
to reach our camp, after marching at least half that distance in pursuit of
the enemy during the morning. It was severe, I assure you. We marched
upon the Sound side of the beach and of course a great part of the way,
across the little inlets, through water 2 and 3 feet deep. I marched till mired
down, then I took off my pants, shoes and socks—which made me much
lighter. Most of us did this, and most of us can walk with difficulty yet
because of sore feet. Those that took it barefooted stood the march the best.
It was said to be the Monticello that attacked us. Of course we could offer
no resistance, for they kept 3 or 4 large sized guns belching forth death and
destruction at us without any compunctions and we had to march down
the beach and take it. The distance is only ¾ mile at the point that we
were attacked. So you can judge of the chance they had at us. Our steamers
were several miles off, inside the Sound, and of course were no protection to
us as they could not reach the enemy that distance and across the island.
The men, all, behaved well so far as I could see. The flag presented us
by the school girls was carried bravely through the terrible fire, unhurt in
the hands of Crawford Reen, whom I was near on the march.[32]

The "Chicamacomico Races" ended with the Confederates returning
to Roanoke Island and the Federals abandoning their advance base and
returning to Fort Hatteras. "Undoubtedly both sides were convinced
that they had successfully foiled a major offensive movement of the
enemy."[33]

Just the same, Colonel Hawkins was severely reprimanded by his
superiors for the Chicamacomico affair and was replaced by Brigadier
General J. K. F. Mansfield.[34] The Colonel maintained, nevertheless, that
his course of action was the correct one. By dividing his forces, he felt
that he had not only stopped the enemy but also had provided protection
for the large number of "natives" at Chicamacomico "who had taken
the oath."[35]

Hawkins' policy, upon assuming command at Hatteras, had been to create friendly relations with the inhabitants. He assumed that since "they were mostly of a seafaring race, they could not have much sympathy with the revolt against a government which had been their constant friend."[36] His assumption seemed correct. Within ten days after the capture of the inlet, 250 of the residents took an oath of allegiance to the United States and promised to keep the Federals informed of Confederate movements on the mainland. They declared that secret Union meetings were being held in the counties bordering Pamlico Sound and that many citizens were ready to avow the Union cause openly.

Colonel Hawkins suggested to his superiors that a popular convention be held under the protection of the Federal army. Such a convention, the Colonel thought, would restore a third of the state to the Union at once.[37]

There was sufficient evidence of Union sympathy on the mainland to give Hawkins encouragement. William S. Pettigrew of "Belgrade" plantation in Washington County, wrote the governor: "Myself and those of our friends with whom I have conversed are of the opinion that it would be well not to commission any of the Militia Officers elected in our county . . . until you are further advised."[38] The chairman of the Committee of Safety in Beaufort County was convinced his own county was in a "deplorable condition" especially in the lower part where there was "a perfect indifference to the state of our country."[39] A Confederate naval officer on duty at the mouth of the Neuse River reported that he had the names of sixty persons residing on Black River in Craven County who were "treasonably dis-affected towards the Confederate States Government."[40]

It must be remembered, however, that the population of many eastern counties was sparse and almost entirely unprotected from the Federal armies. Young men loyal to the Confederacy were already in the army. "Those at home were Unionist in feeling, partly through genuine dislike of the war and a desire to avoid military service for the Confederacy, and partly also by fear of the Federal forces, at whose mercy they were placed on account of the lack of any adequate coast defence."[41]

Such was the state of affairs when Marble Nash Taylor and Charles Henry Foster appeared on the scene. These two men were the self-constituted leaders of Union sentiment in eastern North Carolina. They hoped to organize a "loyal government" in which they both would play a leading role. Not a great deal is known about the background of this lively pair. Taylor had been assigned to the Cape Hatteras Mission on December 11, 1860, by the North Carolina Methodist Conference. But one year later he was unceremoniously voted out as "a traitor to his Conference, his State, and the Southern Confederacy."[42] Foster, a graduate of Bowdoin College in Maine, left his native New England in 1857. After serving as editor of two daily newspapers in Norfolk, Virginia, he purchased the *Citizen,* a Democratic weekly in Murfreesboro, North Carolina. Seemingly sympathetic to the Southern cause, Foster was readily accepted by the local citizens. Secession and war, though, brought about a change of heart for the editor, and he was expelled from Murfreesboro at a public meeting.

Foster's activities after leaving Murfreesboro are uncertain, but in early November he was in New York furthering the scheme for a provisional government in North Carolina. Taylor and Chaplain T. W. Conway of the New York Zouaves also appeared in the big city where, on November 7 at Cooper Institute, they addressed a large gathering. Their appeal was "for the Union men of Hatteras," and their cause was helped more than a little by the following endorsement from President Lincoln: "I have no doubt that the gentlemen are true and faithful, and that their mission of charity is most worthy and praiseworthy." At the conclusion of the meeting a committee of relief was established to collect funds for purchasing food, clothing, and supplies for the Unionists on Hatteras Island.[43] At Washington, D.C., on their way back to the Outer Banks, Foster and Taylor received "authority" to call a convention for the purpose of establishing a provisional government in North Carolina. They were authorized to represent nearly thirty counties by proxy. So persuasive was this pair that "in a time when transport between Hampton Roads and Hatteras was at a premium and important dispatches had to wait for ships to carry them . . . [Foster and Taylor] came back to Hatteras on a vessel put at . . . [their] disposal by the Navy. . . ."[44]*

A so-called convention was held at Hatteras on November 18. The minutes of the meeting list forty-five counties as being represented.

* A correspondent for a North Carolina newspaper, however, had this to say about Taylor: "Marble Taylor is emphatically a small man—small in stature, small in mind, small in morals. His tallow complexion resembles a whited sepulchre, and his eyes, mouth, and chin resemble dead men's bones." D. H. Hill, *North Carolina in the War Between the States—Bethel to Sharpsburg* (Raleigh: Edwards and Broughton, 1926), I, 180.

Only a handful of persons, however, composed the convention, "Taylor and Foster holding what they called proxies for the rest of the counties named. These so-called proxies were authorized by no meetings of citizens, but merely by individuals, who, in most instances, lived in other states." An ordinance proclaimed Taylor provisional governor of North Carolina, and another declared the ordinance of secession null and void and instructed the governor to issue a call for a Congressional election. The election was held, and under highly questionable circumstances Foster was elected to Congress.[45] So fraudulent was this provisional government that Foster was never seated, and Taylor's duties as governor were short-lived.

The Federal authorities, while attempting to restore North Carolina to the Union, were at the same time attempting to raise troops in the eastern counties. From reports of informants on the mainland, Colonel Hawkins was led to believe it would be a fairly simple matter to enlist North Carolinians for military service in the state. He suggested that the Federal government, as a pledge of good intentions, compensate all the inhabitants whose property had been plundered by Federal soldiers.[46] In this effort the Colonel was greatly hindered by the continued depredations of the Twentieth New York under Colonel Weber. The conduct of these men was so bad that on one occasion Hawkins threatened to use his artillery against them if the plundering did not cease.[47] To strengthen further the Union cause in North Carolina, Colonel Hawkins issued the following proclamation addressed to the people of the state:

The colonel commanding the Federal forces now in North Carolina, having heard of the erroneous impression which exists among the inhabitants as to the object and purpose of said forces, would state that it is no part of the object of said forces to pillage and plunder. We come not to destroy, but to secure peace and uphold the law of the United States. The rights of property and persons will be protected and respected, and any Federal soldier infringing upon them will be most severely punished. It is no part of our intention to war against women and children; on the contrary, they shall be protected with all the power under our control. Loyal citizens can enjoy their homes and property without fear of molestation. No law will be abrogated or interfered with unless it comes in conflict with some law of the United States or the Constitution; all others will be obeyed and respected. It is with traitors and rebels in arms who are destroying peace and order and inciting rebellion that the Federal forces are to deal with. We come to give you back law, order, the Constitution, and your rights under it, and to restore peace. We call upon traitors and rebels in arms to lay them down, and upon good citizens, who respect the law, to aid us in our undertaking.[48]

Copies of this proclamation were scattered through all the country along Pamlico Sound. State officials were greatly concerned over this development, but were unable to do anything about it.[49]

President Lincoln, acting on Hawkins' suggestions for raising troops, requested General Scott to frame an order for recruiting North Carolina volunteers at Fort Hatteras. Although leaving it up to the General to select the officers for the proposed regiment, the President said that Secretary William A. Seward's nephew, Clarence, "would be willing to go and play Colonel and assist in raising the force."[50] As a result, fifty or sixty islanders were organized into Company I, First North Carolina Union Regiment and assigned to garrison duty at Forts Hatteras and Clark.[51] Across the sound on the mainland the chief aid the Federal recruiters received was from certain parties whom the Confederates called "Buffaloes." Although the "Buffaloes" considered themselves Union men, very few ever did any fighting. Their activities were confined primarily to robbery and pillage. When the Federal authorities called them "to the field," most of them "took to the woods" instead.[52]

The failure of the Hatteras government and the attitude of the "Buffaloes" convinced the federal government by late 1861 that its objectives in North Carolina, for the time being at least, should be military rather than political. This conclusion had been reached in some military circles long before the close of the year. Only a few days after the capture of Hatteras Inlet, Commander S. C. Rowan of the United States navy was urging his superiors to follow up this initial success. In one letter to Assistant Secretary of Navy, Gustavus V. Fox, Rowan outlined a plan of action later followed by the Burnside expedition.[53] At the same time Colonel Hawkins wrote General John E. Wool, commanding the Department of Virginia, a letter in which he suggested that "Roanoke Island be occupied at once" and that a small force be stationed at Beacon Island. Hawkins was of the opinion that two or three light-draft vessels should be stationed between the mouths of the Neuse and Pamlico rivers to shut off commerce between New Bern and Washington. He also thought that at least eight gun boats should be assigned to Pamlico Sound and that Beaufort "be occupied as soon as possible." The Colonel urged that these proposals be attended to at once, reasoning that "seven thousand men judiciously placed upon the soil of North Carolina would . . . draw 20,000 Confederate troops from the State of Virginia."[54]

General Wool endorsed Hawkins' letter and sent a copy to the Secretary of War. Less than a week later General Wool passed on to the Secretary a second letter from Hawkins urging the authorities to take some action in eastern North Carolina. But the brass in Washington ignored the letters beyond the mere formality of acknowledgment.[55] So, on November 5, Colonel Hawkins was sent to Washington by General Wool to learn if the government intended to hold Hatteras Inlet permanently and, if so, to urge upon the President "the importance of undertaking further operations to hold that position, it being the threshold to the whole inland water system of North Carolina." Upon his arrival in the capital, Hawkins reported to President Lincoln, who asked him to appear before the cabinet.

The Colonel took full advantage of this opportunity, presenting a forceful appeal for more help at Hatteras. After Hawkins sat down the President asked General George B. McClellan, who was sitting in for the Secretary of War, what he thought about keeping the inlet. The General answered to the effect that "the position was an important one to be used as a base for future operations along the coast and in the inland waters of North Carolina." Lincoln listened to McClellan and wisely decided to continue the occupation of Hatteras.[56]

President Lincoln's decision to hold the inlet as a base for future operations caused the citizens of eastern North Carolina to bombard Governor Clark with petitions asking protection for their part of the state. It had now become obvious to these people that a major battle would soon be fought for the control of coastal Carolina. There was little question but that the scene of this engagement would be Roanoke Island. This historic spot, commanding the entrance to Albemarle Sound, was the key to much of eastern North Carolina.[57]

Governor Clark, nevertheless, could promise the people little since the state's coastal defenses were now under the control of the authorities in Richmond.* All he could do was to press the need for troops upon

---

* Governor Clark was unjustly criticized by many North Carolinians for not doing more to protect the coast. John W. Graham thought the Governor "still in a stupor." David Schenck did not question Clark's patriotism but remarked that "his total incapacity is so obvious that it is becoming the subject of everyday remark." John W. Graham to Father, Sept. 22, 1861, W. A. Graham Papers, SHC; David Schenck Journal, Sept. 11, 1861, SHC.

the Confederate officials. He pressed his case in vain. For duty in North Carolina, he was informed that only newly recruited troops and militia were available.[58] President Davis deemed it "highly inexpedient" to withdraw any troops from Virginia for protection of the North Carolina coast. Davis felt that a withdrawal of troops would assure the enemy of success "in their avowed policy to weaken and demoralize the army in Virginia. . . ."[59] A request sent to the War Department for men and arms to defend the coast brought Governor Clark only promises of help, despite the fact that he had pointed out in his request that the "best population" in the undefended eastern counties of the state were now serving in North Carolina regiments stationed in Virginia. Clark also noted for the Secretary: "This state besides arming her own volunteers in Virginia has loaned to the state of Virginia 13,000 (stand of arms). But our liberality has exhausted our supply and I am trying to buy rifles and shot guns."[60] In another letter to the War Department, the Governor stated his case even more emphatically:

I have received various rumors of large fleets and expeditions fitting out in New York and Fortress Monroe, supposed to be designed for our coast. I will make all preparations in my power to repel any invasion, but my resources are now restricted almost to Militia—and they are unarmed, undrilled, and some not yet organized.

We feel very defenseless here without arms, and I will not again report to you that this has been effected by our generosity to others. . . . We see just over our lines in Virginia, near Suffolk, two or three North Carolina Regiments, well-armed, and well-drilled, who are not allowed to come to the defense of their homes—and two of them posted remote from any point of attack. This is not a criticism on their military position, but rather a suggestion of anxiety to have their services when we are so, seriously threatened. . . .

Our forts might resist their attack and landing, but out of reach of the forts we cannot concentrate a force of any magnitude. We have now collected in camps about three regiments without arms, and our only reliance is the slow collection of shotguns and hunting rifles, and it is difficult to buy because people are now hugging their arms to their own bosoms for their defense.[61]*

* The presence of North Carolina troops in Virginia was appreciated by at least a few Virginians. Sally Gratton of Richmond wrote: "I remember what a barren looking [region] North Carolina is. Tar pitch turpintine will stick to the old north state, longer than anything else I reckon. I never thought much of her until she sent so many fine troops to the war. We must not judge by appearances." S. Gratton to A. Brown, Feb. 11, 1862, A. Brown Papers, DU.

Secretary of the Navy Stephen R. Mallory was more sympathetic to North Carolina's plight. He regarded "the affair of Hatteras Inlet as a serious blow demanding energetic action on the part of the Confederate States." He gave Governor Clark permission to take guns that were "rifled for New Orleans" if they were necessary "to repel or keep back the foe."[62]

Unable to supply North Carolina with badly needed troops and arms, the authorities in Richmond did send Confederate officers to take charge of the state's defenses. Major Richard C. Gatlin, who had recently resigned his commission in the United States army, was made a brigadier general on August 19, 1861, and given command of the Department of North Carolina.[63] The popular D. H. Hill was relieved at Yorktown in late September and placed in charge of the defenses of Albemarle and Pamlico sounds. At Wilmington, Brigadier General Joseph R. Anderson of Virginia had taken command on September 7.

Soon after establishing his headquarters at Goldsboro, General Gatlin recommended to the War Department "construction of a number of gunboats, to be placed upon Pamlico Sound. . . ." He suggested the plan be brought to the President's attention since the "only hope for protection to the eastern counties would be to maintain the ascendency upon the sounds and rivers."[64] The plan was approved by the Secretary of War, but the "resources of the state in ship-building" were sadly circumscribed in 1861. It was all the state could do to equip its flood of volunteers. Only a few boats were built and a few purchased. The Confederate navy did undertake, with considerable foresight, to build in the late fall one hundred gunboats "of identical pattern" for costal service. Contracts for similar vessels were also let to private concerns "while some ships of various types were secured and rendered excellent service, the number for the first year especially was small."[65]

Hence General Gatlin, in defending eastern North Carolina, could count on very few boats for duty on the inland waters. The success of his defensive operations depended on Fort Macon, the installations near Wilmington, batteries scattered along navigable rivers, and the incomplete and badly placed forts on Roanoke Island. By attempting to retain these widely dispersed positions with an inadequate force, Gatlin and his superiors left themselves open to the charge of "trying to hold too many points with a few troops at each, instead of maintaining a few strong positions in heavy force."[66]

The validity of this charge was brought home to General Anderson after a September inspection of his extended district. He was appalled not only to find the defenses along the Cape Fear River weak but also to learn that a mere 4,669 men were available for duty. He asked for reinforcements but instead lost two regiments which were transferred to Charleston. Wilmington, destined to become one of the Confederacy's chief ports, could probably have been captured "at any time" up through the "summer or fall of 1862" had the Federals moved against it with a sizable force.[67]

General Hill likewise was startled to find the weakness of the lines he was expected to hold and the scarcity of troops to man the positions. After completing his first tour of inspection, he made the following report to Richmond:

> Fort Macon has but four guns of long range, and these are badly supplied with ammunition, and are on very inferior carriages.
>
> New Berne has a tolerable battery, two 8-inch columbiads and two 32-pounders. It is, however, badly supplied with powder. This is also the condition of Washington.
>
> Hyde, the richest county in the State, has ten landings, and only one gun—an English 9-pounder, of great age and venerable appearance.
>
> Roanoke Island is the key of one-third of North Carolina, and whose occupancy by the enemy would enable him to reach the great railroad from Richmond to New Orleans. Four additional regiments are absolutely indispensable to the protection of this island. The batteries also need four rifled cannon of heavy caliber. I would most earnestly call the attention of the honorable Secretary of War to the importance of Roanoke Island. Its fall would be fully as fatal as that of Manassas. The enemy has now 8,000 men at Hatteras, and Roanoke Island will undoubtedly be attacked. The towns of Elizabeth City, Edenton, Plymouth, and Williamston will be taken, should Roanoke be captured or passed. The inhabitants of those towns have been most criminally indifferent about efforts to fortify them.[68]

Two weeks later, October 27, 1861, Hill wrote again (this time to General Gatlin) concerning the importance of Roanoke Island and urging that reinforcements be sent there immediately.[69]

General Gatlin was sympathetic to Hill's request for troops but had to reply with regret that he had not one soldier to send him. With the exception of one command held in reserve at Goldsboro, every man was already "somewhere on the Coast."[70] General Hill was disappointed to receive Gatlin's message, yet, with characteristic energy, he attempted to make the best of his situation. He ordered all defenses strengthened and everywhere he went "the spade . . . [was] set agoing." A line of defenses was thrown up to cover the approaches to "New Bern, Washington, Hyde, and Roanoke Island." He ordered the relocation of the lower fort on Roanoke Island and directed a line of earthworks to be constructed across the island. Before these defensive moves could be carried out, however, General Hill was transferred to Virginia.[71] His former command was then divided[72] between Brigadier Generals Henry A. Wise* of Virginia and L. O'B. Branch† of North Carolina. Branch was put in charge of the region around New Bern, and Wise, the district extending from Norfolk to Roanoke Island. This latter area, which embraced the counties around Albemarle Sound and Roanoke Island, was separated from North Carolina and incorporated in the Department of Norfolk, commanded by Major General Benjamin Huger.

Though not a professional soldier, General Wise was quick to perceive that the defenses of Roanoke Island were inadequate. He pleaded with General Huger‡ and the Secretary of War to send reinforcements to this vitally important location, but his pleas met with no response.[73] At the same time Governor Clark was vainly importuning Confederate officials to strengthen the coastal defenses, pointing out that the loss of Roanoke Island would be a blow not only to North Carolina but to the Confederacy as well.§ The Governor correctly observed that the loss of the island would mean the abandonment of Norfolk with its important navy yard.[74]

In North Carolina there was only one regiment—Colonel J. V. Jordan's Thirty-first North Carolina—that could possibly be moved, and it was armed so poorly that the Governor hesitated to order it into

---

* General Wise, though not a North Carolinian, was well received in the state. Ann Blount Pettigrew thought this Virginian equal to one thousand men. She understood he talked a great deal but made up for this shortcoming by possessing the boldness of a lion. Ann B. Pettigrew to Brother, Jan. 14, 1682, Pettigrew Family Papers, SHC. See also Henry MacRae to Brother, Jan. 2, 1861, Hugh MacRae Papers, DU.

† Branch was born at Enfield in 1820. He was reared by an uncle (John Branch) who was Governor of North Carolina, congressman, senator, and Secretary of the Navy in Andrew Jackson's cabinet.

‡ Wise was particularly bitter against Huger. After the Battle of Roanoke Island he wrote the chairman of a Congressional investigating committee: "I intend to accuse General Huger of nothing! nothing! ! nothing! ! ! This was the disease which brought disaster at Roanoke Island." *OR*, IX, Ser. I, 121.

§ While the Governor unsuccessfully sought reinforcements for Roanoke Island, the Confederate government was calling on the farmers along the lower Roanoke River to send their corn to Richmond where the troops were in pressing need of it. R. G. Smith to D. Clark, Jan. 15, 1862, D. Clark Papers, NCDAH.

active service. Only after General Huger withdrew Colonel Wright's Georgians from Roanoke Island did Governor Clark send the Thirty-first North Carolina to the coast.* This brought the total number of effectives in Wise's command in early 1862 to slightly less than fifteen hundred men—a mere handful for the task ahead. In addition to the 475 men of the Thirty-first North Carolina, there were on the island 568 men of Colonel H. M. Shaw's Eighth North Carolina and 450 soldiers of Wise's Legion under Lieutenant Colonel Frank P. Anderson—"in all, exclusive of the garrisons in the forts, 1,473 soldiers."[75] "They were," in the General's words, "undrilled, unpaid, not sufficiently clothed and quartered, and miserably armed."[76] Yet their job was to hold Roanoke Island, the key to eastern North Carolina.†

* There was considerable "bad feeling" between the North Carolina and the Georgia troops on Roanoke Island. *OR,* IV, Ser. I, 693; R. C. Gatlin to D. H. Hill, Oct. 28, 1861, Rec. Gr. 109, NA; J. A. Sloan, *North Carolina in the War Between the States* (Washington: Rufus H. Darby, 1883), pp. 3-4.

† All militia colonels in the eastern part of the state were under orders, as soon as the enemy entered Albemarle Sound, "to assume charge of and defend all the navigable rivers in their respective districts." This, of course, resulted in much confusion in some counties. H. T. Clark to W. Edwards, Feb. [?], 1862, H. T. Clark Papers, NCDAH; A. Biggs to H. T. Clark, Feb. 6, 1862, H. T. Clark Papers, NCDAH.

CHAPTER V

The Burnside Expedition

PART I
ROANOKE ISLAND

FEDERAL PLANS for a second strike at the North Carolina coast were made in the fall of 1861. Yet it is difficult to say exactly who originated the idea for this operation. General George B. McClellan maintained that on September 6 he had proposed the formation of an amphibious army division to be composed of New England men "adapted to coast service."[1] On the other hand, Brigadier General Ambrose E. Burnside, who was to command the operation, stated that while recuperating from the debacle of Bull Run, he had suggested to McClellan the organization of an army division numbering "from 12,000 to 15,000 men, mainly from States bordering on the northern sea-coast, many of whom would be familiar with the coasting trade, and among whom would be found a goodly number of mechanics." He also proposed that a fleet of light-draft steamers, sailing vessels, and barges be fitted out to move the troops rapidly "from point to point on the coast with a view to establishing lodgments . . . landing troops, and penetrating into the interior." Such a striking force, Burnside thought, could threaten "the lines of transportation in the rear of the main [Confederate] army, then concentrating in Virginia. . . ."[2]

Regardless of who conceived the idea of an amphibious division, McClellan, as general-in-chief of the Federal armies, was in a position to activate such a force. The Secretary of War was easily won over and General Burnside, McClellan's friend and former business associate,* became the "natural choice for command of the division." He was

* When the war began both men were officials of the Illinois Central Railroad.

authorized to raise fifteen regiments and was given unlimited funds for equipment. Thereby the "first major amphibious force" in United States history was born.[3]*

While his troops were being assembled at Annapolis, Maryland, Burnside labored in New York to secure transports. In this task he was compelled to compete "with an emaciated Navy which had been abruptly aroused from a long period of starvation and given a blank check with which to buy ships needed to carry out the duty of blockading 180 coastal points."[4] As a result, Burnside, though recognized as one "great for dispatching business,"[5] did not get what he wanted and had to settle for what he called a "motley fleet." North River barges and propellers were put into use after they were strengthened "from deck to keelson by heavy oak planks, and [had] water-tight compartments . . . built in them." Each craft was "so arranged that parapets of sand-bags or bales of hay could be built upon their decks, and each one carried from four to six guns." Sailing vessels were fitted out in the same manner, and a number of large passenger steamers, which supposedly drew less than eight feet of water, together with tug and ferry boats, were added to the fleet.[6]

These vessels "had few of the virtues and most of the deficiencies of improvisation." The most damaging defect was a wide range of drafts which became apparent when the ships tried to pass over the swash at Hatteras. Also the mixture of sail and steam made station-keeping very difficult, and maintenance and repair of machinery posed additional problems.[7]

This heterogeneous assortment of vessels was ordered to rendezvous at Fortress Monroe. The transports on their way down were to stop at Annapolis and take on board the troops assembled there. "After most

---

* In November, 1861, Flag Officer Louis M. Goldsborough, commanding the North Atlantic Blockading Squadron, had written the Secretary of the Navy about a way to simplify the problem of blockading Norfolk: "It strikes me that we should command the waters of Pamlico Sound, and this may, I think, be easily accomplished if I can be given a few suitable vessels in addition to those already at Hatteras Inlet. The enemy now have seven or eight small but well armed steamers on those waters, and these I propose to attack and subdue. . . . This done, something further may be attempted in the way of driving the enemy away from Roanoke Island by a combined attack on the part of the Army and the Navy, ascending Albemarle Sound, destroying the lock or locks thereabouts of the canal between it and Norfolk, and thus effectually cutting off all inland communication by vessels between the two places." When Secretary Welles endorsed Goldsborough's plan, it insured the Burnside expedition of the navy's full co-operation. R. W. Daly, "Burnside's Amphibious Division," *MCG*, XXXV (Dec., 1951), 30-31.

mortifying and vexatious delays," the ships finally arrived at the Maryland capital on January 4, 1862. General Burnside, who was extremely anxious to commence operations, started embarking his troops on this date, and according to him, the orders "were received with most enthusiastic cheers from one end of the camp to the other."[8]

Burnside's haste in getting his men aboard ship availed him little for General McClellan had not as yet sent the official orders for the campaign. They were not dispatched from Washington until January 7.

These lengthy instructions outlined the major objectives of the operation:

In accordance with verbal instructions heretofore given you, you will, after uniting with Flag-officer Goldsborough at Fort Monroe, proceed under his convoy to Hatteras inlet, where you will, in connection with him, take the most prompt measures for crossing the fleet over the Bulkhead into the waters of the sound. Under the accompanying general order constituting the Department of North Carolina, you will assume command of the garrison at Hatteras inlet, and make such dispositions in regard to that place as your ulterior operations may render necessary, always being careful to provide for the safety of that very important station in any contingency.

Your first point of attack will be Roanoke Island and its dependencies. It is presumed that the navy can reduce the batteries on the marshes and cover the landing of your troops on the main island, by which, in connection with a rapid movement of the gunboats to the northern extremity as soon as the marsh-battery is reduced, it may be hoped to capture the entire garrison of the place. Having occupied the island and its dependencies, you will at once proceed to the erection of the batteries and defences necessary to hold the position with a small force. Should the flag-officer require any assistance in seizing or holding the debouches of the canal from Norfolk, you will please afford it to him.

The commodore and yourself having completed your arrangements in regard to Roanoke Island and the waters north of it, you will please at once make a descent on New Berne, having gained possession of which and the railroad passing through it, you will at once throw a sufficient force upon Beaufort and take the steps necessary to reduce Fort Macon and open that port. When you seize New Berne you will endeavor to seize the railroad as far west as Goldsborough, should circumstances favor such a movement. The temper of the people, the rebel force at hand, etc., will go far towards determining the question as to how far west the railroad can be safely occupied and held. Should circumstances render it advisable to seize and hold Raleigh, the main north and south line of railroad passing through Goldsborough should be so effectually destroyed for considerable distances north and south of that point as to render it impossible for the rebels to use it to your disadvantage. A great point would be gained, in any event, by the effectual destruction of the Wilmington and Weldon Railroad. I would advise great caution in moving so far into the interior as upon Raleigh. Having accomplished the objects mentioned, the next point of interest would probably be Wilmington, the reduction of which may require that additional means shall be afforded you. I would urge great caution in regard to proclamations. In no case would I go beyond a moderate joint proclamation with the naval commander, which should say as little as possible about politics or the negro; merely state that the true issue for which we are fighting is the preservation of the Union and upholding the laws of the general government, and stating that all who conduct themselves properly will, as far as possible, be protected in their persons and property.[9]

To carry out these orders Burnside organized his forces into three brigades and placed Brigadier Generals John G. Foster, Jesse L. Reno, and John G. Parke in command. These officers were three of Burnside's "most trusted friends," the four of them having been cadets together at West Point. Through the years they had retained the "greatest confidence and esteem" for one another.[10]

The Burnside expedition was but one part of General McClellan's grand strategy for 1862. Besides this strike at the North Carolina coast, Federal plans called for Brigadier General Don Carlos Buell, by rapid marches, to move upon Cumberland Gap and Knoxville in east Tennessee. General B. F. Butler was to reduce the forts on the lower Mississippi and capture New Orleans. Brigadier General T. W. Sherman was to bombard Fort Pulaski, compel its surrender, and "study the problem" of capturing Fort Sumter and Charleston. At the same time, the Army of the Potomac would push with overwhelming force upon Richmond. These moves involving "the operations of all the armies of the Union," were to "be carried out simultaneously, or nearly so, and in cooperation along the whole line."[11]

Aware of the role he was playing in this grand strategy, Burnside, on the morning of January 9, gave the order for his transports to get underway. A rendezvous with the other vessels of the fleet was made at Fortress Monroe the next evening. When the *Picket* with the General aboard arrived several hours later, the men on the anchored transports began a round of cheers for their popular commander. So lusty were their yells that Burnside's secretary remarked that he had never heard anything like it even "from the Yale boys or 'any other man'." Touched by this show of affection the General took off his cap and stood uncovered in the pilot house of the *Picket*.[12]

These soldiers who cheered Burnside so robustly still did not know their destination. With the exception of the General, members of his staff, and the brigade commanders, no one knew where he was going after leaving Fortress Monroe. Ship captains were even given sealed orders to be opened at sea.

The formation of this large expedition, nevertheless, did not go unnoticed. In Washington it caused a great deal of speculation in government circles. President Lincoln afterwards told Burnside that a "public man" had practically demanded that the President tell him where the fleet was going. Finally Lincoln said to him, "I will tell you in great confidence where they are going, if you will promise not to speak of it to anyone." The promise was quickly given and Lincoln said: "Well, now, my friend, the expedition is going to sea." And to sea it went on the night of January 11, Rear Admiral Louis M. Goldsborough commanding the navy vessels in the expedition. General Burnside, thinking of "the great criticism which had been made as to the unseaworthiness of the vessels of the fleet" took for his headquarters ship the smallest vessel in the entire fleet, the little tug *Picket* which had brought him down from Annapolis.[13]

The seaworthiness of this small craft, along with the entire fleet, was soon given a severe test. When the ships rounded Cape Hatteras on the thirteenth, they encountered such rough weather that everything on the decks that was not lashed down was swept overboard. As if the weather were not trouble enough for Burnside and Admiral Goldsborough the captain of one of the ships got "beastly drunk," at this critical time, thus endangering further the lives of the deathly seasick passengers.[14]

Most of the vessels had little difficulty getting over the outer bar at Hatteras Inlet, but "getting across the shallow swash and into Pamlico Sound was something else again."[15] For almost two weeks Hatteras was lashed by one storm after another. The seas became mountainously high, the wind reached gale force, and "the densest of fog set in."[16] Ships anchored near the bar were battered unmercifully. They seemed "principally occupied in smashing and sinking."[17] The night of January 23 was especially harrowing. Henry C. Pardee, aboard the *New Brunswick*, wrote his mother that during the night "the wind blew a

Ships of the Burnside expedition crossing the Hatteras bar, January, 1862.
(From *The Illustrated London News*)

perfect hurricane, and caused many vessels to drag anchor and some to break their cables, and so drift down with the tide, which was at the rate of 8 or 9 miles an hour." Only by keeping up steam all night and "running backwards and forwards" was the *New Brunswick* able to avoid a collision.

Pardee noted also that there was little sleeping done that night but added that their captain and mate had slept but ten hours since they arrived nine days ago. For their "untiring . . . exertions," he said the regiment intended to remember them with a present.[18]

The violent storms of mid-January cost Burnside several of his ships. The *Louisiana* grounded the day she arrived, and the *City of New York* was lashed to pieces on the beach in twenty minutes. Other losses were the *Grapeshot*, which was a floating battery, the *Zouave,* and *Pocahontas,* the latter with one hundred horses aboard.[19]

The violence of these storms made it impossible for the soldiers to get ashore. So aboard ship they amused themselves, as best they could, "by writing letters, making up their diaries, playing cards, and reading old magazines and newspapers. . . ." A few of them even looked at their Bibles. Others gazed longingly at the shore, but what they saw helped very little.* Hatteras Island appeared to take the "premium" for "lonely God-forsaken" places. "It is simply a sand-bar rising a little above the water . . . ," wrote one of the men. "The water is never still and fair weather is never known; storms and sea gulls are the only productions"[20]

It was a thirsty place too, since the storms had driven the water vessels out to sea. On many of the vessels the water supply gave out, and when it did, the men became desperate. Rain water scooped up off the deck sold for as much as seventy-five cents a cup.[21]

The scarcity of food was also a problem. Hard bread, coffee, and "once in a while . . . a little raw pork" was the diet.[22]

Food, weather, and water were not the only tormentors. Adding to the woes of the soldiers were the ever-present "graybacks" or body lice, and the fear of typhoid fever which had already taken the lives of several men.[23]

During these troubled times General Burnside, clad in a blue blouse and slouch hat, became a "familiar figure to all." From aboard the *Picket* he superintended his fleet of transports, performing all of the duties of a harbor master. On more than one occasion his small steamer narrowly escaped being swamped, and according to a reporter for the *London News,* "there is no grade in the Army that he has not filled during the last fortnight so anxious is he for the well-being and comfort of his troops." Burnside's tireless efforts in behalf of his men seemed to have inspired them with courage. When the *Picket* went alongside a vessel with troops aboard, the air was "rent with shouts." One admiring soldier exclaimed that "the men all love him and would fight and work for him as hard as Napoleon's troops would for him." In the minds of the troopers, the long delay at Hatteras, with its many discomforts, was not General Burnside's fault. The navy, they felt, should bear the blame.[24] Admiral Goldsborough, on the other hand, did not see it that way at all. He complained to his wife: "All my force is still kept hanging by the eyelids awaiting the readiness of General Burnside's branch of the Expedition. The sober truth is ever since the 19th inst. I have been prepared to move. . . . In short, we have failed in nothing whatsoever. All of the detentions have been occasional by the other branch of the expedition."[25]

---

* Orison Taft who visited the island did not think it was too bad a place but he found "the ways of the folks . . . real old fashioned. . . ." O. Taft to Father, Jan. 29, 1862, Edwin and Orison Taft Papers, DU.

To the relief of both Goldsborough and Burnside, the weather cleared on the twenty-sixth and the ships began crossing the swash.* By February 4, the entire fleet was safely anchored in the sound, and orders were given for the advance on Roanoke Island.[26]

Confederate authorities failed to take advantage of Burnside's delay at Hatteras, seeming to take the attitude of the *Richmond Examiner,* which stated on February 4: "Nature has prepared a defense for fertile Eastern North Carolina against invasion. . . . The Burnside armada has failed. It has lost its prestige and hope; and henceforth the highest achievement it can accomplish will be that of taking care of itself. . . . As an aggressive demonstration, it is pitiful."[27] A prominent North Carolinian entered in his journal: "God in his mercy has sent the winds to war against our enemies; and has humbled their haughty pride."[28] But W. A. Graham, another well-known citizen of the state, was under no such illusion and neither was General Wise. Graham wrote his wife: "That Post has been strangely neglected by Confederate authorities."[29] And Wise hurried off to Richmond to make a last minute appeal to the Secretary of War and the President for additional troops, but again he was refused.[30] At the same time, Colonel H. M. Shaw was urging Governor Clark to send Negroes to the island to work on the "totally inadequate" fortifications,[31] yet when the Federal fleet finally arrived, the defenses were still woefully weak.†

On the west side of Roanoke Island were three turfed sand forts—Huger, Blanchard, and Bartow—mounting, all told, twenty-five guns. Only the southernmost of these forts, Bartow, became actively engaged in battle, the others being out of range. To protect the east side of Roanoke Island, a two-gun emplacement was erected at Ballast Point. In the middle of the island was an eighty-foot redoubt which commanded the only road running north and south. This three-gun emplacement was flanked by breastworks and deep cypress swamps. Across on the mainland, Fort Forrest, mounting seven guns, was constructed

* This turned out to be quite an operation for the larger ships. In order to get them over the bar the channel had to be deepened. The problem was solved when someone came up with the novel idea of running the vessels into the bar under a full head of steam while the tide was ebbing. An anchor carried forward by a small boat and dropped would hold the ship in position. The strong currents would then wash the sand from beneath the vessel, allowing her to make another run farther into the bar. In this manner a broad channel with a depth of eight feet was opened.

† A member of the prominent Pettigrew family, being completely realistic about the defenses of Roanoke Island, only hoped they were in a better state than a "short time ago." Caroline Pettigrew to J. J. Pettigrew, Jan. 27, 1862, Pettigrew Family Papers, SHC.

on two old barges rammed into the shore. Croatan Sound was obstructed by a double line of sixteen sunken vessels and a system of pilings still being put down when the attack started.[32]

To man these fortifications and defend Roanoke Island, General Wise had an effective force of only 1,435 men, comprised primarily of the Eighth and Thirty-first North Carolina, the Forty-fifth and Fifty-ninth Virginians. A reserve of seventeen companies totaling about eight hundred men were across Roanoke Sound at Nags Head, and an ill-fated battalion of five hundred men from the Second North Carolina landed just in time to be captured.[33]

This paucity of numbers was not the only problem facing General Wise. There was the question of soldier morale.

On the way down from Virginia "a mutinous feeling became evident amongst" some of his troops and two men had to be shot. The North Carolina troops on the island, though not mutinous, were in such weak physical condition and so poorly equipped that they failed to "inspire" the General. The cold, damp, winter weather and lean diet had kept a quarter of them on the sick list. Uniforms were inadequate. No two men dressed alike; clothing consisted of whatever a person could manage. And "weapons were as varied as their owners garb, and ranged from shotguns through superb rifles to gigantic knives."[34]

Notwithstanding the poor condition of his troops, General Wise was anxious to lead them in battle. This honor, though, was denied him. On the day of the assault he was confined to his bed at Nags Head with an attack of pleurisy. The active command of all the troops on Roanoke Island rested on the shoulders of Colonel H. M. Shaw. The Colonel was forty-five years old, slight in figure and medium of height, and was a transplanted New Englander. Unfortunately for Shaw he was not held in high esteem by all of his men. Captain Henry MacRae thought Colonel Shaw was "not worth the powder and ball it would take to kill him" and charged there was not a "meaner officer in the service." He also accused Shaw of spending most of his time in his tent playing chess rather than looking after his men. If MacRae's charges were true, the Colonel could ill afford this indifference to his troops. In holding the island, he faced troubles enough without inviting, through his own actions, low soldier morale.[35]

When the Federal expedition at last got underway on the morning of February 5, Burnside had over thirteen thousand men on his transports and was protected by his gunboats and nineteen naval vessels.[36] "It was a very fine sight," said Daniel R. Larned aboard the *S. R. Spaulding*, "to see these 67 vessels—all gliding on quietly and smoothly, the grand old *'Stars and Stripes'* floating from each vessel." The sky was a bright blue and a gentle breeze was blowing.[37] "All in all it was the grandest sight" a number of the men had ever seen.[38] At 6:00 P.M. the expedition anchored ten miles south of Roanoke Island. No lights were hoisted during the night, but a clear moon made the outlines of the island visible.[39]

February 6, though, opened with rain that settled into a thick fog by noon, postponing all operations for the day. The order "Prepare For Action" was rescinded, and once more the fleet anchored short of its destination. Fearful of a sneak attack by Commodore Lynch's "mosquito fleet," Admiral Goldsborough ordered a watch placed at the mouth of the channel into Croatan Sound.[40]

This was a useless precaution because Commodore Lynch had no intentions of venturing from behind the pilings and sunken vessels separating him from the enemy. His small gunboats—the *Seabird, Appomattox, Curlew, Ellis, Beaufort, Raleigh,* and *Forrest*—were no match for the Federal fleet.

After supper, when it became apparent that Goldsborough's fleet was anchored for the night, Lieutenant W. H. Parker, commander of the *Beaufort*, went aboard the *Seabird* to visit Commodore Lynch. He found the Commodore in his dressing gown, sitting quietly in his cabin reading a novel. After an exchange of pleasantries the two men began a discussion of the impending fight the next day. Neither officer thought success would be on their side, both realizing that "the Federal squadron was too formidable." This dreary discourse was soon dropped, however, and the topic of discussion shifted to literature, a field in which Lynch was well versed. The "delightful evening" was interrupted only when the ship's bell struck eight (midnight). Parker, upon hearing the bells, jumped up, exclaimed he did not know it was so late, and rushed to the gangway. The Commodore's last words were: "Ah! If we could only hope for success but come again when you can."[41]

Ashore in the different fortifications, the small Confederate force also awaited the dawn and battle. During the day the alarm gun had sounded, notifying them of the approach of the Burnside expedition, and for four hours they had "waited anxiously in the rain for some-

thing to happen and then returned to camp to await further orders."
It was 2:00 P.M., February 6, when Lieutenant Julius W. Wright of
the Eighth North Carolina entered in his diary that fifty vessels were
reported eight miles below the lower battery. "Providence seems to be
assisting us, as the heavy rain continues and the sound is quite rough.
God grant that we may be all preserved and achieve a victory." His
entry for February 7 noted that early in the morning it was quite foggy
and cloudy, but around nine o'clock the sun appeared; "so once more
we are laying on our rolls quietly waiting the approach of the enemy."[42]

Long before sunrise the men aboard the Federal transports had been
"astir." Decks were cleaned and sanded in preparation for battle. Rifles
were checked and large quantities of hot coffee, hard tack, and "salt
junk" were consumed.[43] Aboard the *Delaware,* the captain authorized
an extra ration of grog* for his men.[44] Around 7:00 A.M. the fleet got
underway, and as the companies formed in regular order on the decks,
they read the signal displayed on General Burnside's flagship: "Today
the country expects every man to do his duty."[45]

Between 9:00 and 10:00 A.M. the first of the Federal gunboats "began
passing through the Roanoke Marshes Channel, followed by the naval
vessels and transports." At Fort Bartow a Confederate sergeant put
down his pen, after writing: "The enemy are in sight of our battery. . . .
We are all ready for them, and expect to give them a good thrashing
and send them home to their work. The engagement will certainly be
a long and desperate one, but our cause is good; God being, as I firmly
believe, on our side, will give us victory."[46]

At 10:30 A.M. Fort Bartow fired the first shot and the "Ball" was
opened.[47] By noon all of the Federal vessels were in position, some
concentrating their fire on the "mosquito fleet" drawn up in battle formation behind the line of sunken ships and pilings, the remainder
trading shots with the shore batteries.

As the battle progressed, the weakness of the Confederate battery
position became evident. Only Fort Bartow was within effective range,
and of the guns there, Goldsborough nullified all but three by hugging
the shore below the fort. Twice the "mosquito fleet" passed through the

* During the battle one of the gunners on the *Delaware* obtained a key to the "spirits
room," unlocked the door and "helped himself." When the gunner was discovered the
least of his worries was the battle. L. Traver, *Soldiers and Sailors Historical Society of
Rhode Island; Personal Narrative of the Events in the War of the Rebellion. The Battles
of Roanoke Island and Elizabeth City* (Providence: N. Bangs and Co., 1880), Ser. 2, No.
5, p. 20.

line of obstructions, "then turned about and headed north again, trying to lure the Federals through that narrow unmarked channel and into the direct fire of the two more northern forts." But Goldsborough would not be tempted and his vessels continued to pour a heavy fire into Fort Bartow. "To the eye that witnesses such a sight for the first time," wrote a Confederate officer, "it is truly splendent even though conscious that the winged messenger Death and Destruction bear shot and shell to their respective destinations." The officer was proud of the fact that Fort Bartow for seven "long hours" took the fire of the "Yank vessels" and yet still held "her own." Only with darkness did the firing cease.[48]

All through the afternoon Goldsborough's fleet also exchanged shots with Commodore Lynch's gunboats. Around four o'clock, a shot from the Federal flagship *Southfield* struck the hurricane deck of the *Curlew* and went through her decks and bottom as if they were paper. When the captain of the *Curlew,* Commander Thomas T. Hunter, realized that his vessel was sinking, he headed for shore with the intention of grounding her. He was successful in this operation but in so doing went aground in front of Fort Forrest, completely masking its guns.

Commodore Hunter, it seems, was a very excitable person; his friends called him "Tornado." After the battle he admitted to his friend, Lieutenant Parker, that during the fight "he found to his surprise that he had no trousers on." To this Parker replied that he had heard of men being frightened out of their boots, but never out of their trousers.[49]

The *Forrest* was hit, along with the *Curlew,* and forced to retire, but the remaining vessels of the "mosquito fleet" continued in action until they exhausted their ammunition and had to move back up the sound.[50]

Meanwhile the passage of the Federal transports through the narrow channel of the Roanoke Marshes* had been a slow process, and it was not until midafternoon that the last one came to anchor well out of ricochet range of the Confederate guns.† Preparations were immediately made to disembark the troops, as a landing site at Ashby's Harbor, some three miles below Fort Bartow, had already been selected by General

* A series of low islands stretching from the lower end of Roanoke Island to the mainland were known as the "Roanoke Marshes." Today they have for the most part washed away. David Stick, *The Outer Banks of North Carolina* (Chapel Hill: Univ. of N.C. Press, 1958), p. 136.
† One of the Federal ships went aground in passing through the "Marshes."

Burnside. Around noon the General had sent his topographical engineer, Lieutenant W. S. Andrews, in a small boat into the harbor to take soundings and inspect the shoreline. The Lieutenant had with him a six-man squad of soldiers and a Negro boy named Thomas R. Robinson, who had formerly lived on Roanoke Island. Ashore, screened by the dense undergrowth and trees, two hundred of the enemy under Colonel J. V. Jordan awaited them. But for some unknown reason Jordon did not bestir himself until after the Federals had sounded the harbor and actually set foot on the shore, and then it was too late. Andrews made his escape and rowed back out to Burnside with valuable information. His cool competence earned special commendation in the General's report.[51]

Convinced that there was sufficient water available for the approach, Burnside gave the order for the troops to disembark. In light marching order, the men climbed into the surfboats and barges drawn up alongside the transports. The small boats then milled about until they were in precise order to present brigade front immediately upon being put ashore. As each brigade was ready, a light-draft steamer took it in tow and headed for the beach under a full head of steam.[52] After viewing this scene, General Burnside remarked: "I never witnessed a more beautiful sight . . . as the steamers approached the shore at a rapid speed each surfboat was 'let go' and with their acquired velocity and by direction of the steersman reached the shore in line."[53] Henry C. Pardee of the Tenth Connecticut rode in to shore in one of approximately fifty small boats* attached in two lines to the stern of the *Pilot Boy*. He wrote his father that the steamer took them to within about fifty feet of the shore "when the seaman who had been selected rowed smartly to the shore and we jumped on to marshy land where the water and mud was up to our knees, formed in line and marched up to dry ground and to the side of a deserted house where we halted and remained in line for some time. . . ." In the meantime gunboats had come in close, Pardee said, and fired "at a body of Rebels, whose bayonets we could see in the woods a little distance from our landing place although their body's was hid by the high underbrush and the way they scattered was a caution."[54]

Without even firing one shot Colonel Jordon retired. This foolish

---

* Pardee was mistaken in the number of surf boats towed in by each steamer. The number was nearer twenty than fifty. *OR,* IX, Ser. I, 76.

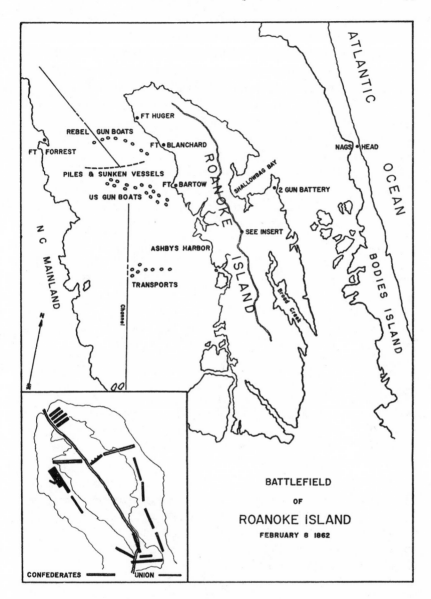

ATLANTIC OCEAN

FT HUGER

REBEL GUN BOATS

FT FORREST

FT BLANCHARD

NAGS HEAD

PILES & SUNKEN VESSELS

FT BARTOW

US GUN BOATS

SHALLOWBAG BAY

2 GUN BATTERY

N C MAINLAND

ROANOKE ISLAND

SEE INSERT

ASHBYS HARBOR

Broad Creek

BODIES ISLAND

Channel

TRANSPORTS

N

BATTLEFIELD

OF

ROANOKE ISLAND

FEBRUARY 8 1862

CONFEDERATES ——— UNION ———

move enabled a six-gun battery and four thousand of the enemy, packed into some sixty-five boats, to land unopposed. No one would seriously argue that Jordon could have prevented the landing, but with two hundred men and two pieces of artillery he could have made the occasion an interesting one, to say the least, for the Federals.[55]*

By midnight, "some 10,000" of Burnside's troops were bivouaced at Ashby's Harbor.† Having come ashore in light marching order, the men did not have any blankets. They kept warm by huddling around "fires built of rails," and with the break of day were ready to move against the island's defensive positions.[56]

The morning was cold and dreary, still the troops moved out in good order. General Foster's brigade was first to move, with the Twenty-fifth Massachusetts in the advance, followed by Midshipman B. H. Porter's six-gun battery. Confederate pickets gave way before their advance, retiring to the redoubt in the center of the island "which, from information received . . . [the Federals] had been led to suppose was there. . . ."[57]

The Confederate line was constructed at the narrowest point on the island and across its only north-south road.‡ "The engineers who laid off the line, the scouts who tried to penetrate their jungles, and the natives who were questioned, all united in pronouncing the vine tangled cypress swamp on the right and left of the works as absolutely impenetrable."[58] A three-gun battery controlled the causeway road as well as several hundred yards of cleared area on either side. Trees were left where they were felled, their branches sharpened above and below the waters. In view of the defensive strength of this position the 400 men in the breastworks and 1,050 in reserve were thought by Colonel Shaw to be sufficient to hold the works.[59] As long as the line could be maintained, the forts, whose guns bore only on the water front, were protected; if this line gave way, then all the defenses were open in reverse.

The fight for this vital position began around eight o'clock. Foster, under orders to make a frontal attack along the causeway, put his artil-

* Colonel Jordan in his official report gives the following reasons for his withdrawal: "Having no horses for our artillery, fearing that we might be cut off, or at least that the shells from the enemy's guns in the sound might confuse and disconcert the men under my command and cause the eventual loss of the field pieces . . . I considered it judicious to retreat." *OR*, IX, Ser. I, 176.

† After the first wave Burnside's organizational work must have stopped. While it took only twenty minutes to land four thousand men and Midshipmen B. H. Porter's battery, it took several hours to get the remainder of the force (around six thousand men) ashore. Daly, "Burnside's Amphibious Division," p. 37; *NR*, VI, Ser. I, 553.

‡ General D. H. Hill, while commander of the defenses between Albemarle Sound and the Neuse River, had recommended that the fortifications be extended through the swamps. Had this been done, the Battle of Roanoke Island might have turned out differently. Hill, *Bethel to Sharpsburg*, I, 205-6.

lery in position and then gave word for the Twenty-fifth Massachusetts to advance.* Lying down to load their rifles and then standing up to fire, the New Englanders inched their way forward.[60] It was slow, tortuous going. There was no place to hide from either the battery or musket fire of the enemy. Realizing that his advance stood little chance of carrying the Confederate position, Foster directed the Twenty-third Massachusetts, followed by the Twenty-seventh Massachusetts, to plunge into the morass on their right "and endeavor to turn the enemy's left."[61] The water in the swamp was knee deep everywhere and waist deep in spots, and the bushes and briars were so thick that "only one man could pass at a time."[62] As these two regiments pushed into the swamp, the Tenth Connecticut was brought up to relieve the Twenty-fifth Massachusetts which "had expended its ammunition and suffered considerable loss." Porter's battery was also running low on ammunition and had experienced some casualties; so Foster ordered its fire to cease.[63]

At this time General Reno arrived with his brigade. He informed Foster that "he would try to penetrate the dense wood to the left and thus turn . . . [the Confederate] right flank. . . ."[64] With the Twenty-first Massachusetts, Fifty-first New York, and Ninth New Jersey regiments, General Reno struck into the swamp, which one of his men called "worse than the Ever Glades of Florida, where we were half the time to our knees in mud and water."[65]

Around 11:30 A.M., the Ninth New York (Hawkins' Zouaves), followed by the Twenty-fourth Massachusetts, came on the field. General Foster immediately ordered the Zouaves, who were in the woods to the rear of the Tenth Connecticut, "to charge down the road into the guns of the enemy and drive them from their works." The soldiers of the Tenth Connecticut lay down, and over their heads the New Yorkers "went, running and yelling like deamons . . . but when they had got about half way there (the distance being about 400 yards) the enemy had left. . . ."[66]

The flamboyant colonel of the Ninth New York, Rush C. Hawkins, always maintained that it was the heroic charge of his regiment that broke the Confederate line, but many people disputed this claim. The Confederate retreat, said General Foster, definitely was not brought on by the charge of the New York Zouaves, "for General Reno had at this

* The colonel of the regiment told his men that "Now that . . . [they could] smell powarder be cool and give them some," O. Taft to Parents, Feb. 13, 1862, Edwin and Orison Taft Papers, DU.

The Ninth New York (Hawkins' Zouaves) and the Twenty-first Massachusetts
storming the Confederate field work on Roanoke Island, February 8, 1862.
(From *The Illustrated London News*)

time turned the enemy's right and was firing into the rear of their
battery and charging at the same time into them. The Twenty-third
Massachusetts . . . sent to turn the enemy's left, had also made its appearance on the other flank."[67]

Marcus Emmons of the Twenty-first Massachusetts, who had strug-
gled through the swamp on the Confederate right flank, was in complete
agreement with General Foster's contention that the Zouaves had not
routed the enemy. Emmons said when the "rebels" heard his colonel,
Alberto C. Maggie, give the order "forward to charge . . . the way they
the Confederates run want slow, the victory was ours the boys rushed
through the water to the battery shouting throwing up their caps and
waving the Stars and Stripes."[68] "Then," added another member of
this Massachusetts regiment, "with our two flags in plain sight upon the
parapet, the fort full of our men, and the last running rebel well out
of sight, the 9th New York [Hawkins' Zouaves] came running up the
narrow corduroy road by the flank, and with a great shout of 'Zou Zou'
swarmed into the battery for all the world as if they were capturing
it."[69]*

* Charles A. Barker, who entered the Confederate battery from the other flank,

The moment the redoubt was flanked, Colonel Shaw considered Roanoke Island lost.[70] With him it was simply a matter of when and where the surrender would take place. The troops in the redoubt retreated up the causeway toward the north end of the island with the Federals in close pursuit. There was one brief encounter when a few of the retiring troops took up a temporary position along the causeway and fired into their pursuers. Then the retreat was resumed. Already messengers were hurrying to the other commands on the island with orders to spike guns, blow up magazines, and retreat to their quarters.

The men at the various batteries were now faced with the "Awful! Awful! Awful!" realization that they were "overpowered" and would have to surrender. Cartridges were thrown in the sand, guns spiked, implements destroyed, and a quick march back to quarters was commenced. When the troops of the Eighth North Carolina reached their camp, they found a white flag flying from Colonel Shaw's tent.[71] The meaning was clear. The fight was over for them.

Earlier in the day, when the cause appeared hopeless, Shaw had sent Lieutenant Colonel Daniel G. Fowle under a flag of truce to ask for terms. At the Federal lines, Fowle was directed to General Foster who stated that "none but those of unconditional surrender" would be acceptable and "that immediately." Major R. H. Stevenson was then detailed by Foster to accompany the flag of truce "back for Colonel Shaw's answer."

Stevenson and the Confederate Colonel found Shaw seated in front of a fire smoking a pipe. Hundreds of soldiers were milling about and

observed a few days after the battle that "they [Hawkins' Zouaves] will probably get most of the credit for the victory, being New York troops, and the illustration papers will I suppose show them up well but the rebels say they didn't fear the Zouaves so much as they did the blue overcoats coming out of the woods." C. A. Barker to "Dear Folks," Feb. 14, 1862, C. A. Barker Papers, EI. Barker's observations proved to be correct. Colonel Hawkins wrote a widely publicized article describing the heroic role of his regiment in breaking the Confederate line. See articles by William L. Welch in Washington *National Tribune*, 1886-87 (Newspaper clippings), Roanoke Island file, NCC. The correspondence of the North Carolina troops in the line reveal that the two flanking movements, not the frontal assault, brought about their withdrawal. *Ibid.* Writing immediately after the battle Hawkins had this to say about the charge of the Ninth New York: "After leading my regiment into a marsh immediately in front of the enemy's entrenchments amidst a steady fire from the enemy of grape and musketry, the order was given to charge the enemy with fixed bayonets. This was done in gallant style, Major Kimball taking the lead—the enemy's works were soon carried and abandoned. All of the officers and men of the Regiment behaved with gallantry and bravery." R. C. Hawkins to J. G. Parke, Feb. 9, 1862, R. C. Hawkins Papers, BU.

"around the door of Head-Quarters was a crowd of officers with very glum countenances." Upon the receipt of Foster's terms, Shaw stood up, gazed into the fire for some moments, then turning around said, "I must surrender," and asked Major Stevenson whether he would re- ceive his sword. The youthful Major replied: "No Sir; General Foster will be here in a very short time to receive it in person," which he did.[72] That night at 9:00 P.M. the Federal fleet at anchor in the sound was signaled that Roanoke Island had fallen and that the Stars and Stripes floated over every battery.[73]

In the aftermath of battle, some of Shaw's troops unsuccessfully tried to escape* in small boats to Nags Head.[74] The next day the Ninth New York was sent there to capture General Wise, but the sick General had long since departed up the Banks.[75]

Losses were not heavy on either side in the Battle of Roanoke Island. Union sources list 37 killed, 214 wounded, and 13 missing;[76] Con- federate casualties were put at 23 killed, 58 wounded, and 62 missing, with approximately 2500 captured.[77]†

Federal military commanders considered the Roanoke Island opera- tions unusually successful. Valuable practice had been gained in making an amphibious landing and lessons were available for review and im- provement. Logistically Burnside had done his job well, but tactically he was weak. His success in the field could be attributed more to his over- whelming numbers, poor Confederate defenses, and three able lieu- tenants than to his thorough planning.[78]

Now that Roanoke Island was in his possession General Burnside could move against the North Carolina mainland. But to gain "absolute control" of the intervening sounds, the Confederate "mosquito fleet"

---

* A few of the men escaped by hiding in the woods. At night they made their way to the beach, seized a boat, and made their way to the mainland. *Harper's Weekly* quoting the Richmond *Dispatch*, Feb. 14, 1862, Extract from *Harper's Weekly*, Folder on Burnside Expedition, NCC.

† Among the troops captured were those belonging to a Confederate relief detachment that had landed on the north end of the island in the morning. E. M. Cox Memorandum Book, [n.d.], UVa. One of those killed was General Wise's son. D. L. Craft to Sister, Feb. [?], 1862, D. L. Craft Papers, DU. The Confederates fought not only with every conceivable type of weapon, but they were attired in everything from the smart uniforms of the "Richmond Blues" to "all sorts of clothes." D. R. Larned to Aunt, Mar. 8, 1862, D. R. Larned Papers, LC; Extracts from *Harper's Weekly*, Folder on Burnside Expedition, NCC; R. C. Hawkins to J. G. Parke, Feb. 9, 1862, R. C. Hawkins Papers, BU; A. S. Roe, *The Twenty-fourth Regiment Massachusetts Volunteers, 1861-1866* (Worcester: Twenty- fourth Veteran's Association, 1907), pp. 63-64; W. F. Draper, *Recollections of a Varied Career* (Boston: Little, Brown and Co., 1908), p. 58.

had to be destroyed first. After expending all of their ammunition in the naval battle of February 8, these small vessels had retired to Elizabeth City, which lay twelve miles up the Pasquotank River from Albemarle Sound and was connected with Norfolk by the Dismal Swamp Canal. Here Commodore Lynch found very little ammunition for his gunboats. So on the ninth he dispatched the *Raleigh* to Norfolk for supplies and, with the *Seabird* and *Appomattox,* started back to Roanoke Island. At the mouth of the river the Commodore learned that the island had fallen but, hoping to rescue the men on the "Croatan floating battery," he continued on. The *Appomattox* and the *Seabird* had gone only a short distance when an enemy flotilla of thirteen ships was seen on the horizon heading straight for the river. Reversing course, the two Confederate vessels hurried back to Elizabeth City.

With battle now imminent, Commodore Lynch made preparations to defend the city. He took the schooner *Black Warrior,* which had been converted into a gunboat for the defense of the town, and moored her across the river from Cobb's Point where a fort had been erected. A short distance up the river from Cobb's Point the gunboats *Seabird, Ellis, Appomattox, Beaufort,* and the tug *Fanny* were lined up from bank to bank so as to obstruct the channel. Negro labor was brought in to work on the defenses and an urgent request for troops was sent to Colonel C. F. Henningsen who, with a small detachment of men, had been in the area since about February 8. After much wrangling with local authorities, the Colonel got the militia called up, but only a handful of men answered the muster.[79]

At 8:06 P.M. on February 9, the Federal flotilla, which had been sighted earlier in the day by Commodore Lynch, dropped anchor in Pasquotank River ten miles below Cobb's Point. Later in the evening the ships' captains went aboard Commander Stephen Rowan's flagship to receive instructions for the next day's engagement. They were told that an inadequate supply of ammunition precluded a heavy bombardment of the fort. Their orders were to "economize ammunition" by running the enemy down and engaging "him hand to hand."[80]

Shortly after daylight on the tenth, Confederate lookouts reported enemy vessels coming up the river. When Commodore Lynch received this word, he decided to go ashore and make a last minute inspection of the fort at Cobb's Point. He found a "wretchedly constructed affair" mounting a four-gun battery. The guns were good enough but poorly

Destruction of Commodore Lynch's "mosquito fleet" by Union gunboats, Elizabeth City, February 10, 1862. (From *Harper's Weekly*)

mounted. Only one was trained to fire across the river, the others down the channel. Even more disturbing was the fact that the garrison consisted of a civilian, a Mr. Hinrick, and only seven militiamen. Since the battery was Lynch's "principal reliance," and the enemy had to pass it before reaching the gunboats, the Commodore decided to "defend the fort in person and sent for Lieutenant Commander Parker, of the *Beaufort,* to bring on shore his ammunition, officers, and crew, leaving only sufficient of the latter to take that vessel up the canal." After reading the Commodore's dispatch, Parker exclaimed: "Where the devil are the men who were in the fort?" The messenger's laconic reply, "All run away," did not satisfy the Lieutenant, but he had no choice but to obey the order.[81]

When the Federal ships came within "long range," the fort and the *Black Warrior* opened fire but inflicted little or no damage. Contrary to Commodore Lynch's expectations, the enemy vessels did not return the fire until they were within three-quarters of a mile of the fort. Then Commander Rowan gave the signal to "dash the enemy." Engineers aboard the Yankee ships pushed throttles wide open and guns flashed for the first time. The *Black Warrior* was disabled and set on fire by her crew who jumped overboard and escaped. The militiamen in the fort deserted, leaving only two guns manned, and these became useless as soon as the Federal column passed the fort. These pieces could not be brought to bear up the river. At this point Lieutenant Parker ordered the guns spiked, the flag lowered, and the fort abandoned. All the while Commodore Lynch stood silently by watching his vessels "destroyed under his eyes."

As the flotillas collided, the *Commodore Perry* rammed the *Seabird*, sinking her.* The *Ellis* was boarded by bluejackets from the *Ceres*. Lieutenant J. W. Cooke of the *Ellis* ordered his crew over the side while he remained aboard with cutlass in hand to meet the enemy. The *Fanny*, aflame, was run aground by her crew and abandoned. Only the *Appomattox* and the *Beaufort*, which was not engaged, escaped up the river. The *Beaufort* made it safely to Norfolk but the *Appomattox* had to be destroyed by her captain when it was discovered that she was "about two inches too wide to enter the mouth" of the Dismal Swamp Canal. The *Forrest*, on the ways at Elizabeth City, was burned at Commodore Lynch's orders.[82]

Commander Rowan, having disposed of the "mosquito fleet," pushed his ships toward Elizabeth City where flames could be seen leaping skyward. "To spite the Yankees" some of the local citizens had set fire to their property. As a result, two city blocks and several buildings on the outskirts of town were aflame when the Union sailors disembarked.†After pushing their way through a large crowd of jubilant Negroes at the wharves, the bluejackets rushed through deserted streets in search of retreating Confederates.

Elizabeth City was a "dead town . . . dead as a graveyard," the inhabitants having fled "in great panic." By the time the Federals arrived, most of them were "on the road," which already was crowded with militiamen "flying before an unseen enemy . . . and minding not the

* When the *Commodore Perry* and the *Seabird* collided, the anchor-fastening on the Union vessel gave way, thus anchoring both ships. The Federal bluejackets became so excited that it was ten minutes before Captain C. W. Flusser of the *Seabird* could get anyone to unshackle the chain. C. W. Flusser to Mother, [n.d.], quoted in S. A. Ashe, "End of North Carolina Navy" (unpublished article), NCC.

† Commander Rowan charged that many of the fires were started by a Lieutenant Scruggs of Wise's Legion under orders from Colonel Henningsen. *NR*, VI, Ser. I, 608. Colonel Henningsen did detach a Sergeant Scroggs "with a detail, to aid the citizens in destroying the place by fire, as I [Henningsen] had been requested to do so by some of the most prominent of them." *OR*, IX, Ser. I, 192. The Federal soldiers fought the fires. Traver, *Battles of Roanoke Island and Elizabeth City*, p. 28.

order of their going." Looking for "asylum in the country," the citizens, "a'foot, shoe tops deep in mud and stuck," were a "muddy, bedraggled, unhappy, wretched" lot.[83]

Back in Elizabeth City the commissary storehouse, at Commander Rowan's orders, was being emptied of "fresh beef, bread and flour." Engineers busied themselves with the task of destroying machinery, boilers, and railroad track, while a detachment of sailors blew up the fort at Cobb's Point.[84]

On February 11, Rowan dispatched Lieutenant A. Murray with a small naval force consisting of the *Louisiana, Underwriter, Commodore Perry,* and *Lockwood* to Edenton. The Lieutenant's orders were to make a reconnaissance and "if he found no fort there to communicate with the authorities and destroy all the public property, but scrupulously to respect that belonging to private individuals."[85] By 8:30 A.M. of the twelfth, the Federal vessels were off from the entrance to Edenton harbor.[86] When Captain G. W. Graves of the *Lockwood* stepped onto the wharf, he was met by James Norcum who introduced himself as a "Union man delegated by the citizens to meet the Federal authorities."[87] Before taking Norcum to Lieutenant Murray, Graves had his men roll several bales of cotton aboard and place them around the ship's boilers for protection.[88] Norcum informed Lieutenant Murray that, upon the arrival of the fleet, parts of two Confederate companies had departed and that the town was undefended except for several antiquated cannons sitting behind the courthouse.[89]* After spiking the cannon, burning a schooner on the stocks, and procuring a few eggs and poultry (which, incidentally, they said "they would return,") the Federals departed.[90]

Soon after Lieutenant Murray's expedition returned from Edenton, Commander Rowan dispatched five vessels "with prize schooners in tow to obstruct the Chesapeake and Albemarle canal." Lieutenant William N. Jeffers was given the immediate task of placing the barriers. Upon reaching the mouth of the canal on the thirteenth, he found that the Confederates had already done his job. But to close the waterway to even the smallest vessels, he sank, "diagonally athwart the canal," a

* At one time these old cannons had been in place behind some earthworks at the foot of the green, but the citizens had objected on the grounds that they were no protection and would only bring on a bombardment. Therefore they were placed behind the courthouse. Mischievous boys would roll them out at night only to have the constable return them to their "hiding" place in the morning. R. Dillard, *The Civil War in Chowan County, North Carolina* (Edenton: Privately Printed, 1916), pp. 27-28.

large dredging machine deserted by the enemy.[91] The completion of this assignment closed out a highly successful week for the Federal forces in North Carolina. In a matter of seven days, the Burnside-Goldsborough command had captured Roanoke Island, occupied two coastal towns, blocked up a vital canal, and destroyed the Confederate navy in the sounds.

In North Carolina the alarm bell sounded. "To arms! To arms!" cried the *North Carolina Standard*.[92] This appeal was heeded, for on February 17 Governor Clark was pleased to announce that the invasion of the state had "infused quite a spirit of volunteering for the war. Within the last two days seven companies have tendered themselves," he said, "and I hear of many more recruiting successfully."[93] Captain William L. Saunders, on recruiting duty in the western part of the state, thought the disasters would "show our determination not to be conquered and not to yield. . . ."[94]* With Caroline Pettigrew of Bonarva Plantation it was "resist to the death . . . even the women."[95]

But patriotic utterances and a rush to the colors could lighten very little the "gloom cast overall" by these defeats.[96] Catherine Devereux Edmondston, at her plantation in Halifax County, "fairly burst into tears" when the mail brought the news of the fall of Roanoke Island.[97] A North Carolina soldier in Virginia, who wanted to see his wife and daughter "more than anything in this world," wrote home that it was not in his power to "git [a] furlow now for the Yankys has tuck Roanoke Island and killed and tuck all of gen Wises Leagion and tuck them priseners all B 7 they got out of the way. . . ."[98] Joseph H. Saunders, stationed at Camp Branch, North Carolina, did not find the island's loss such a personal matter. To him it was a "terrible blow to . . . (the Confederate) cause." He realized that it opened up a "large extent of country" to the enemy.[99] Echoing Saunder's sentiments, the *Richmond Examiner* called "the loss of an entire army at Roanoke Island . . . certainly the most painful event of the war."[100] The editor thought "the Roanoke affair . . . perfectly incomprehensible. The news-

---

* Even though Saunders thought the Roanoke Island defeat would strengthen the South's will to fight, he was disturbed over the fact that the Virginia papers charged the Thirty-first North Carolina with breaking ranks and running. He wrote: "I think the matter has gone about far enough and am heartily tired and disgusted with Virginia and her bragging people. There seems to me to be an ordered design on the part of the Virginian's to slander and abuse our state and for one I am tired of it. For one I would be glad if the Mother of presidents was in the United States. I would be glad for the line to run between Virginia and North Carolina but I have no patience on the subject." W. L. Saunders to Mother, Feb. 14, 1862, W. L. Saunders Papers, SHC.

papers are filled," he wrote, "with extravagant laudations of our valor; the annals of Greece and Rome offer no parallel. Whole regiments were defeated by companies, and we yield only to death. [Yet] our men finally surrender 'with no blood on their bayonets.' "[101] A lady in eastern North Carolina, on the other hand, thought the disaster quite comprehensible. It was the result, she said, of "mismanagement that looks like treachery. . . ." She added that Colonel Shaw was disliked by his men, some even cursing him to his face, and that General Huger's drinking often made him "entirely unfit for business."[102] Not only were the General and the Colonel under fire but also the Governor. The convention, meeting in secret session at Raleigh, discussed the Roanoke Island calamity and the "total incapacity of . . . Governor Clark."[103] At Richmond the Confederate Congress established a committee to investigate and report on the circumstances connected with the surrender of the island.[104]

In Washington, however, the success of the Federal expedition was hailed in all quarters. For Lincoln the winter of 1861-62 had been most discouraging, characterized by military inaction and public despondency. The only welcome news during this period had come out of the West where Major General U. S. Grant had captured Forts Donelson and Henry. In the East, McClellan's cautiousness did little to arouse public enthusiasm. Thus Burnside's victories in eastern North Carolina were joyously received. Victory salutes were fired in the principal northern cities and congratulatory letters were sent to Burnside and Admiral Goldsborough by the President, other high-ranking public officials, and different state legislative bodies. The General Assembly of Rhode Island voted its thanks to Burnside, an adopted son, and then presented him with a sword.[105] The General, wisely, did not rest on his laurels. His orders were to occupy New Bern, the second largest city on the North Carolina coast. As soon as affairs on Roanoke Island could be put in order and the necessary preparations for a new expedition made, it was his intention to proceed at once to the mainland. Approximately a month elapsed before he was ready to get .the New Bern expedition underway. This was a busy thirty-day period for General Burnside, and one of his most pressing problems was the disposition of the more than two thousand Confederate prisoners taken in the Battle of Roanoke Island.* The General finally decided to parole the men when it became

* The prisoners were quite well treated even though some were haughty and acted

evident that transports could not be spared to take them north. It was out of the question to imprison such a large number of soldiers on the island. Had this been done, it would have tied down too many Federal troops. Therefore, on February 20, the prisoners were transported to Elizabeth City and there released.[106]

Burnside enjoyed administering the oath of allegiance to many of the inhabitants on Roanoke Island,* but dealing with the large number of runaway slaves that had made their way across the sound was another matter. The appearance of a Federal fleet in North Carolina waters had caused a considerable number of whites in the eastern part of the state to seek refuge in the interior. At the same time many slaves slipped away to freedom behind the Federal lines.[107] They arrived on Roanoke Island in such large numbers that the General appointed Vincent Colyer (a New York artist) Superintendent of the Poor in the North Carolina Department.[108]

"I commenced my work with the freed people of color, in North Carolina, at Roanoke Island, soon after the battle of the 8th of February, 1862," he reported. "A party of fifteen or twenty of these loyal blacks, men, women and children, arrived on a 'Dingy' in front of the General's Head Quarters, where my tent was located. They came from up the Chowan River. . . ."

Immediately upon their arrival on the island the able-bodied Negro men were offered manual jobs at $8.00 a month and one ration of clothes. By late spring of 1862 there were probably one thousand contrabands in the area.[109]†

Before striking the North Carolina mainland, Burnside and Admiral

---

"like anything but gentlemen." A Federal soldier observed that the Virginia soldiers "talk hard of the North and would go to fighting again if exchanged, but the North Carolina men are as contented as they could wish." There was "much shaking of hands and many goodbys" between the prisoners and their captors on February 20. H. C. Pardee to Father, Feb. 20, 1862, H. C. Pardee Papers, DU; S. H. Putnam, *The Story of Company A, Twenty-fifth Regiment, Massachusetts Volunteers in the War of the Rebellion* (Worcester: Putnam, Davis and Co., 1886), p. 90; Roe, *24 Mass.*, pp. 63-64; C. H. Andrews to Wife, Feb. 23, 1862, C. H. Andrews Papers, SHC.

* Much to the joy of a captured lieutenant of the Eighth North Carolina "the Yankees killed every cow and hog on the Island. I say much to my joy for these miserable traitorous scoundrels on the Island have betrayed us, many acting as Pilots and . . . for months past have been importing knowledge to the Yankees." J. W. Wright Diary, Feb. 9, 1862, Murdock-Wright Papers, SHC.

† Before the war ended Roanoke Island was dotted with Negro settlements. Each family usually had a wooden hut and a garden. J. Schafer, ed., "Intimate Letters of Carl Schurz, 1841-1869," *Publications of the State Historical Society of Wisconsin* (Madison: State Historical Society of Wisconsin, 1928), p. 328.

Goldsborough decided to "sweep Albemarle Sound clean of defenses."[110] In carrying out this plan, they provided for expeditions to dash against any coastal points thought to be armed. Light draft gunboats, carrying infantry, were detailed for these swift blows.[111] Elizabeth City was visited again but suffered little at the hands of the Federals.[112] Winton, a village of three hundred people located up the Chowan River, did not fare so well.[113] On February 18, an expedition of eight gunboats under Commander Rowan started for this small village. Aboard the vessels were approximately one thousand men of Colonel Hawkins' Ninth New York Zouaves and elements of the Fourth Rhode Island Infantry. The purpose of this expedition was to destroy two railroad bridges above Winton and to investigate the rumors of strong Unionist sentiment in the area. By the morning of the nineteenth, the gunboats had entered the mouth of the Chowan* and were proceeding leisurely toward Winton.[114]

With the fall of Roanoke Island, Winton had "taken on significance as a possible base for Union operations in the direction of either Weldon, a key rail junction, or Norfolk." To handle any such moves several militia companies, Lieutenant Colonel William T. Williams' First Battalion of North Carolina Volunteers and a four-gun battery commanded by Captain J. N. Nichols, were rushed to Winton by Confederate authorities. Colonel Williams placed his troops behind the trees and brush at the top of a bluff overlooking the river. (Winton was situated behind the bluff.) By this move the Colonel hoped to give the impression that the town was undefended and thus lure the gunboats up to the Winton wharf "where they would not only be unable to train their artillery on the hill but would be helpless under the Confederate fire." A mulatto named Martha Keen agreed "for a price" to go down to the wharf and try to signal to the "Yankees" that it was safe to dock.

At 4:00 P.M. a Federal gunboat was sighted rounding the bend in the river about a mile below Winton. So spread out were the Federal vessels that the *Delaware*, Commander Rowan's flagship, was all alone when she slowed down and swung to starboard toward the town wharf. Martha Keen stood on the shore waving a piece of cloth as if to assure Commander Rowan "that no danger need be apprehended." When the *Delaware* was within 350 yards of the wharf, Colonel Hawkins, who

---

* Around 2:00 P.M. the fleet passed Coleraine where the wharf was on fire, having been set by "the Southerners themselves." T. C. Parramore, "Burning of Winton," Ahoskie *Daily Roanoke-Chowan News,* Civil War Supplement, 1960, p. 74.

was in the "crosstrees of the main mast," discovered "the glistening of many musket-barrels among the short shrubs that covered the high bank, and farther back two pieces of artillery in position." The Colonel shouted several times to the astonished native pilot at the helm, "Ring on, sheer off, rebels on shore!" At the last moment he changed course, missing the wharf by a mere ten feet.[115] As Hawkins scrambled down from his lofty perch,* the Confederates opened fire with rifles and artillery. The *Delaware* was "pierced like a sieve"[116] by whole volleys of musket fire† but somehow managed to get out into midstream and up past the town. When safely beyond the range of Confederate fire, Commander Rowan turned his large guns on the bluff, causing Captain Nichol's artillerymen to scatter in all directions.[117]

With the Confederate artillery temporarily silenced and aided by the *Commodore Perry* which had come upon the scene, the *Delaware* ran back by the town and escaped downstream. Joined by the other ships in his flotilla, Commander Rowan anchored for the night about seven miles below Winton. During the evening plans were made for a second trip up the river.[118]

In Winton, following a victory celebration, the citizens and soldiers settled down for their first peaceful night's rest in days. But the next morning before many of them had had breakfast, word was received that the gunboats were heading upstream full throttle.[119] Colonel Williams reacted to this news by hightailing it with his small force to the breastworks at Mt. Tabor Church several miles away on Potecasi Creek.‡ At 10:20 A.M. the Union gunboats began to shell the evacuated Con-

---

* Hawkins made it to the deck in such haste that the Confederates reported a lookout in the rigging of one ship fell "persumed dead." H. K. Burgwyn to H. T. Clark, Feb. 22, 1862, H. T. Clark Papers, NCDAH.

† The artillery overshot its mark. *NR*, VI, Ser. I, 654.

‡ It is still a mystery why Colonel Williams did not return to Winton when it became evident that the Federals were not going to advance on his position at Mt. Tabor Church, "unless one prefers to believe simply that courage was not Williams' strongest virtue." Parramore, "Burning of Winton," p. 77. In a letter to Governor Clark, Lieutenant Colonel Henry K. Burgwyn, who was very critical of Confederate leadership at Winton, quotes the lieutenant of a scouting party. The lieutenant thought "the whole affair was badly managed as was to be expected from being under the command of an inexperienced young man of 21 yrs. who had not even a military reputation." Burgwyn, only twenty years old himself, but a graduate of the Virginia Military Institute, seemed to agree with the lieutenant. The youthful Colonel also criticized Captain Nichols for not having his pieces "in position to fire on the enemy. . . . They [the Federals] could have been greatly damaged from a secure position, as the cliff was so steep, their shells must have passed over." H. K. Burgwyn to H. T. Clark, Feb. 22, 1862, H. T. Clark Papers. NCDAH.

federate positions at Winton.* When Commander Rowan was satisfied that the town was no longer defended, the firing ceased and small boats with the Ninth New York headed for shore.

The Zouaves charged up the steep hill into Winton's main street, only to find the town deserted except for a few people. Scouting parties were sent out in several directions, and cannons were placed so as to control the approaches to the town. Colonel Hawkins then made a personal inspection of the buildings in Winton. Concluding that most of them had been used by the Confederates for storage or quarters, he ordered them burned.[120]

After barrels of tar had been rolled into the condemned buildings and set ablaze, the soldiers proceeded to pillage the town.[121] Private Byron G. Still wrote his mother that "court houses, churches, beautifully furnished dwellings with velvet carpets, pianos, etc., all sharing the same fate, and you may be sure that we gave it a pretty good ransacking while the flames were doing their work."[122]

Colonel Hawkins in his official report regretted the burning of Winton, but justified it "upon two grounds—first retaliation for trying to decoy us into a trap at the time of the firing into the Delaware. Second, the buildings fired had been taken possession of and were in the use of the rebel forces as store-houses and quarters. . . ."[123]

The Northern press carried glowing and lengthy accounts of the Winton affair. The editor of the New York *Herald* simply refused to believe that the "act of vandalism," as he termed it, was done other than by the Confederates themselves.[124] The editor of the *North Carolina Standard,* however, knew better. In the March 12 issue of his paper, he printed a letter in which a Winton resident described the pillaging of the town. "After such a statement," the editor questioned, "what confidence can anyone have in the pretenses of Burnside and Goldsborough, as to their designs not to disturb private property?"[125] Other North Carolinians, doubtless, were asking the same question.† Only two days

---

* This bombardment was heard as far away as Gatesville. The cannonading "was so distinct," wrote a young girl to her brother, "it seem to [be] right upon us, and one of the Pickets came in at full speed saying they have landed at the Ferry in large numbers and were making [their way] up the road. It was a public day some four or five hundred men being in the village. Such consternation, such panic as was created you cannot immagine. The women were more composed. . . . Really John we all thought we women make the better soldiers." Sister to "My Dear John," March [?], 1862, Benbury-Haywood Papers, SHC.

† A soldier at Camp Branch had this to say about the actions of the Federals: "The damned white livered Yankees are committing all kinds of depredations on the property

before Winton was leveled, these two Federal officers had issued a proclamation stating that "the Northern people were Christians and would
inflict no injury unless forced to do so."[126]

Columbia, a small village in Tyrrell County, also felt the "Christian"
wrath of Burnside's soldiers, but to a lesser degree than Winton. In
early March, six companies of the Sixth New Hampshire were sent to
Columbia in search of a Confederate regiment said to be recruiting in
the area.[127] No Confederates were found, but a rumor that the local
militia was to be called out was used by the New Englanders as reason
enough to plunder the town.[128] To the delight of the Negroes, the
whipping post was torn down.[129] Then the soldiers broke open the
jail, clerk's office, "and the Dwelling Houses of such as were gone from
home." In the abandoned homes the soldiers partook freely of available
liquor supplies which made "them ripe for more mischief." The ransacking of at least one more home and the depleting of all smokehouses
followed.[130]

By the time the Sixth New Hampshire got back to Roanoke Island,
General Burnside was just about ready to shove off for New Bern. But
these troops were not to be a part of the expedition. Along with the
Ninth and Eighty-ninth New York, they were formed into a new
brigade under Colonel Hawkins and given garrison duty on the island.
The formation of this brigade culminated Burnside's preparations for
the New Bern expedition.[131]

PART 2

NEW BERN

Across the sound at New Bern, Confederate General L. O'B. Branch
had approximately four thousand untried troops, not nearly enough to
man the elaborate set of defenses below the city.[132] Since most of these
fortifications had been constructed before Branch's arrival in November,
1861, he was "for six weeks engaged in making the necessary changes
to contract them. . . ." Branch was greatly hampered in this work by
a scarcity of implements, tools, and Negro labor.* He circulated hand-

---

of our coast friends. They have burned Winton. . . ." O. A. Hanner [?] to J. M.
Harrington, Feb. 26, 1862, J. M. Harrington Papers, DU.

* Adding to General Branch's troubles was a daring and almost successful attempt
by the enemy to burn the Trent River Bridge. J. D. Whitford to H. T. Clark, Mar. 7,
1862, H. T. Clark Papers, NCDAH; S. C. Rowan to L. M. Goldsborough, Mar. 20, 1862,
L. M. Goldsborough Papers, LC.

bills over the state and inserted advertisements in newspapers "calling on the citizens generally to assist" him. But the people failed to respond wholeheartedly. They sent to New Bern a "small party of free negroes without implements" and only one slave.[133] As a result, troops had to be used as laborers. Five hundred men were detailed each day to work on the breastworks, but over half of them had no tools, while the others had only "worn and broken shovels and axes." Despite these difficulties, Branch was still able to strengthen the fortification he intended to hold. He would have preferred, however, more troops to man the entire set of works than laborers and tools to contract them. He repeatedly asked for reinforcements but none were sent.[134]

Below New Bern, about ten miles, was a line of entrenchments running from Fort Dixie on the west bank of the Neuse River for three-fourths of a mile to a dense swamp. This line, known as the Croatan Works, was squarely across the road most likely to be used by the enemy, and it was considered by General Branch as his strongest position. However, because of the small size of his army and the possibility that the works could be taken in reverse by a landing farther up the river, Branch concluded not to make this the point from which to defend the town.[135]

The line over which the battle was to be fought began with Fort Thompson, a thirteen-gun sod installation, anchored on the Neuse, about six miles below New Bern. The placing of the fort's guns—ten bearing on the river and only three on the land approaches to the city—showed the erroneous belief of the engineers that the attack would be mainly by water. Seven forts were designed to protect the town from naval attack; yet not a single heavy gun guarded directly the railroad and the county road that ran along the river and crossed the entrenchments at right angles.[136] A young Confederate officer complained bitterly over the "miserable manner in which our works were constructed. Major [W. B.] Thompson, who has failed in every work he has ever undertaken, made the greatest failure of all, in the construction of those works. They are a disgrace to any engineer."[137]

From Fort Thompson the Confederate line stretched westward for approximately one mile to the Atlantic and North Carolina Railroad. The entrenchments were originally supposed to continue across the railroad to a dense swamp near Brice's Creek. General Branch, when he found it necessary to shorten his lines because of his small force, changed the plan. He dropped the line back 150 yards at the railroad. "Then beginning not very far from the railroad, he constructed westward not a continuous line of breastworks, but a series of redans, just behind Bullen's Branch which flowed into Brice's Creek on his right." This readjustment left an unprotected gap of 150 yards in the defenses at Wood's brickyard along the railroad.[138]

General Gatlin, in company with a board of officers, inspected the New Bern defenses in early March. The recommendations of this inspection party, although calling for more guns than were available, concurred in General Branch's decision to defend only the Fort Thompson line provided the brickyard was protected.[139]

On the day that the inspection party issued its report, March 11, General Burnside completed the embarkation of his eleven thousand troops at Roanoke Island and set sail for Hatteras where a rendezvous with the remainder of his fleet was to be effected.* The fleet arrived at dusk and "for once," a writer observed, "Hatteras had declared a truce." The weather was perfect.[140] The next day General Burnside issued a general order notifying his troops that they were on the eve of an important movement "which would greatly demoralize the enemy and assist the Army of the Potomac in its contemplated move on Richmond."[141] The fleet had barely gotten underway when Admiral Goldsborough received orders to proceed at once to Hampton Roads where the Confederate ironclad *Virginia*† had played havoc with the Federal fleet and come near neutralizing General McClellan's plan for a movement up the peninsula. Disappointed that he would not be able to go on the New Bern expedition, as he "had everything well planned in . . . [his] mind," Goldsborough turned over command of the North Carolina sounds to Commander Rowan and, aboard the *Minnesota*, rushed off for the Virginia waters.[142]

Under its new commander the Federal fleet continued a course toward the North Carolina mainland. The sea was so calm that sailing vessels could not use their canvas.[143] "This is the most beautiful day,"

* The eleven thousand is an approximate figure. The official records are not clear as to the number of men Burnside used in the New Bern operation. *NR*, VII, Ser. I, 118; *OR*, IX, Ser. I, 358. See also D. H. Hill, *North Carolina in the War Between the States—Bethel to Sharpsburg* (Raleigh: Edwards and Broughton, 1926), I, 218-19.

† The *Virginia* was generally known as the *Merrimac*. The *Merrimac* was a United States frigate that had been sunk when the Union forces abandoned the Norfolk navy yard. She was subsequently raised by the Confederates and converted into the ironclad *Virginia*.

wrote a Pennsylvania youth, "I have ever seen. Not a breeze rippled the waves—not a cloud in the sky—all was blue—blue overhead—blue underneath—blue all around."[144]

At 2:00 P.M. the fleet entered the Neuse River which, at its mouth, is an estuary twelve miles wide. The passage of the vessels up the Neuse was an impressive sight. The river was so broad and calm that the transports, their decks crowded with uniformed men, could sail in two parallel lines. The scene reminded one Rhode Island soldier "of our summer steamers with excursionists." Multicolored signal flags fluttering from every halyard added to the color of the occasion.

By 9:00 P.M. the fleet had come to anchor off the mouth of Slocum Creek, about twelve miles below New Bern by water and seventeen by land. At tattoo an order was read to the men stating that they were to land in light marching order. This meant carrying "only rubber and woolen blankets (rolled and worn over one's shoulder like a sash), haversacks and canteens, and sixty rounds of cartridges, forty in the boxes and twenty distributed about" the person.[145]

During the restless night hours many of the soldiers prayed for strength to do their duty.[146] Others evinced in letters home a strong determination to be victorious in the "warm work" ahead, "no matter how great the cost."[147]

The arrival of the Federal fleet was signaled to the Confederate outposts up and down the river by means of large bonfires.[148]* Since the turn of the year the soldiers had been "patiently waiting for Burnside to come up,"[149] but the same cannot be said of the local populace.[150] When Burnside's fleet first appeared in North Carolina waters in January, "it took two extra trains to carry the people away" from New Bern.[151] They were "the worst frightened Dam set I ever saw in my life," said an observer on the scene.[152] Following this exodus, however, things became so dull around the town that a Confederate lieutenant complained that he could hardly write a letter. The Lieutenant's desire for "a little excitement" was more than fulfilled on the morning of March 13.[153] At daybreak on this date, Federal gunboats commenced a bombardment of the shore at Slocum's Creek in preparation for the disembarkation of troops.[154]

---

* Some of the Federal soldiers mistook these fires as indications that the enemy was "destroying what they were afraid might fall into . . . [their] hands." C. A. Barker to "Dear Friend Charlie," C. A. Barker Papers, EI.

The shelling was unnecessary. No Confederates were in the immediate area. To land his troops, General Burnside used the same amphibious techniques followed so successfully at Roanoke Island. Steam vessels with a string of launches in tow headed for the beach full throttle and at a signal released their tows, the momentum sending the launches forward until aground.* The men then jumped overboard into waist-deep water and waded ashore. Once on the North Carolina mainland the soldiers burst into cheers and then started a miry journey towards New Bern. Heavy afternoon rains, "deep sand and thick clay," made it extremely difficult to keep shoes on.[155] The gunboats, advancing slowly ahead of the troops, kept up a steady fire.[156] After splashing six miles, the Federal advance came to the Croatan Works which, much to their surprise, they found deserted.[157] Passing over these formidable works unmolested, Burnside continued his march and that night bivouacked near the Fort Thompson line.† The men built fires and attempted to keep warm but it was difficult to do with the rain now coming down in "torrents."[158] The following parody may have been in many minds that night:

> Now I lay me down to sleep
> In mud that's fathoms deep;
> If I'm not here when you wake,
> Just hunt me up with an oyster rake.[159]

The Confederates in their entrenchments had it no better. The Twenty-seventh North Carolina, under Major John A. Gilmer, was posted with its left touching Fort Thompson. The Thirty-seventh North Carolina, under Lieutenant Colonel William M. Barbour, came next. Extending Barbour's line was the Seventh North Carolina, commanded by Lieutenant Colonel Edward G. Haywood. To the right of the Seventh North Carolina was Colonel James Sinclair's Thirty-fifth North Carolina, and to the right of Sinclair stood the old brick kiln on the

---

* Considerable difficulty was experienced in getting the artillery pieces ashore. The battery arrived at the front too late to fire a shot.

† One of the most uncomfortable individuals that night was Mrs. Kady Brownell, who had accompanied her husband on the march. She attempted to make the march in a pair of ladies "ordinary walking shoes" and thereby blistered her feet badly. C. H. Barney, "A Country Boy's First Three Months in the Army," *Personal Narratives of Events in the War of the Rebellion. Being Papers Read Before the Rhode Island Soldiers and Sailors Historical Society* (Providence: N. Bangs Williams and Co., 1880), Ser. 2, No. 2, pp. 1-47.

side of the railroad. To guard the gap in the line at this vulnerable point, General Branch placed the local militia battalion of Colonel H. J. B. Clark. These militiamen had been in the service for only two weeks, were without uniforms, and carried only shotguns or hunting rifles. On the right of the railroad, Colonel Zebulon B. Vance's Twenty-sixth North Carolina occupied the entrenchments, supported by the "independent company of Captain [?] MacRae" and two dismounted companies of cavalry. Held in reserve was the Thirty-third North Carolina under Colonel C. M. Avery. Two guns of Captain Thomas H. Brem's battery were the only guns on the right side of the railroad, while Captain A. C. Latham's six-gun battery and the remaining four pieces belonging to Brem supported the infantry on the left. Branch put the two wings of his army under the experienced eyes of Colonels Charles C. Lee and Reuben P. Campbell[160]* and then selected for his headquarters a position "about 250 yards from the breastwork and in full view of the enemy." From this vantage point he could view the action along the entire line.[161]

Despite the difficulties of the march on the thirteenth, General Burnside was ready to take the offensive on the morning of the fourteenth. By six o'clock he had all of his generals in the saddle and by seven o'clock the columns were in motion.[162] For the advance Burnside divided his force into three columns. General Foster commanded on the right between the river and the railroad, General Reno on the left of the railroad, and General Parke in reserve along the railroad, ready to aid either column.

Without waiting for General Reno to get into position, Foster made contact with the Confederate left and was greeted with a shell from Latham's Battery.[163] The fight then began "in earnest."[164] From their breastworks Confederate infantrymen opened an "incessant" and "severe" fire.† Simultaneously their artillery raked the front.[165] The three

---

*It is thought that General Burnside knew the exact number of troops in Branch's command and "how they were posted. . . ." It "made no difference," said a Confederate officer, "where the militia had been posted, as he would have attacked them anyhow." G. Lewis to Cousin, Mar. 20, 1862, Battle Family Papers, SHC. Burnside, who had known Colonel Campbell previously, sent him the following message: "Reub quit your foolishness and come back to the Union army." Campbell's reply left no doubt as to where his loyalties rested. "Tell General Burnside to go to the Devil where he belongs." R. A. Ward, "An Amphibious Primer: Battle for New Bern," *MCG*, XXXVI (Aug., 1952), p. 41.

† A member of the Thirty-seventh North Carolina said the enemy never came close enough for the men to use their muskets. Thus "at no time" was the regiment engaged.

Assault of the Union troops on the Confederate defenses below New Bern, March 14, 1862.
(From *Battles and Leaders of the Civil War*)

guns at Fort Thompson that bore on the land were extremely effective. They "mowed gaps in the Yankee line at every discharge. . . ."[166] At this juncture the Confederate gunners received assistance from a totally unexpected source—the Federal gunboats lying in the river. The shells from these vessels were also falling on Foster's line. They "came whizzing over us and all around us," commented one of the Union soldiers.[167] Commander Rowan knew that he was endangering the lives of men in his own army; yet he kept up the heavy fire. In explanation he wrote Admiral Goldsborough: "I commenced throwing 5, 10, 15 second shells inshore, and notwithstanding the risk, I determined to continue till the general sent me word [to stop]. I know the persuasive effort of a 9-inch [shell], and thought I better to kill a Union man or two than to lose the effect of my moral suasion."[168]

His offense stymied, Foster called up reserves. The Eleventh Connecticut replaced the Twenty-seventh Massachusetts which had lost severely and had practically exhausted its ammunition. The Tenth Connecticut was ordered to take position on the extreme left. With "balls

G. Cochran, "Eye-witness Tells How Zeb Vance Bolstered Men's Courage with Brandy," Raleigh *N and O*, June 21, 1936.

and shells whistling over . . .[their] heads," the New Englanders moved up to the safety of a ravine where they remained until the Twenty-third Massachusetts, which had been part of Foster's advance, came "running in every direction" toward the rear. When this happened, the Tenth Connecticut left the ravine, took an exposed position within two hundred yards of the Confederate breastworks, and opened a hot fire on the enemy line. Each man fired "about 3 shots a minute . . . which," said a member of the regiment, "with the Enfield rifle is considered very quick work." Instead of stopping to put the ramrod back in the gun after using it, the Federal soldiers would "stick it in the ground in front of them."[169]* This withering fire still could not break the Confederate line. As a consequence, the Federal offensive on the right came to a standstill.

On the left General Reno also encountered great difficulties, but in moving his brigade up the railroad to attack the enemy's right, his lead regiment, the Twenty-first Massachusetts, discovered the break in the Confederate line at the brick kiln.† No Confederates were on Reno's immediate front for Vance's line did not extend to the railroad.[170] To the right the General could see the flank of the militia with no works or guns protecting it. Seizing the opportunity to flank the Confederate line, Reno formed the Twenty-first Massachusetts at right angles to his line of march and personally led four of its companies in a charge across the railroad against the militia.[171] Upon seeing the enemy on their flank, the militiamen were seized with panic which "exceeded Bull Run," and part of them broke ranks.‡ Colonel H. J. B. Clark of the militia, believing it impossible to reform his line under fire, ordered a retreat that "was succeeded by a stampede."[172]

* Members of the Fifth Rhode Island complained that their ramrods were so rusty that it was impossible to withdraw them "from the pipes." J. K. Burlingame, *History of the Fifth Regiment of the Rhode Island Artillery During Three Years and a Half of Service in North Carolina* (Providence: Snow and Farnham, 1892), p. 45.   Because of the heavy rains many of the muskets carried by General Reno's men would not fire. So on the morning of the fourteenth, before commencing the march, the General ordered his men to "discharge their load, drawing such as would not fire." *OR*, IX, Ser. I, 221.

† The discovery and penetration by the Federals of this break in the Confederate line was the immediate cause of the loss of the battle. General Branch ordered two heavy guns into position to cover this fatal exposure at the brickyard, but the pieces were not in place when the fight started. *OR*, IX, Ser. I, 242; Hill, *Bethel to Sharpsburg*, I, 221.

‡ The flight of the militia must not have come as a great surprise to General Branch. In February he had written the Governor: "I would take great pleasure in discharging all the militia." L. O'B. Branch to H. T. Clark, Feb. 23, 1862, H. T. Clark Papers, NCDAH.

The flight of the militiamen exposed the right flank of Colonel Sinclair's Thirty-fifth North Carolina. When Sinclair saw the militia run, he reported "in much excitement" to Colonel Campbell "that the enemy had flanked him and was coming up the trenches which had been vacated by the militia." Campbell at once ordered the Thirty-fifth North Carolina out of the breastworks "for the purpose of charging bayonets upon the advancing column," but, according to Colonel Campbell, Sinclair "failed to form his men and left the field in confusion."[173]*

General Reno was quick to see the opportunity to bring up reinforcements and sweep down the rear of the Confederate works. However, before he could lead the rest of his regiment across the railroad, Major A. B. Carmichael, commanding Vance's left, opened up a deliberate fire.[174]† General Branch, meanwhile, had ordered Colonel Avery's regiment of reserves to the support of Vance's Twenty-sixth North Carolina and to seal up the break in the line.[175] Four of Avery's companies under Major Gaston Lewis occupied "the hottest part of the battlefield," which was a group of rifle pits near the railroad and almost on Reno's front. In this exposed position, Lewis "behaved most gallantly." He repulsed the enemy time and again, and twice charged them with detachments of companies, and each time made them flee. "Our loss was greater at that point than any other," said Lieutenant Colonel Robert F. Hoke of the Thirty-third North Carolina, "as . . . (Lewis) had to fight to his front, right and left, but still maintained his position . . . no one could have behaved with more coolness, bravery, and determination than he, and he deserves the praise of every true countryman for his actions."[176]

The destructive fire of Lewis and Avery prevented General Reno from throwing more troops across the railroad and forced him to hurry his other regiments into line on Vance's front. This left the four companies of the Twenty-first Massachusetts under Lieutenant Colonel W. S. Clark alone behind the Confederate line. "I was compelled," said Colonel Clark, "either to charge upon Captain Brem's battery or to retreat without anything to compensate for the terrible loss sustained

---

* Colonel Sinclair maintained that in the following words Colonel Campbell ordered a retreat: "You had better take your men out of that as quick as possible." *OR*, IX, Ser. I, 263.

† A member of the Thirty-third North Carolina later charged that the Raleigh *N.C. Standard* played up Vance's role in the battle in the hopes of making him governor. W. G. Lewis to K. P. Battle, April 1, 1862, Battle Family Papers, SHC.

in reaching this point." The Colonel hesitated only a moment. Facing his two hundred men toward Fort Thompson, he gave the command "charge bayonets," and in a matter of minutes two guns of Brem's Battery were in Federal hands.[177] By this time Colonel Campbell had taken the Seventh North Carolina out of the breastworks and ordered it to charge Clark's advancing column.* The order was successfully carried out, with the New Englanders beating a hasty retreat to the railroad.[178]

This feat restored the Confederate front. It was now after eleven o'clock, and the battle had been raging since eight. The right and the left of the Confederate line were still intact, but the unfortified center was seriously menaced by the flight of the militia and the Thirty-fifth North Carolina. Had either one of these regiments been present to step into the deserted line, the day might have been saved.[179] But as it turned out, Colonel Clark, after being driven out of the Confederate entrenchments, reported the defenseless condition of the center to Colonel Isaac P. Rodman of the Fourth Rhode Island. He in turn passed this vital information on to General Parke, whose brigade was being held in reserve. Soon Parke had fresh troops passing through the gap at the brick kiln. The Federals swept along the line where Sinclair's regiment should have been and struck the Seventh North Carolina squarely on its right flank.[180] Seeing what was taking place in the center, General Foster immediately ordered his brigade to charge.[181] The whole line of breastworks between the river and railroad was carried by this combined movement. General Branch, "seeing the enemy behind the breastwork and without a single man to place in the gap through which he was entering," decided his "next care was to secure the retreat."[182] Orders to retire across the Trent River bridge were dispatched to Colonels Avery and Vance, who were still fighting Reno on the right flank and were ignorant of the disaster on the left. Unfortunately for these two courageous officers the couriers never delivered the messages. Therefore Colonel Avery and two hundred of his men were captured while the gallant Major Lewis "had to run the gauntlet to get out. . . ." The remainder of Avery's command, under Colonel Hoke, made it safely to the west bank of Brice's Creek. Colonel Vance, with the Twenty-sixth

---

* Colonel W. S. Clark, Twenty-first Massachusetts, thought his small detachment was saved from annihilation when the Confederates "instead of giving us a volley at once . . . hesitated and then charged upon us without firing." *OR*, IX, Ser. I, 226.

North Carolina, fled across the swamp to his right to escape capture.[183] The remaining North Carolina regiments withdrew across the Trent River bridge into New Bern. The men of the Thirty-seventh North Carolina were instructed to "retreat in order, but," observed Lieutenant George Cochran, "this injunction went in one ear and came out the other. Every man struck out for the bridge . . . as fast as his legs would carry him . . . and the additional spur . . . [they] received from bombs crashing through the timber put . . . [them] to top speed for a three mile sprint." Once across the bridge some of the soldiers did not stop running until they had climbed aboard a westbound train just pulling out of the New Bern depot.[184]

The bridge over the Trent, already prepared for destruction, was set on fire as the last of Branch's command passed over. This halted Foster's brigade which was moving up the railroad in hot pursuit of the retreating Confederates.[185] Commander Rowan's gunboats, however, had successfully passed the obstructions in the Neuse and were abreast of the town as the Confederates filed into New Bern. The *Delaware,* Rowan's flagship, lobbed a few shells in the direction of the depot and then tied up alongside a wharf where "an old darky lady" stood. Rowan asked her where the troops were, and in reply she said: "Lo massa if you believe me they is running as hard as they kin."[186]

Realizing that it would be impossible to hold New Bern, General Branch directed all the officers he could find to conduct the remnants of the army to the rail depot at Tuscarora. There arrangements could be made for their transportation to Kinston.[187] By this time parts of New Bern were aflame. There is little reason to think General Branch ordered the town fired. In his official report he stated that New Bern was "in flames in many places" when he arrived from the battlefield.[188] Adjutant James A. Graham of the Twenty-seventh North Carolina wrote his mother soon after the battle: "We saw we could not hold it and therefore set the town on fire and retreated to this place [Kinston]."[189] From the statements of Branch and Graham, it can be assumed that New Bern was burned by the retreating Confederate soldiers who acted on their own initiative, not on orders from their commanding general. The fires, fortunately for the homeowners, did comparatively little damage. According to a member of the Federal Sanitary Commission, "the retiring rebels . . . left the town to all interests 'almost as good as new.'"

General Branch arrived in Kinston at eleven o'clock on the night of the fourteenth, but it was five full days before his scattered command was in camp at this place.* His troops, "badly demoralized and hungry enough to eat army mules," poured into Kinston from "half a dozen different roads."[190] Only the "muddy, motley and weary" troops of the Twenty-sixth North Carolina seemed to be "in good spirits . . . for Zebulon Baird [Vance] had found a keg of brandy which had restored his soldiers courage and cheered their souls."[191]

New Bern, in the meantime, had been occupied by the victorious Federal army. During the afternoon of the fourteenth, the soldiers were ferried across the Trent River to take possession of their prize. When they reached the city, they found its beautiful tree-lined streets practically deserted and immense volumes of pitchy smoke hovering overhead like "a black pall." Those citizens remaining behind until the last moment in the hope that the city could be saved "had left . . . in the greatest haste leaving everything behind them." Homes were deserted and in many cases doors were neither shut nor locked. No one but Negroes and "poor whites" were around to greet the victors. The Negroes, "hilarious in the employment of their newly found 'Uncle Sam,'" were holding "a grand jubilee." While some "in their rude way" thanked God for their deliverance, others danced in "wild delight" and sang, and still others, "with an eye to their main chance," were pillaging the stores and dwellings. The soldiers and sailors soon joined the Negroes in these acts of lawlessness, and for a day or two after its capture, New Bern was pillaged without restraint. A member of Burnside's staff maintained that the colored people were very adept at plundering because of their ability to carry heavy loads balanced on their heads. This officer said that he saw a young Negro girl no more than ten or eleven years old walk rapidly away from a dwelling with a "server" balanced on her head. On the server was a "pail or pitcher and a small box." In her hands she carried a small card table and a basket filled with small articles, and a bundle was under her arm. After order was restored to the city, the provost marshal sent out details to collect the property stolen by the Negroes. It took only one hour to fill a large wagon with "crockery, furniture, provisions, carpets, clothing, etc."

General Burnside selected a stately old home in New Bern for his headquarters, but when an aide went to get the home in order, he

---

* Confederate casualties (killed, wounded, missing, and prisoners) in the Battle of New Bern totaled 578. *OR*, IX, Ser. I, 247. Federal losses were between 440 and 471. *Ibid.*, pp. 210-11.

found it· in the process of being plundered by soldiers, sailors, and Negroes. One old Negro man was trying his best to make off with all the china ware. Only the threat of putting the vandals in irons got them out of the house. To halt the pillaging in New Bern, General Burnside brought a strong garrison into town and made guards available for those who wanted protection. With order restored, the General instructed the churches of the city to hold special services "of Thanksgiving" on Sunday, March 16, for the victory just gained.[192]

The people of North Carolina were shocked and angry at the apparently easy conquest of New Bern. General Gatlin was so severely criticized that he was removed from command.* His courage was questioned because he was not on the field of battle[193] and his intoxication on the day of the fight was stated as a fact.[194] It so happened that General Gatlin was not drunk or even drinking while the battle was in progress but quite sick at his Goldsboro headquarters. John W. Graham, a member of Gatlin's staff, thought his commanding officer "certainly a man of very good sense, but slow, and somewhat wanting in energy—too indolent . . . for such times as these. . . ." Graham was also of the opinion that Gatlin "committed a great mistake in remaining so much of his time at Goldsboro, and trying to carry on everything entirely by writing."[195] General Gatlin blamed the defeat on the authorities in Richmond who refused his many requests for men and supplies.[196]

The loss of New Bern, regardless of the cause, was a great blow to North Carolina. It did result, however, in the Confederate officials' reevaluating the state scene. A week after the battle General Lee informed President Davis that more Federal troops were sailing for North Carolina and that another Southern "disaster there would be ruinous."[197] Lee, along with certain policy makers, had at last realized that a successful sweep of Burnside's army across North Carolina "would divide the upper Confederacy."[198] These officials were seeing what Lincoln's Assistant Secretary of the Navy, Gustavus Fox, had seen earlier. On February 24, Fox wrote Admiral Goldsborough: "I think that plan

---

* Branch escaped the type of scathing criticism leveled on Gatlin. To most observers he did about as well as could be expected from a "political General." O. A. Hanner [?] to J. M. Harrington, Feb. 26, 1862, J. M. Harrington Papers, DU; G. W. Lewis to "Cousin William," Mar. 20, 1862, Battle Family Papers, SHC. It appears that only Adjutant General Martin of the state's high ranking military figures blamed Branch for the defeat. L. O'B. Branch to H. T. Clark, Mar. 23, 1862, L. O'B. Branch Papers, NCDAH.

(the capture of New Bern and Beaufort) the best, as it gives us a fine base to push any number of troops into the interior, so with North Carolina and Tennessee in our possession, or nearly so, we divide them."[199]

To prevent a Federal push into the interior, Confederate troops were rushed into North Carolina from Virginia. The returns of March 31 show that 24,030 infantry and 142 pieces of artillery were stationed at various posts throughout the State.[200] Had part of these forces been transferred earlier, it is highly possible that the results at New Bern would have been different.[201]

North Carolina's defenses were strengthened further by a change in high command. General Gatlin was relieved from duty.[202] His orders read because "of ill health," but most people knew better.[203] General Lee wanted one of his senior officers, possibly G. W. Smith or James Longstreet, to be intrusted with the vital command of the Department of North Carolina,[204] but Davis gave the post to Major General Theophilus H. Holmes, a native of Sampson County and North Carolina's ranking general in the Confederacy.[205] Brigadier General Samuel G. French* replaced Anderson at Wilmington, and Brigadier General Robert Ransom was brought in from Virginia.

General Holmes organized his troops into four brigades and stationed them, exclusive of garrison details, around Goldsboro. Here they were drilled and instructed in anticipation of Burnside's move inland. Many of these troops were poorly armed when they arrived. But in May, Holmes was happy to distribute 2,400 Enfield rifles brought in through the blockade. This led Lieutenant Tom Branson of the Forty-sixth North Carolina to write his sister: "I am proud of our arms, in fact, of our regiment and the way in which it is being equipped." The Lieutenant went on to say that he had no complaints. "I am as well pleased as I could be anywhere in the Army. If [you] could visit us, you now would be surprised at the air of comfort about our tent. Just imagine us seated around a table furnished with baked chicken, ham, eggs, butter, biscuit, loaf, coffee . . . cake, etc. I tell you we have been living well. . . ."[206] But such was not the case in all the camps. Benjamin E. Stiles complained about "dreadful times . . . so much sickness. Men are dying every day," he told his mother. Yet it was difficult for Stiles

---

* General French was originally ordered to replace Branch at New Bern, but he arrived in North Carolina after the Battle of New Bern. When he replaced Anderson at Wilmington, Anderson was given a brigade in Holmes's command.

to believe men could be as "selfish and indifferent" as were the soldiers in his regiment, "two thirds of . . . [whom] would not wait on the sick if they were not made to do it. They would let them lie and suffer for want of anything." Lieutenant Walter W. Lenoir, encamped five miles east of Kinston, was concerned "with the disaffection" among his troops. He thought it would be a good idea to send them home so their "women . . . would take them and despise them and loathe them."[207]

During this period of watchful waiting by Holmes, General Burnside turned his attention to Fort Macon rather than Goldsboro. Situated on Bogue Banks, Fort Macon guarded Beaufort Inlet, the only entrance through the Outer Banks still not in Federal hands. This Confederate stronghold in Burnside's rear had to be reduced before a move on Goldsboro could be undertaken. As a preliminary to the attack on Fort Macon, Burnside ordered Brigadier General John G. Parke to move down the Atlantic and North Carolina Railroad and occupy Morehead City and Beaufort. An absence of rolling stock* kept Parke from using the railroad for transportation.[208] Still the Federals, with the aid of hand cars to carry supplies, covered the forty odd miles unopposed in two days.[209] Havelock Station was occupied on the twentieth,[210] and the next day Carolina City,† "a village containing from fifty to one hundred inhabitants, a few respectable dwellings and the ruins of a large hotel," was seized.[211] Two companies of the Fourth Rhode Island then moved along the railroad for two and one half miles to Morehead City on the twenty-second, where they found "another small collection of houses and a large railway station and wharves."[212] On the night of March 24, General Parke sent two companies over to Beaufort.[213] The men were rowed across on this dark, wet night in boats manned by Negro fishermen familiar with the waters. Disembarking around 2:00 A.M., the soldiers silently took over dark and deserted streets. The local citizens were greatly surprised the next morning to find their town in

* When the Union fleet first appeared off New Bern, the officers of the Atlantic and North Carolina Railroad used all the locomotives and cars, except a few turned over to the army, to save valuable materials and supplies from the company shops in New Bern. C. L. Price, "North Carolina Railroads" (M.A. thesis, Univ. of North Carolina, 1951), p. 169.

† General Parke said he reached Carolina City on March 22. *OR*, IX, Ser. I, 282. The buildings had been burned by a Confederate raiding party out of Fort Macon. On this same raid the railroad bridge at Newport was destroyed. When Parke's men occupied Newport, which was located between Havelock and Carolina City, crews were put to work at once repairing the bridge. *Ibid.*, pp. 277-78, 282.

Federal hands.[214] From Beaufort, General Parke made contact with the Union blockaders patroling off the harbor entrance. This was accomplished by a party crossing over to Shackleford Banks," and thence in a fisherman's boat to the fleet."[215] Able now to coordinate the land and sea forces, Parke began serious preparations for an assault on Fort Macon.

Back in New Bern, however, General Burnside had other matters on his mind. Word had reached him that the Confederates were building ironclads at Norfolk and intended bringing them to the Albemarle region through the Dismal Swamp and Currituck Sound canals.* To block this supposed move, Burnside ordered General Reno to move up to South Mills on the Dismal Swamp canal, blow up the lock located there, and then "proceed up to the head of Currituck Canal and blow in its banks."[216] Reno left New Bern with the Twenty-first and Fifty-first Massachusetts. Along the way he was joined by Colonel Rush C. Hawkins and three regiments from Roanoke Island, the Ninth New York, Eighty-Ninth New York, and Sixth New Hampshire. The entire command, including a four-gun battery under Colonel W. A. Howard, numbered over three thousand men.[217] Around 1:00 A.M. on the morning of April 19, the transports arrived at Elizabeth City, and by 3:00 A.M. Hawkins' brigade had been disembarked and was on the march. Hawkins, with a mulatto for a guide, took the wrong road and had an extra ten miles added to a normally twelve-mile march. "This detour," said the Colonel, "led to the meeting of the Union commands where the roads joined about three or four miles from the enemy position."[218] The day was extremely warm, and the men, having had little or no sleep and in wet clothing, suffered a great deal. Some fell out from sheer exhaustion. It was a struggle, said Colonel E. A. Kimball of the Ninth New York, for them to "drag one leg after another."[219]

Below South Mills, Reno found his way obstructed by a Confederate force under Colonel A. R. Wright of the Third Georgia Regiment. This able Confederate officer had less than nine hundred men in his command and not all of this number could be placed on the battlefield. To protect his right rear, the Colonel posted two of his companies on the road running along the west bank of the Pasquotank River. In reserve Wright held two more companies of the Third Georgia and most

* Burnside referred to the "Currituck Canal." *OR,* IX, Ser. I, 271. Doubtless, he had in mind that part of the Albemarle and Chesapeake Canal which connected the North River with Currituck Sound.

of Colonel D. D. Ferrebee's First Brigade of North Carolina Militia. The remainder of his command, six companies and some militiamen, Wright posted behind the banks of a long ditch that crossed the road the Federals were advancing on, a road so sheltered by woods that Reno had no idea how many men faced him. Commanding the road were four pieces of artillery under Captain W. W. McComas.[220]

The fight started around noon when Reno's lead regiment, the Fifty-first Pennsylvania, came under brisk fire from McComas' guns. The Pennsylvanians, after taking a few rounds, scurried for shelter in the woods where they dropped "to earth from mere exhaustion and no threats, persuasion, or any other means could induce . . . [them] to rise until they had a rest."[221] As the other regiments came up, General Reno put them on the battle line, but for three hours they were held in check by Confederate fire. Around three o'clock Colonel Hawkins, on his own initiative, decided to have the Ninth New York Zouaves charge the Confederate battery. With a wild yell these colorfully-clad veterans of Roanoke Island started for the Confederate line. They managed to go only a short distance before musket and artillery fire "scattered [them] right and left." In less than two minutes nine Zouaves were killed and fifty-eight wounded.[222] Colonel Wright was able to hold Reno in check for another hour until Captain McComas was killed by a minnie ball. Seeing their gallant commander fall, the artillerymen who, General Huger reported, "for four hours had fought with in-domitable courage became panic-stricken and left the field. . . ." At this moment Reno charged the Confederate line, but somehow Colonel Wright rallied his men and drove the Federals back once again. Taking advantage of the confusion in the enemy ranks, and fearful of being flanked, Wright retired in "good order" to Joy's Creek, two miles in the rear.[223] Reno did not pursue, giving as his reason the exhausted condition of his troops. He might have added that the determination and courage of his adversary, coupled with relatively heavy Federal losses,* were factors also.[224]

The Federals bivouacked on the field that night. Weary from the day's activities, most of them fell asleep even with a heavy rain coming down. Their dampened slumber, however, was of short duration. Around nine o'clock they were awakened by whispered commands to form noiselessly for a night march back to the transports at Elizabeth

---

* Confederate losses were six killed and nineteen wounded. Federal casualties were 13 killed and 101 wounded. *OR*, IX, Ser. I, 307-29.

Top: Ruins of Winton after it was burned by the Union forces on February 20, 1862. (From *Frank Leslie's Illustrated Newspaper*) *Bottom:* Charge of Hawkins' Zouaves on a Confederate battery at South Mills, April 19, 1862. (From *Pictorial War Record*)

City. General Reno, having picked up a rumor that the Confederates were being reinforced from Norfolk, was fearful that the enemy would attack during the night. He instructed his men to march at "quick pace," not "to talk above a whisper and to prevent tin cups and canteens from clashing or making the least noise."[225] Chaplain Thomas W. Conway and Assistant Surgeon Orrin Warren were left behind to care for the wounded and bury the dead.[226]

Despite the official report of General Reno to the contrary,* the Battle of South Mills "was a victory for the South."[227] The locks that the expedition were to destroy remained intact, and it was a weary, if not "dispirited," group of Federal soldiers that returned to New Bern on Tuesday, April 22.[228]

PART 3

FORT MACON

Ashore General Reno's men learned that Burnside had departed early that morning aboard the *Alice Price* for Beaufort harbor.[229] The final phase of the siege of Fort Macon was about to begin, and the Commanding General wanted to be near at hand for the fight.

For a month General Parke had been preparing for a major assault on this Confederate bastion, located on the eastern tip of Bogue Banks.[230] Parke had selected Carolina City for his headquarters because this small village sat opposite the nearest landing point on the Banks. One of the General's first moves, after establishing himself at Carolina City, was to dispatch two officers to Fort Macon with a surrender summons. The fort's commander, Lieutenant Colonel Moses J. White, politely but firmly refused the demand, leaving General Parke no alternative but to commence preparations for a full-scale offensive.[231]

Colonel White's decision to fight rather than surrender was a bold but futile move. He had an inadequate supply of ammunition and a depleted garrison. In February, General Branch had him send nine companies to New Bern, which left only 439 officers and men for duty at the fort. Furthermore this old-style, casemated work was designed primarily to protect Beaufort harbor from an attack by sea, and therefore was vulnerable to a land assault. General Walter Gwynn, when

* General Reno claimed victory on the grounds that he had successfully demonstrated toward Norfolk. But his immediate objective was the destruction of canal locks and this he failed to do.

commanding the Confederate forces in eastern North Carolina, had urged repeatedly that both Bogue and Shackleford banks be occupied by artillery and infantry.[232] D. H. Hill later recommended the same thing, and General Gatlin said that he pleaded with Richmond for troops "until he was ashamed to ask further."[233] Yet Confederate authorities failed to realize how desperate the plight of Fort Macon would be if it were approached by a large land force cooperating with the naval squadron. General Burnside, with more vision, was fully aware of the fort's vulnerability. It was his plan to land troops and artillery on Bogue Banks and then, in conjunction with the war vessels already patrolling off Beaufort Inlet, to reduce the fort.

On March 29, a Federal reconnaissance party of twenty men and one officer secured a beachhead on Bogue Banks, landing under the guns of a Federal warship. "From that time to April 10," says General Parke, "every available hour of night and day was spent in transporting men, siege train and supplies." By the last day of March, the beachhead was firmly established by two companies of the Eighth Connecticut, and a permanent camp was located about eight miles from the fort. Soon signal stations were in operation to communicate with the fleet and the shore towns.[234] Stern-wheel steamers, scows, flat rafts, schooners, and small boats of all kinds were used by General Parke to get his men, artillery, and supplies across the five-mile stretch of water between Carolina City and the landing point on Bogue Banks. During the thirteen days between March 29 and April 10, eight companies of the Fourth Rhode Island, seven companies of the Eighth Connecticut, the Fifth Rhode Island Battalion, one company of the First United States Artillery, and Company I, Third New York Artillery were taken across.[235]

Colonel White's men were equally busy during this period of preliminary maneuvering by the Federals. Demolition crews leveled outside buildings, boats at the dock were burned, sand bags were tarred, and artillery drill was held every day. But in an effort to save powder and shell, Confederate gunners fired very few rounds at the Federal warships. Captain Stephen D. Pool, Tenth North Carolina, was one of the busiest Confederate officers on the Banks these days. To observe the enemy's movements, he maintained a picket station three miles from the fort. From this forward point he relayed his information to Colonel White.[236]

The first clash between the Confederate pickets and the Union troops came on April 8, followed by brisk encounters on the ninth and tenth.[237] The day following the last of these skirmishes General Parke made a reconnaissance in force in the direction of Fort Macon. Driving the Confederate pickets before them, the Federals got within a mile of the work when the guns of the fort opened up. This fire stopped the advance. But the Federal soldiers, instead of returning to their base immediately, took cover behind the sandhills while three of their officers, including a topographical engineer, made a "careful examination of the ground" in search of battery locations. The men retained their advanced position until the sites for the artillery were selected, and then they withdrew under cover of naval guns.[238]

Beginning with April 12, the work on the approaches, trenches, batteries, and rifle pits was vigorously pushed forward night and day by all of General Parke's available force. Under cover of darkness three batteries, well hidden by sandhills, were placed within thirteen to seventeen hundred yards of the fort.[239] Rifle pits were dug about two thousand feet from the works after attempts to move closer were halted by a punishing fire from Colonel White's cannon.[240] While the batteries were being constructed and the rifle pits dug, Confederate guns kept up a desultory fire, ranging from only a few to as many as fifty shells per day.[241] This shelling was not very effective,* as these lines of Colonel White show:

We could only annoy the enemy by the fire of our artillery, which fired horizontally, could do them no damage and only force them to keep behind the sand hills. Not having a mortar in the fort, we mounted six old 32-pounder carronades, which had been placed in the fort for defending the ditch, with 40 degree elevation, and used them for throwing shells behind the enemy's coverings. Two 10-inch guns were used for the same purpose. They (the enemy) were so completely concealed that we could seldom ascertain the position of their working parties, and when driven from them, we could not see when they returned, and from scarcity of shell we could not keep up a continued fire.[242]

* The Confederate fire, though not effective, did keep the Federal soldiers in the pits awake. One of General Parke's men described his experiences as follows: "When our turn came to take our tour of duty in trenches we would proceed along the beach, and when we had approached within range of the guns of the fort, the rebels would send us their compliments in the shape of shot and shell. After taking the places assigned to us in the trenches, one man was stationed on lookout duty near the top of the rifle-pit, while the others would remain below. When the lookout saw the flash of rebel guns he would sing out 'Down' and the men taking to the rifle-pit like a woodchuck to its hole would remain there until the shot had passed over." Burlingame, 5 *R. I.*, pp. 60-61.

Fort Macon was completely invested by the middle of April and all communication with the outside was ended.* The Confederate soldiers became so edgy in their isolated position that dissatisfaction over poorly cooked food resulted in a near mutiny. The trouble was precipitated by Colonel White's refusal to permit the men to draw flour rations and bake their own bread. When General Lee received word of this difficulty on April 15, he considered it serious enough to authorize General Holmes to order an abandonment of Fort Macon if he felt it necessary. Lee was doubtful if "even a tolerable resistance would be made."[243] Evacuation without capture, though, was not possible at this late date. A bloodless surrender to the enemy, on the other hand, was still very much a possibility.

On the afternoon of April 23, Captain Herman Biggs, a West Point acquaintance of Colonel White's, appeared at Fort Macon under a flag of truce. He presented General Parke's second demand for a surrender of the fort, which was refused even though Colonel White probably had fewer than three hundred men fit for duty.[244] The Colonel did request, however, a "conference of higher powers." As a consequence, early the next morning General Burnside met with Colonel White on Shackleford Banks. From the *Alice Price,* the General's secretary, Daniel R. Larned, could see the officers shake hands and then enter into earnest conversation. After no more than fifteen minutes, the conference ended with nothing accomplished. Therefore, observed the secretary, "both parties prepared for battle."[245]

* Two lieutenants, Thaddeus Coleman and Cicero Primrose, did manage, nevertheless, to slip away in a boat one night in "an effort to communicate with Confederate authorities and ask if any relief could be given." R. W. Evans to Mother, Apr. 9, 1862, A. C. Evans Papers, SHC; J. W. Sanders, "Additional Sketch Tenth Regiment," *Histories of the Several Regiments and Battalions from North Carolina in the Great War 1861-'65. Written by Members of the Respective Commands,* ed., W. Clark (Raleigh: E. M. Uzzell, 1901), I, 507. The Confederate steamer *Nashville* also managed to elude the Federals. She arrived in Beaufort harbor with a valuable cargo of rifles but the presence of Burnside in New Bern made it impractical for her to unload. So on the dark, windless night of March 17 she got up steam and slipped past Fort Macon into the open sea. Lookouts on the Federal blockaders spotted her, but with an added burst of steam this sleek blockade-runner outdistanced her pursuers. In the distance the Confederate sailors could hear the cheers of the soldiers in the fort. The escape of the *Nashville* and her subsequent safe arrival in Wilmington was a humiliating experience for Union naval authorities. Assistant Secretary of the Navy Fox wrote Admiral Goldsborough: "It is a terrible blow to the prestige of the Navy and will place us all very nearly in the position we were below our victories. . . . This is not blockade. You can have no idea of the feeling here. It is Bull Run to the Navy." *NR,* VII, Ser. I, 139; M. F. Perry, "Fort Macon's Brief Belligerance," *SM* (Sept. 1920), 6; R. C. Gatlin to S. Cooper, Mar. 4, 1862, Rec. Gr. 109, NA.

Top: Bombardment of Fort Macon by the Union fleet and land batteries, April 25, 1862. *Lower left:* Fort Macon from the upper parapet. *Lower right:* The Fifth Rhode Island entering Fort Macon, April 26, 1862. (From *Harper's Weekly*)

In the clear dawn of April 25, the Federal batteries opened fire on Fort Macon. Ten minutes later, 5:50 A.M., Confederate guns replied and the "ball" was on.[246] For some time the firing on both sides was wild and ineffective. Bursting shells either filled the air with wreaths of smoke or tossed the sand and water in fountain-like columns. The solid shot from the Federal batteries ricocheted along the surface of the water beyond the fort, while Confederate shells glanced harmlessly from one sand hill to another.[247] Without mortars to lob the shells, Colonel White could hope to inflict little damage on the Federal implacements. Horizontally fired cannons were not effective.

The Federal fleet, unaware that the attack was to commence on the twenty-fifth, was late entering the battle. General Parke had intended to notify Commander Samuel Lockwood of the time of bombardment, but pre-dawn high seas prevented any sort of contact with the fleet.[248] Acting on his own initiative, the Commander ordered the battle signals displayed. While the roll of drums called all hands to battle stations, the steamers *Daylight* and *State of Georgia,* the gunboat *Chippewa,* and the bark *Gunsbak* took position and opened fire on the fort. The time was approximately 8:40 A.M. Designed for this type of action, Fort

Macon's guns replied with vigor. The accuracy of this fire, along with rough seas, forced the retirement of the fleet after only one hour.[249]*

Throughout the morning and into the afternoon the Federal land batteries continued to shell the fort. The accuracy of this fire, after the early rounds, was amazing. It is estimated that out of 1,150 shots fired, about 560 hit the fort, and after mid-day, "every shot fired from [the Federal] batteries fell in or near" the target. A total of nineteen Confederate guns were disabled.[250] One shell burst near a cannon on the fort parapet, throwing a soldier twelve feet in the air. Another shot killed three gunners and disabled the same number of guns. The credit for this extraordinary marksmanship must go to Lieutenant W. S. Andrews, the Federal signal officer at Beaufort. Possessing a knowledge of artillery fire, Lieutenant Andrews was able to observe where the shells hit and then forward his corrections by flags to the batteries on the Banks. The only fatality on the Federal side occurred when a shell exploded in front of a mortar battery where a lieutenant and a private were setting out aiming stakes.† The blast tore the private to pieces, "his flesh spattering" into the lieutenant's face.[251]

Some time later in the afternoon Colonel White concluded that further resistance would be futile and ordered "a white flag displayed from the ramparts of the fort." Immediately all firing ceased on both sides.[252] To ascertain the terms of surrender, Colonel White sent Captain H. T. Guion and S. D. Pool under a flag of truce to General Parke. The Federal commander informed the officers that only an unconditional surrender would be acceptable. When Pool and Guion refused to accept the terms, General Parke suggested that the flag of truce remain in effect overnight while he conferred with Burnside.[253] This was agreed to, and before daybreak the next morning General Parke went aboard the *Alice Price* for consultation with the Commanding General. In the ensuing conference aboard ship it was decided that Captain Herman Biggs and Captain J. A. King should be sent to Fort Macon by a small boat with specific terms of surrender. To facilitate the trip of Biggs and King to the beach, the *Alice Price* got underway and proceeded to within a mile of the fort. At this point a small boat was put over the side

---

* The Federal ships did draw enough Confederate fire to allow the Union ground forces to make some repairs on mortar batteries. *NR*, VII, Ser. I, 279.

† The Confederate losses during the bombardment were seven killed and eighteen wounded. Federal casualties other than the one killed were two wounded. *OR*, IX. Ser. I, 284, 294.

and the two officers went ashore. They informed Colonel White that the terms of capitulation were as follows: "The fort, armament and garrison to be surrendered to the forces of the United States.

"The officers and men of the garrison to be released on their parole of honor not to take up arms against the United States of America until properly exchanged, and to return to their homes, taking with them all of their private effects, such as clothing, bedding, books, etc."[254]

These articles were as much as Colonel White could hope for. He accepted them and returned to the General's steamer with Biggs and King. After breakfast aboard ship the Colonel signed the surrender papers. Then the *Alice Price* got up steam and "ran down to the Fort." Much to the chagrin of the ship's crew and the General's staff, Burnside would not allow anyone to leave the vessel. "We were almost mad," said Daniel Larned, Burnside's secretary, and "only confidence in the General," he added, "kept them from being furious." As it turned out, Larned was unduly exercised. The entire proceedings were easily visible from shipboard. He and his companions were able to watch unobstructed as Burnside made preparations to receive the surrender of the fort.[255]

Once on the beach the General's first order was for the Fifth Rhode Island Artillery to form. This artillery battalion, which had just replaced the Eighth Connecticut in the trenches, was given the honor of being the first unit to enter the fort. The battalion's new colors recently sent from home and bearing the words "Roanoke" and "New Bern" were unfurled and handed to color sergeants at the head of the columns. While the Fifth Rhode Island was forming, Colonel White's men, "in all kinds and styles of uniforms," marched out of the fort with their arms and formed in line. The contrast between these troops and the Rhode Islanders was great, the New Englanders "all in good and regular uniforms, their bayonets gleaming." The Federal soldiers proceeded into the fort and formed on one side of the sally port until the Confederate troops re-entered. In a few minutes "the rebel flag" came down* and the Stars and Stripes went up. As soon as "old glory" appeared at "the mast Head," the navy fired a salute and from Beaufort "came the hearty cheers of the Union people." But aboard the *Alice*

---

* The Confederate flag at Fort Macon had been made out of the old garrison flag "with the stars withdrawn to suit the number of revolted states," Burlingame, *5 R. I.,* p. 66. "The red and white stripes had been ripped apart, and arranged into the broad bars of the new dispensation." *RR,* IV, 491.

Price and in the fort "all was quiet as the grave" since General Burnside had requested that "no demonstration be made." This order was promoted by a genuine sympathy on the part of Burnside for Colonel White, who had "manifested much feeling at being forced to surrender."[256]

Once the ceremony was over General Burnside signaled for the officers of his staff to come ashore, "and the way we piled into the boat was not slow," said Daniel Larned. The men found the scene inside the fort "terrible. Guns broken and dismounted—holes in the earth bigger than a hogshead—bricks knocked from the wall. . . . Railroad iron that had been placed up against the doors to protect them bent and broken short off—and the most terrible battering you can imagine."[257]

General Burnside wasted little time in paroling his prisoners. On the afternoon of the twenty-sixth, parts of two companies were taken to Beaufort. The following day the *Chippewa* took on board 150 men for transportation to Fort Caswell at the mouth of the Cape Fear River. At the same time, the *Alice Price,* Burnside's flagship, started for New Bern with Captain Guion's company.[258] As this vessel steamed into New Bern the next day, all the whistles and bells in the harbor sounded. At the dock General Foster and his staff awaited Burnside to escort him through the streets in triumph. At headquarters the reception continued "most enthusiastic." "Everybody," commented an observer, "came in to offer congratulations and laughing and joking with the repetition of the stories and incidents connected with the reduction of the fort was kept up till a late hour."[259]

PART 4

SKIRMISHES

With the capture of Fort Macon, General Burnside completed the three major objectives of his expedition,[260] and, observed his secretary, "we can now go as the General thinks best."[261] Burnside wanted to follow up these successes with a push on Goldsboro and Raleigh. He felt confident that the capture of these two cities would soon put Wilmington and Fort Caswell in his hands.[262]

For the push inland Burnside wanted more men and supplies. He needed in particular at least one mounted unit. This need was taken care of the latter part of April with the arrival of the Third New York

Cavalry under Colonel S. H. Mix. Up to this time the only mounts available to General Burnside belonged to the Rhode Island Battery and the General had learned that artillerymen, even with the best intentions, do not make good horse soldiers.[263] In addition to the cavalry, four infantry regiments and two field batteries had been assigned to the army since its arrival in North Carolina. This gave Burnside approximately a seventeen-thousand-man force, but for the task ahead he thought a larger command was necessary.[264] His hopes for additional reinforcements were dashed, however, when Secretary of War Edwin Stanton wrote him the last of April that no more troops were available for the North Carolina operation. This news was disturbing to Burnside, of course, but not altogether unexpected. On the other hand, he was exceedingly annoyed by the slowness of the Federal authorities in honoring his requisitions for locomotives, so necessary for a move inland. This vexatious delay was difficult for Burnside to understand in view of the fact that he had received the "most flattering approval" from both the President and the War Department that his every request would be filled.[265] On May 17, the General wrote McClellan of his troubles: "I could not muster a train of 25 wagons, which you know would not be sufficient to carry my ammunition, and, as you see, it would be almost fatal to me to make a move into the interior before they arrive."[266]

General Burnside was also hampered in his preparations by orders to correlate his movements with McClellan's Peninsula Campaign in Virginia.[267] On March 17, after months of preparation, General McClellan began the movement of his army by transports from around Washington to Fortress Monroe. And in early April, he started his advance up the Peninsula toward Richmond. McClellan's plans for the cooperation of Burnside in this move were explained in a letter of April 2:

It has now become of the first importance that there should be frequent communication between us, and that I should be informed of the exact state of things with you and in your front. . . . Will you please at once inform me fully, stating how soon you expect to be in possession of Fort Macon, what available troops you will then have for operating on Goldsborough, what can in your opinion, be effected there in the way of taking possession of it, of neutralizing a strong force of the enemy there, and of doing something toward preventing the enemy's retreat from Richmond. . . . You will readily understand that if I succeed in driving the enemy out of Richmond I will at once throw a strong force on Raleigh and open communications with you via Goldsborough. . . . Taking all things into consideration, it appears probable that a movement in the direction of Goldsborough would be the best thing for you to undertake. . . . Great caution will, however, be necessary, as the enemy might throw large forces in that direction. The main object of the movement would be to accomplish that, but it would not do for you to be caught. We cannot afford any reverse at present.[268]

McClellan's advance up the Peninsula, which got underway on April 4, bogged down after only one day when it unexpectedly came upon a Confederate position along the Warwick River. Following a two-day reconnaissance, the General decided on a formal siege "of a position that could have been carried immediately by assault."[269] He wrote Burnside accordingly that no offensive move was to be made into the interior of North Carolina until the issue on the lower peninsula had been determined.[270] His friend replied: "When you start the rebels from Yorktown please let me know at once, and I'll give them a kick in the flank that will make them see stars. . . . You know as well as I that it is easier to turn a flank than face a front."[271] On May 4, Yorktown was evacuated by the Confederates, enabling McClellan to push on towards Richmond. From Tunstall's Station on May 22 McClellan again wrote Burnside, reiterating his desire for cooperation between their forces. But he set no specific date for the North Carolina advance.[272]

While waiting for a specific expression of McClellan's wishes and for transportation, General Burnside continued his practice of sending out expeditions in various directions from his base at New Bern. He started doing this soon after the capture of this North Carolina town and before General McClellan contacted him about the Peninsula Campaign. One of the first of these relatively minor operations resulted in the bloodless occupation of Washington, North Carolina. The defenses of Washington had been abandoned after the fall of New Bern, and the Confederate forces, in accordance with orders, had retired up the Tar River toward Greenville.[273]

The Federal expedition which arrived at Hill's Point, about six miles below Washington, on March 21 consisted of three gunboats, the *Delaware,* the *Louisiana,* and the *Commodore Perry,* commanded by Lieutenant Alexander Murray and the troop ship *Admiral,* with the Twenty-fourth Massachusetts, Colonel Thomas G. Stevenson commanding, aboard. At Hill's Point the expedition was met by Mayor Isaiah Respess, who assured the officers that Washington was not occupied by Confederate troops.* Finding a channel through the obstructions in the Pamlico River at this point, Colonel Stevenson loaded two of his companies on the *Delaware* and steamed up to the town docks.[274]

A correspondent for the Boston *Journal* described Washington as a pleasant little village of 2,500 inhabitants, "some two thirds of whom have seen fit to leave for the interior." The remaining one-third "met the troops with every expression of welcome."[275] Colonel Stevenson noted that "from quite a number of houses we were saluted by waving handkerchiefs, and from one the national flag with the motto 'The Union and the Constitution' was displayed."[276] At the courthouse, to the accompaniment of a Federal air, the United States flag was nailed to a pole.[277] This act signified the complete surrender of the town.†

At six o'clock the Union fleet weighed anchor and started back to New Bern. Colonel Stevenson was happy to report that "while in the city not a man left ranks or behaved otherwise than as if on drill."[278] The Colonel's disciplinary problems, however, were lessened by the fact that the retiring Confederates had "cut to pieces" the gunboat on the stocks and burned all the cotton and naval stores in the town.[279]

The manifestations of Union sentiment in Washington convinced Burnside of the desirability of occupying the town. Therefore, shortly after the return of the Stevenson-Murray expedition, the General stationed a company of the Twenty-fourth Massachusetts and several gunboats at this Beaufort County locality.[280] And it was not long before several Unionist citizens from neighboring Washington County were asking that a Federal force be sent to Plymouth.[281]

It was the "last day of April or first of May" before the Federals got around to visiting this small town located on the Roanoke River. Then three gunboats stopped only long enough to leave a copy of the Burnside-Goldsborough Proclamation addressed to the people of North Carolina.[282] Early on the morning of May 14, Plymouth again received a short visit from three Federal gunboats—the *Commodore Perry*, the *Lockwood*, and the *Ceres* under Lieutenant Flusser. "Finding nothing suspicious" at Plymouth, Flusser "pushed on" up the river. At Jamesville an "unsuccessful search for rebel army stores" was made, but two

---

* After the Federal troops departed, Mayor Respess was taken to Richmond and tried "on a charge of collusion with the Federals." He was acquitted. Hill, *Bethel to Sharpsburg*, I, 317.

† One object of the expedition was to recover the lenses taken from the lighthouse at Hatteras, but they had been moved previously to Tarboro. *NR*, VII, Ser. I, 152.

miles below Williamston the Confederate steamer *Alice,* with a large supply of bacon aboard, was captured. Late in the afternoon Lieutenant Flusser returned to Plymouth with his prize in tow. This time the customhouse was searched, and in it was found the lantern ·from the "light-boat" at the mouth of the Roanoke River, but, said the Lieutenant, "there was no other United States property in the town and none belonging to the rebels."[283] So the next day Flusser departed from Plymouth and proceeded to Windsor on the Cashie River. Here the "tearful prayers of a poor widow" kept the Lieutenant from burning some cotton and beans.[284] The following day, May 17, Flusser was back at Plymouth. Commander Rowan, who had arrived there in the meantime, ordered Flusser to remain at Plymouth.

Through interviews with the town authorities, Rowan had learned that "the most rabid of the secessionists . . . including all the ministers of the gospel, except the Baptist" had left Plymouth. He learned also that the Unionists were being "disturbed" by certain Confederates in the area. Consequently it was "at the earnest entreaty of the Union inhabitants of Plymouth" that Commander Rowan "decided to keep a vessel there."[285] In the middle of June, Company F of the Ninth New York arrived at Plymouth to assist the navy in holding the place.[286]

During the intervening weeks between Colonel Stevenson's expedition to Washington and the permanent occupation of Plymouth by a portion of the Ninth New York, a number of minor engagements took place in eastern North Carolina. One of the earliest of these occurred on April 7 near Newport when a company of the Second North Carolina Cavalry charged a detail from the Ninth New Jersey, killing one man and capturing nine.[287]

On the day of the skirmish at Newport portions of two regiments stationed on Roanoke Island boarded steamers for Elizabeth City. The next day these troops surprised a Confederate militia camp near the town and captured seventy-three militiamen along with fifty stands of arms and considerable ammunition.[288]

A more serious affair took place at Gillett's farm in Onslow County. There, on the bright moonlit night of April 13, a portion of the Second North Carolina Cavalry, led by Lieutenant Colonel W. G. Robinson, attacked two hundred men of the One Hundred Third New York, Colonel Baron Egloffstein commanding. "Three separate and rather desultory charges" were made on the Federals who were encamped in and around the home of Thomas Gillett. The last charge was led by Colonel Robinson with only twenty to thirty men, and resulted in the wounding and capture of the Colonel. Whereupon his command withdrew. Soon after the skirmish General Holmes, commanding the Department of North Carolina, had Brigadier General Robert Ransom investigate the charges that "the engagement was not creditable to the regiment." Ransom drew up a very critical report which Holmes endorsed. The matter was then referred to General Lee who approved Ransom's finding, but added that it appeared from the report of the detachments engaged that some of the companies had very few men present. "For the bad behavior of a few, it would not appear just to punish the whole. I would suggest that these men be stationed at some point, if possible, where their drill could be perfected, as it would seem that their unfortunate behavior was attributable in a large measure to lack of drill and discipline."[289]

Following the skirmish at Gillett's farm, the Second North Carolina Cavalry was given ample opportunity to redeem itself. Stationed at Wise's Forks five miles south of Kinston, the regiment was assigned the duty of picketing the three roads from Kinston to New Bern. Patrolling in as close to New Bern as circumstances would permit, detachments of the Second North Carolina were ofttimes drawn into action with the enemy. Lively encounters took place in April and May near Haughton's Mill, at Young's Cross Roads and in the vicinity of Trenton and Pollocksville. A Federal soldier at New Bern, in writing his sister about one of these skirmishes, aptly described them all when he said he had not "learnt" the particulars but the "story goes that there were a few killed on both sides. . . ."[290]*

The engagement at Tranter's Creek on June 5 between the Forty-fourth North Carolina and the Twenty-fourth Massachusetts was somewhat larger than the skirmishes referred to by the soldier at New Bern. The latter part of May, Colonel E. E. Potter, commanding at Washington, received word that Colonel George B. Singletary, with the Forty-fourth North Carolina, was in the neighborhood of Pactolus. Potter was afraid that Colonel Singletary would attack Washington since he

---

* During May, Colonel C. C. Dodge with the "First New York Mounted Rifles" left Norfolk for a raid through northeastern North Carolina. "The object of this expedition was to open communication with Elizabeth City and to obtain information in relation to the topography of the country between . . . [Norfolk] and certain points in North Carolina, the conditions of the roads, and the general sentiment of the people in that region." *RR*, V, 478. The Dodge raid was not part of the Burnside expedition.

The fight at Tranter's Creek near Washington, June 5, 1862. (From *Harper's Weekly*)

"was a reckless man who would not likely be restrained by prudential considerations." Therefore Potter ordered the Twenty-fourth Massachusetts under Lieutenant Colonel F. A. Osborn to move on Pactolus, some twelve miles from Washington.

After a hot march on June 5, the Federal soldiers arrived at "Myers or Crime's Mill" over Tranter's Creek. The mill consisted of three buildings, about thirty feet apart and open at the lower story. Through these buildings the Tranter's Creek bridge ran. The floor of the third of these buildings had been torn up by the Confederates and made into a barricade on "the opposite side" of the creek. From this well protected position Colonel Singletary's men, approximately four hundred in number, poured a steady fire into the Twenty-fourth Massachusetts. Unable to advance across the bridge, Colonel Osborn called up his artillery and shelled the Confederates out of the barricade, killing Colonel Singletary. Their leader dead, the Confederates retired from the field, but the Federals did not pursue. After loading his dead and wounded on wagons, Colonel Osborn returned to Washington.[291]

During this period, while Burnside's troops were engaged in minor military activity, President Lincoln, for the second time since the war began, attempted to establish "a loyal government" in eastern North

Carolina. Union sentiment such as that manifested in the Washington and Plymouth areas induced the President to appoint Edward Stanly military governor of the state with headquarters in New Bern.[292]

The new governor was a native of Beaufort County and for many years had been a prominent "old line North Carolina Whig."[293] But at the time of his appointment, Stanly was living in California. Secretary Stanton's instructions to the new governor were rather vague, although, in a letter dated May 20, the Secretary did make it clear that the "great purpose" of Stanly's appointment was "to reestablish the authority of the Federal government in the state of North Carolina." Confronted with the monumental task of leading a state that had nearly fifty thousand men under arms back into the Union, the Governor wrote Stanton: "My difficulties are greater than you suppose."[294]

General Burnside, fully cognizant of the difficulties facing Stanly, welcomed his coming "as a relief from many perplexities." At New Bern on May 26, the General gladly turned over to the Governor the jurisdiction of all civil and political affairs, assuring him at the same time of the full cooperation of the military.[295]

No sooner had Stanly arrived in North Carolina than he was confronted with the "slave problem." Since its capture in March, New Bern had been a haven for runaway slaves. They flocked into the town in such large numbers that one Federal soldier, "sick, tired and disgusted with the sight" of black folk, wanted "to be transported to a place where niggers are unknown."[296] A few days after occupying New Bern, General Burnside reported to the Secretary of War: "They are now a source of very great anxiety to us. The city is being overrun with fugitives from the surrounding towns and plantations."[297] As the Negroes continued to come in, the General put many of them to work on fortifications. Organized into a pioneer corps, they marched to work under a battered flag to the music of a fife. Others were sent into the surrounding countryside both to forage and to watch Confederate troop movements.[298]

Vincent Colyer, whom Burnside had appointed Superintendent of the Poor, moved his office from Roanoke Island to New Bern in an effort to supervise these destitute blacks, and whites as well. One of his first moves was to establish a school for Negro children. While approving all Colyer had done to feed and clothe the indigent, Stanly maintained that he could not approve the school because he "had been sent to restore the old order of things." Governor Stanly actually felt the school "would do harm to the Union cause."[299] The Governor also took a stand on the return of runaway slaves that antagonized the extremists in the North. It was his policy to return all slaves to owners who would take an oath of allegiance to the Union.[300] For his policies on the slave question, Stanly was accused of being sympathetic to the South. The United States House of Representatives, on June 3, passed a resolution "asking the President to furnish information as to the powers confined on Stanly by his appointment, whether he had interfered to prevent the education of children, black or white, and if so, by what authority."[301]

In addition to these difficulties, it took Governor Stanly only a short while to realize that Unionist sentiment in eastern North Carolina had been exaggerated. In late June, hoping to arouse some national feeling, he visited several towns occupied by Federal troops. But Stanly's speeches accomplished little for he was generally regarded with hatred and as a traitor to his state.[302]

The *Western Sentinel* reported these visits in its June 27 issue.[303] However, by this time attention in the state was once more focused on General Burnside. Two days earlier he had received orders from General McClellan to advance on Goldsboro immediately with all of his forces.[304] Two locomotives, fifty cars, and a large wagon train had previously reached Beaufort;[305] so Burnside was prepared to move. Just as the Federal army commenced its march, the General was startled to receive the following message from President Lincoln: "I think you had better go, with any reinforcements you can spare, to General Mc-Clellan."[306] In the three days between the two messages, McClellan had been driven from the Chickahominy. "Burnside, instead of striking at a fleeing foe," was being called upon to "strike for a fleeing commander. . . ."[307] On July 6, Burnside, in command of seven thousand troops, left his base in North Carolina to reinforce McClellan on the Peninsula. General Foster, with over nine thousand men, was left in charge of the Department of North Carolina.[308]

Burnside's transfer to Virginia removed the immediate pressure on Lee's flank; yet May and June had been anxious times for the Confederate General. In order to contain McClellan's ponderous army it had been necessary for Lee to withdraw most of General Holmes's command from North Carolina. When the Seven Day's Battles before Richmond started on June 25, Lee became greatly concerned that Burnside would break away from his base at New Bern and move on Goldsboro. Every night he telegraphed General James G. Martin* at Kinston: "Any movements of the enemy in your front today."[309] On the night of the sixth day's fighting, even General Martin's brigade was ordered to Virginia.† This left in North Carolina only two infantry regiments and one of cavalry and three of artillery. The other forty-seven were in Virginia. Here was "North Carolina's contribution to the spring campaign of 1862."[310]

Lee's victory over McClellan was magnificent and far-reaching in its results. Still it must be balanced against General Burnside's victories in eastern North Carolina. To the Confederacy, the results of these Federal operations in North Carolina were far greater than authorities ever anticipated. "The occupation of this territory in the rear of General Lee's army by a mobile force that could be safely increased by water in a few hours was a constant menace to operations in Virginia." From this time forward, whenever the Army of Northern Virginia planned a strategic blow, "it had to be thought out with the possibility of a counterstrike from the easily enlargeable army squatted behind the fortifications of New Bern and within a few hours by open sea of the Confederate capital." Moreover, large numbers of troops urgently needed by Lee for offensive warfare had henceforth to be detailed to hold the Federal army at its North Carolina bases. In addition, the loss of supplies from

* Martin assumed command of a brigade on March 1, 1862. J. G. Martin to T. H. Holmes, June 17, 1862, H. T. Clark Papers, NCDAH. Around the middle of May, General Lee made Martin a brigadier general in the Confederate States Army and put him in command in North Carolina. A. Gordon, "Organization of the Troops," *Histories of the Several Regiments and Battalions from North Carolina in the Great War 1861-'65. Written by Members of the Respective Commands,* ed. W. Clark (Raleigh: E. M. Uzzell, 1901), I, 10. Since September, 1861, Martin had been a major general in the militia. E. J. Warner, *Generals in Gray* (Baton Rouge: Louisiana State Univ. Press, 1959), pp. 213-14.

† General Martin arrived too late to participate in the fighting around Richmond; so he put his brigade in camp near Drewry's Bluff. Gordon, "Organization of Troops," p. 12. General Lee soon ordered Martin (but not his brigade) back to North Carolina to take command in the state. Martin returned to Raleigh and assumed the double duty of adjutant general and commander of all troops on duty in the state. The General's orders dated Aug. 18, 1862, actually assigned him to the District of North Carolina which comprised all the territory from the Roanoke River to the South Carolina line. *OR,* IX, Ser. I, 480. These orders were "by command of" General D. H. Hill who had replaced Holmes as commander of the Department of North Carolina on July 17, 1862. *Ibid.,* p. 476. Then on September 19, 1862, Major General G. W. Smith was put over all the "country" lying south of General Lee's line, including the Department of North Carolina. *Ibid.,* XVIII, Ser. I, 748.

one of the richest farming regions in the Confederacy was irreparable; "supplies, too, that had been accessible through inland waterways safe from molestation by the unopposed Federal fleet and without throwing additional traffic on the already overburdened railways of the South." Nor should the effect on blockade-running be overlooked. While Beaufort and the inlets on the Outer Banks were in Confederate hands, the blockade-runners had a choice of several ports on the North Carolina coast. Hereafter they had only Wilmington, and soon the Federal fleet concentrated around that port so thickly that, as one disgusted blockade-runner phrased it, "the very waves grew tired of holding up their ships."[311]

CHAPTER VI

Raids in Eastern North Carolina

WHEN BURNSIDE departed for Virginia with two divisions, General Foster at New Bern was left with an insufficient number of troops to make the long contemplated move on Goldsboro. Therefore, he turned his attention to strengthening the fortifications at New Bern and the other places in his command. Foster, by education and training an admirable engineer, intended to protect the vital base at New Bern by a complete system of works that would render the place defensible by a minimum number of men. Many Negroes along with regular details of soldiers were put to work on the entrenchments and breastworks. The work was "not very hard," since two men were available for every shovel, and in a few weeks much was accomplished. By the last of August, New Bern was probably "one of the best fortified towns in the United States," so thought at least one observer. A continuous line of earthworks, stretching from the marshes along the Trent River all the way to the Neuse, was anchored by Forts Totten, Rowan, and Dutton. And every day an "awful" looking armored train pulled out of town to patrol the tracks of the Atlantic and North Carolina Railroad.[1]

Long before the fortifications at New Bern were completed, Federal land and naval forces were reconnoitering the surrounding country. On July 9, Commander Rowan, in charge of the United States Naval Forces, Inner Waters of North Carolina, ordered Lieutenant C. W. Flusser, with three gunboats, to ascend the Roanoke River "to ascertain whether the enemy was fortifying the river banks or building men-of-war at the small towns in the interior." Along the way, Lieutenant Flusser had the unique experience of being vigorously attacked by Confederate cavalry. "We were under fire for two hours," said the Lieutenant, "running very slowly and keeping a bright lookout for a battery." At Rainbow Banks, a high bluff about two miles below Hamilton, Lieutenant A. B. Andrews of the First North Carolina Cavalry had stationed forty-one of his men. Their orders were to fire, reload, and fire "again as rapidly as possible." So effectively did these dismounted cavalrymen carry out their orders that Lieutenant Flusser was obliged to put his men under cover. Still this gallant young officer managed to run the gauntlet of fire and reach Hamilton where he captured a Confederate steamer and temporarily occupied the town. The day's action, nevertheless, cost the Federals two killed and nine wounded, and prompted a Confederate general to remark: "This was one of the boldest and most successful attacks on gunboats that I know of during the war."[2]

Shortly after the Hamilton raid, General Foster sent out various detachments to reconnoiter the Trenton-Pollocksville area as well as the region between Washington and Greenville and the country south of New Bern.[3] Other than the destruction of private property, these raids accomplished very little.[4]* Typical of these expeditions was one described by a Massachusetts soldier in a letter to his sister dated August 29, 1862: "Anchored off a little village called Swansboro—went ashore—captured one 'Reb'—several dozens of chickens—cows, pigs, potatoes and numerous other articles too tedious—as the auctioneer says my share of the spoils was a double-barrell gun and a trace of pullets."[5]

Raids, drill, guard duty, and work on the fortifications took up much of the Federal soldier's time but not all of it. Foster's men still found hours for relaxation. Companies formed literary and glee clubs. Barracks rang to banjo music and dancing. Sometimes the music and dancing were provided by the Negroes but more often by the men themselves. Comfortable quarters, which ranged from deserted town mansions to warm tents, good food, and some whisky helped to keep the spirits up. New Bern, crowded as it was with soldiers and Negroes, was considered by many "to be quite a pleasant" town. A young soldier from Maine was correct when he stated: "We of this department are having the same easy time, doing plenty of some kinds of work but little of the 'real.' "[6]

---

* To inconvenience the enemy, Foster had various saltworks along the sounds destroyed. Sometimes reports of the destruction of saltworks were discounted by local citizens. They thought these reports were started by the salt makers in order to raise the price of that scarce item. J. W. K. Dix to D. MacRae, Aug. 18, 1862, Hugh MacRae Papers, DU.

Although Foster's activities during July and August were strictly of a minor nature and the soldiers had time for play, the period proved very trying for the state authorities in Raleigh. Governor Clark was afraid that the Federals might at any moment break away from their base at New Bern and move on Goldsboro, which was practically unprotected. The Governor thought that General Lee, even though he had removed most of the Confederate troops from the state, still appreciated the importance of holding the railroad at Goldsboro. But he doubted seriously if the General had "any idea of the individual and state loss" in property and crops to the Union forces. He urged General Lee to send an expedition to eastern North Carolina at once to drive the enemy out of New Bern, Plymouth, and Washington, "now swarming with Yankees, Negroes and Traitors."[7]

The Confederate military chief replied that, after witnessing the depredations of the Union army in Virginia, he could fully appreciate the injuries suffered by North Carolinians and that he certainly was not unmindful of the importance of the railroad. "But it is impossible with the means at our command," he continued, "to pursue the policy of concentrating our forces to protect important points and battle the principal efforts of the enemy, and at the same time extend the same protection we desire to give to every district."

The General went on to point out to Governor Clark that "the safety of the whole State of North Carolina as well as of Virginia depends in a measure upon the results of the enemy's efforts in this quarter, which if successful, would make your State the theatre of hostilities far more injurious and destructive to your citizens than anything they have yet been called upon to suffer."

He concluded by noting that "to prevent effectually the enemy's gunboats from ascending navigable rivers would require not only batteries, but adequate land forces to defend them which would lead to a subdivision of our forces from which we could anticipate nothing but disaster." In view of this reasoning, about all Lee could do was promise the people of North Carolina that he would refer Governor Clark's letter to D. H. Hill. This popular North Carolinian had replaced Theophilus Holmes as commander of the troops in the state.[8]

General Lee's refusal to weaken his lines in Virginia meant that any Confederate offensive operations in North Carolina would have to come from the small commands already in the state. The first such move came on the morning of September 6 when Colonel S. D. Pool, with detachments from the Seventeenth, Fifty-fifth, and Eighth Carolina regiments, and seventy men from the Tenth Artillery acting as infantry, surprised the Federal garrison at Washington. Concealed by a heavy early morning fog, the Confederates passed unnoticed by the Federal pickets and galloped into town from several directions. "Their demoniac yells" as they charged up and down the streets could be heard "far and near." Sleepy Federal soldiers bolted out of their beds. Grabbing the nearest weapon at hand, they poured out into the streets, soon to be joined by frightened women and children. But "a garrison surprised is a garrison confused—there are no orders—there is for a time no head."

Confusion reigned in the Union camps until the fog began to lift and two Federal gunboats, the *Picket* and the *Louisiana,* opened fire on the Confederates. Then suddenly the magazine on the *Picket* accidentally exploded, sinking the vessel and killing the captain along with nineteen members of the crew. This brought on Confederate shouts of victory. "Little Washington is ours, Little Washington is ours," the men exclaimed. But the claims of victory were premature. Federal reinforcements were to turn the tide of battle.

Colonel Edward E. Potter, First Regiment North Carolina Union Volunteers, commanding at Washington, was at the time of the attack on his way to Plymouth* with five companies of cavalry and one battery of artillery. Close enough to hear the firing, he halted his command and ordered an immediate return to Washington. After two and a half hours of "hard fighting," the Colonel managed to drive the raiders out of town.[9] The day's skirmish cost the Federals seven killed and forty-seven wounded. Confederate losses were slightly higher,[10] but the capture of three "brass field guns," ample supplies, and the accidental destruction of the *Picket* indemnified Pool for his casualties.[11]

Bold exploits such as this raid on Washington were not confined to the outnumbered Confederates during the fall of 1862. On November 23, the *U.S.S. Ellis,* Lieutenant William B. Cushing† in command, en-

---

* A Confederate attempt to take Plymouth had occurred a few days earlier. It failed when a Union sympathizer in the region disclosed the presence of the raiders to the Federal garrison in town. W. C. Humphrey, *The Great Contest: A History of the Military and Naval Operations During the Civil War in the United States of America 1861-1865* (Detroit: C. H. Smith and Co., 1886), pp. 475-76; W. P. Jacocks, "Federal Operations in Eastern North Carolina During the Civil War" (M.A. thesis, Univ. of North Carolina, 1905), p. 8; *OR,* XVIII, Ser. I, 1.

† By this time Cushing's deeds had become almost legendary. In early October, 1862,

tered New River Inlet and started up the river. According to Cushing, his object was "to sweep the river, capture any vessels there, capture the town of Jacksonville, or Onslow Court House, take the Wilmington mail, and destroy any salt works that I might find on the banks." Amazingly enough, the young Lieutenant accomplished all of his objectives and more and would have escaped unscathed had his pilots been more careful. On her way back down the river with prizes, the *Ellis* ran hard aground not far from a high bluff. Certain that the Confederates would attack as soon as they discovered the plight of the *Ellis,* Cushing stripped his vessel of everything valuable and loaded it on one of the captured schooners. He next ordered his crew to board one of the prizes and make their way down the inlet. Before the crew disembarked, the Lieutenant asked for, and got, six volunteers to remain with him on the *Ellis.* Early the next morning the enemy on the river bank opened fire on the grounded vessel and soon had it in a helpless condition. Forced to abandon the *Ellis,* Cushing and his six men clambered into a small boat and bent to the oars. Escaping a Confederate detachment which sought to intercept them at a bend in the river, they rowed safely out to sea. "Because he had lost his ship, Cushing asked for a court of inquiry; instead, he was commended for his courageous and successful escape."[12]

The destruction of the *Ellis* by Confederate troops was fortuitous, certainly, but not so for the capture of Plymouth during the second week in December. As early as October 22, plans were being drawn up "to drive the enemy out of Plymouth and give the people of Martin, Wash-

---

as executive officer aboard the *Perry,* he had performed heroically in the attack on Franklin, Virginia. The young officer wrote his cousin on October 18: "You see I have sort of a roving commission and can run around to suit myself. . . . If under these circumstances I can not stir the rebels up in more places than one, it will be strange indeed." In just a few days he "stirred up the rebels" by steaming into New Topsail Inlet and capturing the *Adelaide* which was loaded with "600 barrels of spirits of turpentine and 36 bales of cotton and some tobacco." This exploit was followed by the Jacksonville raid, described above. Cushing's next adventure came in early 1863 when he attempted to capture some of the pilots who guided the blockade-runners in and out of Wilmington. *NR,* VIII, Ser. I, 106-13, 150-52; T. W. Haight, *Three Wisconsin Cushings,* Original Papers No. 3 (Madison: Wisconsin Historical Commission, 1910), pp. 60-61; C. E. McCartney, *Mr. Lincoln's Admirals* (New York: Funk and Wagnalls Co., 1956), p. 202; R. J. Roske and C. Van Doren, *Lincoln's Commando: The Biography of Commander W. B. Cushing, U.S.N.* (New York: Harper and Brothers, 1957), pp. 113-48; *Message of the President of the United States and Accompanying Documents, to the Two Houses of Congress, at the Commencement of the First Session of the Thirty-Eight Congress* (Washington: GPO, 1863), pp. 41-42.

ington and Tyrrell counties an opportunity to bring out their produce."
Writing from Petersburg, Major General S. G. French urged Governor
Clark to say nothing of this move "as secrecy is the soul of success in
cases of this kind."[13] When the attack finally materialized it caught the
Federals by surprise. Lieutenant Colonel John C. Lamb, with several
companies from the Seventeenth North Carolina, a squadron of cavalry,
and "Moore's battery," reached the picket stations outside of Plymouth
just before daybreak on December 10. Colonel Lamb captured all of
the Union sentinels but one. The soldier who escaped had enough foresight, however, to fire his rifle as he ran, thus warning the Federal garrison of the approach of the enemy.

When the Confederates reached Plymouth, they found the enemy
formed in a line across Main Street. After sizing up the situation,
Colonel Lamb ordered his cavalry "to charge these men, which was
done in good style and with a full allowance of the rebel yell." The
enemy fired one volley and then broke in all directions.[14] Next the
Colonel turned his artillery on the *Southfield,* the only gunboat in the
river on this date. A few shots disabled her and she dropped downstream. Captain Barnabas Ewer, commander of the Plymouth garrison,
upon seeing the *Southfield* "fall back, got frightened, left his men, and
went on board." When asked where his men were, he replied "he did
not know, but hoped most of them were in the swamp." Ewer, whose
actions on this day were considered "disgraceful" by his superiors, later
reported that the Confederates burned half of the town before retiring.
"All the principal buildings on the street where the hotel was situated
are gone," he wrote. "Everything in headquarters was burned, including the record of those who had taken the oath of allegiance, and some
muster and pay rolls which were to be forwarded to other garrisons in
this part of the state."[15]

The December attack on Plymouth was heartening to the people of
eastern North Carolina, but it was only a raid and not sufficiently strong
to put General Foster on the defensive. During the fall months reinforcements, chiefly Massachusetts nine-month volunteers, had poured
into New Bern in such numbers that the General was no longer confined to his fortifications.[16] In November he had conducted a sizable
raid in the direction of Tarboro. The purpose of this expedition was
to capture three Confederate regiments reported to be gathering forage
in the eastern counties.[17]

On the morning of November 2 a five-thousand-man Federal force, including twenty-one pieces of artillery, left its base at Washington for Williamston. In command was General Foster.[18]

"Our route lay through a level country," wrote a reporter for the Boston *Transcript,* "the soil sandy . . . [was] extremely difficult to march on. An unbroken forest of pines . . . lay on either side. In some places the road was covered with water a foot deep. . . . The day was extremely warm, and our progress was necessarily slow, many of the troops, both the old and new regiments, falling out of ranks from exhaustion."[19] By 4:00 P.M. the Federal advance had reached a point about six miles from Williamston. Here the Confederates were encountered in position on the opposite bank of a small coffee-colored stream called Little Creek. Belger's Rhode Island battery was immediately ordered to the front and, while it shelled the enemy works, the lead regiments prepared to ford the stream.* For many of the new arrivals from Massachusetts, this was their first taste of combat. Some of the men had never even loaded their muskets before and did not know which end of the cartridge went first. Fortunately for these green recruits, the Confederates, after one hour, retired to their rifle pits at Rawls's Mill, one mile distant.[20]

At Rawls's Mill there followed a "spirited engagement" of half an hour with the Confederates being driven from their works and across a bridge which they burned. This little skirmish was a "trying experience" for regiments like the Forty-fourth Massachusetts, which had been organized only sixty days previous.[21] "And that a grateful posterity . . . [might] better understand the situation," a New England soldier entered in his diary:

> Then the muels strove and tugged
> Up the hillsides steep and rugged,
> Till they came into a mudhole;
> This was nary a common puddle,
> One it was without a bottom,
> Into which the muels, rot 'em,
> Got so very far deluded

* When the firing ceased, the members of the Fifth Massachusetts were standing at the water's edge in various stages of undress. A good many of the men, in preparing to ford the stream, had taken off their pants, while others had removed all of their clothing with the exception of their shirts. A few stood in drawers alone. A. S. Roe, *The Fifth Regiment Volunteer Infantry* (Boston: Fifth Regiment Veteran's Association, 1911), p. 142.

Nothing but their ears potruded
Picturing in a situation
Well Abe's administration.[22]

That night, while the pioneers repaired the bridge, the Federal soldiers bivouacked in a corn field near the rifle pits. The next day around noon the army arrived at Williamston. A fight was expected at this place, but the men found it practically deserted; so they proceeded to make themselves "at home." In some of the residences men in blue could be seen "lying on sofas resting themselves and smoking contraband cigars; in others they were sitting at tables enjoying turkey, chickens and sweet potatoes. Everything that could not be taken was destroyed." One soldier arrayed himself in a hoop skirt and with a parasol in hand, "created quite a sensation," to put it mildly.[23]

Resuming its march in the afternoon, the Federal army encamped for the night in a field five miles from Williamston and, moving again on the morning of the 4th, proceeded without opposition to the abandoned Confederate fortifications at Rainbow Banks. From here the troops marched three miles into Hamilton,* which, like Williamston, was practically deserted. In violation of General Foster's orders, the troops wantonly destroyed a great deal of property. Many of the deserted homes were set on fire, "presenting," said a "Yankee" reporter, "a sad spectacle of the ravages of war." As the army marched out of town during the evening, its way was lighted by the glare of the conflagration.[24] Three miles beyond Hamilton the army encamped on a large plantation where an abundance of pigs, poultry, corn, and sweet potatoes were found "for the subsistence of the troops and horses."[25]

The next day, November 5, the Federal advance got within a few miles of Tarboro,† but reports of heavy Confederate troop concentrations in the area‡ caused Foster to abandon his plan of pursuing the enemy into the town.[26] By the tenth, the Federal army was back at Plymouth where it was "re-embarked" for New Bern.§

* The navy cooperated with Foster during this raid, and at Hamilton five gunboats awaited him. *OR*, XVIII, Ser. I, 22.

† In his official report General Foster states that he got within ten miles of Tarboro on the sixth. But other accounts have him there on the fifth. This latter date appears correct since there is no evidence to indicate that the army remained at Hamilton an extra day.

‡ Train whistles heard in the direction of Tarboro helped convince General Foster that Confederate reinforcements were arriving almost hourly. *RR*, VI, 193.

§ While Foster was away from his home base, a Confederate detachment, on Novem-

This raid accomplished very little other than the freeing of a large number of slaves and the destruction of much private property.[27] General Foster failed in his major objective to capture the Confederate regiments foraging in the eastern counties.[28] The five prisoners captured at Little Creek and Rawls's Mill hardly represented three regiments. Charles A. Barker, a Massachusetts soldier, gave a concise account of the expedition when he wrote: "We have . . . burned their houses, stole their whiskey and brought home their horses, mules and other contraband articles. . . . [We got] the best of the country, especially as we left it when we got ready although our departure may have been somewhat hastened by the rebels. . . ."[29]

Following the Tarboro raid, Foster did not remain idle long. Before a month passed, he had his troops on the move again. The Federal army, double in size, had as its destination the important railroad bridge over the Neuse River at Goldsboro. This expedition was timed to coincide with General Burnside's advance on Fredericksburg.* Foster wrote General Halleck that, even if he did not succeed in his "expectations," he hoped the movement might "be useful as a demonstration in favor of the Army of the Potomac."[30]†

The force that the General led out of New Bern on the "splendid wintry morning" of December 11 consisted of 10,000 infantry, 40 pieces of artillery, and 640 cavalry.[31] Taking the Trent Road (a road running a few miles west of the Trent River and almost parallel with it) Foster moved his men about fourteen miles before he found his way obstructed by felled trees. The General bivouacked for the night in order that the pioneers might clear the obstructions.[32]

---

ber 11, paid "the Yankees around Newbern a visit." After driving in some pickets about five miles from town, the raiders captured and thoroughly plundered a hastily evacuated Federal camp. Then they returned to their base at Kinston. J. Evans to Father, Nov. 15, 1862, J. Evans Papers, SHC; D. L. Craft to "My Dear Friend," Nov. 13, 1862, D. L. Craft Papers, DU; *OR*, XVIII, Ser. I, 24-31.

* Following McClellan's Peninsula Campaign, the major battles in the east had been Second Manassas (Bull Run) in August, 1862, and Antietam in September, 1862. In both of these engagements North Carolina soldiers fought well. At Second Manassas the state's losses were 70 killed and 448 wounded. For the invasion of Maryland the reports listed 335 North Carolina soldiers killed and 1,838 wounded. D. H. Hill, Jr., *North Carolina*, ed., C. A. Evans, *Confederate Military History* (Atlanta: Confederate Publishing Co., 1899), IV, 105-31.

† Had Foster not encountered such stiff opposition on this march, he doubtless would have attempted not only to destroy the bridge but also to hold the vital rail junction at Goldsboro. The size of the Federal army seems to uphold this contention. J. L. Stackpole, "The Department of North Carolina under General Foster, July, 1862—July, 1863," *MHSM* (Boston: Military Historical Society of Massachusetts, 1912), IX, 90.

At five o'clock the next morning, Friday, the twelfth, the drum beat roused the men from their slumbers. It was a bitter cold winter's morning—so cold, in fact, that the water in the canteens froze. But roaring fires soon had the containers thawed and the men warm. After gulping down a breakfast of hard bread and steaming coffee, the troops resumed their march.[33] Moving rapidly over a level countryside covered with pine forests, the Federal advance was able to reach a crossroads by noon. The right fork of this intersection led directly to Kinston. At this point General Foster ordered three companies of cavalry to make a demonstration on the Kinston road, while the rest of the army continued its advance along the road to Goldsboro. The main column pushed on another four miles and encamped for the night.[34]

To the weary soldiers it seemed as though they had scarcely retired before reveille put them on the march again. It was Saturday the thirteenth. During the morning the head of the main column came to a crossroads which, at a very sharp angle, led back in a northeasterly direction toward Kinston. Taking this road, Foster advanced as far as Southwest Creek, where he found the bridge across the stream destroyed and a Confederate force, under Colonel James D. Radcliffe's Sixty-first North Carolina, posted on the opposite bank. Since the creek was not fordable at this point, Foster ordered the Ninth New Jersey and the Eighty-fifth Pennsylvania to cross as best they could and flank the Confederate position. With the aid of felled trees, some fragments of the bridge, an old mill dam, and a bit of swimming, these two regiments crossed the stream and dislodged the enemy. Brigadier General N. G. Evans, who had arrived on the field in the meantime and assumed command of the Confederate troops, ordered his men to fall back toward the Neuse River.[35]

He stopped the retreat and dug in about two miles from the Kinston bridge. Evans posted his men in a strong wooded position, "taking advantage of the ground, which formed a natural breastwork." His right flank was protected by a deep swamp and his left by a bend in the river.[36] But to man this well-chosen position, General Evans had only the "Seventeenth, Twenty-second, Twenty-third, and Holcombe Legion South Carolina Volunteers; Colonel Radcliffe's Sixty-first Regiment North Carolina Troops; Major [Peter] Mallett's battalion; Captain R. Boyce's light battery South Carolina Volunteers; Captains [S.R.] Bunt-

Union expedition under General J. G. Foster from New Bern to Goldsboro, December 11-20, 1862. *Top:* Engagement at Goldsboro, December 17. 1862. *Center:* Engagement at Kinston, December 14, 1862. *Bottom:* Engagement at Whitehall, December 16, 1862. (From *Harper's Weekly*)

ing's and [J.B.] Starr's batteries North Carolina troops"—in all, 2,014 men.[*37]

On the morning of December 14, General Evans, with his South Carolinians on the left and the North Carolinians on the right, awaited Foster's attack. It commenced around nine o'clock. The Ninth New Jersey in the lead was deployed as skirmishers in the woods on both sides of the road.[38] The Federal soldiers advanced calmly when "almost simultaneously the whistling of grape shot and crashing of boughs over . . . [their] heads" caused them to hit the dirt at once.[39] The Confederates were so effectively concealed in the woods that hardly a man could be seen, and for a while it was a "blind battle of invisible foes."[40] When the firing started, the two lines were within seventy-five yards of each other" and shots flew thick and fast.[†] "It was a time to try the soul," said a South Carolina soldier, "the balls whizzing past and men falling around."[41]

General Foster placed his artillery in a large field on the right of the road about three-quarters of a mile in the rear of his line of attack.[42] As the regiments arrived at this point, Foster ordered them into the woods on either side of the road. A good many of the troops were volunteers who had never been under fire.[43][‡] In the excitement of battle some of them fired on their comrades by mistake and,[44] in turn, had their own artillery drop shells in their ranks. E. T. Hale, a new recruit in the Forty-fifth Massachusetts, described his experiences as follows:

> At about ten we left the main road and marched into a corn-field, crossing which we entered a swampy piece of woods where there was not the least vestige of a road. The swamp became deeper as we advanced, until in many

* General Evans also had Colonel S. D. Pool's battalion of heavy artillery which "commanded the intrenchments at the obstruction's below Kinston." A fleet of gunboats was supposed to cooperate with Foster on this expedition, but a combination of low water and Colonel Pool's guns kept them from reaching Kinston. *OR*, XVIII, Ser. I, 105, 113.

† A soldier in the Ninth New Jersey said his regiment "gladly retraced its steps out of the swamp, where it was constantly assailed by a rattling shower of grape and leaden hail. . . ." J. M. Drake, *The History of the Ninth New Jersey Veteran Volunteers* (Elizabeth: Journal Printing House, 1889), p. 102.

‡ One hesitant soldier, as he entered "the gloomy recesses of the swamp at Kinston," could recall only "a line of black faces behind . . . out of the range of shot. . . . They were officer's servants and camp-followers, attached in various ways to the column. They were not at the time supposed to possess sufficient courage to fight." E. H. Rogers, *Reminiscences of Military Service in the Forty-third Regiment, Massachusetts Infantry* (Boston: Franklin Press, 1883), p. 101. The heavy firing caused some of the Federal soldiers to break ranks and run. C. A. Barker Diary, Dec. 14, 1862, EI.

places it was up to our knees, in some cases it was waist deep. We had to struggle along as best we could; several times I became so enlaced in the vines and shrubbery that I found it almost impossible to extricate myself. We had not gone far in this way before we were obliged to pass under the fire of one of our own batteries; of course we felt perfectly safe in doing this, not supposing that we would be shot by our own men, when to our unspeakable horror, the first shot from the battery carried away half the head of a man in Co. D . . . killing him instantly, and the regiment passed on. Our Company after witnessing this, was obliged to pass directly in range of this same battery, however, they were loading at the time, so we escaped. Company K, which comes next behind us came up in season for the next fire, and had had several men wounded, and this from our own gunners. Shortly after this, we began to notice an occasional bullet whistling through the trees toward us, and soon the order came, "Lie down." Just as we were and wherever we happened to be we lay down and commenced firing in the direction from which the shots came. Then the order came "Rise up and advance." We rose and advanced until we got into a furious fire of musketry, when the order was again to lie down and that each man should seek the best protection he could find and there do battle. The only shelter I could see at first was some evergreen boughs which amounted to little or nothing as protection against bullets, but before long I spied a tree about as large as I could clasp with both hands, so I crept behind it and remained there during the rest of the fight.[45]

While young Hale was pinned to the ground by the heavy fire of the North Carolinians on his front, his comrades across the road managed to turn the Confederates left, causing the South Carolinians to retire across the bridge. The center and right of the Confederate line, for some unexplained reason, received no orders to retreat. General Evans, nevertheless, mistakenly assumed that all of his command was safely across the river and ordered the bridge burned. He then opened fire with his artillery upon the Confederate right and center, thinking these were enemy positions.[46] Under this bombardment and mounting Federal pressure, the isolated Confederate line gave way, the extreme right under Colonel Peter Mallett the last to leave the field. The retreat was orderly until the troops came within sight of the burning bridge "crowded with men endeavoring to cross." Panic ensued.[47] The soldiers broke ranks and rushed toward the bridge. "It was an awful scene." W. W. Sullivan, a member of one of the South Carolina regiments, said he could feel his hair being singed as he raced across the burning structure. About midway on the bridge the soldier in front of Sullivan stumbled, causing a terrible pile-up. "I never came so near being mashed to

death and suffocated in my life," he wrote a friend. "I thought my time
had come and that I had passed the balls only to perish miserably on
that burning bridge, but at last I dragged myself out and hobbled across
the bridge," dropping exhausted on the other side.[48] So near were the
pursuing Federals that about four hundred of Evans' command were
unable to cross the bridge* and were captured.[49]

General Evans reformed his broken ranks and, joined by the Forty-
seventh North Carolina which had just arrived on the scene, prepared a
new line of battle about two miles beyond Kinston. Soon a messenger
arrived from General Foster with a demand for surrender, to which the
Confederate officer replied: "Tell your General to go to h--l."[50] Upon
receipt of Evans' reply, Foster made ready for an attack. However, before he could get into position, the Confederates withdrew.† The Union
General decided not to pursue and that night bivouacked his troops in
a field near the town. While here General Foster learned not only that
Burnside had been defeated at Fredericksburg but also that Confederate
reinforcements were being rushed to North Carolina.[51] Despite this
disturbing news, Foster decided to move on to Goldsboro and do as
much damage to the railroad as possible before returning to New Bern.
The next morning, the fifteenth, the Federals recrossed the Neuse on
the partially destroyed bridge and took the river road for Goldsboro.
They left behind a thoroughly ransacked town,‡ Kinston.[52]

The Federal troops advanced to within four miles of Whitehall, a
small village on the south side of the Neuse about eighteen miles from
Goldsboro. After halting for the night, General Foster sent three com-

* When the Federal soldiers reached the bridge the sight of "two dead bodies lying
in the fire" was a shocking experience. Z. Gooding to Brother, Dec. 27, 1862, Z. Gooding
Papers, SHC. A bucket brigade extinguished the flames before great damage was done.

† Many of the officers in General Evans' command were critical of their superior's
actions at Kinston and petitioned that he be removed. One of them wrote: "Any private
in the ranks could have carried out things better than Gen. Evans. It was disgraceful
the way he acted and sacrificed his men. He was drunk as usual, and it seems he did
not know what he was about. He was not too drunk, however, to keep in a safe place,
and he did not show himself once on the battlefield. He kept on this side of the bridge."
W. W. Sullivan to "My dear Friend," Dec. 27, 1862, Lalla Pelot Papers, DU.

‡ Four days after the battle, the wife of a prominent Kinston physician wrote her
brother about her experiences while the Federal army was in town. She managed to get
guards, she said, for her house, but "Calvin and Adams [servants] had to help them,
for the soldiers were carrying on the most wholesale robbery. . . . At Delia's . . . they
took every article of bed clothing, knives and forks, sugar, honey, preserves, table cloths—
in fact everything." The writer concluded by saying: "I felt more like crying than I had
for the day." Mary E. Miller, "Letter from Mrs. Mary Ellen Miller to John Jameson—
Kinston, N.C., December 18, 1862," *NCHR*, V (Oct., 1928), 452-57.

panies of cavalry and several pieces of artillery to make a reconnaissance in the direction of Whitehall. The horsemen arrived just in time to see a Confederate force retire across the river and apply the torch to the bridge. The Federal artillery was brought into position immediately, and it shelled the Confederate position until after dark. In order to reveal "every movement of the enemy," two thousand barrels of turpentine were seized by the Federal cavalry, piled in an immense heap on the river's bank, and set on fire. "Such a bonfire mortal eyes have seldom seen," said a Northern reporter. "Vast sheets of billowy flame flashed their forked tongues to the clouds. The whole region for miles around was lighted up." Aided by this light, a private in the Third New York Cavalry swam the river to put the finishing touches on a partially completed Confederate boat already hit by several shells. The private got across the stream and returned safely, but Confederate rifle fire kept him away from the boat. After this rather daring exploit, Major Jeptha Garrard marched the entire command back to camp.[53]

The next morning—December 16—the main Federal column reached Whitehall.* Finding the bridge over the Neuse burned and "the enemy in some force, with infantry and artillery on the other side," General Foster decided "to make a strong fight, as if to rebuild and cross," and then to continue his march along the main road to Goldsboro. The Ninth New Jersey and Colonel Thomas J. C. Armory's brigade were sent forward and posted on the bank of the river "to engage the enemy."[54] In this exposed position the Federals were to suffer rather heavy casualties. The woods, free of underbrush, offered little protection, while the Confederates were "screened by the rank growth on their side of the river, whose autumn coloring fairly matched the color of their garments."[55] General Foster also ordered up several batteries and posted them on a hill overlooking the Confederate entrenchments.

In command of the Confederate line was Brigadier General B. H. Robertson of Evans' command. Under him were the Eleventh North Carolina, Colonel Collett Leventhorpe; the Thirty-first North Carolina, Colonel John V. Jordan; six hundred dismounted cavalrymen from

---

* On this same morning General Foster ordered Major Jeptha Garrard with five companies of the Third New York Cavalry to proceed to Mt. Olive station on the Wilmington and Weldon Railroad. Garrard arrived at the depot around 3:00 P.M. He found the ticket agent selling tickets and passengers loitering around waiting for cars. The Major put everyone under arrest, cut the telegraph wires, and sent out detachments to tear up the track. *OR*, XVIII, Ser. I, 69; W. W. Howe, *Kinston, Whitehall and Goldsboro Expedition, December, 1862* (New York: W. W. Howe, 1890), pp. 31-34.

D. D. Ferrebee's and Evans' regiments; and a section of J. W. Moore's battery, under Lieutenant N. McClees.[56] Owing to the range of hills on the Whitehall side of the river, the Federal troops had the advantage of position, and since the "point occupied by . . . [Foster's] troops was so narrow, not more than one Confederate regiment at a time could advantageously engage him." Robertson, therefore, held Leventhorpe, Ferrebee, and Evans in reserve. This left the artillery, Thirty-first Regiment and two picket companies in front. The cannonading from the enemy's batteries became "so terrific" that the Thirty-first North Carolina withdrew from its position without orders, necessitating the advance of Leventhorpe, who moved up with "alacrity."[57] Louis Warlick, a member of the Eleventh North Carolina, knew there were bigger battles than Whitehall "by a great deal," but he did not think any regiment "since the war commenced" was under heavier fire than the Eleventh. He maintained that the only thing that saved them "from all being killed was the heap of logs on the river bank. . . ."[58] Another North Carolina soldier with similar sentiments wrote his sister that, had it not been for the large number of "saw logs" along the banks, "it would have been murder."[59] So deadly was the Federal artillery fire that the dense woods on the opposite side of the river were mowed down, said one observer, "as the scythe mows the grass. For a quarter of a mile back from the river, and for a mile up and down the banks scarcely a tree was left standing."[60]

After the fight at Whitehall, Foster moved on toward Goldsboro. His men gaily sang "Rally Round the Flag, Boys, Rally Once Again," as they marched along.[61] By the morning of the seventeenth, this high-spirited army had reached the railroad a few miles south of Goldsboro. From this point General Foster sent a detachment of cavalry to nearby Dudley Station and Everittsville to destroy railroad property.[62] At the same time he ordered five regiments to move down the track and burn the railroad bridge over the Neuse.[63] This important crossing was guarded by Confederate troops under Brigadier General Thomas L. Clingman. At or near the bridge were the Eighth, Fifty-first, and Fifty-second North Carolina. In position on the north side of the Neuse, "commanding the immediate approaches to the railroad," were three companies of the Tenth Artillery, acting as infantry, one company from the Fortieth Artillery also serving as infantry, and Starr's battery, all under Colonel S. D. Pool. There were other troops in the vicinity but for various reasons, including lack of transportation, they did not become engaged in the battle.[64]*

The Federal attack fell heaviest upon the Fifty-first and Fifty-second North Carolina "on the southwest side of the bridge" and on Colonel S. D. Pool's companies on the north side of the crossing. The two North Carolina regiments, unable to hold their own against the heavy Federal fire, broke and fell back across the country bridge that spanned the river about one quarter of a mile from the railroad bridge and that was on a road nearly parallel with the track.[65] As these regiments re-treated, a Lieutenant Graham of the Twenty-third New York Battery rushed forward under heavy fire and put the torch to the railroad bridge. To prevent a Confederate effort to save the structure, General Foster brought "all of . . . [his] artillery to bear" on the bridge. Satisfied after a short while that "the fire was doing its work," the General ordered a countermarch for New Bern. He left Colonel H. C. Lee to form a rear guard.[66]

Lee was forming his brigade to leave the field, thinking the fight was over, when he happened to notice there were enemy regimental colors across the railroad. Before he could get his men into a defensive position, wildly cheering Confederates emerged from behind the high roadbed and charged the unsuspecting Federals. The gray-clad soldiers were able to get within a few hundred yards of Lee's brigade before artillery fire shattered their ranks, forcing them to retire.[67] This heroic little charge ended the day's fighting for both sides and, along with it, the Goldsboro raid.†

General Foster considered the expedition "a perfect success,"[68] a con-clusion not accepted by all those who made the tiresome march, however. The object of the expedition "is said to have been accomplished," wrote one soldier, "but the return of all the forces to this place [New Bern] has a . . . [demoralizing] effect."[69] Another trooper considered Decem-ber 21—the date his battered regiment returned from the expedition—

---

* The Sixty-first North Carolina and Evan's brigade of South Carolinians arrived on the field in time to take part in the afternoon fighting. Also, when General Evans reached the bridge, he took over command from Clingman.

† Like the skirmish at Whitehall the fight at Goldsboro was small when compared to some of the battles in Virginia. But, said a North Carolina soldier, it "quite satisfied all who were engaged in it." To him the incessant roar of the cannon resembled the peal of thunder "while volly after volly of grape whizzing along and then tearing up the ground on their errand of death played beautiful the part of a whirlwind. . . ." Cousin [?] to Catherine Buie, Jan. 21, 1863, Catherine (McG.) Buie Papers, DU.

the "saddest day" he had "seen in the army."[70] A member of the Fifth Rhode Island Heavy Artillery, in commenting on the operation, could only point to the fact that much private property, namely "fences . . . houses . . . cattle, hogs, poultry . . . sweet potatoes . . . and corn," had been "swept away in a few days."[71]*

Even though the countryside had been terribly devastated, this was not the primary purpose of the expedition. Foster set out to destroy the Wilmington and Weldon Railroad in the Goldsboro area. Including the loss of the Neuse River bridge, the damage to the line was only superficial and was repaired in a few days. Confederate work crews soon had a temporary structure built over the Neuse, and the road was operative again before the new year rolled around.[72]

On the evening of December 31, a Confederate soldier in camp near Weldon wrote his sister:

The last day of the old year is just passing away and tomorrow the usherer in of the new will soon be upon us. How great the contrast in the condition of our young Republic do we see now when compared to what it was twelve months ago. Then, the fall of Fort Donelson, Roanoke and Newbern and the continued successes of our foes had cast gloom over the whole Confederacy. . . . These reverses, though, . . . called forth more energy and we have the happy result in the present, bright, prosperous state of our affairs. The victory at Fredericksburg has sent the Abolition army "reeling back from its third attempt upon Richmond"; our Capitol is still safe. Foster, indeavoring to cut our line of communication with the south at Goldsboro, did no material damage and fled hastily back to his fortifications at Newbern.

In concluding, the writer admitted that the fortunes of war were uncertain but he was quick to add: "I live in hope."[73] This was an optimism shared by many in the Confederacy and aptly expressed by another soldier when he said: "The sky is brighter to-day . . . than it has been since the inception of the revolution."[74]†

---

*Another soldier in describing the march back to New Bern through the burning pine woods noted that "all the foliage was burned off, and the blackened tree trunks, in places ashy-white, looked like ghosts in the smoky atmosphere." Barker Diary, Dec. 18, 1862, EI.

†A soldier from New England expressed well the feelings of some of the men in blue: "And 1863 will soon be here! Would that it could be a happy new year to the people of the once United States. Darker and darker grows the day! defeat after defeat! Are we to go down? Must this once great nation sink into nothingness? I hope not but these are trying times for us all." N. C. Delaney, "Letters of a Maine Soldier Boy," *CWH*, V (March, 1959), p. 58.

CHAPTER VII

D. H. Hill Takes Command

AFTER HIS great victory at Fredericksburg, General Lee detached Lieutenant General James Longstreet with two divisions and sent him to the south side of the James to defend against any possible Federal move on Richmond from that direction.[1] A week later, February 25, 1863, Longstreet took on added responsibilities when he replaced Major General Gustavus Smith as commander of the Department of Virginia and North Carolina, with headquarters at Petersburg.* The new commander was a fighter and had no intention of "lying still to await the enemy's" first move.[2] It was Longstreet's intention to protect the supply lines in eastern North Carolina and at the same time gather provisions from that fertile region. This plan was agreeable to Lee,† who badly needed the supplies.[3] In order that the Confederate supply trains could move unmolested through the rich corn country, especially that east of the Chowan River, it was necessary to keep the enemy confined to his bases in tidewater Virginia and eastern North Carolina. In pursuance of this plan, Longstreet organized in Virginia a move on Suffolk, while D. H. Hill, his subordinate in North Carolina, planned demonstrations on New Bern and Washington.[4]‡

---

* General Longstreet's orders read: "You are by special orders, this day assigned to the command of the department recently made vacant by the resignation of Maj. Gen. G. W. Smith." *OR*, XVIII, Ser. I, 895. Smith's command had embraced "that part of the country lying south of the line of operations under General R. E. Lee, including the Department of North Carolina." *Ibid.*, p. 748. On January 27, 1863, General Smith was called to Richmond and Major General S. G. French was put in temporary command of the department. *Ibid.*, p. 861.

† General Lee, however, could see little to be gained at this time from a major offensive. "The enemy's positions in North Carolina have always appeared to me to be taken for defense," he wrote Longstreet, "and if driven from them they can easily escape to their gunboats. Unless, therefore, they will come out into the country I do not know how you can advantageously get them." *OR*, XVIII, Ser. I, 907.

‡ Longstreet also felt that "a forward movement would be a diversion in favor of

General Hill assumed command of the troops in North Carolina on February 25[5] and immediately addressed "a few words of exhortation" to his troops. Urging his men to do their "full day," he promised "those who . . . [had] never been in battle . . . the novel sensation of listening to the sound of hostile shot and shell, and those who . . . [had] listened a great way off . . . [the chance] to come some miles nearer, and compare the sensation caused by the distant cannonade with that produced by the rattle of musketry."[6] From most of his men these words brought a "Hurah! for old Daniel H."[7]

The Raleigh *Progress*, in commenting on Hill's appointment, had this to say: "We have had vastly too much strategy, too much science, and too much ditching and digging in North Carolina. Had we less of these and more fighting things might have been different, than at present; and as General Hill has established a reputation for being one of the best fighting men in the service, we may expect a change in management if not a change in base, in North Carolina."[8] Major John C. Haskell, who was sent to North Carolina "to organize the artillery and incidentally, to command it," described Hill as "a man of considerable capacity and always seemed to go from choice into the most dangerous place he could find on the field. He was as earnest in his Puritan beliefs as was Stonewall Jackson, who was his brother-in-law. . . . He had a high and well deserved reputation as a fighter."[9]

General Hill found it difficult to live up to his "reputation as a fighter" because he considered his force too small "to assume offensive operations." He wrote Longstreet:

Charleston [S.C.] . . . ." *OR*, XVIII, Ser. I, 903. The year 1863 opened with the prospect of another invasion of North Carolina by Federal forces. Toward the end of January a force of about twelve thousand men was assembled at Beaufort, North Carolina, to assist in a joint land and naval attack on the defenses of Wilmington. General Lee, still faced by Burnside's army, which was "increasing rather than diminishing," was unable to answer calls for aid. He did offer to detach General D. H. Hill, "a native of North Carolina, and most valuable officer," and send him to Raleigh "to enspirit or encourage the people." The threat of invasion, though, passed away in early February when authorities in Washington decided to attack Charleston, South Carolina, rather than Wilmington. Ten thousand of the Federal troops in North Carolina were sent to Port Royal, South Carolina, to assist Major General David Hunter and Rear Admiral S. F. Dupont in operations against Charleston. *OR*, XVIII, Ser. I., 819, 823-24; J. A. Seddon to Z. B. Vance, Jan. 17, 1863, D. H. Hill Papers, NCDAH; J. A. Sloan, *Reminiscences of the Guilford Grays, Co. B, Twenty-seventh North Carolina Regiment* (Washington: R. O. Polkinborn, 1883), pp. 60-64; G. J. Fiebeger, *Campaigns of the American Civil War* (West Point: U.S. Military Printing Office, 1914), p. 186.

With the addition of a single good Brigade I could drive the enemy to his strongholds, and get out immense supplies of corn and bacon from the rich eastern counties. The presence of this force too would secure confidence to the planters and protect that planting interest so essential to our very existence another year. If the planters are not protected in the east, we must lose next year the richest and most valuable portion of the Confederacy. The question of supply is getting to be a very serious one and we cannot afford to lose the crops in Pitt, Bertie, Edgecomb, etc. The planters are now at a loss to know what to do and will not pitch another crop until the presence of a competent force in North Carolina will guarantee protection. . . . A forward movement too at this time would distract the enemy's attention from South Carolina, detain his forces here and perhaps compel him to send others. I am strongly impressed with the importance of harassing the yankees here and have written to the Secretary of War on the subject but a single word from you would have more effect than all I could say in a month.[10]

This letter crossed in the mails with one from General Longstreet expressing "almost precisely" the same views,[11] and in compliance with General Hill's request for more troops, Longstreet instructed Brigadier General W. H. C. Whiting at Wilmington "to prepare himself to reinforce . . . [Hill with] 4000 men." This additional force, Longstreet estimated, would bring Hill's command up to fourteen or fifteen thousand men.[12]

In arranging his forces to protect the supply trains in the eastern counties of North Carolina, Longstreet planned for Hill to "make a diversion upon New Bern and surprise the garrison at Washington." Heavy rains and high waters, however, delayed the attack on Washington, forcing Hill to make a strong demonstration on New Bern first.[13] General Hill's strategy for this latter operation called for a three-pronged push on the city. The attack was to be launched from Kinston where four different roads, besides the railroad, led to the coast. Hill instructed Brigadier General Junius Daniel's brigade to move on New Bern by the "lower Trent road"; the cavalry under Brigadier General B. H. Robertson was ordered to proceed along "the south side of the Trent River," and Brigadier General James Johnston Pettigrew, with the artillery under Major John C. Haskell, was to approach the city near Barrington's Ferry. Robertson's orders were to break up the Atlantic and North Carolina Railroad. Pettigrew's instructions were to shell Fort Anderson and the enemy gunboats in the river.[14]

The opening round in the Confederate attack on New Bern occurred on Friday, March 13,* when General Daniel's scouts, moving along the "lower Trent road," encountered enemy pickets about ten miles from the city. The Federals were easily pushed back two miles to a line of works at Deep Gully. Then the "excitement commenced." Following a bombardment of the Federal position,[15] General Daniel led four companies in a successful charge on the enemy works.[16] "We run them out of their intrenchments," remarked a North Carolina soldier.[17] Before the end of the day the Federals were "heavily re-enforced";[18] still, they made no attempt "at a recapture of Deep Gully" until daybreak the next morning.[19] Repulsed in this attempt, the Federal troops retired under orders to the main defenses at New Bern.[20]

* In early January, 1863, General Foster had approximately twenty-four thousand men in his department. Ten thousand of these, however, he took to South Carolina in February to participate in the attack on Charleston. See above p. 150n. Following a quarrel with General David Hunter, Foster returned to North Carolina later in the month. But he had to leave his troops behind. Thus, when General Hill made his move, the Federal forces in eastern North Carolina numbered no more than fourteen thousand.

The attack on New Bern, though the first major offensive move by either side in 1863, was not the only activity up to that time. January, February, and March saw much reconnaissance work on both sides and a number of minor skirmishes. A Federal reconnaissance from New Bern to Pollocksville, Trenton, and Young's Cross-Roads, January 17 to 21, was little more than a mud march and one participant complained: "[we] fired only two guns, as the rebels had run, not being reinforced." *OR*, XVIII, Ser. I, 127-30; E. H. Rogers, *Reminiscences of Military Service in the Forty-third Regiment, Massachusetts Infantry* (Boston: Franklin Press, 1883), 110-18; C. F. Pierce, *History and Camp Life of Company C, Fifty-first Regiment, Massachusetts Volunteer Militia, 1862-1863* (Worcester: Charles Hamilton, 1886), p. 97; *RR*, VI, 394-96. At Sandy Ridge, near Kinston, on February 13 the Fifty-eighth Pennsylvania skirmished with a detachment from the Eighth North Carolina, killing one, wounding four, and capturing forty-three North Carolinians. *OR*, XVIII, Ser. I, 153-54. A Federal expedition to Hyde County the first part of March was especially destructive. A member of the One Hundred Third Pennsylvania stated that the "object of this expedition was in the nature of a reprisal for the action of a number of citizens of this county who had formed a home guard and in an ambushcade had killed several of the 3d New York cavalry the previous week." The writer admitted that "during this trip, from the time the Regiment debarked until it re-embarked at the landing, a half-mile from Swan Quarter, no attempt was made to keep discipline. . . . There is no doubt," he said, "that this raid was the most discreditable affair in which the 103d Regiment participated during nearly four years of service." L. S. Dickey, *History of the One Hundred Third Regiment Pennsylvania Veteran Volunteer Infantry, 1861-1865* (Chicago: L. S. Dickey, 1910), p. 42; E. T. Hale to Mother, Feb. 27, 1863, E. T. Hale Papers, SHC; *OR*, XVIII, Ser. I, 180-83.

The Confederate and Federal pickets in eastern North Carolina did a lot of fraternizing as their posts frequently were almost in sight of each other. A Confederate soldier on duty below Kinston wrote a friend about how some men of his company, under a flag of truce, had visited a "Yankee" camp and got "as much good lickar as they could drink and plenty of good things to eat." W. McLeod to J. M. Harrington, Feb. 22, 1863, J. M. Harrington Papers, DU; C. Hackett to J. C. Hackett, Feb. 28, 1863, J. C. Hackett Papers, DU.

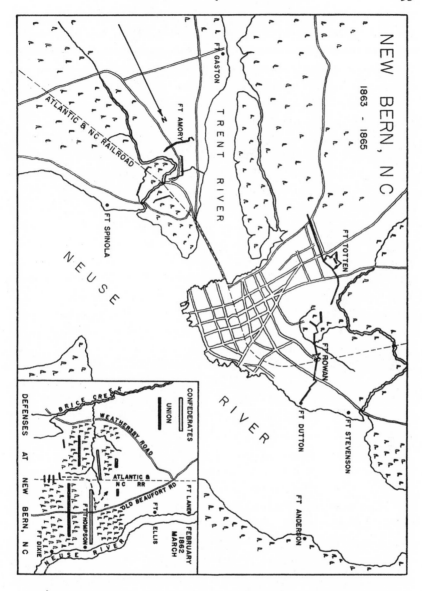

General Daniel's victory at Deep Gully failed to assure Hill of a successful expedition. Difficulties encountered at Fort Anderson were to doom the Confederate chances of taking New Bern. General Pettigrew had hoped "to carry the work by moonlight on Friday morning" and with that objective in mind he had pushed his men night and day. He got them within a short distance of the Neuse River, but ahead of his wagons, and too hungry and exhausted to move to the attack. For twenty-eight hours the Confederate troops lay within a few miles of the enemy at Fort Anderson. Fortunately for Pettigrew, the Federals "never seemed to suspect trouble" until the fight actually started on the morning of the fourteenth.[21]

Fort Anderson, which was garrisoned by the Ninety-second New York, Lieutenant Colonel Hiram Anderson, Jr., commanding, was an earthwork on the north bank of the Neuse directly opposite New Bern. It was flanked on both sides by swamps and was approachable only in front along a narrow causeway. At dawn on the morning of the fourteenth, General Pettigrew rushed his command across this causeway and, with the light batteries, opened "a rapid and well directed fire" on the fort.* After several minutes of intense firing, the General sent an aide, Lieutenant Louis G. Young, to the fort with a demand for its surrender. Fearful that a charge on the Federal works would cost him between fifty and a hundred men, Pettigrew had decided to deploy his force, demoralize the enemy by a heavy fire, and then demand a surrender. By these moves he planned on saving his own men "and not unnecessarily killing theirs."[22]

The surrender demand proved a serious mistake. Colonel Anderson had no intention of surrendering his garrison. To gain time for the Federal gunboats to get into position, he asked for a cease fire. The Colonel made his request under the pretense of consulting with General Foster at New Bern about capitulation. Against the advice of Major Haskell and Lieutenant Young, Pettigrew granted the truce. But when it became evident that Anderson was merely stalling, the General ordered his artillery to resume its "rapid and terrific fire." So many shell fragments fell in the river behind Fort Anderson that a New England journalist decribed the water as resembling "a pond in a hailstorm." Those shells

* When the firing started, the Federal garrison in New Bern thought it was in honor of the capture of the city which had occurred a year ago that day. A "gay time" had been planned—reviews, salutes and "plenty of beer." But the news that the firing came from the enemy soon put an end to all thoughts of revelry. The Federal soldiers formed in "light marching order" before breakfast, and "it looked," said one of their number, "as if our breakfast as well as our beer would get stale." J. J. Wyeth, *Leaves from a Diary Written While Serving in the Department of North Carolina from September, 1862, to June, 1863* (Boston: L. F. Lawrence and Co., 1878), p. 41; A. S. Roe, *The Fifth Regiment Volunteer Infantry* (Boston: Fifth Regiment Veteran's Association, 1911), p. 204.

not over-shooting their mark completely riddled the camp in the fort and kept the Federal soldiers pinned down to their positions. This heavy Confederate fire lasted until the Union gunboats arrived on the scene.[23]

Although late getting into the fight, these vessels,* along with a battery on the New Bern side of the river, soon made the Confederate position tenuous.[24] General Pettigrew had only four guns with range enough to reach the gunboats. Of these, one exploded, another broke down and the shells from the others "burst just outside the guns." So, rather than sacrifice his men by storming the works with infantry, Pettigrew decided to withdraw. The Twenty-sixth North Carolina and its youthful commander, Henry King Burgwyn, left the field with much reluctance, having waited since daylight to assault the fort.[25]

General Robertson, under orders to cut the railroad, fared little better than Pettigrew in achieving his objectives.[26] Because of this he was severely reprimanded by the Commanding General: "Robertson sent me out a lieutenant, who partly cut the railroad. He sent out a Colonel who saw some Yankees and came back. Robertson did not go himself. We must have a better man."[27] The failure of the cavalry should not have come as a surprise to General Hill for a month earlier he had called Robertson's brigade "wonderfully inefficient"† and requested that the Secretary of War send Wade Hampton's cavalry‡ to North Carolina.[28]

The failure of Robertson and Pettigrew to carry their objectives caused General Hill to withdraw his forces from New Bern. Although the Confederate movements had done little more than harass the enemy, Southern newspapers carried reports of a Confederate victory in which fifteen hundred prisoners were taken. Hill's men not only knew this was untrue but many of them also had serious doubts as to whether their Commanding General had any "real object" in mind when he started the expedition.[29] Young Walter MacRae, who was in the skirmish at Deep Gully, wrote his brother:

* The *Hunchback* was aground and the other two vessels needed repairs.

† Hill put very little faith in any cavalry, once offering a reward to anyone who would find him a dead man with spurs on. J. W. Ratchford to D. H. Hill, [?], D. H. Hill Papers, NCDAH. For North Carolina's mounted units General Hill had practically no use. He wrote his wife on March 8, 1863, following some skirmishing below Kinston: "Our men except the cavalry behaved well. Cavalry is always cavalry and our North Carolina cavalry seems to be peculiarly so." D. H. Hill to "My Dear Old Woman," Mar. 8, 1863, D. H. Hill Papers, NCDAH.

‡ At this time Wade Hampton of South Carolina was commander of a brigade of J. E. B. Stuart's Cavalry Corps of the Army of Northern Virginia.

Repulse of D. H. Hill's troops at New Bern, March 14, 1863. (From *Harper's Weekly*)

Nobody hurt on either side—one of our horses killed. The 1500 prisoners captured at Deep Gully have dwindled down to *one* cross-eyed Yankee and a Buffaloe! No one down here knows what General Hill intended to do . . . although the papers confidently assert that he accomplished his object. To the admirers of Daniel H., it would not seem exactly oxthodox to say he had no definite object in view when he set out from Kinston; but I must say it looks very like it to a man up a tree. These big generals don't always have such deep laid plans as people give them credit for.[30]

Immediately after the New Bern fiasco, Hill turned his attention to Washington. General Lee had already advised against a full scale attack on the town because of the loss it might entail.[31] Longstreet, who agreed with Lee that a frontal assault would be unwise, suggested to Hill that he withdraw from Washington if he found that the reduction of the garrison "at any point" would take "too much time." But, if at all possible, Hill was first to get the supplies out of the eastern counties.[32] Additional "objects" of the expedition were "to harass the Yankees . . . and to make a diversion in . . . favor" of General P. G. T. Beauregard at Charleston.[33]

By March 30, Hill had Washington under siege. Along the Pamlico River, east of the town, he erected batteries to engage the Federal gunboats and to check any attempt to reinforce the enemy garrison by water. The fort on the south bank of the Pamlico at Hill's Point, constructed by the Confederates at the start of the war, was seized and guns were placed at Swan's Point, which was further up and on the north bank of the river. The Rodman's Point battery, armed with Whitworth guns, guarded the south bank a short distance below Washington. In addition to the various batteries, rows of piles cut off below the water and sunken hulks made river travel a hazardous undertaking. To prevent the relief of the Washington garrison by the Federal forces at New Bern which could move overland, General Hill placed the brigades of Pettigrew and Daniel between the Chockowinity crossroads and Blount's Creek. Across the river, Brigadier General R. B. Garnett's Virginians* invested the town.[34]

When General Foster learned that the Confederates planned an attack on Washington, he immediately left New Bern with several members of his staff for the Tar-Pamlico River town, arriving there just ahead of Hill's forces. He found that the Federal garrison numbered approximately twelve hundred men drawn from the Forty-fourth and Twenty-seventh Massachusetts, First North Carolina (Union) Volunteers, Third New York Cavalry, and Third New York Artillery. Supporting these ground forces were the gunboats *Commodore Hull, Ceres,* and *Louisiana,* anchored in the river.†

Immediately upon his arrival in Washington, Foster began to strengthen existing fortifications and to build new ones. Strong forts and blockhouses were located within the town, along the river, and at key road intersections. In order that anyone assaulting the fortifications would have to pass over open terrain, the woods in front of the entrenchments were leveled for half a mile.[35]

Since General Hill was under orders to take his objective by siege, most of the fighting at Washington consisted of an exchange of artillery

---

* At the time of the New Bern attack, General Garnett's brigade at Greenville was under orders to invest Plymouth in order that the surrounding countryside could be foraged. Although it was late in getting started, a sizable force numbering 2500 men, one battery and a regiment of cavalry, "sat quietly down in a couple miles of Plymouth" and remained there from Wednesday, March 18, until Saturday. During this period Confederate supply wagons brought out of Washington and Tyrrell counties 35,000 pounds of bacon, and a great deal of corn, potatoes, and lard. J. T. Ellis to "Dear Charles," Mar. 26, 1863, G. W. Munford Papers, DU; G. P. Erwin to Mother, Mar. 24, 1863, G. P. Erwin Papers, SHC.

† Foster strengthened his garrison by arming some of the Negroes at Washington. E. R. Hutchins, *The War of the Sixties* (New York: Neale Publishing Co., 1912), p. 384.

fire.* Every day during the siege Confederate guns engaged the Federal forts and gunboats.[36] A surgeon in the Forty-fourth Massachusetts wrote on April 2, 1863: "The face of events has greatly changed since last I wrote and at present we are regularly besieged; cut off from the world outside and surrounded more or less by batteries, which boom away at intervals, to keep us constantly aware of their existence."[37] And when the band of the Forty-fourth Massachusetts played "Dixie," the Confederate bombardment always seemed to intensify.[38]

General Garnett in a report to Hill said he gave "the enemy a dose of artillery every morning" but, fearing that he might exhaust his ammunition, the fire had "to be somewhat broken." He could not perceive that he had produced "any effect other than to make the Yankees keep very close behind their breast-works."[39]†

The Federal fleet in the Pamlico River below Hill's Point had a calliope, and every day after dinner someone would play it; then the vessels would shell the Confederate position for an hour or two. A Confederate soldier remarked: "They never did any real harm; it was almost as if it were done for an evening's entertainment."[40] Up the river nearer Washington the firing was heavier.[41] Here the Federal gunboats lying safely near the bridge exchanged shots daily with the Confederate batteries.[42]

Frequently during the siege Hill would go to Major Haskell, his artillery officer, to tell him that he thought General Foster lived in a certain part of town and ask that few shells be thrown in that direction. Haskell "always declined" since Hill "never gave . . . [him] positive orders." Furthermore, it would have been impossible, the Major said, "to throw shells . . . [into Washington] and not hit noncombatants."[43]

After a week in the lines one of Hill's soldiers summed up his expe-

---

* Confederate cavalry did a good bit of reconnoitering, especially at night. In an effort to deceive the enemy, the cavalrymen would tie cow bells around their mounts' necks. But soon the Federals caught on to the ruse and began shooting "at bells." S. F. Blanding, *Recollections of a Sailor Boy or the Cruise of the Gunboat Louisiana* (Providence: E. A. Johnson and Co., 1886), p. 281.

† General Garnett's Virginians were not very happy in North Carolina. John T. Ellis had written: "I am hearty tired of this country and long to return to old Va the land of the free and enlightened." J. T. Ellis to "Dear Charles," Apr. 11, 1863, G. W. Mumford Papers, DU. Earlier the writer had described the people of eastern North Carolina as "grossly ignorant squalid and such specimens of humanity I have never met before in all my travels. . . . Children and pigs abound at every homestead and beauty among the ladies is unheard of." J. T. Ellis to "Dear Charles," Mar. 26, 1863, G. W. Mumford Papers, DU.

riences this way: "We are heare in thre miles of Washington. We expect to march evrry day on the enemy. We have bin a canonading evry day fore the last weak they try to run up the river with their gun boats but we beat them back we have got the river Blockadded we have got the sity serrounded so they can't reinforce . . . . our army is in site of the sitty our Picket guard is in fifty yards of none another. But they ar not aloud to shoot at none another the citisson has ris white flags all in the sity and evy house."[44]

While the artillery duel was in progress, Hill's troops were gathering large amounts of corn and bacon from the neighboring counties.[45] To assist in this operation by protecting the Confederate supply trains, Longstreet detached Brigadier General Henry L. Benning's Georgians and sent them to North Carolina. General Benning was to limit his movements to those of the supply trains and move on only as the trains "exhaust the sections of the country." But Longstreet wisely added to Benning's orders: "Don't confine to these instructions when you see circumstances arise that were unforseen by me but use your own good judgment in acting promptly to meet emergencies as they arise."[46]

Although the fighting at Washington was not heavy, General Foster found himself in a precarious position from the first. One Federal soldier put it this way: "There is very little doubt but that we are surrounded and besieged. We have come down to very small rations (small enough before) of pork and bread, and no beef; and limited to half a dipper of coffee at a meal, while the work is increasing and hard work, too."[47] The "Lord only knows how . . . [we are] to get away," wrote another of Foster's men.[48] As for the General, he planned to break the siege by bringing in reinforcements from New Bern. In his appeals for relief, Foster left it to the discretion of the officer who was to command the relieving force whether to land at Hill's Point, take the Confederate battery there and proceed up the Pamlico River, or whether to march overland from New Bern.

Foster did not know it, but the management of affairs in New Bern during his absence had reached such a state that any relief column moving out of the city stood little chance of success, regardless of the route it took. Second in command of the Department of North Carolina was Brigadier General Innis N. Palmer, a regular army officer of good standing. Under him was Brigadier General Henry Prince, also a professional soldier. The third brigadier was General F. B. Spinola, who

Union steamer *Escort* running the Confederate batteries east of Washington on April 13, 1863. (From *Harper's Weekly*)

was far more familiar with politics than with the army. Of these three officers, General Prince was designated to command the first relieving column. He took a steamer to the mouth of the Pamlico River, got a good look at Fort Hill, became sick at his stomach, and retired ingloriously to New Bern.

To the surprise of every interested man in the Department, the next expedition was led by General Spinola. Up to this time the General had never even "set a squadron in the field." While the two regular army officers, Palmer and Prince, remained behind at New Bern, Spinola went to the relief of Washington.[49] At Blount's Creek on April 9, he encountered a portion of Pettigrew's brigade and, in the ensuing skirmish, artillery fire alone sent the Federals "skidaddling" back to New Bern. Spinola tarried long enough only to fell trees to cover his retreat.[50] This embarrassing affair still failed to take General Spinola out of the field. A short while later, he was sent on a "reconnaissance in force" which, to the surprise of very few people, gained "no additional information."[51]

It is little wonder that General Foster concluded that, in order to lift the siege of Washington, he must run the blockade and put himself at the head of a relieving force. His opportunity to get away came on the fifteenth.* Two evenings previous the steamer *Escort*, with hay bales protecting her decks and machinery and the Fifth Rhode Island aboard, had run the Confederate batteries.†

Under cover of darkness on the thirteenth, the white hulled *Escort* had started her treacherous run up the Pamlico. She was abreast of Fort Hill before the Confederates were aware of her intentions. Although slowed by the obstructions in the river, aground once, and under almost constant fire, the steamer made it safely to Washington. The soldiers crouched below decks were more than relieved when the chaplain's voice in the companionway announced their arrival at the municipal wharf.[52]

Foster promptly put the Fifth Rhode Island in the line of works and then made preparations to leave Washington aboard the *Escort* the night of the fourteenth. The pilot advised against making the run at night, so the departure of the steamer was delayed until daybreak. Having heard that the pilot, a Captain Pedrick, was disloyal and would arrange to have the vessel captured, Foster stood in the pilot house, revolver drawn, as the *Escort* steamed down the river. Afterwards the General told a friend: "We were passing the last obstruction and Pedrick had just said to me: 'I reckon we're all right now,' when he was shot. He exclaimed, 'I'm killed, General, but by God, I'll get you through!' Colonel, I couldn't help it; I cried like a baby."[53]

As the *Escort* successfully ran the Confederate batteries for the second time,‡ General Hill began the withdrawal of his forces. The arrival of Federal reinforcements and supplies had made the capture of Washington by siege extremely unlikely.§ Some of the soldiers were keenly disappointed at leaving Washington in the hands of the enemy, having gone there with the confident expectation that the town would

---

* There is some confusion over the date General Foster left Washington on board the *Escort*. In his official report the General says it was the fifteenth. *OR*, XVIII, Ser. I, 215. Naval records put the date as the fourteenth. *NR*, VIII, Ser. I, 683.

† Two schooners carrying ammunition and commissary supplies also made it safely by the Confederate batteries. *OR*, XVIII, Ser. I, 215.

‡ Foster arrived safely at New Bern even though the *Escort* was hit approximately forty times. *OR*, XVIII, Ser. I, 215; E. T. Hale to Sister, Apr. 15, 1863, E. T. Hale Papers, SHC.

§ General Longstreet wrote Hill on the fifteenth: "We cannot afford to keep the large force that you have watching the garrison at Washington." J. Longstreet to D. H. Hill, Apr. 15, 1863, D. H. Hill Papers, SLR.

be theirs.[54] Others more bitter called the expedition a failure that would "detract from General D. H. Hill's heretofore reputation of a great military leader."[55] Company K of the Thirty-second North Carolina, expressed its sentiments in the following notice conspicuously posted at Hill's Point: "Yankees we leave you, not because we cannot take Washington but because it is not worth taking; and besides, the climate is not agreeable. A man should be amphibious to inhabit it."[56] It was raining "like fury" when the members of Company K tacked up their notice, and the march they were about to commence was not soon forgotten. "We fell in the mud several times," said one of the men, "and were certainly beautiful objects to look at with suits of mud, for we were covered with it."[57]

For his two months in command of the troops in North Carolina, Hill had very little to show other than the removal of corn and bacon from the eastern counties. He had coordinated his movements before New Bern very badly, and at Washington he had shown little imagination. Still, he talked of successes and explained to the Governor that only an absence of reserves prevented him from following up his victories.[58]

In a letter dated May 25, General Lee thanked Hill very kindly for his harassment of the enemy "during the past months" and expressed the wish that the forces in North Carolina were strong enough to drive the Federals from the state.[59] Yet, as Lee wrote these lines, he was withdrawing troops from Hill's command. Following his victory at Chancellorsville, May 1 to 4, 1863,[60] General Lee had begun preparations for an offensive across the Potomac and therefore had urgent need for the troops stationed in North Carolina.[61] The resulting transfer of large numbers of men to the Army of Northern Virginia put Hill on the defensive and at the same time provided General Foster at New Bern with an opportunity to venture beyond his fortifications.

By the middle of May, Foster had decided that he could easily make a demonstration inland along the Atlantic and North Carolina Railroad. In his first move the General ordered Colonel J. Richter Jones "to endeavor to surround the enemy at Gum Swamp,"* a Confederate out-

---

* An earlier attempt, on April 28, to capture the Confederates in this area had failed. This affair was called by various names—Wise's Cross-Roads, Dover Cross-Roads, and First Gum Swamp. For an account of this action see *OR*, XVIII, Ser. I, 343-53; R. D. Graham, "Fifty-sixth Regiment," *Histories of the Several Regiments and Battalions from North Carolina in the Great War 1861-'65. Written by Members of the Respective Com-*

post about eight miles below Kinston. Jones, commander of the Fifty-eighth Pennsylvania, was reinforced by the Fifth, Twenty-fifth, Twenty-seventh, and Forty-sixth Massachusetts Regiments, three pieces of artillery and a battalion of cavalry. The plan called for three regiments with the cavalry and artillery to advance along the railroad and Dover Road to attack the Confederate works from the front while the Fifty-eighth Pennsylvania and Twenty-seventh Massachusetts, under the immediate command of Colonel Jones, took an unfrequented path through the swamp to the Confederate rear. Both columns were to arrive at the enemy's entrenchments as near daybreak as possible on the morning of the twenty-second and there make a joint attack front and rear.[62]

The main column, with Colonel George H. Pierson, Fifth Massachusetts commanding, met the Confederate pickets at daybreak on the twenty-second, drove them back to their entrenchments and commenced an attack on the front. Colonel Jones, who was supposed to be on the Confederate rear when Pierson commenced his attack, did not get into position until around 9:30 A.M. because of his "defective knowledge of the ground." But on reaching his station, Jones immediately deployed his regiments, opened fire, and advanced. At the same time, Colonel Pierson intensified his attack on the front.[63] "With . . . the enemy in our rear, on the left and in front . . . we had no other course left," said a Confederate officer, "but to take to the swamp on our right." The Federals in close pursuit captured 165 men of the Fifty-sixth North Carolina. Many of those who managed to escape were forced to take "up lodgings with the musquitoes that night," the swamp being "almost unpenetrable."[64]

When the men of the Fifty-sixth at last rejoined the rest of their regiment, they learned that Confederate reinforcements had driven the Federals back toward New Bern and that on the afternoon of the twenty-third, at Batchelder's Creek, the Federal troops had stopped their retreat to make a stand. But in the skirmish that followed, their gallant commander, Colonel Jones, had lost his life.[65]

The death of Colonel Jones could hardly be balanced against the

---

mands, ed. W. Clark (Goldsboro: Nash Brothers, 1901), III, 323-24; E. T. Hale to Mother, May 5, 1863, E. T. Hale Papers, SHC; H. A. Cooley to Father, May 8, 1863, H. A. Cooley Papers, SHC; A. B. McDougald, a Confederate soldier in this fight, wrote a friend: "I may be in 40 fights [but] I never Expect to be in any hotter Place than I was on the Evening of the 28th April." A. B. McDougald to J. M. Harrington, May 15, 1863, DU.

humiliation at Gum Swamp. The officers and men of the Fifty-sixth North Carolina were rightly concerned about what General Hill might think about their conduct.* "But," observed Captain Robert D. Graham, "I think any sensible man will acknowledge we did as well as could be expected." Furthermore, Graham was certain that their brigade commander, General Robert Ransom, who himself had barely managed to escape capture, would take up for his "favorite" regiment.[66] But Graham was mistaken, as shown in the following letter to his mother: "I had thought that Ransom would have generosity enough about him to explain the whole matter in an official report, but he is not willing to make any sacrifice at all, to save us from ignominy. . . . Ransom in a day has lost the popularity that he had been making for months."[67]

The expedition to Gum Swamp was followed by a lengthy period of inactivity on both sides. June saw little or no fighting in eastern North Carolina, and it was the middle of July before Foster made another offensive move.

This time Brigadier General Edward E. Potter, Foster's chief of staff, led a sizable cavalry force out of New Bern for a raid on Greenville, Tarboro, and Rocky Mount.† July 19 found the Union General within twelve miles of Greenville, where he surprised and captured a fifteen-man picket detail. Potter then proceeded unopposed to the "pretty little village" of Greenville. He found it "completely surrounded by a strong line of intrenchments" but there were no Confederate troops, except a few convalescents, to man the works. During their three-hour stay in town, Potter's men destroyed an estimated $300,000-worth of property, robbed the citizens "of everything of value," got drunk in the local taverns, and burned the bridge over the Tar River.[68]

---

* The author has uncovered no record of what Hill thought of the Fifty-sixth North Carolina at Gum Swamp, but it is known that the General had the highest praise for the "parts of two Brigades" that ran the "Yankees into their works" at Batchelder's Creek. "I never saw men behave better than [John R.] Cookes skirmishers and all manifested the utmost coolness and in fact eagerness," said Hill. "I want no better troops whatever fighting civilians may think." D. H. Hill to Z. B. Vance, May 31, 1863, Z. B. Vance Papers, NCDAH.

† The primary objective of the Potter raid was the destruction of the railroad bridge at Rocky Mount. A successful raid had been carried out on the Wilmington and Weldon Railroad on July 5 when Lieutenant Colonel G. W. Lewis with 640 men had destroyed over a mile of track at Warsaw. *OR*, XXVII, Ser. I, Pt. II, 859-60; C. L. Price, "The Railroads of North Carolina During the Civil War" (M.A. thesis, Univ. of North Carolina, 1951), pp. 176-77.

The Federal march was resumed at 6:00 P.M. and by midnight Potter was at Sparta, some eight miles from Tarboro. At this point the advance was halted in order that Major Ferris Jacobs' battalion could proceed to Rocky Mount to "destroy the railroad bridge and Government property" located there. It was around three in the morning when Jacobs pulled out, and two hours later the main column resumed its march on Tarboro, arriving there between 7:00 and 8:00 A.M., July 20. Charging into town, the Federals "met a few of the enemy, who fired some hurried shots and fled across the river." In Tarboro, General Potter found an iron-clad on the stocks and two steamboats, all of which were destroyed along with "some railroad cars, 100 bales of cotton, quartermaster's subsistence and ordnance stores." Afterwards the Federal "wretches" (so called by the local residents) repaired to the local hotel and dined. During the day, General Potter learned that the enemy "in considerable force" were on the opposite side of the river, so he decided to return to New Bern by the same road which he had "taken in coming." Late in the afternoon the bridge over the Tar was burned, and the command started its return march.[69]*

Shortly after leaving Tarboro, the Federal column was rejoined by Major Jacobs with his detachment. Jacobs maintained that he had "been completely successful in his operations at Rocky Mount."[70] His report read:

The advance captured a train of cars, although in motion, upon which were 5 officers, viz, 1 captain, 2 second lieutenants, 2 first lieutenants, and 10 privates. This train of cars together with the depot, railroad and telegraph officers; country bridge . . . railroad bridge; cotton-mills, employing 150 white girls, built of stone and six stories high; one Government flouring mill (four stores); 1,000 barrels of flour, and immense quantities of hardtack (already manufactured staple cotton and manufactured goods filled the storerooms of the cotton factory); a machine-shop filled with war munitions; several separate storehouses; three trains of Government wagons (one, 14

---

* Wilson was not visited on this raid, but when word was received that Federal troops were in the area, the local citizens "flew to their trunks and wardrobes, [and] the militia . . . to the woods." Only the "Hospital Defenders" from General Military Hospital No. 2 took up arms. This "glorius band," said a Confederate surgeon, rallied "in defense of their bunks, their rations, their homes, and all they . . . [held] dear." They were "composed of the halt and the maimed and the blind, of those who had diverse miseries in the bowels, in the back and especially in the breast. . . ." This feeble group was "stationed . . . to guard the bridge . . . which was the key to the situation." S. S. Satchwell to "Surgeon Graves," July 25, 1863, W. A. Holt Papers, SHC.

wagons; one, 11 wagons, and another, 12 wagons), loaded with all manner of stores and supplies, these latter being collected for burning (fell into our hands). Several Confederate soldiers emerged, and became prisoners of war. The destruction of property was large and complete.

At 11 A.M. I marched leisurely back toward Tarborough, burning large quantities of cotton and a train of 5 wagons, on the way. Cotton destroyed exceeded 800 bales.[71]

Potter's entire force now moved on "without interruption" as far as Sparta. But a short distance past this place, the Federal advance was fired on, and "the fun commenced in earnest." From this time until they safely reached New Bern on July 23, the Union horsemen fought a running skirmish with the pursuing Confederates. On most occasions, however, the Federals escaped by showing "a clean pair of heels" to the enemy.

In many respects Potter's raid was a remarkable small-scale cavalry operation. For six days and five nights of marching the Federal cavalry-men carried only three days' rations for themselves and two feed bags of oats for their mounts. So closely pursued were they by the enemy on the return march that sleep was almost unheard of. Yet Potter not only destroyed communication lines* and vast quantities of supplies but also managed to arrive at New Bern with one hundred prisoners, three hundred horses and mules, and some three hundred "contrabands." His losses in killed, wounded, and missing did not exceed seventy-five.[72]†

The aroused citizens of eastern North Carolina pled with the Governor for help. One resident pointed out that the raid "cost the Government and individuals too much to allow another" and that it was far "better to submit to a dozen false alarms than to one surprise."[73] This admonition went unheeded for in less than a week a Federal cavalry detachment, under Colonel Samuel P. Spear, came close to pulling off another surprise raid—this time on the railroad bridge at Weldon.

The raid on the Weldon bridge had its beginning on the hot, Sunday afternoon of July 26, 1863, when Federal ships anchored off Winton and began disembarking several hundred soldiers belonging to the

---

* The officials of the Wilmington and Weldon Railroad kept a large labor force on duty to repair any damage done to the line by raids. A temporary bridge was constructed at Rocky Mount by this force, and the road was in operation again by August 1. Price, "North Carolina Railroads," p. 177.

† The Federal losses, doubtless, would have been larger had not Confederate cavalry-men stopped from time to time to help themselves to "what they found along the road." C. Elliott to J. N. Whitford, July 25, 1863, Rec. Gr. 109, NA.

Twenty-fifth, Seventeenth, and Twenty-third Massachusetts, the Eighty-first New York, the Ninth New Jersey, and Belger's First Rhode Island Battery. These regiments, all under the command of General Foster,* were to support a large body of cavalry, expected hourly from Virginia. Once it reached North Carolina, the cavalry was to proceed to Weldon and destroy the important rail junction there, thus interrupting the flow of supplies to the Army of Northern Virginia.[74]

The first regiments ashore at Winton were the Ninth New Jersey and the Seventeenth Massachusetts, whose assignment was to march to Hill's Bridge on Potecasi Creek between Winton and Murfreesboro and hold that point until further notice. The New Jersey soldiers formed their ranks on shore and moved quickly up the steep hill "and through the town which . . . [was] now only a collection of houseless chimneys." Before the men had marched a full mile it was ascertained that they had taken the wrong road and would have to countermarch. Meanwhile, the Seventeenth Massachusetts disembarked, proceeded up the hill, and took the correct route out of town, unaware that it was not following the Ninth New Jersey. For this reason no pickets were sent ahead to reconnoiter the road. When it got about three miles beyond Winton, the Massachusetts regiment was ambushed by Major Samuel J. Wheeler's Murfreesboro home guard, which numbered approximately two hundred unmounted cavalrymen. This surprise attack halted but momentarily the Federal advance. Recovering quickly from the "shower of bullets," the Seventeenth drove the Confederates back to a line of works on the right bank of Potecasi Creek. Here, aided by the Ninth New Jersey which had finally gotten on the right road, the New Englanders routed the home guard and captured thirty prisoners.[75]

While the two regiments were mopping up at Hill's Bridge, Federal troops continued to come ashore at Winton. They encountered no opposition but on the outside of a store building the men found the following note: "You——Yankees are a——set of Pillfering Rogues." A member of the Eighty-first New York did not bother to deny the charge. He merely added: "Which Now is King, cotton or corn, since Lee went into Pennsylvania? How do you like Meade since Gettysburg?"

* On July 15, 1863, the Departments of Virginia and North Carolina were united into one and Foster was assigned to command. *OR*, XXVII, Ser. I, Pt. II, 919. Major General John L. Peck became commander of the District of North Carolina on August 14, 1863. M. W. Boatner, *The Civil War Dictionary* (New York: David McKay Co., 1959), p. 629.

As soon as the troops came ashore detachments were formed to scour the countryside and occupy strategic crossroads.[76]* Early on the morning of the twenty-seventh, the long awaited cavalry, under Colonel Spear, began to arrive on the Gates County side of the river. These troops were ferried across the Chowan during the day. Once across the river, they "set out" for Weldon by way of Hill's Bridge, which had been repaired the previous evening.[77]

Confederate intelligence on this occasion was on the alert. The same afternoon that Colonel Spear's cavalry crossed the Chowan, General Whiting, new commander of the Department of North Carolina,† wired Confederate authorities at Petersburg: "The enemy are reported advancing . . . toward Weldon. If you have any available force, send down and intercept them."[78] Immediately Matt Ransom's brigade was ordered to Garysburg. The Thirty-fifth North Carolina left that afternoon by mailtrain, arriving that night. Brigadier General Matt W. Ransom followed in the evening, reaching Garysburg at daybreak. At this place the General found a section of artillery with two guns. These he ordered to Boone's Mill, seven miles on the "country road" from Garysburg to Jackson. Four companies of the Twenty-fourth North Carolina, under the command of Lieutenant Colonel John L. Harris, had preceded the artillery to the mill. The Thirty-fifth Regiment was sent to defend another route to Garysburg and Weldon.[79]

After leaving orders for all troops arriving at Garysburg to proceed at once to Boone's Mill, General Ransom and his staff departed for Nashville "to obtain information on the enemy's movement." About 12:30 P.M. Ransom left Jackson to return to Boone's Mill, where the pond and swamp would give him a defensive advantage over the enemy who were "reported rapidly advancing." When the General had gotten no more than a half mile out of town, he heard a great shout to his rear. He stopped to learn the cause, and suddenly the enemy cavalry

---

* While the Federal troops were in the Winton area (July 26 to 30), the *U.S.S. Whitehead* and *Valley City*, with landing parties aboard, visited Murfreesboro on the Meherrin River. Here the Union soldiers burned the bridge and pillaged the town. "These are the cute political brothers," wrote a resident of Murfreesboro, "sent to win us back to a former Union." T. C. Parramore, "Five Days in July, 1863," Ahoskie *Daily Roanoke-Chowan News*, Civil War Supplement, 1960, pp. 89-90; *NR*, IX, Ser. I, 790; Fragments of letter in W. N. H. Smith Papers, DU.

† On July 1, 1863, General Hill was "assigned temporarily to command of troops in the Department of Richmond." *OR*, XVII, Ser. I, Pt. II, 4. Major General William H. C. Whiting was "assigned to command of the Department of North Carolina" on July 14, 1863. *Ibid.*

charged into sight over a hill about 250 yards away. "It was now a question as to whose horses were the fastest, as two miles or more lay between the Confederate commander and his men. . . ." Putting spurs to their rested mounts, Ransom and his staff stayed safely in front of their pursuers, "though in reach of and subject to the enemy's fire all during the pursuit."

As the General came within sight of his position at Boone's Mill, he was dismayed to find most of his infantry bathing in the warm waters of the mill pond. So, "no sooner had his horse thundered across the loose planking of the mill stream bridge," than he barked orders for the removal of the structure's planking. These commands, together with the appearance of the onrushing "Yankees," brought the bathing infantrymen running from the pond.*

Colonel Spear of the Union cavalry, instead of charging the disorganized Confederates, halted to reform his columns and bring up his artillery. It was only after he had shelled Ransom's position for "an hour or more" that Spear dismounted his cavalry and attempted to advance down the mill road. This move was checked, as were subsequent attempts to turn the Confederate flanks. Having failed to carry out his mission, Colonel Spear withdrew his command late in the day.[80] "With a brigade of cavalry, nine pieces of artillery and a supporting force of infantry at Winton, all totaling about 5,000 men, [Spear] had been repulsed by not more than two hundred Confederate infantry with two pieces of artillery."[81]

Although it involved comparatively few men, the fight at Boone's Mill was "a brilliant military achievement" for General Ransom. A defeat here would have resulted in the destruction of the railroad bridge over the Roanoke River at Weldon.[82] The Wilmington and Weldon Railroad, "the lifeline of the Confederacy"[83] had to be kept open to carry vital supplies to the battered Army of Northern Virginia, regrouping after the disaster at Gettysburg.†

Boone's Mill brought to an end all but minor skirmishing in eastern

---

* The battle was fought on Ransom's plantation. His home was less than two miles from where the fighting occurred and his wife and children could hear the roar of combat. Parramore, "Five days in July, 1863," p. 93.

† At Gettysburg, North Carolina troops reached "the pinnacle of military greatness. . . . Of the 15,301 Confederates killed and wounded . . . [in this battle] 4,033 wore North Carolina uniforms." R. D. W. Connor, *North Carolina Rebuilding an Ancient Commonwealth* (New York: American Historical Society, 1929), II, 245.

North Carolina for the year 1863, and eleven months were to pass before the Federals attempted another raid on the important Wilmington and Weldon line.*

*In June, 1864, five hundred men under Colonel James Jourdan, U.S.A., attempted unsuccessfully to burn the large covered bridge over the "Northeast Cape Fear River" and to destroy as much of the track of the Wilmington and Weldon Railroad as possible. *OR*, XL, Ser. I, Pt. I, 817-19; Price, "North Carolina Railroads," pp. 177-78.

CHAPTER VIII

"Awful Times" in the State

EVEN THOUGH MILITARY activity was at a minimum in North Carolina during the summer and fall of 1863, the times were gloomy. Lee's defeat at Gettysburg* and the capture of Vicksburg cast a spell of despondency over the state.[1] One prominent North Carolinian concluded that "only the hand of providence" could now save the Confederacy.[2] A farmer in Person County entered in his diary on July 10: "Yankees took Vicksburg. Yankees taking the South—awful times."[3] A few days later a soldier in camp at Raleigh, upon learning that Lee had "crossed the Potomac" with the Federals in pursuit, added in a letter to his sister that times were "very darke," and dark they were.[4] But defeats on the battlefield were not solely responsible for this gloom. Peace movements, desertion of state troops† and enemy raids all combined to make the future look dreary. Editor W. W. Holden of the Raleigh *Standard* certainly contributed to this despondency by carrying on an active campaign in 1863 to bring the war to a close. At first he merely urged that peace negotiations be opened by the Confederacy, but failing to make any impression on President Davis, he shifted his ground to a demand for peace by separate state action.[5] In western North Carolina

---

* William T. Loftin, a member of a North Carolina regiment, wrote his mother: "This Gettysburg fight was the most awful slaughter that ever my two eyes beheld . . . which will be remembered by me for a long time to come." W. T. Loftin to Mother, Aug. 29, 1863, W. T. Loftin Papers, DU. Federal soldiers in North Carolina took the news of Gettysburg as being "too good to be true." D. L. Craft to Sister, July 7, 1863, D. L. Craft Papers, DU.

† During the four years of war some 23,000 North Carolina soldiers deserted, but more than 8,000 of these later returned to their posts. The percentage of desertion of North Carolina troops, about 20 per cent, was no higher than that of other states in the North and South. Hugh T. Lefler and A. R. Newsome, *North Carolina: The History of a Southern State* (Chapel Hill: Univ. of N.C. Press, 1954), p. 446.

a veritable civil war existed between the Confederate troops on the one hand and organized deserters and "bushwackers" on the other.* At the same time, the Federals in the eastern part of the state were stripping the "region of everything of value that was movable."[6]

The eastern counties, lying open to the Federals, were subject to numerous enemy raids[7] which "nearly cleaned the county."[8] For the planters, these raids always "meant [a] loss of stock, provisions . . . [and] slaves."[9] Besides gathering supplies, the Federal soldiers in their forays into the country committed depredations of all sorts. A youthful Confederate trooper who scouted the Trenton-Pollocksville area found the latter place "almost entirely deserted, only one family there," and its

. . . many fine dwellings . . . mostly all destroyed, the Yankees having knocked to pieces those which they could not burn—chairs, sofas, bedsteads, wash-stands, bureaus, and all sorts of furniture are broken up, and scattered broad-cast over the streets and fields. On our road to Pollocksville we passed several of the finest farm houses I have ever seen, and they were all ruined. I noticed one in particular. The Yankees had destroyed a mill near it, burned the kitchen, broken open the cellar doors, windows, etc. and to "capall" (no not to cap all) had broken open the plastering and built a big fire between the walls; fortunately it went out, before the house took fire—"To cap all" really, they had killed all the stock on the farm, and the house and yard were full of buzzards, some of [them] regaling on a dead horse before the front door, and some . . . perching in the parlor and on the peazza. The walls of all the houses were scribbled on, and writing generally was of a mean character. . . If every person in the South could witness the useless ruin that the Yankees have caused in Jones and adjoining counties, the name and sight of Yankee soldier would be hated throughout all eternity, and it would help to show what an abandoned and Godless foe we have to contend against.[10]

The "Godless foe" not only pillaged but seemed to be pleased with his work: "If you could see," wrote a member of the Tenth Connecticut stationed at New Bern,

. . . the ruin devastation and utter abandonment of villages, plantations and farms, which but a short time ago was peopled fenced and stocked. Houses

* There were organized bands of deserters in the eastern part of the state at this time but nowhere near as many as in western North Carolina. One of the bands in the east operated in Robeson County where it committed "the most outrageous depredations upon the families of absent *soldiers*." M. Swann to W. H. C. Whiting, Feb. 11, 1863, Z. B. Vance Papers, NCDAH. A Confederate soldier stationed at Weldon wrote his mother that recently six deserters were shot and another branded with a "D." E. Phifer to Mother, Oct. 13, 1863, Phifer Papers, SHC.

once comfortable that are now either burned or deserted, barns in ashes all along the road side, fences destroyed for miles and over thousands of acres, no cows horses mules sheep or poultry to be seen where ever the Union army advances, and you would see conclusively the destitution for the coming year is to be four fold greater than the past year. This whole country for purposes of maintenance for man or beast, for the next twelve months is a *desert* as hopeless as *Sahara* itself, If this *war* continues another twelve months this country will be little else than a "howling wilderness" and the "abomination of desolation" will be written on every "gait post."[11]

For protection against the outrageous conduct of the enemy, the citizens of eastern North Carolina, mostly women, children, and old men, appealed to state authorities. Troops, however, were not available even "to protect so . . . important a region."[12] The home guard, sometimes referred to as "guerrillas" or "partisan rangers" by the Federals, harassed the raiders but could do little else.*

The deplorable conduct of the Federal troops, together with Lincoln's Emancipation Proclamation, caused Edward Stanly, the Union Governor of North Carolina, to resign his position. He sent his resignation to President Lincoln on January 15, 1863,[13] stating that he was no longer able to assure the people of the state that the administration was only trying to secure their rights and to restore the Union. Regarding the Emancipation Proclamation,† the Governor said: "It is enough to say I fear it will do infinite mischief. It crushes all hope of making peace by any conciliatory measures. It will fill the hearts of Union men with despair and strengthen the hands of the detestable traitors whose mad ambition has spread desolation and sorrow over our country. To the negroes themselves it will bring the most direful calamities."[14] Stanly reviewed his course as military governor and said concerning it: "That I have offended some is probable; but they were those whose schemes

---

* A Federal soldier complained that these "guerilla bands" did "not attack . . . except they find a small squad alone somewhere." N. Lanpheur to L. C. Newton, June 15, 1863, N. Lanpheur Papers, DU. See also R. M. Sherrill to H. T. Clark, Apr. 29, 1862, H. T. Clark Papers, NCDAH; Pugh, *Three Hundred Years Along the Pasquotank*, pp. 173-88; (Anon.), "Old Times in Betsy," Elizabeth City *Economist*, Sept. 14, 21, Oct. 19, 1900. For more on the home guard see also above pp. 20, 167, and below pp. 192ff.

† Many of the Federal soldiers and Unionists in eastern North Carolina were willing for the Negroes to be freed "provided they . . . [were] removed from the county." J. A. Hedrick to D. R. Goodloe, Oct. 21, 1862, B. J. Hedrick Papers, DU. A soldier from New England, after calling slavery a "wrong, a curse," went on to say that "we cannot have the negro in this country unless we give him one or two states and let them go it, they and the whites never can get along together. I can't bare them." N. C. Delaney, "Letters of a Maine Soldier Boy," *CWH*, V (March, 1959), 54-55.

of plunder I defeated—whose oppressions of the innocent and helpless I resisted—whose purposes seemed to have been to join or follow the troops and to encourage and participate in the most shameful pillaging and robbery that ever disgraced an army in any civilized land."[15]*

The horror of Federal occupation was intensified by the activities of "bands of armed negroes [who] domineer in the homes of their masters and spread terror over the land."[16] A lady in Elizabeth City wrote in early 1863 that over two hundred armed Negroes daily went out "to maraud the country," which added greatly "to the terror and alarm of the women and children."[17]

Aside from the armed bands of Negroes, native Union "bushwackers" known as "Buffaloes"† terrorized the countryside.[18] In gangs of usually a dozen or so men, they infested the swamps, emerging at night to visit their former neighbors, especially those "who sympatize[d] with the South," and to perpetrate every type of violence and crime.[19]

In August, 1862, the "Buffaloes" established themselves at Wingfield, the estate of Dr. Richard Dillard, seventeen miles above Edenton on the east bank of the Chowan River. Dr. Dillard was absent with his family in Virginia at the time. The farm offered two natural advantages for

---

* In a letter to Charles Sumner the Governor was even more caustic: "Had the war in North Carolina been conducted by soldiers who were christians and gentlemen, the state would long ago have rebelled against rebellion. But instead of that, what has been done? Thousands and thousands of dollars worth of property were conveyed North." *A Military Governor Among Abolitionists: A Letter from Edward Stanly to Charles Sumner,* Pamphlet, NCC.

† As the war progressed and more and more areas of eastern North Carolina suffered from the pillage of the robbers, the term "Buffalo" became synonymous with murder, thievery, and desertion. D. G. Coward to W. Pettigrew, Dec. 19, 1862, Pettigrew Family Papers, SHC. The term "Buffalo" was used before the war. The Raleigh *Register* of January 9, 1856, spoke of the "Buffalo know nothings." T. C. Parramore, "The Roanoke-Chowan Story—Chapter 9. Roanoke-Chowan Plays Rare Role in War," Ahoskie *Daily Roanoke-Chowan News,* Civil War Supplement, 1960, p. 98. Even the Federals referred to this lawless group as their "Home Guard thieves." *NR,* VIII, Ser. I, 78. The term "Buffalo" was also used to denote North Carolinians who signed up for service in the First and Second North Carolina (Union) Volunteers. The First North Carolina (Union) Volunteers was organized in June, 1862, under Colonel E. E. Potter and the Second in early 1863 under Lieutenant Colonel C. H. Foster. Parramore, "Roanoke-Chowan Plays Rare Role in War," p. 98. Writing from Beaufort, North Carolina, October 13, 1863, a Unionist described a company of North Carolina Union Volunteers as looking "first-rate with their sky-blue pants and dark blue coats and hats on. I believe that they make a better appearance than the Yankee soldiers do. Their uniforms make them appear so large that the people call them 'Buffaloes' I think that they like to be called buffaloes. They go about in gangs like herds of buffaloes." J. A. Hedrick to B. J. Hedrick, Oct. 13, 1862, B. J. Hedrick Papers, DU.

the intruders. First, it was relatively easy to defend from land attack, and second, its location on the river's edge meant that they could be protected by Federal gunboats. There was, however, little danger of a Confederate attack since the regular Confederate infantry had abandoned the region in the summer and because Federal cavalry was still on hand to patrol the countryside.

It did not take long for Wingfield to become the rendezvous "of fugitive negroes, lawless white men, traitors and deserters from the Confederate army." The encampment was under the command of John A. (Jack) Fairless, "a hard-drinking, fast-living Gates county farm boy from Mentonville" who had deserted from the Fifty-second North Carolina. Fairless and his group pillaged, plundered, burned, and decoyed off slaves in their forays into Chowan and the neighboring counties of Bertie, Perquimans, Hertford, and Gates.[20] So undisciplined were Fairless and his men that they became the concern of both the local citizens and the Federal authorities.

Lieutenant Commander Charles W. Flusser, chief of the Union naval force in the Albemarle Sound region, decided to investigate the truth of the reports he had been receiving about Fairless. On September 18, he dispatched the gunboat *Shawsheen,* under Lieutenant Thomas J. Woodward, to visit Wingfield, and Woodward's report confirmed the worst of the rumors:

. . . I found, out of sixty three recruits, only twenty present; the others had gone to their homes or elsewhere as they chose. The Captain was in a state of intoxication, threatening to shoot some of the remaining men, and conducting himself in a most disgraceful manner by taking one man's horse and making other people pay him the money to pay for them, and this, too, from people who are well disposed toward our Government. . . . He has no control over his men and [by] the manner in which he conducts himself he is doing much injury to the U. S. Government.[21]

Shortly after Lieutenant Woodward submitted his report, Jack Fairless ceased to be a problem for anyone. In October, while on a reconnaissance with eight men, the "Buffalo" leader got into an argument with a private named Jim Wallace and was killed. Fairless fired at Wallace but missed, "he being so drunk, and before he could fire again the said private shot him dead."[22]

Jack Fairless' untimely but unmourned death brought Lieutenant Joseph W. Ethridge, a Roanoke Island resident newly recruited into

Union ranks, to Wingfield as its new commander. The Lieutenant encountered at the base the old problems of low morale and general disorganization, now aggravated by the growing numbers of Confederate "guerrillas" or "partisans" who infested the area.[23]

A small number of these "partisans," together with about twenty Confederate regulars under Captain Ned Small of Edenton, staged an unsuccessful attack on Wingfield on November 17.* Although the assault was easily repulsed, it did reveal to the "Buffaloes" a weakness in the defensive arrangements about their camp.[24] As a result, an expert was brought in the next month to strengthen existing fortifications and to build new ones. Employment for the large number of Negroes in and around the plantation was found by having them fell trees, erect breastworks, and construct blockhouses. An ancient cannon was brought up from Edenton and placed inside the fort, which was "a log structure 75 feet square atop a mound of earth." The fortification rested about two hundred yards from the river. Thus Wingfield became the "only Federal military base established in the interior of the Roanoke-Chowan region during" the war.[25]

The strengthening of the fortifications at Wingfield made it clear to the Confederate authorities that this "Buffalo" camp must be destroyed. In accordance with this decision, Lieutenant Colonel John E. Brown, Forty-second North Carolina, with a force of three hundred men, "partisan" and regular, attacked Wingfield at daybreak on the morning of March 23.† A frontal assault across the open field outside the "Buffalo" camp stampeded the Wingfield defenders. One of them gamely fired the old cannon twice and then joined his comrades in a mad dash for the blockhouses on the river bank. The Confederates rushed into the interior of the camp but, having no artillery, they were unable to storm the blockhouses in which the "Buffaloes" were trapped. Colonel Brown's

---

* Back in September a group of civilians from Chowan and adjoining counties formulated plans for an attack on Wingfield, but the operation never got underway. Union sympathizers around Edenton tipped off the Federals. Parramore, "Jack Fairless and Wingfield Buffaloes," Ahoskie *Daily Roanoke-Chowan News,* Civil War Supplement, 1960, p. 112.

† An earlier attempt to surprise the camp had failed when one of the "Buffalo" pickets spotted Colonel Brown's men and warned the fort. Federal gunboats then shelled the Confederate position, forcing Colonel Brown's men to retreat. T. J. Brown, "Forty-second Regiment," *Histories of the Several Regiments and Battalions from North Carolina in the Great War 1861-'65. Written by Members of the Respective Commands,* ed. W. Clark (Goldsboro: Nash Brothers, 1901), II, 789-807.

men had to be content with destroying the fort "and, to the sorrow of all, [with] setting fire to the handsome home which had served as Buffalo headquarters." Only one of the defenders was said to have died in the fighting. The others escaped by Federal gunboats.[26]

Having done their job well, Colonel Brown's troops retired across the river.[27] The "Buffaloes" later returned to their base, only to abandon it permanently in early spring. On April 17, the Forty-first North Carolina appeared before the Wingfield barricades and found the "quarry gone forever." A search of the camp produced a pencilled note that had been stuck onto the side of one of the blockhouses. The words read: "A leetle too late."[28]*

The abandonment of Wingfield by the "Buffaloes" was wonderful news to the suffering people of the Roanoke-Chowan region. But their troubles were not ended. Worse days were yet to come. On November 11, 1863, Major General B. F. Butler superseded General Foster in command of the Department of Virginia and North Carolina.[29] This change was welcomed neither by the local citizens nor the Federal soldiers in the department. Foster was popular with his men,[30] and, in addition, it was said the new commander had "nigger on the brain." Rumors made the rounds of the Federal camps that General Butler would "punish a man for looking crosswise at any of the Sable-brethern."[31] So it surprised no one when Butler, on December 5, ordered Brigadier General Edward A. Wild with two regiments of Negro troops into the northeastern counties of North Carolina. Butler gave as the purpose of the raid: "Our navigation on the Dismal Swamp canal had been interrupted, and the Union inhabitants plundered by the guerrillas."[32] However, General Wild was under instructions "to clear the country of slaves and procure recruits for his brigade. . . ."[33]

Wild marched his eighteen hundred Negro soldiers from the Norfolk area to Elizabeth City by way of the canal road through the Great Dismal Swamp.[34] Two small steamers loaded with rations were to accompany the columns along the route "but by some unaccountable blunder they were sent astray through the wrong canal." At South Mills the General learned of this error and decided to proceed without the steamers. After living off the country for several days, during which

* The "Buffalo" company now under the command of Lieutenant James J. "Jemsey" McLane remained intact for the remainder of the war, but Wingfield was no longer an active base.

time he "judiciously discriminate[d] in favor of the worst rebels," Wild arrived in Elizabeth City.[35]* The seven days of Federal occupation (December 9 to 16) that followed were for the local citizens ones of "perpetual panic," many of them having never seen Negro troops before. Even though the Union General was a Harvard educated M.D., he was, in the eyes of many white residents, a "monster of humanity" for his use of colored troops.[36] From his headquarters in the home of a local physician,[37] this "cousin to Beelzebud" (as Wild was also called) "sent out expeditions in all directions, some for recruits and contraband families, some for guerrillas, some for forage [and] some for firewood, which was scarce and much needed. . . ."[38]

The raiders brought in approximately twenty prisoners, all of whom "had the benefit of a drumhead court martial." Eight were found guilty of various offenses and ordered to be taken to Norfolk; two were retained as hostages. The rest, with the exception of Daniel Bright of Pasquotank County, were ordered released.[39] The unfortunate Bright was afterwards hanged, placarded thus: "This guerrilla hanged by order of Brigadier General Wild."[40] The execution of Bright was in accordance with what the General called "a more rigorous style of warfare." He wrote his superiors: "Finding ordinary measures of little avail I . . . burned their houses and barns, ate up their live stock, and took hostages from their family."[41]†

* In his official report General Wild fails to give the date of his arrival in Elizabeth City. It appears, however, that he arrived on the ninth. *RR*, VIII, 298. The journey through the Great Dismal Swamp left a memorable impression on everyone. A correspondent wrote: "We were in the dreariest and wildest part of the Dismal Swamp, the darkness was dense, the air damp, and the ghostly silence was broken only by the hooting of owls and crying of wild cats. For two hours we rode through the Stygian darkness of the forest, when we arrived at South Mills. . . . Here we left the canal and descended into another swamp of Hades. The narrow crooked road was flooded with water and crossed with innumerable little rickety bridges, over which our horses made their way with great caution and reluctance." *RR*, VIII, 298.

† Without question General Wild did "his work with great thoroughness" but, concluded General Butler, "perhaps with too much stringency." *OR*, XXIX, Ser. I, Pt. II, 596. Confederate officers, on the other hand, were not so restrained in their references to activities of the commanding general of the "Colored Brigade." Colonel Joel R. Griffin, writing from Franklin, Virginia, in January, 1864, had this to say: "Probably no expedition, during the progress of the war, has been attended with more bitter disregard for the long established usages of civilization or the dictates of humanity than your late raid into the country bordering the Albemarle. Your stay, though short, was marked by crimes and enormities. You burned houses over the heads of defenceless women and children, carried off private property of every description, arrested non-combatants, and carried off ladies in irons, whom you confined with negro men.

"Your negro troops fired on Confederates after they had surrendered and they were

Upon leaving Elizabeth City, General Wild divided his command into three columns and moved eastward across Camden and Currituck counties to Currituck Court House.[42] The four-hundred-man column under Colonel Alonzo G. Draper encountered sizable "guerrilla" forces at Shiloh, Sandy Hook, and Indiantown in Camden County. On the nineteenth, the day following the skirmish at Indiantown, Draper was joined by General Wild's column. The combined forces then drove the Confederate "guerillas" back to their camp in the swamp which, "after much trouble," was found and burned by the Federals. From Indiantown, Wild marched to Currituck Court House where he was met by the other column of his command and two Federal steamers sent to pick up the large number of Negroes following the expedition. While the "contrabands" were being placed aboard ship for transportation to Roanoke Island, detachments of troops under Colonel Draper searched for "guerrilla" camps in the area. The activities of Draper and the movement of the Negroes continued until reports reached Currituck that Confederate troops were moving in force in that direction. This news sent General Wild scurrying back toward Norfolk, where he arrived on December 23.[43]

The General estimated that 2,500 Negroes were "released" as a result of his raid. The exact number, he admitted, was "impossible to count as they were constantly coming and going. . . ." It is a matter of record, however, that nine boat-loads of Negroes were sent to Roanoke Island and two to Norfolk, "besides 4 long trains over land." As for the other accomplishments of the raid, General Wild reported:

We burned 4 guerrilla camps, took over 50 guns, 1 drum, together with equipment, ammunition, etc.; burned over a dozen homesteads, 2 distilleries, etc. Took a number of prisoners, including 6 Confederate soldiers, provided with furloughs, some with a printed clause stipulating that they should provide themselves with horses before returning; also 4 hostages for our men taken prisoners, 3 women and 1 old man. Hanged 1 guerrilla, captured 4 large boats engaged in contraband trade, and took many horses.[44]

---

only saved by the exertions of the more humane of your white officers. Last, but not least, under pretext that he was a guerilla, you hanged Daniel Bright, a private of Company L. Sixty-second Georgia regiment [cavalry] forcing the ladies and gentlemen whom you held in arrest to witness the execution. Therefore, I have obtained an order from the General commanding, for the execution of Samuel Jones, a private of Company B. Fifth Ohio, whom I hang in retaliation. I hold two more of your men—in irons—as hostages for Mrs. Weeks and Mrs. Mundin. When these ladies are released, these men will be returned and treated as prisoners of war." "Recent Expedition to Elizabeth City," Milledgeville, Ga., *Southern Recorder*, Jan. 19, 1864, Newspaper clipping, NCC.

Negro troops of General E. A. Wild liberating slaves in eastern North Carolina, December, 1863. (From *Harper's Weekly*)

The real significance of the raid rests not upon the number of slaves freed, homes burned, and hostages taken but upon the fact that this was the first raid "of any magnitude undertaken [solely] by negro troops since their enlistment was authorized by Congress. . . ." A Northern reporter, who accompanied General Wild on this expedition, concluded that "by it the question of their [the Negroes'] efficiency in any branch of the service has been practically set at rest." He noted that the Negro troops were "thoroughly obedient to their officers [and] performed in the enemy's country all the duties of white soldiers—scouting, skirmishing, picket duty, guard duty, every service incident to the occupation of hostile towns, and best of all, fighting."[45]

Confederate accounts gave an entirely different picture of the Negroes' conduct. From the Milledgeville, Georgia, *Southern Recorder* came the report that "the negro ran riot during the Yankee stay in the Albemarle country" and when fired upon "fled like wild deer."[46]

The Negro soldier, brave or not, was almost universally detested by the whites in eastern North Carolina. His departure from the upper sound region of the state was, therefore, hailed in all quarters by the local citizens. But trying times were ahead for the residents of the northeastern counties. General Butler, in his efforts to "exterminate all guerrillas East of the Chowan River," threatened the people with more "visitations from the colored troops" if they did not assist him in driving the "Partisan Rangers" out of the region. "You will never have any rest from us so long as you keep guerrillas within your borders," Butler told the citizens of Currituck, Pasquotank, Perquimans, Gates, and Chowan counties.[47] As a result, public meetings were held in several counties and resolves were passed "asking instructions, claiming protection, appointing delegates and committees, etc., taking action against guerrillas, against rebel conscription, etc."[48] At Elizabeth City, 523 citizens of Pasquotank County signed a petition urging the governor to either "remove or disband" the "Rangers."[49]*

Many of those unwilling to sign the petitions sought refuge in the central part of the state, but this region, along with the western counties, was also experiencing difficult times.† By the close of 1863, disaffection in these areas had reached an alarming stage. As early as November, 1861, Governor Clark had become concerned over conditions in western North Carolina. On this date he wrote the authorities in Richmond that he was receiving "numerous communications from the North Carolina counties bordering on East Tennessee" requesting help against traitors.[50] When the Governor proposed moving Colonel R. B. Vance's regiment from the mountains to Raleigh, the infuriated cry arose that Vance was needed "to look after the Lincolnites in East Tennessee."[51]

Although the mountain people owned very few slaves and had opposed secession, they showed great loyalty at the outbreak of war by furnishing an undue portion of volunteers.[52]‡ Companies were formed in an atmosphere of "feverish excitement."[53] Former Unionists flocked to public meetings and loudly called for action to repel "the usurpations of Lincoln."[54] A resident of Mitchell County later explained his own

---

* On this date Elizabeth City was full of Union men and "Buffaloes." The few "secessionists" still around dared not voice themselves because "a negative vote would have meant death at a yard arm." (Anon.), "Old Times In Betsy," *Elizabeth City Economist*, Aug. 31, 1900.

† The planter generally took his slaves with him when he moved. And, observed a Confederate colonel on duty in eastern North Carolina, the "Negroes, who, from being producers, became consumers and add to our calamaties." W. J. Clarke to Z. B. Vance, Nov. 27, 1863, Z. B. Vance Papers, DU; W. Pettigrew to Sister, Oct. 8, 1862, Pettigrew Family Papers, SHC.

‡ "From Ashe to the Georgia line the thirteen mountain counties, with 68,000 population, had furnished by the last of October, 4,400 soldiers, one in fifteen, while the remaining counties furnished only one in nineteen." S. A. Ashe, *History of North Carolina* (Raleigh: Edwards and Broughton, 1925), II, 660-61.

reaction by saying that "when the war come, I felt awful southern."[55]*
By July, 1861, Burke County had about 400 men under arms or in
training out of a voting population of 1,100.[56] By late fall of the same
year, Caldwell County had an even higher percentage. "Former Union
men apparently were as zealous for the Confederacy as those who originally advocated secession."[57] And the Cherokee Indian nation was "exceeded by no one in patriotism and loyalty to the South."[58] Among the
home guard units, the Indian groups were "the most active and dependable in guarding prisoners."[59] Patriotism such as that manifested in
Burke and Caldwell counties and among the Cherokees, however,
stripped many areas of all young men, making it almost impossible for
the mountain folk to protect themselves against native Unionists, east
Tennessee raiders, and various outlaw bands that had collected in the
area to rob and steal.[60]

The troubles of the mountain folk were eased none by the elections
of 1862. The bitter party spirit that developed in that year helped to
increase the dissatisfaction and disloyalty in both the central and western
counties. W. W. Holden, the influential newspaper editor, vigorously
attacked Governor Clark's policy of "the last man and last dollar," if
necessary, to win the war. He charged that it was a "rich man's war
and a poor man's fight"† and urged the election of "peace men" to state
and Confederate offices. For the governor's chair, Holden supported the
youthful colonel of the Twenty-sixth North Carolina, Zebulon B. Vance,
against William J. Johnston, the pro-Davis and Confederate party man.
Vance was referred to in the North as the "Northern or Federal Candidate."[61]

The agitation of the disgruntled elements paid dividends. As early
as March, 1862, it was necessary to send troops into Chatham County
to arrest deserters.[62] On every side it was said that extreme disloyalty
existed in Davidson, Forsyth, Randolph, Moore, and Guilford counties.[63]
Large numbers of deserters collected in this central region, knowing
that the Quakers living there opposed the war.[64] In Yadkin and Wilkes
the disaffected men threatened to interfere with coming elections, mak-

---

* Asheville and Buncombe County became a concentration point for troops. Fortifica-
tions, as well as a hospital, armory and supply center, were located in the area. J. P.
Arthur, *Western North Carolina: A History from 1730-to 1913* (Raleigh: Edwards and
Broughton, 1914), pp. 601-3; F. A. Sondley, *A History of Buncombe County, North
Carolina* (Asheville: Advocate Printing Co., 1930), II, 689-92.

† Governor Z. B. Vance was to make the same charge later against President Davis.

ing it necessary for Captain D. G. McRae, enrolling officer in Wilkes, to ask for arms and men to "arrest the large number of deserters and conscripts skulking about. . . ."[65] Farther west in Madison County, Major General E. Kirby Smith had troops to deal with the large number of deserters. For three days in April, Confederate detachments unsuccessfully attempted to wipe out resistence in the Laurel Valley, "a district in Madison County long known as a general resort and hiding place for outlaws."[66]

When the election was held, Vance won a convincing victory over Johnston by a vote of 54,423 to 20,448. In the central and western counties as well as in the army, Vance's margin of victory was great. The strong vote in the disaffected area, nevertheless, did not mean that the new governor wanted "Unionist" support. Not once during the campaign did he state that he agreed with the "peace" sentiments of Holden. For the Fayetteville *Observer,* Vance expressed views to the contrary. In a letter to the paper he said: "Believing the only hope of the South depended upon the prosecution of the war at all hazards and to the utmost extremity so long as the foot of the invader pressed Southern soil, I took the field at an early day, with the determination to remain there until an independence was achieved. My convictions in this regard remain unchanged."[67]

While the gubernatorial campaign of 1862 was in progress, the Confederate government passed the first of three laws that were to be particularly obnoxious to the mountain people. It was the Conscription Act of April, 1862, calling into service for three years all white males between eighteen and thirty-five years of age. The other two laws that brought the war forcibly home to the region were the tax-in-kind and impressment acts passed in 1863. The first of these was a tithe to the government, under which farmers were compelled to give one-tenth of all their produce for distribution by the authorities at Richmond. The second law gave specific committees the right to take livestock, slaves, provisions, and wagons for use by the Confederate army and to set the price that should be paid for them. For mountaineers, accustomed to individual freedom, these acts were especially galling. Of the three pieces of legislation, the conscription act was the most detested.* Having

* Originally secessionists admitted that conscription was a drastic step but thought it was necessary if troops were to be kept in the field. However, by 1862 volunteers were not coming forward in sufficient numbers. H. T. Clark to B. Craven, Feb. 25, 1862, Trinity College Papers, DU. A few people did not take the "draft very seriously." H.

responded so generously to the early call for troops, the mountain region was pretty well depleted of young blood by the time conscription went into effect. This additional demand for troops, therefore, met with considerable opposition.

A writer in Stokes County, protesting the call for more men, pointed out that the county had already enrolled thirteen hundred men, of whom eleven hundred were in the service. The deprivations suffered by the women and children, he said, were almost unbelievable. The corn, wheat, rye, and oat crops were short, and the few men who had corn were afraid to let it go, for they did not know at what moment they too would have to leave their family to care for themselves. "If all the conscripts from my county are taken off," the writer continued, "it will be impossible for those left behind to make support for another year."[68]

Thomas W. Atkin "and other citizens of Western North Carolina" pointed out to the Secretary of War that "the safety and security of . . . [their] homes and property . . . [were] seriously menaced and openly assaulted by herds of disloyal citizens and gangs of deserters from the Confederate army," and they went on to say, "in the event, the conscripts . . . are taken into Confederate service, we shall doubtless fall an easy prey to the malicious hands of marauders, which now openly parrade themselves in the different counties, west of the Blue Ridge."[69]

The use of conscription, with its accompanying threat of privation and violence, was without question a very potent cause of discontent in the mountains. In the lower house of the Confederate Congress the two votes in opposition to conscription in the North Carolina delegation were cast by men from the western district.[70] The exemption provisions of the bill, added subsequent to its passage, were disliked and allowed the poorer classes to believe that it was, indeed, a "rich man's war and a poor man's fight."[71] A mountaineer in Alexander

---

Proffit wrote from camp that he was of the opinion that the "law will, but seldom if ever, be rigidly enforced over the entire Confederacy, particularly in N.C. . . ." H. Proffit to A. J. Proffit, May 10, 1862, Proffit Family Papers, SHC. Another soldier asked his sister to urge "Harrison to stay at home and attend to his farm he will find that camp life is a hard life more than that he ought to take care of things at home." C. Mills to Sister, Feb. 26, 1862, E. Amanda Mills Papers, DU. Despite the attitude of such men as Proffit and Mills, Governor Clark intended "to carry out the Conscription Act fairly and to the fullest extent of the wants of the Country." H. T. Clark to G. W. Randolph, Apr. 24, 1862, H. T. Clark Papers, NCDAH.

County complained that "everyone who was making money by speculation" seemed to be exempted.[72]

Another aspect of conscription that met with great disapproval was the appointment in 1863 of Colonel Thomas P. August, a native of Virginia, to the office of commandant of conscripts in North Carolina. Governor Vance protested the appointment as both "unjust and impolitic." He wrote Secretary Seddon: "I wish to say in all candor that it smacks of discourtesy to our people, to say the least of it. . . ."[73]

To escape conscription many eligible males hid out in the mountains, swearing "they would dye at home before they would be forced off. . . ." "When the time came for them to go," wrote R. G. Armfield from Yadkinville, "perhaps nearly one hundred in this county took to the woods, lying out day and night to avoid arrest, and although the militia officers have exerted themselves with great zeal, yet these skulkers have always had many more active friends than they need, and could always get timely information of enemy movement to arrest them and so avoided it."[74]

Those not hiding out in the woods resorted to all sorts of devices to stay out of the army. As one soldier put it, ". . . the die is cast and the dog is dead and the baby is born and his name is conscription . . . but you must know that all men between those ages of 18 and 35 years will have more broken arms and legs. . . ."[75] Also, fingers were cut off, skin scaled to produce bad sores, and a great variety of diseases feigned. One individual told a surgeon he had "a confliction of diseases as great as any man ever had." Another complained of a "very dirty" affliction that he did not like to name. A soldier with dark skin professed to being part Negro. More than one alleged impotence, while some professed "being affected periodically, like the female sex." Family birth records in Bibles were changed, and in the more remote places men even assumed the garb of women and worked in the fields.[76]

It was not an uncommon practice, however, for males over the conscript age to be forced into the service. Three men in Cherokee County were arrested by a detachment of Georgia troops and were given the option of going to prison or joining the Confederate army. Governor Vance, upon learning of this instance, threatened to call out the militia and shoot any person who tried it again.[77]

In early 1863, conscription reached a critical stage when twenty to thirty conscripts lodged themselves in a Yadkin County schoolhouse and fought a pitched battle with a small squad of militia, each side suffering a few casualties.[78]* Following this little affair, the situation in the mountains got practically beyond the control of the military. "Plundering and robbing became so serious that soldiers had to be sent to protect loyal Confederates. The militia was powerless against the combined forces of deserters and desperadoes. . . . Alleghany County was the scene of pitched battles, and a lawless element continued to terrorize the countryside. Confederate officers now faced the possibility of being shot even at their own homes. . . ."[79] A one-hundred-member gang, pillaging Cherokee County in July, 1863, would disarm soldiers trying to return to their regiments and send them home. This same gang raided the town of Murphy in "broad daylight" and shot up the courthouse. A few days later in Yancey County, another gang killed the sentry guarding some deserters at the house of "Squire Hearington" and rescued their companions. In Henderson County, Confederate officials had virtually no control. A sixty-five-member band of desperadoes, "all armed and daily increasing," was in command.[80]

An inspector of conscription, writing from Salisbury in the late summer of 1863, stated that in Cherokee County a large body of deserters and those resisting conscription "had assumed a sort of military occupation, taking a town" and that "in Wilkes County they had organized, drilling regularly, and were intrenched in a camp to the number of 500." The report indicated also that three or four hundred deserters were organized in Randolph County and that there were large numbers in Catawba, Yadkin, and Iredell. "Those who were liable to conscription," the Inspector said, "lagged behind in proportion to those deserting." As a result of this situation, the enrollment officers went

* After the skirmish, Lieutenant Colonel W. A. Joyce of the militia urged Vance to send "as soon as possible a detachment of 40 or 50 men to scour the county [Yadkin]. It would not only inable us to execute speedily but might save some valuable lives. We intend at all hazards to execute the law." However, in executing the law, the militiamen usually found themselves faced by conscripts better armed than they were. Mrs. M. B. Moore, writing from Madison County later in the year, gives a good picture of why local military units experienced great difficulty in rounding up conscripts: "Our Home Guard called out yesterday to attempt to arrest . . . these deluded men. The Regiment consisted probably of one hundred men, horse and 'infantry; a few had good arms, many with inferior ones, and some without any; while some were on horse back, some on foot and some in buggies." W. A. Joyce to Z. B. Vance, Feb. 16, 1863, Z. B. Vance Papers, NCDAH; Mrs. M. B. Moore to Z. B. Vance, Sept. 10, 1863, Z. B. Vance Papers, NCDAH. See also L. S. Gash to Z. B. Vance, Dec. 25, 1863, NCDAH. There were charges that some of the militia officers were disloyal. R. R. Crawford to Z. B. Vance, Feb. 28, 1863, Z. B. Vance Papers, NCDAH.

about their work "with only hope that they would reach their goal by means of a military force."[81] Unfortunately for these officers, sufficient troops for this type of duty were seldom available.

In addition to conscription, there were many things to arouse discontent in the mountains.* The people were also irate over the assignment of North Carolina troops to regiments of other states† and the placement of Virginia officers over North Carolina troops. "I protest against the appointment of *any* Virginian to command N. Carolina forces . . . ," wrote one J. T. Mitchell.[82] On several occasions Governor Vance corresponded with Lee about the objection of the North Carolina officers "to a Virginia brigadier." An exception was the case of Brigadier General Raleigh E. Colston, the adopted son of a Virginia physician and Virginia Military Institute graduate. When General Lee removed him from command of some North Carolina troops because of a complaint from Vance, the officers of the First and Third North Carolina Regiments signed a "memorial" requesting that Colston be left in "the command which . . . [he had] so gallantly sustained to the general satisfaction of the officers and men of the First and Third Regiments."[83]

Most injurious to a feeling of state pride was the impression that North Carolina troops were not getting the good publicity they deserved. On November 17, 1862, Governor Vance addressed the General Assembly on this matter. He pointed out, with considerable justification, that officers from the state were not receiving deserved promotions. In proportion to the number of troops in the field, North Carolina was entitled to 128 general officers, but only a fraction of that figure were ever so promoted.[84]

---

* A great deal of concern was manifested over the collection of the "tithe tax" and especially odious was the fact that a Virginian had been selected as "tithingman" for North Carolina. In some quarters resistance "to the bitter end" was advocated rather than pay "any such monarchial tax." W. D. Cotton, "Appalachian North Carolina— A Political Study, 1860-1889" (Ph.D. dissertation, Univ. of North Carolina, 1954), p. 123. See also Raleigh *N.C. Standard*, July-Aug., 1863.

† Hoping to encourage procurement of men, Governor Vance insisted upon an order allowing conscripts to choose their regiments, and as a result many came in voluntarily. Yet at the enrolling camps they were not given a choice of regiments. Vance, who thought he had an understanding with President Davis and other officials on this matter, wrote in disgust that he would not assist in "duping the soldiers" or participate in "bad faith toward the soldiers on the part of the government." R. E. Yates, *The Confederacy and Zeb Vance,* ed., W. S. Hoole, *Confederate Centennial Studies* (Tuscaloosa: Confederate Publishing Co., 1958), No. 8, pp. 39-42. See also Cotton, "Appalachian North Carolina," pp. 114-15.

Another source of discontent was the belief that "the rights of individuals were being subordinated to temporary expediency and that the wealthy classes were riding roughshod over the poor." Holden did much to promote these beliefs by calling for certain changes in the tax and conscription laws. His proposals appealed to the poor, non-slaveholding class.[85] From Madison County, P. Black wrote: "Our pore class of men are all gonn to the ware to fighte to save our countrey and the rich man negroes . . . are all at home."[86] A soldier, concerned over the wickedness abounding in the country, was afraid that the "speculator and extortioner" would "be the ruin of the Confederacy. . . ." He was convinced that every one exempt from service had become insane "for the love of the almighty dollar."[87] Soldiers and civilians alike complained about the repudiation of Confederate currency. And residents of one western county felt that they were subjected to postal discrimination.[88] In Salisbury a food shortage brought "a mob of females, accompanied by a number of men" to the business establishment of Michael Brown. When their demands for flour were not met, the mob took hatchets and knocked the door down. The group dispersed only when the proprietor agreed to deliver ten barrels of flour. Brown was greatly disturbed over the fact that the "mayor and some of the commissioners of the town were present, together with various citizens, and [yet] no resistance was offered, no effort made to end and prohibit the illegal and forcible seizure."[89]

Adding to woes of the mountain people in particular was the presence of Confederate troops and horses in areas already suffering from short crops. In early 1863, it was reported that a "large lot of broken down cavalry horses" were being quartered and fed in Wilkes, Yadkin, Ashe, Watauga, Caldwell, McDowell, and Surry counties. Complaints arose that the soldiers were "frequently breaking open granaries, drinking . . . insulting citizens, and making themselves a terror to the whole population." The supply officer, it was said, would demand corn of the farmer and offer to pay only two dollars a bushel. If the owner refused to sell, then the crib was broken open and the corn scattered on the ground for the horses to eat. Upon departing, the officer would leave with the farmer "an order on someone who they . . . [said was] coming on behind to pay him" at only a dollar and a half per bushel.

The Confederate War Department defended its action on the grounds that these were regular cavalry horses being built up for the next campaign. Also, it frequently happened that families of the men in service complained about "their more wealthy neighbors . . . not sell[ing] to them" and suggested that the authorities send in horses to eat up all the forage "belonging to wealthy people." Later in 1863 a cavalry detachment impressed horses in Madison, and in "Wilkes and other counties Confederate soldiers plundered and drove off cattle, pocketing the receipts while they were supposedly arresting deserters." Near the end of the year Governor Vance wrote Secretary Seddon that depredations of cavalry units on detached service in illegally seizing property and other acts had become "grievance, intolerable, damnable, and not to be borne!" It was enough, he confessed, "to breed a rebellion in a loyal country against the Confederacy."

If God Almighty had yet in store another plague—worse than all others which he intended to have let loose on the Egyptians in case Pharaoh still hardened his heart, I am sure it must have been a regiment or so of half armed, half disciplined Confederate cavalry! Had they been turned loose on Pharoah's subjects with or without an impressment law, he would have become so sensible of the anger of God, that he never would have followed the children of Israel to the Red Sea. No, sir, not an inch!! Cannot officers be reduced to the ranks for permitting this? Cannot a few men be shot for perpetrating these outrages, as an example? Unless something can be done, I shall be compelled in some sections to call out my militia and levy actual war against them. I beg your early and earnest attention to this matter.[90]

The discontent of the mountain folk over the presence of cavalry mounts on their lands was manifested in part by an increase in the number of desertions of western North Carolina troops.[91] The problem of desertion, however, was an old one. It arose during the first weeks of the war and got progressively worse. The fighting had scarcely been going on a month before thirty "Black Mountain Boys" from Yancey County "became dissatisfied and went home." A McDowell County company lost so many men through desertion that the remainder marched home. A "large number of deserters" from Company B, Fifty-fifth North Carolina, returned to Wilkes County in 1862, demonstrating "determination to resist efforts to return them to their company."[92]

Desertion became such a serious problem by the latter part of 1862 that early in the new year Governor Vance issued a proclamation in which he appealed to the deserters to return to their commands. He promised to "share the last bushel of meal and pound of meat in the State" with the wives and children of the men in the army. But this failed to produce the desired effects. Most of the absentees remained in hiding, and soon they were enjoying the company of an ever-increasing number of fellow deserters.[93]

By the spring of 1863, disloyalty in the Army of Northern Virginia was so great that General Lee became concerned. He informed the Secretary of War on April 18 that there had been "frequent desertions from the North Carolina Regiments."[94] The soldiers continued to leave in such numbers that, in May, General Lee again wrote the Secretary about this matter, stating that unless desertions could be stopped immediately, the number of North Carolina troops in the army would be greatly reduced.[95] From northern Virginia deserters usually followed the mountain ridges southward into western North Carolina or other mountain areas. They generally traveled in bands as they left the army and were heavily armed, which made it almost impossible for the home guard to cope with them.[96]

There were many causes for desertions,* but, undoubtedly, communications from home had much to do with soldiers' leaving the ranks.[97] A letter from Martha Revis to her husband in a Madison County regiment is a good example of those received by the North Carolina troops. After telling her husband that she had good crops and plenty to eat, she continued: "You said you hadn't anything to eat. I wish you was here to get some beans for dinner. . . . The people is generally well hereat. The people is turning to the Union here since the Yankees has got Vicksburg. I want you to come home as soon as you can after you git this letter. . . . That is all I can think of, only I want you to come home the worst that I ever did. The conscripts is all at home yet, and I don't know what they will do with them." Thomas Hunter, who was cutting oats for Mrs. Revis, added: "I am well, and is right strait out for the Union, and I am never going in the

---

* Disloyalty to the Confederacy was a factor in causing desertion, but battle fatigue, homesickness, unredeemed promises of furloughs, and inability to choose the regiment in which to serve were much more important in causing a soldier to leave the ranks. Desertion was also encouraged by the fact that in many counties the deserter faced no hostile sentiment and would be harbored and protected. Violent dislike for commanding officers was also a factor at times, as was the feeling that the war was being fought for the benefit of the rich man. In addition many were confident that the Confederacy would collapse "and the Union would be restored by Christmas of 1863." Cotton, "Appalachian North Carolina," p. 133.

Confederate deserters in the mountains. (From *Pictorial War Record*)

service anymore, for I am for the Union for ever and ever, Amen. . . .
There was 800 left to go to the North, so will tell you all about it in
the next letter. . . ."[98]

General D. H. Hill, in an address delivered after the war, told the
story of Edward Cooper, who at his court martial read the following
letter:

My Dear Edward——

I have always been proud of you, and since your connection with the
Confederate army I have been prouder than ever before. I would not have
you do anything wrong for the world, but before God, Edward, unless you
come home we must die. Last night I was aroused by little Eddie's crying.
I called, "What's the matter, Eddie?" and he said, "Oh, Mama, I'm so
hungry." And Lucy, Edward, your darling Lucy, she never complains, but
she is growing thinner and thinner, and Edward, unless you come home we
must die.

Your Mary.[99]

Such letters as this, and the one of Martha Revis, could do nothing but
weaken morale.

Governor Vance estimated that there were twelve hundred deserters
in the mountains of western North Carolina in 1863.[100] All mountain
localities had some deserters and conscripts hiding out. But in Henderson and Cherokee counties the number was so large that these areas fell
under the virtual control of a lawless element.[101] This situation led

J. A. Campbell, Assistant Secretary of State, to write that the "condition of things in the mountain districts of North Carolina, South Carolina, Georgia, and Alabama menaces the existence of the Confederacy as fatally as either of the armies of the United States."[102] To cope with the vast numbers of deserters in the western counties, Vance asked General Lee to "send one of our diminished brigades or a good strong regiment to North Carolina. . . ."[103] Lee honored the request by sending Brigadier General Robert F. Hoke with two regiments and a squadron of cavalry to the state.[104]

During the fall of 1863, General Hoke operated in the western and central counties. He discovered that Davidson, Randolph, Moore, and Montgomery were especially troublesome.[105] Back in February, General James G. Martin had found it necessary to send a small detachment of troops into Randolph County to round up deserters. Patrols on foot captured eighteen deserters in four days and sent them to Raleigh for assignment to regiments. But, lamented Lieutenant W. A. Pugh, "before I got back to Raleigh on my return two thirds of those men had returned to their homes. . . ."[106] When Pugh's detail was removed, conditions in Randolph County became "desperate." Deserters were so bold and numerous that a "loyal" man or woman dared not travel even a short distance alone.[107] Lieutenant Colonel S. G. Worth of the Randolph County home guard described the situation to Vance in a letter dated September 3, 1863: "I regret that it becomes my duty to make a very unfavorable report of operations, thus far, in this county. I find it impossible under existing circumstances to get the men subject to duty in the Home Guard to come out to arrest deserters and conscripts." Since the deserters and conscripts had "taken every gun" they could "get their hands on" and were committing "all sorts of depredations," Colonel Worth urged that a "company of regular troops" be sent into the county. He goes on to say that there "are so many who sympathize with them that it is difficult to get information on their activities." He notes for the Governor, however, that "quite as many deserters, who are in Randolph at present, belong to Chatham, Moore, Montgomery and Davidson." The Colonel explained this by the fact that Randolph County had "more . . . that sympathize with them."[108]

The deserter in the central counties, having neither the swamps of the east nor the mountains of the west for refuge, "like all hard run creatures naturally took to earth." The underground homes of the fugitives

. . . were burrowed in some low hillside to avoid moisture, or hollowed below the flat earth, if necessary. The entrance to the burrow was effected by means of a trapdoor in the roof, which was cunningly concealed by boughs, dirt, and leaves most carefully arranged to look as if they had never been disturbed. The telltale freshly turned red clay from the excavation (usually six by eight feet, though often larger) was first thrown into a bed quilt, and then carried away in buckets and piggins by the faithful hands of old men, women, and children, to be thrown into a running stream near by, which obligingly carried away the evidence which would have betrayed the fugitive. A fallen log or mass of carelessly strewn stones formed a pathway to the entrance so as to render impossible the wearing of a path while a charred tree stump or dead tree, apparently still smoking, placed ingeniously just at the mouth of the chimney, would arouse no suspicion of a fire below the surface of the earth and so awaken no dangerous question in the mind of a passing guard, alert for the presence of deserters. Much more reasonable was it to attribute the smoke to a recent negro possum-hunt. The damp cave was made habitable by a fireplace cut into the earthen wall, by a carpet of pine-needles, and by a bed of pine boughs spread on a pole frame erected on trestles of forked stakes. Occasionally there was even a cupboard cut into the earthen wall. Except for the fact that the caves were merely places of refuge during a search, life in their chilly, grave-like recesses would have been intolerable, and so for the most part their occupants used the caves only as sleeping places, and ventured out into the woods in daytime, trusting to their sharp eyes and swift legs to escape capture even if detected. For greater safety, a band would have several caves in different places, to which they could make progressive brief visits. An onion or odorous herb, rubbed on the soles of the feet, was quite adequate to confuse the dogs when set on their trail. The fugitive was fed by his wife or by some female member of the family. As the latter were soon suspected by the officers and their movements watched, they became very adept smugglers in concealing provisions about their persons.

The tedium of cave life . . . was broken by practical jokes which the men played upon each other. One trick was for several deserters to don the uniforms of Confederate soldiers, proceed to the vicinity where a cave was known to be located, prod and beat the ground systematically to locate the cave, finally triumphantly pull open the trapdoor, and sternly order out the deserter. It was sometimes part of the game to chase the poor victim around his haunts for several days before the hoax was revealed. The negro's native instinct for woodcraft was often a great help to the master through cunning suggestions, while his innocent responses to the guard usually threw the latter off the right scent. He even helped to keep his master well provisioned.[109]

In view of the deserter's ingenuity in hiding out, and the sympathy he received from certain elements in the local populace, it is little wonder that military authorities found it extremely difficult to round up the defectors. Major John W. Graham of Hoke's command said: "There is very little use in hunting the rascals, the only way to get them is to seize their property and keep it until they surrender. I have found several times, by pressing a horse, that a man who has not been seen or heard of by his family in six months can be produced in three hours."[110]* Usually forage for the animal and a wagon were also taken but with the promise that the horse would be returned and the forage paid for when the deserter surrendered. Graham maintained that he could not have captured one out of thirty defectors had he not followed this policy.[111]

The local citizens complained bitterly about the conduct of the soldiers detailed to bring in the deserters.[112] "They are doing no good," said a resident of Randolph County, "going from house to house, desturbing the people all they can killing dogs and chickens and stealing eggs. . . ."[113] An officer of the Fifty-sixth North Carolina readily admitted there was "indiscriminate plunder of property belonging to deserter's families, (such as wearing apparel and watches) and depredations on property of good citizens."[114]

In the late fall of 1863, General Hoke returned to Virginia convinced that the presence of troops in North Carolina had "had a fine effect."[115] He even went so far as to say that "Wilkes is now the truest and most loyal county in the state."[116]† Despite the fact that he rounded up many deserters and recusant conscripts,‡ little was really accomplished toward clearing the mountains and the piedmont of disaffected bands. A prominent North Carolinian and admirer of the General's put it this way: "There is a good deal of work to do yet to clear the state. . . ."[117]

Hoke's men deeply regretted that they could not "get at" W. W.

* Graham called his duty "the most disagreeable business I have ever engaged in." J. W. Graham to Father, Nov. 21, 1863, W. A. Graham Papers, SHC.

† As soon as the troops were removed from Wilkes County, the deserters returned to their old hideouts. P. F. Faison to Z. B. Vance, Jan. 4, 1864, Z. B. Vance Papers, NCDAH.

‡ General Hoke got a good many deserters to give themselves up voluntarily. He did this by promising them furloughs to get their domestic affairs in order. Then they would be sent to Raleigh. E. J. Hale Jr. to Mother, Oct. 7, 1863, E. J. Hale Papers, NCDAH. One writer complained, nevertheless, that many of those who came in voluntarily "are now writing from prison, being lodged at Castle Thunder." J. A. Parks to Z. B. Vance, Nov. 16, 1863, Z. B. Vance Papers, NCDAH.

Holden before they left the state. In their eyes this leader of North Carolina's peace movement was even more disloyal than the deserters they were hunting. But Vance prevented any retaliatory action when he wrote Hoke requesting the General "to restrain" his men as they had been called into North Carolina at the Governor's request. Furthermore, the men had the satisfaction of knowing that Holden had already been taken care of once. On the night of September 9, 1863, soldiers belonging to H. L. Benning's Georgia brigade broke into the *Standard* office and completely wrecked it. Holden's papers were scattered about and the type either dumped into the street or carried away. Upon learning of the mob action, Vance contacted Lieutenant Colonel W. S. Shepherd, Second Georgia Regiment, who had his quarters in a local hotel, and the two of them rushed to the scene. They found soldiers inside and outside the office but little difficulty was experienced in restoring order. Vance addressed the soldiers on the freedom of the press. They listened respectfully, gave the Governor three cheers, and then marched off. When Vance returned to the governor's mansion, "he found the frightened editor of the *Standard* seeking protection from a possible attack on his person. Holden praised Vance's bravery and quieted his own nerves with brandy which Vance had thoughtfully provided."

Early the next morning the town bell was rung and some two hundred of Holden's followers gathered in the streets of Raleigh. "Led by one Mark Williams, a strong Union Man, they marched to the office of the State Journal, which was the Confederate administration paper, and without interference from either the mayor or police, completely demolished the office." Once more the Governor hastened to the scene and prevailed upon the crowd to disperse. He then wired President Davis, asking him to "order immediately that troops passing through here shall not enter the city." Davis promptly complied.

On the following day Raleigh's peace was again disturbed, this time by an Alabama regiment, "threatening murder and conflagration." Once more the weary Governor restored order, after which he turned on President Davis: "This thing is becoming intolerable. For sixty hours I have traveled up and down making speaches alternately to citizens and soldiers, without rest or sleep almost, engaged in the humiliating task of trying to defend the law and peace of the State against our own bayonets. Sir, the means of stopping these outrages I leave to you. If not done, I shall feel it a duty which I owe to the dignity and self-respect of the first State in the Confederacy in point of the numbers and good conduct of her soldiers and all the natural resources of war to issue my proclamation recalling her troops from the field to the defense of their homes."

President Davis promptly issued strict orders to troops moving through Raleigh, and September 15, Vance was able to wire the President: "The troops are now passing quietly and no further disturbance apprehended. Quiet is restored."[118]*

Federal authorities failed to capitalize on the critical state of affairs in the central and western parts of the state. No large-scale military operations took place in these areas during 1863. On the other hand, skirmishes accompanied by extreme violence and cruelty had marked the scene in the mountains since early in the war.

In September, 1862, several companies of the Sixty-ninth North Carolina were ordered to Powell's Valley in east Tennessee, between Cumberland Gap and Jacksboro. This regiment, better known as Thomas' Legion, was raised in the mountains of North Carolina by Colonel William H. Thomas of Jackson County and had in it two companies of Cherokee Indians. On this march to Powell's Valley, one Indian company engaged "some Federals, killing, wounding, and driving back their force." But in the charge, "Lieutenant Astooga Stoga, a splendid specimen of Indian manhood and warrior" was killed. This infuriated the redmen "and before they could be restrained, they scalped several of the Federal wounded and dead. . . ."[119]†

* Most of the loyal soldiers in the Confederate army hated Holden. In August, 1863, men from the North Carolina regiments in Virginia held meetings in which they denounced Holden and appointed delegates to a general convention to be held at Orange Court House on August 12. Ashe, *N.C.,* II, 841-42; Tatum, *Disloyalty in Confederacy,* p. 121; "Proceedings of a Meeting Held by Sixth North Carolina Troops, August 8, 1863, Orange Court House Virginia," A. W. Mangum Papers, SHC; J. R. Davis, "Cleveland Men Respond," Shelby *Daily Star,* Cleveland Centennial Edition, Aug., 1940. Those loyal to the Confederacy but not in the army held equally strong sentiments against Holden and his newspaper. D. P. Johnstone of Transylvania County called the *Standard* "a fire brand and a curse to the land and its editor," he thought, "should be hung. . . ." D. P. Johnstone to Z. B. Vance, Sept. 11, 1863, Z. B. Vance Papers, NCDAH. Another western Carolinian thought the editor a "son of Belial" who ought to be "hewed in pieces before the Lord." Laura Norwood to "Dear Uncle James," July 11, 1863, J. Gwyn Papers, SHC.

† Although this skirmish took place in Tennessee, the author recorded it because it touched on the issue of scalping. Members of Thomas' Legion, writing after the war, give contradictory statements on whether the Indians followed the practice of always scalping their victims. W. W. Stringfield says that the "savage" came out in redmen only once. W. W. Stringfield, "Reminiscences" (unpublished reminiscence), W. W. Stringfield

The Sixty-ninth North Carolina, since its inception in the summer of 1862,[120] had been on duty in east Tennessee, its companies scattered along the railroad from Chattanooga to Bristol. But in January, 1863, Colonel Thomas and two hundred of the Legion were put in a provisional force, commanded by Brigadier General William G. M. Davis, and ordered from Strawberry Plains, north of Knoxville, Tennessee, to Madison County in North Carolina. This move was made under orders from Brigadier General Henry Heth, whose command then included the mountains of western North Carolina.[121] The purpose of the operation was to investigate reports that "organized bands of armed men" were terrorizing the region.[122]

Madison County, since the first months of the war, had been a haven for deserters, "bushwackers," and "tories," as Union sympathizers in western North Carolina were called. In early 1862 Captain Dave Fry, "ring-leading bridge burner," and a band of men had fled from Greene County, Tennessee, and found refuge "on the head of Laurel" Creek in Madison County. Soon the Captain and his followers were conducting raids back across the state line, "taking money, powder, threatening death, and on occasion beating Southern men." In response to an outcry from both Tennessee and North Carolina to suppress this "den of marauding thieves," Confederate troops made an attack on the "head of the Laurel." A few of Fry's men were killed, but the results of the skirmish were negligible. Several days later a detachment of state militia conducted a more successful operation. By obstructing several passes, the militiamen were able to capture between thirty and forty of the "tory" ringleaders. Following these skirmishes, many men in Shelton Laurel (the local name for Laurel Valley) promised to be loyal to the South and joined the Confederate army. Before long, though, most of them deserted.[123]

During the early winter of 1863 brutality in the mountain struggle probably reached its height. In January of that year a band of men from Shelton Laurel raided Marshall, the county seat of Madison County, to get salt supposedly being withheld from them because of their Unionist sympathies. The raiders broke into several stores and took what they wanted. They also pillaged the home of L. M. Allen, a colonel in the

Papers, NCDAH. J. W. Terrell says, on the other hand, that "throughout the war they did scalp every man they killed if they could get to him, which they generally managed to do. . . ." Terrell, "Reminiscences" (unpublished reminiscence), J. W. Terrell Papers, DU.

Sixty-fourth North Carolina.[124] On hearing of the Marshall raid, Governor Vance appealed for military aid from General Heth at Knoxville.[125] Heth immediately dispatched Davis' provisional force to Madison County.[126] The report of General Davis, dated January 20, 1863, stated that his men killed twelve "tories" and captured twenty more but that the extent of disloyalty in the area had been greatly exaggerated.[127]

Subsequent communications to Governor Vance indicated that the General did not know the whole of the Shelton Laurel story. These letters told how Lieutenant Colonel J. A. Keith, a native of Marshall and member of the Sixty-fourth North Carolina, had captured thirteen old men and boys and had them shot under the most cold-blooded circumstances. Although the records are not clear on these points, it appears that the killings took place in February and that periodically since late 1862, Colonel Keith, with a two-hundred-man detail, had been on duty in Madison County. During this period the soldiers were constantly "bushwacked from behind every shrub, tree or projection on all sides of the road," and, wrote one of the men, "only severe measures will stop it." Colonel Keith's resort to the extreme action not only failed to stop "bushwacking," but brought about his own removal from command.[128]

When Governor Vance heard the "rumors and reports of a brutal mass murder of prisoners" at Shelton Laurel, he requested an official investigation. Keith was allowed to resign, but only on the grounds of incompetency. In self defense he maintained that General Heth gave him verbal orders not to take any prisoners. Heth "vigorously denied" this accusation. While the controversy raged over what happened at Shelton Laurel, militia units were chasing "marauders" elsewhere in Madison and Yancey counties.[129]

The spring of 1863 had been a "tense violent season" in the mountains,[130] and the picture was to brighten not a bit with the capture of east Tennessee by the Federals in the fall of the same year. This left western North Carolina open to the threat of constant raids "by the miserable thieves and Toryes" and possibly a major invasion by Union troops.[131] In the words of W. W. Stringfield of Thomas' Legion, the Federals now had a "walk over" and "we Confederates had only to 'walk out.'"[132] Knoxville was entered by the Union forces under General Burnside on September 2, 1863. When this happened, the Great Smoky Mountains became the chief barrier separating western North

Carolina from the enemy.[133] Judge Augustus S. Merrimon of Asheville, one of Vance's chief informants in western North Carolina, wrote: "This section is in a threatened condition owing to the fact that the enemy occupy East Tennessee, and our people are in a really distressed condition. . . ."[134]

On the same day that General Burnside occupied Knoxville, Colonel Thomas, with several hundred men of his Legion, evacuated the Confederate base at Strawberry Plains and started falling back toward the North Carolina line. In close pursuit was a Federal cavalry detachment under Colonel F. W. Graham. When the Union Colonel was forced to give up the chase after a short distance, Thomas made his escape into the lofty reaches of the Great Smokies. His pursuer had hoped the local citizens would "blockade" the Confederate line of retreat, but this failed to materialize. Colonel Thomas continued on through the mountains and, in accordance with instructions, blocked all the passes between Paint Rock in Madison County and Ducktown, Tennessee.[135]

In late October, Captain C. H. Taylor and twenty-five of Thomas' Indians joined a small detachment of Confederate cavalry and the Cherokee County home guard in pursuit of the "tory" Goldman Bryson, who had been raiding the county with a force of approximately 150 men. About fifteen miles from the town of Murphy, Bryson was overtaken, and in the skirmish that followed the "tory leader" had two men killed and seventeen captured and lost most of his horses and arms. Bryson then fled into the mountains with the remainder of his force. Only a portion of the home guard and the Indians continued the chase, and the raiders, with the exception of their leader, made it safely back to Tennessee. Bryson was "tracked" to his home, where he was killed. Some of the Indians were later seen on the streets of Murphy wearing various pieces of the bloody, bullet-riddled uniform of the dead man.[136]

Farther north in Madison County, Confederate operations were not even partially successful. A 150-man force sent out in October by Brigadier General Robert B. Vance, brother of the Governor and commander of the newly formed Western Military District of North Carolina, was so soundly beaten that it was feared Asheville, or even Greenville, South Carolina, would soon be taken.[137] The fears, however, were not justified and by the second week in November, General Vance was able to write his brother: "I have raided Cocke County [Tennessee] and a part of Greene pretty thoroughly, and brought out safely 800 hogs and some horses and cattle. . . . I am not only saving property for the Government, but threatening the enemy on his lines, and keeping him uneasy, and drawing some of his force away to watch me."[138]

Governor Vance forwarded this letter to the War Department with a request that his brother's command be increased "if possible."[139] But General Vance's forces were never appreciably enlarged, for in November the attention of authorities at Richmond was focused on Knoxville where the very able James Longstreet had the city invested.[140] The Confederate high command had decided that "this Federal establishment in a vital area had to be dislodged. . . ."[141]

The assault failed, nevertheless, and in December the Confederate army went into winter quarters at Greeneville, Tennessee. Longstreet, who had tried in vain to have Vance join him at Knoxville,[142] now wrote the General "requesting him to put his troops at Newport" in east Tennessee. Longstreet thought that by this move Vance could still "give . . . protection to his own district . . . at Warm Springs, and . . . at the same time guard . . . [the Confederate] left [in Tennessee] and protect in a measure . . . [the] foraging wagons."[143]

Despite Longstreet's request, Vance kept his command based on the North Carolina side of the mountains. However, in early January, 1864, he did conduct a raid into east Tennessee, which, had it been successful, would have taken him as far as Newport. In bitterly cold weather, General Vance, with one section of artillery and approximately five hundred cavalry and infantry, "crossed Smoky Mountain from Jackson County . . . to East Tennessee." Little difficulty was experienced in pulling the artillery up the mountain, but serious problems arose in getting the ordnance down the other side. Guns had to be dismounted and "dragged naked . . . down the steep mountain" slope. At the same time, the wheels and axles of the carriages were taken apart, divided among the men and carried to the foot of the mountain, where they were reassembled.

After reaching the foot of "Smoky mountain on its western side," General Vance sent Colonel Thomas and his Indians, and Lieutenant Colonel J. L. Henry with his mounted troops, to Gatlinburg four miles away. With the remainder of his force, 180 cavalry, the General proceeded to Seviersville where, on January 13, he captured a train of seventeen wagons. From this place he started for Newport, but he never reached his destination. The next afternoon at Schultz's Mill on Cosby Creek (Cocke County, Tennessee), Vance and most of his command were surprised and taken prisoners by a force of the enemy's cavalry.[144]*

* Colonel Thomas "commanding the party left at Gatlinburg, had been ordered to

War in the mountains. (From *Harper's Weekly*)

The command of the Western District now fell upon Colonel John B. Palmer* of the Fifty-eighth North Carolina.[145] This officer inherited a most difficult task. The year 1863 had closed with things in a critical condition in the mountains, and General Vance's capture, before the new year was a month old, had added only gloom to an already dark picture. Nor was the situation brighter in the eastern part of the state where the Federal troops still controlled much territory. North Carolina, in the last weeks of 1863, was truly in a "deplorable" condition at the mercy of the enemy.[146] "Our unfortunate troubles must be closed in some way soon," wrote a correspondent of Governor Vance's on Christmas Day, 1863, "or we shall close out, all signs indicate it too plainly to be mistaken. But you have no patience with croakers and want something encouraging to stimulate you, whether true or not, I must confess I am unable to help you any."[147]

fall back with his infantry and to send Lieutenant-Colonel Henry with his cavalry and artillery to Schultz' Mill, where they were directed to take up position and await the arrival of General Vance." Instead of obeying orders Henry fell back with Colonel Thomas. For this Colonel Henry was put under arrest "for disobedience of orders. . . ." *OR*, XXXII, Ser. I, Pt. I, 76.

*Palmer had temporarily held the command before. On November 18, 1863, he had replaced Vance as commander of the District of Western North Carolina. *OR*, XXXI, Ser. I, Pt. III, 711. Then on December 4, 1863, Vance resumed command of the district. *Ibid.*, XXIX, Ser. I, Pt. II, 860.

CHAPTER IX

Pickett Fails at New Bern

ON JANUARY 2, 1864, General Lee, aware of the critical state of affairs in North Carolina and having his own army in winter quarters, wrote President Davis:

The time is at hand when, if an attempt can be made to capture the enemy's forces at New Berne, it should be done. I can now spare the troops for the purpose, which will not be the case as spring approaches. . . . New Berne is defended on the land side by a line of intrenchments from the Neuse to the Trent. A redoubt near the Trent protects that flank, while three or four gun-boats are relied upon to defend the flank on the Neuse. The garrison has been so long unmolested, and experiences such a feeling of security, that it is represented as careless. The gun-boats are small and indifferent and do not keep up a head of steam. A bold party could descend the Neuse in boats at night, capture the gun-boats, and drive the enemy by their aid from the works on that side of the river, while a force should attack them in front. A large amount of provisions and other supplies are said to be at New Berne, which are much wanted for this army, besides much that is reported in the country that will thus be made accessible to us.[1]*

* Henry P. Gibson, who lived near Williamston, would have been pleased to learn of any plans to run the Federals out of eastern North Carolina. In a letter dated January 13, 1864, Gibson described conditions in his area: "It is a hard thing to do for many to get bread down here. . . . There is nothing new but the first of a new year, and in the commencement it is dreary and dull, and the prospects for peace and prosperity look much more gloomy than ever. We are along here in what I call the Yankee lines, and no prospect of being out of them soon unless we move out and that won't do for there is no possible chance for any more people to live up above as provisions are so very scarce." H. P. Gibson to J. W. Smith, Jan. 13, 1864, Williamston *Enterprise*, Aug. 19, 1941. The early part of 1864 saw considerable activity by the "Buffaloes." In January a party consisting of "Buffaloes" and Federal troops raided Windsor and "carried off three local citizens." This was probably done in retaliation for the arrest of some "Buffaloes" which had occured earlier. "The raid caused great excitement in town, as well as in the country." J. L. Taylor to P. H. Winston [?], Feb. 1, 1864, R. W. Winston Papers, SHC. See also J. B. Chesson to W. Pettigrew, Apr. 8, 1864, Pettigrew Family Papers, SHC; J. R. Griffin to Z. B. Vance, Feb. 4, 1864, Z. B. Vance Papers, NCDAH.

Davis knew about conditions in North Carolina and willingly approved of Lee's plan, even going as far as to suggest that the General himself take command of the operation.[2] Lee was hesitant to accept the position and suggested North Carolinian Robert F. Hoke as the best man for the job. Despite Lee's recommendation, Hoke was not given the command. He was only a brigadier general, and it was thought that an officer of higher rank was needed to conduct a campaign of such large proportions. Thereupon, Major General George E. Pickett was selected for the task. For command of the cooperating naval force President Davis selected his own aide, Commander John Taylor Wood.[3]

A force of approximately thirteen thousand men and fourteen navy cutters were soon concentrated at Kinston, North Carolina.[4] Pickett divided his troops into three columns and, on the morning of January 30, moved off in the direction of New Bern.* His plan of operation was basically that suggested earlier by Hoke to Lee. It called for Brigadier General Seth M. Barton, "with his own brigade and that of [Brigadier General J. L.] Kemper, and three regiments of [Matt] Ransom's, eight rifled pieces, six napoleons, and 600 cavalry," to cross the Trent River near Trenton and proceed on the south side of this body of water to Brice's Creek below New Bern.† After crossing the creek, he was to take the forts along the Neuse and Trent rivers and enter New Bern by way of the railroad bridge. This would prevent any reinforcements either by land or water from the Morehead City and Beaufort area. Colonel James Dearing, commanding a column composed of the Fifteenth and Seventeenth Virginia, Colonel J. N. Whitford's regiment, three pieces of artillery and three hundred cavalry, was "to move down north of the Neuse . . . [and] capture Fort Anderson at Barrington Ferry. . . ." General Hoke, accompanied by Pickett and the remainder of the force, planned to "move down between the Trent and the Neuse, endeavor to surprise the troops on Batchelder's Creek, silence the guns in the star fort and batteries near the Neuse, and penetrate the town in that direction." A simultaneous assault by these three columns on the defenses of New Bern was planned for Monday morning,

---

* In command of the Federal District of North Carolina with headquarters at New Bern was Major General J. J. Peck. Major General Benjamin F. Butler still commanded the Department of Virginia and North Carolina. His headquarters were at Fortress Monroe. *OR,* XXXIII, Ser. I, 916. See also above p. 177.

† Brice's Creek flows into the Trent River a short distance before its confluence with the Neuse below New Bern.

February 1. The night before this move, Commander Wood was to descend the Neuse, "endeavor to surprise and capture the gun-boats in that river" and then cooperate with the land forces in their attack on New Bern.

On the day of the general assault, General Whiting, commanding at Wilmington, was to have a force in position to threaten Swansboro "so as to fix the attention of the enemy at" Morehead City. "Everything," General Lee wrote Pickett, "will depend upon the secrecy, expedition, and boldness of your movements. . . . If successful, everything in New Berne should be sent back to a place of security. In that event, too, it is hoped that by the aid of the gun-boats water transportation can be secured, the enemy driven from Washington, Plymouth, etc., and much subsistence for the army obtained. I wish you, therefore, to follow up your success. It will also have the happiest effect in North Carolina and inspire the people."[5]

In accordance with this ambitious plan, General Hoke went into camp on the night of the thirty-first at Steven's Fork, a point approximately ten miles from New Bern and two from a Federal outpost. The men camped without fires until 1:00 A.M., at which time the march was resumed. Hoke moved forward "with all speed" in order to reach Batchelder's Creek* before the bridge could be taken up. But he arrived too late. The firing of the pickets had warned the enemy of his approach. Finding the bridge destroyed and the enemy strongly entrenched at this point, the General decided to await the dawn before continuing his advance.†

With the break of day, General Hoke "threw some trees across the creek and crossed two regiments over. . . ." This detail was to keep the Federals occupied so that repairs on the bridge could be made. By this maneuver the General hoped "to avoid the loss of men by storming." The operation did not go exactly as planned because the enemy, in the meantime, had received reinforcements from New Bern and was in a position to offer stout resistance. Still Hoke "routed them" once he got his troops across the creek. Following this engagement, the

---

* Batchelder's Creek is sometimes referred to as Bachelor's Creek.

† Hoke expected and wanted the enemy "to throw troops by cars across the creek on the railroad and . . . [get in his] rear." If this happened, he planned to rush forward toward New Bern, cut the track, capture the train, and enter the city by rail. The Federals did as Hoke anticipated, but the General missed his prize by five minutes. Warned by telegraph of Hoke's moves, the enemy rushed the train back to New Bern. *OR,* XXXIII, Ser. I, 96.

Confederates moved on to within a mile of New Bern, where a halt was called to await the sound of Barton's guns from the opposite of the Trent River. Hoke waited in vain all day for some sign of activity to the south. He suspected the worst, for during the day two trains arrived in New Bern from Morehead City. This could not have happened had General Barton gained his objectives.[6]

Barton had conducted his command well until he reached Brice's Creek on the morning of February 1. Before leaving Kinston, he strengthened the picket line between the Neuse and the Trent and had cavalry detachments out covering all the roads and paths south and east of Kinston. He hoped "to prevent information reaching the enemy of any movements likely to create suspicions."[7] Also, orders were issued to take Negroes "into custody" to prevent them from running ahead with news of the expedition.[8] So well did Barton conceal his movements that when a "blockhouse" several miles from New Bern was taken, there was only one Federal soldier awake at the time. At another enemy post, "all [were] surprised, and of course left everything."[9] Captain Henry A. Chambers, Forty-ninth North Carolina, said it was only when fortifications, church spires, and houses could be seen in the distance did Barton's men themselves realize their destination and purpose. "We all now knew that Newbern was just before us and we formed more tangible ideas respecting the object of the expedition."[10]

When the enemy works came into view around 8:00 A.M. on the first, General Barton immediately advanced a line of skirmishers close to Brice's Creek.[11] However, instead of capitalizing on the element of surprise by dismounting his large cavalry force and having it join the infantry in an assault on the Federal works, he brought up his artillery[12] and then, in company with General Matt Ransom and Colonel William R. Aylett, made a reconnaissance. According to Barton's official report the three officers found:

An open plain, varying from 1 mile to 2 miles in breadth, reaching to Brice's Creek; this very deep and about 80 yards wide, with marshy banks, the timber upon which had been cut down, a temporary bridge, on the east bank a blockhouse and breast-works, behind which a camp; at confluence of creek with Trent River, 1,000 yards distant, a field-work mounting ten guns; 300 yards east another work with eight guns; one-half or three quarters of a mile east, near railroad bridge, and about 1 mile from Brice's Creek bridge, another very large work; south on Neuse River, about 2 miles from Brice's Creek bridge, a very large fort for land and river defense; a line of breastworks extending from this west to Brice's Creek, and terminating in a field work 1 mile above the bridge, other works of less importance covering the plain and connecting the forts; on north side of Trent, here 700 yards wide, two field-works commanding those on south side.[13]

General Barton concluded that he was "unprepared to encounter obstacles so serious" and therefore "was forced to the conviction that they were insurmountable by the means at . . . [his] disposal." He immediately dispatched "several messengers, scouts, and couriers to General Pickett, informing him of the posture of affairs and asking instructions. . . ."[14] In the meantime, a lively artillery duel had started that was to last throughout that day and into the next.[15] "The shot and shell now went screaming and shrieking throughout the air over our heads," jotted a Confederate officer in his diary. "The aim of the enemy was pretty good," he conceded, "many of their shells bursting in rather unpleasant proximity to our position."[16]

It was Tuesday morning before one of Barton's couriers managed to get across the Trent to contact General Pickett. Upon receipt of Barton's message, the Commanding General dispatched Captain Robert A. Bright of his staff to communicate with the brigade commander in person. General Barton informed Bright that "he had been entirely misinformed as to the strength of the place, and that he pronounced the works as too strong to attack and that he had made no advance and did not intend to, and that he had sent out twice his cavalry to cut the railroad and they returned without accomplishing it." Captain Bright then, by Pickett's direction, ordered Barton to join the troops before New Bern for an assault on that front. To get across the Trent, Barton had to retrace his steps to Pollocksville, at which place on February 3 he received new orders directing him to Kinston.[17]*

General Pickett had decided to abandon the entire New Bern opera-

---

* General Barton certainly thought the fortifications at Brice's Creek were impregnable. Pickett, on the other hand, felt that his subordinate should have attacked the works and asked for an investigation of "his want of co-operation." *OR,* XXXIII, Ser. I, pp. 94, 98-99. General Hoke hid his disappointment over Barton's actions by stating: "Being junior officer it does not become me to speak my thoughts on the move." *Ibid.,* p. 96. However, at least one foot soldier, John L. Stuart of Moore County, agreed with General Barton that the Federal position could not be taken. He wrote home: "I tell you I was relieved the most you ever saw for we thought we would have to charge the city but our Generals found it was too strongly fortified." J. L. Stuart to Mother, Feb. 5, 1864, J. L. Stuart Papers, DU. Earlier Stuart had written: "We was ordered by the commanding General to charge the town but our General that was with us said it could not be done for there was two Bridges to cross and three batteries to take." J. L. Stuart to Mary A. Harper, Feb. 5, 1864, J. L. Stuart Papers, DU.

tion when he learned that Barton could not join him until the fourth, if then. Also, Colonel Dearing, whose orders were to take Fort Anderson, reported that the fortifications on his front were too powerful to storm. Faced with the failure of two of his columns, the General withdrew his forces from New Bern on the third.[18] Although the enemy failed to give chase, the march, because of the mud, was long remembered by the Confederate soldiers, especially those belonging to Barton's command.[19] The low, swampy country had been bad enough on the way down, but the rain and passage of troops "rendered it terrible" on the way back. The road was "one vast mudhole about the consistency of batter and about shoe-mouth deep as a general thing, with frequent places of much greater depth." The night was extremely dark and this darkness was "inhanced" by the thick swamps on either side of the road. Orders to keep the ranks closed up were unnecessary "as the discharge of firearms towards the rear answered . . . [the] purpose." Assuming the enemy was close behind, the men plunged through the mud without stopping, except those who stuck so fast that they had "to be pulled out." Wagons stalled and several horses and mules had to be killed. Along the road pine trees that had been notched for turpentine were lighted, illuminating the night sky. "It was a picturesque scene," wrote a Confederate officer, "this rush of muddy men along an illuminated muddy road."[20]

Pickett bungled the New Bern operation.[21] The co-ordinated attack on the city, as outlined by Hoke, never materialized. The Commanding General blamed this failure on the "lack of co-operation" by two of his subordinates,[22] but many felt that the expedition would have succeeded had Hoke been in command.[23] He was certainly "the moving spirit" of the operation,[24] and he was congratulated by Lee: "You and your gallant brigade accomplished your part of the work."[25]

The results of the expedition were summed up by General Pickett as follows:

[Federal] Killed and wounded, about 100; captured, 13 officers, 284 privates, 14 negroes, 2 rifled pieces and carssons, 300 stands of small-arms, 4 ambulances, 3 wagons, 103 animals, a quantity of clothing, camp and garrison equipage, and 2 flags. . . . Our loss about 45 killed and wounded.

The present operation I was afraid of from the first, as there were too many contingencies. I should have wished more concentration, but still hope the effect produced by the expedition may prove beneficial.[26*]

* Among those captured by the Confederates were some members of the First and

If anything proved "beneficial" about the operation, it was the work of Commander Wood and his detachment of sailors and marines who were assigned the task of attacking the gunboats at New Bern.[27] Even though the small boats, which were to be used in this operation, did not arrive in Kinston by rail until the morning of January 31, Wood had his entire force afloat by that afternoon. Lieutenant B. P. Loyall, with the boats and men from the James River Squadron, had arrived at 2:00 A.M. on this date,[28] but it was approaching noon before Lieutenant George W. Gift arrived from Wilmington* with 2 heavy launches, 2 rowboats and approximately 135 officers and men.[29] Rather than lose time by waiting for the heavy launches to be taken off the cars, Commander Wood put all the light boats in the water at once and started down the Neuse. Lieutenant Gift and eighty-two men in the two launches were to follow "as soon as possible." It was no easy task to get the cumbersome boats off the cars and to the river. It took two mules and a great deal of man power to accomplish the job by 3:00

Second North Carolina Union Volunteers. Twenty-two of these prisoners, having formerly been in the Confederate army, were hanged for desertion. The execution took place at Kinston in February, 1864. A great many Northerners considered this "wholesale murder." "Cold Blooded Murder," Broadside, NCC; Unidentified newspaper clipping, B. S. Hedrick Papers, DU. There were a few "Yankees" who did not go along with this line of thinking. A member of the Twenty-fifth Massachusetts, for one, thought the Federal government was at fault for allowing "deserters from the enemy to enlist into our army." Denny, *Wearing the Blue,* p. 250. Most Southerners naturally felt that these men received their just reward. Chaplain John Paris, C.S.A., visited each of the condemned men and then preached a sermon that was later printed and given. wide circulation. In this sobering message he warned that these men had all been good, honest citizens before they were "victimized by mischievous home influences." The culprits, he said, were "civilian croakers" who advocated peace and spread their "poisonous contagion of treason" among the soldiers. In conclusion the Chaplain called for a revival that would set the Confederacy free. He based the plea upon the fact that "Patriotism and Christianity walk hand in hand." J. W. Silver, *Confederate Morale and Church Propaganda,* ed., W. S. Hoole, *Confederate Centennial Studies* (Tuscaloosa: Confederate Publishing Co., 1957), No. 3, p. 76. For an account of the controversy arising over the execution of these men see United States War Department, *Murder of Union Soldiers in North Carolina,* 39 Cong., 1 Sess., House of Representatives Executive Document No. 98 (Washington: GPO, 1866); R. C. Hawkins, *An Account of the Assassination of Loyal Citizens of North Carolina for Having Served in the Union Army Which Took Place at Kinston in North Carolina in the Months of February and March, 1864* (New York: Privately printed, 1897).

* Lieutenant Gift's late arrival was caused by difficulties encountered at Wilmington. He complained of "endeavoring to perform impossibilities in the way of procuring materials, etc. for . . . the expedition." He said "the army people monopolize everything and yield up nothing. I have run from office to office looking up stores, munitions and with such poor success that I am not only tired bodily but mentally disgusted. I am almost at the point of quitting." G. W. Gift to Ellen Shackelford, Jan. 29, 1864, Ellen S. Gift Papers, SHC.

P.M., at which time, remarked the Lieutenant: "We left the landing cheered by a great many pretty girls." Commander Wood's entire force was now afloat. It consisted of approximately 250 select seamen, 25 marines, 35 officers, and 14 boats.[30]

By 3:00 P.M. the Commander's party, bending silently to muffled oars, had moved far down the river. The distance by rail between Kinston and New Bern was about thirty miles. Nevertheless, the "tortuous and circuitous course which the river took" made the journey by water at least twice that length. For the men, the trip down was of little interest. Gnarled cypress trees, whose great branches hung over the water's edge, formed a wall on either side of the river, and not a sign of life was visible, save an occasional flock of wild ducks which, startled at the approach of the boats, would rise suddenly from the water. Except for this sound and the steady splash of the oars, little else broke the stillness. Just before dark the boats "were hauled alongside each other to receive instructions." This done, Commander Wood offered "fervent prayers" for the success of the operation. And once more the twelve boats "were wending [their way] down the Neuse." Night fell and with it came a heavy fog that made it difficult to see the banks of the river. Wood did not have a pilot, and not a soul in his party had ever been down the "lonesome river" before. These facts registered fully with the Commander around three o'clock in the morning when he found himself in "the open country above Newbern. Here the Neuse widened and the shore disappeared into marshy lowlands, making navigation difficult. It took an hour to get opposite the town, and even then little could be seen because of the fog and darkness. Still, Commander Wood searched for the Federal gunboats until the break of day forced him to move up the river to Batchelder's Creek. After hiding the boats in the tall grass of a small island, the men threw themselves upon the ground for a well-deserved rest.[31] During the day Lieutenant Gift, with the two launches, joined Commander Wood and plans were made to capture the *Underwriter,* the only gunboat in the Neuse on February 1.* "We had to content ourselves with her," complained the Lieutenant.

* The *Underwriter,* a side-wheel steamer, was the largest gunboat at New Bern. She mounted four guns and carried a crew of seventy-two men and twelve to fifteen officers. She had engaged in the fight at Roanoke Island and other encounters in North Carolina waters. *NR,* IX, Ser. I, 452; T. J. Scharf, *History of the Confederate States Navy from its Organization to the Surrender of its Last Vessel* (New York: Rogers and Sherwood, 1887), pp. 395-96.

The vessel lay about five hundred yards below Fort Stevenson and approximately five hundred yards from a Federal battery, both on the west bank of the Neuse. Directly across the river from the battery was Fort Anderson.[32]

Once darkness came, preparations were begun in earnest for what each member of the party knew was "a perilous interprise." Arms were inspected, ammunition distributed, and everything made ready for embarkation. In order to distinguish himself in the dark from the enemy, every man wore a white badge on his left arm and made a mental note of the password, "Sumter." Sometime before midnight the boats were put in the water. Immediately Commander Wood arranged them in two divisions, the first commanded by himself and the second by Lieutenant Loyall. After coming into parallel position, the two divisions pulled rapidly downstream.[33]

At 2:30 A.M. they were near Fort Anderson "peering into the darkness" when the striking of a ship's bell and a faint light in the distance located the *Underwriter.* "So the long column turned its head and struck out steadily and noiselessly for . . . [its] victim. As I stood up and watched the line," wrote Lieutenant Gift, "it looked like a naval funeral procession. Not a sound could be heard save the dipping of the oars. Every ear was wide open for the first sound of alarm." In a few minutes, from the *Underwriter* came the hurried cry "boat ahoy," followed by a call to quarters which brought the Union blue jackets rushing up on deck.

As soon as his columns were hailed, Commander Wood stood up in his boat and ordered his men to "give way" and "lay him aboard." The sailors sprang to their oars and the boats "shot forward to the attack"[34] in the face of musket and pistol fire that "lighted up the night sky."[35] When the boats struck the sides of the *Underwriter,* the grapnels were thrown on board, and immediately the Confederate sailors sprang to the deck with a rush, their wild cheer ringing across the waters. First to board the Union gunboat was the brave Lieutenant Loyall, followed closely by Commander Wood.[36] The vessel was carried in a few minutes, but not before some bloody close-quarter fighting. The "sharp quick reports of pistols, and the clash of cutlases could be heard in all directions. . . ."[37] After the surrender of the *Underwriter,* Wood's men commenced plundering their prize and much confusion ensued. The looting was of short duration for, once the firing stopped, the Federal batteries knew the vessel had been taken and opened fire on her.[38] This not only put a stop to the Confederate plundering but forced Commander Wood to abandon all efforts to move the gunboat. Further complications arose when it was discovered that there was not enough steam in the ship's boilers to get her underway. Thus, after removing the wounded and the prisoners, the gallant Commander burned his prize and returned safely up the river.[39] Even though the *Underwriter* had to be destroyed, its capture was the chief accomplishment of General Pickett's otherwise ill-fated expedition.*

While the fighting was in progress around New Bern, a detachment of troops from the Wilmington area was enjoying complete success at Newport Barracks, a Federal depot on the railroad some twenty miles south of New Bern. On January 28, General James G. Martin, leading a force comprised of infantry, artillery, and cavalry, marched out of Wilmington to threaten the enemy's positions at Morehead City. This move was designed to draw attention away from New Bern and was made in accordance with Lee's instructions to General Whiting dated January 20, 1864.[40] Martin moved unopposed until around noon on February 2, when he encountered enemy pickets and blockhouses at Gales Creek and Bogue Sound. Easily pushing aside this opposition,[41] the General moved on to within two miles of Newport Barracks[42] where he "had quite a serious engagement from 4 to 6 o'clock."[43] It ended with the Federals' being "completely routed" and making "a gallant retreat" to Beaufort.[44] As they broke and fled toward the Newport River, they set fire to stables, storehouses, and the railroad bridge.[45]† We fired into them "so clost," wrote a North Carolina soldier, "that tha never went in to their fourts tha sot the best of their stoers on fier and grat quantities of provishens was burnt [we] captued thousands upon thousands but wee could not git much of it A way it looked like a pittey to destroy their quarters, poor fellows tha was living so well aney thing a man wanted tha had it the peple of Salesbury never lived as well as tha Yankee soldiers did" at Newport Barracks.[46] This semi-

---

* Northern journalists attempted to explain the loss of the *Underwriter* by saying that the vessel's captain, Jacob Westervelt, held secession in very "high esteem and regard." *RR*, VIII, 360.

† The Confederate soldiers were able to extinguish the fire on the "railroad bridge . . . [but] later in the evening [General Martin] judged it best to burn it. It was now too dark to follow the enemy." *OR*, XXXIII, Ser. I, 85. By destroying the bridge and cutting the railroad, General Martin did much of the job that had been assigned to General Barton. See above p. 206.

literate soldier from western North Carolina was correct about the vast quantity of supplies seized in this engagement. These included quartermaster, commissary, and ordnance stores. In addition, General Martin reported the destruction of three railroad bridges and the capture of four heavy dirt forts, three blockhouses, and approximately eighty prisoners.[47]

Following his victory at Newport Barracks, General Martin anxiously awaited instructions for his next move. He was totally ignorant of the failure at New Bern;[48] furthermore, he had accomplished the major objective of his mission which was to focus attention on Morehead City and the surrounding country.* Finally, at 7:00 P.M. on February 3, he received a three-line dispatch from General Barton ordering him to fall back since the Confederate troops were being withdrawn from around New Bern. The next morning the return march to Wilmington was commenced.[49]

The expedition to Newport Barracks had been "well managed and well fought."[50] It was "an entire success,"[51] a most satisfying victory for all North Carolinians, but it could hardly compensate for Pickett's defeat at New Bern.†

* John A. Hedrick, collector of customs at Beaufort, bore out the truth of this statement when he wrote on February 6: "We have just passed through one of the greatest panics that has happened during the war." J. A. Hedrick to B. S. Hedrick, Feb. 6, 1864, B. S. Hedrick Papers, DU.

† Following the New Bern expedition there was some minor skirmishing in eastern North Carolina. General Matt Ransom with his brigade and a cavalry force drove the Federals out of Suffolk, Virginia, on March 9. This fighting was preceeded by some skirmishing along the Dismal Swamp Canal in North Carolina. Chambers Diary. Mar. 1, 1864, NCDAH; J. W. Graham to Father, Mar. 13, 1864, W. A. Graham Papers, SHC; *OR,* XXXIII, Ser. I, 237-39. Also, Confederate batteries on the Chowan River "trapped" the Union steamer *Bombshell* and came close to capturing her. For an interesting account of this little episode see T. C. Parramore, "The Roanoke-Chowan Story—Chapter 9. Roanoke-Chowan Plays Rare Role in War, "Ahoskie *Daily Roanoke-Chowan News,* Civil War Supplement, 1960, pp. 101-4.

CHAPTER X

The Confederate Goliath

AFTER THE failure of the New Bern expedition, Pickett returned to Virginia and General Hoke took over command of the army.* Immediately upon assuming his new duties, Hoke made plans for an attack on Plymouth. This strategic little town, situated on the south bank of the Roanoke River near its mouth, was an important supply depot for the Federal land forces in eastern North Carolina. Its 2,834-man garrison, Brigadier General W. H. Wessells commanding, consisted of four infantry regiments, two companies of the Second North Carolina Union Volunteers, a detachment of cavalry, six guns of the Twenty-fourth New York Independent Battery, and two companies from the Second Massachusetts Heavy Artillery. These soldiers manned a series of forts that ringed the town on its land side. The fortifications were connected by strong redoubts, breastworks, and formidable obstructions. On the west side of Plymouth was a small earthwork called Battery Worth. Extending south from this installation ran a line of breastworks to the southwest corner of town. Here it turned at right angles and continued to the southeast edge of Plymouth. Together with the river to the north, the line surrounded Plymouth on all sides except the east. This open stretch, however, was guarded by several strong fortifications, and it was thought low, marshy ground made an attack from the east impracticable. Fort Williams, which was the strongest of the works, stood in the south center of the defenses. Less than a mile to the southwest of this anchor fortification and detached from the main works was Fort Wessells, also known as the Eighty-fifth Redoubt. Two and a half miles up the river was another

---

* There was very little change in the size and composition of the army when Hoke took command.

detached work, Fort Gray, which was separated from the main line by Welch's Creek and its marsh. On the east side of town, Fort Comfort and two redoubts covered the Columbia Road. In the river Commander C. W. Flusser had the gunboats *Miami* and *Southfield,* plus two smaller vessels, the *Whitehead* and *Ceres.*[1]

In order to capture Plymouth, so strongly fortified, General Hoke felt it necessary to have both ground and naval forces at his disposal. Opportunely for him, the Confederate navy had under construction at this time, at Edwards Ferry on the Roanoke River, an ironclad ram named the *Albemarle.* In response to appeals from Hoke, Confederate authorities authorized the ram to participate in the attack on Plymouth.

"No vessel was ever constructed under more adverse circumstances," said Gilbert Elliott.[2]* In the spring of 1863, this nineteen-year-old engineer-inventor from Elizabeth City contracted with the Confederate Navy Department to build an "iron-clad gun-boat, intended, if ever completed, to operate on the waters of Albemarle and Pamlico Sounds." To supervise construction, John L. Porter, Chief Constructor of the Confederate navy and designer of the *Albemarle,* arrived at Edwards Ferry. Porter, who had helped convert the *Merrimac* into the ironclad *Virginia* at the Norfolk navy yard, was shocked to find the "Edwards Ferry Yard" a corn field. None of the usual facilities such as engines, derricks, pulleys, and power tools were available. Work started anyhow. Peter E. Smith of Scotland Neck, owner of the "cornfield," was in charge of actual construction. This energetic and resourceful individual soon had lumber mills brought up the river and established for the cutting of heavy timbers necessary in the *Albemarle.* A blacksmith shop supplied badly needed tools. With Smith "necessity was the mother of invention." He designed and made a twist drill that reduced the time needed to bore holes in iron plates from twenty minutes to four. There was such a shortage of this metal that young Gilbert Elliott had to spend much of his time scouring the state in search of abandoned railroad ties, in fact, scrap iron of any size down to nuts and bolts. At the Tredegar Works in Richmond and the Clarendon Foundry at Wilmington, the iron that Elliott managed to scrape up was smelted and rolled into plate.[3]†

---

* In contemporary correspondence the name Elliott is spelled both with one "t" and two "t's."

† The armament of the ram consisted of two rifled Brooke guns, mounted on pivot carriages, and working through three portholes. G. Elliott, "The Career of the Confederate Ram 'Albemarle,'" *B and L,* eds. R. U. Johnson and C. C. Buel (New York: The Century Co., 1888), IV, p. 421.

In spite of the herculean efforts of Elliott and the others at Edwards Ferry, progress on the *Albemarle* was slow and Confederate authorities became impatient. To speed up construction, Commander James W. Cooke was sent to replace Porter. The Commander brought with him additional tools and men. He wanted "with all his heart" to finish the vessel, and for him no problem was insurmountable.[4] When informed that iron was scarce, he sent raiding parties to all the farms in the neighborhood to gather scrap.* Soon Commander Cooke was known as the "Ironmonger Captain."[5]

By spring of 1864, the *Albemarle* was nearly complete and a formidable vessel she was. Her two engines, though built out of odds and ends, were two hundred horsepower each. She was 152 feet long, 45 feet in the beam, and drew 8 feet of water. Her frame was made of yellow pine timbers "8 by 10 inches thick dovetailed together and fastened with iron and treenails." She was sheathed in yellow pine, four inches thick. Her sixty foot octagonal shield was covered with "two courses" of iron plating two inches thick. The eighteen-foot prow, which was to be used as a ram, was built of oak and was covered with iron plates.[6]

Toward the end of March "it was thought judicious" to move the *Albemarle* about two miles down the river to Hamilton, where the work could be completed and the "finishing touches" applied. While moored in the river off this small town, the ram was visited by General Hoke who had ridden up to Hamilton to inquire of Commander Cooke when he could expect the cooperation of the *Albemarle*. At first the Commander said it would be impossible for him to have the vessel ready in time to participate in the attack on Plymouth. But the General's persuasive powers won out, and he departed with Cooke's promise that the ram, complete or not, would take part in the assault.[7]

Assured of assistance from the *Albemarle,* Hoke confidently put his army in motion for Plymouth. At 4:00 P.M. on Sunday, April 17, his advance reached a point five miles from the town. Some enemy pickets were captured here and a detachment of cavalry was scattered. Hoke

---

* It was very difficult to get the iron out of Wilmington; so Commander Cooke sent Elliott to the coast to expedite matters. At Wilmington the young engineer-inventor found that most of the trouble centered around Flag Officer Lynch. He called this officer "incompetent, inefficient and almost imbecile." Gilbert Elliott to Z. B. Vance, Jan. 27, 1864, Z. B. Vance Papers, NCDAH; J. W. Hinton to Z. B. Vance, Feb. 4, 1864, Z. B. Vance Papers, NCDAH.

then proceeded to invest Plymouth on its land side. The Federals answered with artillery fire, which lasted until night fell.[8] In the Confederate lines "all was quiet during the evening, but in Plymouth great commotion existed through the night." The steamer *Massasoit,* loaded with frantic women, crying children, Negroes, and other non-combatants, departed for Roanoke Island. The local citizens remaining behind knew that escape by land was now impossible. They could only hope that the water route remained open.[9]

The next morning the fight commenced in earnest. At daylight "a severe cannonade was opened against Fort Gray." The Federal garrison remained firm, but the transport *Bombshell,* which was in communication with the fort, received several hits below her waterline and barely made it back to Plymouth, sinking at the wharf.[10]*

Late in the afternoon General Hoke decided that his brigade would assault Fort Wessells while Matt Ransom, with fourteen pieces of artillery, moved to the right and demonstrated in force against the enemy line east of Fort Williams. Ransom started his attack around six o'clock and kept it up until 10:00 P.M. In the face of artillery fire that illuminated the night sky, the Confederates managed to advance within a few hundred yards of the enemy works. "It was a wild sight, and the ground shoke with the explosion of shells" as "the lines . . . advanced." Such a heavy "dose of iron" was thrown at Ransom's men this night that, around 1:00 A.M., they withdrew to their position of the morning.[11]

In the meantime, Hoke's brigade had captured Fort Wessells. Several times the infantry charged the fort only to be repulsed by heavy musket fire and hand grenades. In one of these charges Colonel John T. Mercer, in command of Hoke's brigade, fell mortally wounded at the head of his column. Captain Nelson Chapin of the Eighty-fifth New York, commanding in the fort, also lost his life in the fight. The capture of Fort Wessells provided General Hoke with a good position for his artillery, but he knew that capture of Plymouth still depended on the cooperation of the *Albemarle,* which had not arrived.[12] "Bitterly disapointed" that the ram had not made its appearance and fearful that it would not, many of Hoke's men "fell to sleep, deeming it more probable that the morrow would bring orders for Tarboro! than for Plym-

---

* The *Bombshell* was later raised by the Confederates and put into service. J. C. Long to Sarah MacKay, May 30, 1864, MacKay-Stiles Papers, SHC.

outh."[13] The enemy, however, harbored no such thoughts. Commander Flusser, aboard the *Miami* on the evening of the eighteenth, wrote: "We have been fighting here all day. About sunset the enemy made a general advance along our whole line. They have been repulsed. . . . The ram will be down to-night or tomorrow. I fear for the protection of the town."[14] These were prophetic words, for, on the evening of the seventeenth, the *Albemarle* had cast off from her moorings at Hamilton and started slowly down the river.[15]

As the ram steamed downstream, workmen still swarmed over her decks, and a small boat with a portable forge followed behind. The forge was put to good use when the ship's engines failed and the rudder head broke. These misfortunes caused a ten-hour delay but failed to stop the *Albemarle*. She finally dropped anchor around 10:00 P.M. on the eighteenth, three miles above Plymouth at Thoroughfare Gap. Since the Union forces had obstructed the river at this point, a detail was sent out to learn the extent of the obstructions. It returned in two hours and the lieutenant in charge reported that mines, sunken vessels, and other obstructions made the river impassable. Commander Cooke banked the fires on the ram and most of the hands turned in for a night's sleep.

Gilbert Elliott, who had come along as a volunteer, could not sleep. He was disturbed over the lieutenant's report on the obstructions. He asked Commander Cooke for permission to take a look for himself and started off with three men in a small boat. When Elliott returned, he reported that a "remarkable freshet" then prevailing had deepened the channel and that ten feet of water was now over the obstructions. Upon receipt of this encouraging word, Cooke ordered the *Albemarle* to get underway. The time was 2:30 A.M., Tuesday, April 19.[16]

Fort Gray opened fire. The *Albemarle* disdained to answer, the shot and shell of the enemy sounding to those aboard "no louder than pebbles thrown against an empty barrel."[17] Having passed the obstructions and the fort without difficulty, the ram slipped on down the river until suddenly, looming out of the darkness ahead, were two Federal steamers.

They were the *Miami* and the *Southfield,* which "were lashed together with long spars, and with chains festooned between them." Charles W. Flusser, who was in command, hoped to get the ram caught between the two Union vessels and there batter her to pieces with gunfire at close range. Commander Cooke, seeing what his opponent had in mind, ran the *Albemarle* in close to the south shore and then suddenly turned into the middle of the river. With throttles wide open, the ram dashed her prow into the *Southfield,* making a hole large enough to carry the Union vessel to the bottom. For a moment, however, it looked as though the victim would take the victor to the bottom with her. The chainplates on the forward deck of the *Albemarle* had become entangled in the frame of the *Southfield,* pulling the ram's bow down until water poured into the portholes. But as the Union vessel touched bottom in the shallow river and turned over on her side, the *Albemarle* was released and came up on an even keel.

As soon as the ram was free of the *Southfield,* she opened fire on *Miami* which was "right alongside." So close together were the vessels that a shell with a ten-second fuse fired by the *Miami* rebounded off the ram and landed on the deck of the Union ship. The explosion killed Commander Flusser where he stood, lanyard in hand, by the gun that had fired the shot. The death of this gallant officer left Lieutenant Charles A. French in command of the *Miami.* French, who had survived the sinking of the *Southfield,* had had enough fighting for one day. He headed the *Miami* downstream and sped to safety, followed by some smaller Union ships that had not been engaged in the fight.[18] Having successfully carried out his part of the operation, Commander Cooke awaited instructions from General Hoke. Word came to move close to shore and shell the enemy fortifications. This was done with vigor well into the night.[19]

The land fighting on the nineteenth consisted primarily of an exchange of artillery fire, but in the late afternoon Ransom's brigade was ordered to cross Conaby Creek to the east, "make a detour of four or five miles around to the Columbia road," and attack the town from that direction. This change of position took until midnight, and for that reason it was necessary to delay the attack until the next day, and the men were "told to rest till day-break."* Rolling themselves up in their blankets against the chilly night air, the weary soldiers lay down

---

* A sergeant in the Eighty-fifth New York described conditions within the Union lines on the night of the nineteenth as follows: "During the evening I went out on the line of works and delivered the men their rations. The men seemed in good spirits and said the rebs could never take their works in front, but we all knew it was only a question of time for we were completely surrounded on the land and the ram had command of the river and could hold it against any force. . . ." N. Lanpheur, "Fall of Plymouth" (Unpublished reminiscence), N. Lanpheur Papers, DU.

for a few winks of precious sleep.[20] At daybreak they were aroused and the line of battle was formed. A signal rocket notified General Hoke that the attack was about to commence. The skirmishes under the gallant Captain Cicero Durham, fighting quartermaster of the Forty-ninth, moved forward and drove the enemy pickets before them. The infantry then advanced "at quick time." Soon it became "double quick" and yells broke from the entire line. The Confederate artillery from its position on the left opened fire upon the fortifications ahead which lay on both sides of the Columbia road. At this moment, General Hoke, on the west side of town, opened with his artillery and his men sent up yell after yell as if about to charge. The Virginians facing the enemy line to the south followed suit.

Steadily Ransom's men pushed forward. They carried the fortifications and entered the town, driving the enemy into Fort Williams. The Eighth North Carolina, flushed with victory, charged the fort, only to be repulsed with heavy losses. General Hoke had not authorized this foolhardy attack and sent word that "no further charging" would be necessary. He felt this anchor position could be "compelled by artillery." This news brought a sigh of relief to the men. They had fought well and the town was now entirely theirs except for Fort Williams.[21]

Hoping to avoid further bloodshed, Hoke demanded the surrender of the fort, and when it was refused by General Wessells, Confederate artillery opened up a terrific fire. What followed is best described in the words of Wessells:

I was now completely enveloped on every side, Fort Williams, an enclosed work in the center of the line, being my only hope. This was well understood by the enemy, and in less than an hour a cannonade of shot and shell was opened upon it from four different directions. The terrible fire had to be endured without reply, as no man could live at the guns. The breastheight was struck by solid shot on every side, fragments of shells sought almost every interior angle of the work, the whole extent of the parapet was swept by musketry, and men were killed and wounded even on the banquette slope. A covered excavation had been previously constructed, to which the wounded were conveyed, where they received sufficient medical attention. This condition of affairs could not be long endured without reckless sacrifice of life; no relief could be expected, and in compliance with the earnest desire of every officer, I consented to hoist a white flag and at 10 A.M. of April 20 I had the mortification of surrendering my post to the enemy with all it contained.[22]*

* In his official report General Wessells also made note of the fact that "a considerable

According to a Richmond newspaper, General Wessells surrendered approximately 2,500 men, 28 pieces of artillery, 500 horses, 5,000 stands of small arms, 700 barrels of flour, "with other commissary and quartermaster supplies, immense ordnance stores," and most important, the "strong position of Plymouth." This little town could now serve as a port for the ironclad to drive the enemy gunboats out of Albemarle and Pamlico sounds.[23]

General Hoke, who was only twenty-seven, treated his elderly prisoner with "kindness and courtesy."[24] The young officer was in a happy frame of mind, and well he might be, for President Davis had made him a major general "from the date of the capture of Plymouth."[25]* The victory was especially gratifying to Governor Vance "because it was accomplished by troops under the command of two distinguished sons of North Carolina—Brigadier, now Major General Hoke, commanding the land forces, and Commander Cooke, with the steam ram *Albemarle*."[26]

The fall of Plymouth led to the Federal evacuation of Washington. Hoke laid siege to Washington on April 27,[27] but he made no effort to storm the defenses since reports indicated that the enemy was abandoning the place. Unfortunately for the local citizens, while Hoke bided his time for three days, the evacuating Federal troops thoroughly sacked the town.

On the evening of April 26, Brigadier General Edward Harland, in command at Washington, had received orders to evacuate his base. The intended evacuation seems to have become generally known by the next day, for during the afternoon of the twenty-seventh there were some instances of theft, and before morning pillaging commenced.

---

number of North Carolina soldiers (many of them deserters from the enemy and all of them fearing bad treatment in the event of capture) left their companies without authority, escaping in canoes, being picked up, as I have understood, by our boats in the sound." *NR*, IX, Ser. I, 655. It was rumored in Federal circles that during the afternoon of the surrender the sharp crack of "Rebel rifles" could be heard—"persumedly shooting Buffaloes and Negroes." A. S. Billingsley, *From the Flag to the Cross; or Scenes and Incidents of Christianity in the War* (Philadelphia: New-World Publishing Co., 1872), p. 69; J. A. Hedrick to B. S. Hedrick, Apr. 25, 1864, B. S. Hedrick Papers, DU. A small number of Wessells' men were not in Fort Williams when it surrendered. These troops fought on for a short while. W. M. Smith, "The Siege and Capture of Plymouth," *Personal Recollections of the War of the Rebellion. Addresses Delivered before the New York Commandery of the Loyal Legion of the United States* (New York: Published by the Commandery, 1891), I, 338-41.

*The Confederate Congress voted a resolution of thanks to Hoke and Cooke "for the brilliant victory over the enemy at Plymouth, N.C." *OR*, XXXIII, Ser. I, 305.

"Government stores, sutler's establishments, dwelling houses, private shops, and stables suffered alike. Gangs of men patrolled the city, breaking into houses and wantonly destroying such goods as they could not carry away. The occupants and owners were insulted and defied in their feeble indeavors to protect their property." This lawlessness lasted until 4:00 P.M. of the thirtieth, when the last of the troops boarded steamers for New Bern.* As these final detachments prepared to embark, fires broke out in town. The flames quickly spread from the riverfront warehouses to the northern limits of Washington, and before the conflagration could be brought under control fully one-half of the town lay in ashes.[28]

So outrageous was the conduct of the Federal soldiers that one of their officers wrote: "While the troops of this command may exult and take just pride in their many victories over the enemy, yet a portion of them have within a few days been guilty of an outrage against humanity, which brings the blush of shame to the cheek of every true man and soldier."[29]

When the Confederate troops finally entered Washington, they found it a "ruined City . . . a sad scene—mostly . . . chimneys and Heaps of ashes to mark the place where Fine Houses once stood, and the Beautiful trees, which shaded the side walks, Burnt, some all most to a coal."[30]† This was a depressing sight for Hoke's men. Still, it made them all the more anxious to get on with the work at hand—the capture of New Bern. Leaving the Sixth North Carolina behind to garrison Washington and help the citizens restore order, Hoke pushed on for the big Federal base at the confluence of the Trent and the Neuse.[31]

Hoke's plan of attack once again called for cooperation from the *Albemarle*. General P. G. T. Beauregard, who on April 23 had assumed command of the newly created Department of North Carolina and Cape Fear, had suggested that the ram be used.[32] He told Hoke that with the assistance of this vessel the expedition should meet with "complete success."[33] General Hoke concurred and approached Commander Cooke with the idea. The Commander agreed to take part in

---

* During this period the First North Carolina Union Volunteers, their families, and other "loyal North Carolinians" were evacuated to New Bern. *OR*, XXXIII, Ser. I, 312; Thompson Diary, Apr. 28, 1864, DU. The "poor Negroes" were "flying for protection in every direction." Jesse Harrison to Mother, Apr. 28, 1864, Jesse Harrison Papers, DU.

† After the Confederates entered Washington, a fire was started accidently. It destroyed even more of the town. James Evans to Father, May 10, 1864, James Evans Papers, SHC.

the operation, although he knew the risks were great. To reach New Bern, the ironclad would have to cross Albemarle, Croatan, and Pamlico sounds and then steam up the obstructed Neuse River. But a great deal was at stake, and for this reason Cooke agreed to the undertaking.[34]

Late in the afternoon of May 5, the *Albemarle* got up steam, weighed anchor, and together with the *Bombshell* and[35] and *Cotton Plant* started down the Roanoke River. The ultimate destination of the three vessels was New Bern. But at the head of Albemarle Sound the ironclad and her two consorts were attacked by seven Union warships under Captain Melancton Smith.*

Late in April, Captain Smith had been sent down specifically to take care of the *Albemarle*. Smith's plan of attack, which was worked out soon after he arrived in North Carolina waters, called for the large vessels of his fleet, the double-enders *Mattabesett, Sassacus, Wyalusing,* and *Miami*,† "to pass as close as possible to the ram without endangering their wheels," to deliver their fire, and then, after reloading, to come around for a second volley. The smaller vessels, *Whitehead, Ceres,* and *Commodore Hull,* were to attack "the armed launches" that were expected to accompany the ironclad. The *Miami* carried a torpedo attached to a boom to be exploded under the ram and a net to foul her propellors. Ramming was optional with each commander.[36]

The *Albemarle* opened the fight shortly before 5:00 P.M.‡ Her second shot took away part of the *Mattabesett's* rigging and wounded six seamen. The ram followed up this initial success by steaming straight for the Union flagship, but she missed her target and, in so doing, took at close quarters a broadside of "solid 9-inch shot" from the *Sassacus.* "The [Federal] guns might as well have fired blank cartridges, for the shot skimmed off into the air and even the 100 pound solid shot from the pivot-rifle glanced from the sloping roof [of the ironclad] into space with no apparent effect." The *Sassacus,* seeing that her heavy guns had failed "to make any mark" on the adversary, turned her attention to the *Bombshell,* which lay off the port quarter of the ram. The Union double-ender gave the little Confederate vessel the starboard

---

* On April 29, the *Albemarle* had steamed down to the mouth of the Alligator River and escorted a captured Union vessel back to Plymouth. While the ram was on this run, the Union fleet made no move to intercept her.

† Double-enders were side-wheel vessels able to steam in either direction.

‡ The *Cotton Plant* was not involved in the battle. When the enemy was first sighted, she turned around and went back up the river. *NR,* IX, Ser. I, 768.

The *U.S.S. Sassacus* ramming the Confederate ironclad *Albemarle,* May 5, 1864.
(From *Battles and Leaders of the Civil War*)

battery and got her surrender. This action took the *Sassacus* some distance from the *Albemarle,* but for Lieutenant Commander F. A. Roe, captain of the Union ship, this was the "decisive moment." He decided to ram the Confederate ironclad lying broadside to him about four hundred yards away. Commander Roe yelled to his engineer, "Crowd waste and oil in the fires. . . ! Give her all the steam she can carry!" To Acting Master Charles A. Boutelle he said, "Lay her course for the junction of the casemate and the hull!" Then came four bells, and with full steam and open throttle, the ship "sprang forward like a living thing." Straight as an arrow the *Sassacus* shot for the ironclad and, with a crash that resembled "an earthquake," she struck "full and square on the iron hull." The collision damaged the bow of the *Sassacus* and ripped and strained her timbers at the waterline. The *Albemarle,* as a result of the crash, heeled over and shipped a good bit of water, causing many of her crew to fear that she was about to sink. But the Captain's calm voice restored order.* "Stand to your guns," he said, "and if we must sink let us go down like brave men."[37]

Following the crash, the *Sassacus* was stuck fast to the ironclad. This afforded the grimy Confederate gunners an opportunity to send a hundred-pound rifle shot through the starboard boiler of the Union vessel and into her wardroom. Escaping steam filled every part of the *Sassacus* from the hurricane deck to the fire room, and cries of the

* A member of the *Albemarle's* crew conceded that his captain, at the time of the collision, "looked kinda scared like." *NR,* IX, Ser. I, 769.

scalded men could be heard even above the roar of battle. But when the steam cleared, Commander Roe found himself free of the iron monster. Although battered the *Sassacus* continued to fire at her adversary, as she drifted helplessly downstream, until the range became too great.[38]

The ramming might have been more successful if the other Union ships had closed in while the two vessels were engaged. But they did not, and so the battle continued until 7:30 P.M.* It was apparent by this time the *Albemarle* was in no condition to continue the voyage to New Bern. Her colors were shot away, her steering mechanism damaged, and her smokestack so riddled with holes that it was difficult to keep up steam. Only by throwing butter, lard, and bacon into the boilers was it possible for the crippled ironclad to raise enough steam to limp back to Plymouth.[39]

Commander Cooke was disappointed that he had failed to reach New Bern although justly proud that, after engaging the enemy fleet, he was yet able to bring his ship safely back to port. And there was some comfort in the news of the sixth that revealed that Hoke's attack on New Bern had been stopped, not because the *Albemarle* failed to arrive, but on orders from Richmond.

General Hoke, on the evening of May 4, had driven in the enemy pickets at Deep Gully some eight miles from New Bern. Leaving the Sixty-seventh North Carolina behind to hold this position on the Trent Road, the General then marched down the Trent River on its south side to below New Bern. Here, on the fifth, he engaged the enemy batteries, "both army and navy," and a "railroad iron-clad monitor." During the day Brigadier General James Dearing's cavalry and some artillery captured the blockhouse on Brice's Creek that, a few weeks earlier, General Barton had considered such a Gibraltar.[40] At this point, General Hoke was confident of victory even though the *Albemarle* had not yet arrived.[41] If a demand for surrender were refused by General I. N. Palmer,† commanding at New Bern, Hoke intended a full-scale assault on the city. This "intended" attack, however, failed to materialize. Much to his dismay, Hoke received an urgent message from

---

* Commander Roe complained that the other vessels had not supported him, He later wrote: "In the Sassacus, in the sounds of N.C.—I left the Line of Battle, I attacked single handed the terror of the South. I disabled the Ram, and defeated her, tho without glory to me." F. A. Roe to "Dr. Benjamine," n.d., a note accompanying a picture of Rear Admiral F. A. Roe, SHC.

† On April 19, 1864, Brigadier General I. N. Palmer replaced General Peck as commander of the District of North Carolina. *OR*, XXXIII, Ser. I, 916.

Beauregard ordering him "to repair forthwith to Petersburg, no matter how far his operations might have advanced. . . ."[42] In northern Virginia, Grant was poised to strike Lee and, on May 4, President Davis, fearful of the threat posed by Grant's offensive, had ordered Beauregard to send Hoke north with all speed.[43] This recall to Virginia was one of Hoke's "greatest disappointments," but he obeyed the order promptly, arriving at Petersburg on the tenth.[44]

After Hoke's withdrawal, New Bern was never again attacked in force by Confederate troops.* However, the fortunes of war in the summer of 1864 gave rise, in Confederate quarters, to the hope that the town might fall without a fight. Northern morale reached a low ebb in July and August of that year, and north of the Potomac there was talk of peace.† In the spring, Grant had pushed Lee from the wilderness west of Fredericksburg to behind his defenses at Petersburg, but, in so doing, Federal casualties mounted to 55,000 men. This price was almost too much for the country to stand. Furthermore, as the summer dragged on, the Union commander, in the eyes of his critics, became stagnant behind his fortifications.[45] He was no closer to Richmond in August of 1864 than McClellan had been two years earlier. And the news from Georgia was not good. Major General William T. Sherman, under orders to "break . . . up" the Confederate Army of Tennessee and move into the interior of the Confederacy, was still north of Atlanta and faced by an army that was very much intact.[46] The outlook was so

---

* The correspondence of Henry J. H. Thompson, a self-righteous soldier from New England, gives a colorful description of life in New Bern during 1864. For Thompson, New Bern was a sinful town overrun with Negroes, whom he did not like, and drunken soldiers. Fights, which sometimes turned into full-scale race riots occurred almost every day. And "of all the places for bad women," he wrote his wife, "I guess this caps all, from white down 2 the blackest. . . ." The New Englander found the stores in New Bern very "curious . . . if we should want ribons or anything in that line we should very apt 2 find it in a hardware store . . . go in 2 a dry Goods shop and you will find anything you want in the Grocery line. . . ." In his letters he also made note of the yellow fever epidemic that raged from August to November and took several hundred lives. Tar and pitch were burned in great quantities to ward off the fever, and whisky and quinine were prescribed twice daily for all people remaining in New Bern. The quinine went "down hard" wrote Thompson, implying that the whisky did not. See Henry J. H. Thompson Papers, DU.

† In the South there was general optimism. William Pettigrew, a planter in eastern North Carolina wrote: "The Confederate prospects are decidedly brightening; justifying the hope, I think, that the war is drawing near its close and that the South is to be a free and independent people." W. Pettigrew to J. C. Johnston, Aug. 9, 1864, Hayes Collection, SHC.

gloomy by the last weeks of August that President Lincoln became reconciled to defeat in the fall elections.*

At New Bern, Private Henry J. H. Thompson of the Tenth Connecticut expressed, in a letter to his wife dated August 17, 1864, some very decided ideas on the forthcoming presidential election and the depressing military picture as well. Thompson was a strong "McClellan man." He told his wife that a vote for "old Abe" would mean twenty more years of war and the expenditure of a great deal of money. The Private came to this conclusion by a curious line of reasoning: "Every niger that has been freed has cost four thousand dollars and some white man's life thus far and according to that, we shall loose one million of lives and every thousand nigers cost four million of dollars and there is three million of nigers yet to free, if the north thinks they can stand that all I have got to say is vote for old Abe and they are sure 2 get it. . . ." Thompson followed this unique observation with some comments on the military: "Two years ago or more we were going to take richmond, since that Grant one of the best Generals had undertaken the job with all the men that could be obtained with all the equipment and can't take the little city of Petersburg." If Grant could not take Petersburg, Thompson reasoned, how could he hope to capture Richmond? The Private also wanted to know who was going to fill the ranks, since one-third of the men stay "on the sick list." Then, turning to matters in the North Carolina theater, he made note of the loss of Plymouth "and the large number of good troops captured" there, as well as the fact that the "rebels have got a navy at Plymouth and have built one heavy Iron Clad Ram. . . ." In conclusion, Thompson raised a question for all readers of his letter: "Shall we continue in this bloody strife till another million is laid under the sod and the crime enough to darken the Heavens in the blackest dye, or shall we look to a more calm cooler way." In his mind the "calm cooler way" was, of course, the path advocated by the Democrats.[47] But following the November elections, the disappointed soldier could only write that he was pleased that at least some of the states and the city of New Haven had gone for his candidate, McClellan.[48]

In early September, the tide of anti-war feeling in the North had be-

* The correspondence of the Federal soldiers stationed in eastern North Carolina reveal that the presidential election of 1864 created a great deal of interest in the camps. As early as March, 1864, the election became "all the talk" at New Bern. H. J. H. Thompson to Wife, Mar. 27, 1864, H. J. H. Thompson Papers, DU.

gun to ebb. Atlanta fell to Sherman on September 2.* The effect above the Mason-Dixon line was electric. To most Northerners, weary of war and heavy losses of manpower, the fall of Atlanta was the most important military achievement of the year 1864, and to Lincoln, especially, it was a godsend. The victory assured his re-election. Not long after this heartening news from the deep South came word that Major General Philip Sheridan had defeated Jubal Early in the Shenandoah Valley. The South's hope that the people of the North would get tired and quit was fast becoming a matter of wishful thinking.

In eastern North Carolina, though, a spirit of optimism still prevailed in some quarters. The *Albemarle* was moored safely at Plymouth and, as long as the ram remained afloat, the people knew she was a threat to Federal supremacy of the sound region.† Union naval officers recognized this fact also and were in agreement that the Confederate Goliath had to be destroyed—but how and by whom?‡ The job finally was given to young William B. Cushing, whose daring exploits in North Carolina waters had brought him to the attention of his superiors.[49]

Lieutenant Cushing reported at once to Rear Admiral S. P. Lee aboard the *Minnesota.* The youthful Lieutenant informed the Admiral that he had two plans in mind, either of which he was willing to undertake. Both involved torpedo attacks. One called for an India-rubber boat to be transported through swamps around Plymouth and launched at a point across the river from the *Albemarle's* berth. In the other, the attacking party "was to be conveyed in two low-pressure and very small steamers, each armed with a torpedo and howitzer."[50] Admiral Lee thought the latter plan a good one and sent Cushing to Wash-

---

* At New Bern a one-hundred-gun salute was fired in honor of Atlanta's fall and by order of the War Department all work was suspended for a day. Thompson Diary, Sept. 9, 1864, DU.

† Soon after the engagement with the *Sassacus,* Captain Cooke left the *Albemarle.* His successor was Captain John N. Maffitt, another North Carolinian. But Maffitt was not allowed to take the ram into action. Brigadier General L. S. Baker, commanding the Second District, Department of North Carolina and Southern Virginia, was afraid another head-on encounter with the Union fleet would mean the loss of the ram and open the door for the recapture of Plymouth. The General convinced authorities that the ram should remain at Plymouth, at least until additional naval units could be secured to aid her. Under these circumstances Commander Maffitt was happy to turn over command of the *Albemarle* to Lieutenant A. F. Warley. *NR,* IX, Ser. I, 624, 718, 719; A. F. Warley "Note on the Destruction of the 'Albemarle,'" *CM,* XXXVI (May-Oct., 1888), 439; L. S. Baker to J. M. Maffitt, July 6, 1864, J. N. Maffitt Papers, SHC.

‡ The Federal navy did not have an ironclad with shallow enough draft to cross the Hatteras bar. Also disturbing to the Federal officials was the failure of a "boat expedition" from the *U.S.S. Wyalusing* to destroy the *Albemarle. NR,* X, Ser. I, 95-96.

Destruction of the *Albemarle* at her moorings at Plymouth, October 27, 1864.
(From *Harper's Weekly*)

ington to submit it to the Navy Department. Gustavus Fox, Assistant
Secretary of Navy, doubted the merits of the project but agreed to go
along with it, and he ordered Cushing to New York to "purchase suitable vessels." At the navy yard in Brooklyn, the Lieutenant found
some boats being constructed for picket duty. He selected two and
proceeded to outfit them. "They were open launches about thirty feet
in length, with small engines and propelled by a screw." A twelve-
pound howitzer and a spar with a complicated torpedo device attached
to it* were fitted to each craft.[51]

Sometime after the middle of September, when all work was completed, the launches started south for Roanoke Island along inland water routes. The boats were commanded by two of Cushing's junior
officers, the Lieutenant having received permission to spend a few days
at home. On October 10, he rejoined the party at Hampton Roads,
Virginia, to learn that only one of the launches had made the trip successfully. The other boat had been lost on the way down. Still undaunted, Cushing set out from Norfolk on the twentieth by way of the
Albemarle and Chesapeake Canal. In addition to himself, there were
six men aboard the launch. Three days later they arrived at Roanoke

---

* The torpedo device was extremely complicated. Cushing described it as follows:
". . . A boom was rigged out some fourteen feet in length, swinging by a gooseneck
hinge to the bluff of the bow. A topping lift, carried to a stanchion inboard, raised or
lowered it, and the torpedo was fitted into an iron slide at the end. This was intended
to be detached from the boom by means of a heel-jigger leading inboard, and to be
exploded by another line, connecting with a pin, which held a grape-shot over a nipple
and cap." W. B. Cushing, "The Destruction of the 'Albemarle,' " *CM*, XXXVI (May-
Oct., 1888), 433. See also *NR*, X, Ser. I, 622-23.

Island but remained there only a few hours. During the night, Lieutenant Cushing and his companions slipped away to join the Union fleet guarding the mouth of the Roanoke River.[52]

The impatient young officer, after reporting to Commander W. H. Macomb aboard the *Shamrock*, wasted no time in preparing for the hazardous job ahead. Around 11:30 on the chilly, dark night of October 27, a launch with a cutter in tow entered the river.* It was raining hard and the twenty-five men in the boats under the command of Lieutenant Cushing shivered in silence. They had been warned not to talk lest a Confederate sentry on the river bank hear them and give the alarm. The little engine had been boxed and covered with a tarpaulin to muffle its noise. In the inky blackness of the night, Cushing could hardly see the hands on his watch. But when he saw, on one of his periodic checks, that it was two o'clock, his heart quickened a beat. The half-submerged wreck of the *Southfield* should be visible any minute. Reports had indicated there were pickets stationed on the hulk and a schooner anchored nearby. The Lieutenant did not think he could possibly pass these two vessels without being noticed, but if he could, he had a plan in mind. It called for landing at a wharf downstream from the ram. From this point he would lead his heavily armed crew in a surprise attack on the *Albemarle* from the shore. After the ironclad was captured, her hawsers would be cut so she would drift downstream. There would be ample time, he knew, to start the engines and, with the Stars and Stripes at the masthead, steam triumphantly into the sound.

For a while it looked as though Lieutenant Cushing would have the chance to try his bold plan. The launch and its tow somehow managed to pass unnoticed between the *Southfield* and the schooner, and just two miles up the river was Plymouth. The minutes ticked off; still the enemy had not seen them. Then suddenly, as the launch swept around a bend in the river, the huge silhouette of the *Albemarle* was distinguishable in the darkness. Cushing decided in a split second to try the plan and headed for the shore. As the launch neared the wharf, a dog's bark awoke a dozing sentinel and the challenge "Who goes there?" broke the stillness of the night. The chance to board was lost. So, as quickly as he had decided on the plan, Cushing abandoned it.

* Cushing started up the river on the night of twenty-sixth but his launch grounded, forcing him to return.

He ordered the cutter, which was still in tow, to cast off and "go down and get those pickets on the schooner." In practically the same breath, he ordered "all steam" for the launch and went at the dark mountain of iron in front of him. The launch lept forward into a hail of bullets. Suddenly a huge bonfire on the bank blazed up, throwing light on a semicircle of cypress logs "around the *Albemarle,* boomed well out from her side" to protect against a torpedo attack. This "unfortunate" revelation failed to discourage the Lieutenant. He took the launch in close to get a good look at the logs and then, in a hail of bullets, fled across the river. Cushing now concluded that the only way to get in close to the *Albemarle* was to strike the logs squarely at right angles, trusting they had become slimy enough to enable the launch, under full headway, to slip over them into the pen with the ram. "This was my only chance of success," he wrote afterwards, "and once over the obstruction my boat would never get out again; but I was there to accomplish an important object, and to die, if needs be. . . ."

Having reached a decision on what had to be done, Cushing ordered the launch to head back across the river. As it sped toward the ram, there was a momentary lull in the firing and again the Confederate challenge, "What boat is that?" The men gave comical answers while the Lieutenant replied with a dose of canister. In another instant the launch struck the boom of logs. The bow rose, slid forward a short distance and came to rest on the boom. Cushing, standing forward in the bow, his uniform "perforated" by bullets, calmy lowered the spar with the torpedo attached and exploded it under the *Albemarle.* The ram went down with a "hole in her bottom big enough to drive a wagon." But the immense volume of water thrown up by the explosion of the torpedo crashed into the launch, and it seemed "to flatten out like a pasteboard box on the logs." It was now every man for himself. Cushing tore off his shoes and coat, dropped his sword and revolver, and dived into the cold waters of Roanoke River. He swam a long distance downstream and gained the opposite bank, where he lay exhausted until the morning sun awakened him. Having gained sufficient strength by this time to proceed, Cushing plunged into the swamp along the river bank. About two o'clock in the afternoon, he stumbled upon a Confederate picket station. Awaiting his opportunity, he stole the soldier's skiff and made it to the mouth of the river. Then he rowed for hours toward a light that proved to be that of the Federal picket vessel, *Valley*

City. Of the Lieutenant's companions on the torpedo launch, two were drowned, one escaped and the rest were taken prisoners.[53]

In one daring exploit Lieutenant William Baker Cushing put to naught the victories so handsomely won by Commander Cooke and General Hoke. As a result of the *Albemarle's* destruction, Plymouth was recaptured by the Federals on October 31. Washington fell shortly thereafter. Thus the sound region of North Carolina once again fell under enemy domination.*

* The Federal troops continued their raids in eastern North Carolina. One of the largest of these was a four-hundred-man expedition to Southwest Creek below Kinston, December 10-15, 1864. *OR*, XLII, Ser. I, Pt. I, 1027; T. M. Wilson to Wife, Dec. 13, 1864, Mary Ann C. Wilson Papers, SHC; James Evans to Father, Dec. 17, 1864, James Evans Papers, SHC; Thompson Diary, Dec. 13, 1864, DU.

CHAPTER XI

War in the Mountains, 1864

IN WESTERN North Carolina during 1864, Confederate officials were extremely fearful of cavalry raids from east Tennessee on the vital rail lines east of the mountains. With much of east Tennessee in Federal hands, and widespread disloyalty and Unionism in the western counties, authorities had every reason to be concerned.[1] Colonel J. B. Palmer, commanding in western North Carolina with less than five hundred regular Confederate troops, had to rely heavily upon the home guard in defending against raids. These citizen-soldiers were not dependable fighters, and in time of an emergency they were very difficult to rally.[2] "We are in a truly deplorable condition," wrote a resident of Franklin. "There is no reliable forces in the country or between us and the enemy. Col. Thomas had been pretending to picket the passes at the Smokey mountains, but to no purpose as recent facts go to prove."[3] The writer of these lines was referring to a recent raid on Quallatown, Jackson County, in which part of Thomas' Legion was surprised by a Federal cavalry detachment.

The cavalry belonged to Brigadier General S. D. Sturges' command at Maryville, Tennessee. When this Union officer learned that "the force of Indians and whites commanded by the rebel Thomas . . . [was] lying around" at Quallatown, he ordered Major Francis M. Davidson's Fourteenth Illinois to surprise the Confederates and destroy their force, if possible. On February 2, Davidson moved up the Tuckaseegee River road, robbed, "and captured Col. [T. P.] Siler and passed on to Thomas' camp and into the camp amongst his Indians before they or anyone else had any warning of their approach." In the lively skirmish that followed, the redmen "fought nobly . . . until their ammunition failed," and they were forced to retire.

Having broken up the Confederate base, the raiders started back to Tennessee. They took along twenty-two Indian and thirty-two white prisoners, including Colonel Siler. On this return trip the Federals stopped once again at the home of the Colonel, "where they carried away all his corn, poured his rye in the sand, took his wife's money and all the arms and horses they could find. . . ." Siler looked on helplessly as his property was destroyed, but that night he enjoyed the satisfaction of making his escape. The other prisoners, however, were taken on to Knoxville. Here, according to the *Daily Confederate,* they "were flattered and feasted. . . . They were promised their liberty and *five thousand dollars in gold,* if they would bring in *the scalp of their chief, Col. William H. Thomas!* The Indians . . . agreed to the proposition. They were released, returned to their native mountains, sought the camp of their Chief, told him all, and have ever since been on the warpath—*after Yankee scalps.*"[4]

The Quallatown raid confirmed the general belief of the local inhabitants that western North Carolina was unprotected* and it was assumed by all that more raids were to come.[5] Many of the residents wrote Governor Vance about their plight, and at least one of their number, Colonel T. P. Siler, decided to consult with the Governor in person "on the best means to defend . . . [the western] section of the state from Yankees and Tories. . . ."[6] Yet, before the Colonel could reach Raleigh, news reached him that Major Nathan Paine, with 250 men of the First Wisconsin Cavalry, had moved unmolested through Cherokee County.[7] And in June, while the passes through the mountains were still undefended, Colonel George W. Kirk led a daring raid all the way from east Tennessee to Camp Vance near Morganton, North Carolina. Kirk, a native of Greene County, Tennessee, was considered a "bushwacker" by the Confederates. But among the Federals, he was known as an officer who could conduct the guerrilla warfare necessary in the mountains.

On June 13, 1864, Kirk, with about 130 men, including 12 Indians, left Morristown, Tennessee, for the raid on Morganton.† Each man

---

* This low state of morale found expression among the people in the sentiment that they were "lible to be overrun at anytime by bands of Robbers and Tories from E. Tennessee. . . ." W. Horton and others to Z. B. Vance, June 24, 1864, Z. B. Vance Papers, NCDAH.

† Some observers put Kirk's force at nearer three hundred. J. P. Arthur, *Western North Carolina: A History from 1730 to 1913* (Raleigh: Edwards and Broughton, 1914), p. 626.

was on foot and carried his own rations, blankets, and arms.[8] Moving swiftly, the raiders, in less than two weeks, passed through Bull's Gap, Greeneville, and Crab Orchard, all in Tennessee; crossed the state line; forded the Toe River about six miles south of the Cranberry Iron Works in North Carolina; and "scouted through the mountains" toward the Linville River, which was crossed on the afternoon of the twenty-sixth. The previous day Kirk had picked up a guide, Joseph V. Franklin, who was reared near Linville Falls and "knew the country like a book." On the twenty-seventh, Franklin led the expedition through such a long "stretch of mountains" that it took most of the day to cross. But instead of camping, Kirk decided to push on and just at dark crossed Upper Creek. This put him on the road leading to Morganton, twelve miles distant. By keeping in the woods and marching all night, Kirk arrived at Camp Vance in time to hear reveille.[9]

This Confederate base was used to train conscripts and, on the morning of the twenty-eighth, there were "some 240 of the Junior Reserves* . . . besides the officers present."[10] The camp's commanding officer, Major James R. McLean, however, was not on the post at the time. He had departed the previous day, leaving Lieutenant W. Bullock in charge "with instructions to organize and arm the three remaining companies of Junior Reserves. . . ." The Lieutenant found it impossible to arm and organize three companies in one day, so he postponed issuing the rifles, intending to do so in the next twenty-four hours. "But," wrote a Confederate soldier, "ere the sound of reveille hushed in camp it was resumed by an unknown hand, and a squad, under cover

---

* On February 17, 1864, the Confederate Congress passed an act "by which the military age, previously 18 to 45, was extended to embrace all from 17 to 50. Those from 17 to 18 years of age, known later as Junior Reserves, were embodied into companies in April and May, and in May and June were formed into battalions and later on into regiments—forming a total in . . . [North Carolina] of three regiments and one batallion, which became the Junior Reserves Brigade in [R.F.] Hoke's Division, [W.J.] Hardee's Corps." C. W. Broadfoot, "Seventieth Regiment," *Histories of the Several Regiments and Battalions from North Carolina in the Great War 1861-'65. Written by Members of the Respective Commands,* ed. W. Clark (Goldsboro: Nash Brothers, 1901), IV, 9. At the same time the Confederate Congress placed in the reserves "those between the ages of . . . 45 and 50." These became known as the Senior Reserves. Their organization, however, was postponed a few weeks to enable them "to make and save their crops and make arrangements for the care of their families." *Ibid.;* W. Clark, "Organization of Reserves," *Histories of the Several Regiments and Battalions from North Carolina in the Great War 1861-'65. Written by Members of the Respective Commands,* ed. W. Clark (Goldsboro: Nash Brothers, 1901), IV, 2.

of a flag of truce, proceeding to headquarters, demanded an unconditional surrender of the camp, by order of Colonel . . . [G. W.] Kirk,
commanding a detachment of the Third Regiment North Carolina
Mounted Infantry Volunteers. . . ." Lieutenant Bullock, his men scattered all over the post and unarmed, decided to surrender without a
fight. This decision saved lives but not property. The Federal soldiers
took over the camp and proceeded to burn every building except the hospital. "The surgeons by their blarney and ingenius persuation" managed
to save this lone structure "intact."[11]

The main purpose of the raid, though, was not the pillage and destruction of Camp Vance. Kirk hoped to capture a train on the Western North Carolina Railroad, make a swift dash to Salisbury to release
Federal prisoners and possibly to burn the important railroad bridge
over the Yadkin River just north of town.* However, before he could
cut the telegraph line, a warning was sent to Salisbury, and a force of
home guards and prison guards was raised to pursue him.[12] With his
plan foiled, the Colonel took "a few men and went down to the head
of the railroad [Morganton]," where he burned the depot, destroyed
four railroad cars, and damaged one engine. He then started back to
Tennessee, taking with him approximately 130 prisoners, some recusant
conscripts released from the camp stockade, 32 Negroes, and a number
of horses and mules.[13]

Following a skirmish with a small party from Morganton,† the
Federals crossed the Catawba River and camped for the night. The
next morning, the twenty-ninth, Kirk resumed his march, crossing
John's Creek.‡ At Moore's Crossroads in Burke County, his rear guard
was overtaken by a small scouting party headed by George W. F. Harper
of Lenoir. Harper and his "party of nine men" charged the Federals,
"capturing one prisoner (Hollifield), 2 mules, 2 carbines, 2 pistols and
a lot of cotton yarn, tobacco, shoes, etc. . . . and [then] fell back to avoid
capture from [a] flanking party."[14]

Later in the afternoon Kirk was attacked at Brown's Mountain, fourteen miles from Morganton. In taking a defensive position, the crafty

---

* Kirk brought along a locomotive engineer in case he captured a train and made the
run to Salisbury. Arthur, *Western North Carolina*, p. 606.

† Those who escaped capture at Camp Vance were given a few minutes warning "by
a neighboring family, the Lowdermilks." The escapees went to Morganton, six miles
away, and gave the alarm. Nancy Alexander, *Here Will I Dwell: The Story of Caldwell
County* (Salisbury: Rowan Printing Co., 1956), p. 137.

‡ Also referred to as John's River.

Confederate prison at Salisbury, 1864. (Courtesy of the North Carolina Collection, University of North Carolina)

but unscrupulous Union Colonel put fifteen or twenty of his prisoners in the front line, one of whom was killed and another wounded. Above the firing, he was heard to shout: "Look at the damned fools, shooting their own men." Fortunately for the prisoners the skirmish lasted only a short while, after which the pursuers, some "sixty-five men and boys,"[15] withdrew. Kirk continued across Upper Creek and went into camp at the top of "Winding Stairs road," which was little more than a narrow path near the top of "Jonas Ridge."* He had now come approximately twenty-one miles from Morganton.

At daybreak the Federal pickets reported, "Confederates approaching." It was Colonel H. S. Brown† with the Salisbury detachment, a few regular soldiers on furlough, and the home guard "hurriedly gathered from the counties of Burke, Caldwell, Catawba and Rowan." Kirk was not particularly disturbed to get this report. He knew his position on top of the ridge was a strong one. Stationing his men so they could pour an enfilading fire into the Confederates as they approached along

* "Winding Stairs road" was also identified as being near Piedmont Springs. *OR*, XXXIX, Ser. I, Pt. I, 263; G. W. F. Harper to W. W. Lenoir, July 11, 1864, G. W. F. Harper Papers, SHC.

† At least one account has Colonel Thomas G. Walton in command of the Confederate force. Arthur, *Western North Carolina*, pp. 607-8.

the narrow path, Kirk was able to repulse the enemy with ease. The Union fire took such a heavy toll of the Confederate advance that Colonel Brown had to abandon the attack before all of the men even reached the scene of action.[16]

Following this little skirmish along "Winding Stairs road" no further efforts were made to harass the raiders, and in early July, the Federal command at Knoxville was pleased to announce that Kirk had "just returned from a highly successful expedition into Western North Carolina."[17] Across the mountains at Asheville, Colonel Palmer tried to explain why Kirk had not been detected in his march to Camp Vance. "It appears . . ." he said, "Kirk, with a small band of Indians, negroes and deserters . . . travel[ed] in the night . . . avoiding all roads."[18] Regardless of whether the Federals traveled by night or by day, the raid served as additional proof to those living in the mountains that the passes were unguarded.

Many Unionists now felt that it was safe to come out of hiding. After years of living under tension, they returned home without the constant fear of capture or death.[19]* Among the number was "Keith" Blalock, who was even bold enough to appear in his native county in Federal uniform, fully armed.[20]† John Preston Arthur, in his *History of Watauga County,* says: "It might seem almost as if the history of the Civil War in Watauga were inextricably interwoven with the life and adventures of W. M. Blalock, commonly called 'Keith' Blalock."[21] This fascinating character and his wife, born Malinda Pritchard, were living "under the Grandfather"‡ when the war started and both joined "Zeb" Vance's Twenty-sixth North Carolina Regiment; he as W. M. and she as Sam Blalock. Malinda (or Sam) wore a private's uniform, tented with "Keith," and even watched the men "when they went in swimming," although never going in herself. "Keith" was a Union man and joined the Confederate army only to avoid conscription and in the

* The actions of the loyal Confederates, at the same time, tended to become violent in opposition to the Unionists. A. H. Jones, *Knocking at the Door. Member-Elect to Congress: His Career Before the War, During the War, and After the War* (Washington: McGill and Witherow, 1866), pp. 21-23.

† During the war two Union mounted regiments were raised in western North Carolina and large numbers of natives joined Tennessee, Kentucky, and Northern regiments. F. Phisterer, *Statistical Record of the Armies of the United States* (New York: Charles Scribner's Sons, 1883), p. 16; Jones, *Knocking at the Door,* pp. 32-33; J. P. Arthur, *A History of Watauga County, North Carolina, with Sketches of Prominent Families* (Richmond: Everett Waddey Co., 1915), p. 159.

‡ Grandfather Mountain.

hope that he might escape to the Union lines. When the fortunes of war took him to eastern North Carolina, "Keith" decided he must devise a means to get out of uniform. He hit upon the idea of deceiving the medics and to do this he covered himself with poison oak. When the army surgeons saw Blalock, they were puzzled as to his condition and agreed that he should be discharged. "Sam" then presented "himself" to the Colonel and with little difficulty convinced Vance "that he was no longer fit for duty, his lawful tentmate and messmate having been discharged."* The two Blalocks then returned to their home "under the Grandfather." But once "Keith's" poison oak cleared, Confederate enrolling officers attempted to arrest him. Blalock consequently fled to Tennessee and became the recruiting officer for a Michigan regiment. When not on recruiting duty, "Keith" spent much of his time traveling back and forth across the mountains to keep Federal authorities informed of conditions around his "old home."[22] On some of his trips back to Tennessee, Blalock, doubtless, gave assistance to escaped Union prisoners attempting to make their way to the Union lines.

This type of work was one of the "dramatic and dangerous" activities of the Unionist. Food, shelter, and clothing were generously furnished, and guides were provided for the trip across the mountains. The Union sympathizers in Wilkes and Yadkin counties were especially active in this work, and at Bat Cave in Henderson County, an "underground station" was maintained throughout the war.[23] One escape route led through Watauga County to Johnson County, Tennessee. Another passed through Rutherford and Henderson counties, "flanked Asheville," and followed the French Broad River through the mountains.[24] Guides such as Lewis Banner and William Estes were remarkably successful in piloting the escaped Union soldiers over the intricate mountain paths.† "One man in Mitchell County hid and fed four men for two weeks and then guided them to Union lines in Tennessee one night; the next morning, he was at work as usual at the Cranberry Iron Works."[25]

The escapees, in their efforts to get to the Union lines, were some-

---

* In Moore's *Roster of the North Carolina Troops,* "Keith's" name is listed as L. M. Blaylock and Malinda's as Mrs. L. M. Blaylock—beside the notation is "discharged for being a woman." J. W. Moore, *Roster of the North Carolina Troops in the War Between the States* (Raleigh: Printed by the state, 1882), II, p. 386.

† The reward for this hazardous work was frequently the creation of a lasting friendship between the guide and the Federal soldier. W. D. Cotton, "Appalachian North Carolina—A Political Study, 1860-1889" (Ph.D. dissertation, Univ. of North Carolina, 1954), p. 128.

Unionists escaping across the mountains into east Tennessee. (From *Harper's Weekly*)

times aided by the home guard. Late in the war many of these units were infiltrated by men who were either lukewarm to the Confederacy or were from the "outlier class"* and tired of living in caves. When "rallied," they would usually arrest deserters and "tories," but, if circumstances permitted, they would allow "and even aid prisoners to escape." In Stokes, where it was feared by late 1864 that recusant conscripts and deserters would "very soon overrun the county," it was extremely hazardous for the home guard to be overly zealous in apprehending deserters; "as a result, these units operated in a perfunctory and ineffective manner."[26]

By this time the question of troop reliability was not confined to the home guard. Considerable "Unionist sentiment" was also found "among officers serving in or near the mountains."[27] Governor Vance charged Colonel William H. Thomas with disobeying orders,[28] while others accused him of doing "as he had always done—virtually no good."[29] Colonel J. B. Palmer was also regarded by many as incompetent and harboring "disloyal" men.[30] Colonel G. N. Folk was thought

* The "outliers" were Unionist, deserters, or persons eligible for conscription who hid out to avoid arrest.

to be a drunkard who "tyrannizes" over his men.[31]

As all semblance of Confederate control vanished in large areas of the mountains, "Robbers and Bushwackers" became "more violent" and aggressive. "We never go to bed without thinking they may come before morning." The writer of this line feared, along with many others, that western North Carolina would soon "be ruled by Bushwackers— Tories and Yankees."[32]

In April, 1864, violence reached "a new stage" when the "tory" Montrevail Ray and about seventy-five of his followers raided Burnsville, headquarters for the home guard. The bulk of the local troops, on the day of the raid, were in Madison County to defend against Colonel Kirk, who had appeared in the Shelton Laurel section with a band of men. At Burnsville, Ray's men broke open the magazine and removed all the arms and ammunition, pillaged a store, and abused the local enrolling officer. Following the raid, the commander of the home guard, Brigadier General John W. McElroy could only remark: "The county is gone up."[33]

"Bushwackers" were active in all of the counties. Most of them were heavily armed and on the alert. "Observers noted that although such men were normally quiet and rational, their eyes showed the glare of hunted men."[34] The Church brothers in Wilkes County, and the Vance brothers in Henderson, committed every type of crime.[35] A lawless band in Surry County was strong enough to assemble near the courthouse, break into the jail, and free the prisoners.[36] Killing became frequent. "Old Adam Brewer," a "hot head Seses," was shot down in cold blood,[37] as were "Stol and John H. Farmer."[38] C. G. Memminger reported from Henderson County in December, 1864, that a state of anarchy existed except where troops were stationed in sufficient force to provide protection.[39]

As if brutal harassment by Unionist and "bushwackers" were not trouble enough for the mountain people, the Confederate War Department had men and horses from Longstreet's command "eat . . . out the country."[40] W. W. Avery wrote Vance from Morganton that his county was overrun with artillery and cavalry horses, "consuming what little surplus provisions are left. . . ."[41] Tod R. Caldwell, also from Morganton, complained that "men professing to be impressing agents from Longstreet's army and elsewhere are getting to be as thick in this community as leaves in Vallambrosa."* Scarcely a week passes, he said, without a new and hungrier group showing up.[42] In Watauga County there were not enough "provisions" to sustain the people. And, according to Lieutenant J. C. Wills, Thirty-third North Carolina, "our great reason of the scarcity, is owing to [Brigadier] Gen. [J. C.] Vaughn's† command having passed through recently and pillaged the country as they went." Wills spoke with authority, for he had witnessed Vaughn's cavalry on the march. He described the disheartening experience in a letter to the governor, dated April 29, 1864:

> In crossing the Blue Ridge, on my way here, on the 16th inst. I met Gen. V. and two or three other officers (of his staff I presume). Half a mile behind him I met some half doz. of his soldiers, and I continued to meet them in squads, of from two to twenty, all the way to this place (Boone)— stragling along without the shadow of organization or discipline. In this manner, they continued to come through for ten days. The whole command (some seventeen or eighteen hundred men) just disbanded, and turned loose, to pillage the inhabitants, and thoroughly did they perform their work. It was not merely stealing but open and above board highway robery. They would enter houses violently breaking open every door, and helping themselves to what suited their various fancies—not provisions only, but everything, from horses down to ladies breast pins."[43]

General Vaughn regretted the actions of his men, blaming this depredation on "Brandy" which they found "in too many famlys." He maintained if "those citizens could only see how E. Tenns. have suffered they would not Grumble half so much. . . . E. Tenn. no people in this Confederacy has suffered as our Relations and friends have. They are all robbed and Imprisoned—not allowed the libertys of negros."[44] However, for western Carolinians there was little solace in the knowledge that their friends on the other side of the mountains were also having

---

* The cavalry not only "cleaned out" Burke but also McDowell, Caldwell, and Wilkes counties. C. J. Cowles to Z. B. Vance, Apr. 4, 1864, Z. B. Vance Papers, NCDAH; [E.] Jones to "Dear Samuel," May 3, 1864, Lindsay Patterson Papers, SHC; T. York to Z. B. Vance, May 5, 1864, Z. B. Vance Papers, NCDAH.

† General Vaughn fought at Vicksburg and was captured along with the rest of the Confederate army in July, 1863. He was, however, "soon exchanged and sent with a brigade of mounted men to operate in east Tennessee and southwest Virginia." In the late spring of 1864, he moved into the Valley of Virginia to oppose Major General David Hunter. He was with Jubal Early on his Washington raid and "being wounded . . . was furloughed and returned to Bristol, Tenn." After the death of Brigadier General John Hunt Morgan in September, 1864, Vaughn "took command of the forces in east Tennessee." J. D. Porter, *Tennessee,* C. E. Evans, ed., *Confederate Military History* (Atlanta: Confederate Publishing Co., 1899), VIII, 340.

it hard. Conditions were too difficult at home for them to give much thought to the problems of others.

Joining the Unionists, "bushwackers," and Confederate cavalry in acts of lawlessness were the deserters, who continued to flock to western North Carolina. In 1864, the mountains were so full of those leaving the ranks that very little social stigma was attached to desertion, and the warm welcome accorded many a wayward soldier caused the area to fill up with the disloyal from all the Southern states.[45]

Although Governor Vance sympathized with the deserters, he realized they were jeopardizing the Confederate war effort, and he used "every imaginable step" to return them to their commands.[46] Yet in this work he was greatly handicapped by R. M. Pearson, Chief Justice of the North Carolina Supreme Court. Judge Pearson believed the conscription law to be unconstitutional and held that it was no crime to resist arrest for desertion. He readily issued writs of habeas corpus that secured the release of both deserters and conscripts.*

The attitude of the Chief Justice, together with the numerical strength of the "peace" men in the state, gave W. W. Holden good reason to believe he could defeat Vance in the gubernatorial election of 1864. The Governor and his erstwhile political ally had parted ways in late 1863 over Holden's "peace" activities. And in the elections of 1864, the two men opposed each other in the race for governor. Holden, the "peace party" candidate, was forewarned of defeat on July 28—the date the soldiers went to the polls. Of the 15,033 army votes cast, he received only 1,824. Governor Vance, running on a platform of "fight the Yankees and fuss with the Confederacy," carried the day. The victory was made complete on August 4 "when the citizens increased Vance's ballots to a total of 57,873, giving Holden only 14,432."[47]

Vance's re-election dispelled the fear that North Carolina might leave

* Shortly after his inauguration, Vance began using the militia to arrest deserters. However, Judge Pearson held that the Governor had no authority to arrest deserters or recusant conscripts. The execution of Confederate laws (such as the Conscript Act), Pearson said, was the duty of the Richmond government. Therefore, Vance sought to have the legislature pass a law authorizing him to arrest deserters and conscripts. In July, 1863, the Governor got the legislation he wanted, but in the same session of the legislature a law was passed abolishing the militia and substituting the Guard for Home Defense (home guard). Vance, however, chose to believe that the lawmakers intended for him to use the home guard as he had the militia. So up to the close of the war, the Governor, despite Judge Pearson's rulings, used the home guard to arrest deserters. R. E. Yates, *The Confederacy and Zeb Vance*, ed., W. S. Hoole, *Confederate Centennial Studies* (Tuscaloosa: Confederate Publishing Co., 1958), No. 8, pp. 45-47.

the Confederacy, but it failed to stop or even slow down the desertion of North Carolina troops. Shortly after the election, Vance issued a proclamation promising that all deserters who returned voluntarily within thirty days would receive only nominal punishment. This promise of amnesty was, nonetheless, generally unsuccessful.* Desertions continued to mount, and in some mountain localities loyal Confederates were forced to leave their homes and seek safety elsewhere. The mountain people were truly in a "deplorable condition."[48]

On the day after Christmas, 1864, a young girl living near Lenoir wrote her brother a letter: "I wish you could be at home now like you were a year ago. I have thought of it very often since yesterday, and thought of what a pleasant time we all had together then, forgetting the past and looking forward to the future with bright anticipations. Alas! What changes in one short year. May not the future be brighter. I hope so."[49] The depression and concern expressed by this young girl, as the year 1864 drew to a close, was widespread among the people of North Carolina. Practically all the males of conscript age were either in the service or in hiding. Lawless bands roamed almost at will in the central[50] and western counties. Much of the coastal region, with the exception of the Cape Fear defenses, was under Federal control. In Georgia, General William T. Sherman was preparing for a move through the Carolinas, after a successful "march to the sea," and in Virginia, General Grant, after bloody engagements at the Wilderness, Spotsylvania, and Cold Harbor, had Lee pushed back to Petersburg.

* J. F. Hill was "happy to report," on the other hand, that under General Lee's Order No. 54 and the Governor's "wise and timely proclamation" between forty and fifty deserters from Stokes county "came forward." J. F. Hill to Z. B. Vance, Sept. 5, 1864, Z. B. Vance Papers, NCDAH.

CHAPTER XII

"Gray Ghosts in the Night"

THE SIEGE OF Petersburg emphasized for the Federals the importance of the port of Wilmington to Lee's army. By late 1864, Wilmington was possibly the most important city in the South, with the exception of Richmond.[1] General Lee, confined to his fortifications at Petersburg, was largely dependent upon this Cape Fear River port for supplies. The Wilmington and Weldon Railroad, which joined the Petersburg Railroad at Weldon, provided Lee with a direct line to the North Carolina coast. But when the Union forces occupied the northern end of the Petersburg Railroad in August, 1864, the Wilmington and Weldon became useful only as a local supply road. The direct connection between the Confederate capital and Wilmington was broken and supplies brought in through the blockade had to be transported north along a more circuitous route.[2]

In 1862 the Burnside expedition had cost the Army of Northern Virginia the corn and bacon from many of the agriculturally rich counties in eastern North Carolina, and Federal victories in the west a year later cut off the food supplies and cattle from the trans-Mississippi region. These disasters were followed in 1864 by Sherman's march through Georgia. This move disrupted communications and crushed all hope General Lee had of getting assistance from the deep South. Furthermore, Mobile and Charleston were so tightly blockaded by December of the war's fourth year that they had "virtually lost contact with the outside world." Wilmington alone remained, "the South's last port of entry for munitions from Europe."[3] But as long as blockade-runners could slip in and out of this vital port, Lee had a chance to survive.

At the outset of war the Federal navy had undertaken the herculean task of blockading the Confederate coast from Virginia to Texas. On April 19, 1861, five days after the evacuation of Fort Sumter, President Lincoln proclaimed a blockade of the Southern states then out of the Union. Eight days later he issued another decree extending the blockade to include Virginia and North Carolina. This made the blockade of the South complete, but only on paper.

At the time it was impossible for the Federal government to enforce a blockade of a coastline measuring almost four thousand miles and containing 189 harbors. Lincoln's able Secretary of the Navy, Gideon Welles, had but forty-two ships in commission when the war started—a far cry from the number necessary to close the Confederate ports.[4] In May, 1861, only two vessels guarded the entire coast of North Carolina,[5] and it was not until July 20 that the blockader *Daylight* took up station off the Cape Fear River.[6] Twelve months later Rear Admiral S. P. Lee, in command of the North Atlantic Blockading Squadron, had three cordons of blockaders guarding the mouth of the Cape Fear. Still, he found it impossible to prevent vessels from coming in and going out. "It is greatly to our mortification, after all our watchfulness to prevent it . . . ," reported one of the Admiral's staff. "None can be more vigilant than we are—the officer of the watch, with the quartermaster, always on the bridge, lookouts on each bow, gangway, and quarter. For myself I never pretend to turn in at night, and am frequently on deck during the night inspecting the lookouts in person, taking what sleep I can get in my clothes ready for a moment's call. And I believe it is the same with all the commanding officers."[7]

Wilmington, 570 miles from Nassau and 674 from Bermuda, was ideally situated for blockade-running. Located twenty-eight miles up the Cape Fear River, it was free from enemy bombardment as long as the forts at the mouth of the river remained in Confederate hands. Moreover, there were two navigable entrances to the Cape Fear. These channels were separated by Smith's Island, which was about ten miles long and located directly in the mouth of the river. North of the island was New Inlet, and south of it was Old Inlet. The distance between the passages was only six miles, but lying between and jutting out into the Atlantic Ocean for about twenty-five miles was Frying Pan Shoals; therefore, a fleet guarding the two entrances had to cover a fifty-mile arc and at the same time stay out of range of Confederate shore batteries. Protecting New Inlet, the passage preferred by most blockade-runners,

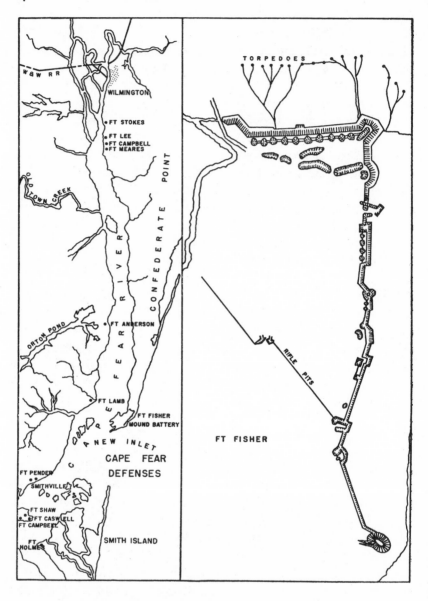

was the extensive work known as Fort Fisher.[8] This mammoth installation was sprawled along the beach of Confederate Point, a narrow strip of land that separated the river from the ocean. The big guns of the fort offered protection to incoming vessels by keeping the Union fleet several miles out to sea. Forts Caswell[9] and Campbell* on the mainland guarded the lower passage, as did Fort Holmes on Smith's Island. Up the river's west bank at Smithville† and "Old Brunswick,"[10] respectively, stood Forts Johnston‡ and Anderson. The latter installation, "a beautiful and substantial structure of turf" was designed as part of the defenses for the city of Wilmington and thus was too far up the river to have a bearing on blockade-running.[11]

The strength of these fortifications,§ along with the natural advantages of Wilmington for blockade-running made the absolute closing of the port probably more difficult for the Federals than the problem of slipping in and out was for the blockade-runners. These sleek, shallow-draft steamers were designed for speed, their chief reliance for success. They were totally unfit to brave the storms of the Atlantic; yet, the rougher the weather, the better chance they had to escape detection. Their hulls were painted gray to match the horizon at night, and telescopic funnels and hinged masts could be lowered close to the deck. Small boats were carried square with the funnels, and when available, anthracite coal was used to keep down tell-tale smoke.

On dark nights it was extremely difficult to see the low gray hulls of the blockade-runners and on "moonlight nights, as a rule . . . few ships ventur[ed] to run the gauntlet. . . ." Under no circumstances were lights used at sea. "Everything was in total silence and darkness." Anyone speaking above a whisper or striking a match was subject "to immediate punishment." To lessen the noise, canvas curtains were dropped to the water's edge around the paddles, and steam was blown off under water.

An outward-bound steamer, after taking on its cargo, would proceed

* Fort Campbell was an "earthwork of beautiful proportions" about a mile west of Fort Caswell. J. R. Randall to "Kate," June 3, 1864, J. R. Randall Papers, SHC. It was also referred to as Battery Campbell. See also James W. Albright Diary, Jan. 22, 1864, SHC.

† A resident of Wilmington called Smithville (present day Southport) a "pretty considerable village having a Court House, Church and Hotel." The writer was additionally impressed by the large number of beautiful shade trees. J. R. Randall to "Kate," June 3, 1864, J. R. Randall Papers, SHC.

‡ This installation, also referred to as Fort Pender, was called "one of the prettiest forts on the river." W. Calder to Mother, Feb. 18, 1864, SHC.

§ In addition to the forts there were numerous batteries along the river. A "ponderous chain" across the Cape Fear and marine torpedoes further strengthened the Wilmington-Cape Fear defenses. J. R. Randall to "Kate," Feb. 26, Apr. 8, 1864 J. R. Randall Papers, SHC; J. Sprunt, *Chronicles of the Cape Fear River, Being Some Account of Historic Events on the Cape Fear River* (Raleigh: Edwards and Broughton, 1914), pp. 449-500.

On board the *Lillian* running the blockade into Wilmington. (From *The Illustrated London News*)

down the river a short distance to be "searched and smoked" for stow-aways. The fumigation of the blockade-runners by a "smoking apparatus" proved most effective in flushing out the stowaways. But for the captain whose vessel was loaded with inflammable cotton the practice "seemed most astonishing."

This irritating regulation out of the way, the blockade-runner would drop down the Cape Fear to Smithville and anchor. From this vantage point the captain could scrutinize the Federal squadrons which were "distinctly" visible just beyond each of the rivers two inlets. When the tide and moon were favorable for the run "through . . . the gauntlet," the "grand master of the ship," the pilot, would come aboard. Having observed the number and latest position of the blockaders, he would select his course and await nightfall. Since the outward voyage was to be made with the ship blacked out, the binnacle had to be covered with canvas, and to put the pilot in communication with the helmsman wires were rigged fore and aft. If all went well, only "a deep sigh . . . from the [ship's] engines" would break the stillness of the night and the swell of the sea would indicate when the bar had been successfully passed.

The usual plan of the blockade-runners on the inward voyage was to strike the coast thirty or forty miles above or below the inlets, depending on which bar they intended to cross, and then hug the coast so close that they were invisible against the heavily wooded shore line. They did not have to worry about noise because the surf drowned out the sound of the paddle wheels. Sometimes a blockade-runner would deliberately pass right through the middle of the enemy fleet. This was done upon the assumption that not many rounds would be fired during the passage, lest a shell hit another blockader.

The principal dread of the blockade-runner captains, once they were close off shore, was the hazards of navigation, not the presence of the fleet. All lighthouses had been discontinued and there were very few artificial shore marks to aid the navigator. The most conspicuous object for miles around was the "Mound," a huge pile of sand rising sixty feet above the beach. It was a part of Fort Fisher. The blazing salt works that dotted the shore were of help also, and range lights were available when an inbound steamer requested them. Still "the dangers of navigation were tremendous; and as pilots became scarcer toward the end of the war (a captured pilot was never exchanged), the problem of getting over the bar was really more acute than that of getting through the enemy fleet."

Admiral Lee attempted to blockade the two harbor entrances by dividing his command into three sections. The first line was semicircular, reaching along the coast in either direction and far out to sea. In this cordon he placed sluggish, barely seaworthy vessels whose orders were not to give chase but to signal the position of blockade-runners to the faster vessels patrolling in the second group, or to the few cruisers even farther out. Captain John Wilkinson, one of the most successful and famous of the blockade-runner captains, thought that if the number of vessels concentrated off the two bars had been decreased and "a cordon of fast steamers stationed ten or fifteen miles apart, inside the Gulf Stream, the number of captures would have been tremendous."

To run the blockade successfully was an exciting experience but one usually filled with moments of extreme anxiety. Captain Wilkinson on one occasion, when foul weather prevented him from crossing the bar at New Inlet, anchored for the night within rifle range of twelve Federal blockaders. Yet at the break of day he got underway and steamed safely into the harbor. On another occasion Wilkinson found himself hard pushed by a Federal cruiser. His coal was bad, and only by using cotton dipped in turpentine could he stay ahead of his pursuer. By nightfall the Federal cruiser was only four miles away and gaining. Under these circumstances the Confederate captain decided to try a ruse. He directed his engineer to make as much black smoke as possible. At the same time he posted lookouts with telescopes to report the moment the enemy ship became invisible in the deepening twilight. When the report came, Wilkinson had the smoke cut off by closing the dampers. The helm was put hard to starboard, and the blockade-runner shot off into the darkness while the cruiser continued its course in pursuit of a shadow.

Captain Wilkinson also used rockets to great advantage in eluding the enemy vessels. After several trips through the blockading fleet, he observed that as soon as a Federal ship sighted a blockade-runner, a gun was fired and a rocket sent up in the general direction "of the offending craft." As a consequence of this observation, the enterprising Captain obtained some rockets of his own. Each time he was fired upon, he sent signals indicating a course at right angles to the one he was following.

The thrills at sea were sometimes matched by the excitement that accompanied the end of a successful voyage. The revelry started as the blockade-runner, in ascending the Cape Fear, came abreast of the "dram tree." Since early colonial days, sailors on inward bound vessels had followed the custom of taking a drink when they passed this ancient cypress standing on the river's edge two miles below Wilmington. For weary seafarers, this landmark symbolized the end of all worries and dangers. The Englishman Augustus Charles Hobart-Hampden wrote after the war that it was difficult to erase the memory of the excitement "of the evening we made our little craft fast alongside the quay at Wilmington. . . . The congratulations we received, the champagne cocktail we imbibed, the eagerness with which we gave and received news. All these things combined with the delightful feeling of security from capture and the glorious thought of a good night's sleep in a four poster bed, wound one up into an inexpressible state of jollity."[12]

Many of the blockade-runners that made it safely into Wilmington were indebted to Colonel William Lamb, the commanding officer at Fort Fisher. This fine soldier was immensely popular with the officers and sailors and became regarded as their guardian angel. "And it was no small support in the last trying moments of a run," said Captain Thomas E. Taylor of the *Banshee,* "to remember who was in Fort Fisher." Shortly after taking command of his new post in the summer of 1862, Lamb recovered from the wreck of the blockade-runner *Modern Greece* four Whitworth rifle guns that had a range of five miles. With these pieces he made the blockading fleet move its anchorage from two and one-half to five miles from the fort. So many vessels were saved by these guns that they soon had a reputation throughout the South, and three of them were transferred to other commands.

In August, 1863, the steamer *Hebe,* carrying a valuable cargo of drugs, coffee, clothing, and foodstuffs, was run ashore to prevent her capture, a practice followed by many captains when hard pressed by the enemy. In an effort to save the crew and cargo of the *Hebe,* Lamb sent a company of troops to her relief. They arrived just in time to sink the boats of a boarding party sent out from one of the blockaders. The troops remained behind with a Whitworth gun and another artillery piece to guard the wreck until its cargo could be unloaded. This proved to be a mistake, for the small party lost its Whitworth gun and barely escaped capture themselves when the Federals came ashore and attempted to salvage the *Hebe.* General Whiting, at his Wilmington headquarters had this to say: "I have met with a serious and heavy loss in that Whitworth, a gun that in the hands of the indefatigable Lamb, has saved dozens of vessels, and millions of money to the Confederate States." Whiting urged the Secretary of War to have two of the guns originally saved from the *Modern Greece* returned to Fort Fisher. He added: "Could I get them with horses, we could save many a vessel that will now be lost to us."

Colonel Lamb's friends among the blockade-running commanders came to the rescue. At the suggestions of Captain Tom Taylor a battery of six Whitworth guns was subsequently presented to the Colonel, "and good use he made of them in keeping the blockaders at respectful distance." He would gallop them down the beach "by the aid of mules" and open fire on the Federal vessels when they were least expecting it.

Despite the heroic efforts of Colonel Lamb and his Whitworths, more than thirty blockade-runners came to grief on the shores in the vicinity of the Cape Fear. One of the last steamers lost was the *Ella,* which was wrecked off Smith's Island in December, 1864. No sooner had the firing stopped, than boats filled with garrison personnel "flocked

The steamer *Hansa* running the blockade under the guns of Fort Fisher.
(From *Harper's Weekly*)

from every direction like vultures over a carcass. The scene that followed was shameful," said William Calder, stationed at Fort Caswell.
"Men seemed perfectly crazy, and officers high in command were
beastly drunk. . . . The sacredness of the day (Sunday) not regarded
at all, and men flocked from all directions to plunder and traffic. On the
steamer the men seemed perfectly wild with excitement, and drunken
with liquor. Nothing was heard but blasphemous oaths, and a perfect
babel of eager voices of avarious men."[13]

For every blockade-runner destroyed on the beach, at least one other
was captured at sea by the Federal naval forces. Union sailors much
preferred to capture the vessels because of the large prize money involved. When the *Aeolus* pounced on the *Hope* off Wilmington in
October, 1864, "the master won $13,164; the assistant engineer, $6,657,
or more than four years' pay; the seamen, over $1,000 apiece; the cabin
boy, $532.60." This was big money, but it did not approach the profits
piled up by the blockade-runners.[14]

With cotton selling in the Confederacy for 3¢ a pound and in England for the equivalent of 45¢ to a $1.00 a pound, investors were more
than willing to hazard the blockade in order to reap enormous dividends. Many successful steamers piled up millions in profits. A blockade-runner carrying one thousand bales of cotton sometimes realized a
profit of a quarter of a million dollars on the inward and outward run
within two weeks. The *R. E. Lee,* under Captain Wilkinson, ran the
blockade at Wilmington twenty-one times and carried aboard nearly
seven thousand bales of cotton, worth about $2,000,000 in gold; "and
she also took into the Confederacy equally valuable supplies." The most
successful of all the blockade-runners, the *Siren,* made sixty-four trips
through the Federal fleet, running her profits up into the millions.
Captain Tom Taylor estimated that the *Banshee* "earned her stock-

holders 700 per cent on her eight trips. . . ."[15] In a twelve month's period Captain Daniel Martin made and lost two fortunes, suffered capture and imprisonment, bought a rice plantation, and even had time to be reunited with his wife from whom he had parted five minutes after their marriage.[16] Armistead Plummer had interest in one steamer which netted him profits "not far short of" $1,000,000. "He can get tomorrow," said a kinsman of his, "over five hundred thousand dollars for his shares. . . . I speak knowingly of what I have asserted."[17] Even a purser on a blockade-runner could expect to make "about $20,000 a trip, from commissions and perquisites."[18]

In accordance with an act of the Confederate Congress, every steamer that left port had to carry a certain amount of government cotton. This requirement was, of course, unpopular with private shippers, but few thought that it would bring on "an open demonstration" between "the military and naval authorities" at Wilmington.

In March, 1864, when a steamer attempted to leave port without complying with law, Flag Officer W. F. Lynch, in charge of naval defenses, sent marines aboard her and took possession. General Whiting resented this action and considered it an unwarranted interference with his authority as departmental commander. He, in turn, marched in a detachment of troops and ejected the marines. The steamer was moved upstream and moored to a wharf. "Old Lynch" said he did not care how far General Whiting took the vessel up the river, but he vowed that if any attempt was made to take her to sea, he would use his guns. Excitement ran high in Wilmington and for a short period it looked as though "our own men [are] going to fight." The worker in the Clarendon Iron Works, who expressed these sentiments, "was gladd," as were most other people, when the dispute was settled without "a collision."[19]*

Long before this incident "an ugly feeling" had existed between the army and navy. "Old Lynch's" fleet was the laughing stock of the army, and many were the jeers that the Confederate "mudcrushers" let off at

* Another clash between the army and the navy occurred in September, 1864, when the Confederate raiders *Tallahassee* and *Chickamauga* were ready to put to sea from Wilmington. General Whiting objected and wrote Governor Vance: "Should they leave on this service [commerce raiding] the few vessels they might destroy would be of little advantage to our cause, while it would excite the enemy to increase the number of blockading squadron. . . ." Whiting, therefore, wanted the raiders to remain at Wilmington "for the defense of his place." He kept them there for a while by refusing to turn on the range lights. W. H. C. Whiting to Z. B. Vance, Sept. 26, 1864, Z. B. Vance Papers, NCDAH; G. W. Gift to Ellen Shackelford, Oct. 6, 1864, Ellen S. Gift Papers, SHC.

his two ironclads. One of these iron rams, the *North Carolina,* drew so much water that she could not pass over the bars at the mouth of the Cape Fear. As a consequence she spent the war stationed off Smithville. Finally, rotten with sea worms, the *North Carolina* weakened and sank at her moorings. The *Raleigh,* not completed until 1864, had a slightly more illustrious career. One night she steamed out among the blockaders and frightened them badly, but on her return trip through New Inlet, she grounded and broke in half.[20]

While the soldiers might laugh at the Confederate navy, they were much impressed by the blockade-runners that slipped through the Federal fleet "like gray ghosts in the night."[21] The years 1863 and 1864 saw the height of maritime activity in Wilmington.[22] There are various estimates as to the number of ships that entered the port during this period, but it is doubtful if correct information is available on the subject. One source states that 397 ships visited Wilmington during the first two and a half to three years of the war, which is proof enough that the traffic was heavy.[23]

Of all the ships running the blockade, the steamer *Advance* was among the best known for she was owned by the State of North Carolina.[24] The state entered the blockade-running business at the suggestion of Adjutant General James G. Martin, who in the dog-day heat of July, 1862, "began to shiver with apprehension" lest he could not find uniform material for the 67,000 North Carolinians under arms. In August, he approached Governor Clark with his problem and asked permission to buy supplies abroad and a ship to transport them. Governor Clark's term was about to expire; so he requested that the matter lie over until Vance took office. The newly elected governor, after much persuasion from Martin, authorized the purchase of a ship and supplies. John White of Warrenton was selected as the state's purchasing agent abroad and Thomas M. Crossan, a former naval officer, was given the duty of finding a vessel suitable for blockade-running.

After considerable searching in England, Captain Crossan found his ship, the *Lord Clyde,* "a long-legged steamer," capable of making seventeen knots. Crossan rechristened her the *Advance.* In the meantime White had secured the English firm of Alexander Collie and Company as agents for the state. This well-established firm handled the blockade-running affairs of North Carolina up to the time of Wilmington's capitulation.

On her maiden voyage as a blockade-runner, the *Advance* successfully avoided the Federal fleet and entered the mouth of the Cape
Fear on June 26, 1863. From this date until her capture at sea by the
Santiago de Cuba, a little over a year later, she contributed "much to
the welfare of the war-harassed state and was regarded in an affectionate
personal way by a half million people. . . ."25*

The loss of the *Advance* was a blow to North Carolina's war efforts,
but for the Union sailors aboard the *Santiago de Cuba* the capture of
the blockade-runner was a thrilling experience. Except when a chase
developed, the life of the Federal bluejacket aboard the blockading vessels was a "perfect hell" of exasperation and monotony. For hours
crews would stand wearily at their guns, "waiting, watching, cursing,"
until the order came to secure. "We go below," grumbled one officer,
"and throw ourselves, clothes and all, on the bunk. . . ."26

Ashore the garrison life of the Confederate soldier was equally mo-
notonous.27 In early December, 1864, a marine captain at Fort Fisher
faked a raid on the base just to liven things up a bit and made a boast-
ful adjutant of General Whiting's staff the butt of the joke. One dark
night when the Adjutant was out riding along the beach, three of the
Captain's cohorts, posing as Federal raiders, stopped him. They dis-
armed the Adjutant, relieved him of his watch, made him take an oath,
and then released him under the threat of death if he failed to keep
his "parole." The badly frightened officer, "got cleer and run his hors
up to Col Lambs quarters. . . ." And according to one of the soldiers
in the fort, he told the Colonel

> . . . their was Yankees in the garrison it friten him nerly to death he
> run out and had the long role beat and every man was soon under arms. . . .

* Governor Vance regarded the success of the venture of state blockade-running as
one of the most important achievements of his administration but considerable controversy
developed between him and President Davis over this activity.

"The Confederacy allowed the states complete freedom to own and use ships for
running the blockade; but blockade-runners which were privately owned—as most of
them were—or those owned in part by the states, were required to carry one-half their
cargoes 'on Confederate account.' This policy irritated Vance, who accused the Confederate government of hampering his efforts to supply North Carolina soldiers and
citizens with essential goods. He declared that the port of Wilmington was 'more effectually blockaded from within than from without,' that the Confederate policy would
cause blockade-runners 'to incur a loss on every voyage,' and that in respect to the
blockade-runners partially owned by the state, he would 'fire the ships' rather than submit to the requirement concerning the carriage of a fixed quota of goods for the Confederacy." Hugh T. Lefler and A. R. Newsome, *North Carolina: The History of a Southern State* (Chapel Hill: Univ. of N. C. Press, 1954), pp. 444-45.

l tell you thair was quite an excitement in the garrison for two hours Adams was a running a rown having the horses hitched Som of the drivs could not find their bridles I tell you evy thing was excitement I got my horse and sadle him all redy if we had to run I tell you I always look out for number one. . . . it friten him nerly to death and he had bin a bradging that he *would* never surrender he die first but he surrendered quick time."[28]

The Adjutant, unquestionably, had made a fool of himself, but he had good reason to be on edge. A few months back, "Lincoln's commando," Lieutenant William Baker Cushing, and about twenty bluejackets in two boats had rowed up the Cape Fear River to Smithville in a daring attempt to capture Brigadier General Louis Hébert. The General who was in charge of the heavy artillery for the Cape Fear Department, escaped capture only because he happened to spend Monday night, February 29, 1864, in Wilmington. He usually spent Mondays at his Smithville residence and the Federals knew this. So to find him gone was vexatious in the extreme for Lieutenant Cushing, but the young Lieutenant was not to be thwarted completely. He captured Hébert's chief engineer, a Captain Kelly and barely missed getting another member of the General's staff, W. D. Hardman. Luckily for Cushing, Hardman mistook the noise of the raid for a garrison mutiny and took to the woods in his nightclothes. Had he sounded the alarm rather than running, it is probable the raiders would have been captured and the glamorous career of Lieutenant Cushing would have ended at Smithville. But Hardman did not give the alarm, and Cushing escaped to return for more remarkable exploits.[29]

In late June the Lieutenant led a reconnaissance mission almost to Wilmington in an effort to get information on the Confederate ironclad *Raleigh*. His party left the *Monticello,* which lay off the mouth of the Cape Fear, about sunset and rowed up the river past Fort Anderson. At daybreak they pulled into a spot on the right bank and hid the boat.

During the day Cushing learned from some fishermen that the *Raleigh* had fallen apart. This story was hard for him to believe, and furthermore he did not want to return quite yèt to the *Monticello*. Using the fishermen as guides, the Lieutenant pushed on to the Wilmington-Fort Fisher turnpike, where he stationed his men in the underbrush along the road to await developments.

Shortly after sunrise an unsuspecting hunter was captured and then a Confederate courier. In the soldier's mailbag were hundreds of letters, some of them containing valuable information on the number of men, supplies, and guns at the various forts. With this knowledge Cushing started back to the fleet. He had now been in enemy territory for two days and his situation was serious. Not only was he a long way from the *Monticello,* but he had been spotted, and the prisoners taken along the way encumbered his movements. Nevertheless, by a combination of daring, skill, and luck Cushing made it back safely. When he tumbled into his bunk the next afternoon, he had been without sleep for sixty-eight hours.[30]

The exploits of Lieutenant Cushing on the Cape Fear were widely acclaimed in the North and certainly respected throughout North Carolina. In Wilmington there was great concern over what he might try next. General Whiting even felt compelled to place a guard at his house in town, but the port city had long since been turned "topsy turvy" by the war.[31]

Before the outbreak of hostilities Wilmington was "very gay and social. But the war . . . sadly changed the place," remarked a Confederate officer. Many of the old families moved away and those remaining "either from altered circumstances or the loss of relatives in battles," lived "in retiracy."[32] Also, a "fierce and illegitimate commerce" brought into Wilmington "a gang of foreign and domestic ruffins" who made a livelihood out of robbery and murder.[33] It was unsafe to venture into the suburbs at night, and "even in daylight there were frequent conflicts in the public streets, between the crews of the steamers in port and the soldiers stationed in the town, in which knives and pistols were fully used; and not unfrequently a dead body would rise to the surface of the water in one of the docks, with marks of violence upon it."[34] The situation became so bad that the civil and military authorities were almost "powerless to prevent crime."[35] A local paper frankly advised the citizens to carry arms with them or to keep a loaded weapon handy.[36]

James Randall, a shipping firm employee, had the unpleasant experience of being "treated to a murder" directly under his window. He saw a sailor from one of the blockade-runners shot by a "notorious" barroom keeper. The next day Randall was invited to dine aboard the *Lynx* and there, to his surprise, on the ship's forecastle was the dead man, his shipmates "munching their breakfast around him with the most perfect indifference." Randall passed on into the wardroom, but, as he said, his appetite was "paralyzed."[37]

Wilmington swarmed with foreigners, "Jews and Gentiles," during the war years. "In fact," observed a contemporary writer, "going down the Main street or along the river, you might well imagine you were journeying from Jerusalem to Jericho." In reference to the "English blockade-running fraternity," he said:

> At every turn you "met up" . . . with young Englishmen dressed like grooms and jockeys or with a peculiar coachmanlike look. . . . These youngsters had money, made money, lived like fighting cocks and astonished the natives by their pranks, and the way they flung the Confederate "stuff" about. . . . They occupied a large flaring yellow house, like a military hospital at the upper end of Market Street. . . . There these youngsters kept open house and spent their pa's and the company's money, while it lasted. There they fought cocks on Sundays, until the neighbors remonstrated and threatened prosecution. A stranger passing the house at night, and seeing it illuminated with every gas jet lit . . . and hearing the sound of music, would ask if a ball was going on. Oh no! it was only these young English Sybarites enjoying the luxury of a band of negro minstrels after dinner. They entertained any and everybody, from Beauregard and Whiting . . . down to the most insufferable sponge or snob who forced his society upon them.[38]

Speculators from all over the South joined the "foreigners" at Wilmington and congregated to attend the auctions of luxury items brought in through the blockade. When a steamer arrived, men, women, and children rushed down to the wharves "to buy, beg or steal something." Everyone wanted to know if their "ventures" (the proceeds of the bales of cotton or boxes of tobacco sent out) had come in. The women were the most excited of all as they looked for "gloves, parasols, hoop-skirts, corsets, flannels, and bonnets, silks and calicoes." The first people aboard always were the agents—"on such occasions very big men." Then on swarmed the local officials, army and navy officers, "friends," and "bummers" hunting for anything from drinks and dinner to a bunch of bananas.

Many of the local residents despised the "whole crew of money-getters." Just the same, they did some speculating themselves. One such individual wrote his sweetheart that had her father sent him the money requested he "could have cleared $10,000 easily. Calicoes went off for $3.75 and hats for $26.00. Six hours after the sales, these bargains were resold for $7.00 and $50.00 respectively." But in closing he said: "When I allowed myself to be led into a scheme for gain, I feel as if I had sullied the whiteness of my aspiration."[39]

Blockaders, to the sorrow of many people, did not always bring in auctionable goods. The little steamer *Kate* arrived in Wilmington from Nassau on August 6, 1862, bringing with her the dread disease, yellow fever. Almost overnight it spread throughout the city. Deaths reached as high as eighteen in a single day, and at one time there were five hundred cases reported. The panic that seized the people added to their suffering. Those who were able left town. Business came to a standstill. Even train and telegraph service were stopped for a period. Finally, with the arrival of cool fall weather, the fever abated. But it left in its wake almost five hundred dead—10 per cent of the native population.[40]

Numerous costly fires also plagued Wilmington. Many people believed that "incendiaries" were "abroad." In May, 1863, a fire destroyed 1,016 bales of cotton, and in July of the same year another blaze consumed several warehouses containing cotton and naval stores. A conflagration in the spring of the following year damaged property valued at several million dollars. The situation became so bad that sizable rewards were offered for information leading to the arrest of those responsible for the fires.[41]

More spectacular than these fires in town was the burning of the pine forests around Wilmington. A soldier on duty at Lockwood's Folly entered in his diary: "I have seen the mountains on fire—have read of prairies on fire—but a fire in an old turpentine orchard, overgrown with rank grass and weeds—every tree coated with rosin for ten or twenty feet from the ground presents an awful and sublime sight. I never knew what a power—uncontrolled fire was before. The roar of the flames could be heard a great distance—as the fire leaped from tree to tree— 20 feet or more above the ground—like living bodies all aflame. Never read of anything more grand or terrific."[42]

Salt was a very scarce item in the Confederacy, and as the only possible way to manufacture it was by evaporating sea water, numerous saltworks sprang up along the coast. Wilmington was "full of people" from Georgia, South Carolina, and the western part of North Carolina, "all wanting" this precious commodity. "Salt is the rage now," wrote a resident of Wilmington in 1862. "The demand increases daily. . . ." The fires used to boil the salt water were kept going twenty-four hours a day. At night they were easily visible to the Federal fleet off shore. To disrupt operations, the works were sometimes shelled by the Union ships, and occasionally a raiding party would come ashore to destroy them entirely. In April, 1864, the extensive saltworks near Masonboro Inlet were burned by boat crews from two Federal blockaders. The raiders took fifty prisoners, among them two newlyweds. When the husband was captured, the wife asked to go along as a prisoner also.[43]

The citizens of Wilmington, with the exception of those engaged in blockade-running, suffered toward the end of war from a lack of adequate food. Prices skyrocketed and, as one hard pressed individual put it, "gouging is the order of the day and night."[44] Mayor John Dawson wrote, February 10, 1864: "The supply of provisions in this market is not equal to the wants of the community. A very large majority of the people of Wilmington are living upon short rations. This is true of all excepting the blockade runners who are able and willing to pay ruinous prices for everything which they buy, while the poor are in actual want, and would suffer extremely but for private and public charity."[45]

One of the earliest charitable organizations in Wilmington was the Ladies' Soldiers' Aid Society. Since the port city was located on one of the main rail lines between the Virginia battlefields and the Southern states, countless trains filled with sick and wounded soldiers passed through Wilmington. When a train pulled into the depot, the ladies would come aboard to dress the wounds of the men. Those who were able to leave the cars found tables of food in the station yard. Mrs. Armand J. deRossett was influential in the success of the Society, serving as its president throughout most of the war.[46]

However, Miss Mary Ann Buie was known as the "soldier's friend." A sharp businesswoman, she made a considerable amount of money speculating. But she was most generous with her earnings, willing to share them with the soldiers or, for that matter, with most any male nice enough to call. Her "squat body, long mouth, twitching chin, oyster eyes and preposterous nose" made a social visit almost prohibitive. Nevertheless, those brave enough to risk it were usually showered with valuable gifts. One caller, after a visit with Miss Buie, wrote his fiancée that he was now out of debt and had $100 in his pocket, thanks to the generosity of his hostess. Miss Buie also presented her caller with handkerchiefs, a towel, and one pound of coffee. After this windfall, the recipient remarked that he could no longer criticize "the soldier's friend" even though her gifts were accompanied with "egotism and trumpet blowing."[47]

Miss Buie was extremely critical of anyone who refused to donate to the soldiers' relief fund, and well she might have been, having on one occasion fitted out an entire company at her own expense. Her "great annoyance" was Colonel Crenshaw of Richmond, "a large owner of ships engaged in blockade running." On one occasion she told him that she "wished his next ship to enter would be last." About two days after "this pious prayer," Crenshaw lost the *Hebe.* The Colonel still would not "subscribe to her fund," so Miss Buie imprecated all kinds of vengeances upon Crenshaw "reminding him of the *Hebe* and asking God to destroy the next vessel of his" that attempted to pass through the blockade. "Well *on last night,*" wrote an acquaintance of the "soldier's friend," "the old *witch was gratified.* Crenshaw's fine steamer "Venus" was chased ashore and burned *precisely on the same shoal where the "Hebe" was wrecked.* Old Buie has cast the Witch of Endor completely into shame."[48]

Fortunately for General Lee, who needed all the supplies he could get, most steamship owners gave generously to the soldiers' relief fund, thereby avoiding Miss Buie's hex and at the same time keeping their vessels afloat. By late 1864, the Army of Northern Virginia was getting possibly half its foodstuffs through the blockade at Wilmington.[49] In August of that year, following the Federal victory in Mobile Bay, Lee wrote Governor Vance that the importance of the port of Wilmington was "such that every effort should be made to defend it. . . ."[50] A few months later, he was saying that "if Forts Fisher and Caswell were not held, he would have to evacuate Richmond."[51] It was obvious to Federal commanders that they could strike General Lee no more effective a blow than by an attack on Wilmington. The capture of this vital port, contemplated since 1862, had now become an absolute necessity.[52]

CHAPTER XIII

Fort Fisher

On the evening of August 30, 1864, Lincoln's Secretary of the Navy, Gideon Welles, made the following entry in his diary: "Something must be done to close the entrance to Cape Fear River and port of Wilmington. . . . I have been urging a conjoint attack upon Wilmington for months. Could we seize the forts at the entrance of Cape Fear and close the illicit traffic, it would be almost as important as the capture of Richmond on the fate of the Rebels, and an important step in that direction. But the War Department hangs fire, and the President, whilst agreeing with me, dislikes to press matters when the military leaders are reluctant to move. . . ."[1]

Secretary of War Edwin M. Stanton was willing "in a lukewarm way" to cooperate with Welles but doubted if Grant would favor an expedition that might drag on. Welles, though, was not to be denied. He had his able Assistant Secretary, Gustavus V. Fox, contact both President Lincoln and General Henry W. Halleck, the army's chief of staff. The President was agreeable but, like Stanton, deferred to Grant. Nevertheless, on September 2, the War Department consented, with some reservations, to a joint operation against the defenses at the mouth of the Cape Fear.

In agreeing to this undertaking, Grant set one condition, and it was that Admiral Samuel P. Lee should not head the expedition. The commander of the North Atlantic Blockading Squadron was not energetic enough for the General or, for that matter, for Secretary Welles, whose first choice was Rear Admiral David Farragut.

In view of the Secretary's feelings Farragut was offered the command first, but for reasons of ill health he declined it. Next to be considered was Rear Admiral S. F. DuPont, but he was passed over because many high-ranking officers felt that he had "failed miserably" at Charleston the year before. The name of Rear Admiral John A. Dahlgren, commander of the South Atlantic Blockading Squadron, also came up. Welles thought Dahlgren had "some good qualities" but lacked the "great essentials" and therefore could not be "thought of" for the command. This left Rear Admiral David D. Porter "the best man for the service. . . ." "Porter is young," the Secretary wrote, "and his rapid promotion has placed him in rank beyond those who were his seniors, some of whom it might be well to have in this expedition. But again personal considerations must yield to the public necessities. I think Porter must perform this duty."

So, on September 22, Admiral Porter was detached from the Mississippi Squadron and ordered east. After stopping off in Washington for briefing on his new assignment, the Admiral formally relieved S. P. Lee, who turned over to him a full report on the preliminary arrangements for the expedition.[2]

The selection of an army commander was also a problem. The War Department suggested Major General Quincy A. Gillmore, but he did not get the command. It went instead to Benjamin F. Butler whose "pen was mightier than his sword." Nor were the chances of the proposed expedition enhanced by the fact that Butler and Admiral Porter thoroughly disliked each other.[3]

Ignoring these difficulties, Secretary Welles went ahead in his characteristically energetic way to assemble a fleet. While he was busy with this task, General Butler came up with the idea of a powder ship and went directly to President Lincoln with the plan. He told the Chief Executive about reading a newspaper account of the explosion of an ammunition dump in England. The blast, which occurred on the banks of Thames River near London, destroyed three cottages, split two barges into fragments, leveled an embankment, and shattered glass windows for miles around. If a great explosion could wreak such devastation, Butler pointed out to the President, why could not an old steamer filled with powder be exploded next to Fort Fisher? He felt certain the resulting blast would smash the fort's walls, dismount the guns, paralyze the garrison, and make simple the matter of occupancy. Despite Butler's arguments, President Lincoln apparently remained noncommittal. Welles did not think much of the idea, and neither did Major General Richard Delafield, the army's able Chief of Engineers, but there were other "experts" who were more than willing to go along with the plan. Among this number was Admiral Porter who thought it was at least "an experiment worth trying."[4]

"Casting about him for the best means to prosecute the enterprise," the Admiral selected from his fleet the *Louisiana,* an "old war-worn propeller of about 250 tons" which had seen considerable duty in the sounds of North Carolina. This "old tub" was admirably suited for the job of powder ship. She was flat-bottomed, drew only five or six feet of water, and was fast becoming worthless. Said one romantic soul: "It was, too, a fitting end for the old war-worn steamer, that she should go from the ranks of the fleet, not into the degrading servitude of some speculating contractor, as an old race-horse ends his days in a cart; nor even into the dull but honorable retirement of a Navy-yard hulk; but into the very forefront of the battle; and then gloriously expire in one brilliant flash; slaying, like Samson of old, more at her death than done during her whole life-time."[5]

The *Louisiana* was ordered from the North Carolina waters to Norfolk where her officers and crew were transferred to other vessels, and gangs of workmen at once commenced transforming her into a "torpedo."[6] An intricate firing mechanism was designed to detonate the 185 tons of powder to be stored aboard, and "to make the explosion a certainty" a fire, to be lit at the last moment, was laid in the stern.

From Norfolk the powder boat was towed to Craney Island at the mouth of the Elizabeth River. Here Commander Alexander C. Rhind and Lieutenant Samuel W. Preston took charge.[7]

Meanwhile, fall had turned to early winter and Grant was urging Butler to get started. At last on December 7, Butler began embarking at Bermuda Hundred, Virginia, a force of approximately 6,500 men. Two days later Butler wired Admiral Porter from Fortress Monroe that "the Army portion of the conjoint expedition against Wilmington was ready to proceed."* Porter, however, was far from sanguine about the success of the expedition. He thought Butler had only a vague idea of what he was going to do, "depending on the explosion to do all the work."[8]

---

* General Butler wanted the Federal troops at New Bern to engage in a cooperative movement at the time of his attack on Fort Fisher. It was to consist of an attack on Rainbow Bluffs, followed by a "forced march" on Tarboro. For an account of this operation see W. P. Derby, *Bearing Arms in the Twenty-seventh Massachusetts Regiment* (Boston: Wright and Potter Printing Co., 1883), pp. 446-57.

When it became evident to Confederate authorities that an attack on the Cape Fear defenses was being planned, President Davis sent General Braxton Bragg to Wilmington to "exercise immediate command over the troops and defenses of . . . [the city] and its approaches."[9]* Bragg wisely left General Whiting "as second in command, in discharge of his former functions of administration and detail."[10] Whiting had commanded the area defenses since November, 1862, and was popular with both his men and the local citizens. A Richmond paper gave expression to the feeling of many people in the curt paragraph: "Bragg has been sent to Wilmington, good-bye Wilmington."[11]

Fort Fisher, the mammoth earthwork at the tip of Confederate Point, was the key to the Cape Fear defenses.[12] It was begun in April, 1861, with the construction of Battery Bolles, which later became a part of the larger works. In July of the following year, Major (later Colonel) William Lamb assumed command at Fort Fisher and began construction in earnest on what was to become one of the strongest installations in the world. When this able Virginian undertook his new duties, he found the fort to consist of no more than "several detached earth-works," so he immediately "went to work and with 500 colored laborers, assisted by the garrison, constructed the largest earth-work in the Southern Confederacy. . . ."[13]

Fort Fisher was shaped like the letter "L," with the angle pointing out to sea in a northeasterly direction. The north, or land front, which extended some 682 yards across the peninsula, was the horizontal arm. The east, or sea face, running approximately 1,898 yards down the beach, was the vertical arm. At its southern extremity was the famous Mound Battery,[14] whose two long-range guns protected many a blockade-runner. Battery Buchanan was about a mile from the "Mound" and near the tip of Confederate Point on the river side. Although the battery was separated from Fort Fisher, it was considered a part of the main works. To the rear of Fort Fisher proper was a line of rifle pits designed to protect the fort in the unlikely event of an enemy approach from the river.

*On November 11, 1864, President Davis constituted "the State of North Carolina east of the Blue Ridge" a military department under General Bragg. D. C. Seitz, *Braxton Bragg, General of the Confederacy* (Columbia: The State Co., 1924), p. 465. On November 22, Bragg was ordered to Augusta, Georgia. But, by December 17, he was back in Wilmington. *Ibid.*, pp. 469-79.

Colonel Lamb, in designing his fort "to withstand the heaviest artillery fire," constructed it primarily out of sand and marsh grass. The land and sea fronts were, in general, earth-work parapets, "sandbagged and revetted, 20 feet high [and] 25 feet thick." Between the gun chambers containing one or two guns were heavy traverses made of earth, sand, and sodded with grass. Thus a shell falling into a gun chamber would injure only the men at that particular battery. In addition, the traverses protected against an enfilading fire. Altogether there were forty-eight guns in the fort. The land approach was further protected by a shallow ditch and a log palisade in front of which was an electrically controlled mine field. Within the fort there were bomb-proofs where personnel could take shelter during a heavy bombardment. Magazines deep in the earth protected against explosions.[15]

People called Fort Fisher the Gibraltar of the South, and it is little wonder that Federal military chieftains were hesitant to attack this massive earthwork. As Admiral Porter put it: "No one could form the slightest conception of these works—their magnitude, strength, and extent—who had not seen them, and General Whiting . . . must have had an abiding faith in the Confederacy when he expended so many years of labor on them." The construction of Fort Fisher had taken nearly four years, and on the day Admiral Porter's fleet arrived off the mouth of the Cape Fear, work was still in process.[16]

The army transports arrived at the rendezvous point twenty miles off New Inlet on the evening of December 15, and for three days waited for the navy in weather that was the "finest possible." Admiral Porter, who had stopped at Beaufort for ammunition, arrived with his fleet on the evening of the 18th.* The powder ship *Louisiana* was intended to go in that night, but General Butler requested that the explosion be delayed. It was just as well because, after a week of good weather, the "wind sprang up freshly," making it impossible to land troops.

Upon the advice of Admiral Porter the fleet of transports turned back to Beaufort to ride out the storm and to take on coal and water. The weather continued bad until the twenty-third. But when it broke, Butler sent a member of his staff on a fast steamer to Porter to advise him that the army would be at the rendezvous point on the evening of

* A Confederate soldier wrote: "The fleet has come . . . that long-talked-of, much-dreaded monster now lies calmly at anchor off Ft. Fisher, and any hour may see the commencement of the siege so full of . . . woe to us." W. Calder to Mother, Dec. 20, 1864, W. Calder Papers, SHC.

the twenty-fourth and ready to commence the assault, weather permitting.[17]

Admiral Porter decided not to await Butler's arrival to begin the attack. The weather was "clear and fine" on the night of the twenty-third, so he directed Commander Rhind "to proceed and explode the [powder] vessel right under the walls of Fort Fisher."[18] Previously Sub-Assistant J. S. Bradford of the United States Coast Survey had made an extensive beach reconnaissance and reported that a vessel with a seven-foot draft could be placed "right on the edge of the beach."* Although the *Louisiana* still had steam, she was towed by the *Wilderness* "to a point within a short distance of her station." Upon signal the *Wilderness* cast off the powder boat and anchored. The *Louisiana,* carrying a crew of thirteen men and two officers, steamed in unaided to within three hundred yards of the beach and dropped her anchors. Commander Rhind and Lieutenant Preston wasted little time once the anchors took hold. They triggered the mechanism designed to explode the powder and started the fire already laid in the ship's stern. Then joining the volunteer crewmen in a small boat drawn up alongside, they raced back to the *Wilderness,* reaching her precisely at midnight. The *Wilderness,* with the Commander's party aboard, steamed off at full speed for almost an hour, hove to, and waited.[19]

In order to be absolutely safe, Admiral Porter had pulled his whole fleet back twelve miles. In his detailed instructions to Commander Rhind, the Admiral had optimistically predicted that "houses in Wilmington and Smithville will tumble to the ground and much demoralize the people, and I think if the rebels fight after the explosion they have more in them than I give them credit for."[20]

At 1:40 A.M. the powder boat went up. A huge column of fire shot skyward, followed by four loud explosions at intervals of about half a second, "and all was darkness." Twelve miles away Admiral Porter hardly felt the shock. Commander Rhind, aboard the *Wilderness,* turned to some officers and quietly remarked, "There's a fizzle," and went below. A young sentinel walking the parapet at Fort Fisher "reckoned one of them Yankee gunboats off thar had done busted her biler." Colonel Lamb reported the explosion to his superiors as a Federal blockader that had run aground and destroyed herself.[21]

* By sending Bradford ashore, Admiral Porter was in some respects anticipating modern underwater demolition team usage. E. H. Simmons, "The Federals and Fort Fisher—Part I," *MCG,* XXXV (Jan., 1951), 57.

Since the walls of Fort Fisher had not come tumbling down as expected, Admiral Porter made preparations to use his guns, nearly six hundred in number, against this Gibraltar. In the clear dawn of December 24, the Admiral got his fifty vessels underway.[22] This was "the largest collection of combatant ships ever assembled under the American flag up to this date." As fast as the vessels came into line, they anchored, "until the whole formed nearly a semicircle, distant about half a mile from the . . . [shore.]"[23]

All was quiet and calm in the fort. The men were at their guns. Colonel Lamb, standing on the parapet with watch in hand, noted the time of the first shot.[24]

At 11:30, Porter gave the order "to engage the forts."[25] "A flash—a curl of smoke, and a loud report, followed by the shrieking noise of shell" announced to the garrison that the battle had commenced.[26] The bombardment was "tremendous . . . shot and shell fell like rain in [Fort] Fisher."[27] A soldier who witnessed the action from Fort Caswell, thought it "to be the most awful bombardment that was ever known for the time."[28] Another member of the Caswell garrison wrote his mother that the naval attack was "unparalleled in the annals of the war for fierceness. Inside the fort, and for miles up and down the beach, the ground . . . [was] literally covered with fragments of iron. . . ."[29]

Late in the day Butler's fleet arrived from Beaufort. But it was too late to attempt a landing[30] and at nightfall Porter broke off the attack. It became "as quiet as Sunday and I assure you," remarked a sailor on the *Wilderness,* "it is a great relief to the head and nervous system."[31]

Despite the heavy Union shelling, Fort Fisher suffered very little damage and few casualties. "Never since the invention of gunpowder," wrote Colonel Lamb, "was there so much of it harmlessly expended as in the first days attack on Fort Fisher."[32] Admiral Porter's losses were far greater than Colonel Lamb's. This was not, however, because of the volume (672 projectiles)[33] and accuracy of the Confederate fire but because of the faulty construction of the Federal guns. During the day, six "Parrott 100-pounders" exploded.[34] On the *Ticonderoga* one accident alone killed eight sailors and wounded twelve.[35] These guns were obviously unfit for service and calculated, so Admiral Porter thought, to kill more Federals than Confederates.[36]

Just about the time firing stopped, General Whiting arrived at Fort Fisher, having taken a steamer down from Wilmington.[37] His presence seemed to give the small Confederate garrison, numbering approximately nine hundred men, a lift.[38]* The soldiers worked energetically to repair the damage to the fort and daylight, Christmas morning, found them at their posts awaiting a renewal of the attack.

It came around 10:30 A.M. when the guns of the fleet opened fire. The Federal strategy on this date called for Porter to shell the fort while Butler's ground forces assaulted its land face.[39] In accordance with this plan the Federal troops began coming ashore above Fort Fisher about noon. Two small Confederate batteries manned by Junior Reserves guarded the beach at this point, but they surrendered without firing a shot. However, Butler learned from his prisoners that part of General Robert F. Hoke's division had recently arrived in Wilmington from Virginia. Lee, knowing full well that his own ability to stay in the field depended to a large extent on keeping the port of Wilmington open had, on December 20, dispatched Hoke and six thousand veteran troops to strengthen the Cape Fear defenses. This was chilling news to Butler but he decided to continue the fight.[40]

By 4:00 P.M., Major General Godfrey Weitzel, Butler's chief lieutenant, had moved his skirmish line to within fifty yards of Fort Fisher and Admiral Porter had increased the tempo of the bombardment. The thunder of the guns became deafening. A "torrent of missiles" either fell into, or burst over, the fort. The Admiral was convinced that "it was impossible for anything human to stand" such fire. "Now is the time for the assault," he cried. "Where are the troops?" With his spyglass he could see General Weitzel making observations and the soldiers scurrying about, but there was no assault, only a bit of firing from the skirmishers on both sides. Then suddenly the three thousand Federal troops turned their backs on the enemy and marched up the beach. Admiral Porter could not believe his eyes. Butler was retreating rather than advancing. A close look at Fort Fisher had taken the General's courage.[41]

Butler afterwards explained his loss of initiative on the grounds that it was getting dark, the weather was threatening, and, as far as he could

---

* When the fleet was sighted, Colonel Lamb's effective force numbered not over five hundred men, but on the twenty-third, reinforcements, which included some Junior Reserves, raised the total to nine hundred. W. Lamb, "The Defense of Fort Fisher," *B and L*, eds., R. V. Johnson and C. C. Buel (New York: The Century Co., 1888), IV, 267. One reason the Confederate garrison was so small was that Bragg had sent five companies of the Thirty-sixth North Carolina to Georgia to oppose Sherman. *Ibid.*

tell, the fort had suffered no material damage. His conclusion was that nothing short of a regular siege could reduce the massive work and he was not authorized to conduct such an operation. Therefore, the orders were issued for the troops to re-embark on the transports that would take them back to Fortress Monroe.[42]

Butler was so anxious to get off the beach that he left a sizable detachment behind with only his word that naval gunfire would protect the men. The next day Admiral Porter sent a dispatch to Captain James Alden on the *Brooklyn,* ordering him "to get those poor devils of soldiers off today or . . . lose them." He added: "And won't I be glad to get rid of them; ain't a soldier troublesome?"[43] Bad weather delayed things, but Alden had the men off by the twenty-seventh. All the while thirteen hundred of Hoke's men* at Sugar Loaf, a short distance up the beach, were "strangely stagnent." In fact they were digging in rather than preparing for an advance. So, on this strange note the first battle of Fort Fisher closed.[44]

Captain Franklin E. Smith of the United States navy, writing to his daughter on Christmas night, 1864, summed up the expedition in a few words: we have had "two days of hard fighting and I am sorry to say we seem to have accomplished but little. . . . [Fort Fisher] after enduring the most terrific assault of the very heaviest guns ever before employed in war, still holds out." Smith was disturbed because he felt that the fort could have been taken had the troops been well commanded.[45] His fellow naval officer, David Porter, was in hearty agreement.† He told Grant to send him the same soldiers with another general and the fort would be his.[46] Captain Charles Steedman of the *Ticonderoga,* on the other hand, felt that Grant should bear part of the responsibility "for the distressing fiasco—as he was perfectly aware of the character and attributes of that humbug and thief Butler. . . ."[47] Anyway, all the navy agreed it was a "fussy fight" without any great results.[48]

Ashore, the Confederates were jubilant. General Bragg congratulated his officers and men for their "successful defense of Fort Fisher

* Most of the men belonged to Brigadier General W. W. Kirkland's Command. *OR,* XLII, Ser. I, Pt. I, 1021.

† One bright spot for Porter in the expedition was the work of Lieutenant W. B. Cushing. On Christmas day the Admiral sent Cushing out to buoy the channel since it was inaccurately marked on Union maps. This brave officer performed his duty well. Even though he was under fire for six hours and at times very close to the beach, he suffered nothing more than a wet uniform. *NR,* XI, Ser. I, 258.

Union soldiers and sailors landing above Fort Fisher, January 18, 1865.
(From *Harper's Weekly*)

against one of the most formidable naval armaments of modern times. . . ." He was especially complimentary of General Whiting* and Colonel Lamb.[49] These same officers, however, were not lulled into apathy by the praise of the Commanding General. They appealed for more guns, men, and supplies. Even though the fleet had sailed northward, they knew it would return.[50] Bragg did not agree. At least, he thought it would be quite some time before the Federals would try the "inhospitable coast of North Carolina" again.[51] "Bragg the Confederate was in some ways almost as inept as Ben Butler the Federal."[52]

On January 8, 1865, Colonel Lamb's intelligence reported that Federal transports were rendezvousing with Admiral Porter's fleet at Beaufort before clearing for the mouth of the Cape Fear. Yet, on this date Bragg ordered Hoke's men north from Sugar Loaf to a camp above Wilmington where they staged an elaborate review.† Four days later the Federal fleet was plainly in sight as it passed observers on the coast east of Wilmington. Still Bragg did not consider it his duty to warn Colonel Lamb at Fort Fisher. The Colonel's own mounted pickets had to bring him the news. That night, January 12, he watched with heavy heart the return of "the great Armada."[53]‡

* General Whiting was of the opinion that the fort could have been carried by assault on December 24 and 25. W. H. C. Whiting to J. A. Seddon, Jan. 1, 1865, Rec. Gr. 109, NA. On the twenty-fifth Whiting wired Bragg: "If you can send re-enforcements . . . to attack in the rear, we can hold out." W. H. C. Whiting to B. Bragg, Dec. 25, 1864, Rec. Gr. 109, NA.

† Hoke opposed the withdrawal of the troops from Sugar Loaf, but General Bragg overruled him. J. G. deR. Hamilton, "General R. F. Hoke and His Military Career" (Unpublished article in possession of J. G. deR. Hamilton estate, Chapel Hill, N.C.).

‡ Colonel Lamb's wife and two children occupied a rustic cottage in back of the

Shortly after dawn the next morning, the gallant Colonel inspected the fort to make certain everything was in order and ready for action. Gray-clad gunners stood by their pieces. Overhead the Confederate banner fluttered in the breeze. Except for the wash of the surf and the scream of the sea gulls, an ominous silence hovered over the vast fortification. Then with startling suddeness the Union "Armada" opened fire, the *New Ironside* spouting her flame and thunder first. The sky was rent by the sound and the "very earth and sea" seemed to tremble. Confederate guns answered "with a deep throated roar." The second battle of Fort Fisher was on.[54]

During the day Colonel Lamb received around seven hundred reinforcements which brought his complement up to only 1,500 men. An unexpected, but welcome, arrival was General Whiting, who took a steamer down to Battery Buchanan and then walked up to the fort. He found the Colonel on the ramparts. "Lamb, my boy," he shouted above the roar of battle, "I have come to share your fate. You and your garrison are to be sacrificed." Seeing that Whiting was greatly upset, Colonel Lamb replied: "Don't say so, General; we shall certainly whip the enemy again." But Whiting knew better. He had come from Wilmington where Bragg was loading his wagons and "looking for a place to fall back upon." Lamb offered General Whiting command of the garrison. "I will counsel with you," replied the General, "but I will leave you to conduct the defense."[55]

The deadly battering by the Union ships continued all day and into the night. The fire of the big guns was directed primarily at the land face of the fort and with remarkable effectiveness. Admiral Porter, who still commanded the fleet, wanted to weaken the sandy walls to clear the way for another grand assault, which he felt would succeed now that Butler had been replaced by Major General Alfred H. Terry.[56]

The landing of the Federal troops on January 13 was a well-executed, yet sometimes humorous, operation. Promptly at 8:00 A.M., General Terry started putting his men and supplies ashore. The boats on approaching the beach would throw out small anchors "and then let themselves work shorewards" on the waves. The crafts usually grounded short of the beach, so the men got wet in disembarking. On

fort but on the twelfth the Colonel had them evacuated across the river. Mrs. J. H. Anderson, *North Carolina Women of the Confederacy* (Fayetteville: Privately printed, 1926), p. 56; H. Cochran, *Blockade Runners of the Confederacy* (New York: Bobbs-Merrill, 1958), p. 315.

shore they would remove their clothing to dry and watch their comrades come in. It was an "amusing sport" to see a soldier step carefully into knee deep water and find it suddenly somewhere about his ears.* Laughter from those on the beach rivaled the roar of the ocean, and the landing became "a scene of meriment that would do no discredit to the jolliest of picnics." Despite this revelry rolls were somehow called, regiments formed, and pickets thrown out. A few scattered shots from Confederate outposts provided the only opposition.† By 3:00 P.M. General Terry had large quantities of supplies and eight thousand men ashore, each soldier with three day's rations and forty rounds of ammunition.[57]

Before landing, Terry had selected the general area for the strong defensive line which he planned to construct across the peninsula. Such a position, facing north, would protect his rear while he operated against Fort Fisher. His maps, though, proved to be faulty, and it was 2:00 A.M. before he located a suitable defensive spot just two miles from the forbidding land face of the fort.

But morning found the Union troops behind a "thoroughly respectable breastwork" thrown up during the last hours of darkness. From this position Terry had Brigadier General Martin Curtis' brigade push forward to feel out the front. When the New Yorkers reached the outworks of Fort Fisher, several hundred yards from the parapet, they were joined by General Terry, who wanted to get a careful look at the land face. As a result of his observations, the General decided that the assault could be made the following day.

That evening Terry visited Admiral Porter aboard the *Malvern* to work out plans for the next day's attack. The two officers decided that

---

* While the unopposed landing was taking place, it dawned on some of the men, all at once, that there they "were on an open beach with the big fort on one side and a veteran division of 5,000 Confederates on the other." L. R. Thomas, *The Story of Fort Fisher, N.C., January 15, 1865* (Ocean City: Privately printed, 1915), p. 6.

† General Bragg, who joined Hoke at his headquarters on the thirteenth, gave two reasons for the failure to attack Terry on the beach. First, the swamp and water limited his room to maneuver. Second, the fire power of the fleet was too great. *OR*, XLVI, Ser. I, Pt. 432; B. Bragg, "Letter of Braxton Bragg to Thomas Bragg—January 20, 1865," SHSP, X (Aug.-Sept., 1882), 346-49; W. Lamb, "Account of Colonel William Lamb," SHSP, X (Aug.-Sept., 1882), 350-68; Simmons, "Fort Fisher," Pt. I, p. 52. Once the troops were ashore, Admiral Porter swore that "if those soldiers want to go back to their ships, they'll have to swim, for I'll be d - - d if I'll let them have any boats to come off in." J. Parker, "The Navy in the Battles and Capture of Fort Fisher," *Personal Recollections of the War of the Rebellion. Addresses Delivered before the New York Commandery of the Loyal Legion of the United States* (New York: G. P. Putnam's Sons, 1897), II, 110-11.

Interior of Fort Fisher during the second bombardment, January 13-15, 1865.
(From *The Confederate Soldier in the Civil War*)

a heavy bombardment would begin in the morning and last up to the moment of the assault.* At a given signal a column of sailors and marines would strike the "northeast bastion" (where the land and sea faces join) while the army hit the western half of the land front. Satisfied that this was a good plan, Terry returned to his base and retired for the evening. But sleep was out of the question as the navy continued to pound Fort Fisher all night.[58]

The shelling had been so fierce during the day that Colonel Lamb had found it impossible to repair damages. He scarcely had time to bury his dead. The "damaging and overwhelming" fire literally paralyzed the fort. "It was beyond description," said General Whiting, "no language can describe that terrific bombardment."

Colonel Lamb, from his headquarters at a battery on the sea face about one hundred yards from the northeast salient, weathered the fire with General Whiting at his side. On the fourteenth, as an estimated one hundred shells a minute were bursting among the guns and trav-

---

* At least one officer on each ship understood the army code. Therefore Terry could communicate with Admiral Porter "though nearly a mile apart and amidst the din of battle." Simmons, "Fort Fisher," Pt. II, 50.

erses, Whiting, at Colonel Lamb's request, wired Bragg to come to the rescue of the fort.[59]* In response to this appeal General Bragg immediately sent eleven hundred "veteran infantry" down the river by steamers, but the transports went aground and less than half the men reached the works. Colonel Lamb put the figure at 350 South Carolinians of Johnson Hagood's brigade† who did not arrive until the early afternoon of the fifteenth.[60]‡

These few reinforcements did little more than replace the Confederate killed and wounded, numbering by the afternoon of the fifteenth, three hundred. The casualties left Colonel Lamb with no more than twelve hundred men to defend the works. And on the land face but one heavy gun remained serviceable, the others having been smashed by shell fire. To replace them, Lamb could bring forward only a few small pieces. The situation was now extremely critical for the Confederate garrison and through the smoke the men could see Union soldiers, sailors, and marines forming for an assault.[61]

The bluejackets on the beach were from the various ships of Admiral Porter's fleet. Stiffened by marines and armed with "well sharpened" cutlasses and revolvers, they numbered some two thousand in all. Their orders were to "board the fort [at its northeast salient] on the run in a seaman-like way." The marines had instructions to form in the rear and to support the assault with their muskets.[62]

On the opposite side of the peninsula, four-thousand troops under Brigadier General Adelbert Ames also formed for an attack. The remainder of General Terry's force, mostly Negro troops, commanded by Brigadier General Charles J. Paine, manned the defensive line which stretched from the ocean to the river.[63]

It was mid-afternoon when Confederate sentinel Arthur Muldoon

* Even though Colonel Lamb failed to receive a reply from Bragg, he felt certain the General intended to attack. So ten companies were put in readiness for a sortie, and a scouting party was sent out to locate the position of the enemy. Lamb, "Defense of Fort Fisher," pp. 225-26. General Bragg maintained that he replied to Whiting's wire. *OR*, XLVI, Ser. I, Pt. I, 433.

† General Bragg reported that 500 reinforcements reached the fort and that this number raised Lamb's force to 2300. (Colonel Lamb said he never had this many men.) As Bragg saw it, all the Fort Fisher garrison had to do was to hold out until the first bad weather drove the fleet out to sea. This would make Terry's force easy prey for Hoke. B. Bragg, "B. Bragg to T. Bragg, Jan. 20, 1965," pp. 346-49; Lamb, "Account of Colonel Lamb," pp. 350-68; *OR*, XLVI, Ser. I, Pt. I, 432-34; Simmons, "Fort Fisher," Pt. II, 52.

‡ With the dawn of January 15, the fire on the land face of the fort had redoubled. *NR*, XI, Ser. I, 439.

called out to Lamb that "the enemy are about to charge." General Whiting, who was nearby and heard the report, decided to send another appeal to Bragg at Sugar Loaf: "The enemy are about to assault; they outnumber us heavily. We are just manning our parapets. Fleet have extended down the sea front outside and are firing heavily. Enemy on the beach in front of us in very heavy force, not more than seven hundred yards from us. Nearly all land guns disabled. Attack! Attack! It is all I can say and all you can do."[64]*

No sooner had General Whiting dispatched his message than all the naval bombardment ceased and every Union vessel offshore sounded its steam whistle. This was the signal for the land forces to attack. Navy gunners, no longer blinded by smoke, watched their comrades ashore dash for the fort. The soldiers struck the western end of the land face, while the tars, under Lieutenant Commander Randolph Breese, headed for its eastern tip.†

"Come on, come on," shouted an officer at the head of the naval column, waving his sword as he ran forward. In reply the fort's one big gun and Lamb's small pieces opened up with grapeshot and canister, "ploughing lanes in the ranks," but the bluejackets charged on gamely. At the angle formed by the joining of the land and sea faces, they halted to allow the rear to catch up. Crowding and confusion developed and, with rifle fire from the parapet "terrific," the scene became a "slaughter-house." The sailors fell back in panic,‡ leaving their dead and wounded, over three hundred in number, on the beach.[65]

As shouts of victory went up from his men, Colonel Lamb turned

---

* Hoke's troops were deployed for an attack on Paine's line, but after a few feeble probings the attack was halted. The excuse this time was that Bragg, learning of the repulse of the navy landing force, thought that the Federal assault had failed. *OR*, XLVI, Ser. I, Pt. I, 424, 433-34; B. Bragg, "B. Bragg to T. Bragg, Jan. 20, 1865," *SHSP*, 346-49; B. Bragg to Z. B. Vance, Jan. 15, 1865, Telegram, Z. B. Vance Papers, NCDAH.

† The marines were not in position when the sailors moved out, Therefore, they had a very small role in the fight. Simmons, "Fort Fisher," Pt. II, 50-51.

‡ Admiral Porter thought the works would have been carried "but for the infernal marines who were running away when the sailors were mounting the parapets, and every man fighting like a lion. . . ." D. Porter to G. V. Fox, Jan. 21, 1865, G. V. Fox Papers, NYHS. The failure of the assault, however, could not be attributed solely to the marines. The entire operation was handled badly. Very few of the officers and men had had any experience on land. Furthermore, the final orders for the charge were not issued until the men were ashore. When the army attack jumped off, the sailors were not ready, and instead of advancing in three lines, as planned, the bluejackets merged into one and rushed down the beach. A party under the indomitable Lieutenant W. B. Cushing did, somehow, manage to charge through a gap in the palisades and reach the wall, but this position could not be held.

Admiral David Porter's fleet celebrating the surrender of Fort Fisher.
(From *Harper's Weekly*)

to look at the western salient, and there, to his "astonishment" were three Federal battle flags crowning the works. While the naval force had engaged the attention of Lamb, a column of Terry's men had gained a foothold at the west, or river end, of the parapet.

General Whiting saw the flags and roared for a counterattack to drive the enemy out. A savage hand-to-hand battle developed, the fighting swirling back and forth between the traverses. Cursing men, locked together, rolled in the sand. Bayonets, knives, and gun butts came into play.

"Surrender!" yelled the men in blue. "Go to hell, you Yankee bastards!" shouted General Whiting in reply. But with these words he sank to the sand, critically wounded.

Colonel Lamb ordered what cannon he had left to swivel around and fire point blank into the mass of bluecoats. Then he rallied his men to sweep the Federals from the land face. Several gun chambers were retaken and enemy battle flags disappeared from the ramparts. For a moment it seemed as though the tide of battle was turning in favor of the Confederates. Then suddenly the naval bombardment, which had been confined to the sea face, turned again to the land front with "deadly precision."

The "remorseless fleet" had come to the rescue of the faltering Union troops in time. Admiral Porter delivered support within fifty yards of Terry's advancing lines.* This fire swept everything before it, including Colonel Lamb who fell, a bullet in his hip, while leading his men in a final desperate charge.[66]

The command now develoved upon Major James Reilly. "It was from traverse to traverse," he afterwards wrote, "from traverse to the main magazine, from there to the breastwork where the last and most determined stand was made, and we [did] not leave until we were attacked on both flank and front. . . . Our march was directed to Battery Buchanan where we expected to reform our shattered ranks, and to be in a position to engage the enemy under more favorable circumstances. The command was badly disorganized from the position they were placed in and the mode of fighting we had to resort to . . . [we] were subject to the demoralizing effect of the destructive fire of the enemy's fleet. . . ."

A short distance from the battery, Reilly halted his troops and sent a messenger ahead to warn the post of his arrival. He did not wish to be mistaken for the enemy. The Major also sent along instructions to Captain R. F. Chapman, commanding the small installation, to have "his men and armament ready for action." The messenger returned shortly with the word that "Captain Chapman and command was gone with few exceptions, the Battery abandoned and the guns spiked. . . ." This was disturbing news. Yet Reilly had no alternative but to proceed with his original plan. At Battery Buchanan he attempted to get his men "in some order," only to learn that three-fourths of them had no arms. Offering even token resistance to the Federals, advancing rapidly down the beach, was now out of the question.

In company with Major James H. Hill and Captain A. C. Van Benthuysen of the Marine Corps, Reilly went up the beach a short distance to await the enemy.† He carried a white flag. Around 10:00

---

* The phenomenally close support given Terry by the navy guns can be explained by three factors: "First, the naval gunfire ships were in the ideal position of firing at right angles to the axis of the Federal advance so that errors in range did not endanger the friendly troops greatly; second, Civil War shells, although potent, did not have the lethal radius of today's projectiles; third, the Confederate system of traverses and lateral fortifications formed compartments which protected not only the defenders but the attackers as well." Simmons, "Fort Fisher," Pt. II, 52.

† Earlier in the evening Bragg had received the following wire from General Whiting: "The enemy are assaulting us by land and sea. Their infantry outnumbers us. Can't you help us? I am slightly wounded." Bragg's idea of help was to send Brigadier General A. H. Colquitt down to the fort to take command. When the General arrived at Battery

P.M., the Federal advance appeared. Major Reilly stepped forward and, to the Captain in charge, said: "We surrender." With this laconic statement, the second battle of Fort Fisher came to an end. One of the most important engagements of the war was over.[67]

To celebrate the victory, the ships of the Union fleet set off a brilliant pyrotechnic display. "Battle lanterns, calcium lights, magnificent rockets, blue lights and every description of fireworks" lit up the heavens.[68] But inside the fort the scene was horrifying—"the dead and wounded, the fragments of shells, dismounted guns, splintered carriages, earthworks ploughed in furrows, devastation, ruin, death in every attitude and every form. . . ." These are the things, wrote a Federal officer, that "we lose sight of when the pride, pomp and circumstances of Glorius war are mentioned."*

When the telegraph announced the next day the fall of Fort Fisher, the seal of doom was put on the Confederacy. The loss of the mouth of the Cape Fear River destroyed the last major contact of the South with the outer world.† Although late in acting, the Federal high command had chosen its objective well.[69]

General Whiting, who was to die shortly after the battle from his wounds, attributed the loss of Fort Fisher "solely to the incompetency, the imbecility and the pusillanimity" of Braxton Bragg. "He could have taken every one of the enemy," Whiting wrote, "but he was afraid. After the fleet stopped its stream of infernal fire to let the assaulting columns come on, we fought them for six hours from traverse to traverse and parapet to parapet, 6,000 of them. All that time Bragg was within two and a half miles, with 6,000 of Lee's best troops, three batteries of artillery and 1,500 reserves. The enemy had no artillery at all. Bragg

---

Buchanan and saw the state of things, he tarried only long enough to inform Colonel Lamb, whom he found lying on a stretcher, that he had brought neither reinforcements nor a plan of evacuation. Then with his staff Colquitt hurried back to his rowboat and headed upstream to report the disaster to Bragg. *OR,* XLVI, Ser. I, Pt. I, 434-35, 442-44; Lamb, "Defense of Fort Fisher," pp. 234-35.

* Reilly regretted that he could not put up a fight at the battery. It was clear night and the "Yankees" coming down the beach would have made good targets. J. Reilly, "Report on the Battle of Fort Fisher" (Battle report), W. L. de Rosset Papers, NCDAH.

† The daredevil W. B. Cushing, at the time of Fort Fisher's fall, managed to capture some of the pilots who guided the blockade-runners over the bar, and by forcing them to display the usual signals, he was able to capture two vessels that sailed up the river unaware that the fort had fallen. R. J. Roske and C. Van Doren, *Lincoln's Commando: The Biography of Commander W. B. Cushing, U.S.N.* (New York: Harper and Brothers, 1957), p. 263.

was held in check by two negro brigades while the rest of the enemy assaulted and he didn't even fire a musket."[70]

Many of the Confederate soldiers shared General Whiting's sentiments. D. A. Buie thought: "Had Genl. Bragg let Genl. Hoke attack the enemy when he asked him to do so," Fort Fisher would still be in Southern hands. "Bragg has had bad luck wherever he has been and always will, he is too fond of retreating or too fearful of being taken by the enemy."[71] Another soldier wrote: "The people in Wilmington seem to think the enemy can take possession whenever they are ready. They have no confidence in Genl. Bragg, and in fact the army has as little. I am not given to croaking about our generals but I must say that the blame of the fall of Fort Fisher rests on his shoulders. The enemy should have been attacked by Hoke whether he could carry the works or not."[72] And Chaplain John Paris said: "The Confederate General Bragg manifested as much timidity as the Yankee did boldness, according to the declarations of many of the officers."[73]

As soon as General Terry could find time to count his spoils and take a muster, he reported the capture of 169 pieces of artillery, 2,000 stand of small arms, considerable quantities of ordnance and commissary supplies, and prisoners totaling 112 commissioned officers and 1,971 enlisted men.[74]* His own casualties numbered 659 in killed, wounded, and missing.[75] Admiral Porter's losses, including those resulting from the explosion of a magazine in Fort Fisher subsequent to its capture, were approximately four hundred.[76] The records are not clear, however, on Confederate casualties, but the number was probably between four and five hundred, and most of these were the result of the naval fire.[77]†

With Fort Fisher in enemy hands, General Bragg was forced to abandon the other defenses at the mouth of the Cape Fear. Around 7:00 A.M. on the sixteenth, Confederate troops marched out of Forts Caswell and Campbell "and wound their way with heavy hearts down the

* When the fort was assaulted on the afternoon of the fifteenth, Colonel Lamb put the strength of his garrison at only 1550 men. Lamb, "Defense of Fort Fisher," p. 226. Also see above p. 275.

† In his official report Admiral Porter estimated that the fleet had "expended in the bombardment about 50,000 shells." "Compilers can account for 20,271 projectiles weighing 1,275,299 pounds in the first attack, 19,682 weighing 1,652,638 pounds in the second attack, and estimate that these totals to be 90 to 95 percent complete. Taking the length of the fort as 2,580 yards this yields a ratio of well over 1,000 pounds of metal and explosive for every linear yard." Simmons, "Fort Fisher," Pt. II, 52; NR, XI, Ser. I, 441.

beach." They halted after six miles to await the demolition teams left behind to demolish the forts. All day, and well into the night, they waited. Finally, at 1:30 A.M., several terrific explosions indicated the job was done. In an instant, the works "were one mass of shapeless ruins." Everything inflammable "was consumed to ashes." "The Yankees made a barren capture in Forts Caswell and Campbell," remarked a Confederate soldier, and he could have said the same of Forts Holmes and Johnston, which were also leveled by the evacuating forces. Once the works were destroyed, the Confederate troops proceeded up the west bank of the Cape Fear to Fort Anderson.

Directly across the river at Sugar Loaf, Hoke was entrenched, his left resting on Masonboro Sound and his right on the Cape Fear. The Federals considered Hoke's line impregnable and made no effort to breach it until the second week in February. By this time, Union General John M. Schofield had arrived from the west with a portion of the Twenty-third Army Corps to take command of the Department of North Carolina.[78]

Without waiting for the arrival of the remainder of his troops, Schofield decided to move against Hoke. On February 11, he advanced Terry's line close enough to the enemy "to compel him to hold . . . [it] in force." He then made preparations to send a fleet of "Navy boats and pontoons" up the coast. At a designated landing spot, two army divisions, having moved up the beach at night, were to meet them, transport the boats and pontoons across the narrow sand strip to the sound, "and cross the latter to the mainland in rear of Hoke's position." On paper, this was a very good plan, but foul weather made its execution impossible. The expedition "got stuck in the deep sand . . ." on the night of the fourteenth.[79]

As a consequence of this failure, Schofield decided to try the west bank of the river, where he would have more room to maneuver. Two divisions were ferried across the Cape Fear to Smithville. Here they were joined by an additional brigade, all under the command of Major General Jacob D. Cox. The Federal plan called for a joint army-navy advance on Fort Anderson. Since the vessels of the fleet had, from time to time, already engaged the fort at long range, Admiral Porter was to order the fire renewed when the land forces advanced.

On the morning of the seventeenth, Cox's troops marched out of Smithville. About three miles beyond the town Confederate pickets

Bombardment of Fort Anderson by Union vessels, February 11, 1865.
(From *Harper's Weekly*)

started a running skirmish that they kept up until they were pushed back to within two miles of the fort. Cox stopped the skirmishing here, dug in, and opened communications with Admiral Porter.

A reconnaissance the next morning revealed to the General that, in addition to the main fort "immediately by the river," a line of breastworks ran at right angles from the bank to Orton Pond (a lake several miles long). This gave Fort Anderson a front that could not be turned "except by a long detour." In accordance with his orders, Cox had two brigades invest the works from the south, while two others marched for the head of Orton Pond. The detour necessitated a march of about fifteen miles, so it was almost night when the causeway through the marsh at the head of the pond was reached. Confederate cavalry put up stout resistance at this point but was pushed back. At this point General Cox did not pursue, having received a message from General Schofield ordering him to encamp for the night.

In the meantime Federal gunboats and monitors had made Fort Anderson "anything but comfortable" for its defenders. One Confederate soldier said the fort was "knocked out of all shape." And when it was learned that a Federal column was approaching from the rear, the men were not unhappy to evacuate the works.[80]

Early on the morning of the nineteenth, the Confederate garrison fell back to Town Creek, some eight miles north, and took position in the breastworks there.* Shortly before dusk "a sharp little fight" developed with Cox's advance. In this skirmish the Confederates were pushed back across the bridge, but they managed to burn it in time to stop the Federal attack. The following day Cox had one of his brigades demonstrate on the Confederate front, while the remainder of his troops crossed the creek downstream, near where it emptied into the Cape Fear. By 4:00 P.M. the Federals had the enemy position flanked, making it necessary for General Johnson Hagood, in command of the Confederate forces, to order a retreat toward Wilmington. In the "hurried flight from the trenches [that] followed," Hagood suffered a considerable loss of 350 men killed, wounded, and captured.

Continuing his advance up the west bank of the Cape Fear, Cox was across the river from Wilmington on February 21, which, in General Bragg's words, "rendered our continued occupation of the town very hazardous to the whole command. . . ." Accordingly he instructed Hoke to abandon his position below Wilmington. And in the city naval stores, cotton, and tobacco were set on fire.[81]

Since the Second Battle of Fort Fisher, the citizens of Wilmington had known they were at the "mercy of the enemy."[82] Some packed up at the last minute and went inland, but most of them decided to remain at home. Yet, as one resident put it: "I am completely heartbroken, can't eat, or sleep. God have mercy on me, I feel that it will kill me."[83]

The times were especially trying for those soldiers of Bragg's command who were natives of Wilmington. William Calder wrote in his diary, February 21, 1865: "I think this has been one of the saddest days of my life. I never had such a hard thing to do as leave all my old friends and home where my childhood's days were spent. I procured a horse in the afternoon and rode over the town for the last time."[84] He found the stores closed "and people . . . [gathered] together in groups with sadden hearts and woeful faces."[85] "Zac" Ellis, who was to be killed in battle a few weeks later, at first could not express how he felt, "knowing that . . . [his] good old town was doomed."[86] Despite a strong desire to remain behind both Ellis and Calder reported at nightfall to their commands which they found busily preparing to evacuate the city. Before the break of day, the two men, along with the remainder

* When the Confederate garrison fell back to Town Creek on the nineteenth, General Hoke, who was still across the river, fell back also. He retired to a position on the east bank of the Cape Fear, opposite the mouth of Town Creek.

of the Confederate troops, went into camp on the "North side of the Northeast River."* General Bragg's withdrawal of the army to this spot was hardly in accordance with Lee's wire to "be bold and judicious."[87]

Back at Wilmington, "a mass of black smoke had settled like a pall over the silent town; in its extent and density suggestive of the day of doom."[88] No one knew what to expect. The local citizens could only hope for the best and wait in suspense for the conquerors of Fort Fisher. They did not have long to wait. Hardly had the last squad of Confederate cavalry dashed out of town when a small company of blue-clad horsemen galloped down Market Street to where a small group of people was standing. One of the riders politely asked for the mayor. "His Honor, John Dawson," being in the group, stepped forward and said: "I am the man." The officer then stated that General Terry would meet the Mayor and commissioners at the city hall in five minutes. The Reverend Mr. Burkhead, who witnessed the meeting between Mayor Dawson and Terry, afterwards wrote:

Here [city hall] we stood for perhaps half an hour, during which time horsemen were dashing in hot haste through all the streets picking up the Confederate stragglers who had fallen behind General Hoke's retreating veterans. Then came General Terry at the head of a column up Front Street with the strains of martial music and colors flying. Leaving the main column at Market Street, heading a column of splendidly equipped men mounted on superb charges—every horse a beautiful bay—he dashed up to the City Hall, instantly dismounted, and said, "Is this the Mayor?" The Mayor replied, "It is." Whereupon General Terry took off his hat; the Mayor did likewise, and they shook hands with formal and graceful cordiality and together ascended the steps of the City Hall. The troops came pouring through the city, white and colored, and marched directly toward "Northeast" in pursuit of . . . [General Bragg.][89]

The Federal soldiers took the fall of Wilmington as a good omen since it occurred on George Washington's birthday.[90] "I think we celebrated the day well, don't you?" one of them wrote.[91] But for the residents of Wilmington it was a time of sadness, not celebration. The omen was bad, not good. The Confederacy, without supplies from abroad, surely could not stand much longer.

* There was some skirmishing at Northeast River on the twenty-second. Calder Diary, Feb. 22, 1865, DU.

CHAPTER XIV

Sherman Enters the State

Upon assuming command of the Department of North Carolina, General Schofield was under orders to make Goldsboro his ultimate objective and, as soon as possible, to open railroad communication between that city and the coast. Schofield was also to accumulate supplies for Sherman's army and to make junction with that fighting force at or near Goldsboro.[1] Sherman at the time was marching northward through South Carolina.[2]

At Wilmington, General Schofield found very little rolling stock and few wagons. These shortages compelled him to operate from New Bern alone for the capture of Goldsboro. He first reinforced the New Bern garrison and ordered General I. N. Palmer to move immediately "with all his available force, toward Kinston, to cover the workmen engaged in repairing the railroad." When, on February 25, Schofield learned that Palmer had not moved "as was expected," he sent General Cox to take command at New Bern and to "push forward at once."[3]

By March 6, Cox had two divisions—those belonging to Palmer and Brigadier General S. G. Carter—in motion for Goldsboro. A third division, Major General Thomas H. Ruger commanding, was to follow.* Altogether Cox had an effective force of over thirteen thousand men.[4] At Southwest Creek below Kinston on the seventh, the Federals encountered Bragg with Hoke's division.[5] The Confederates were strongly entrenched on the west bank of this sizable stream which flowed into the Neuse from a southwesterly direction about three miles east of

* This was a "provisional corps." Palmer's and Carter's divisions were made up from troops that had been on garrison duty in eastern North Carolina. Ruger's command was the First Division, Twenty-third Corps.

Kinston. Here General Bragg hoped to delay, if not halt, the Federal advance.

For a long time Confederate authorities had considered the creek as the main defensive line against attacks from the east. All of the wagon roads leading from Kinston to New Bern crossed Southwest Creek, as did the Wilmington road and the Atlantic and North Carolina Railroad. The Neuse road ran near the south bank of the river, going east. Next came the railroad, following nearly a straight line to New Bern. The Dover road branched off from the Neuse road not far from the town and took "a devious way" through the swamps in the same general direction. "The upper Trent road ran more nearly south toward Trenton, and followed the course of the Trent River" into New Bern. The upper Trent road did not cross Southwest Creek. Starting at Trenton, it ran almost directly north to the Neuse road, striking it just east of the stream. The intersection of the upper Trent and Dover roads was known as Wise's Forks.[6] When General Cox reached Southwest Creek, he found the numerous bridges over the stream either "destroyed or dismantled." So he moved his two divisions up to the edge of a swamp at Wise's Forks; Palmer on the right, covered the railroad, and Carter on the left, protected the Dover road. An interval of a mile separated the two. The Twelfth New York Cavalry was used to patrol the roads to the left and to watch the various crossings of the creek. An old road, known as the British road, ran parallel to the creek about a mile in front of the Federal position, and where it crossed the Dover road, Colonel Charles Upham was stationed with two regiments.[7]

There was some exchange of artillery fire on the seventh, but little else. Bragg used the time to prepare an attack for the next day. Since D. H. Hill was expected to arrive momentarily with reinforcements,[*] the plan called for Hill to relieve Hoke's division in the line while Hoke crossed the creek and struck the Federal left flank. At the sound of Hoke's attack, Hill was to cross over and hit the enemy's right flank.[8] Before dawn on the eighth, Hill's troops, some two thousand in number, including both veterans of the Army of Tennessee† and Junior Re-

---

[*] It was not a pleasant task for Hill to report to General Bragg for duty. The officers had had a bitter quarrel during the Chickamauga campaign. However, in deference to his superiors Hill put aside his personal differences "for this emergency." *OR*, XLVII, Ser. I, Pt. II, 1338; J. W. Ratchford to D. H. Hill, Jr., n.d., D. H. Hill Papers, NCDAH.

† Only the shell of the Army of Tennessee remained. At Nashville, Tennessee, in

serves,* were in the trenches. Bragg's forces now numbered between eight and ten thousand men.[9]

Hoke moved out early in the morning of the eighth. After crossing Southwest Creek, he struck the British road and turned northward, which put him on Colonel Upham's flank. The Colonel, upon learning of the enemy's approach, hurried the Twenty-seventh Massachusetts to the British road and formed it in a line about a quarter of a mile south of the Dover road. He also ordered to this point a section of artillery and a battalion of his own regiment, the Fifteenth Connecticut. "These orders were judicious, but the odds were too great to make them successful." Far outflanked on both sides, the Masachusetts regiment was put to flight. The artillery never got into position, passing "on the run under a very hot musket fire," and, complained Colonel Upham afterwards, "I have not seen the officer in command of it since." All the horses at one gun were killed, and even though the men cut the traces in trying to save the piece, it too had to be abandoned.[10]

At the sound of Hoke's engagement (around noon) Hill crossed Southwest Creek in an attempt to turn the Federal right flank. His hodgepodge command advanced "with very good courage, but exceedingly bad order." The Junior Reserves, who had been on the skirmish line since early morning, moved "handsomely for a time, but at length one regiment . . . broke, and the rest lay down and could not be got forward." The remainder of the troops, however, continued their advance, "intercepting the right battalion of Upham's Connecticut regiment, which "ran in the wildest confusion." At this critical moment, as Hill prepared to press forward in the direction of Hoke's firing, Bragg ordered him to proceed along the Neuse road to its intersection with the

---

December, 1864, it had been cut to pieces by a Union force under Major General George H. Thomas. In returning from this disastrous expedition the Army of Tennessee had halted in Northeastern Mississippi. Here Lieutenant General J. B. Hood, commanding the army, furloughed many of his men. But when Sherman's army invaded South Carolina in February, 1865, "General Beauregard ordered those remaining on duty to repair to that state." The first detachment arrived in time to oppose Sherman's crossing of the Edisto River but these troops engaged in no other fighting in the state. They were then ordered to march to Charlotte, and after this the other detachments of the Army of Tennessee were directed on into North Carolina. General Hill commanded the group that arrived at Smithfield, North Carolina, from Charlotte in early March. Bragg had Hill join him at Southwest Creek. J. E. Johnston, *Narrative of Military Operations, Directed, During the Late War Between the States, by Joseph E. Johnston, General, C.S.A.* (New York: D. Appleton and Co., 1874), pp. 373-79. Also see below p. 329n.

* The Junior Reserves, added to Hill's command on the morning of the eighth, were under Brigadier General L. S. Baker.

British road and here to intercept the retreating Federals. Hill moved immediately, reaching the intersection at 4:30 P.M. but he failed to see any evidence of a fleeing enemy, and the distant firing indicated that Hoke was not advancing. Shortly, another message arrived from the Commanding General, suggesting that he "return, if too late to strike a blow." Hill was now five miles from his improvised bridge over Southwest Creek, held only "by a picket," and Federal cavalry had appeared on his front. In view of these circumstances General Hill followed Bragg's "suggestion" and marched rapidly back to his position of the morning.[11]

Although the main Federal line had remained intact and Hill had been sent off on a wild-goose chase, the first day of the Battle of Wise's Forks had gone for the Confederates. Generals Hill and Hoke captured together almost a thousand prisoners.[12] A private in the Fifteenth Connecticut, who fortunately for himself had missed the fight, wrote home: "I am obliged to tell that the brave Fifteenth are no more, they were nearly all taken prisoners . . . they were surrounded by a Division of rebs and they fought bravely and were slaughtered at the onset, the rebs pouring 3 voleys in to them 8 rods of . . . we lost our Lieutenant Colonel Major and most of our officers killed, there is from 75 to 120 of the old members left. . . . It is rather a sad affair. . . ."[13]

These Federal losses were more than made up for with the arrival of Ruger's division. Shortly before dark it took position between Carter and Palmer. In preparation for a renewal of the battle the next day, General Cox had his troops construct a continuous line of breastworks along the whole front. His intention was to fight defensively, at least for a while. General Schofield, who had arrived in New Bern on the eighth, had directed him "to maintain a watchful defensive" until the remainder of the Twenty-third Corps arrived. It was, at the time, marching up from Wilmington.[14]

March 9 found the Confederates occupying a line of breastworks along the British road and another nearly at right angles to it covering the railroad down to Southwest Creek. The Junior Reserves were in the trenches along the creek. After their first day's performance, it was thought best to keep them in the fortifications "waiting for the Yanks while the old soldiers . . . [did the] fighting."[15]

During the day Hoke attempted to flank the Federal right "but finding the Yankee strongly intrenched did not attack. . . ."[16] Despite

The Battle of Wise's Forks near Kinston, March 8, 1865. (From *The Soldier in Our Civil War*)

this reverse, Bragg still felt he could dislodge the enemy from his entrenched position. And with more troops from the Army of Tennessee expected, he ordered Hoke to make a flank movement to the right, while Hill demonstrated on his front.* The attack was set for the morning of the tenth.[17]

Around 3:00 A.M. on this date Hoke started working his way around the Federal left. Everything went off "quietly and safely." Only the sound of falling rain broke the suspicious stillness. The Federal soldiers, shivering in their trenches, began to wonder whether the enemy had retreated. But "this suspicion . . . was ruthlessly dispelled shortly after noontime" by the noise of artillery fire and that "wild and peculiar yell of the Southerners." Private Henry Thompson had just crawled out of his tent when the Confederates "riz up and fired and then made a charge on . . . the breastworks. . . ." The startled Private was not "long in taking out . . . into the swamp," the "balls spoting into the trees all round" him. His only concern was a fear "some of the balls

* Hill was not ordered to assault the main Federal works. He was to make only a demonstration. This, doubtless, was because Hill's officers "had stated to . . . [him] the unwillingness of the men to attack earthworks, their experience in the late campaign not being favorable to such an undertaking." D. H. Hill to "Colonel," Mar. 29, 1865, D. H. Hill Papers, NCDAH.

might make a mistake and take . . . [him] for a tree." Happily for General Cox, very few of Thompson's comrades joined him in flight.[18]

Hoke's attack was the signal for Hill to advance. Hill's troops moved forward "with alacrity," taking an entrenched line of Federal skirmishers. This advance, however, threw the Confederate line of battle so far forward that reserves had to be brought up. Also, "a considerable Yankee force" was now visible outside of their works. While contemplating his next move, Hill learned that Hoke was retiring after finding the Federals strongly entrenched and getting one brigade "roughly handled." When this news was reported to General Bragg, he ordered Hill to fall back also. That night the Confederate troops crossed the Neuse and encamped near Kinston. Cox made no effort to pursue.[19]

The resistance offered by the Confederate forces at Wise's Forks, "though inspiring" and resulting in the temporary halt of the Federal advance, "was on too small a scale to produce important results." In order to resume his march on Goldsboro, General Schofield had only to repair the railroad bridge over the Neuse River at Kinston and bring up pontoons for a wagon crossing. These tasks were completed in something like ten days, after which the Federal army was ready to roll again.*

In the meantime Bragg's troops had retired to Goldsboro, their commander having preceded them there to await orders from his immediate superior, General Joseph E. Johnston.

On February 22, 1865, Lee had ordered Johnston to assume command of the remnants of the Army of Tennessee and all of the troops in the Department of South Carolina, Georgia, and Florida and to "concentrate all available forces and drive Sherman back." Two weeks later

---

* The Confederate navy had an ironclad, the *Neuse*, at Kinston, but it was not engaged in the fighting at Wise's Forks. Bragg did want, nontheless, to use the vessel to cover his retreat. He hoped Captain Joseph Price of the *Neuse* would "move down the river by way of diversion and make the loss of his vessel as costly to the enemy as possible." This failed to materialize, and on the fourteenth, General Cox reported the "ram is burned; her wreck is in sight. . . ." The ironclad had been destroyed by the retreating Confederates.

General Cox enjoyed no more success than Bragg in getting help from the navy. His efforts to have several steamers move up the Neuse River from New Bern to cooperate with him fell through. Various reasons, including shallow water, were responsible for this. W. T. Rutledge, "Battle of Wise's Forks or Battle of Southwest Creek, North Carolina" (Unpublished article in possession of the author); *OR*, XLVIII, Ser. I, Pt. I, 1366; *Ibid.*, Pt. II, 696, 707, 802, 814-15, 1079; *NR*, XI, Ser. I, 754; *Ibid.*, XII, 67.

Johnston also had all of "the troops serving in North Carolina" added to his command.[20]

The General's first problem, on assuming his new duties, was to unite his meager forces that were scattered from Mississippi to Virginia. He hoped to concentrate them at some place in North Carolina and there strike one of General Sherman's columns on the move. The Federal order of march, by wings, gave support to this idea.

Sherman had divided his army into two wings. Major General Oliver O. Howard commanded the right wing which was composed of the Fifteenth and Seventeenth Corps, commanded respectively by Major Generals John A. Logan and Francis P. Blair, Jr. The left wing was under the charge of Major General Henry W. Slocum. The Fourteenth Corps, under Major General Jefferson C. Davis, and the Twentieth Corps, under Brigadier General Alpheus S. Williams, composed this wing. The cavalry was led by Brigadier General H. Judson Kilpatrick.

Giving battle to Sherman's entire army was out of the question because of the great disparity in the size of the two fighting forces, but it was Johnston's ultimate aim to join Lee when and if he should abandon Richmond and with their combined forces fall upon Sherman.[21]

While Johnston mapped out his strategy, South Carolina was suffering the horrors of total war at the hands of Sherman's men. This unique concept of warfare had been developed by Sherman in the fall of 1862 while he was on duty at Memphis, Tennessee. It called for making war "so terrible" that the South would exhaust all peaceful remedies before commencing another struggle.[22] Considering all the people of the South as enemies of the Union,[23] Sherman planned to use his military forces against the civilian population as well as the armies of the enemy. He believed that this plan of action would not only demoralize the noncombatants but the men under arms as well. The Southern armies in the field, he felt certain, could be disheartened by attacks on the civilian population as easily as by defeats on the battlefield. Sherman's program of total war also called for the destruction of the enemy's economic resources. By paralyzing the Confederate economy he hoped to destroy the South's ability to supply its fighting forces with war materials. In bringing war to the home front he hoped to destroy both the South's capacity to wage war and its will to fight.[24]

"Collective responsibility," the theory upon which total war rests,

Sherman's foragers starting out in the morning. (From *Harper's Weekly*)

made possible a new mode of warfare in which the accepted rules of
the time were transgressed. The effect was a certain disregard for human rights and dignity, but with Sherman "war . . . [was] war and
not popularity seeking."[25] He thought the South, for its part in bringing on the conflict, deserved "all the curses and maledictions a people
can pour out."[26] Nevertheless, he held out to his enemies the sincere
promise of a helping hand if they would lay down their arms and rejoin the Union. It was not a sense of cruelty and barbarism that
prompted Sherman to formulate his theory of total war. This conception was the outgrowth of a search for the quickest, surest, and most
efficient means to win a war. Victory, he determined, could be won
more easily by moving troops than by fighting. Strategy had become
to him the master of tactics. The purpose of his strategy was to mini-
mize fighting by striking at the supply lines and the morale of the enemy.[27]

The full application of this new philosophy of war had been made
by Sherman first in campaigns through Mississippi and Georgia. When
the Georgia operations ended at Savannah on December 21, 1864, all the
accepted rules of strategy called for the immediate transfer of Sherman's
sixty thousand veterans from the Georgia coast to Richmond where
Grant had Lee bottled up behind fortifications.[28]* General Grant was
desirous of this move,[29] but much to his dismay Sherman voiced strong
objections to such a plan. He hoped to march on to Richmond by way

---

* Grant's strategy for the 1864 campaign called for attacks on Lee's army, on Richmond, and several subsidiary offensives. Sherman's march into Georgia was one of the
subsidiary operations.

of Columbia and Raleigh in the Carolinas.[30] Every step northward from Savannah, Sherman felt, was as much a direct attack on Lee as though he were operating within sound of the artillery of the Army of Northern Virginia. He was firmly convinced that an application of total war in the Carolinas would have a direct bearing on the outcome of Grant's struggle around Richmond.[31]

The combination of Sherman's persistence and the news of Thomas' devastating victory over Hood at Nashville[32] persuaded the reluctant Commanding General to grant permission for the move through the Carolinas.[33]

Sherman's plan of campaign called for feints on both Augusta and Charleston, a march directly on Columbia, and from there to Goldsboro, North Carolina, by way of Fayetteville on the Cape Fear. Goldsboro was chosen as the destination because of its rail connections with the coast. By this circuit the Federal force could destroy the chief railroads of the Carolinas and devastate the heart of the two states.[34]

Sherman planned to cut himself off completely from his base in Savannah; hence, he could expect no government supplies until he reached the Cape Fear River in North Carolina. His wagons could carry only limited provisions, and the army of sixty thousand would have to "forage liberally on the country during the march." To regulate the foraging parties, very strict orders were issued.[35]

These instructions were in complete compliance with the accepted rules of warfare. Yet there was wide discrepancy between the orders and the actions of some of the men. In Georgia many of the foraging parties had degenerated into marauding bands of mounted robbers which operated not under the supervision of an officer but on their own. These groups committed every sort of outrage. Most of the pillage and wanton destruction of private property in the two Carolinas was the work of the "bummers," "smoke house rangers," or "do-boys," as this peripheral minority of self-constituted foragers was called.[36]* The majority of officers and men in Sherman's army neither engaged in indiscriminate looting nor condoned the actions of those who did. The

---

* On most occasions these foragers were referred to as "bummers." The origin of the term is obscure, but it was in use at the time of the "march to the sea." A member of Sherman's staff termed the "bummer" as "a raider on his own account, a man who temporarily deserts a place in the ranks and starts upon an independent foraging mission." H. S. Commager, ed., *The Blue and the Gray: The Story of the Civil War as Told by Participants* (New York: Bobbs-Merrill, 1950), II, 952.

foragers, who many times absented themselves from their commands for several days at a time, always returned with a peace offering in the form of the choicest spoils of the land. Lieutenant Charles Booth of the Twenty-second Wisconsin wrote:

Imagine a fellow with a gun and accoutrements, with a plug hat, captured militia plume in it, a citizen's saddle, with a bed quilt or table cloth, upon an animal whose ears are the larger part of the whole. Let us take an inventory of his stock as he rides into camp at night. Poor fellow! he had rode upon that knock-kneed, shave tail, rail fence mule over 30 miles, had fought the brush and mud, and passed through untold dangers, and all for his load, which consists of, first, a bundle of fodder for his mule; second, three hams, a sack of meal, a peck of potatoes, third, a fresh bed quilt, the old mother's coffeepot, a jug of vinegar, and a bed cord. You call him an old, steady bummer. I'll give you one more picture. Here comes a squad of eighteen or nineteen, no two alike. Look at the chickens, geese, beehives; see that little fellow with a huge hog strapped upon his nag's back. There rides the commander, a Lieutenant, completely happy for the day had been a good one, and his detail has got enough for a day's good supply for his regiment.[37]

Having previously been stationed in South Carolina, Sherman was familiar with the treacherous topography of the region he was about to enter. He was aware of the fact that heavy rainfall would make the existing roads almost impassable. The success of the campaign, he knew, would depend largely upon the efficiency of the pioneer corps whose duty it was to build and repair roads and bridges. In order that this large army might remain on the move, every division and brigade had a regularly organized pioneer corps.[38]

This corps performed a remarkable engineering feat in maintaining the roads through the swampy and sandy areas of the Carolinas. To keep the roads in a usable state, they made extensive use of the corduroy process whereby logs were laid transversely across the muddiest part of a roadway to give it foundation. The pioneer was so successful at this work that one Confederate soldier remarked: "If Sherman's army had gone to hell and wanted to march over and there was no other way, they would corduroy it and march on.[39]

The strength of Sherman's army was approximately 60,079 men. The trains were made up of about 2,500 wagons and 600 ambulances[40] under the charge of teamsters, who, undoubtedly, were the most profane group in the service. David P. Conyngham, a reporter for the *New York*

Herald, felt certain they had a contract to do all the swearing for the army. He was not too sure they did not pray in oaths.[41] The wagons carried an ample supply of ammunition for a great battle but forage for only seven days and provision for twenty days.[42] On good roads these trains stretched out twenty-five miles. Consequently, it was necessary for each corps to move upon a separate road. To shorten further each corps' column, roads were reserved exclusively for wheels, the troops marching alongside but outside of the roads.[43]

Sherman commenced his march through the Carolinas the latter part of January, 1865, and by February 7 the major part of his army had penetrated, without difficulty, well into South Carolina and was encamped along the Charleston-Augusta Railroad.[44] Five days later Orangeburg, to the north, was in Federal hands.[45]

As the army had pushed deeper into South Carolina, foraging had become more of a vital necessity to the success of the campaign. Although Sherman had ordered that officers command all foraging parties,[46] scores of foragers roamed about under no supervision, intent only on plunder. Largely because of the activities of this group, much of the lower part of the state lay in smouldering ruins by the second week in February.

From Orangeburg the army moved out in the direction of Columbia, destroying the railroad as it went. This capital city, crowded almost to suffocation with refugees, was the scene of confusion and turmoil when the booming of cannon gave strength to the rumors of Sherman's proximity.[47] Early on the morning of the seventeenth, Columbia fell to the Federal troops, and that night the soldiers, crazed by whiskey, burned the city to the ground.

Sherman's orders for the campaign of the Carolinas contained no instructions concerning the molestation of private property in Columbia.[48] But in the long run the General felt that the burning of private homes was a trifling matter compared to the manifold results that soon followed. "Though I never ordered it and never wished it, I have never shed any tears over the event, because I believe that it hastened what we all fought for, the end of the war."[49] This brief statement generally sums up Sherman's sentiments on the burning of Columbia.

The army remained in the city for two days, destroying, under orders, public and railroad property.[50] On February 20, to the accompaniment of hisses and boos from the people along the streets, the army resumed its march north toward Winnsboro.[51]

This historic old town, as well as Camden to the south and Cheraw to the east, suffered much at the hands of the Federal troops. At Cheraw, the army's last stop in South Carolina, Sherman learned that his former opponent, Joe Johnston, had replaced Beauregard as commander of the Confederate forces in North and South Carolina. He concluded that the battle he wished to avoid was now unavoidable.[52]

While Sherman contemplated his next move, General Judson Kilpatrick, his cavalry commander, was skirmishing with the enemy just across the line in North Carolina. On March 3, at Phillips Cross-Roads, a portion of Kilpatrick's command engaged some of Major General Joe Wheeler's Confederate horsemen.* The Federals were on the verge of being routed when their artillery was brought into play and the day was saved.[53]

Before this engagement started, a scouting party of one hundred men from the Ninth Michigan cavalry, under the command of Major J. G. McBride, had been sent to Wadesboro with instructions to "clean out the town." The Major carried out his orders by destroying a gristmill, sawmill, tannery, large government stables, and other public property.[54]

Wadesboro, however, had already been pillaged the previous day by detachments of Kilpatrick's scouts under Captain T. F. Northrop.[55] Thomas Atkinson, Episcopal Bishop of North Carolina, wrote of how, at the point of a gun, he was robbed of watch, clothes, jewelry, and horse. He said that every house where there seemed to be anything worth taking was robbed. The soldiers broke open the storehouses and took what they wanted. Atkinson went on to state that in some instances defenseless men were shot for plunder: "A Mr. James C. Bennett, one of the oldest and wealthiest men in Anson County, was shot at the door of his own house because he did not give up his watch and money, which had been previously taken from him by another party."[56]

Monroe, twenty-five miles to the west, had been visited even earlier, probably on March 1, either by Kilpatrick's men or foragers from one of the other corps. Building were not leveled as in Wadesboro, yet the usual looting took place. The most lucrative prize was ten fully loaded wagons belonging to an unfortunate party of refugees from Chester,

*Wheeler's cavalry had opposed Sherman both in Georgia and South Carolina.

South Carolina, who arrived in Monroe almost simultaneously with the Federals.[57]

Following the skirmish at Phillips Cross-Roads, both Wheeler and Kilpatrick crossed the Pee Dee River and moved toward Rockingham with Wheeler in the lead. On March 7, the Confederate General took a few of his scouts almost to this North Carolina town, where he "attacked and killed or captured thirty-five" of the Federals, most of whom were foragers from Sherman's Fourteenth and Twentieth Corps. Another skirmish was going on in Rockingham at this time between Union foragers and a brigade of Lieutenant General Wade Hampton's cavalry.* The Confederate horsemen had been ordered to remain in the town as a rear guard for W. J. Hardee's troops, who, after evacuating Charleston on February 18, had been moving north just ahead of Sherman's army. When Kilpatrick's advance guard appeared on the scene, the fighting developed into a considerable skirmish, but by 11:00 A.M. the Confederates had been driven out of town.[58]†

On the day before the skirmish at Rockingham, General Sherman had crossed the Pee Dee at Cheraw and had all of his army marching for Fayetteville, North Carolina, approximately seventy miles northeast.[59]

As early as January, 1865, the North Carolina newspapers had begun to prepare the people of the state for invasion,[60] but with the fall of Fort Fisher and the occupation of Wilmington, the people of North Carolina had almost surrendered themselves to a wave of despondency.[61] Late in February, General Lee declared that the despair of the North Carolinians was destroying his army. He wrote to Governor Vance: "Desertings are becoming very frequent and there is reason to believe that they are occasioned to considerable extent by letters written to the soldiers by their friends at home."[62] The diaries and letters of the men in the lines around Richmond show that Lee had reason to be con-

---

* In January, 1865, Lee had detached Major General M. C. Butler's division of Wade Hampton's cavalry and ordered it to South Carolina. He also allowed General Hampton to return to his native state (South Carolina) to assume command of all of the cavalry in operations against Sherman. Hampton was made a lieutenant general on February 16, 1865, the day before he became chief of cavalry. His command consisted of Wheeler's Corps, between four and five thousand strong, and Butler's division which numbered between one thousand and fifteen hundred men. *OR,* XLVII, Ser. I, Pt. I, 1132. Wheeler actually outranked Hampton but was his junior in service.

† The Federal soldiers destroyed the Great Falls Cotton Mill at Rockingham. J. Robertson, *Michigan in the War* (Lansing: W. S. George and Co., 1880), p. 500.

cerned.[63] "Deserters increase . . . we had three more last night" is a February entry in the diary of Samuel Hoey Walkup of the Forty-eighth North Carolina Regiment.[64] On March 6, Walkup expressed the sentiments of those soldiers whose homes were in Sherman's path: "I am in agony of suspense to hear from home. It has been nearly a month since I left them and have received no letter since. The Yankees were there. Between them and our forces I can only look Heavenward for comfort."[65]

General Sherman entered North Carolina with the confident expectation of receiving a welcome from its supposedly large number of pro-Union citizens.[66] Thus he had his officers issue orders for the gentler treatment of the inhabitants. General Slocum's orders read: "All officers and soldiers of this command are reminded that the State of North Carolina was one of the last states that passed the ordinance of secession, and from the commencement of the war there has been in this state a strong Union party. Her action on the question of secession was undoubtedly brought about by the traitorous acts of other states, and by intrigue and dishonesty on the part of her own citizens. The act never even met the approval of the great mass of her people. It should not be assumed that the inhabitants are enemies to our Government, and it is to be hoped that every effort will be made to prevent any wanton destruction of property, or any unkind treatment of citizens."[67]

When the state line was crossed, new orders were also issued regulating foraging. This practice was not stopped, however, even though Sherman had originally planned to issue a non-foraging order when the army reached North Carolina.[68] Faced with the prospect of battle and having many new mouths to feed in the refugee train, Sherman still found foraging a necessity. He could expect no Federal supplies until he met provision ships at the crossings of the Cape Fear and the Neuse rivers ahead. Neither could he expect much success from foraging operations between the Pee Dee River and Fayetteville. In the first place, the line of march of his troops led partially through a sandy, rolling, barren country. Secondly, the retreating Confederates were also having to subsist on this thinly populated countryside.

General Blair, after witnessing the "bummer's" work in South Carolina, thought the foraging system was "vicious and utterly deplorable" and wanted it changed, especially since the army was about to enter North Carolina.[69] Upon Blair's insistence, General Howard issued the following orders: "Hereafter but one mounted foraging party, to consist of sixty men with the proper number of commissioned officers, will be allowed for each division. The division commanders will be careful to select reliable officers for the command of these parties, who shall be held strictly accountable for the conduct of their men; whenever it may be necessary to send a party from the main body, a commissioned officer will be sent in charge, but in no case will it be allowed to go in advance of the advance guard of the leading division, or more than five miles from either flank of the column. All surplus animals will be disposed of by the corps quartermasters for the benefit of the artillery, bridge train, etc."[70] General Blair made his orders on foraging stricter still. No one was to be permitted to enter dwelling houses under any circumstances. The parties were allowed to take only animals, food for the command, and forage for the stock. The provost marshal was to arrest all men other than authorized foragers found away from their commands.[71] Blair thought the desire to be mounted would cause a strict compliance with the order. For any disobedience the offender could be sent to his place in the line.[72]

But no orders were issued prohibiting the burning of the great pine forests within North Carolina. So, "as the flames from buildings grew less frequent, smoke from burning forests grew heavier." The state's turpentine forests blazed in fantastic "splendor as 'bummers' touched matches to congealed sap in notches on tree trunks." The territory between the Pee Dee and Cape Fear river was one, vast, extensive pine forest, and on nearly every stream there was a factory for the making of turpentine, rosin, and tar. Seldom would the soldiers pass up an opportunity to fire these factories because burning rosin and tar created a spectacle of flame and smoke that surpassed in grandeur anything they had ever seen.[73]

By March 7, Sherman's entire command had not crossed the state line into North Carolina. However, by noon of that day advance units of the Twentieth Corps reached Marks Station on the Wilmington, Charlotte, and Rutherford Railroad. Here Major General J. W. Geary's division destroyed three-quarters of a mile of track and a large quantity of new iron rails.[74] Sherman had ordered the railroad destroyed. To the commander of his left wing, Henry W. Slocum, he wrote: "En route break the railroad which is known as the Wilmington and Charlotte. . . . It is of little importance, but being on it, we might as well use up some of its iron."[75]

On this same date the depot and temporary railroad shops at Laurinburg were burned.[76]* This probably was done by Captain William Duncan's scouts who were reported on March 7 to have reached the railroad and destroyed some trestlework.[77]

On March 8, North Carolina for the first time felt the full weight of Sherman's army, the right wing having crossed the state line on that date. The two columns of the Fifteenth Corps united at Laurel Hill,† five miles west of Laurinburg, and went into camp. The remainder of the wing bivouacked along the banks of the treacherous Lumber River, called Drowning Creek in its upper reaches.[78]

North Carolinians shuddered to think what was in store for them. They were fully aware of South Carolina's treatment at the hands of an army that applied total war in its severest terms. As a "Yankee" private put it: "South Carolina will be no more till she is rebuilt. What a terrible curse has she been visited with. She was deserving of it certainly, but I sincerely wish I had not been a spectator of her devastation, or one of the army that invaded her. . . . Oh! I have seen too much of war already."[79]‡

* The railroad shops had been moved to Laurinburg in the hope that they would be safe from the Federal forces besieging Fort Fisher. R. H. Cowan to J. R. Hawley, Apr. 24, 1865, J. F. Boyd Papers, DU. Several residents of Wilmington also moved to Laurinburg, thinking they would be safe from the invaders.

The reports of Federal officers do not mention the destruction of any property in Laurinburg. It is known, however, that a new railroad shop was built in the town soon after the war was over and that it was built on the site of the old shop. *Proceedings, Stockholders of the Wilmington, Charlotte and Rutherford Railroad Company* (Wilmington: William H. Bernard's Printing and Publishing House, 1866), p. 24.

† The soldiers destroyed the Murdock Morrison gun factory which was nearby. D. Brown, "Sherman Closed Tar Heel Business," Raleigh *N and O*, July 26, 1953.

‡ Lieutenant C. S. Brown, Twenty-first Michigan, expressed similar sentiments: "South Carolina may have been the cause of the whole thing, but she has had an awful punishment." C. S. Brown to "Etta," Apr. 26, 1865, C. S. Brown Papers, DU.

CHAPTER XV

"Kilpatrick's Shirt-Tail Skedaddle"

GENERAL SHERMAN was traveling with the Fifteenth Corps on March 8 when it crossed the line into North Carolina, and that evening both the General and the corps went into camp near Laurel Hill Presbyterian Church, a region his soldiers thought looked "real northern like. Small farms and nice white, tidy dwellings."[1]

The torrential rains that set in on this date, making it one of ". . . the most disagreeable . . . of the whole campaign" continued the following day.[2] The roads soon became a sea of mud and water, almost impassable for troops and trains. The most formidable obstacle in the path of the army was the dark swirling water of Lumber River and its adjacent swamps.[3] This region brought from Sherman the remarks: "It was the damnest marching I ever saw."[4]

The wagons and artillery could only be dragged along by the mules with the assistance of soldiers who either tugged at ropes ahead of the teams or put their hands to the wheels.[5] The teamsters, reins in one hand, constantly punctuated the air with a dexterous whip lash to remind each poor mule of his "black military heart" and endless faults. Every sentence was ordained with an oath.[6] "Such a wild scene of splashing and yelling and swearing and braying has rarely greeted mortal eyes and ears," wrote one Ohioan of Sherman's army. After darkness the work was carried on in the eerie light of thousands of torches and blazing pine trees.[7]

General Sherman, still riding with the Fifteenth Corps, took refuge on the night of March 9 from a "terrible storm of rain" in a little Presbyterian church called Bethel.[8] Refusing the bit of carpet one of his staff had improvised into a bed on the pulpit platform, the General stretched himself out on one of the wooden pews for the night.[9] Outside in the cold and rain were the men of the Fifteenth Corps, many of them without shoes or blankets. Those fortunate enough still to have their rubber ponchos used them primarily to shield their pine-knot fires from the rain.[10] Someone left a momento of Sherman's visit to Bethel in the form of a few suggestions for the preacher. Pencilled in the church Bible are the following lines: "Mr. McNeil will please preach a sermon on the illusions of pleasure and hope—Mr. McNeil will please prove the absurdity of the universalist doctrine—Mr. McNeil will please preach a sermon from the First Epistle of John 4 chapter—Mr. McNeil will please pray for old Abe—By Order—W. T. Sherman—Major General Commander—U. S. Forces."[11]

Not far from Bethel Church, at the meeting hall of the Richmond Temperance and Literary Society,* could be found another reminder of Sherman's visit. J. M. Johnson, secretary of the society, entered in the minutes, April 22, 1865:

> After a considerable interruption, caused by the unwelcome visit of Sherman's thieves, the Society meets again. And, of course, when God's own house is outraged by the Yankee brutes, temples of morality and science will not be respected.
>
> We find the ornaments of our fair little Hall shattered and ruined; our book shelves empty; the grove strewn with fragments of valuable, precious volumes; the speeches and productions of members who are sleeping in silent graves, torn and trampled in the mire, "as pearls before the swine."
>
> Ye illiterate beasts! Ye children of vice! Ye have not yet demoralized us. Today we marshall our little band again; and with three cheers for Temperance and literature, unfurl our yet triumphant banner to the breeze.[12]

Before General Blair ordered the Seventeenth Corps to move from Campbell's Bridge on March 9, he sent a mounted infantry regiment to Lumberton,† some thirty miles east, with orders to burn all bridges and railroad property in the area. Since late February the people of Lumberton had been in a dilemma as to Sherman's destination. The Methodist minister in town, Washington S. Chaffin, said that each day

---

* The old Temperance Hall still stands outside of Wagram in Scotland County. (In 1865 Scotland was a part of Richmond County.)

† Lumberton was not the only town in Robeson County visited by Sherman's men. A resident of the village of Philadelphus, after passing through "the ordeal of brutal, inhuman and merciless Yankieism," wrote: "They visited us in torrents" and acted like "escaped fiends from the lower regions. . . ." [?] to Kate McGeachy, Mar. 27, 1865, Catherine (McG) Buie Papers, DU.

brought a different rumor as to Sherman's whereabouts.[13] It so happened that Chaffin had just entered in his diary on March 9: "The Yankees are said to be in two different places near here. I am incredulous. . . ." when shouts of "The Yankees are coming, the Yankees are coming" were heard in the distance. Dropping his pen, the minister rushed to the window where he saw the streets instantaneously fill up with troops. In front of his very door, Chaffin saw a neighbor of his fired upon twice when he tried to run. Before the pastor fully realized what was happening, a cavalryman had robbed him of Mrs. Chaffin's watch and stolen his horse, Kate.[14] In this raid the Federals destroyed the wagon and railroad bridges over the Lumber River, the rail depot, six box cars, and about one mile of track.[15] Following their usual custom, the soldiers entered many houses and committed many depradations. After the troops departed, the clergyman completed the entry in his diary which had been so rudely interrupted. His chief concern seemed not to be for his wife, "who was greatly excited," but for Kate whom he had owned for "five years, 11 months, 17 days—she had never been sick—I traveled with her on horseback, etc., 17,102 miles."[16]

Nightfall of this same day found the Seventeenth, Fourteenth, and Twentieth Corps encamped at Raft Swamp between the fifteen and twenty-mile posts on the Fayetteville plank road and near McFarland's Bridge over the Lumber River.* The day's march, because of heavy rains, had been extremely difficult for all. Practically every foot of the way had to be corduroyed with fence rails and split saplings.

The Federal cavalry under General Kilpatrick had crossed the Lumber River on the night of March 8 and at Solemn Grove (Monroe's Cross-Roads), a crossroads around ten miles north of Love's Bridge, had struck the rear of Lieutenant General W. J. Hardee's column, capturing a number of prisoners.[17] From these prisoners Kilpatrick learned that General Hampton's cavalry was a few miles in the rear and marching rapidly for Fayetteville. An examination of his map showed Kilpatrick that Hampton could be moving on any one or more of three different roads. Hoping to intercept the Confederate cavalry, Kilpatrick assigned each of his brigades the corner of a triangle that not only crossed the possible enemy lines of march but also made it feasible for the brigades to protect one another.[18]

* On the tenth, General Blair had the Rockfish Textile Mill (318 looms) destroyed. It was located between the Lumber River and Fayetteville. *OR*, XLVII, Ser. I, Pt. I, 382.

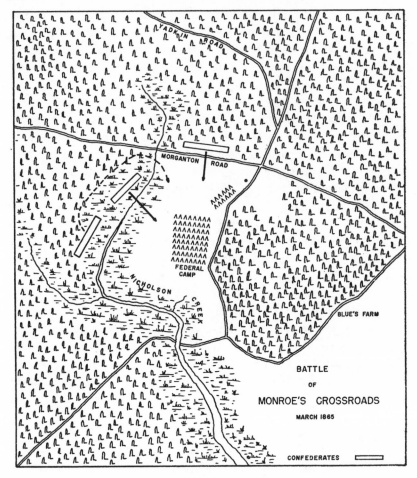

BATTLE
OF
MONROE'S CROSSROADS
MARCH 1865

The excitement and graveness of an expected clash with Hampton caused the Federal commander to spend much of the afternoon passing from one of his detachments to another. For consolation in such troubled times, "Litle Kil" shared the carriage of a beautiful young lady accompanying the army north. Made to walk behind the carriage was a Confederate prisoner, Lieutenant H. Clay Reynolds, who was able to view from close range the entertaining spectacle of the General lying with his head in his lady friend's lap.[19] That night Kilpatrick made his camp with Colonel George E. Spencer's brigade north of Solemn Grove.

About dusk the Confederate cavalry, lead by Major General M. C. Butler's division of Hampton's command, approached the vicinity of Solemn Grove. Captain M. B. Humphrey's squadron, Sixth South Carolina cavalry, was the advance guard of the column, and Wheeler's division brought up the rear. At the intersection of one of the Fayetteville roads, Humphrey noticed that a heavily mounted column had just passed. He reported the fact to Butler, and while they were discussing the situation, a squad of thirty Federal cavalrymen of the Fifth Kentucky appeared on the road. By a bit of trickery, Butler was able to capture all of them without firing a shot,[20] with the exception of General Kilpatrick, who was with the detachment at the moment but managed to escape with his staff.[21]

Hampton, upon learning that Kilpatrick was near, decided to atatack the Federal camp at daylight the next morning, March 10. During the early part of the evening, one of Kilpatrick's officers mistakenly rode into the Confederate lines and was brought immediately to General Butler for questioning. Butler was able to learn from this officer the location of Kilpatrick's headquarters, which were in the Charles Monroe dwelling. Around midnight Butler reconnoitered the Federal position and learned that Kilpatrick had posted no pickets to protect his rear. This enabled Butler and his men to ride almost up to the camp fires without being noticed. Kilpatrick had moved around the head of a swamp and pitched his camp in front of it. His rear and right were protected by the swamp, but his left was entirely exposed.

With this information Generals Hampton, Wheeler, and Butler formed their plan of battle. The attack, which was to commence at daylight, was to be led by Butler. He was to move when the head of Wheeler's column appeared in the rear. He was to follow the road taken by Kilpatrick, move around the head of the swamp, and fall suddenly on the Federal camp from the west. Wheeler had instructions to move through the woods to the right and attack from the rear. Captain Bostick of Young's brigade was given the task of capturing General Kilpatrick. He was instructed upon entering the Federal camp at daylight to rush straight for the house in which Kilpatrick had his headquarters. He was to surround the building and hold his position until assistance came.[22]

By nine o'clock on the evening of March 9, Brigadier Generals Thomas J. Jordan and Smith D. Atkins, commanding Kilpatrick's First and Second Brigades respectively, discovered that while Hampton had been amusing them in front, he was passing with his main force on a road to his right. These officers at once made every effort to reach Kilpatrick before dawn but failed to do so, owing to bad roads and almost incessant skirmishing with the Confederates, who were marching on a parallel road at some points not a mile distant.[23] The Confederate and Federal columns were so close that some of the time they became mixed together. One of Wheeler's men said that on this particular night he happened to glance up one time and discovered, much to his surprise, that a number of Federal cavalrymen were riding by his side and that by the time he had reported this to his captain at the head of the column, the Federals had disappeared, taking with them as prisoners the Confederate rear guard.[24]

The night hours dragged by for Butler's men who halted in the woods near the enemy camp. The period was passed in complete silence and darkness. All conversation was prohibited. No fires were allowed. Each man sat on the ground holding the bridle-rein of his saddled mount and wondering what the morning held for him.[25] Occasionally passing through the mind of a trooper was the intriguing thought that he might get a close look at Kilpatrick's fair lady.[26] Just before the break of dawn, Colonel "Gid" Wright of Butler's division gave the long-awaited command to mount up, and with the first rays of daylight, he struck Kilpatrick's camp, which was found to be without a picket or camp guard. Following immediately in his rear was General Butler with the other brigades. Riding into a sleeping camp, the Confederate cavalrymen were able to put the entire Federal command, including the General himself, to flight in less than a minute. For a moment it looked like a cyclone had struck the encampment. Blankets were flying in the air and men in their night clothes were running in every direction. A stampede on foot was underway.[27] Kilpatrick called this attack "the most formidable cavalry charge I have ever witnessed."[28] Although his headquarters were taken, the General managed to avoid capture and reached his camp a few hundred yards to the rear, where a fight was going on between his men and the Confederates for possession of the camp and animals.*

* A detail of twenty men had been picked from Hampton's ranks and given instructions to slip into the Federal camp to capture Kilpatrick before the general charge started. This detail was within twenty yards of the General's headquarters when the

General Judson Kilpatrick recapturing his headquarters at Monroe's Crossroads after being routed by Confederate cavalry. (From *Harper's Weekly*)

To make his escape "Little Kil" had to spring from the warm bed of his lovely lady.[29] The first thought to enter his mind at the sound of piercing "Rebel" yells was not the embarrassment of having such a delightful nocturnal slumber abruptly interrupted but that his four years of hard fighting for a major general's commission were going up with the surprise attack. The initial shock of this unexpected visit did not completely separate the cavalry commander from his wits, however. While standing in front of his headquarters, a Confederate rider dashed up to Kilpatrick and asked him if he had seen the General, to which he replied, "There he goes on that black horse," pointing to a man making off on such a mount. Thereupon the soldier pursued the figure pointed out to him. Kilpatrick, clad only in his night clothes, then jumped upon the nearest horse and made a hasty departure.[30]*

By this time, chance bullets were fast perforating the weatherboards of the headquarters house. This was sufficient to bring the General's forsaken damsel to the doorway.† For a moment she looked disconsolately at her carriage as if the vague idea were dawning that it was time for her to be leaving. This was followed by a short period of mute despair when it became apparent to her that the carriage would not

fighting commenced. P. Hamilton, "The Effort to Capture Kilpatrick," *Confederate Veteran*, XXIX (Sept., 1921), 329.

* In his official report Kilpatrick states that he made his escape on foot. *OR*, XLVII, Ser. I, Pt. II, 786.

† The true identity of Kilpatrick's lady companion was never determined. In all probability it was the beautiful Mary Boozer who had traveled north with Sherman's army from Columbia, South Carolina. See J. G. Barrett, *Sherman's March through the Carolinas* (Chapel Hill: Univ. of N.C. Press, 1956), pp. 93, 97.

move without horses. The strange apparition of a lovely young woman in scanty night dress on the field of battle brought one Confederate captain's horse to a fast halt. Southern chivalry rose to the occasion. Dismounting, the cavalryman led the distressed one to the safety of a nearby ditch.[31]

Shortly thereafter Kilpatrick and his cavalrymen were driven back some five hundred yards to the swamp. The Confederates, however, did not follow up this initial success. General Kilpatrick said they stopped to plunder and this gave him time to rally his men.[32] General Butler explained this loss of initiative by the fact that Wheeler was unable to cross the swamp and attack from the rear[33]* and that Brigadier General E. M. Law's brigade, which he ordered to move up and take possession of the camp after Wright's command had been scattered, had been, without his knowledge, ordered to some other point by General Hampton.[34] No matter what the cause, the fact remains that the Confederate cavalry did not follow up their surprise attack. This enabled the Federals to rally and, with the aid of rapid-firing Spencer carbines, to retake their camp and artillery.† The artillery they turned on the disorganized Confederates, driving them out of the camp.

About eight o'clock, Brigadier General J. G. Mitchell's brigade of the Fourteenth Corps came to Kilpatrick's assistance. Although the fighting was over, this infantry brigade moved into position and remained with Kilpatrick until 1:30 P.M.

The casualty reports of this skirmish are both confusing and contradictory. Kilpatrick reported that he lost 4 officers killed and 7 wounded, 15 men killed and 61 severely and several slightly wounded, and 103 officers and men taken prisoners. He further stated that over 80 Confederate dead and a great number of wounded were left in his

---

* General Butler is mistaken in his statement that Wheeler's command was not engaged in the fighting at Solemn Grove. See W. G. Allen, "About the Fight at Fayetteville, N.C.," *Confederate Veteran*, XIX (Sept., 1911), 433-34; J. A. Jones, "Fayetteville Road Fight," *Confederate Veteran*, XIX (Sept., 1911), 434; S. Bennett, "Another Brief Account," *Confederate Veteran*, XIX (Sept., 1911), 434. General Kilpatrick in his official report mentions two of Wheeler's divisions as being engaged in the action. *OR*, XLVII, Ser. I, Pt. II, 787. Wheeler in reporting the engagement lists the wounded in his command. *Ibid.*, Pt. I, 1130.

† Lieutenant Colonel Joseph F. Waring of Hampton's cavalry thought it was to the enemy's credit that they rallied so "promptly after the first surprise." J. F. Waring Diary, Mar. 10, 1865, SHC. See also W. S. Nye, "Monroe's Creek Fight," Fayetteville *Observer*, Nov. 15, 1939.

camp and that 30 prisoners and 150 horses were captured. The horses had been abandoned in the swamp.[35]

Wheeler said he took over 350 prisoners.[36] General Johnston put the figure at 500 plus 173 Confederate prisoners that were freed.[37]

Kilpatrick's escape on the morning of the surprise attack is as controversial a subject as the number of casualties suffered on each side. The Union General told M. C. Butler after the war that on this particular morning he had walked out of his headquarters in his slippers about daylight, as was his usual custom, to see that his horses were fed.[38] Such a habit was certainly the exception rather than the rule for most high-ranking officers. A Confederate soldier who participated in this surprise attack presumed Kilpatrick to be the only example from Joshua to the nineteenth century of a major general who would walk out of a warm room in cold weather only partially dressed to see horses fed one hundred yards away.[39]

Captain T. F. Northrop, Kilpatrick's chief scout, said he saw General Kilpatrick before he had a chance to change his clothes and that the General had on shirt, vest, trousers, and slippers or shoes, but he was without hat, coat, and probably boots. He states emphatically that no nightshirt was in evidence.[40] However, J. W. DuBose, in his article "The Fayetteville (N.C.) Road Fight," quotes Sergeant A. F. Hardee, one of Wheeler's scouts, as follows: "General Kilpatrick left his hat, coat, pants, sword, and pistols, etc."[41]

The General did lose around thirty valuable horses from his headquarters.[42] Among them were his two fine stallions, one a small spotted horse and the other a large black.[43]

There will be disagreement always as to who actually got the better of the fighting at Solemn Grove (Monroe's Cross-Roads), contemptuously tagged by the Federal infantry as "Kilpatrick's Shirt-tail Skedaddle."[44] Yet, the fact stands that by engaging Kilpatrick in battle, Hampton was able to open the road to Fayetteville, which the Federal camp had blocked. The Confederate cavalry joined Hardee near Fayetteville that night. But there was little rest in store for the weary horsemen.

Early on the morning of March 11, General O. O. Howard, commander of Sherman's right wing, ordered Captain William Duncan to take all of the available mounted men at his headquarters to scout toward Fayetteville.[45] Finding a by-road not picketed by the Confederates, Duncan entered the city and surprised General Hampton. Had it not been for one of Hampton's best scouts, Hugh Scott, the General might have been captured. Scott was able to warn Hampton in time for the General to rally seven followers—two members of his staff, three privates from Company K of the Fourth South Carolina cavalry, Scott, and one man said to have been from Wheeler's command whose name is unknown—and charge Duncan, who had drawn up his command of sixty-eight in a nearby street.[46] Confused by the suddenness of the attack, the Federals wheeled about and ran, but less than one hundred yards down the street was a sharp turn to the left into the by-road by which they had entered the city and by which they must escape. Here they became jammed together, and in the confusion all organization was lost. Eleven Federals were killed and twelve were captured. Among those taken prisoner were Captain Duncan and a Federal spy, David Day, who was dressed in a Confederate uniform.[47] Two of these casualties were reported as having been inflicted by General Hampton himself, but this failed to impress the Confederate General, Lafayette McLaws, who by this time, was fed up with tales of South Carolina heroism. In his order book he wrote: "Report says he killed two with his own hand, but the chivalry have fallen so deep into the pit of 'want of chivalry' that they are constantly inventing Munchausen as to the prowess of those from that state, of defaming others in order that thereby they appear elevated by the contrast."[48] Had McLaws known it, he could have ridiculed another South Carolinian, E. L. Wells, who boasted of having cleaved in one fellow's head with his saber in addition to using his pistol freely.[49] As far as is known, the only Confederate casualty was a handsome, well-bred mare ridden by one of the privates.[50]

After this street fight, General Butler could sympathize with Kilpatrick in his embarrassment of fleeing, not fully clothed, before the enemy. Captain Duncan's surprise visit to Fayetteville caught Butler and Lieutenant E. Thornton Tayloe sound asleep in a private home while a Negro woman behind the house scrubbed the only uniforms and underclothes they possessed. They were awakened when a courier burst into their room shouting, "The Yankees, the Yankees!" The two officers then had no option but to spring into the three pieces of wearing apparel available for each—boots, overcoats, and hats. Butler and Tayloe galloped off at a fast clip, though not in the direction of the firing.[51]

Major General G. A. Smith, commanding the Fourth Division of Sherman's Seventeenth Corps, sent two hundred mounted men to the assistance of Duncan's scouts, but they arrived too late to help the Captain.[52] Aided by General Howard's escort, also ordered forward, this detachment got possession of Arsenal Hill and undertook to save the bridge over the Cape Fear. While they were engaged in this, General Smith's leading brigade entered the city.

By this time the Confederate cavalry had, for the most part, withdrawn across the river, placed a section of a battery of artillery in position, and opened fire on the Federal skirmish line. Even in the face of the fire the Federals were able to get within two hundred yards of the bridge before it was fired.[53] This can be attributed in part to the high mettle of a captured horse General Smith's adjutant was riding. With the sudden blast of a brass band, the adjutant's horse ran away and headed straight for the bridge. The Federal skirmishers, thinking this a bold attempt to save the crossing, followed the runaway horse and its frightened rider in the direction of the river,[54] but the Confederates had piled large quantities of rosin upon the bridge, and it was already in flames and burning "beautifully" when the squad reached it.[55]

Mayor Archibald McLean made a formal surrender of the city to Lieutenant Colonel William E. Strong of Howard's staff and then to General Slocum who arrived shortly thereafter. Next, the United States flag was raised over the market place.[56]

General Sherman reached Fayetteville on March 11,* and set up headquarters in the old United States Arsenal, whose cream colored buildings comprised the handsomest structures in town and whose well-kept grounds served as a municipal park.[57] On the same day immediate preparations were made to lay two pontoon bridges across the

---

* While at Laurel Hill, Sherman had selected three enlisted men and given them a dispatch to deliver to the Commanding General at Wilmington. It read: "We are marching for Fayetteville, will be there Saturday, Sunday and Monday, and then march for Goldsboro. If possible, send a boat up Cape Fear River, and have word conveyed to General Schofield that I expect to meet him about Goldsboro." OR, XLVII, Ser. I, Pt. II, 713; *Ibid.*, Pt. I, 203; J. Pike, *The Scout and Ranger: Being the Personal Adventures of Corporal Pike of the Fourth Cavalry* (Cincinnati: J. R. Hawley and Co., 1865), p. 382. On Sunday, March 12, a boat arrived in Fayetteville with a reply from General Terry at Wilmington. "The effect was electric," Sherman wrote, "and no one can realize the feeling unless like us, he had been cut off from all communications with friends. . . ." W. T. Sherman, *Memoirs of General W. T. Sherman* (New York: D. Appleton and Co., 1875), II, 295. See also G. B. McMillian Diary, Mar. 12, 1865, HSW; G. T. Spaulding to Wife, Mar. 13, 1865, G. T. Spaulding Papers, HSW.

Cape Fear, one near the burned bridge, and another about four miles down the river.

While at Fayetteville, Sherman took the opportunity to replace all rejected animals of his trains with those taken from the local citizens and to clear his columns of the vast crowd of white refugees and Negroes that followed the Federal army. He called these followers "twenty to thirty thousand useless mouths."[58] To General Terry he wrote: "They are dead weight to me and consume our supplies."[59] On March 12, Sherman wrote Grant that he could leave Fayetteville the next day were it not for the large crowd of refugees that encumbered his army.[60]

Major John A. Winsor, One Hundred and Sixteenth Illinois, was detailed to conduct this refugee train to Wilmington. A guard of one hundred men from each wing of the army was sent along as escort for the train.[61] Fenwick Y. Hedley, in his book *Marching Through Georgia,* gives an interesting description of this refugee train as it left Fayetteville for the coast:

The white refugees and freedmen traveled together in the column, and made a comical procession. They had the worst possible horses and mules, and every kind of vehicle, while their costuming was something beyond description. Here was a cumbersome, old-fashioned family carriage, very dilapidated, yet bearing traces of gilt and filagree, suggesting that it had been a very stylish affair fifty years before. On the driver's seat was perched an aged patriarch in coarse plantation breeches, with sky-blue, brass-buttoned coat very much out of repair and his gray grizzled wool topped off with an old fashioned silk hat. By his side rode mater-familias, wearing a scoop-shovel bonnet resplendent with faded ribbons and flowers of every color of the rainbow, a silk or satin dress of great antiquity, and coarse brogans on her feet. The top of the carriage was loaded with featherbed, two or three skillets, and other "plunder." From the glassless windows of the clumsy vehicle peered half a score of pickaninnies of all sizes, their eyes big with wonder. Elsewhere in the column a pair of "coons" rode in a light spring wagon, one urging the decrepit horse to keep up with the procession, while the other picked a banjo and made serious attempts to sing a plantation song, which was almost invariably of a semi-religious character. Those who traveled on foot, men and women, of all colors from light mulatto to coal black, loaded down with bedding, clothing and provisions, were legion. Occasionally, a wagon was occupied by white refugees, who, being unionist, had been despoiled by the Confederates. These were sad and hopeless. The colored people, on the contrary, were invariably gay hearted, regarding their exodus as a pleasure trip, and evidently strong in the faith of their lot, on "gittin to freedom," was to be one of bliss.[62]

Overlooked by Hedley in his description was what General Slocum called the "best way of transporting pickaninnies." This unique procedure came to the attention of the refugees one day when a large family of slaves came through the fields to join the trains of the left wing. Mounted on a mule was the head of the family and safely stored away behind him, in bags attached to a blanket covering the animal, were two small Negro children, one on each side. The next day more than one mule appeared in column covered by a blanket, which in some instances had as many as ten or fifteen bags tacked to it. Nothing was visible of the mule except head, tail, and feet, all else being covered by the black, wooly heads and bright shining eyes of little children. Occasionally a cow was substituted for the mule. This was a decided improvement as the cow furnished rations as well as transportation.[63]

General Sherman especially wanted to reach Fayetteville so that he could retake the arsenal located there,[64] assuming the United States government would never again trust North Carolina with such property to appropriate at her pleasure.[65] He assigned the First Regiment of Michigan engineers the task of thoroughly demolishing the arsenal and its machinery.[66] Early on the morning of March 11, however, the Confederate authorities had shipped out of Fayetteville by rail some of the arsenal's machinery and stores. The machinery was hidden at the Egypt Coal Mines in Chatham County, while many of the stores were carried on to Greensboro by wagon.[67] Also escaping Sherman's destructive order were a few Enfield rifles passed out to Hardee's troops during their short stay in Fayetteville.[68]

Specific instructions were issued by General Sherman as to what property was to be destroyed in town. In Special Field Orders, No. 28, he directed General Slocum to lay pontoons for crossing the Cape Fear, "but in the meantime . . . [to] destroy all railroad property, all shops, factories, tanneries, etc. and all mills save one water-mill of sufficient capacity to grind meal for the people of Fayetteville."[69] All of this property was destroyed and much more.[70] E. J. Hale, Jr., son of the editor of the *Fayetteville Observer,* estimated that his father's property, before the war, was easily convertible "into $85 to 100,000 in specie," but after Sherman's departure he had "not . . . a particle of property" which would bring him "a dollar of income. . . . In fact," the younger

Hale wrote, "he has nothing left, besides the ruins of his town buildings and a few town lots which promise to be of little value hereafter, in this desolate town. . . ."[71]

Besides the actual firing of property, there was considerable pillaging, but this plundering of private property was done, for the most part, before Major General Absalom Baird took command of the city and garrisoned it with his three brigades. After guards were posted at public building and at nearly every private house, good order was established and maintained.[72] Baird stated in his report that, upon his arrival in the city, he found stragglers from all portions of the army who had pushed in with the advance guard and committed "many disorders" before he could clear them out.[73] These "bummers" did a very thorough job of pillaging during their short stay in Fayetteville. An eye witness to this chaotic scene was certain that every house and store in town, except where guards were promptly obtained, was entered and robbed "of everything valuable or fit to eat. . . ."[74]

For over a week the "bummers" had been happily anticipating the spoils awaiting them in Fayetteville. Many of them had not reported to their commands since leaving Cheraw, preferring to camp each night with the extreme advance. Five of this number became so bold as to venture into town the day before it was taken. Such foolhardiness cost one life and brought no plunder. The morning of March 11, though, found scores of "bummers" hovering around the outskirts of Fayetteville, impatiently watching for the lead columns that they planned to join as skirmishers. But once inside the limits it was plunder, not the enemy, that these men "went for."[75] They were a happy group to greet the occupying forces of General Baird's division. On one corner stood a big strapping soldier beside a barrel of whiskey. With gourd in hand, he made a valiant effort to treat the entire Fourteenth Corps as it marched by. On another corner stood a "bummer" who, from a large box of tobacco, would throw a plug to anyone asking for a chew. Upon some columns it "literally rained tobacco. . . ." Meeting with less success than his two companions, but still enjoying himself tremendously, was a third soldier who gave away books from a large stack by his side.[76]

Despite all this lawlessness, very little personal violence was inflicted upon the people of Fayetteville. The exceptions occurred when two or three of the local gentlemen were forcibly divested of their pants, boots, and watches.[77]

Houses in the suburbs and vicinity suffered more severely than those in town.* The nights were illuminated by the glare of blazing houses all through the pine groves for several miles around Fayetteville.[78]

The diary of James Evans, a planter living near Fayetteville, chronicles well these hectic days:

March 12, 1865—clear and cool, Yanks in my house about 11 o'clock A.M. March 13, 1865—clear, over 1000 Yanks in my house during the day and niggers in vast numbers, in the yard and out-houses, stole all of my provisions, and a large amount of other things, all my cattle, horses, mules, Buggy Wagons, Hogs. . . . March 14, 1865—very cloudy. Thousands of Yanks in the yard and house all day. March 15, 1865—very rainy, Thousands of Yanks in house and yard and field, plantation entirely covered with them, from one side to the other, burnt one hundred thousand rails.[79]

The first chance he got, Evans sat down and itemized his "losses by the infernal Yanks." The items ranged from four "demi Johns" valued at $5.00 to sixty-eight shares of "Bridge Stock" worth $2,500. All told, Evans estimated his losses at $6,391. "Besides," he wrote, "they cut many of my apple trees and some of the shade trees and took many small articles that I have not enumerated. The 9 negroes were a curse to me, yes, a real and substantial scourge."[80]

The food situation became acute for the citizens of Fayetteville soon after Sherman's troops arrived in the city. The invading army found

*A lady living near Fayetteville told the following story of a visit from Sherman's men: "There was no place, no chamber, truck, drawer, desk, garret, closet, or cellar that was private to their unholy eyes. Their rude hands spared nothing but our lives. . . . Squad after squad unceasingly came and went and tramped through halls and rooms of our house day and night. . . . At our house they killed every chicken, goose, turkey, cow, calf, and every living thing, even to our pet dog. They carried off wagons, carriage, and horses, and broke our buggy, wheelbarrow, garden implements, axes, hatchets, hammers, saws, etc., and burned the fences. Our smoke house and pantry, that a few days ago were well stored with bacon, lard, flour, dried fruit, meat, pickles, preserves, etc., now contain nothing whatever except a few pounds of meal and flour and five pounds of bacon. They took from old men, women, and children alike, every garment of wearing apparel save what he had on, not even sparing the napkins of infants, blankets, sheets, quilts, etc., such as it did not suit them to take away they tore to pieces before our eyes." Unidentified newspaper clipping, Emma Mordecai Diary, 1864-65, SHC. See also C. P. Mallett to C. P. Spencer, Mar. 22, 1865, C. P. Spencer Papers, SHC; C. P. Spencer, *The Last Ninety Days of the War in North Carolina* (New York: Watchman Publishing Co., 1866), pp. 67-68. Some of the planters had already suffered from the depredations of Confederate deserters. J. C. MacRae to D. MacRae, Apr. 3, 1865, H. MacRae Papers, DU.

much flour and corn and immediately proceeded to take most of it, as well as making a clean sweep of all pantries and smokehouses that they had time to plunder. It was doubtful if all of Fayetteville, the day after the entrance of the Federal troops, could have contributed a bushel of meal to the relief of the Confederate army, so completely had every house in town been visited.[81] A well-known gentleman of the city wrote on March 14: "There will not be left more than fifty head of four-footed beasts in the country and not enough provisions to last ten days. Many, very many families have not a mouthful to eat. We have meal and meat to last two weeks, by eating two meals a day."[82] Captain Dexter Horton, an observant young Federal officer of the Fourteenth Corps, entered in his diary on March 13, that all of the residents were out of "grub." The next day he wrote that he had seen many sad sights, such as weeping mothers with babies in their arms begging for meal.[83] The hungry had to apply to the Federal commissary for meal and then go to one of the mills to get it. Not only the civilians but also Confederate officers on parole had to beg sustenance.[84] The city's grist mills were operated as long as the Federal troops occupied the city, but when they left, all but one were destroyed.[85]

After a week in North Carolina, the invading army had found booty and destroyed property, but they had found little evidence of the supposedly strong Union sentiment among the people. One of Sherman's aides, Major George W. Nichols, wrote: "Thus far we have been painfully disappointed in looking for the Union sentiment in North Carolina about which so much has been said. Our experience is decidedly in favor of its sister state; for we found more persons in Columbia who had proved their fealty to the Union cause by their friendliness to our prisoners than all this state put together. The city of Fayetteville was offensively rebellious. . . ."[86]

Theodore Upson, One Hundredth Indiana, agreed with Major Nichols. He wrote in his diary that he heard a good sermon in Fayetteville on the subject of loving one's enemies but that he thought the South had a long way to go in this respect.[87]

Captain Horton, to the contrary, thought that there was a considerable amount of affable social intercourse between the Federal army and the civilian population of the invaded city. Extracts from his diary bear out this fact.

Capt. White and myself took rooms at Mrs. Ockletra's and shall have nice beds to sleep on. Seems to be a nice lady. . . . Make [made] the acquaintance of several ladies. Certainly we are enjoying ourselves hugely. . . . Went in evening with Charlie Jones and called on Misses Lily. Spent the evening very pleasantly. Pretty girls and very talkative. . . . Had heaps of fun all day. . . . Called with Charlie Jones at Mr. Lily's. Carried them some tea, coffee, and meal. How thankful they were. The girls were very interesting and shook our hands heartily when we left. . . . Received a written order to move at about one o'clock. I had gone to bed at Mrs. Ockletra's. Guard woke me up. I bid them goodbye. They really felt bad to see me go. The old lady shed tears and said let us part as friends and hoped I would reach my family in safety.[88]

By March 15, Sherman had his entire army across the Cape Fear, and the march on Goldsboro had begun. The Seventeenth Corps, followed by the Fifteenth, marched on the right. The Fourteenth and Twentieth Corps were on the extreme left, with the cavalry acting in close concert. Sherman was in a happy frame of mind as he watched his troops move out. The campaign was running like clockwork. Goldsboro, he felt sure, would be his in a few days.[89]

CHAPTER XVI

Averasboro and Bentonville

UNTIL HE reached Fayetteville, Sherman had succeeded in interposing his army between the scattered Confederate forces and had prevented any concentrated action by Johnston. After crossing the Cape Fear, however, he was faced with the fact that most of these Confederate troops had reached North Carolina and, under the able Joe Johnston, made up an army comparable to his in cavalry* and formidable in artillery and infantry. Hence he must use caution on his march to Goldsboro.† He planned to keep his columns as compact as possible.[1]

General Kilpatrick was ordered to move up the plank road to and beyond the small village of Averasboro on the east bank of the Cape Fear. He was to be followed by four divisions of the left wing, with as few wagons as possible. The rest of the train, under escort of the two remaining divisions of that wing, was to take a shorter and more direct road to Goldsboro. In like manner, General Howard was instructed to send his trains, under good escort, well to the right toward Faison's Depot and Goldsboro and to hold four divisions light, ready to go to the aid of General Slocum's wing if it were attacked while in motion.[2]

---

* Kilpatrick's cavalry numbered 5,659. W. T. Sherman, *Memoirs of General W. T. Sherman* (New York: D. Appleton and Co., 1875), II, 334. Estimates of Hampton's command range from 4,000 to 6,726. J. E. Johnston, *Narrative of Military Operations, Directed, During the Late War Between the States, by Joseph E. Johnston, General, C.S.A.* (New York: D. Appleton and Co., 1874), p. 372; *OR*, XLVII, Sec. I, Pt. I, 1060.

† Sherman greatly overestimated the Confederate forces opposing him at 37,000 infantry and 8,000 cavalry. This was one reason he felt that it would be unwise to leave a small detachment behind to garrison the arsenal and to save this Federal property. He thought all available forces should be at hand to cope with Johnston. *OR*, XLVII, Ser. I, Pt. II, 794, 800.

Uncertain as to whether Sherman's destination after leaving Fayetteville was Raleigh or Goldsboro, Johnston selected Smithfield, a small
town about midway between the two places, as the concentration point
for his different commands.* General Bragg's troops, along with the
scattered commands of the Army of Tennessee, were ordered to Smithfield. Hardee, who was keeping just in front of Sherman's army, was
instructed to follow the road from Fayetteville to Raleigh, which for
thirty miles was also that to Smithfield. Since March 11, Hardee had
kept scouts on the west side of the Cape Fear in order to keep Johnston
informed of any Federal troops movements. It was Johnston's plan to
have Hardee's movements conform to those of Sherman, so a force
would always be at hand to delay the Federal advance if possible. If
Sherman moved on Raleigh, Bragg's troops were to be brought up and
combined with Hardee's. If Sherman, on the other hand, decided to
move on Goldsboro, Hardee was to join Bragg.[3] Hampton placed
Wheeler's cavalry division on the Raleigh road and Butler's on that to
Goldsboro.

On March 15, Kilpatrick's cavalry, preceding the left wing on the
Raleigh road, slowly pushed back Wheeler's command, which was acting as a rear guard for Hardee's corps.[4] General Hardee, encamped at
the time in the vicinity of Smith's Mill a few miles from Averasboro,
abandoned his original intention of resting a day and began to deploy
for battle. He made this decision in spite of the fact that his small
force, slightly less than six thousand strong, had been reduced both by
desertions and the withdrawal of the brigade of South Carolina militia
by Governor A. G. Magrath.† By giving battle, General Hardee hoped
to ascertain whether he was followed by the whole of Sherman's army
or a part of it and what was its destination.[5]

He ordered Colonel Alfred Rhett's brigade of Brigadier General
William B. Taliaferro's division into position in the rear of an open
field on the right of the Raleigh road. Breastworks were erected, a few
hundred yards in front of which a strong infantry skirmish line was
established.

* Sherman intended to feint strongly on Raleigh but swing rapidly on Goldsboro
when his wagons were well toward Faison's Depot. Johnston was not sure of Sherman's
intended movements even though Beauregard had written him on March 14 that Sherman was moving "doubtless to form a function with Schofield's forces around Goldsboro." *OR*, XLVII, Ser. I, Pt. II, 834-35, 1392.

† A. R. Wright's division never left the State of South Carolina.

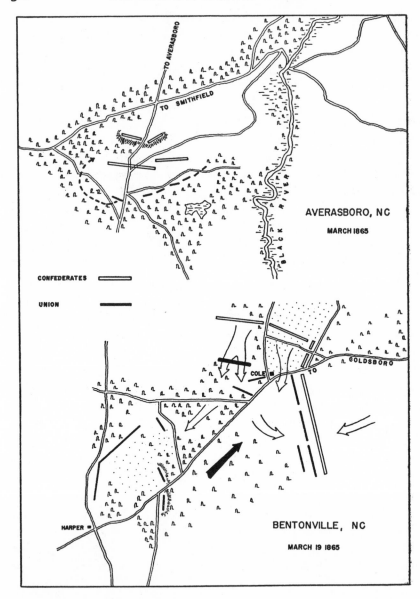

AVERASBORO, NC

MARCH 1865

CONFEDERATES

UNION

BENTONVILLE, NC

MARCH 19 1865

Hardee intended for Rhett's brigade to check only temporarily the advance of the Federals. It was his design to hold them until he was reasonably sure Taliaferro's trains were out of danger, at which time Colonel Rhett was to retire his brigade a half mile to the rear and join the brigade of Brigadier General Stephen Elliott, Jr.[6]

Around three o'clock in the afternoon Kilpatrick's column, with the Ninth Michigan in advance, struck the Confederate skirmish line. General Atkins, commanding Kilpatrick's First Brigade, deployed the Ninth Michigan on foot and succeeded in driving the Confederate skirmishers back into their works, but in so doing he drew Confederate artillery fire. While the Ninth Michigan continued to skirmish, Kilpatrick ordered Atkins to put the remainder of his brigade and the other brigades, as they came up, into position and to build barricades. When the barricades were finished, the Ninth Michigan was withdrawn. Taliaferro's troops felt out the Federal position strongly during the afternoon, but the Federal artillery kept them at a good distance most of the time.[7]

At General Kilpatrick's request, Slocum sent forward Colonel William Hawley's brigade to assist in holding the barricades. During the night Hawley took position in the center of the cavalry command, with his left resting on the main road.[8]

The day's skirmishing cost Taliaferro the services of one of his brigade commanders. Colonel Rhett was captured when he mistook a party of Federal cavalry for his own.* The Federals called on Rhett to surrender and ordered him "in language more forcible than polite" to turn and ride back. He first supposed these men to be of Hampton's cavalry and threatened to report them to their commanding officer for disrespectful language. But upon learning their true identity, Rhett surrendered.[9]

There was no skirmishing on the night of March 15 between Kilpatrick and Taliaferro, but early the next morning, Lieutenant Colonel F. A. Jones's Eighth Indiana cavalry moved on Taliaferro. Colonel Jones succeeded in driving the Confederate skirmish line back into the

---

* The capture of Colonel Rhett caused quite a stir within the Federal lines. Besides owning the handsomest boots in the Confederate army, he was a South Carolina aristocrat. The fact that Colonel Rhett had for some time been in command at Fort Sumter also contributed to the strong feeling among the Federal troops against him. A Federal officer wrote: "From the conversation of this Rebel Colonel, I judge him to be quite as impracticable a person as any of his class." Another officer called Rhett incarnate, selfish, and a "devil in human shape, who is but a type of his class and whose polished manners and easy assurance made him only more hideous to me [Major Henry Hitchcock] and utterly heartless and selfish ambition and pride of class which gave tone to his whole discourse." The officer admitted, however, that all "Southern Gentlemen" and all Confederate officers were not like Rhett. M. A. deW. Howe, ed., *Marching with Sherman: Passages from the Letters and Campaign Diaries of Henry Hitchcock, Major and Assistant Adjutant General of the Volunteers, November, 1864-May, 1865* (New Haven: Yale Univ. Press, 1927), pp. 289-90; G. W. Nichols, *The Story of the Great March from the Diary of a Staff Officer* (New York: Harper and Brothers, 1865), p. 254; Sherman, *Memoirs*, II, 301.

works. This, however, made further operations on horseback impossible and forced Jones to dismount his command and send his lead horses to the rear. The Colonel next ordered his lines to reconnect with the infantry brigade of Hawley. At this time Taliaferro attacked in force, and soon the entire Federal line was under heavy fire.

By ten o'clock Kilpatrick's dismounted cavalrymen, running dangerously low on ammunition, were close to having their right flank turned. Disaster was averted when portions of the Twentieth Corps arrived on the field just in time to stem the Confederate attack.

Three batteries of artillery were immediately placed in a commanding position by Major J. A. Reynolds, chief of artillery, Twentieth Corps. While these guns vigorously shelled the Confederate line, the Federals took the offensive. Two brigades pressed Taliaferro's front while a third, under command of Colonel Henry Case, moved in a diagonal direction toward the right of the enemy's works. Case succeeded in turning the Confederate flank, which forced Rhett's brigade, now commanded by Colonel William Butler, to fall back to the second line of defenses.[10]*

The First and Third Divisions of the Twentieth Corps followed up Case's success by advancing upon the second line of Confederate defenses. General Mitchell's brigade of the Fourteenth Corps joined them, forming to the left. At the same time, Kilpatrick was ordered to draw back his cavalry and mass it on the extreme right and to feel forward for the Goldsboro road.[11]

The cavalry moved forward under the immediate direction of General Kilpatrick, whose scouts soon reported to him that a road leading off to the right circled around to the rear of the Confederate position. Accordingly, the General ordered the Ninth Ohio cavalry to move out on that road. After advancing a short distance, the Ninth Ohio was attacked by Colonel G. P. Harrison's brigade of Lafayette McLaws' division, which was moving through underbrush so dense that the Federal cavalry did not notice it until the brigade was within a few yards of their column. The Ninth Ohio was driven back two hundred yards to high ground. There it reformed its lines and held Harrison in check until

---

* The Confederate losses were heavy during the morning's fighting. Rhett's brigade, suffered especially heavy casualties when it was routed by Case. It must be remembered, however, that Rhett's troops had previously done only garrison and artillery duty at Charleston, and this was their first experience in infantry fighting in the open.

The Battle of Averasboro, March 16, 1865. (From *Harper's Weekly*)

relieved by a brigade of infantry, at which time the Confederates withdrew.[12]

In danger of being flanked and hard pressed on his front, Taliaferro withdrew his division to the main line of defense. He took position "to the right, and left of the main road." McLaws' division was on his left and Wheeler's dismounted cavalry on his right. Most of Rhett's brigade, which had been so severely engaged all day, was held in reserve a few hundred yards in the rear of the line of works.[13]

The Federals pressed Hardee hard all afternoon and up into the early part of the evening, but they were unable to carry the Confederate works. Around 8:00 P.M., Hardee started withdrawing his troops and artillery on the Smithfield road as General Johnston had ordered.[14] Wheeler's dismounted cavalry was left behind to cover the retreat.

Generals Slocum and Kilpatrick reported their casualties for the day's fighting, called the Battle of Averasboro, at 682 killed, wounded, captured, or missing. Of the casualties, 533 were wounded.[15] This was a serious loss because none of the wounded could be left behind.* Every injured man had to be carried in an ambulance.[16]

Major Henry Hitchcock of Sherman's staff was one of the few soldiers on the field who never once had occasion to think he himself might be listed as a casualty at the day's end. The Major had spent his time with Sherman "lying around in the woods . . . while the fight . . . was going on." Much to Hitchcock's disgust, the General never ventured very near the front line. On one occasion some canister shot did splash "the mud not far off," and on another "a bullet pattered among the branches overhead." But newspaper accounts of "Tecumseh directing the battle under a warm fire" the Major knew to be "just so much poetry."[17]

* Commands with empty wagons were ordered to send them to the battlefield to carry off the wounded. W. McK. Heath Diary, Mar. 17, 1865. OHS.

The Battle of Averasboro was actually fought in a section of Harnett County called Smithville, so named after a prominent family of Smiths living in that rural neighborhood. The three homesteads belonging to Farquard, John, and William Smith survived the battle primarily because they were utilized in some capacity by both armies.[18] Janie Smith, a seventeen-year-old in the Farquard Smith home, wrote her friend Janie Robeson a lengthy and rather fiery letter on April 12, 1865, giving her impressions of the Federal soldiers and her reaction to the sight of battle. In discussing the carnage of the battlefield, this young girl declared that "the scene beggars description. The blood lay in puddles in the grove, the groans of the dying and the complaints of those undergoing amputation was horrible. I can never forget it. . . ." But to her the battlefield did not compare in stench with "such fiends incarnate as fill the ranks of Sherman's army." She also told her friend how the Federal soldiers "left no living thing in Smithville but people, and one old hen, who played sick, thus saving her neck but losing her biddies." Having lost all of her personal effects to the pillagers, Janie further declared: "If I ever see a Yankeewoman I intend to whip her and take the clothes off her very back. . . . When our army invades the North, I want them to carry the torch in one hand and the sword in the other. I want desolation carried to the heart of their country; the widows and orphans left naked and starving, just as ours were left."[19]

Janie Smith's letter, of course, told only one side of the story. There were acts of kindness on the part of the men in blue. Federal surgeons took care of the many Confederate wounded left behind at Smithville, and Sherman in person visited a makeshift hospital in one of the Smith residences while the surgeons were at work. To get inside he had to step over arms and legs left lying in the yard and on the porch. In one of the rooms was a handsome young captain named McBeth who, upon seeing the General, identified himself as having been a boy when Sherman visited in his father's home in Charleston. After inquiring of the young officer's family, Sherman enabled him to write a note to his mother, which was later mailed to her from Goldsboro.[20]

The Battle of Averasboro was little more than a skirmish, although to the soldiers involved it was "quite an engagement."[21] The battle is significant because the stout resistance put up by Hardee stopped the advance of the Twentieth Corps while General Howard's right wing, still moving on the extreme right, continued its march on Goldsboro.

As a result the columns of Slocum's left wing became strung out and the distance between the two wings of the army increased. These developments made it possible for Johnston to start preparations for battle. His plan was to isolate and crush one of the Federal columns before Sherman could get his army back in compact form.

On the morning of March 17, Kilpatrick, in accordance with Sherman's order of march, crossed Black River and moved out upon the Smithfield road to the left and front of the Fourteenth and Twentieth Corps, which were moving upon the direct road from Averasboro to Goldsboro. The distance marched by the Fourteenth Corps on March 17 was not more than six or eight miles because of the bogs and swampy creeks that lay across the way. A soldier, after patiently wading waist deep in a seemingly shoreless stream, was heard to remark: "I guess Uncle Billy has struck this stream endwise."[22] The Twentieth, following the Fourteenth Corps, moved up to Black River on the afternoon of March 17 and encamped on the west side.[23] General Howard, uncertain as to the result of the Battle of Averasboro the day before, moved the right wing only six miles on March 17.* This closed, somewhat, the distance between it and the left wing.[24]

It was almost daybreak on March 18, when information came to Johnston from his chief of cavalry, Wade Hampton, that the Federal army was definitely marching toward Goldsboro.[25] According to Confederate cavalry reports, Sherman's right wing was approximately half a day's march in advance of the left wing. With this information in mind Johnston calculated that the heads of the two columns were about a day's march from each other.

To be prepared to attack the head of the left Federal column the next morning, the troops at Smithfield and Elevation were ordered to march immediately to Bentonville, a small town approximately twenty miles west of Goldsboro, and to bivouac that night between the town and the road on which Slocum's column was marching.[26] At Smithfield, General Bragg had Hoke's division of North Carolinians, and Lieutenant General A. P. Stewart had a portion of the Army of Tennessee. At Elevation, General Hardee's command was encamped.

---

* The Seventeenth Corps moved out on the Clinton road. When it was within six miles of Clinton, the Ninth Illinois was sent forward to cover the refugee train moving from Fayetteville to Wilmington by way of Clinton. *OR,* XLVII, Ser. I, Pt. I, 383. Clinton suffered the unhappy fate of being pillaged by the "bummers." J. L. Stewart to C. P. Spencer, Jan. 1, 1867, C. P. Spencer Papers, SHC.

Following the Battle of Averasboro, Hardee had stopped at this village. He intended to give his troops several days of badly needed rest as many of them had had nothing to eat since the night of March 15 and were exhausted after the hard fight.[27] Nevertheless, at 8:50 A.M. on March 18, he sent Johnston a dispatch stating that he was putting his command in motion for Bentonville but that he was ignorant of the road Johnston had designated for him to take.[28]*

By General Johnston's map, the distance from Elevation to Bentonville was but twelve miles. This assured Johnston of the arrival of Hardee's command on the night of March 18. The map proved to be incorrect, however, and deceived Johnston greatly in relation to the distance between the two roads on which the Federal columns were marching.[29] It exaggerated considerably the distance between Howard and Slocum, and it reduced the distance between Elevation and Bentonville.[30] General Hardee found the distance too great for a day's march. He was still six miles from Bentonville by nightfall of the eighteenth. Bragg and Stewart reached the village during the night.[31]

Johnston wrote General Lee on March 18 that his effective totals, infantry and artillery, were: Bragg, 6,500; Hardee, 7,500; Army of Tennessee, 4,000.[32]† These totals, plus Hampton's cavalry, made up an army considerably less than the forty thousand troops Sherman thought opposed him.

Johnston was compensated in part for this paucity of manpower by the large number of able captains present at Bentonville. Besides Johnston and Bragg, who were both full generals, three officers—Hampton, Hardee, and Stewart—carried the rank of lieutenant general.

To give Johnston time to concentrate his forces, Hampton moved out on the eighteenth to meet the Federal advance. Fighting dismounted, his troops stopped the enemy skirmishers short of the spot selected for the battle next day.[33]

During the evening of the eighteenth, Hampton gave General Johnston all the necessary information on the position of the Federal troops. He also described the ground near the Goldsboro road, about two miles south of Bentonville, as favorable for the surprise attack. Slocum's column was moving upon this single road. The ground suggested for

---

* Johnston ordered Hardee to move from Elevation to Bentonville on a road not shown on the map. He had learned of the road from the sheriff of Johnston County.

† These figures are probably a little high. Most returns put Johnston's entire army at not more than twenty thousand effectives.

the battle was the eastern edge of an old plantation that extended a mile and a half to the west and lay principally on the north side of the road. It was surrounded east, south, and north by dense thickets of "blackjack." In the thickets were many marshes from which streams ran in all directions.[34] The Federal camp on this night was several miles nearer that ground than Hardee's bivouac, and it was only because of Hampton's vigorous efforts that the head of the Federal left wing was not past Bentonville.

Since General Johnston had not been able to examine the ground, Hampton suggested to him such disposition of the forces as he thought "would be most advantageous." The proposed plan called for the cavalry to move out at daylight and to occupy "the position held by it the previous evening." The infantry was then to be deployed "with one corps across the main road and the other two . . . to the right of the first." As soon as these positions were occupied, Hampton was to fall back and pass to the rear of the infantry line and take position on the extreme right. All offensive movements were to be delayed until Hardee should reach his position.[35]

Sunday morning, March 19, dawned clear and beautiful. For the unsuspecting Federal soldiers, everything seemed to forecast a Sunday of peace and quiet. The weary soldiers anticipated the rest that would be theirs once they reached Goldsboro. "It is a long campaign we have had," one staff officer noted in his diary, ". . . and repose would be welcome."[36] Unknown to this soldier, Hampton had moved out with his cavalry in the early morning hours to his position of the previous evening and had posted pickets within a mile of the Federal advance. Almost immediately his pickets became engaged with foragers of the Fourteenth Corps,* who were greatly surprised to find Confederate cavalry giving ground grudgingly and even being inclined to fight. So an expression of the Atlanta campaign, "They don't drive worth a damn," was brought into use again.[37] One group of foragers, under command of Major Charles Belknap, somehow managed to advance far enough to ascertain that a large Confederate force was entrenching itself on Slocum's front. Belknap dispatched one of his best men with this information to Brigadier General William P. Carlin, commanding the First Division of the Fourteenth Corps, but the messenger never reached the General.[38]

---

* The foragers always left camp several hours before the troops moved.

The Civil War in North Carolina

The movements of the Federal left wing on March 19 began at 7:00 A.M., with Carlin's division in the lead. Numerous indications on the eighteenth that a battle was in prospect prompted Carlin to prepare for the occasion.* All wagons and pack mules marched in the rear of the troops. The General even put on his newest uniform so there would not be any doubt as to his rank in the case of his capture or death.[39] Carlin advanced his troops up the road until he overtook his foragers, still skirmishing with the Confederate cavalry. At this point he was joined by General Slocum.

Although his foragers had never before been checked so near their camp, Slocum still did not suspect that Johnston had concentrated his entire army only a few miles up the road. Slocum seemed to have overlooked this indication of battle and put his faith in the report of an escaped Federal cavalry officer. This officer had reported to him that Johnston was concentrated at or near Raleigh. Consequently Slocum believed the force in his front to consist only of cavalry with a few pieces of artillery. He sent a dispatch to this effect to General Sherman, who had left his column during the morning to join Howard.[40] Sherman did not anticipate an attack. He could not see how Johnston would risk a fight with the Neuse to his back† "All signs enduced me to believe," Sherman put in his official report, "that the enemy would make no further opposition to our progress, and would not attempt to strike us in flank while in motion."[41]

The deployment of the Confederate forces was a slow process. Their

* On the eighteenth, Carlin had stopped at a farmhouse for dinner and through conversation with the head of the household learned that he was very much frightened at the prospect of a battle being fought on his farm. Carlin stated his suspicions to General Jeff Davis who repeated them to Sherman. General Sherman replied: "No Jeff, there is nothing there but . . . [Confederate] cavalry. Brush them out of the way. Good morning. I'll meet you tomorrow at Car's Bridge." Major E. C. Belknap, one of Carlin's foragers, also gained information from local citizens and Confederate wounded that Johnston planned to make a stand near Bentonville. This information was sent to General Sherman, but he did not credit it. C. E. Slocum, *Life and Services of Major General Henry Warner Slocum, Officer in the United States Army* (Toledo: Slocum Publishing Co., 1913), p. 274; W. P. Carlin, "The Battle of Bentonville," *Sketches of War History of 1861-1865. Papers Read before the Ohio Commandery of the Military Order of the Loyal Legion of the United States* (Cincinnati: Robert Clark and Co., 1888-1908), III, 235; C. E. Belknap, "Bentonville: What a Bummer Knows About It," *War Papers Read before the Military Order of the Loyal Legion of the United States, Commandery of the District of Columbia* (Washington: Published by the Commandery, 1893), No. 12, p. 6.

† Kilpatrick's poor reconnaissance work completely misled Sherman. The cavalry commander reported that "Joe Johnston [was] collecting his old Georgia army this side of Raleigh." *OR*, XLVII, Ser. I, Pt. II, 886.

march was confined to a single road through the dense "blackjack" lying between Bentonville and the battlefield.[42] Hoke's division was the first on the ground. It was formed across the Goldsboro road almost at right angles. In this line were the North Carolina Junior Reserves, "the seed corn of the Confederacy."[43] The Army of Tennessee, commanded by General A. P. Stewart, was formed to the right of Hoke, its right strongly thrown forward, conforming to the edge of the open field.* The center of Johnston's position, therefore, was not on the Goldsboro road but at the corner of the plantation, approximately a quarter of a mile north. The two wings went forward from the point, the left crossing diagonally the road on which Major General Jefferson C. Davis' Fourteenth Corps was advancing; and the right, partially hidden in a thicket, reached forward ready to envelop any force that might attempt to turn the flank.† General Hardee, who was to hold the position between Hoke and Stewart, had not reached the field when these two corps went into position. His absence left a gap in the center of the Confederate line that had to be filled by two batteries of horse artillery.

In the meantime Carlin's skirmishers were pushing Hampton back, but as their progress was slow, Brigadier General H. C. Hobart, commanding Carlin's First Brigade, was directed to deploy half of his force and move in line against the Confederates until something was developed. Just before Hobart advanced, Brigadier General G. P. Buell's Second Brigade, at the suggestion of Slocum, was sent to the left of the road to attack the Confederate right flank. The advance of Hobart had reached the Cole house in a large open field when the Confederates

---

* The remnants of this once proud Confederate army, as it marched into position, was divided into three corps—Stewart's, Lee's, and Cheatham's—commanded respectively by Major Generals W. W. Loring, D. H. Hill, and W. B. Bate. Neither Lieutenant General S. D. Lee nor B. F. Cheatham were on the field this day. Lee, severely wounded at the Battle of Nashville, had been unable to lead his corps northward from Augusta, and Major General C. L. Stevenson had done this for him. Cheatham and his division did not arrive at Bentonville until after the battle was over. The delay was at Salisbury, North Carolina, where, by March 11, men and supplies clogged the rail yard to such an extent that Cheatham's departure was delayed until March 19. R. C. Black, *The Railroads of the Confederacy* (Chapel Hill, Univ. of N.C. Press, 1952), pp. 274-78. The troops under Bate's command belonged to R. R. Cleburne's and his own divisions, constituting the only part of Cheatham's corps present on March 19.

† The ground on Johnston's front, north of the road, was clear; that south of the road was covered with thickets. *OR*, XLVII, Ser. I, Pt. I, 1056. With Johnston were four very able engineers to assist in the construction of breastworks. Mrs. J. H. Anderson, "Memorial on the Battlefield of Bentonville," *Confederate Veteran*, XXXV (June, 1928), 367.

opened with a heavy fire of artillery and musketry. The open field had to be abandoned by Hobart, so he moved three regiments to the left and front of the field into a pine thicket where light entrenchments were thrown up. The other three regiments of Hobart's First Brigade, under command of Lieutenant Colonel M. H. Fitch, were placed in position on the right of the road supporting a battery of artillery,[44] which had been ordered up and placed in position 350 yards in the rear of the Cole house. Carlin's Third Brigade, Lieutenant Colonel D. Miles commanding, was placed on the right of Colonel Fitch's three regiments. At the same time General Buell was ordered to return and form on Hobart's left. This order was issued because Buell had diverged too far to the left of the main road.[45]

It was General Slocum's plan to make repeated assaults at different points along the Confederate front. As soon as Buell reached his assigned position, General Davis ordered him to attack again on the enemy's right. In order to multiply the chances of success, Carlin instructed Colonel Miles to hit the Confederate left. Carlin also had the part of the brigade on the left of the road join Buell in his advance. The heaviest fighting centered on Hoke's position, which was charged "again and again." The attack here was so vigorous that General Bragg, never the most steadfast of battlers, thought that Hoke, slightly entrenched, would be driven from his position. He therefore urgently applied for strong reinforcements. General Hardee, the head of whose column was just appearing on the battlefield, was directed by Johnston, "most injudiciously," to send his leading division, McLaws', to Hoke's assistance.[46]* The other division, Taliaferro's, moved on to its position in the line on the extreme right. McLaws moved up very slowly, having to pass through a dense thicket or swamp. The officers sent to him as guides lost their way several times, and the division did not reach the

---

* General Hampton considered this initial Federal attack to be one of those incidents that so often change the fate of battles. This one interrupted the Confederate battle plan just at the crisis of the engagement. Hampton thought the Federals struck Hoke's division at the moment when Johnston, in accordance with the plan agreed upon, should have thrown his forces on the disorganized Federals.

Hampton was also of the opinion that Johnston made only one mistake at Bentonville: that was in ordering McLaws to Hoke's assistance. He believed that had Hardee been in the position originally assigned him at the time Hoke repulsed Miles, Hardee's and Stewart's commands could have been thrown on the flanks of the retreating Federals, probably driving the Fourteenth Corps back in disorder. W. Hampton, "Battle of Bentonville," *B and L*, eds. R. U. Johnson and C. C. Buel (New York: The Century Co., 1887), I, 703-4

ground to which it was ordered until after Hoke had decisively repulsed the Federal attack.[47]

The attack on the Confederate right was also repulsed.[48] In this fight "the Rebs held their fire," said one of Buell's young officers, "until all were within 3 rods of the works when they opened fire from all sides and gave us an awful volley. We went for them with a yell and got within 5 paces of their works. . . . I tell you it was a tight place. . . . Men pelted each other with Ramrods and butts of muskets and [we] were finally compelled to fall back. . . . [We] stood as long as man could stand and when that was no longer a possibility we run like the duce."[49]*

As Carlin's troops fell back to their former position, three soldiers left the Confederate lines and came over to the Federals. They asked to speak to someone in authority and were soon brought to General Slocum for questioning. The spokesman claimed that he and his companions were former Union soldiers who had enlisted in the Confederate army to avoid prison. He stated that behind those Confederate lines waited General Johnston with his entire army. Slocum was inclined to doubt the truth of the man's story until an aide, Major W. G. Tracy, rode up and recognized the deserter and confirmed his identity. Slocum now decided to take a defensive position and communicate with Sherman. He entrusted this important message to Major Joseph Foraker. With instructions to ride far to the right and not to spare the horse, the young officer dashed off in the direction of Howard's columns. Slocum also sent word for the two light divisions of the Twentieth Corps to hasten forward.[50]

By this time the Second Division, Fourteenth Corps, under the command of Brigadier General J. D. Morgan, had gone into position on Carlin's right, south of the Goldsboro road. John G. Mitchell's and W. Vandever's brigades formed in front and B. D. Fearing's Third Brigade to the rear.[51] Both Mitchell and Vandever deployed their respective brigades in two lines. Sturdy log works rapidly thrown up in front of these four lines had a great deal to do with the success of Morgan's command later in the day.[52] General Carlin went so far as to say that these fortifications probably saved Sherman's reputation.[53]

In response to Slocum's urgent message that the light divisions of the Twentieth Corps move forward, Major General A. S. Williams, commanding the corps, dispatched his advance, the First Division, at

* General Hill said the enemy broke in "great confusion." D. H. Hill to W. D. Gale, Mar. 31, 1865, D. H. Hill Papers, NCDAH.

double quick toward the noise of battle. It was shortly after two o'clock when the Third Brigade of this division, Brigadier General J. S. Robinson commanding, appeared on the field. Robinson was ordered to fill the gap in Carlin's line between Hobart and Miles with three of his regiments. He complied with these instructions, but three regiments were not enough to close the breach.[54] Robinson's two remaining regiments dug in to the left and rear of the Fourteenth Corps line.[55]

Between 2:30 and 2:45 P.M., Johnston was ready to take the initiative. General Hardee* was directed to charge with the right wing, composed of the Army of Tennnessee and Taliaferro's division, and General Bragg was to join in the movements with the troops of Hoke and McLaws. Johnston had already lost much valuable time when he had not immediately followed up the success of Hoke and Stewart in their repulse of Miles, Hobart, and Buell. Nevertheless, the advance was postponed another thirty minutes. Major General W. B. Bate, after a personal reconnaissance, reported that the left of the Federal line did not extend connectedly beyond his right. He urged that Taliaferro's division, lying in reserve in his immediate rear, make a detour so as to fall upon the Federal left flank. This suggestion was adopted and the division was given half an hour to get into position.[56]

Although Taliaferro had not completed his flanking movement, the Army of Tennessee moved forward in two lines at 3:15 P.M.[57] Rebel yells once more pierced the air from these tattered veterans of the disaster at Nashville. They were determined to redeem their reputation on the field of battle this day.[58] It was the renewal of "acquaintance with . . . [their] old antagonist of the Dalton and Atlanta Campaign."[59] Several of the officers "led the charge on horseback . . . with colors flying and line of battle in such perfect order . . . it looked like a picture. . . ." But for the men in Bragg's trenches, who for some reason had not been ordered forward by their commander, "it was a painful sight to see how close their battle flags were together, regiments being scarcely larger than companies and a division not much larger than a regiment should be."[60]

Passing "over the bodies of the enemy who had been killed in the [initial Federal] assault and whose faces, from exposure to the sun, had turned black," the long gray line kept advancing until it received Carlin's first volley.[61]

* During the early part of the afternoon, Johnston had put Hardee in temporary command of the Army of Tennessee.

Staggered only momentarily by this fire, the Confederates resumed the attack. In a few minutes the entire Federal left "broke panic stricken, throwing away 'guns,' 'knapsacks' and everything and all running like a flock of sheep." Miles's brigade took refuge within the lines of Morgan's division. Buell, Hobart, and Robinson (three regiments) fell back in confusion upon the Twentieth Corps,* which was just moving into position approximately a mile to the rear.[62] In this retreat Buell's men showed "the Rebs as well as the outside some of the best running ever did. . . ."[63] A Federal officer making his way to the front at this time was met by "masses of men . . . falling back along the Goldsboro road and through the fields and woods. . . . Minnie balls were whizzing in every direction." The officer checked his horse just long enough to catch a glimpse of the "rebel regiments in front in full view, stretching through the fields to the left as far as the eye could reach, advancing rapidly, and firing as they came. . . . The onward sweep on the rebel lines was like the waves of the ocean, relentless."[64] When Miles was driven from his position, all connection between Carlin and Morgan, on the Federal right, was broken. Luckily for the Federals, Morgan was not hit in this initial advance. Bragg's slowness in getting underway spared this division. Of the Fourteenth Corps, Morgan's command alone remained intact after the Confederate charge.[65]

One of the critical moments of the battle had arrived. The Confederate right, flushed with success and excitement, doubtless could have continued its advance.[66] Hardee thought, however, that now was the time to reform his lines. In carrying the Union defenses, his troops had become "considerably broken and confused"; the men were exhausted. The General, therefore, halted his advance long enough to regroup his forces, after which he renewed the attack.[67]

As the Confederate columns moved across the Goldsboro road they collided with a fresh brigade of Union infantry. In order to check Hardee's advance, Jeff Davis, commanding the Fourteenth Corps, ordered Morgan to move his reserve brigade (Fearing) to the left in an effort to plug the gap opened by Carlin's retreat. Arriving just as Fearing was ready to charge, Davis shouted: "Advance to their flank, Fearing. Deploy as you go. Strike them wherever you find them. Give

---

* General Carlin escaped capture at this time. Carlin, "Bentonville," pp. 242-47. The emblem of the routed Fourteenth Corps was the acorn, so members of the Twentieth Corps referred to Bentonville as the "Battle of Acorn Run." N. C. Hughes, "The Battle of Bentonville, March 19-21, 1865" (Unpublished article in possession of the author).

them the best you've got and we'll whip them yet." The men caught up the words "we'll whip them yet." They pushed on to the Goldsboro road and succeeded in blunting the Confederate columns. They held their position until assaulted by overwhelming numbers in front and on the right. The brigade then retreated some three hundred yards to the rear where a new line, with its left resting on the Goldsboro road, was formed.[68]

Fearing's withdrawal created a gap between his brigade and the rest of Morgan's division. Before this break in the Federal line could be closed, three brigades of Hardee's wing smashed through and moved against the rear of Morgan's breastworks. Hoke, who had finally been ordered forward by General Bragg, wanted to exploit this breakthrough by throwing his division into the breach. Bragg, however, restrained him, ordering instead a frontal assault.*

A "desperate" fight developed in this isolated position south of the Goldsboro road.[69] The "roar of musketry" was "continuous and remorseless" as men clubbed each other in dense thickets and swampy woods.[70] Veterans of the Army of Northern Virginia called "it . . . the hottest infantry fight they had ever been in except Cold Harbor."[71] For a brief period, Union General William Vandever was in doubt as to whether the occupants of his works were friend or foe, so thick was the rifle smoke and fog that had settled over the battlefield. But a Confederate demand for surrender dispelled all doubts. The Federals answered with a "go to hell" and charged out of their works, firing into what had been their rear.[72]

General Davis, some distance behind the lines, sat uneasily in his saddle. Twice he remarked to an aide: "If Morgan's troops can stand this, all is right; if not the day is lost. There is no reserve—not a regiment to move—They must fight it out."[73] At this crucial moment Brigadier General William Cogswell's brigade[74] of the Twentieth Corps arrived and Davis immediately ordered it forward to Morgan's assistance. Plunging through a tangled swamp, Cogswell's tired troops stumbled upon Hardee's men as they assaulted Morgan's rear lines.† "With a yell . . . [Cogswell's] brigade went at them and after a sharp

---

*Both General D. H. Hill and Johnson Hagood thought Bragg's order was a bad one, causing the attack to fail. D. H. Hill to W. D. Gale, Mar. 31, 1865, D. H. Hill Papers, NCDAH.

† Cogswell's timely arrival was certainly one of the turning points in the battle. J. S. Robinson to L. T. Hunt, Apr. 20, 1865, J. S. Robinson Papers, OHS; J. Luvaas, "Bentonville—Johnston's Last Stand," *NCHR*, XXXIII (July, 1956), 346.

fight pushed the Confederates back to the Goldsboro road."[75] In front, Hoke was being repulsed with heavy losses. One of his regiments, the Thirty-sixth North Carolina, in attempting to carry Morgan's breastworks, suffered 50 per cent casualties in a matter of minutes.[76]

While Morgan beat off the attacks on his front and rear, the Confederate divisions of Bate[77] and Taliaferro, on the north side of the Goldsboro road, engaged the Twentieth Corps. General Williams had placed his line approximately one and a half miles in the rear of Carlin's original position. His right, resting on the Goldsboro road, was composed of Robinson's three regiments which had been forced back by the original Confederate onslaught.[78] Four hundred yards to the left, across an open field, rested Colonel William Hawley's brigade. The gap between Robinson and Hawley was covered by artillery. Colonel J. L. Selfridge's brigade was held in reserve, and as the troops of the Third Division arrived, they were placed as an extension of Hawley's line.[79]

The fight on the north side of the Goldsboro road reached its climax late in the afternoon when General Bate, reinforced by a portion of McLaws' command, launched a series of violent attacks against the Twentieth Corps in a final effort to break the Union line.* Five times the Confederate General tried desperately to drive a wedge between Hawley and Robinson, but each time he had to fall back before heavy small arms and artillery fire.[80] "The raging leaden hailstorm of grape and canister literally barked the trees, cutting off limbs as if cut by hand." A North Carolina sergeant was certain that there was no place "in the battle of Gettysburg as hot as that place."[81]

The last charge occurred just at sundown. "Gradually the firing died away as dusk faded into darkness and night separated the weary combatants."[82] The Confederates, after hastily burying their dead, withdrew to the positions they had occupied earlier in the day. On the battlefield ". . . natural darkness was much increased by the smoke of battle and of thousands of smoldering pine stumps and logs. . . ."[83] The troops "lay or sat shivering on the wet ground, most without food, all without fires. The undiscovered wounded remained in the low swampy places and in the thick underbrush, wet to their hips from crossing the swamps, drenched by the rain, and very cold,—their suffering intense. Nature's

---

* Bate had asked for reinforcements earlier in the afternoon. He thought that if these fresh troops had been thrown in an hour earlier, when he had called for them, a Confederate victory might have been possible. *OR*, XLVII, Ser. I, Pt. I, 1107.

peculiar noises blended with the metallic clank of the spade and the muffled footsteps of those moving up to the line. . . ."[84]

It was late in the evening before Sherman learned of Johnston's bold gamble. When the courier arrived with the news, the General was resting in Howard's tent at Falling Creek Church. In his excitement Sherman rushed out to a camp fire without waiting to put on his pants. He presented a ludicrous appearance standing in ashes up to his ankles, hands clasped behind him, with nothing on but a red flannel undershirt and a pair of drawers. Nevertheless, as he barked his orders, there was immediate "hurrying to and fro and mounting in hot haste." The General's instructions for Slocum were to fight a defensive action until the remainder of the army could be rushed to his aid.

Anticipating the arrival of Sherman's right wing, Johnston charged his position. Otherwise, Hoke would have been hit from behind by the Federal reinforcements moving westward on the Goldsboro pike. Johnston bent back his left so as to form a bridgehead with Mill Creek and a single bridge to his rear. This put his line roughly in the form of a "V."

By noon of the twentieth, nearly all of the Fifteenth Corps was on the ground. The Seventeenth Corps, which was following the Fifteenth, arrived during the afternoon. Both of these commands went into position facing Johnston's left. Slocum's wing was across from the right line of the Confederate "V."

As Sherman deployed his troops, Johnston ascertained that his left was very far overlapped by the Federal right. Therefore McLaws' division was ordered to Hoke's left. Johnston was so outnumbered that he had to deploy much of his cavalry as skirmishers on McLaws' left. This was the only way in which he could show a front equal to that of the Federals.[85]

Sherman did not feel disposed to invite a general battle on March 20. He was still uncertain of Johnston's strength, his foodstuffs were low, and during the day he had received messages from General Schofield at Kinston* and General Terry at Faison's Depot. Both officers had assured him in their reports that they would be in Goldsboro by March 21.[86] To Slocum, Sherman wrote: "Johnston hoped to overcome your wing before I could come to your relief. Having failed in that I cannot

---

* Schofield did not occupy Kinston until the nineteenth. Bragg's troops had destroyed the bridge over the Neuse following the Battle of Wise's Forks. See above p. 290.

see why he remains and still think he will avail himself of night to get back to Smithfield. I would rather avoid a general battle but if he insists on it, we must accommodate him."[87] Johnston remained on Sherman's front after March 19 only to cover the removal of his wounded.* Bad roads and poor means of transportation compelled him to devote two days to the operation.[88] Captain J. M. Robinson, engineer in charge of railroads, was ordered to dispatch as many trains as possible to Smithfield to carry off the wounded. A medical officer of field experience was sent to the same place to take charge of matters, as Johnston had received several complaints concerning the treatment of the wounded when they were brought to the rear lines.[89] Sherman, not guessing why Johnston remained on his front, sent his trains to Kinston to get supplies that would be needed in case he had to fight the next day.[90]

The fighting on March 20, although of a relatively minor nature, did encompass a heated afternoon duel between Howard and Hoke. Between noon and sunset the Federals made repeated attacks on Hoke's division.[91] Holding an important position in this Confederate line were the North Carolina Junior Reserves who, in General Hoke's words, "repulsed every charge that was made upon them with very meagre and rapidly thrown up breastworks."[92] Major Walter Clark, the seventeen-year-old commander of the brigade's skirmish line which twice turned back the enemy, saw the afternoon's affair "as a regular Indian fight . . . behind trees."[93] The skirmishers to the right and left of Clark gave ground, but not once did these North Carolina youths fall back.†

* Johnston did not show sound military judgment in remaining on the field after both wings of Sherman's army had united. His explanation for remaining—to remove the wounded—was a humane policy but scarcely defensible from a military standpoint since he was "jeopardizing" one of the few remaining Confederate armies "for the sake of a few hundred wounded." Luvaas, "Bentonville" p. 356. In his official report dated March 27, 1865, Johnston stated: "On the morning of the 20th, as the enemy had three of his four corps present and well entrenched, the attack was not renewed. We held our ground, however, in the hope that his greatly superior numbers might encourage him to attack. . . ." *OR*, XLVII, Ser. I, Pt. I, 1056.

† Far from the line of fire, in fact safely situated "in the rear of the reserves," one could find General Sherman and his staff. When not receiving messages and sending orders, Sherman nervously paced back and forth under the shade of some large trees. The cigar in his mouth was more often out than burning. Once he stopped an officer who was smoking and asked for a light. The officer obliged by handing him his own smoke. As the General lit his cigar, he seemed to be oblivious of those around him. His mind was on the noise of battle. Suddenly he turned, dropped the officer's cigar on the ground, and walked off puffing his own. The startled soldier looked at him a moment, then laughed, picked up the cigar, and continued his smoke.

Even though he was intent on every detail of battle, Sherman was not disposed to

On March 21, there was heavy skirmishing along the entire Confederate front. Stewart and Taliaferro's skirmishers pushed forward far enough to learn that Sherman had drawn back his left and entrenched it as well.[94] Detachments from E. C. Walthall's and Bate's divisions drove the Federals from the vicinity of the Cole farm house and burned all buildings to prevent their further use by enemy sharpshooters.[95] But the most important development of the day was an impromptu dash on Johnston's extreme left flank by J. A. Mower's First Division of the Seventeenth Corps, in position on the Federal right. Around four o'clock this audacious officer put his command in motion along a road to his right, which he understood crossed Mill Creek by a ford and would enable him to flank Johnston. After crossing a very bad swamp, Mower struck and easily pushed back the thin line of dismounted cavalry that joined Johnston's left on this part of the field. He rapidly approached the road and bridge across Mill Creek, Johnston's sole line of retreat.[96]

General Hampton was the first to report the Federal move to Johnston, who immediately ordered Hardee to unite Taliaferro's division and a small detachment of infantry reserves, both of which were moving to the left at the time, and to oppose Mower. The Federal advance, however, was so sudden that the union could not be accomplished. Fortunately for the Confederates, General Hampton, while leading a cavalry reserve to meet Mower, saw Alfred Cumming's brigade of Georgians, under command of Colonel R. J. Henderson, moving to the left and directed it toward the scene of action. Hardee, who had brought up a few members of the Eighth Texas cavalry, ordered Henderson to strike Mower in the front. The Eighth Texas, whose ranks had been thinned by two days' fighting and was now commanded by "a mere boy," Captain "Doc" Mathews, hit the Federal left flank. Hampton, coming up on the other side with Pierce Young's brigade of cavalry, commanded by Colonel Gilbert J. Wright, charged Mower's right flank. Wheeler, at a considerable distance from this point, assailed

ride forward and view firsthand the tide of events. This characteristic of the General disturbed Major Henry Hitchcock no end. He was by now convinced that the safest position in the army was the one he now held, a place on Sherman's staff. As commander of a large army Sherman's place was not on the front line, as the Major seemed to think, but in the rear where he could conduct the over-all operation of battle. Howe, *Marching with Sherman*, p. 284; M. Grigsby, *The Smoked Yank* (Sioux Falls: Bell Publishing Co., 1888), p. 237.

General J. A. Mower's impromptu charge on the Confederate flank at Bentonville, March 21, 1865. (From *The Soldier in Our Civil War*)

the rear of the Federal column in flank with a part of Brigadier General William Allen's brigade of Alabamians.[97]

Mower's movement had been made without authority of, or consultation with, any of his superior officers, and when Sherman learned of this, he immediately ordered Mower to return to his original position. The General feared that a Confederate concentration might cut Mower off from the rest of the Seventeenth Corps.[98] This move was characteristic of Sherman who never had the "moral courage to order his whole army into an engagement."[99]

The simultaneous attacks upon a numerically stronger Federal column had been skillfully and bravely executed, and it is only natural that the Confederates, after such a display of valor, should be slow to admit that Mower retired under orders.[100]

In the gallant charge of the Texas cavalry, General Hardee's sixteen-year-old son, Willie, fell mortally wounded. Only a few hours before the fight Hardee had reluctantly given his son permission to join the Texans. The news of Willie's death was sent through the Federal lines to General Howard who had once been the young boy's tutor and Sunday School teacher. For Willie's sake, and in response to a letter from the youth's sister, Howard went out of his way to protect friends and relatives of the Hardees' in North Carolina.[101]

During the night of March 21, all of the Confederate wounded that could bear transportation were removed and Johnston, learning that Schofield had reached Goldsboro, ordered his army to cross Mill Creek by the bridge at Bentonville and retreat on Smithfield.[102] The extreme darkness of the night and the heavy woods caused the Confederate troops to move very slowly. At sunrise the rear of Johnston's army was still in Bentonville. General Wheeler, covering the retreat, found it necessary to dismount most of his men in order to check the Federals sent in pursuit.[103] Wheeler attempted to burn the bridge at Mill Creek,* but the Federals who were in close pursuit managed to extinguish the flames and save the bridge.[104] By ten o'clock the Confederate cavalry had fallen back to Hannah's Creek,† where it crossed the Smithfield road. Here a lively skirmish took place in which three Federal color bearers fell within fifty feet of Wheeler's line.[105] At this point the pursuit of Johnston was stopped, and the Federal troops returned to Mill Creek.[106]

General Johnston's strategy at Bentonville was bold and skillfully executed at times, but he lacked the number necessary for a decisive victory. His lieutenants performed both brilliantly and poorly on the battlefield. Of these subordinates, Hardee seems to have been the guiding spirit. He led the initial charge on the nineteenth and was instrumental in stopping Mower on the twenty-first. Hampton and Wheeler, too, performed well at Bentonville. Hampton selected the site and suggested the plan of battle, while General Wheeler's rear-guard action made possible Johnston's safe withdrawal from the battlefield. On the other hand, Braxton Bragg figured in two unfortunate incidents that had a bearing on the first day's fight. By calling for reinforcements that were not needed, he delayed the initial Confederate assault. And by

* According to T. F. Upson, One Hundredth Indiana, there was another bridge crossing Mill Creek at this point, one made of rosin and capable of holding up men. In his journal Upson entered: "We saw a curious sight at Mill Creek. There was a great pile of rosin—I cannot tell how much—[and] we set it on fire. It melted and ran out over the water; the rain finally put out the fire, and there was a bridge of rosin from shore to shore. Some of our boys crossed it." O. O. Winther, ed., *With Sherman to the Sea: The Civil War Letters, Diaries, and Reminiscences of Theodora F. Upson* (Baton Rouge: Louisiana State Univ. Press, 1934), p. 160.

† Wheeler said he skirmished with the Federals at Black Creek, but evidently he was mistaken because the Federal pursuit was stopped at Hannah's Creek which was east of Black Creek.

restraining Hoke from exploiting the breakthrough behind Morgan's lines, he jeopardized the chances of success on that part of the field. On the whole Confederate staff work was poor but this can be explained, at least in part, by the fact that Johnston's army was only recently organized and had never fought before as a unit.*

One important object was gained, however. Confidence was restored to the Confederate troops.[107] To many of them Sherman had come out "second best" in this struggle.[108] Before the battle the morale of Johnston's men had been very low. They had not been paid for quite some time, and the prospects of their getting paid in the near future were very dim.[109] Furthermore, the defeats which parts of the Confederate army had suffered in Tennessee, at Wilmington, and at Kinston had caused them to lose confidence in themselves. The Army of Tennessee especially redeemed itself. Johnston wrote Lee on March 23: "Troops of Tennessee Army have fully disproved slanders that have been published against them."[110] The battle, however, did not restore confidence to all of Johnston's troops. Some went straight home from the battlefield and were never heard of again.[111] Others probably went into Bladen, Brunswick, and Columbus counties to join the band of Confederate deserters which was raiding the countryside in that region.[112]

General Sherman claimed victory at Bentonville on the grounds that he was in possession of the battlefield when the fighting ceased and that Johnston had failed in his attempt to crush the Federal left wing.[113] Still the General had little to boast about. His force was more than

* "Even if Johnston had defeated the Left Wing before the Right Wing arrived with assistance, would it have affected the final outcome of Sherman's Carolina Campaign? Probably not," states Jay Luvaas in his excellent account of the Battle of Bentonville. "Johnston still would have had to face the combined forces of Howard, Schofield, and Terry—better than 60,000 men—for it would have been impossible to prevent their junction at Goldsboro. Moreover, it is extremely unlikely that he could have defeated the Left Wing. By 1865 the Civil War armies had become very proficient in the art of constructing field works, and it was a rare occasion when either side achieved a decisive victory. At Bentonville, Slocum alone commanded at least as many and probably more troops than Johnston, and he had only to dig in and hold off the Confederates until help arrived. If Morgan's division had been defeated as decisively as the troops under Carlin, the 14th corps might have been crippled, but there was still the 20th corps to contend with. It is inconceivable that this corps, posted behind strong breastworks and supported by both cavalry and artillery, could not have held its ground until reinforced the following morning." One is forced to agree with General Jacob D. Cox, who, when informed by rebel citizens that Slocum had been whipped, noted in his journal: "We suspect that his [Sherman's] advance guard may have received a rap, but know the strength of his army too well to believe that Johnston can whip him." Luvaas, "Bentonville," p. 355.

twice the size of his opponents. Yet on March 19, the Federals tottered on the brink of a resounding defeat. Sherman's conduct at Bentonville bears out the truth in General Howard's statement: "Strategy was his strongest point. Take him in battle and he did not seem to me to be the equal of Thomas or Grant."[114]

From Savannah to Fayetteville, Sherman had moved his army in flawless fashion, but from this latter place to Goldsboro his operations were definitely characterized by carelessness in the management of a large army. From Fayetteville he had written: "I will see that this army marches . . . to Goldsborough in compact form."[115] But this resolve was soon forgotten, and when Johnston made his bold gamble, the Federal columns were strung out over a considerable distance. This is all the more significant when one considers the fact that Sherman supposed the Confederate forces to be stronger than either one of his wings alone.[116] Neither would he give credence to the reports that the enemy was concentrating on his front.[117] In the General's defense, however, it can be said that a combination of adverse weather, topography, and poor roads in part explain why the divisions were so widely separated.

On the field of battle, Sherman erred on two occasions. First, he failed to follow up Mower's breakthrough of Johnston's flank on March 21.* Secondly, he did not pursue the Confederate forces after the battle. Sherman readily admitted he was wrong in halting Mower's charge. Concerning this movement he said: "I think I made a mistake there, and should rapidly have followed Mower's lead with the whole of the right wing, which would have brought on a general battle, and it could not have resulted otherwise than successfully to us, by reason of our vastly superior numbers. . . ."[118] Sherman lacked that element of "confident boldness or audacity" necessary to all great field commanders. But it is possible that the awareness of his own impulsive nature made him unduly cautious when under great responsibilities or emergencies.[119]

The General's explanation to Grant as to why he pushed on to Goldsboro rather than after Johnston leaves something to be desired.[120] In this communication he does not claim that his men were short of food or ammunition, "the only adequate excuse" for halting. He seemed

---

* Sherman definitely made a mistake in not crushing Johnston after Mower's break-through. "But this opportunity was not actually as golden as even Sherman believed. Mower had actually retreated before receiving Sherman's orders, and if he had been permitted to advance a second time he would have found the Confederates heavily re-inforced on his front." Luvaas, "Bentonville," p. 357.

to consider shoes, which were noticeably absent among the men, his most essential need. But the scarcity of footwear did not warrant a delay at this time. The Confederate soldiers were also without shoes.*

Sherman, who took his campaigns in stages with a pause to wash and "fix up a little," felt that his men deserved a rest. For several weeks he had "constantly held out to the officers and men to bear patiently the want of clothing and other necessaries, for at Goldsborough awaited . . . [them] everything."[121] This promise he did not wish to break. He was a very popular officer with the soldiers and desired to remain so.[122]

By going into camp at Goldsboro, Sherman knew that it would give Johnston time to lick his wounds, but he assumed that his adversary would remain inactive. This assumption proved correct, but under sound military judgment Sherman had no right to count on it. Two days after the battle, General McLaws was writing to his wife that Johnston would soon be in a position to chase General Sherman out of the state.[123]

The *Official Records* show the total Federal losses at Bentonville in killed, wounded, captured, and missing as 1,527.[124] The Confederate casualties are listed at 2,606.[125] These figures are not completely reliable because there are wide discrepancies in all of the Federal and Confederate tabulations. For instance, General Howard reported that the right wing alone took 1,287 Confederate prisoners.[126] Yet Confederate returns show Johnston's total loss in captured and missing as only 673.[127]

Most of the Federal wounded were gathered in a building near the battlefield. Colonel William Hamilton, Ninth Ohio Cavalry, gives an interesting description of this makeshift hospital: "A dozen surgeons and attendants in their shirt sleeves stood at rude benches cutting off arms and legs and throwing them out of the windows, where they lay scattered on the grass. The legs of infantrymen could be distinguished from those of the cavalry by the size of their calves, as the march of 1,000 miles had increased the size of the one and diminished the size of the other."[128]

Sherman directed General Howard and the cavalry to remain at Bentonville through March 22 in order to bury the dead and remove the wounded.[129] He himself rode to Cox's Bridge over the Neuse, where he met General Terry.

---

* Although Sherman did not claim a shortage of food, he did tell Grant that he planned to pick up rations in Goldsboro. *OR*, XLVII, Ser. I, Pt. I, 950; A. H. Burne,

On March 23, the two Generals rode into Goldsboro. There they found General Schofield, thus effecting a junction of all three armies, as originally planned. Colonel S. D. Pool, Confederate commander at Goldsboro, had evacuated the town at 4:00 P.M.[130] on March 21, amidst the confusion of an excited citizenry and burning cotton.[131] He had been able to offer little resistance to Schofield. The unpleasant task of surrendering the city fell to Mayor James H. Privett.[132]

The left wing came in during March 23 and 24, and the right wing followed on the twenty-fourth, on which day the cavalry moved to Mount Olive and General Terry went back to Faison.

Sherman's army as it approached Goldsboro presented a comical picture. The soldiers trudged along in company with pets acquired along the line of march. It was not an unusual sight to see a squirrel perched on a knapsack, a coon on a string, or a fighting cock in hand. Many of the men, mounted on mules or horses, generally of the plug variety, had little to occupy their attention, while others on foot were busy tending to the large number of sheep, cattle, and hogs that were distinctive to this fighting force. In every column was at least one wagon loaded with geese, turkeys, and chickens, all adding voice to the noisy occasion.[133]

At Goldsboro, Sherman held a review for the benefit of Generals Schofield, Terry, Cox, and other newly arrived officers. "Laughing and cursing, the men made clumsy attempts to close files that had been open for months." An Indiana soldier recorded the event in his diary as follows:

> We marched in platoons, and I doubt if at any time the troops of the rebel army were more ragged than we. Probably one man in a dozen had a full suit of clothes, but even this suit was patched or full of holes. . . . Many were bareheaded or had a handkerchief tied around their head. Many had on hats they had found in the houses along the line of march, an old worn out affair in every instance—tall crushed silk hats, some revolutionary styles, many without tops, caps so holely that the hair was sticking out, brimless hats, brimless caps, hats mostly brim. Many men had no coats or wore buttonless blouses, and being without shirts their naked chests protruded. Many a coat had no sleeves, or one only, the sleeves having been used to patch the seat or knees of the trousers. . . . Generally both legs of the trousers were off nearly to the knees, though now and then a man more fortunate had only one leg exposed. Socks had disappeared weeks before,

---

Lee, Grant and Sherman: A Study in Leadership in the 1864-65 Campaign (New York: Charles Scribner's Sons, 1939), p. 179.

and many a shoeless patriot . . . kept step with a half-shod comrade. But the men who had cut off the tails of their dress coats "to stop a hole to keep the wind away," though bronzed and weather-beaten, marched by General Sherman with heads up. . . .[134]

As the troops swung past, General Blair remarked: "See those poor fellows with bare legs." To this remark Sherman replied: "Splendid legs! Splendid legs! I would give both of mine for any one of them." The review, nevertheless, turned out to be a failure, and after two regiments had passed, Sherman halted it.[135]

The contrast in personal appearance between Schofield's and Sherman's men was quite in evidence to all that saw them together. Sherman's unkempt veterans were not indisposed to chaff their newly uniformed comrades from the coast. The heroes of the "march to the sea" called them "bandbox soldiers."[136]

The final arrival of the Federal armies in Goldsboro was in one sense welcomed by the local citizens.[137] For weeks they had been living in frightful expectation of the day when the men in blue would appear.[138] Now the suspense was over, and they turned out in large numbers to view the enemy. Joining them on the streets were throngs of Negroes, who sang for General Sherman's benefit a little ditty that went like this:

> Brave Sherman, sent by God's decree
> Has led the Yankees through the South
> And set four million "niggers" free.[139]

Very few of Goldsboro's residents had fled the city, but among those doing so was John Spelman, editor of the *Goldsboro State Journal*. And it is probable that he saved his skin by running. One Northern writer had termed him a "little, dirty, nasty, howling, snarling hypocritical, demagogical seccesh" who had done his best to involve the country in a fratricidal war.[140]

At Goldsboro, General Sherman found neither the railroad from New Bern nor the one from Wilmington fully repaired and no supplies awaiting him.* In an angry mood he wrote his Quartermaster General L. C. Easton:

I have made junction of my armies at Goldsborough a few days later than I appointed, but I find neither railroad completed, nor have I a word or

---

* The absence of supplies at Goldsboro made Sherman's decision not to pursue Johnston look very bad.

sign from you or General Beckwith of the vast store of supplies I hoped to meet here or hear of. We have sent wagons to Kinston in hopes to get something there, but at all events I should know what has been done and what is being done. I have constantly held out to the officers and men to bear patiently the want of clothing and other necessaries, for at Goldsborough awaited us everything. If you can expedite the movement of stores from the sea to the army, do so, and don't stand on expenses.[141]

Although provisions for the army had not arrived from the coast, Sherman decided to change the foraging system. All foragers were ordered dismounted and placed in the ranks. A considerable number of horses and mules were turned over to the quartermaster corps. "About half of this army are mounted," wrote a Federal soldier before this order went into effect. "It rather don't care to do much more walking. Nearly everyone has his own coach, cab, buggy, cart or wagon, drawn by horses or mules—blind or lame—colts or old worn out horses or mules. . . . General Sherman could now advertise a livery stable extensive enough to supply the whole country, provided they were not choice as to rigs."[142]

Nevertheless, the "corn-crib" and "fodder-stack" commandoes could look back upon a plentiful harvest between Fayetteville and Goldsboro. The countryside had supplied them with more forage, in some instances, than they could carry away. Meat and meal had been found in abundance. So skillfully had the "bummers" covered this region that the rooster no longer crowed in the morning because he no longer existed. Had the rooster escaped with his life, there would have been no fence rail for him to stand on. Such was the opinion of a newspaper correspondent.[143]

As vital as the forager had been to the success of the campaign, General Morgan regretted that he had to exclude him from praise and credit. He wrote:

I regret that I have to except anyone from praise and credit, but I have some men in my command . . . who have mistaken the name and meaning of the term foragers, and have become under that name highwaymen, with all of their cruelty and ferocity and none of their courage; their victims are usually old men, women, and children, and Negroes whom they rob and maltreat without mercy, firing dwellings and outhouses even when filled with grain that the army needs, and sometimes endangering the trains by the universal firing of fences. These men are a disgrace to the name of soldier and the country. I desire to place upon record my detestation and abhorrence of their acts.[144]

Sherman's arrival had been announced by the columns of smoke which rose from burning farm houses on the south side of the Neuse.[145] Elizabeth Collier, an eighteen-year-old girl of Everittsville, entered in her diary:

On Monday morning, the 20th, the first foraging party made their appearance at Everittsville. We were of course all very much alarmed. They asked for flour and seeing that we were disposed not to give it, made a rush in the house and took it himself—the cowardly creature even pointed his gun at us—helpless women. Looking out, we soon found that poor little Everittsville was filled with Yankees and that they were plundering the houses. After a while we succeeded in getting a "safe guard" and for a week we got along comparatively well. But in the meantime everything outdoors was destroyed—all provisions taken—fences knocked down—horses, cows, carriages, and buggies stolen, and everything else the witches could lay their hands on—even to the servants clothes.[146]*

Within Goldsboro itself the "bummers" had little chance to pillage and destroy, as they had done in the surrounding countryside, because Schofield had occupied the town two days before they arrived and had guards stationed to prevent outrages.[147] The Federal officers took forcible occupancy of the town's best homes, however, and the Wayne Female College was turned into a hospital.[148] But beyond the loss of fences and outhouses torn down for fire wood and depredations on poultry yards and smokehouses, this Wayne County town suffered little at the hands of the occupying forces.[149]

In return the local inhabitants were generally "pleasant" to the Federal soldiers. Sergeant Theodore Upson found "them very poor as a general thing but very kind and hospitable with none of the treachery

---

* The small town of Pikeville to the north of Goldsboro fared much the same as Everittsville at the hands of the Federal foragers. Both the tavern and inn were destroyed and much damage was done to the property of Sarah Pike, widow of the Nathan Pike for whom the town was named, as well as to the property of others.

Around Faison, where General Terry had his camp, Sherman's "bummers" managed to make an unwelcome appearance. In general, though, Terry kept good order in the vicinity. His troops were well behaved and he himself mingled freely with the local people. His considerations went so far as to have one of the Federal bands play "Dixie" at an afternoon concert.

In the face of the outrageous conduct of the "bummers," a few rural souls managed to retain a sense of humor. At "Ravenswood," a plantation south of Goldsboro, the lady of the house burst into laughter when a soldier appeared dressed in her nephew's best suit of clothes. The resemblance between the rightful owner and wearer of the suit was so striking it was amusing to her. R. P. Howell, "Memoirs" (Unpublished memoirs) R. P. Howell Papers, SHC; Goldsboro *News-Argus*, Oct. 4, 1947; Raleigh *N and O*, Mar. 11, 1923.

found in other places."[150] Still, the people of Goldsboro, according to H. M. Dewey of that town, were of the unanimous voice that the number of gentlemen in Sherman's army was exceedingly small.[151]

By March 25, repairs on the railroad from New Bern were finished, and the first train from the coast arrived in Goldsboro.[152] This completed the task Sherman set out to do upon leaving Savannah. His army was united at Goldsboro with those of Schofield and Terry. Large supply bases on the North Carolina coast were available by rail, and the countryside from Savannah to Goldsboro, for an average breadth of forty miles, had been laid waste. Writing in December, 1865, Sherman had this to say about his Carolinas campaign: ". . . no one ever has and may not agree with me as to the very great importance of the march north from Savannah. The march to the sea seems to have captivated everybody, whereas it was child's play compared with the other."[153]*

The General now decided it was time to discuss with Grant the plans for a junction of their armies around Richmond. Sherman was a national hero as a result of his successful and self-devised campaigns in Georgia and the Carolinas, and as yet the climactic battle of the war had not been fought.[154] Sherman still hoped to share the glory of capturing Richmond with Grant. All the while his army was pushing through the Carolina swamps, Sherman had his eyes focused on the capital of the Confederacy where Grant and Lee were stalemated. He was almost obsessed with the idea of being present at Lee's surrender, but now he was acutely aware that Grant no longer needed his help in dealing with the depleted Confederate forces. So the primary purpose of a talk with the Commanding General was that of persuading him

---

* One of Sherman's soldiers writing on March 28, 1865, echoed the General's words: "We have come to light . . . at this place [Goldsboro] after being emmersed for nearly two years in the heart of the Confederacy . . . The campaign just closed has thrown the Georgia campaign far in the shade." J. K. Mahon, "Letters of Samuel Mahon," *IJH* (July, 1953), p. 260. Another tired soldier commented: "Since I wrote you last we have marched 500 miles subsisting almost entirely from the enimey's country." R. B. Hoadley to Cousin, Apr. 8, 1865, R. B. Hoadley Papers, DU. General Howard wrote Governor Lamb of Maine: ". . . less than a year ago, we were hovering about Chattanooga, with a hostile force obstructing the avenue to Georgia. Atlanta, Savannah, Charleston and Wilmington were held with elaborate works and strong garrisons. Today our army is quartered about Goldsboro, N.C. The history of its triumphant march is already chronicled over the land, and the humble heart beats high with expectation . . . for what everyone deems the final encounter." O. O. Howard to W. Lamb, Mar. 31, 1865, O. O. Howard Papers, BC.

not to make a move until the armies at Goldsboro could cooperate. This intense desire on Sherman's part to march into Virginia was also the general sentiment of the army, as shown by the soldier who one day called out to Sherman, "Uncle Billy, I guess Grant's waiting for us in Richmond."[155]

Late in the day of March 25, the General boarded a train for City Point, Virginia, Grant's headquarters. Schofield was to be in command of the army during his absence.[156] In a jesting mood before departure, Sherman told friends that he planned to see Grant in order to "stir him up" for he had been behind fortifications so long "that he had got fossilized."[157]

CHAPTER XVII

Stoneman's Raid

THE DAY previous to Sherman's departure for City Point, Major General George H. Stoneman left Morristown, Tennessee, for a raid through southwest Virginia and western North Carolina.[1]* The primary purpose of this operation was to disrupt the Virginia and Tennessee Railroad in Virginia,† the North Carolina Railroad, and the Danville-Greensboro line (Piedmont Railroad) in North Carolina.‡

* The military operations in western North Carolina in 1865, other than Stoneman's raid, were strictly minor in nature. In January several hundred Indiana cavalrymen captured a small body of Confederates near Bryson City. This skirmish was followed by Colonel G. W. Kirk's visit to Waynesville. Kirk sacked the town and burned the jail and one residence. Then on April 3, Colonel Isaac M. Kirby, One Hundred First Ohio, conducted a "scout in the direction of Asheville." He left east Tennessee with approximately nine hundred men and by the sixth was on the outskirts of the city. But he was easily turned back by Colonel J. B. Palmer's brigade. OR, XLIX, Ser. I, Pt. I, 31-32; W. W. Lenoir to "Dear Joe," Mar. 1, 1865, Lenoir-Norwood Papers, SHC; W. W. Stringfield, "Memoirs" (Unpublished memoirs), W. W. Stringfield Papers, DU; W. C. Allen, The Annals of Haywood County, North Carolina (Waynesville: Privately printed, 1935), pp. 80-91; F. A. Sondley, A History of Buncombe County, North Carolina (Asheville: Advocate Printing Co., 1930), I, 693-97; Ina W. Van Noppen, "The Significance of Stoneman's Last Raid," NCHR, XXXVIII (Jan.-Oct., 1961), 39-40; J. G. Martin to C. P. Spencer, June 11, 1866, C. P. Spencer Papers, SHC. The dates given for Kirk's raid on Waynesville vary from early February to April, 1865. In all probability it occurred the last of February or the first of March.

† Major General George H. Thomas, Stoneman's immediate superior, thought the cutting of the Virginia and Tennessee Railroad would be like "dismantling the country to obstruct Lee's retreat," Van Noppen, "Stoneman's Raid," p. 28.

‡ General Stoneman's original instructions were to "penetrate South Carolina well down toward Columbia, destroying the railroad and military resources of the country. . . ." He was "to return to East Tennessee by way of Salisbury, North Carolina" and there "release some of . . . [the Federal] prisoners of war in rebel hands." However, before Stoneman could organize his command and get underway, Sherman took Columbia, burned it, and moved on, making it no longer necessary for him to operate in South Carolina. OR, XLIX, Ser. I, Pt. I, 616.

Stoneman's command consisted of the cavalry division of Brigadier General Alvan C. Gillem. The first brigade of this force was commanded by Colonel William J. Palmer. Brigadier General S. B. Brown had the second brigade while the third was headed by Colonel John K. Miller.[2] The entire division, numbering approximately six thousand men, was a veteran outfit, well mounted, battle hardened, and well led. Except for one ambulance and four ammunition wagons, it was a completely mounted force "stripped down for fast action."* The men carried bacon and coffee in their haversacks, one hundred cartridges, an extra set of horseshoes and nails, and their carbines.[3]

The advance guard of this force, a detachment of the Twelfth Kentucky, hit Boone, North Carolina, on March 28.[4] Unaware there was a Federal cavalryman within fifty miles, the local citizens were taken by complete surprise.[5] A few men belonging to a company of home guards did manage, however, to grab their guns and fire a few shots at the raiders, precipitating a fight.† Mrs. James Councill, on hearing the ruckus, stepped out on her porch only to be greeted by "a volley of balls [which] splintered into the wood all around her." She escaped unhurt, but not Calvin Green who was shot down and left for dead. Another casualty was Jacob M. Councill. Although this local resident had taken no part in the skirmish, he was killed in the field where he was plowing. Steel Frazier, a lad of fifteen, was more fortunate. When he was charged by a squad of Federal cavalry, he took careful aim from behind a fence rail and killed two of the raiders. Then he hightailed it to the safety of the woods.

General Gillem had the jail at Boone destroyed, and all of the Watauga County records were burned.[6] There was, nevertheless, little

---

* To protect Stoneman's rear, Brigadier General Davis Tillson, commanding the Fourth Division, Department of the Cumberland, was to occupy the mountain passes in northwestern North Carolina. *OR*, XLIX, Ser. I, Pt. I, 337.

† "Just a few weeks earlier at Camp Mast (Sugar Grove) where . . . two companies of Home Guards had alternated in service, one company remaining in camp while members of the other returned home to catch up with their farm work, Captain James Champion of the Thirteenth Tennessee Cavalry, United States Army, had assembled about twenty-five union men on leave in Watauga County with their war equipment, and fifty scouts with muskets, shotguns, and hog rifles. Having built a line of campfires at daybreak, long enough to warm a large army, the invaders surprised the sleeping camp and misled the Home Guards into believing that they were being attacked by a formidable force; the camp voted for surrender and marched out in military formation, only to discover that two-thirds of their captors were their neighbors." Van Noppen, "Stoneman's Raid," pp. 36-37.

damage to private property. That came later when Colonel George W. Kirk occupied the town after Stoneman had moved on.*

At Boone, General Stoneman divided his command. The First Brigade, accompanied by the General, proceeded through Deep Gap to Wilkesboro. Brown's brigade and the artillery moved by way of the Flat Gap road to Patterson, not far from Lenoir. Colonel Miller's brigade followed.[7] The Federals, not expected at Patterson, "were right in the streets before . . . [anyone] knew of their approach.[8] And "in a few minutes, the people around were under guard and the command encamped."[9] The time was 9:00 P.M., March 28.

In this fertile section of the Yadkin Valley the Federals found not only a sizable cotton mill to burn but also an ample supply of corn and bacon to eat. After men and mounts were fed and rested, the march was resumed the next morning at 11:00 A.M. A detail was left behind to guard the forage until the arrival of Colonel Miller, "who had orders, after supplying his command, to destroy the remainder and burn the factory."[10] With "great coolness and method" the Colonel carried out the instructions of his immediate superior,[11] General Gillem, a "home Yankee" (native of Tennessee) who was always quick to light the torch, a fact that brought him into conflict with Stoneman more than once.†

The split force, with the exception of Miller's brigade, was united at Wilkesboro by the evening of March 29.‡ And in order to obtain forage, it was decided to cross over to the north side of the Yadkin. Palmer completed the move early on the morning of the thirtieth. However, before the Second Brigade, along with Generals Stoneman and Gillem,

---

* Kirk's task, upon arriving at Boone on April 6, was to barricade the roads in Watauga County over which the Confederate cavalry might pursue Stoneman. For an account of Kirk's activities in and around Boone see Van Noppen, "Stoneman's Raid," 39-44; J. P. Arthur, *A History of Watauga County, North Carolina, with Sketches of Prominent Families* (Richmond: Everett Waddey Co., 1951), pp. 180-81; R. L. Beall to C. P. Spencer, n.d., 1866, C. P. Spencer Papers, SHC. In her article Mrs. Van Noppen has an interesting breakdown of Kirk's command by counties. Her findings show that "all of mountainous counties" of North Carolina were represented in the Second and Third North Carolina Mounted Volunteer Infantry regiments. These units were under Kirk. Van Noppen, "Stoneman's Raid," p. 40.

† It was said that Stoneman regretted both the burning of the Boone jail and the Patterson factory. R. L. Beall to C. P. Spencer, n.d., 1866, C. P. Spencer Papers, SHC. Other than the burning of the factory there was little destruction of private property at Patterson. J. C. Norwood to "Dear Walter," Apr. 2, 1865, Lenoir-Norwood Papers, SHC.

‡ The Twelfth Ohio drove the "enemy from Wilkesborough, compelling them to leave their stores and a number of horses behind." *OR*, XLIX, Ser. I, Pt. I, 331; J. C. Norwood to "Dear Walter," Apr. 2, 1865, Lenoir-Norwood Papers, SHC.

could make the crossing, the river became impassible, thus dividing the command once again.[12]

While General Palmer, on the north side of the river, was making an effort to protect private property, the Federal troops south of the Yadkin were "carrying off all the horses and mules, and burning the factories." In Wilkesboro, General Gillem seized the home of Augustus Finley for his headquarters and "captured" and "paraded" a horse that had belonged to Brigadier General James B. Gordon, one of Jeb Stuart's lieutenants.[13]

April 1 found Palmer at Elkin's factory and Stoneman at Jonesville on the bluffs just across the river from the mill. The following day Stoneman forded the Yadkin and turned north towards Virginia. His command was united once again, as Miller's brigade had joined the column on the thirty-first.[14]

The cavalry passed through Dobson and Mount Airy on its way to Hillsville, Virginia.[15*] North Carolinians, thinking the raid was over, breathed a sigh of relief.[16]

When Stoneman reached Hillsville on April 3, he feinted toward Wytheville and then, swinging to the northeast, struck at Christiansburg, an important depot on the Virginia and Tennessee Railroad. Along the way detachments were sent out to raid up and down the line. Colonel Miller with five hundred picked men went as far west as Wytheville, while Major William Wagner and two regiments of Tennessee cavalry tore up track to within four miles of Lynchburg.[17] Satisfied that the Virginia and Tennessee line was sufficiently broken, Stoneman reunited his scattered troops in North Carolina. On April 9, the day Lee surrendered at Appomattox, the Federal cavalry went into camp at Danbury in Stokes County. The following day it moved south to Germanton. Here Stoneman cleared his ranks of the large "number of negroes who were following the column." They were sent to east Tennessee, where those fit for military service were enlisted in the One Hundred Nineteenth United States Colored Troops.[18]

At Germanton on April 10, Colonel Palmer was again detached, this time to visit Salem. His orders read: "Destroy the large factories engaged in making clothing for the rebel army, and thence send out parties to destroy the railroad south of Greensborough and Danville. . . ."[19]

---

* Stoneman's men overtook a Confederate wagon train headed for Virginia and burned it. *OR*, XLIX, Ser. I, Pt. I, 331; J. G. Hollingsworth, *History of Surry County or Annals of Northwest North Carolina* (Greensboro: Privately printed, 1935), p. 150.

For several days the residents of Salem had "excitedly prepared for the invasion." Money, jewels, and other valuables were hidden in cellars. Horses were taken to the woods, and cotton and cloth were stored in private homes.[20]   At Winston, a neighboring town and county seat of Forsyth County, court was supposed to be in session on the tenth. However, neither the presiding judge nor lawyers showed up; so the clerk of the court, John Blackburn, tumbled the most valuable of the records into a sack and rushed out of the courthouse. He first went across "the street to the Widow Long's house to deposit with her the sack, and then on to Mrs. Emily Webb's and to Franklin L. Gorrell's with his other documents."[21]

With the safety of the court records off his mind, the clerk joined a delegation going out to ask protection for the towns. When the alarm had sounded the approach of the Federal cavalry, the Reverend Robert de Schweinitz, principal of the Salem Female Academy; Joshua Boner, mayor of Salem; Thomas J. Wilson, mayor of Winston; and R. L. Patterson took white handkerchiefs and started walking in the direction of the approaching troops. A short distance north of Winston they met the Federal advance and there in the rutted road the peace commissioners officially surrendered the towns. In return they were assured that private property would be protected and that no pillaging would be allowed. Following these formalities Colonel Palmer and his staff allowed the commissioners to escort them to Salem, where the army encamped.[22]*

"Had it not been for the noise of their horses and swords . . . it

* The Federal advance actually rode through the commissioners in pursuit of some Confederate pickets. But Colonel Palmer and his staff arrived shortly thereafter and accepted the surrender. Van Noppen, "Stoneman's Raid," pp. 163-64. Tradition has it that the Reverend Mr. de Schweinitz, on being ignored by Palmer, cried out, "I am de Schweinitz!" Palmer replied, "I had a teacher of that name when I was at school at Lititz," And because of his pleasant memories of the Moravians in Pennsylvania the Colonel spared Salem. There are many different accounts of this story, but the point in all of them is the same—Palmer spared Salem because of some previous association with the Moravians. Adelaide L. Fries and others, *Forsyth: A County on the March* (Chapel Hill: Univ. of N.C. Press, 1949), pp. 53-54; D. LeT. Rights, "Salem in the War between the States," *NCHR*, XXVII (July, 1950), p. 287; Van Noppen, "Stoneman's Raid," p. 166. The implication of this legend—that Palmer would have sacked the town except for memories of the past—is unfair to the Colonel. Throughout the raid both Stoneman and Palmer tried to prevent the wanton destruction of private property. The same, though, cannot be said of General Gillem who was called by one North Carolinian "supercilious, insulting and unfeeling." R. L. Beall to C. P. Spencer, n.d. 1866, C. P. Spencer Papers, SHC.

would have been hardly noticed that so large a number of troups were passing through our streets," wrote a member of the Moravian congregation in Salem. "The strictist discipline was enforced, guards rode up and down every street and very few comparatively were the violations of proper and becoming conduct on the part of the soldiers."[23] Contrary to Colonel Palmer's orders, several troopers did enter a large cotton factory and begin to pillage it "to some extent." But as soon as the Colonel heard of this action, he put a stop to it. Govenment stores and a number of horses and mules were seized by Palmer's men but little else.[24] They only laughed when they rode past the home of C. L. Rights, and the town clerk's son yelled, "You can't get our horses, we got 'em hid in the celler." Neither did they bother two handsome black horses owned by the Academy and hidden under "the Main Hall." The valuables that the students and faculty had placed under a stone in the cellar of the principal's home also were untouched.[25]

From Salem, Colonel Palmer sent out hard-riding bands in all directions. A hundred-man detachment burned the bridge over Reedy Fork on the tenth. This was a vital link in the Piedmont Railroad which connected Danville and Greensboro. Jefferson Davis, fleeing with what was left of his government and treasury, came down this road a little earlier on the same day. Palmer's men missed bagging the entire Confederate government by a narrow margin; some say by as little as a half hour.[26]

Lieutenant Colonel Charles M. Betts, commander of the Fifteenth Pennsylvania, marched toward Greensboro. He got within two miles of the city and in so doing routed the Third South Carolina cavalry and burned the bridge over Buffalo Creek.[27]

Other detachments cut the track of the North Carolina Railroad at various places. At High Point the depot and seventeen hundred bales of cotton were burned. An important bridge at Jamestown was destroyed, and at nearby Florence a lieutenant with five men leveled a factory that manufactured small arms for the Confederacy.[28]

The raiders on several occasions encountered "considerable" opposition from Confederate cavalry. Nevertheless, Colonel Palmer was able to execute his orders to the "entire satisfaction" of General Stoneman. On April 11, he reunited his command and moved out of Salem to rejoin the main body of troops.[29]*

---

* Lexington and Thomasville were saved when Confederate cavalry drove the raiders back to Salem. R. L. Beall to C. P. Spencer, n.d., 1866, C. P. Spencer Papers, SHC.

The previous day General Stoneman, with the Second and Third Brigades of his command, had marched from Germanton to Bethania, another of the old Moravian towns. Here the troopers broke up the Easter week religious services, ate everything in sight, and then moved on to Shallow Ford, on the Yadkin west of Winston.[30]

A Confederate detachment posted at the ford was taken by surprise at daybreak on the eleventh. The defenders put up "feeble resistance" and then fled, leaving Stoneman with one hundred new muskets.[31] From Shallow Ford the Federal march was almost directly south. At Mocksville the home guard heard that the Federals were coming and, thinking it was a minor raid, ran out to give the intruders "a warm reception." They came back through town at an even faster clip when they discovered it was the enemy in force.* Stoneman remained in Mocksville only long enough to feed his troops, as he was in a hurry to reach Salisbury.[32] On the night of the eleventh, his cavalry bivouacked in the road twelve miles north of this important railroad junction.†

Salisbury was a town the Confederacy could ill afford to lose. It was a major military depot, housing the trainloads of materials that had been sent south from Richmond and rushed north before Sherman. Fearful that Raleigh would fall, Governor Vance had sent large quantities of state property to the Salisbury warehouses. In addition, the town contained several military hospitals, an ordnance plant, and a state district headquarters for the Commissary of Subsistence.[33]

For Stoneman's cavalrymen this Rowan County town was particularly attractive because of the large Confederate prison located there. In November, 1861, a vacant cotton factory in Salisbury had been turned into a military prison. By late 1864, over ten thousand men crowded its six-acre compound, which was large enough to handle only a fraction of that number. This over-taxing of facilities and a shortage of supplies had resulted in a staggering mortality rate. As a consequence of these

* Because of the shots fired by the home guard there was some talk among the Federal soldiers of burning Mocksville, but Stoneman prohibited it. Van Noppen, "Stoneman's Raid," p. 172; C. P. Spencer, *The Last Ninety Days of the War in North Carolina* (New York: Watchman Publishing Co., 1866), pp. 198-99.

† Had Stoneman proceeded from Wilkesboro to Salisbury, rather than taking a swing into Virginia, he probably would have encountered more trouble than he was seeking. A sizable Confederate force was in Salisbury at the time. However, by the second week in April there were few troops available to defend the city, A. Roman, *The Military Operations of General Beauregard in the War Between the States 1861-1865. Including a Brief Sketch and Narrative of Service in the War with Mexico* (New York: Harper and Brothers, 1884), II, 658-59; Van Noppen, "Stoneman's Raid," pp. 353-55.

conditions Confederate authorities decided to remove the prisoners as soon as a safe place could be found for them. The news of Stoneman's raid and the government's need for workshops hastened the move. By March, 1865, all of the prisoners, except the infirm, had been evacuated. Nevertheless, the tales of the camp with its high plank wall, one deep well, "dead house" (where the bodies of the prisoners were placed to await burial), and "cornfield" burying ground were the goads that spurred Stoneman's troopers on towards Salisbury.[34]

Brigadier General Bradley T. Johnson was in command of the Confederate forces at Salisbury. However, on the morning of April 12, he was absent* and the job fell to Brigadier General W. M. Gardner.[35] This officer had, perhaps, between five and eight hundred men to hold the town.[36] Some two hundred of the number were "galvanized" Irishmen. ("The Yank recruiters caught the immigrant Irish as they came off the boat, the Rebs captured them in battle and then re-recruited them from the prison camps.") Most of the rest were mechanics from the railway shops and home guard. Gardner was fortunate, none the less, in that he had at least one experienced officer to rely upon. Caught in Salisbury at this time was Colonel John C. Pemberton, an ordnance inspector who had formerly held the rank of lieutenant general while commanding at Vicksburg.[37]

Gardner put his force, which included several pieces of artillery, across the Mocksville road along Grant's Creek, a few miles north of Salisbury. He removed the boards from the bridge and awaited the enemy. At daylight on the twelfth, they appeared with startling suddenness.

Finding his way blocked by Gardner's men, Stoneman sent detachments up and down the creek to cross and hit the Confederate rear. Simultaneous with these moves details from the Eighth and Thirteenth Tennessee Union Cavalry relaid the flooring on the bridge. This allowed Miller's brigade to charge across and hit Gardner in the center. Within twenty minutes it was all over. The small Confederate band scattered through the town and to the woods beyond.[38]

Salisbury was a rich prize. Stoneman took it over quickly, placing guards at various points to enforce his orders against pillaging. For quite some time the citizens had been expecting the raiders. Since the last week in March the "excitement" in town had been "almost per-

* Johnson had been ordered to Greensboro with most of the Salisbury garrison.

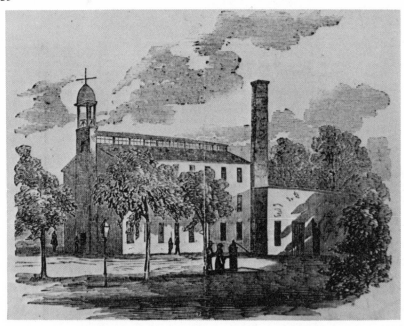

The main building of the Confederate prison at Salisbury, burned by General George Stoneman during his raid, April 12-13, 1865. (From *Harper's Weekly*)

petual." Each day brought a new rumor of Stoneman's closeness and those townspeople who expected no clemency because of the prison in their midst "drowned" themselves "in feeling of profound dispair."[39]

Soon after entering Salisbury, General Stoneman sent out a strong detachment to capture the long railroad bridge over the Yadkin River, some six miles above town. From strong entrenchments on the north side of the river, a hastily assembled Confederate force of approximately a thousand men defended the bridge. This enemy position on the bluffs overlooking the trestle appeared so formidable to the Federals that they decided against a major assault. After feeling out the defenses and receiving in return strong Confederate artillery fire, the cavalrymen pulled back to Salisbury.[40] Since they left the long bridge intact, their return to town was not marked by "wild cheers" or "war whoops of victory."[41]

On April 12 and 13, General Stoneman destroyed the public buildings and military stores he had captured in Salisbury. But first he had the contents of the Confederate supply depot thrown into the streets so that the "poor whites" and Negroes could get what they wanted. Then all that was not carted away was burned.[42] Also destroyed were the Confederate prison,* four cotton mills, seven thousand bales of cotton, an extensive steam distillery, railroad shops, fifteen miles of track, a tannery, and ordnance works.[43] General Gillem listed the destruction of the following stores: "10,000 stand of arms, 1,000,000 rounds of ammunition (small), 10,000 rounds of ammunition (artillery), 6,000 pounds of powder, 3 magazines, 6 depots, 10,000 bushels corn, 75,000 suits of uniform clothing, 250,000 blankets (English manufacture), 20,000 pounds of leather, 6,000 pounds of bacon, 100,000 pounds of salt, 20,000 pounds saltpeter, 50,000 bushels of wheat, 80 barrels turpentine, $15,000,000 Confederate money, a lot of medical (supplies) . . . worth over $100,000 gold."[44]†

As flames engulfed the large quantity of ordnance stores, the air was rent by the noise of exploding shells. Columns of dense smoke marked the city by day, while huge flames leaping skyward made the conflagration plainly visible at night for miles around.[45] It was a fearful piece of destruction, but it was limited, except in a few instances, to legitimate military booty. A resident of Salisbury wrote: "[The] people will always hold Stoneman in grateful remembrance for the strict control exercised over his troops. Again and again he stated that no private property should be plundered—and his officers seconded him—whether willingly or not."[46]

On the thirteenth, his work done, Stoneman turned west toward Tennessee. His advance reached Statesville at night on the same date. Here the soldier's pattern of action remained unchanged. It was a mixture of good and bad. The Confederate stores and the railroad depot were

* The men of the Twelfth Ohio were given the "grateful" duty of leveling the Salisbury prison. F. H. Mason, "General Stoneman's Last Campaign and the Pursuit of Jefferson Davis," *Sketches of War History of 1861-1865. Papers Read before the Ohio Commandery of the Military Order of the Loyal Legion of the United States* (Cincinnati: Robert Clarke, 1888-1909), II, 29. Most of the town's citizens were glad when the soldiers "made a bonfire of the evil smelling empty, dolorous prison, the scene of so much unalleviated suffering and so many deaths." H. S. Chamberlain, *This Was Home* (Chapel Hill: Univ. of N.C. Press, 1938), p. 119.

† On the day of the attack several trains loaded with Confederate supplies were able to get out of Salisbury before the Federals arrived. One passenger train was captured by the Union troops and among the passengers was the widow of Confederate General Leonidas Polk. R. L. Beall to C. P. Spencer, n.d., 1866, C. P. Spencer Papers, SHC. Even though $100,000 worth of medical supplies were captured in Salisbury, one of the Federal surgeons made a local doctor turn over half of his scarce supply of medicine. Spencer, *Ninety Days*, p. 205.

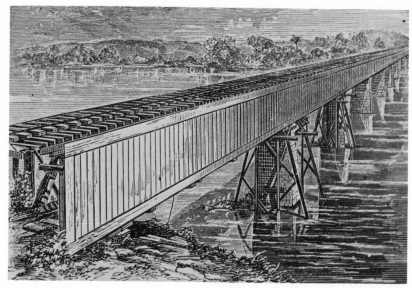

Railroad bridge across the Catawba River south of Charlotte, destroyed by Stoneman's raiders in April, 1865. (From Lossing's *Pictorial History of the Civil War*)

burned, as was the office of the *Iredell Express*,* and there was some pillaging. The soldiers beat up one of the local residents in an effort to get him to disclose the hiding place of some gold. But, at the same time, Mrs. Zebulon Vance, who had taken refuge in Statesville, was treated with meticulous courtesy by the raiders. Colonel Palmer compelled his men to return the clothing, silver, and money they had taken from a trunk belonging to Mrs. Vance, even though the trunk was "captured" outside of town.[47]

At Statesville, Palmer was instructed to leave the main column and proceed to Lincolnton in order "to watch the line of the Catawba."[48] He followed the Lenoir road as far as Taylorsville and then turned south. The cavalry passed through Newton on the fifteenth,† stopping long

---

* The flames touched off a private home and came close to firing the entire town. R. L. Beall to C. P. Spencer, n.d. 1866, C. P. Spencer Papers, SHC.

† One account has Palmer, or at least a part of his command, still in Taylorsville on the fifteenth. This same account also states that "at Hickory, a station on the road, the rebels destroyed a large amount of stores and cotton." H. K. Weand, "Our Last Campaign and Pursuit of Jeff Davis," *History of the Fifteenth Pennsylvania Volunteer Cavalry*, ed. C. H. Kirk (Philadelphia: Society of the Fifteenth Pennsylvania Cavalry, 1906), pp. 504-5. See also C. J. Preslar, Jr., ed., *A History of Catawba County* (Salisbury: Catawba County Historical Association, 1954), pp. 279-83.

enough to burn the jail and large commissary building. "Ours was a little village," wrote an eighteen-year-old girl, "It did not take long to overrun the place."[49]

The next day Palmer's brigade occupied Lincolnton, where it was to remain for a week.* The townspeople had to feed the men and horses; and the Negroes, taking advantage of the presence of Union troops, refused to work, "lounging around the streets by the hundreds and acting as spies to discover hidden horses or food." But, admitted a leading resident, ". . . we were magnanimously treated in our persons and homes, both of which were protected from violence or molestation."[50] The Colonel kept his men so busy watching "the line of the Catawba" River that they had little time to plunder. A detachment of the Twelfth Ohio turned back some Confederate cavalry at Tuckasego Ford, about ten miles west of Charlotte.† Another detail from this regiment crossed over the line into South Carolina and destroyed a big railroad bridge over the Catawba. These Ohioans not only burned this Charlotte and South Carolina Railroad trestle but captured the "bridge guard" of 7 officers and 223 men, and returned to camp without the loss of a man.[51]

While Palmer was raiding along the lower Catawba, General Stoneman, with the brigades of Miller and Brown, proceeded to Lenoir by way of Taylorsville. Mrs. George W. F. Harper of Lenoir entered in her diary, April 15, 1865: "At sunset the Yanks rushed in on us. We obtained a guard about our house after they came in, and fared better than some others. Did not undress nor sleep all night."[52] The sixteenth was Sunday and it was a bright, warm day, "but Oh! how unlike the Holy Sabbath," thought Mrs. Harper, "excitement, confusion and hurry all day. Our poor prisoners seemed almost starved."[53]

* A Federal account has the cavalry arriving in Lincolnton on the seventeenth. Weand, "Our Last Campaign," p. 505.

† Captain H. A. Ramsay, in charge of the Charlotte Navy Yard, said that after Stoneman raided Salisbury, the Federals were expected daily in Charlotte. Therefore he was furnished with three hundred muskets and directed to form two companies from the employees of the navy yard. V. G. Alexander, "The Confederate States Navy Yard at Charlotte, N.C., 1862-1865," *NCB*, XXIII (Jan., Apr., July, Oct., 1926), 4. Stoneman was expected because the "Confederate treasure" had arrived in the city on the eighth and was stored in the mint. Actually there were two separate and distinct funds that were brought away from Richmond under the same guard and on the same train. One was the public fund of the Confederate government and the other was the private property of certain Virginia banks whose officers decided to seek safety and protection for their funds under the same escort provided for the Confederate "treasure." O. Ashmore, "The Story of the Confederate Treasure," *GHQ*, II (Sept., 1918), 121-22; W. H. Parker, *Recollection of a Naval Officer, 1841-1865* (New York: Scribner's Sons, 1883), p. 355.

The prisoners Mrs. Harper referred to were the nine hundred that Stoneman brought.with him to Lenoir and confined in the Saint James Episcopal Church and about the grounds. Many in this number were old men past conscript age. Others were boys in their teens and some were Confederate soldiers "in feeble health or maimed, who had been captured at their homes." Although completely exhausted by the march, they were given nothing to eat until around 10:00 A.M. Sunday. And adding to their troubles was General Gillem's order to shoot any man who tried to escape. Because of what they considered the brutal treatment of the prisoners, the citizens of Lenoir long remembered Stoneman's visit, and numerous acts of lawlessness in the town added to these unpleasant memories.[54]

On April 17, Stoneman left Lenoir with troops enough to guard his prisoners and returned to Tennessee by way of Blowing Rock and Boone.* Gillem was instructed to take the Second and Third Brigades and proceed to Asheville.

At Rocky Ford, a mile or two from Morganton, General Gillem encountered stiff resistance from a small band of Confederates numbering no more than three hundred men (the Federal estimate)[55] and certainly no less than fifty (the Confederate figure).[56] Colonel T. G. Walton of the Burke County home guard[57] had placed his men behind slight earthworks on the south side of the Catawba. A howitzer on the crest of a hill commanded the approach to the bridge some 250 yards away. When the head of the Federal column got almost to the ford, a shell from the field pieces dispersed the troopers right and left "in double quick time." Several times Gillem's cavalry tried to cross the Catawba, but on each attempt the men in the trenches, the howitzer, and "the citizens . . . posted on a wooded hill near the river bank" emptied several saddles. This stubborn resistance forced Gillem to send the Eighth Tennessee up the river about two miles with instructions to cross over and to get in the enemy's rear. At the same time the General dismounted part of his command to keep the Confederates busy in front. When Colonel Walton received word that the Eighth Tennessee was approaching from the rear, he ordered a withdrawal. Enemy fire had already knocked out his cannon, and in front the dismounted Federal

---

* General Stoneman was blissfully unaware on the seventeenth that Jefferson Davis would cross the Yadkin near Salisbury on this date. Two days earlier the Confederate President had left Greensboro for Charlotte. J. T. Wood, Diary, Apr. 15-17, 1865, SHC. For the national uproar occasioned by Davis' flight, see below p. 390.

cavalrymen were charging "across the bridge on the sleepers." These moves overwhelmed the "little band" of home guard defenders. They "scattered in every direction, fleeing to the woods and mountains."[58]

The road to Morganton was now open for Gillem's raiders. They dashed into the deserted streets of the town "cursing and swearing vengeance on the damed rebels." In half an hour's time "the work of destruction and devastation had commenced."[59] A lady from western North Carolina put it succinctly when she wrote: "[In Morganton] they plundered and pillaged as in every town." But there was little ransacking of the houses. The soldiers, instead, "exercised their ingenuity in searching for hidden treasure out of doors. It seemed to have been understood that the Morganton people, warned of their approach, had 'cached' most of their valuables. The 'caches' were hunted up with unremitting vigor, and most of them were discovered and rifled."[60]

On the nineteenth, Gillem reached Pleasant Garden in McDowell County. Here his men followed their "usual program of plunder." Emma Rankin, "a school ma'am" in the home of Colonel Logan Carson, said the "horrid blue coats" swarmed in, through and around her employer's house, but she noted that the intruders found little in the way of spoils. Anticipating the Federal raid, the Carson household had engaged in "the biggest burying . . . [Emma had] ever attended." What could not be placed underground was hidden either in the woods or in a deserted cabin. Still the raiders searched the house and grounds for loot. At one time it seemed to the Carsons and Emma that "there were about a million of them" roaming the premises.[61]

From Pleasant Garden, Gillem continued west toward Asheville, but at Swannanoa Gap on the twentieth, he found his way "effectually blockaded and defended" by a Confederate force with artillery.[62]

When General James G. Martin, commander of the District of Western North Carolina,[63] learned that the Federal cavalry was headed for Asheville, he moved his entire command, consisting of J. B. Palmer's brigade* and J. R. Love's regiment,† to the vicinity of Swannanoa Gap. He placed Love's troops in the gap and ordered them to obstruct the way. The men cut down some trees and "made a few other arrangements" that were sufficient to repulse the Federal attack "with ease."[64]‡

---

* Colonel J. B. Palmer's brigade consisted of the Sixty-second, Sixty-fourth, Sixty-ninth North Carolina, and a South Carolina battery.

† Colonel J. R. Love's regiment belonged to Thomas' Legion.

‡ Emma Rankin quoted a Federal soldier as saying: "It would take a month to clean

It did not take Gillem long to realize that it would be next to impossible for him to effect a passage through the mountains at this point. So he moved forty miles south to Rutherfordton and by sundown on the twenty-second had passed the Blue Ridge at Howard's Gap in Polk County.[65]

General Martin was not deceived by this move. He ordered Palmer's brigade to meet the Federals at Howard's Gap. The men, however, refused to obey the order, having picked up a rumor that Johnston and Sherman had signed an armistice.[66] This was no rumor. Sherman and Johnston had negotiated a truce on the eighteenth,[67] but the news was slow in reaching the mountains. Martin did not learn of these negotiations until the twenty-second, and it was the following afternoon before he was able to contact General Gillem who was advancing on Asheville from Hendersonville.[68]* A formal meeting between the two officers on the twenty-fourth resulted in an agreement that the Federal cavalry would "go through Asheville to Tennessee" under a flag of truce and would be furnished nine thousand rations from the Confederate commissary.[69]

Gillem arrived in Asheville on Tuesday, April 25. "Everything went off quietly and in order," wrote Martin. "The Genl. and one Staff Officer dined with me." That night the Union commander left his men and went on to Greeneville, Tennessee.[70]†

At nightfall the next day, for some unexplained reason, General S. B. Brown, with a portion of the same troops that had just passed through Asheville, returned and thoroughly ransacked the town.[71]‡ General Martin, a witness to the scene, had this to say:

out the road." E. L. Rankin, "Woman's Experiences in the War between the States as Described in Stoneman's Raid (Unpublished reminiscence), NCC.

* Gillem entered Hendersonville at daylight on the twenty-third. OR, XLIX, Ser. I, Pt. I, 335. At Hendersonville the Union troops captured three hundred stand of arms. Van Noppen, "Stoneman's Raid," p. 513. See also Sadie S. Patton, The History of Henderson County (Asheville: Miller Printing Co., 1947), pp. 128-29.

† During the day Colonel Kirk arrived in Asheville, but finding Gillem there he moved on. Spencer, Ninety Days, pp. 228-29. When General Gillem returned to Tennessee he was granted "leave of absence to enable him to go to Nashville to be a member of the Tennessee Legislature, just assembling." Van Noppen, "Stoneman's Raid," p. 520.

‡ Mrs. Van Noppen advances the following theory as to "why, after Gillem left them, the Second and Third Brigades returned to Asheville. The most logical reason is that they were obeying orders which they received subsequent to Gillem's departure. On April 24 General Thomas wrote to General Stoneman at Knoxville: 'The terms of surrender of Johnston to Sherman have been disapproved by the President, and Sherman is ordered to push his military advantages. [See below p. 385.] Direct your cavalry to

. . . I have heard of no worse plundering any where. . . . I believe no one escaped entirely—I was arrested and taken to Genl. Brown and after an absence of less than an hour I returned to my house in charge of a United States Officer. When we reached the house I found Mrs. Martin and my daughters going over the house with a squad of Federal soldiers holding candles for them to examine all the trunks and for such things as they fancied and to such things they helped themselves. The Officer ordered them out of the house immediately, and they obeyed. The same men had been before or were immediately after detained as a guard for my house, but the officer remained also till the troops left. This I believe was the experience of all the houses in town, where the ladies remained to face the soldiers. Some faced [worse treatment] when the men were able to get liquor. Some [homes] were evacuated and of course were searched much worse. No one was prepared for so speedy a return after seeing them pass through the day before, the twenty-fifth of April, under a flag of truce. . . .

I ought to have said some houses were searched and plundered as already described by two or three squads in succession before they were able to get an officer or a detailed guard. . . .

Mrs. Polk, wife [of the] Capt. and a Sister of the Captain were met in the street and Mrs. Polk's ring was taken from her. Miss Polk was also searched but they found nothing—Mrs. Middleton, an English lady wife of a S. C. Gentleman lost her silver, etc. She with many others applied to Genl. Brown for the property that had been taken from them. He promised . . . all and did nothing to keep his promises. Some very hard stories were told of Genl. Brown, but I think I had better say nothing more.

At the home of Judge John L. Bailey "the actions of the soldiers were most extreme." The men rode their horses up the steps onto the piazza, broke the glass doors, and proceeded through the house to the room where the family was gathered. Each trooper had a flaming torch in his hand. When the Judge threatened to fire on the intruders, they gave him a blow on the head. After taking all of the silver and jewelry the "thieves" departed.[72]*

For all practical purposes, Stoneman's raid ended in Asheville on April 26.† This lengthy ride through a hostile land was in many respects

---

act in concert and do all in its power to bring Johnston to better terms.' The truce was broken, probably in conformance with the above directions." Van Noppen, "Stoneman's Raid," pp. 520-21; *OR*, XLIX, Ser. I, Pt. I, 31-33.

* When Brevet Brigadier General W. J. Palmer, who had been promoted to the command of the cavalry division, learned of Martin's arrest, he ordered him released "on a parole of honor to report to General Stoneman." At this time Palmer was approaching Asheville on the Rutherfordton road. *OR*, XLIX, Ser. I, Pt. II, 491; Spencer, *Ninety Days*, pp. 232-33.

† Even though Stoneman's raid through southwest Virginia and western North Caro-

a "brilliantly destructive military feat,"[73] But it was overshadowed by the rush of momentous events that brought about the collapse of the Confederacy. As Stoneman's cavalry moved through the mountains of Virginia and North Carolina tearing up railroad track and burning property, the armies of Sherman and Grant* were applying the death blows to the South.†

---

lina came to an end at Asheville, the Federal troops were not through riding. On April 27, General Stoneman received word that Jefferson Davis was fleeing south with the Confederate treasury. He immediately ordered Colonel Palmer to pursue the Confederate president "to the ends of the earth." *OR*, XLIX, Ser. I, Pt. I, 545-47. For an account of the pursuit of Davis see *ibid.*, pp. 547-57.

* The raid came too late to be of much help to either Grant or Sherman.

† Deserters from Stoneman's command stayed active after the war. Some of them formed outlaw bands and harassed the people in the western part of the state. In Wilkes County a lawless band led by two desperate men named Wade and Simmons terrorized the countryside. W. R. Gwaltney, *Capture of Fort Hamby: A Thrilling Story of the War* (Taylorsville: Published by the Mountain Scout, 1903), p. 1; G. W. F. Harper, *Reminiscences of Caldwell County, N.C., in the Great War of 1861-65* (Lenoir: G. W. F. Harper, 1913), p. 45.

CHAPTER XVIII

Bennett's Farmhouse

GENERAL SHERMAN, as has been previously pointed out, had visited Grant at his City Point headquarters during the latter part of March in the hope of organizing a joint offensive against Lee.* The mission proved futile as the Commanding General was not willing to delay his own push against the Confederates at Richmond until the Federal troops could arrive from Goldsboro.† March 29, the date set by Grant for his offensive, was at least two weeks earlier than Sherman's planned departure from his North Carolina base.[2] Thus Sherman had no alternative but to return to Goldsboro and address himself to the task of

* General Howard wrote Governor William Lamb of Maine: "Grant and Sherman have already joined hands and with silent pressure pledged support and sealed the plans of future work. Their very attitude with hand joined in hand, beneath the eye of our revered President, affords us a touching and graphic scene and may we not regard it as beautifully prospective, just at the dawn of great events." O. O. Howard to W. Lamb, Mar. 31, 1865, O. O. Howard Papers, BC.

† Grant had two reasons for not wanting Sherman with him. First, he felt he no longer needed Sherman's help to defeat Lee. Second, he thought the Army of the Potomac should have the honor of vanquishing its old enemy, the Army of Northern Virginia. Sherman's troops were mostly Westerners while Grant's were Easterners. With this fact in mind Grant told Lincoln: "If the Western armies should be even upon the field, operating against Richmond and Lee, the credit would be given to them for the capture. . . . Western members might be throwing it up to the members of the east that in the suppression of the rebellion they were not able to capture any army, or to accomplish much in the way of contributing toward that end, but had to wait until the Western armies had conquered all the territory south and west of them and then come on to help them capture the only army they had been engaged with." U. S. Grant, *Personal Memoirs of U. S. Grant* (New York: Charles L. Webster, 1886), II, 460; J. G. Barrett, *Sherman's March Through the Carolinas* (Chapel Hill: Univ. of N.C. Press, 1956), p. 196. See also A. Ames to "My Dear General," Mar. 28, 1865, W. H. Noble Papers, DU; C. B. Tompkins to Wife, Apr. 7, 1865, DU; T. H. Capron, "War Diary of Thaddeus H. Capron, 1861-1865," *JISHS*, XII (Oct., 1919), 330-407.

reorganizing his army* and replenishing depleted stores.³ His next move would depend upon how Grant fared at Richmond. If Lee managed to hold out, Sherman would get his chance to engage the Army of Northern Virginia; otherwise, he would move against Johnston.†

After the battle of Bentonville, Johnston was uncertain whether Sherman's march to Virginia would be through Raleigh or by the more direct route through Weldon; consequently, he located his army in and around Smithfield. From this small town northwest of Goldsboro, Johnston was in a position to place his army in front of Sherman on either one of the roads he chose to follow. Also, by doing this, Johnston made possible a junction with the Army of Northern Virginia should Lee abandon his entrenchments around Richmond in order to fall upon Sherman with the combined Confederate forces. The cavalry, at the same time, was placed in close observation of Sherman's army.‡ Wheeler's division was encamped to the north and Butler's to the west of the Federal camps around Goldsboro.⁴

Johnston learned from Federal prisoners that Sherman planned to remain in his present camp for some time, to rest his troops and get supplies. This pause afforded him by Sherman proved very beneficial to Johnston. Besides providing an opportunity for the Quartermaster and Commissary Corps to bring up supplies, it enabled several thousand troops of the Army of Tennessee, who were coming up from Georgia in independent detachments, to rejoin their commands. Most of them had been united into one body at Augusta by Lieutenant General S. D. Lee and led to Smithfield. Upon arrival a great majority of them had no arms, and by April 10, more than thirteen hundred were still without arms.⁵ During this period of inaction Johnston had Lieutenant General Theophilus Holmes confer with Lee on the subject of joining forces against Sherman.⁶

Johnston was given time also to reorganize his hodgepodge forces.⁷

* The addition of Schofield's troops made the reorganization of Sherman's army necessary. As of April 10, 1865, the total force numbered 88,948 men. Sherman, *Memoirs*, II, 334.

† Grant did not forbid Sherman to join him in Virginia. He merely stated he would not delay the planned attack on Lee. Therefore, upon his return to Goldsboro, Sherman issued special Field Orders No. 48: "The next grand objective is to place this Army . . . north of the Roanoke River, facing west . . . and in full communication with the Army of the Potomac, about Petersburg. . . ." Sherman, *Memoirs*, II, 341-42.

‡ The Confederate cavalry had several skirmishes with Federal patrols operating from Sherman's bases in and around Goldsboro.

After the reorganization was completed, a big review was held. Governor Vance and several ladies from Raleigh came out to view the troops who "once more . . . began to look like soldiers." Hoke's division of North Carolinians naturally received the loudest cheers from the women. Morale was high among the men.[8] Horse races were held every day in a field outside Smithfield, and although no thoroughbreds ran, a considerable amount of Confederate money changed hands after every race.[9]

On April 5, rumors began to circulate around the Confederate camps that Richmond had fallen, and with this disheartening news spirits began to wane. "Heaven the gloom and how terrible our feelings," wrote a member of General Stewart's staff.[10] Another soldier, who spent most of his time trying "to talk good cheer into the hearts of some of the despondent," admitted there were "some badly whipped men around" him.[11] Desertions increased by leaps and bounds. General McLaws had to send out two patrols every day to arrest men absent from camp. In an effort to keep the soldiers close at hand, as many as five divisional roll calls were held per day.[12]

Discouraging as the picture was, young Walter Clark of the North Carolina Junior Brigade could write his mother: "While I am able for service I intend to stand by the cause while a banner floats to tell where Freedom and freedom's sons still support her cause." His was the voice of that group willing to fight to the bitter end.[13]

Between April 5 and 9, Johnston received several dispatches on Lee's activities in Virginia, but for some unknown reason was not officially notified of Richmond's fall. He states: "There was nothing . . . to suggest the idea that General Lee had been 'driven' from the position held many months with so much skill and resolution." The last dispatch, one from the Secretary of War dated April 9, indicated, however, that Lee was encountering difficulties in attempting to move southward.[14]

Johnston, although badly misinformed or uninformed on the fighting in Virginia, did receive good intelligence on Sherman's activities. On April 9, General Hampton informed him that the country people living near the Federal camps reported that the soldiers expected to move on Raleigh the next day. This report enabled Johnston to put his army in readiness to move at the first sign of Federal activity.

The fall of Richmond had killed all hopes that Sherman harbored of marching into Virginia. This news reached him at Goldsboro on

April 6,* and two days later he wrote Grant: "On Monday at daylight all my army will move straight on Joe Johnston, supposed to be between me and Raleigh, and I will follow him wherever he may go."[15] In accordance with this plan, the Federal troops broke camp on the tenth and started their march. Sherman's movements were reported to Johnston, who immediately put his army in motion for Raleigh.[16]

Federal progress on this date was slow. Most of the roads needed considerable corduroy and in some areas the Confederate cavalry put up a "determined resistance."[17] This stubborn rear guard action by Johnston's retreating forces continued on the eleventh, keeping the advance of the Fourteenth Corps from reaching Smithfield until around noon. And more opposition was encountered in the streets of the town. The Confederates fought behind barricades until they were driven across the Neuse.[18]

Federal troops burned little in Smithfield other than the wooden stocks near the jail which a member of General Sherman's staff called "that comfortable institution for the improvement of criminals." Escaping the torch, but thoroughly rifled, were the Masonic Lodge, Odd Fellow Hall, churches, and courthouse. At the latter place the contents of all shelves were dumped on the floor, and soon the archives of Johnston County lay "in confusion amongst the dirt."[19]

During the night General Sherman learned of Lee's surrender. At 5:00 A.M. he wired Grant: "I hardly know how to express my feelings, but you can imagine them. The terms you have given Lee are magnanimous and liberal. Should Johnston follow Lee's example I shall of course grant the same."[20] To his men, Sherman announced: "Glory to God and to our Country, and all honor to our comrades in arms, toward whom we are marching. A little more labor, a little more toil on our part, the great race is won, and our Government stands regenerated after four long years of bloody war."[21] Horsemen took the news through

---

* A Federal soldier wrote: "When Richmond fell from Rebel power, I felt relieved. It seemed as if a heavy·weight had fallen from our shoulders and that we could take a long breath once more. We received the news on the 6th and I tell you the blue jackets made old North Carolina ring for once with cheers. . . ." J. B. Foote to Sister, Apr. 9, 1865, J. B. Foote Papers, DU. See also A. R. Mead to "Folks at Home," Apr. 7, 1865, R. Mead Papers, LC; "Oscar" to "Dear Parents," Mar. 30, 1865, E. O. Kimberly Papers, HSW. On the sixth, Sherman took time to send his wife a seal that she could label: "Official seal of the colony of Georgia at the time of General Oglethorpe—taken at Milledgeville by a soldier of Sherman's Army November, 1864." W. T. Sherman to Wife, Apr. 6, 1865, W. T. Sherman Papers, UM.

drowsy camps, bellowing, "Lee's surrendered!" "Begod," cried an Irish private in the Eighty-fifth Illinois, "You're the man we have been lookin' for the last four years!"[22]

This news brought rampant joy to the Federal camps and "certain knowledge" to General James S. Robinson "that several drinks were taken soon after the receipt of the dispatches."[23] This officer's reference to drinking was the understatement of the day. At a division head-quarters of the Fifteenth Corps "a great big bowl" was placed on a camp table and everyone from Major General C. R. Woods to the members of the band helped themselves to the "never ending supply of punch."[24] The Second Division of the Twenty-third Corps was near an open field when the messenger arrived with the official word that Lee had surrendered. In a letter to a friend a soldier described what followed:

> The command was at once closed . . . and the order read amid profound silence by [Major] General [D. N.] Couch and then rose . . . cheer upon cheer—men shook hands, threw up their hats until the sky was black with them. Some threw up their cartridge boxes and their knapsacks—occasionally one shouted glory to God—Officers cheered—waved their hats shook hands—hugged each other. The band struck up the "Star Spangled Banner" which they turned into "Yankee Doodle" the martial bands struck up (13 of them) cheers upon cheers! When quietude again occured the band gave us "Home Sweet Home" and I tell you there was many a quivering lip and glistening eye but the order is march! and with three cheers for the "banner" and three for Major General Couch as he galloped through the mass of men waving his hat—the grandest, wildest and most glorious pageant I ever witnessed was concluded.[25]*

In the Confederate camps the news of Lee's surrender was at first met with skepticism.†[26] The parolees from the Army of Northern Virginia who brought this news were called liars and deserters.[27] Some were put under guard until their stories could be verified.[28] General

---

* An officer of the Twenty-third Corps clapped his heels together and with a wild yell turned a complete somersault in the road. A. J. Ricks, "Carrying the News of Lee's Surrender to the Army of the Ohio," *Sketches of War History, 1861-1865. Papers Read before the Ohio Commandery of the Military Order of the Loyal Legion of the United States* (Cincinnati: R. Clark and Co., 1888-1908), I, 240.

† Johnston received the news of Lee's surrender at 1:00 A.M. on April 11 while encamped at Battle's Bridge. He did not make an immediate announcement to his troops. J. E. Johnston, *Narrative of Military Operations, Directed, During the Late War Between the States, by Joseph E. Johnston, General, C.S.A.* (New York: D. Appleton and Co., 1874), p. 396.

Hampton called the surrender news "a rumor he did not believe" and announced he would lead the corps westward across the Mississippi.[29] To the boys in Johnston's army, such as Lieutenant Bromfield Ridley, the rumors of Lee's surrender meant little. An entry in Ridley's journal shows what occupied his thoughts at the time: "Camped three miles west of Raleigh, on Hillsboro Road. . . . As we passed the female seminary in Raleigh the beautiful school girls greeted us warmly. Each one had a pitcher of water and goblet. We drank, took their addresses and had a big time."[30]

On April 12, the soldiers in Sherman's army were in a hilarious mood, even as the march went forward. They sang, they shouted, and they fired muskets in the air. Chaplain J. J. Hight, who had been unsuccessful in his efforts to hold a church service in honor of Richmond's fall, gave up all thought of doing anything religious on this date.[31] Toward this army was coming a Confederate locomotive drawing one passenger car which carried the peace commissioners. From the cowcatcher of the engine waved a white flag. Four days earlier David Lowry Swain, former governor of North Carolina and at the time President of the University at Chapel Hill, wrote W. A. Graham, also a former governor, suggesting they meet with Governor Vance in Raleigh on Monday, April 10, to discuss "the state of public affairs."[32] Having only recently discussed this topic with Vance, Graham did not think it necessary, perhaps not advisable, to accompany Swain to Raleigh; but he suggested that Swain stop by his home at Hillsboro on the way to the Capital City to discuss the best mode of effecting their common purpose—peace.[33] Swain spent April 9 with Graham and a course of action was agreed upon which was presented to Governor Vance the next day.

Swain suggested to the Governor that he convene the legislature, have it pass resolutions expressing a desire to stop the war, and invite the concurrence of the other states. This body should elect commissioners to treat with the United States government and report to a convention that would be called. If, in the meantime, Sherman advanced upon Raleigh, the Governor should send a commission to him to ask for a suspension of hostilities until final action of the state could be ascertained.[34] Vance agreed to the latter part of this plan on the condition that General Johnston's approval be obtained, but before he put the plan into effect, he wished to have another interview with Graham.

Vance consulted Johnston "as to what is best for me to do." Johnston, who arrived in the capital on the eleventh, frankly advised Vance to remain in Raleigh, to communicate with Sherman, and if the General would agree to treat him "with respect," to stay and do the best he could.[35]

The Governor wired Graham on April 11, to join him that night in Raleigh, since the city "will not hold longer than tomorrow."[36] At three o'clock on the morning of April 12, Graham arrived in the city, and after an early breakfast Vance, Swain, and Graham repaired to the Capitol, where the following letter to Sherman was composed over Vance's signature:

> Understand that your army is advancing on this capital, I have to request, under proper safe-conduct, a personal interview, at such time as may be agreeable to you, for the purpose of conferring upon the subject of a suspension of hostilities, with view to further communications with the authorities of the United States, touching the final termination of the existing War. If you concur in the propriety of such a proceeding I shall be obliged by an early reply.[37]*

The Governor then appointed Graham and Swain as commissioners to visit General Sherman and to deliver this letter to him.

Armed with a permit from General Hardee[†] and the letter from Vance, the two commissioners boarded their special train at 10:30 A.M., April 12. They were accompanied by Dr. Edward Warren, Surgeon General of the State, Colonel James G. Burr, an officer of the State Guards, and Major John Devereux of Vance's staff. On the streets of Raleigh army officers were heard to say that "such cowardly traitors ought to be hanged."[38] The two old men were not to be intimidated, however, and shortly after ten o'clock started their journey.

A short distance down the track the special train was halted by General Hampton and ordered to return to Raleigh.[39][‡] The train backed slowly for a mile or two, only to be stopped by Federal cavalrymen

---

* Twenty-five years later Vance thought his letter requested not only an interview with Sherman but also asked that the city and state records be spared, adding that Swain and Graham were authorized to treat with him on these matters. C. Dowd, *Life of Zebulon B. Vance* (Charlotte: Observer Publishing and Printing House, 1897), p. 483.

† In the meantime, Johnston had been called to Greensboro by President Davis, See below p. 378.

‡ Probably President Davis directed Johnston to send the commissioners back to Raleigh. R. E. Yates, *The Confederacy and Zeb Vance*, ed., W. S. Hoole, *Confederate Centennial Studies* (Tuscaloosa: Confederate Publishing Co., 1958), No. 8, p. 117.

who escorted the commissioners to Sherman's headquarters at Gulley's (Clayton).[40]

The General met Swain and Graham at the station and conducted them to his tent. So it was that the old men arrived at their destination. Captured by Hampton, rescued by Kilpatrick, they stood before Sherman, as he observed, "dreadfully excited" by their experiences.[41]

The commissioners presented Vance's letter and were gratified to find Sherman ready to make "an amicable and generous arrangement with the State Government."[42] In a letter addressed to Governor Vance the General stated: "I will aid you all in my power to contribute to the end you aim to reach, the termination of the existing war." With this communication went an enclosure that ordered the Federal troops to "respect and protect" the governor of North Carolina and other state officials, as well as the Mayor and civil authorities of Raleigh, provided no hostile act was committed against the invading army between Gulley's and Raleigh.[43] The commissioners had hoped to return to the capital on the afternoon of the twelfth, but as a result of various delays and impediments, this was impossible.

In the meantime, Vance was anxiously waiting in Raleigh. Since the commissioners had left well before noon, he expected their return by 4:00 P.M. at the latest. "It was extremely important that they should return by that time," he later said, "for the city of Raleigh was to be completely uncovered that night and the remaining of the Governor and all state officers in the discharge of their duties depended on the reply which was expected from General Sherman."[44] Late in the day Wheeler informed Vance that the commissioners had been captured. No longer expecting their prompt return, he accordingly wrote Sherman a letter, saying that Mayor William H. Harrison had been authorized to surrender the city and requesting that the charitable institutions, the Capitol, and the museum be spared from destruction.[45] Vance lingered in Raleigh until midnight; then, unwilling to trust himself to Sherman's hands without terms as long as eight thousand of General Hoke's North Carolina troops remained under arms, he mounted his horse and rode out to Hoke's camp,* about eight miles west of the city.[46] In his flight the Governor was accompanied by two volunteer aides.[47] He later

---

* In neither Georgia nor South Carolina had the governor of the state fallen into Sherman's hands, and Vance apparently had no desire to be the first to try "this interesting experiment." R. E. Yates, "Governor Vance and the End of the War in North Carolina," *NCHR*, XVIII (Oct., 1941), 330.

wrote Cornelia Spencer of Chapel Hill: "Many of my staff officers basely deserted me at the last. . . . I rode out . . . at midnight without a single officer of all my staff with me! Not one. I shall hit the deserters some day, hard."[48]

At sunrise on April 13, the commissioners began their return trip to Raleigh. They intended to meet Governor Vance, consult with him, and return to General Sherman with Vance's answer before the Federal troops should enter the city.[49] Five miles from Raleigh their train was stopped by General Kilpatrick who informed the commissioners that they might proceed under the flag of truce but issued the warning that "we will give you hell" if any resistance is met in Raleigh.[50] Within a mile of the capital flames could be seen rising from the railway station, which had first been plundered and then set on fire by General Wheeler's troops who were evacuating the city at the time.[51] General Hardee had led all but Wheeler's cavalry out the day before.* The commissioners found Raleigh nearly deserted. Scarcely a person was to be seen on the streets. All shops were closed, the Governor and state officials gone. At the Capitol they found only a faithful Negro servant who had been entrusted by Governor Vance with the keys to the building. After a hasty consultation, the commissioners decided that Swain should remain at the Capitol until the Federal army entered the city and Graham should make his way, as well as he could, to Hillsboro where it was supposed the Governor had stopped.[52] Thus Raleigh, without defenders and without a government, awaited the invaders.

The city, which on the eleventh had been "in a great stir," now presented less external appearance of terror and confusion than might have been supposed. Most of the citizens had decided it would be best to remain quietly at home with their families.[53] Some were nursing the Confederate wounded from the battles of Averasboro and Bentonville who filled many private residences, the unfinished building for Peace Institute, and the basement of the First Baptist Church.[54]

That Sherman would arrive in Raleigh in the course of his march had been anticipated since the day he entered the state,[55] and the local papers had kept the citizens posted on the progress of his march. This fact and wild stories of Federal atrocities circulated by Wheeler's men

* Stewart's and Lee's Corps, with Butler's cavalry as a rear guard, moved on the Hillsboro road. Hardee marched his troops on the road through Chapel Hill. Johnston, *Narrative*, p. 400.

were not very comforting thoughts for the local inhabitants.[56] Following the general practice of those Carolinians caught in Sherman's path, the citizens of Raleigh hid their possessions in an effort to save them. Former Governor Charles Manly placed a portion of his possessions in a heavy wooden box and buried it three miles from the city. "It was a terrible job," he declared. "I laid on the ground perfectly exhausted before I could gain strength to mount my horse."[57] Soon after the Federal occupation of Fayetteville, Vance began the transfer of state records and huge military stores he had accumulated. To Graham, Greensboro, and Salisbury were transferred forty thousand bushels of corn, six thousand scythe blades, and large quantities of cotton cloth, yarns, cotton cards, and imported medical stores.[58] The last train out of Raleigh with supplies, records, and state officials aboard left the depot shortly before 9:00 P.M. on April 12.[59]

"God save us from the retreating friend and advancing foe," wrote Bartholomew F. Moore, a distinguished jurist of Raleigh.[60] This line by Moore expressed the feelings of the citizens who feared the arrival in the city of both Confederate and Federal troops. Charles Manly voiced this fear in two letters to David L. Swain. On March 29, he wrote: "The enemy as well as our own stragglers and deserters search every house and cottage and Negroes cabins and take everything they find. . . . Between the two fires desolation, plunder, and actual starvation await us."[61] April 8 he wrote again: "I don't know what to do. I think it pretty certain that Johnston and Sherman will both pass over this place. Utter and universal devastation and ruin will follow inevitably. There is no difference in the armies as to making a clean sweep wherever they go of provisions, stock and everything dead or alive."[62] A few stores were broken into by Wheeler's men and disorder marked their conduct in the suburbs and about the depot where the commissary stores were kept.[63] The weathercock atop Christ Church was probably the first and only chicken Wheeler's troops saw which they could not reach.[64] But there was no universal destruction of property as Manly and Moore had feared.

April 13 had dawned under threatening skies. By the time the Mayor and his party set out to meet the Federal advance, rain was falling in torrents. A mile outside of Raleigh this peace delegation was stopped by Kilpatrick. At Mayor Harrison's request, Kenneth Rayner made a short speech formally surrendering the city to the cavalry commander and asking his "forebearance and protection of private persons and private property. . . ."[65]

From the Capitol, Swain watched General Kilpatrick ride into the city at the head of his division. With banners and guidons unfurled and a band playing, the Federal cavalry rode up Fayetteville Street. When the advance was within one hundred yards of the "old New-Berne bank," a resounding "God damn 'em," accompanied by five shots scattered the troops. A rash young Texan of Wheeler's command by the name of Walsh, who had suspended his retreat in order to plunder, had emptied his revolver at the approaching Federals. Walsh, after firing the shots, wheeled, put spurs to his black mare, and galloped up Morgan Street, closely pursued by twelve Federal horsemen. Turning a corner, his horse fell. He remounted but was soon overtaken and brought back to General Kilpatrick, who ordered his immediate execution. The young Confederate soldier pleaded in vain for five minutes' respite in order to write his wife. The General assured Swain that he did not hold the act against Raleigh or the Confederate army, so there was no act of reprisal.[66]

After chopping down the flag pole on the Capitol grounds and raising the United States flag over the statehouse dome, Kilpatrick pushed forward in pursuit of Wheeler, who was retreating toward Chapel Hill. He left behind one regiment to act as guards for the city until the main body of troops arrived.[67]

At approximately 7:30 A.M., General Sherman, traveling with the Fourteenth Corps, reached Raleigh and immediately set up headquarters in the governor's mansion, which Major Nichols called "a musty old brick building . . . in derision called the 'Palace.'" It had been "skinned" of its furniture and consequently was almost uninhabitable. From the "Palace," Sherman wired Grant of his entry into Raleigh and of his intention to move next on Asheboro and Salisbury or Charlotte.[68]

Hoping to forget the rigors of war, the General went visiting on the morning of April 14. In company with a member of his staff, Sherman paid a call on Thomas Bragg, former governor of the state and brother of General Braxton Bragg, Sherman's intimate prewar friend. After inquiring about the welfare of his brother and allaying his host's anxieties about the fate of Raleigh, Sherman terminated his visit.[69]

On the way back to his headquarters he was stopped by one of Kilpatrick's couriers who had just ridden in from Morrisville. The breathless rider dismounted and handed Sherman a brief note stating that Kilpatrick was in possession of a letter from General Johnston addressed to the Commanding General and delivered under a flag of truce. These few lines conveyed to Sherman the certainty that Johnston's message embodied more than routine military matters. He felt it was the preliminary to surrender.[70] Elated with the thought, he ordered the message sent to him at Raleigh and later in the day he received the following letter from Johnston, dated April 13:

> The results of the recent campaign in Virginia have changed the relative military condition of the belligerents. I am, therefore, induced to address you in this form the inquiry whether, to stop the further effusion of blood and devastation of property, you are willing to make a temporary suspension of active operations, and to communicate to Lieutenant-General Grant, commanding the armies of the United States, the request that he will take like action in regard to other armies, the object being to permit the civil authorities to enter into the needful arrangements to terminate the existing war.[71]

General Johnston, on the afternoon of the eleventh, had received a telegram at Raleigh directing him to leave his troops under General Hardee's command and report immediately to President Davis at Greensboro. Johnston arrived in Greensboro around 8:00 A.M. on April 12. There he was met by General Beauregard who accompanied him to Davis' office. In later years, Johnston had the following to say about this first meeting with the President: "We had supposed that we were to be questioned concerning the military resources of our department in connection with the question of continuing or terminating the war. But the President's object seemed to be to give, not to obtain information; for, addressing the party, he said that in two or three weeks he would have a larger army in the field. . . . Neither opinions nor information was asked, and the conference terminated."[72]

During the afternoon Major General John C. Breckinridge arrived in Greensboro with the official announcement that the Army of Northern Virginia had capitulated. The news of this disaster fully convinced Johnston that the Confederacy was doomed. His small army, its ranks growing thinner by the day, was no match for Sherman. Young Bromfield Ridley of the Army of Tennessee noted in his diary: "Desertions every night is frightful. . . . Our army is getting demoralized. A band of marauding soldiers visited our camp and coolly helped themselves to some leather and other goods that we had quietly secured from the Quartermaster Department."[73]* Against this small force the Federal authorities could have marshalled troops outnumbering Johnston twelve or fifteen to one. Johnston knew that with such odds against him and "without means of procuring ammunition or repairing arms, without money or credit to provide food," it would be impossible to continue the war "except as robbers." The consequence of prolonging the struggle, Johnston felt, "would only have been the destruction or disposition of . . . [the South's] bravest men and great suffering of women and children by the desolation and ruin inevitable from marching of 200,000 men through the country."[74]

In Johnston's opinion President Davis had only one governmental power left, that of terminating the war, and he thought this power should be exercised immediately.[75] At a meeting of the President's cabinet on the morning of the thirteenth, the General was able to get Davis, after much discussion, to authorize him to send Sherman the communication of April 14 asking for a suspension of hostilities.[76]†

* On the home front it was: "Get rid of all your Confederate money and hold on to your cotton." G. Elliott to "My Dear Friends," Apr. 17, 1865, P. E. Smith Papers, SHC.

† Secretary of Navy S. R. Mallory was present at this cabinet meeting. He described it as follows: "After some informal conversation Davis turned to Johnston: 'I have requested you and Genl. Beauregard, Genl. Johnston, to join us this evening that we might have the benefit of your views upon the situation of the country. Of course, we all feel the magnitude of the moment. Our late disasters are terrible; but I do not think we should regard them as fatal. I think we can whip the enemy yet. . . .' A pause ensued, Genl. Johnston not seeming to deem himself expected to speak; when the President said 'we should like to have your views General Johnston.' Upon this the General, without preface or introduction, his words translating the expression which his face had worn since he entered the room, said in his terse, concise, demonstrative way, as if seeking to condense thoughts that were crowding for utterance. 'My views are Sir, that our people are tired of war, feel themselves whipped, and will not fight. Our country is overrun, its military reserves greatly diminished, while the enemy's military power and resources never greater, and may be increased to any extent desired. We cannot place another large army in the field, and, cut off as we are from foreign intercourse, I do not see how we can maintain it in fighting condition, if we had it. My men are daily deserting in large numbers, and are stealing my artillery teams to aid their escape to their homes. Since Lee's defeat they regard the war as at an end. If I march out of North Carolina her people will all leave my ranks. . . . My small force is melting away like snow before the sun. . . .'

"When he stopped speaking a pause of two or three minutes insued. The President, who during . . . [the] delivery, had sat with his eyes fixed upon a scrap of paper which he was folding and refolding abstractedly and who had listened without a change of position or impression, broke the silence by saying in a low even tone, 'What do you say Genl. Beauregard.' 'I concur in all Genl. Johnston has said.' Another pause more eloquent of the full appreciation of the condition of the country than words could have

Sherman replied by letter that he was "fully empowered to arrange . . . any terms for the suspension of further hostilities."[77] In view of this, Johnston, through his cavalry chief, Wade Hampton, suggested a meeting at a point on the Hillsboro road an equal distance between Durham and Hillsboro.[78]* This was agreeable with Sherman, and on Monday morning, April 17, he prepared to board a special train that would take him from Raleigh to Durham. His departure was delayed when the operator at the depot rushed up to him and said that at that instant he was receiving a coded message from Morehead City that he thought Sherman should see. The General held the train for almost thirty minutes while the message was decoded and written out. It was the announcement of Lincoln's assassination.[79] Fearing the effect this news would have on his troops, Sherman swore the operator to secrecy before commencing his trip.[80] Around eleven o'clock, the train—composed of an engine of the Raleigh and Gaston line and two cars—pulled into Durham. There the General and his staff were met by Kilpatrick, who escorted them to his flag-draped headquarters in the home of a Dr. Blackwell. At 11:20 the party set out to meet Johnston. In the lead was a soldier with a white flag. He was followed by a small platoon of cavalry. Next came the official party of Sherman and Kilpatrick with their respective staffs. Bringing up the rear was Colonel Michael Kerwin, Thirteenth Pennsylvania cavalry, with the remainder of the escort.[81]

From the west a party of gray-clad cavalrymen was slowly approaching. In the advance was General Hampton's orderly, Wade H. Manning, glumly carrying a flag of truce. To his rear were Generals Johnston and Hampton with a few members of their respective staffs. The Fifth South Carolina cavalry was the acting escort.[82]

The Federal party had ridden approximately five miles when the white flag of the Confederate detail was seen in the distance. Soon the

been succeeded, during which the President's manner was unchanged. . . . Without raising his eyes from the slip of paper between his fingers [President Davis said], 'Well, General Johnston what do you propose. You speak of obtaining terms. You know, of course, that the enemy refuse to treat with us. How do you propose to obtain terms?' " Mallory, "Reminiscences" (Unpublished reminiscence), S. R. Mallory Papers, SHC.

* Johnston had left Greensboro on the evening of the thirteenth to rejoin his army. He received Sherman's reply on the morning of the sixteenth "when the [Confederate] army was within a few miles of Greensboro. . . ." He rushed off to Greensboro to see Davis but learned that the President had departed for Charlotte on the fifteenth. Johnston, *Narrative*, p. 40. P. G. T. Beauregard to Z. B. Vance, Apr. 15, 1865, Z. B. Vance Papers, NCDAH. During these days Davis was "making tracks with his headquarters in a haversack." N. G. Dye to Friends, Apr. 7, 1865, N. G. Dye Papers; DU.

The James Bennett house where the Johnston-Sherman surrender negotiations took place, April 17-18, 26, 1865. (From *Harper's Weekly*)

two flag bearers met and word was passed back to Sherman that Johnston was near at hand. Sherman then rode forward and for the first time met in person the Confederate general who had been his chief opponent for many months and for whose military ability he had great respect. In personal appearances the two officers were in marked contrast. General Johnston, his graying beard and mustache well-groomed, was neatly dressed in his gray uniform, coat buttoned to his chin. He carried his slight frame with full military bearing. The younger and taller Sherman, with his unruly red hair, shaggy beard, and untidy dress, resembled more the private soldier than the conquering general. After shaking hands and introducing their respective aides, Sherman asked if there was a place nearby where they might talk in private. Johnston replied that he had passed a small farmhouse a short distance back. Side by side the two generals rode to the small log home of James Bennett.

The two officers dismounted in the road, turned their mounts over to orderlies, and walked toward the house. They were met at the door by Lucy Bennett. They requested and received her permission to use the house, and Lucy with her four children retired to one of the two outhouses in the yard.

This historic homestead, although not pretentious in any respect, was sturdy, sufficient, and scrupulously neat. Its log exterior, shingled roof, and massive chimney provided comfort for the Bennett household. The interior consisted of a single downstairs room approximately eighteen by eighteen feet, and an attic over it which was adjoined to the main floor by some form of stairway, probably a crude ladder. Among the pieces of furniture in the home were a bed, desk, wing table, candle table, and chairs. It is probable that one officer sat by the candle table near the center of the room, while the other sat at the leaf table toward the west side.[83]

When the generals closed the door to the Bennett home behind them, there were no witnesses to their conference. However, both Sherman in his *Memoirs* and Johnston in his *Narrative* state that much time was spent in discussing the terms that might be granted the seceded states upon their submission to Federal authority. Also, there was debate over the disposition of President Davis and his cabinet. No decision was reached on this latter point by midafternoon, so it was decided to meet again the next morning at the same place.*

When Johnston and Sherman emerged from the house, all eyes turned in their direction for some word of greeting, but none was forthcoming. Johnston lifted his hat to the Federal soldiers gathered in the yard, then mounted his horse, and rode off in the direction of Hillsboro. Sherman's usually expressive face showed no emotion. Preying on his mind was Lincoln's assassination and the fear that the news would leak out before he could return to his headquarters.

That night in Raleigh, Sherman officially announced Lincoln's death.[84] This startling news caused a great stir among the Federal troops. Many of them swore *"eternal vengence against the whole southern race."* A few went so far as to say they would "reinlist for

---

* Sherman afterwards told a group of officers that Johnston told him that he had known for several months that the Confederate cause was hopeless. J. S. Robinson to L. T. Hunt, Apr. 20, 1865, J. S. Robinson Papers, OHS. In the yard of the Bennett home the soldiers in blue and gray mingled freely. But around two figures, in particular, most attention centered—the heavily bearded Hampton and the red-sideburned Kilpatrick. These two were incapable of friendly conversation. W. F. Waring Diary, Apr. 17, 1865, SHC; G. W. Pepper, *Personal Recollections of Sherman's Campaign in Georgia and the Carolinas* (Zanesville: Hugh Dunne, 1866), pp. 409-11; U. R. Brooks, *Butler and His Cavalry* (Columbia: The State Co., 1909), p. 288; G. W. Nichols, *The Story of the Great March From the Diary of a Staff Officer* (New York: Harper and Brothers, 1865), p. 311; D. P. Conyngham, *Sherman's March Through the South with Sketches and Incidents of the Campaign* (New York: Sheldon and Co., 1865), pp. 364-65.

forty years to exterminate the Southern race" and still others threatened
to burn the place to the ground.[85] Fearful that the soldiers would re-
act violently to the announcement, Sherman instructed the general in
command of the Raleigh garrison to carry out certain precautions for
safeguarding the city.[86]

During the evening of April 17 and the morning of the eighteenth,
Sherman talked with Generals Schofield, Slocum, Howard, Logan, and
Blair, and without exception they urged him to make terms with John-
ston. They expressed dread at the thought of another long march.
Johnston could be defeated they were positive, but forcing him to do
battle was another matter.[87]

From Hampton's headquarters in the home of a Dr. Dickerson, two
miles east of Hillsboro, Johnston wired John C. Breckinridge to join
him at once. He hoped that General Breckinridge's[88] close association
with President Davis, as Secretary of War, would enable him to influence
the President favorably on any terms that might be agreed upon the
next day. Breckinridge, in company with Postmaster General John H.
Reagan, arrived at Hampton's headquarters shortly before daybreak on
April 18. Johnston immediately informed them of his conference with
Sherman and repeated, as well as he could, the terms they had agreed
upon. Reagan suggested that the terms be put in writing to facilitate
discussion at the next meeting. Before this could be done, Johnston and
Breckinridge had to depart for the Bennett house. They left behind in-
structions that the paper, including a general amnesty clause protecting
Davis and his cabinet members, be forwarded there immediately.[89]

Relieved that no violence had occurred during the night, Sherman
boarded his special train for Durham on the morning of April 18. There
Kilpatrick again conducted him to his headquarters. On this occasion
the band of the Third Kentucky serenaded the General while the horses
were being saddled. As the party rode out in the direction of Hillsboro,
the men, sensing the importance of the occasion, lined the roadside to
view their commanding general who without belt, saber, or pistol, and
attired in his usual untidy manner, was astride a white charger. "An
old, low crowned, round topped, faded black felt hat sat clapped close
on his head," and his unbuttoned coat flapped in the breeze. The vain
Kilpatrick presented an entirely different appearance. He could not resist the opportunity to bedeck himself in all his finery. Belted, sashed,
and sabered, he rode next to his chief.[90]

Sherman reached the Bennett home around noon but General Johnston had not arrived. It was not long before a courier appeared with the word that the Confederate General was on his way. When Johnston arrived and the conference commenced, it was on the same cordial level of the previous day. During the afternoon Breckinridge was invited to join the discussion.[91]

Soon after Breckinridge entered the room, Sherman stepped to the door and called for his saddlebags. The soldiers in the yard, as they watched the orderly take the bags to the door, thought this was a request for pen and paper. An agreement must be near at hand, they reasoned. They were mistaken. It so happened that Sherman was thirsty and desired a drink of whiskey. The sight of the whiskey bottle brought a sparkle to Breckinridge's eyes. It was like manna from heaven for this gentleman from Kentucky who had been without his daily toddy for quite some time. After pouring himself a healthy drink, Breckinridge addressed Sherman in a most eloquent and persuasive manner for some six or eight minutes, quoting "law of war, laws governing rebellion and laws of nation" with such force and eloquence that Sherman pushed his chair back and exclaimed: "See here, Gentlemen, who is doing this surrendering anyway? If this thing goes on, you'll have me sending an apology to Jeff Davis."[92]

When Breckinridge sat down, Johnston, who had been sitting by a window intently watching the soldiers plucking leaves and flowers for souvenirs, addressed Sherman on the possibility of an amnesty that would specifically include Davis. But Sherman turned a deaf ear to him.[93]

The talks were still in progress when a courier arrived from Hillsboro with Reagan's memorandum on the previous day's meeting. Johnston and Breckinridge examined the paper and after a short consultation between themselves turned the memo over to Sherman. He read the terms Reagan had proposed but announced they were too general and verbose to be acceptable. Sherman then sat down and began to write. After a few minutes he arose, slowly walked over to his saddle bags, and drew out the whiskey bottle. Breckinridge prepared himself for another stiff drink by throwing away his chew of tobacco. But General Sherman, with his mind on the terms he was writing, poured only one drink and that for himself. To the Kentuckian this was inexcusable. General Sherman was "a hog. Yes, sir, a hog!" Breckinridge exclaimed afterwards.[94] In a short while Sherman handed a paper to Johnston, stating he was willing to submit it to President Johnson.

A defeated foe could ask little more than Sherman's terms contained—orderly disbandment of the Confederate army; recognition of the existing state governments "by the Executive of the United States"; the re-establishment of federal courts; the guarantee of political, property, and personal rights "as defined by the Constitution of the United States and of the States respectively"; freedom from molestation because of participation in the war; adjudication by the United States Supreme Court of the legitimacy of rival state governments, where they existed; and lastly, for a general amnesty "so far as the Executive can command."[95] These terms restored to the South a large measure of its *status quo ante bellum*. Sherman had now kept his oftmade promise to befriend the people of the South once they laid down their arms. Through the Carolinas he had reiterated this statement, and at Bennett's farmhouse he had proved his words.[96]

On the evening of April 18, Sherman sat down at his desk in the governor's mansion to write letters to Grant and Henry W. Halleck which contained the momentous events of the day. The General was satisfied that in his dealing with Johnston he had acted "honestly and conscientiously, without assuming more authority than he had good reason to believe had been granted to him."[97] He urged speedy action on the agreement as it was "important to get the Confederate armies to their homes. . . ."[98] But Sherman, neither politician nor lawyer, was unaware of the full political and legal implications of his concessions.* Thus he was taken by surprise when Grant arrived in Raleigh early on the morning of April 24, bearing the news that civil authorities had turned down the agreement signed at the Bennett home.†

* In a letter to his wife Sherman expressed relief that the "cruel war" was over and soon he could come home to her for at least a month. M. A. deW. Howe, ed., *Home Letters of General Sherman* (New York: Charles Scribner's Sons, 1909), pp. 344-45.

† Sherman's troops, bivouacked in and around Raleigh, found North Carolina's capital very pretty. They called it "beautiful Raleigh city of oakes." The town was fortunate in that there was no interval between the departure of the Confederates and the arrival of the Federals in which the "bummers" could ply their thievery. Other than the destruction of the printing establishments of two newspapers, little else was harmed in the city. At nearby Chapel Hill, General Smith D. Atkins' brigade of Kilpatrick's cavalry was encamped. While his troops were in the college town, General Atkins courted and won the hand of Eleanor Swain, daughter of President D. L. Swain of the University of North Carolina. For a full account of this courtship see Barrett, *Sherman's March*, pp. 245-66.

Greatly disappointed, but with little show of emotion, Sherman sat down and addressed two notes to Johnston.* In the first, he informed the Confederate General that the suspension of hostilities would cease forty-eight hours after the note reached his lines. This was in accordance with the first article of their agreement of April 18. In the second dispatch, penned shortly after the first, Sherman informed Johnston that he was empowered to offer only the terms Grant gave Lee at Appomattox. This dispatch was rushed to Kilpatrick in Durham for immediate delivery to the Confederate lines. Later in the day Sherman issued orders for all commands to be ready to move within forty-eight hours.[99]

On the afternoon of April 24, Johnston, who had been in Greensboro since the meeting at Bennett's farmhouse,† received a wire from President Davis, then in Charlotte,‡ approving the terms of April 18.[100]

---

* The New York newspaper that Sherman read on the twenty-third prepared him slightly for the possibility that the terms would be rejected.

† While in Greensboro, Johnston had a first-hand view of a dying nation. The scene was described by a local newspaper as follows: "As April 1865 dawned upon the world, Greensboro was no longer the beautiful, quiet, delightful place of yore. . . . The streets were swimming in mud. . . . Tramp, tramp, tramp was heard at all hours, day and night. . . . Horses and horsemen were dashing through the mud from street to street. . . . Lee's men were coming in rapidly, broken down, hungry, ragged and careworn. . . . The main streets were crowded with desperate soldiers who were reckless because of their final defeat. . . ." These "desperate" men turned to general rioting and plundering. They stormed a Confederate quartermaster warehouse and pillaged it, leaving only when a "Major rushed into their midst with a flaming torch, crying that he would set fire to a barrel of powder" if they did not get out. On another occasion Wheeler's cavalry raided a state quartermaster depot, and before order could be restored several men were killed. Even the women of Greensboro, during the last days, tried to storm the warehouse. Finally, in order that the supplies would not fall into Federal hands, the "great houses of commissary and quartermaster stores were thrown open" and the contents distributed to the Confederate soldiers. J. Sloan to Z. B. Vance, Apr. 15, 1865, Z. B. Vance Papers, NCDAH; A. B. Bowering, "Reminiscences" (Unpublished reminiscences of A. B. Bowering in possession of Chester Goolrick, Lexington, Va.); J. B. Cole, *Miscellany* (Dallas: Press of Ewing B. Bedford, 1897), pp. 10-16; Greensboro *Patriot*, Mar. 23, 1866, quoted in Ethel S. Arnett, *Greensboro, North Carolina: The County Seat of Guilford* (Chapel Hill: Univ. of N.C. Press, 1955), pp. 394-96.

‡ Davis arrived in Charlotte on the nineteenth. And "in a day or two the town was filled with unattached officers, disbanded and straggling soldiers, the relics of the naval forces, fleeing officials and the small change of the Richmond bureaus." Brigadier General Josiah Gorgas, chief of Confederate Ordnance, writing long after 1865 had this to say about Charlotte during the closing days of the war: "The labors and responsibilities of my department closed practically at Charlotte, North Carolina, on the 26th of April, when the President left that place. . . . My last stated official duty, that I can recall, was to examine a cadet in the Confederate service for promotion to commissioned officer. On the afternoon of the 25th of April I received due formal notice from the Adjutant-General's office . . . [stating that three officers] constituted a Board of Examiners on Cadet——. We met a little before sundown, in the ample upper story of a warehouse in Charlotte, North Carolina, and by the waning light of the last day

Before Johnston could communicate this news to Sherman, he received the latter's two dispatches. The contents of these communications were wired immediately to Charlotte, and on the morning of April 25, Davis' reply was in Johnston's hands. The President ordered the disbanding of the infantry to meet again at some appointed location. As for the cavalry and all soldiers who could be mounted, Johnston was ordered to organize this conglomeration into an escort for the President in his flight through the South. Johnston, more convinced than ever that it would be a great crime to prolong the war, "deliberately disobeyed these orders." Instead of joining Davis, he suggested to Sherman that they meet again to discuss terms of surrender.[101] Sherman answered that he would meet Johnston at the Bennett house at noon on April 26.[102]

The armistice had created a hopeless disciplinary problem in the Confederate army. "Officers of all ranks and from every quarter . . . [went] home."[103] General Johnston estimated that, between April 19 and 24, over four thousand from the infantry and artillery deserted and almost as many from the cavalry.[104] A Northern newspaper correspondent was near the truth when he expressed the opinion that if the terms were not agreed upon soon Sherman would have to lend Johnston some men to surrender.[105] During these last days all of the quartermaster and commissary depots not held by the enemy were raided by the Confederate soldiers. "Southern Independence had gone up," wrote a member of Davis' cabinet, and these men wanted their "sheer" of whatever was left. They swarmed like "locusts into well filled warehouses struggling, cursing, yelling, everyone for himself in utter disregard of all authority." All of this was not without the ludicrous touch, however. One cavalryman emerged from a navy warehouse "with a mariner's compass under his arm and a quadrant in his hand, declaring that he wanted them to find his way to Texas."[106]

General Baird reported to Sherman that large numbers of Johnston's men, passing into his line on their way home, reported that no objec-

of the Confederate Government, we went through all the stages of an examination of an expectant Lieutenant of the Confederate armies. . . . Altogether there is no little incident in my Confederate career that I have mused over oftener than that twilight examination of the last Confederate cadet." J. Gorgas, "Notes on the Ordnance Department of the Confederate Government," *SHSP*, XII (Jan.-Feb., 1884), 91; Nora M. Davis, "Jefferson Davis's Route from Richmond, Virginia, to Irwinville, Georgia, April 2-May 10, 1865," *Proceedings of S.C. Hist. Assoc.*, XI (1941), 12; B. W. Duke, *Morgan's Cavalry* (New York: Neal Publishing Co., 1916), pp. 436-37; J. T. Wood Diary, Apr. 19, 1865, SHC.

tions were made by the Confederate officers to their leaving.[107] Colonel Wright of Hampton's cavalry allowed his men to desert so they might avoid the humility of surrender, but there was absolutely no surrender in Hampton. This popular cavalry leader rallied his men by personal appearances. To help his troops divert their minds from home, he approved camp tournaments such as the one held by Colonel J. F. Waring's brigade on April 22, and witnessed by females from "far and near." For many of Hampton's staff, as well as the General himself, the truce was a "bitter pill." The army could revive again and the South "yet be free," they felt sure.[108]

Sherman once more went to Durham by rail. There he was met by Kilpatrick and escorted to the place of meeting. After the usual salutations, Sherman and Johnston retired to the one downstairs room of the Bennett house. They were inside "a long time" before Sherman called Schofield, who had accompanied him. Schofield was informed by his commander that they had been unable to reach an agreement. Johnston objected to the terms' being based solely on those given to Lee by Grant on April 9. He pointed out that the disbanding of Lee's army at Appomattox, without sufficient provisions for subsistence or arms for protection and no transportation to their homes, had turned the parolees into a band of robbers. Sherman, on the other hand, felt that any terms not based on Lee's terms of the ninth would be disapproved in Washington. Schofield solved this dilemma by pointing out that he would be departmental commander after Sherman's departure and could then take care of any difficulties that might arise with the disbanding of the army. This solution to their problem suited both generals. So Schofield wrote the Military Convention of April 26, which was agreed to by Johnston "without difficulty" and Sherman, "without hesitation." By the terms of this short agreement, Johnston's army was to be mustered at Greensboro, where ordnance supplies were to be deposited and men paroled to their homes.[109]

Still in the company of Johnston, Schofield sketched a series of six supplemental terms in which he assured Johnston that transportation would be provided for the majority of the troops on their way home. He also agreed that each Confederate brigade or group could keep one-seventh of their arms until they reached respective state capitals. Both officers and enlisted men were to be allowed retention of their private property and horses. This agreement was dated April 26 and was signed by Johnton asnd Schofield, not Sherman. The next day Sherman instructed Schofield to facilitate in any way he could the return of the Confederate soldiers to their homes. He was ordered to furnish this disbanded army with enough rations for ten days. In carrying out these instructions, Schofield was able to furnish the Confederate troops 250,000 rations and wagons to haul them. These rations in a large measure kept the Southern soldiers from subsisting on the already depleted countryside as they returned to their homes.

After leaving Bennett's farmhouse, Johnston announced the termination of hostilities in two dispatches; one to the governors of the states, the other to the Confederate army.[110]

Early in the evening of the twenty-sixth, Sherman reached Raleigh. He proceeded directly to his headquarters in the governor's mansion. A band outside was serenading the large crowd of officers standing on the front patio, but Sherman was in no mood to stop and mingle with this group. He hastily entered the house, for he wished to show Grant the terms he had in his pocket. Upon Sherman's request the General wrote his approval on the terms. Grant remarked that the only change he would have made would have been to put Sherman's name before Johnston's. The next morning, with the original of this agreement in his possession, Grant departed for New Bern.[111]

News of the final surrender did not bring the "exciting freshness" that accompanied the first announcement of the previous week.[112] There was no triumphant show put on by the victorious troops of Sherman's army.[113] The absence of boasting did not mean that the news was accepted without celebration. Fireworks blazed in the streets of Raleigh, torchlight processions were numerous, bands played, and everyone sang and cheered.[114] In fact the celebration continued for several days. When the *Raleigh Standard* went to press on Friday, April 28, rockets were still going off, bands still playing, and the soldiers were yet rejoicing at the thought of peace.[115]

Having placed upon Schofield the responsibility of carrying out the surrender terms, Sherman prepared to leave for Savannah, Georgia. There he planned a short conference with Major General J. H. Wilson, and then it would be a quick return to his troops at Richmond.

His plans for departure were temporarily interrupted with the arrival in Raleigh of the New York newspapers of April 24. As he read the *New York Times,* his face became flushed and his anger began to rise. Prominent in the paper's columns, banded in heavy mourning for Lincoln, was an official War Department bulletin published over Stanton's signature.[116] This bulletin implied that Sherman had deliberately disobeyed Lincoln. More besmirching of Sherman, yet more absurd, was Stanton's implication that the General, for "bankers gold," might allow Davis to escape.[117] On April 21, Halleck had wired Stanton that Davis was fleeing south with a large amount of specie, hoping to make terms with Sherman or some Southern official for the continuance of his flight to Mexico or Europe.[118] This news, coupled with the knowledge of Sherman's order of April 18 to Stoneman to join him near Raleigh,[119]* caused the jumpy Secretary to reason that Sherman was deliberately allowing Davis to escape.

Sherman's order to Stoneman was issued in complete indifference to Davis' flight. He merely hoped, in accordance with the truce of April 18, to halt Stoneman's devastation of the western part of the state.† Had Stanton known the intent of Sherman's order, it is doubtful he would have accepted it. He had deliberately deleted the following sentence from Halleck's wire of April 21: "Would it not be well to put Sherman and all other commanding generals on their guard in this respect."[120] The deletion of this line made it appear that Halleck also suspected Sherman's motives. In view of the fact that Davis left Greensboro for Charlotte on April 15 and that Sherman did not wire Stoneman until the evening of the eighteenth, Stanton's accusation seems all the more ridiculous.

Bitter at Northern politicians and the press, Sherman now considered as his best friends the defeated Confederates and the soldiers of his own army. In a letter to Chief Justice Salmon P. Chase, Sherman voiced a strong feeling for the people of the South. He told the Judge that, in case of war against a foreign foe, he "would not hesitate" to mingle with the Southerners and lead them in battle.[121] In the same temper he wrote his wife, Ellen: "The mass of the people south will never trouble us again. They have suffered terrible, and I now feel disposed to befriend them—of course not the leaders and lawyers, but the armies who have

---

* Stoneman never received the order. By the eighteenth, he had left his command and was on his way to Tennessee. See above p. 362.

† On April 18, General Gillem was at Morganton and Palmer at Lincolnton. Had Stanton bothered to examine a map he would have seen that these two commands would have crossed Davis' path to reach Raleigh. See above pp. 361, 363.

fought and manifested their sincerity though misled by risking their persons."[122]

On April 28, Sherman summoned to his headquarters in the governor's mansion all corps and army commanders. He explained to them their duties after his departure. The necessary orders were completed and on April 29, Sherman departed by rail for Wilmington. He could leave Raleigh knowing that he had honestly endeavored to shorten the road to reunion. If the terms first offered Johnston had been accepted, the Southern people would have resumed the place they held in the Union in 1860, and the evils of Congressional reconstruction might have been forestalled.

Sherman's departure from Raleigh brought to an end the Campaign of the Carolinas. The Federal march north from Savannah had been a bold, imaginative stroke, masterfully executed. Rail communications were disrupted and large quantities of the South's dwindling supplies had been destroyed. But this aspect of total war had little bearing upon Appomattox and Bennett's farmhouse. It was Sherman's undermining of Southern morale by the use of a military force against the civilian population that hurt Lee and Johnston most. Total war produced a defeatist psychology both on the home front and on the battlefield. Lee's ranks were thinned daily by the desertions of North Carolina soldiers who went home to protect their families living in the line of Sherman's march. It was in this respect, primarily, that the Carolinas campaign had an effect on the end of the war.

There was some skirmishing in the mountains of western North Carolina in late April and early May, but the affairs were isolated and minor in nature. Union Colonel George W. Kirk, after riding out of Asheville on April 25, raided Franklin in Macon County,[123] and near Waynesville in early May, a small Confederate force belonging to Thomas' Legion engaged a detachment of Federal cavalry.* The shots

* The dates for this skirmish vary almost by the account, as do the details of the fight. The action probably took place sometime between May 1 and 10. Confederate Colonel J. R. Love seems to have been there. The Federal troops were probably part of Colonel C. G. Bartlett's command. W. W. Stringfield, "Memoirs" (Unpublished memoirs), W. W. Stringfield Papers, DU; W. W. Stringfield, "Sixty-ninth Regiment," *Histories of the Several Regiments and Battalions from North Carolina in the Great War 1861-'65. Written by Members of the Respective Commands*, ed. W. Clark (Goldsboro: Nash Brothers, 1901), III, 760-61; D. H. Hill, Jr., *North Carolina*, ed., C. A. Evans, *Confederate Military History* (Atlanta: Confederate Publishing Co., 1899), p. 281; W. C. Allen, *The Annals of Haywood County, North Carolina* (Waynesville: Privately printed, 1935), p. 91; Lincolnton *Times*, Oct. 7, 1935.

exchanged this day between Thomas' troops and the Union horsemen were the last to be fired on North Carolina soil.

From the Battle of Hatteras to the skirmish at Waynesville, four long and trying years, North Carolina served as a battleground for the armies of a divided nation. Although the numbers involved in these engagements were comparatively small, the battles themselves were not unimportant in the big military picture. Lee's operations in Virginia were controlled to a large extent by the fact that North Carolina was a chief source of supply. His ability to remain in the field during the closing months of the war depended in many ways upon the success of the blockade-runners at Wilmington. When this vital port was lost following the Battles of Fort Fisher, the days of the Confederacy were numbered. The Federal occupation of much of the state's coastal region after 1861 was also of vital concern to General Lee, since Union troops in this area posed a constant threat to the vital communication lines running south from Richmond. Lee's dependence upon North Carolina, both for supplies and for protection to his rear, led to Stoneman's raid and Sherman's march in 1865. And with the latter came the horrors of total war and the pangs of defeat. Struck by land and sea—invaded from the east, the west, the north, and the south—North Carolina played an important but frequently overlooked role in the grand strategy of the war.

Abbreviations

REPOSITORIES

BC—Bowdoin College Library
BU—Ann Mary Brown Memorial Library, Brown University
DU—Manuscript Division, Duke University Library
EI—Essex Institute, Salem, Massachusetts
EU—Emory University Library
HSW—State Historical Society of Wisconsin
LC—Library of Congress
NA—National Archives
NCC—North Carolina Collection, University of North Carolina
NCDAH—Manuscript Division, North Carolina Department of Archives and History
NYHS—New York Historical Society
OHS—Ohio Historical Society
SHC—Southern Historical Collection, University of North Carolina
SLR—State Library, Richmond, Virginia
UM—Clements Library, University of Michigan
UVa.—Alderman Library, University of Virginia
VMI—Virginia Military Institute
WRHS—Western Reserve Historical Society

PUBLICATIONS

AHQ—Alabama Historical Quarterly
AM—Atlantic Monthly
B and L—Battles and Leaders of the Civil War
CM—The Century Illustrated Monthly Magazine
CWH—Civil War History
GHQ—Georgia Historical Quarterly
HNMM—Harper's New Monthly Magazine
*HM—The Historical Magazine and Notes and Queries Concerning the Antiques, History
    and Biography of America*
IJH—Iowa Journal of History
IMH—Indiana Magazine of History
JISHS—Journal of the Illinois State Historical Society
JSH—Journal of Southern History
MCG—Marine Corps Gazette

MHSM—*Papers Read Before the Military Historical Society of Massachusetts*
MR—*The Medical and Surgical History of the War of the Rebellion*
MVHR—*Mississippi Valley Historical Review*
N and O—Raleigh *News and Observer*
NCB—*North Carolina Booklet*
NCHR—*North Carolina Historical Review*
NJHS—*Proceedings of the New Jersey Historical Society*
NR—*Official Records of the Union and Confederate Navies in the War of Rebellion*
OHQ—*Ohio Historical Quarterly*
OR—*The War of Rebellion: A Compilation of the Official Records of the Union and Confederate Armies*
PMHS—*Proceedings of the Massachusetts Historical Society*
RR—*Rebellion Records,* edited by Frank Moore
SAQ—*South Atlantic Quarterly*
SHQ—*Southwestern Historical Quarterly*
SHSP—*Southern Historical Society Papers*
SM—*State Magazine*
TCHSP—*Trinity College Historical Society Papers*
TISHS—*Transactions of the Illinois State Historical Society*
USNIP—*United States Naval Institute Proceedings*
WMCQ—*William and Mary College Quarterly*

Notes

CHAPTER I

1. In 1860 North Carolina had 34,658 slaveholders out of a white population of 629,942. This group owned 331,059 slaves or an average of 9.6 to each owner. *Eighth Census of the U.S., Population* (Washington: GPO, 1864), pp. 348-63.

2. Hugh T. Lefler and A. R. Newsome, *North Carolina: The History of a Southern State* (Chapel Hill: Univ. of N.C. Press, 1954), p. 45; Annie W. Garrard, "John W. Ellis" (M.A. thesis, Duke Univ., 1930), p. 78.

3. W. K. Boyd, "N.C. on the Eve of Secession," *Amer. Hist. Assoc. Report, 1910,* p. 168.

4. J. W. Ellis Diary, Nov. 5, 1860, SHC.

5. J. C. Sitterson, *The Secession Movement in North Carolina* ("James Sprunt Studies," Vol. 23, No. 2 [Chapel Hill: Univ. of N.C. Press, 1939]), p. 177.

6. Wilmington *Journal,* Nov. 8, 1860.

7. Sitterson, *Secession,* p. 177.

8. *Ibid.,* p. 180.

9. Raleigh *N.C. Standard,* Nov. 10, 1860; J. G. deR. Hamilton, "Secession in North Carolina," *North Carolina in the War Between the States—Bethel to Sharpsburg* (Raleigh: Edwards and Broughton, 1926), I, 18-19.

10. C. B. Harrison to L. O'B. Branch, Dec. 2, 1860, L. O'B. Branch Papers, DU.

11. Garrard, "John W. Ellis," pp. 79-80; J. G. deR. Hamilton, *The Correspondence of Jonathan Worth* (Raleigh: Edwards and Broughton, 1909), I, 135-37.

12. Sitterson, *Secession,* pp. 181-82.

13. *United States Senate Journal,* 1860-61, pp. 11-43.

14. *Ibid.,* p. 126.

15. *United States House Journal, 1860-61,* p. 262.

16. Raleigh *N.C. Standard,* Nov. 28, 1860.

17. Wilmington *Journal,* Dec. 20, 1860. This meeting is said by some to have been the first distinctively secessionist meeting in the state. H. M. Wagstaff, *States Rights and Political Parties in North Carolina, 1776-1861* ("Johns Hopkins Studies in History and Political Science," XXIV [Baltimore: Johns Hopkins Press, 1906]), p. 127.

18. Sitterson, *Secession,* p. 192.

19. T. F. Wood, "Recollections of My Life," Raleigh *N and O,* May 20, 1895; Sitterson, *Secession,* p. 195.

20. J. C. Johnston to J. J. Pettigrew, Jan. 2, 1861, Pettigrew Family Papers, SHC.

21. Sitterson, *Secession,* p. 196.

22. R. G. Gurthy to Z. B. Vance, Jan. 16, 1861, Z. B. Vance Papers, NCDAH.

23. Raleigh *N.C. Standard,* Dec. 1860-Jan., 1861.

24. Garrard, "John W. Ellis," p. 98.

25. *Ibid.*, p. 90; J. W. Ellis Diary, Dec. 31, 1860, SHC.

26. J. W. Ellis to J. L. Cantwell, Jan. 11, 1861, J. L. Cantwell Papers, NCDAH.

27. Wilmington *Herald*, Jan. 5, 1861; Hamilton, "Secession," p. 27; J. L. Cantwell, "Capture of Forts Before the War," *Histories of the Several Regiments and Battalions from North Carolina in the Great War 1861-'65. Written by the Members of the Respective Commands,* ed. W. Clark (Goldsboro: Nash Brothers, 1901), V, 24; Wood, "Recollections," Raleigh *N and O,* May 20, 1895.

28. Wilmington *Herald*, Jan. 9, 1861.

29. Cantwell, "Capture," p. 24.

30. *OR,* I, Ser. I, 474-75. At Smithville, Hedrick was joined by Captain S. D. Thurston, commander of the Smithville Guards, a number of his men and local citizens "but all acting as individuals only. . . ." Cantwell, "Capture," p. 24. J. L. Cantwell to J. W. Ellis, Jan. 15, 1861, J. L. Cantwell Papers, NCDAH.

31. *OR,* I, Ser. I, 476; Cantwell, "Capture," pp. 24-25. According to the Wilmington *Herald* the people of the city were not unanimous in their approval of the seizure of the forts. Wilmington *Herald,* Jan. 11, 1861.

32. J. W. Ellis to J. L. Cantwell, Jan. 11, 1861, J. L. Cantwell Papers, NCDAH. The Governor doubted not for a moment the patriotic motives behind the seizure. But with North Carolina still in the Union he could not sanction such a move.

33. *OR,* I, Ser. I, 475.

34. *Ibid.*, p. 476; J. J. Hedrick to J. L. Cantwell, Jan. 13, 1861, J. L. Cantwell Papers, NCDAH.

35. *OR,* I, Ser. I, 484-85.

36. David Schenck Journal, Mar. 11, 1861, SHC.

37. W. S. Smith, "First Secession Flag," *NCB,* XVI (Apr., 1917) 219.

38. On the very day the Confederate States of America was being formed in Montgomery, Alabama—February 4, 1861—the Washington Peace Conference assembled. Twenty-one states sent representatives, but none of the delegates had enough drive to give the conference necessary leadership. And by the last of February, Louisiana and Texas had joined South Carolina, Georgia, Florida, Alabama, and Mississippi out of the Union. The conference folded on February 27.

39. Schenck Journal, Mar. 11, 1861, SHC.

40. William Calder Diary, Apr. 13, 1861, DU; A. W. Mangum to Sister, Apr. 15, 1861, A. W. Mangum Papers, SHC; Wilmington *Journal,* Apr. 18, 1861.

41. Calder Diary, Apr. 14, 1861, DU.

42. Sitterson, *Secession,* p. 239.

43. Ethel S. Arnett and W. C. Jackson, *Greensboro, North Carolina* (Chapel Hill: Univ. of N.C. Press, 1955), pp. 390-91.

44. Margaret McK. Jones, ed., *The Journal of Catherine Devereux Edmondston, 1860-1866* (Mebane: Privately printed, 1954), p. 25.

45. *OR,* I, Ser. I, 486. The Governor's reply to Lincoln's call for troops met with general approval outside of the state. Garrard, "John W. Ellis," pp. 104-5.

46. Sitterson, *Secession,* p. 239.

47. *OR,* LI, Ser. I, 11. W. Alexander to Chief of Ordnance Department, Apr. 14, 1861, Rec. Gr. 156, NA.

48. *OR,* I, Ser. I, 476-77.

49. R. S. Barry, "Fort Macon: Its History," *NCHR,* XXVII, (April, 1950), 168-69; Laura E. Lee, *Forget-Me-Nots of the Civil War* (St. Louis: A. R. Fleming Printing Co., 1909), pp. 41-43.

50. Barry, "Fort Macon," p. 168.

51. S. J. Person to J. L. Cantwell, Apr. 15, 1861, J. L. Cantwell Papers, NCDAH.

52. Wilmington *Journal,* Apr. 15, 1861.

53. J. L. Cantwell to J. W. Ellis, Apr. 17, 1861, J. L. Cantwell Papers, NCDAH; *OR,*

LI, Pt. I, Ser. I, 1-3; E. S. Martin, "Services During the Confederate War" (Unpublished reminiscence, NCC); J. S. Reilly, *Wilmington, Past, Present and Future* (Wilmington: J. S. Reilly, 1884), p. 17.

54. G. Daves to H. T. Clark, Oct. 2, 1861, H. T. Clark Papers, NCDAH; L. Leon, *Diary of a Tar Heel Confederate Soldier* (Charlotte: Stone Publishing Co., 1913), p. 1; R. C. Todd, *Confederate Finance* (Athens: Univ. of Georgia Press, 1954), p. 12.

55. Major S. S. Anderson commanded the Federal troops at the arsenal. See also above p. 313.

56. *OR*, I, Ser. I, 478-80. The Fayetteville Light Infantry and the Lafayette Light Infantry comprised part of the force that seized the arsenal. Fayetteville *Observer*, Apr. 12, 1954.

57. *OR*, I, Ser. I, 478-80; A. Gordon, "Organization of Troops," *Histories of the Several Regiments and Battalions from North Carolina in the Great War 1861-'65. Written by Members of the Respective Commands*, ed. W. Clark (Goldsboro: E. M. Uzzell, 1901), I, 39-40.

58. J. M. Smith to J. F. Poindexter, Apr. 22, 1861, J. F. Poindexter, Papers, DU. Virginia's withdrawal from the Union on April 17 helped destroy Union sentiment in North Carolina. At Wilmington cannons boomed along the wharves in salute to Virginia's action. Wilmington *Herald*, Apr. 19, 1861.

59. C. Manly to D. L. Swain, Apr. 22, 1861, D. L. Swain Papers, SHC.

60. Sitterson, *Secession*, p. 242.

61. "Louise" to Aunt, Aug. 12, 1861, Jones Family Papers, SHC.

62. E. Conigland to Wife, Apr. 16, 1861, E. Conigland Papers, SHC.

63. Calder Diary, April 18, 19, 1861, DU.

64. C. Dowd, *Life of Zebulon B. Vance*, (Charlotte: Observer Publishing and Printing House, 1897), pp. 441-42.

65. J. W. Ellis to W. H. C. Whiting, Apr. 12, 1861, J. L. Cantwell Papers, NCDAH.

66. Raleigh *N.C. Standard*, May 1, 1861; Sitterson, *Secession*, pp. 242-43; Garrard, "John W. Ellis," p. 105; J. W. Ellis Papers, April-May, 1861, NCDAH. The Hillsboro Military Academy was tendered a recruiting station. Some of the cadets became drill instructors, but many of them went home. Calder Diary, Apr. 15, 1861, DU.

67. H. C. Graham, "How North Carolina Went Into the War," *Blue and Gray*, III (Nov., 1894), 283-84; Leon, *Diary of a Tar Heel*, p. 1.

68. H. M. Wagstaff, ed., *The James A. Graham Papers, 1861-1884* (Chapel Hill: Univ. of N.C. Press, 1928), p. 103; J. M. Smith to J. F. Poindexter, Apr. 22, 1861, J. F. Poindexter Papers, DU; J. A. Sloan, *Reminiscences of the Guilford Grays, Co. B, Twenty-seventh North Carolina Regiment* (Washington: R. O. Polkinborn, 1883), pp. 18-19; Laura E. Lee, *Forget-Me-Nots of the Civil War* (St. Louis: A. R. Fleming Printing Co., 1909), pp. 41-43; E. Wadsworth to "Dear Cousin," Sept. 5, 1861, Confederate States Arch., DU.

69. See Hugh MacRae Papers for a copy of this resolution. DU.

70. Sitterson, *Secession*, pp. 243-44. The call for a convention created a great deal of excitement throughout the state. Sloan, *Guilford Grays*, p. 20.

71. Hamilton, "Secession," p. 39.

72. Schenck Journal, May 19, 1861, SHC; W. T. Loftin to Mother, May 5, 1861, W. T. Loftin Papers, DU; Charlotte *Southern Presbyterian*, May 18, 1861, quoted in Sadie S. Patton, *The Story of Henderson County* (Asheville: Miller Printing Co., 1947), p. 125.

73. Hamilton, "Secession," p. 39; S. E. Penland to "Cornelia," May 26, 1861, C. McGimsey Papers, SHC.

74. Schenck Journal, May 20, 1861, SHC; Calder Diary, Sept. [?], 1861, DU; R. D. W. Connor, *North Carolina, Rebuilding an Ancient Commonwealth* (New York: American Historical Society, 1929), II, 150-51; Lefler and Newsome, *N.C.*, p. 425; Graham, "How N.C. Went to War," p. 285; D. H. Hill, Jr., *North Carolina*, ed., C. A. Evans, *Confederate Military History* (Atlanta: Confederate Publishing Co., 1899), IV, 8-9.

CHAPTER II

1. R. D. W. Connor, *North Carolina, Rebuilding an Ancient Commonwealth* (New York: American Historical Society, 1929), II, 174.

2. D. H. Hill, Jr., *North Carolina*, ed., C. A. Evans, *Confederate Military History* (Atlanta: Confederate Publishing Co., 1899), IV, 5-31; *Eighth Census of the U.S., 1860, Population* (Washington: GPO, 1864), p. 357; *Eighth Census of the U.S., 1860, Manufactures* (Washington: GPO, 1865), pp. 437-38.

3. "Arming the State—Letter of a North Carolinian to the General Assembly During its Session, 1860-1861," Clipping in volume of documents, 1860-61, NCC.

4. See above p. 15.

5. C. S. Powell, "War Tales" (Unpublished reminiscence), C. S. Powell Papers, DU.

6. W. T. Loftin to Mother, May 5, 1861, W. T. Loftin Papers, DU.

7. A. W. Mangum to Sister, May 20, 1861, A. W. Mangum Papers, SHC. According to Cornelia McGimsey of Burke County, Z. B. Vance's command consisted of "96 of the best men in N.C. their average weight is 168 pounds and are about his (Vance's) highth." Cornelia McGimsey to L. Warlick, May 6, 1861, C. McGimsey Papers, SHC.

8. D. H. Hill, *North Carolina in the War Between the States—Bethel to Sharpsburg* (Raleigh: Edwards and Broughton, 1926), I, 63.

9. H. T. King, *Sketches of Pitt County: A Brief History of the County, 1704-1910* (Raleigh: Edwards and Broughton, 1911), pp. 123-24.

10. P. E. Smith, "Scotland Neck Mounted Riflemen" (Unpublished account), P. E. Smith Papers, SHC.

11. "Events of Day," Washington *Daily News*, Aug. 17, 1951, quoting 1861 newspaper.

12. J. Y. Savage, "Sketch of Scotland Neck Cavalry" (Unpublished sketch), P. E. Smith Papers, SHC.

13. Brother to C. (McG.) Buie, Nov. 3, 1861, C. (McG.) Buie Papers, DU.

14. H. C. Graham, "How North Carolina Went Into the War," *Blue and Gray*, III (Nov., 1894), 283; Ethel S. Arnett and W. C. Jackson, *Greensboro, North Carolina* (Chapel Hill: Univ. of N. C. Press, 1955), pp. 389-90.

15. B. N. Smith to J. L. Gorrell, May 4, 1861, F. G. Gorrell Papers, SHC; J. M. Grizzard, "The Militia," *Histories of the Several Regiments and Battalions from North Carolina in the Great War 1861-'65. Written by Members of the Respective Commands,* ed., W. Clark (Goldsboro: Nash Brothers, 1901), IV, 645; W. Clark, "The Home Guard," *Histories of the Several Regiments and Battalions from North Carolina in the Great War 1861-'65. Written by Members of the Respective Commands,* ed. W. Clark (Goldsboro: Nash Brothers, 1901), IV, 649; R. E. Yates, *The Confederacy and Zeb Vance,* ed., W. S. Hoole, *Confederate Centennial Studies* (Tuscaloosa: Confederate Publishing Co., 1958), No. 8, pp. 45-46.

16. M. G. Kidder, "The Old Home Guard," *Overland Monthly and Out West Magazine,* XXXIII (Apr., 1915), 342.

17. A. Gordon, "Organization of Troops," *Histories of the Several Regiments and Battalions from North Carolina in the Great War 1861-'65. Written by Members of the Respective Commands,* ed. W. Clark (Raleigh: E. M. Uzzell, 1901), I, 1-65; Hill, *Confederate Military History,* IV, 12-17; W. Clark, *Memorial Address Upon the Life of General James Green Martin* (Raleigh: n.p., 1916), pp. 9-11.

18. P. R. Hines "The Medical Corps," *Histories of the Several Regiments and Battalions from North Carolina in the Great War 1861-'65. Written by Members of the Respective Commands,* ed. W. Clark (Goldsboro: Nash Brothers, 1901), IV, 623-44.

19. B. E. Wiley, "A Time of Greatness," *JSH,* XXII (Feb., 1956), 25-28; C. J. Presler, Jr., ed., *A History of Catawba County* (Salisbury: Catawba County Historical Association, 1954), p. 275; Mary F. Sanders, "Saved by Mason's Certificate," Raleigh *Morning Post,* Aug. 11, 1905; G. W. F. Harper Diary, May 29, 1861, SHC.

20. J. W. Ellis to D. H. Hill, Apr. 24, 1861, D. H. Hill Papers, SLR; John G. Barrett, *North Carolina as a Civil War Battleground* (Raleigh: NCDAH, 1960), p. 11; Graham, "How N.C. Went to War," p. 285.

21. L. Warlick to C. McGimsey, May 28, 1861, C. McGimsey Papers, SHC.

22. E. J. Hale, "The Bethel Regiment," *Histories of the Several Regiments and Battalions from North Carolina in the Great War 1861-'65. Written by Members of the Respective Commands,* ed., W. Clark (Raleigh: E. M. Uzzell, 1901), I, 75.

23. Graham, "How N.C. Went to War," p. 283.

24. G. P. Erwin to Sister, Mar. 16, 1862, G. P. Erwin Papers, SHC.

25. W. H. Proffit to Brother, July 20, 1861, Proffit Family Papers, SHC; O. Alderman to "Captain Hawes," July 15, 1861, Confederate Papers, SHC.

26. J. L. Gorrell to "Mary," Sept. 5, 1861, R. Gorrell Papers, SHC; J. W. Collins to J. W. K. Dix, May 11, 1861, H. MacRae Papers, DU; T. F. Wood, "Recollections," Raleigh *N and O*, May 20, 1895. At Fort Macon great excitement prevailed when a flag presented to the garrison by the ladies of Morehead City was hoisted and given a nine-gun salute. The firing brought "the boys" on the beach running to the fort. They thought it was under attack. H. M. Wagstaff, ed., *The James A. Graham Papers, 1861-1884* (Chapel Hill: Univ. of N.C. Press, 1928), p. 104.

27. T. W. Wills to Sister, Apr. 30, 1861, G. W. Wills Papers, SHC.

28. R. B. MacRae to Brother, Oct. 1, 1861, H. MacRae Papers, DU.

29. L. Warlick to C. McGimsey, May 12, 1861, C. McGimsey Papers, SHC.

30. David Schenck Journal, Dec. 1, 1861, SHC.

31. J. D. Harris to Mother, June 23, 1861, J. D. Harris Papers, DU.

32. H. T. Clark Papers, 1861, NCDAH.

33. Clark, *Memorial Address on General Martin,* p. 21; Hill, *Confederate Military History,* IV, 14-15; Connor, *N.C.,* II, 194.

34. Hill, *Bethel to Sharpsburg,* I, 159; Connor, *N.C.,* II, 175-77.

35. J. Gorgas, "Notes on Ordnance Department of the Confederate Government," *SHSP,* XII (Jan.-Feb., 1884), 69.

36. Gordon, "Organization of Troops," p. 40; Hill, *Bethel to Sharpsburg,* I, 129; OR, I, Ser. I, 478-79.

37. OR, II, Ser. I, 3-6; *Ibid.,* III, Ser. IV, 987; Gorgas, "Notes on the Ordnance Department," p. 71.

38. *Ibid.,* p. 86; Hill, *Bethel to Sharpsburg,* I, 128; J. Gorgas to H. T. Clark, Sept. 14, 1861, H. T. Clark Papers, NCDAH.

39. Gordon, "Organization of Troops," pp. 42-43; D. Brown, "Sherman Closed Business," Raleigh *N and O*, July 26, 1953; Connor, *N.C.,* II, 194.

40. Schenck Journal, Oct. 23, 1861, SHC; Gordon, "Organization of Troops," p. 42; W. Clark, "The Raising, Organization and Equipment of North Carolina Troops During the Civil War," *NCB,* XIX (July-Oct., 1919), 3.

41. Schenck Journal, Oct. 23, 1861, SHC; Jean Boyd, "Historical Spots of Early Edenton," Newspaper clipping, NCC; Gorgas, "Notes on Ordnance Department," pp. 71-72; Connor, *N.C.,* II, 194-95.

42. OR, III, Ser. IV, 987; Gordon, "Organization of Troops," p. 44; Gorgas, "Notes on Ordnance Department," p. 77.

43. Gorgas, "Notes on Ordnance Department," p. 78; Gordon, "Organization of Troops," p. 46.

44. Hill, *Confederate Military History,* IV, 31; Connor, *N.C.,* II, 195; Gordon, "Organization of Troops," pp. 16-36. Young Henry K. Burgwyn, a former Virginia Military Institute cadet, wrote to Captain William Polk at the Lexington school: "I write to ask concerning a matter of apparently little importance but one which nevertheless troubles me considerably. It appears that I can not get any cadet grey cloth for less than $12 per yard in North Carolina and not wishing to pay that price I should like very much

to get a suit made at V.M.I. and also if possible for the Major and Col. of my regiment. (26 N.C.). My account with the institute is not settled and I should regard it as a great accommodation if I could get the suit made. Please let me know what it will cost me." H. K. Burgwyn to W. Polk, Dec. 27, 1861, H. K. Burgwyn File, V.M.I.

45. See below p. 245.

46. Hugh T. Lefler and A. R. Newsome, *North Carolina: The History of a Southern State* (Chapel Hill: Univ. of N.C. Press, 1954), p. 430.

47. Hugh T. Lefler, *History of North Carolina* (New York: Lewis Historical Publishing Co., 1956), II, 494.

CHAPTER III

1. R. D. W. Connor, *North Carolina, Rebuilding an Ancient Commonwealth* (New York: American Historical Society, 1929), II, 232.

2. D. H. Hill to B. F. Butler, July 5, 1861, B. F. Butler Papers, LC.

3. D. H. Hill to J. W. Ellis, June 11, 1861, Newspaper clipping, Scrapbook, NCC.

4. Warlick to C. McGimsey, June 11, 1861, C. McGimsey Papers, SHC.

5. David Schenck Journal, July 5, 1861, SHC.

6. D. H. Hill, *North Carolina in the War Between the States—Bethel to Sharpsburg* (Raleigh: Edwards and Broughton, 1926), I, 61-62.

7. James C. Harper Diary, July 24, 1861, SHC; Schenck Journal, July 25, 1861, SHC.

8. F. J. Iredell to Cousin, July 10, 1861, Hayes Collection, SHC.

9. Hill, *Bethel to Sharpsburg*, I, 154; T. J. Scharf, *History of the Confederate States Navy from its Organization to the Surrender of its Last Vessel* (New York: Rogers and Sherwood, 1887), p. 368.

10. Hill, *Bethel to Sharpsburg*, I, 155.

11. *Ibid.*

12. See below, p. 265.

13. T. N. Ramsay, *Sketches of the Great Battles in 1861, in the Confederate States of America* (Salisbury: J. J. Bruner, 1861), p. 19; D. Ammen, *The Atlantic Coast* (New York: Charles Scribner's Sons, 1883), pp. 163-64; J. L. Nichols, *Confederate Engineers,* W. S. Hoole, ed., *Confederate Centennial Studies* (Tuscaloosa: Confederate Publishing Co., 1957), p. 15; Hill, *Bethel to Sharpsburg*, I, 156; W. Gwynn to J. W. Ellis, June 14, 1861, Rec. Gr. 109, NA; W. Gwynn to W. Johnston, June 11, 1861, Rec. Gr. 109, NA.

14. W. Gwynn to "Citizens of Currituck County," June 9, 1861, Rec. Gr. 109, NA.

15. B. D. McNeill, *The Hatterasman* (Winston-Salem: J. F. Blair, 1958), pp. 138-39. See also J. W. Rolinson Journal, SHC.

16. *NR*, VI, Ser. I, 79, 713-14; *OR*, IV, Ser. I, 590-92; Schenck Journal, July 2, 1861, SHC; David Stick, *The Outer Banks of North Carolina* (Chapel Hill: Univ. of N.C. Press, 1958), p. 119; J. M. Merrill, "The Hatteras Expedition, August, 1861," *NCHR*, XXIX (Apr., 1952), 207.

17. J. W. Rolinson Journal, May [?], 1861, SHC; McNeill, *Hatterasman*, p. 145; *NR*, VI, Ser. I, 79.

18. Stick, *Outer Banks*, p. 119.

19. *NR*, V, Ser. I, 688.

20. *Ibid.*, VI, Ser. I, 713.

21. Rolinson Journal, May [?], 1861, SHC; J. W. Ellis to L. D. Starke, Apr. 29, 1861, Starke-Marchant-Martin Papers, SHC; *NR*, VI, Ser. I, 140-42. As late as July 22, 1861, General Gwynn was urging state authorities to put more troops along the coast. W. Gwynn to H. T. Clark, July 22, 1861, Rec. Gr. 109, NA.

22. T. Sparrow to Wife, June 23, July 26, 1861, T. Sparrow Papers, SHC.

23. H. T. Clark to W. Winslow, July 11, 1861, H. T. Clark Papers, NCDAH.

24. T. Sparrow to Wife, June 23, 1861, T. Sparrow Papers, SHC; Schenck Journal, June 30, 1861, SHC.

25. T. Sparrow to Wife, June 23, 1861, T. Sparrow Papers, SHC.

26. Hill, *Bethel to Sharpsburg,* I, 158.

27. A. Tredwell, "North Carolina Navy," *Histories of the Several Regiments and Battalions from North Carolina in the Great War 1861-'65. Written by Members of the Respective Commands,* ed., W. Clark (Goldsboro: Nash Brothers, 1901), V, 299; *NR,* VI, Ser. I, 79. Some reports have the *Winslow* mounting only one gun.

28. Tredwell, "N.C. Navy," p. 300.

29. Hill, *Bethel to Sharpsburg,* I, 158; *NR,* VI, Ser. I, 23.

30. W. W. Robinson, Jr., *The Confederate Privateers* (New Haven: Yale Univ. Press, 1928), pp. 101-5; *NR,* VI, Ser. I, 72ff.; T. Sparrow to Wife, July 26, 1861, T. Sparrow Papers, SHC; Schenck Journal, July 2, 1861, SHC; W. Gwynn to W. Winslow, June 28, 1861, Rec. Gr. 109, NA.

31. *NR,* VI, Ser. I, 72; T. Sparrow to Wife, July 26, 1861, T. Sparrow Papers, SHC.

32. *NR,* VI, Ser. I, 78.

33. *Ibid.,* p. 111.

34. *Ibid.,* p. 72.

35. *Ibid.,* p. 110.

36. Merrill, "Hatteras Expedition," p. 209.

37. Stick, *Outer Banks,* p. 120.

38. *NR,* VI, Ser. I, 69-70.

39. *Ibid.,* p. 82; *OR,* IV, Ser. I, 603.

40. R. S. West, Jr., *Mr. Lincoln's Navy* (New York: Longmans, Green and Co., 1957), p. 75.

41. *Ibid.,* p. 77; *NR,* VI, Ser. I, 120; Merrill, "Hatteras Expedition," p. 210. The *Cumberland* was to join the fleet at sea.

42. *NR,* VI, Ser. I, 78-80.

43. *Ibid.,* p. 137; H. T. Clark to W. T. Dortch, Sept. [?], 1861, H. T. Clark Papers, NCDAH.

44. West, *Lincoln's Navy,* p. 77.

45. *NR,* VI, Ser. I, 121.

46. J. A. Marshall, ed., *Private and Official Correspondence of General Benjamin F. Butler during the Period of the Civil War* (Norwood, Mass.: Plempton Press, 1917), I, 227-28.

47. *NR,* VI, Ser. I, 140; T. Sparrow Diary, Aug. 28, 1861, SHC; Robinson, *Confederate Privateers,* p. 113.

48. *RR,* III, 17.

49. *Ibid.,* p. 18.

50. *NR,* VI, Ser. I, 121.

51. *Ibid.,* p. 136.

52. *RR,* III, 18.

53. *OR,* IV, Ser. I, 582, 589.

54. *NR,* VI, Ser. I, 141.

55. *Ibid.,* p. 121.

56. J. B. Fearing, "Federal Attack on Hatteras—Letter of John Bartlett Fearing," *Year Book—Pasquotank Historical Society,* ed., J. E. Wood (Elizabeth City: Historical Society, 1956), II, 110-11.

57. *NR,* VI, Ser. I, 121; *OR,* IV, Ser. I, 582; *RR,* III, 19. Colonel W. F. Martin had the following to say about a flag at Hatteras: "It may be proper to state that no flag was raised upon Fort Hatteras during the day of the 28th. This was a fact, however, that did not attract my attention, and I suppose can only be accounted for from the flag having been torn to pieces by the winds and no new ones procured. . . ." *NR,* VI, Ser. I, 142.

58. *Ibid.,* pp. 134-35.

59. *OR,* IV, Ser. II, 589.

60. *NR,* VI, Ser. I, 121.

61. *RR,* III, 19.

62. *OR,* VI, Ser. I, 589; *RR,* III, 25; R. Tomes, *The War With the South: A History of the Late Rebellion with Biographical Sketches of Leading Statesmen and Distinguished Naval and Military Commanders, etc. By Robert Tomes, M.D. Continued from the Beginning of Year 1864 to the End of the War by Benjamin G. Smith* (New York: Virtue and Yorston, 1862-67), I, 534.

63. Thomas Sparrow Diary, Aug. 27-28, 1861, SHC; *NR,* VI, Ser. I, 139. Barron, as late as April 1861, had been detailed by Lincoln as Chief of the Bureau of Navigation. A. Gleaves, *Life and Letters of Rear Admiral Stephen B. Luce U.S. Navy* (New York: G. P. Putnam's Sons, 1925), p. 73; W. H. Patrick, "The Fall of Hatteras," *The Confederate Reveille* (Raleigh: Edwards and Broughton, 1898), pp. 124-25.

64. Sparrow Diary, Aug. 28, 1861, SHC.

65. *NR,* VI, Ser. I, 143.

66. *Ibid.,* p. 139; T. J. Scharf, *History of the Confederate States Navy from its Organization to the Surrender of its Last Vessel* (New York: Rogers and Sherwood, 1887), p. 375.

67. Sparrow Diary, Aug. 28-29, 1861, SHC; H. T. Clark to S. L. Fremont, Sept. 2, 1861, H. T. Clark Papers, NCDAH.

68. *NR,* Ser I, 121-22.

69. *Ibid.*

70. Sparrow Diary, Aug. 29, 1861, SHC.

71. *Ibid.; NR,* VI, Ser. I, 139; Extracts from *Harper's Weekly,* 1861, Folder, NCC.

72. *RR,* III, 20.

73. *OR,* IV, Ser. I, 583; Merrill, "Hatteras Expedition," p. 215.

74. *OR,* IV, Ser. I, 583-84.

75. *Ibid.,* p. 583; Stick, *Outer Banks,* pp. 127-28; P. F. Mottelay and others, eds., *The Soldier in Our Civil War: A Pictorial History of the Conflict, 1861-1865* (New York: Stanley Bradley, 1880), I, 121; Fearing, "Letter of J. B. Fearing," pp. 110-11.

76. *Report of the Joint Committee on the Conduct of the War* (Washington: GPO, 1863), III, (Hatteras Inlet Expedition), p. 284.

77. Merrill, "Hatteras Expedition," pp. 217-18.

78. *OR,* IV, Ser. I, 585; *NR,* VI, Ser. I, 144.

79. T. Sparrow to Wife, Sept. 1, 1861, T. Sparrow Papers, SHC; R. B. MacRae to Brother, Sept. 1, 1861, H. MacRae Papers, DU; C. H. Doughty, "C. H. Doughty's Record" (Unpublished reminiscence), NCC.

80. Merrill, "Hatteras Expedition," p. 218.

81. E. L. Perkins to H. T. Clark, Sept. 30, 1861, H. T. Clark Papers, NCDAH; "Minnie" to "My Dearest Carey," Sept. 13, 1861, Pettigrew Family Papers, SHC; "Cornelia" to "My Dearest Manerva," Sept. 3, 1861, Pettigrew Family Papers, SHC; R. B. MacRae to Brother, Sept. 1, 1861, H. MacRae Papers, DU; Hill, *Bethel to Sharpsburg,* I, 169.

82. See *Report of the Roanoke Island Investigation Committee* (Richmond: Enquirer Book and Job Press, 1862).

83. Elizabeth Collier Diary, Aug. 30, 1861, SHC; Kate M. Rowland, "T. Rowland Letters," *WMCQ,* XXV (Oct., 1916), 73-74; Schenck Journal, Aug. 30, 1861, SHC; R. B. Creecy to [?], Sept. 1, 1861, Creecy Papers, SHC; Raleigh *Register,* Sept. 11, 1861. Many women and children left eastern North Carolina following the loss of Hatteras.

84. Harrington *Weekly News,* Sept. 4, 1861; Mrs. R. B. Creecy to "Dr. Smedes," Aug. 31, 1861, Creecy Papers, SHC.

85. W. Whitehead Diary, Sept. 1, 1861, SHC.

86. Collier Diary, Aug. 28 [?], 1861, SHC.

87. W. Pettigrew to J. J. Johnston, Oct. 1, 1861, Pettigrew Family Papers, SHC. William Pettigrew also thought the Hatteras affair "a disgraceful page in the history of the state." *Ibid.*

88. *OR*, IV, Ser. I, 584-85; Stick, *Outer Banks*, pp. 128-29.

89. *OR*, IV, Ser. I, 606.

90. R. C. Hawkins, "Early Coast Operations in North Carolina," *B and L*, eds., R. U. Johnson and C. C. Buel (New York, Century Co., 1887), I, 634.

91. *NR*, VI, Ser. I, 782; Hill, *Bethel to Sharpsburg*, I, 172-73. Governor Clark in his report to the legislature stated that the forts were evacuated "under circumstances that cannot be approved." H. T. Clark to W. T. Dortch, Sept. [?], 1861, H. T. Clark Papers, NCDAH; H. T. Clark to J. G. Martin, Feb. 15, 1862, H. T. Clark Papers, NCDAH. See also *NR*, VI, Ser. I, 222-24; Scharf, *Confederate Navy*, p. 376.

92. D. McD. Lindsey to J. G. Martin, Sept. 3, 1861, H. T. Clark Papers, NCDAH; R. B. Creecy to [?], Sept. 1, [1861], Creecy Papers, SHC; Stick, *Outer Banks*, p. 129; Minutes of the Council of War held at Fort Oregon, Aug. 31, 1861, H. T. Clark Papers, NCDAH; E. Morris to W. Winslow, Sept. 5, 1861, H. T. Clark Papers, NCDAH.

93. D. D. Porter, *Naval History of the Civil War* (New York: Sherman Publishing Co., 1886), p. 47.

94. W. H. Parker, *Recollections of a Naval Officer 1841-1865* (New York: Charles Scribner's Sons, 1883), p. 215; Merrill, "Hatteras Expedition," p. 217.

CHAPTER IV

1. B. D. McNeill, *The Hatterasman* (Winston-Salem: J. F. Blair, 1958), p. 162.

2. R. C. Hawkins, "Early Coast Operations in North Carolina," *B and L*, eds., R. U. Johnson and C. C. Buel (New York: Century Co., 1887), 634-35.

3. J. E. Wool to R. C. Hawkins, Sept. 10, 26, 1861, R. C. Hawkins Papers, BU.

4. David Stick, *The Outer Banks of North Carolina* (Chapel Hill: Univ. of N.C. Press, 1958), p. 130; McNeill, *Hatterasman*, p. 162.

5. *NR*, VI, Ser. I, 221-25; J. D. Whitford to H. T. Clark, Sept. 19, 1861, H. T. Clark Papers, NCDAH.

6. Hawkins, "Coast Operations," p. 635.

7. *Ibid.*, pp. 636-37; *OR*, IV, Ser. I, 595-98. Much of Hawkins' information came from runaway slaves who made their way to Hatteras. Hawkins, "Coast Operations," p. 635.

8. T. J. Scharf, *History of the Confederate States Navy from its Organization to the Surrender of its Last Vessel* (New York: Rogers and Sherwood, 1887), p. 378. The garrison on Roanoke Island consisted primarily of the Third Georgia (Colonel A. R. Wright) and the Eight North Carolina (Colonel H. M. Shaw.)

9. Stick, *Outer Banks*, p. 131.

10. D. H. Hill, *North Carolina in the War Between the States—Bethel to Sharpsburg* (Raleigh: Edwards and Broughton, 1926), I, 174.

11. *NR*, VI, Ser. I, 275-80; *OR*, IV, Ser. I, 596-97, 621; Scharf, *Confederate Navy*, p. 379.

12. Part of the valuable cargo consisted of overcoats, dresscoats, pantaloons, and shoes.

13. J. H. Morrison and G. H. Ridgly to R. C. Hawkins, Oct. 1, 1861, R. C. Hawkins Papers, BU; *RR*, III, 155-57. It was hinted in some Northern circles that Morrison had sold out to the Confederates. Extracts from *Haper's Weekly*, 1861, Folder, NCC.

14. W. L. Brown to R. C. Hawkins, Oct. 2, 1861, R. C. Hawkins Papers, BU.

15. *Ibid.*; J. Clark to R. C. Hawkins, Oct. 2, 1861, R. C. Hawkins Papers, BU.

16. J. L. Reid to Wife, Oct. 2, 1861, J. L. Reid Papers, DU; Scharf, *Confederate Navy*, p. 379; Stick, *Outer Banks*, p. 132.

17. Scharf, *Confederate Navy*, p. 380.

18. E. C. Yellowly to J. B. Yellowly, Oct. 2, 1861, E. C. Yellowly Papers, SHC.

19. Scharf, *Confederate Navy*, p. 380.

20. H. T. J. Ludwig, "Eighth Regiment of North Carolina Troops," (Manuscript), H. T. J. Ludwig Papers, SHC; Stick, *Outer Banks*, p. 133.

21. R. B. Creecy to "Betty," Oct. 9, 1861, Creecy Papers, SHC.

22. Scharf, *Confederate Navy*, p. 381.

23. *RR*, III, 168.

24. W. L. Brown to R. C. Hawkins, Oct. 6, 1861, R. C. Hawkins Papers, BU. Confederate vessels shelled the Federal position. It was known as Camp Live Oak. *Ibid*.

25. E. C. Yellowly to Nephew, Oct. 10, 1861, E. C. Yellowly Papers, SHC. Some of the Georgians stopped long enough to pillage the Federal camp before giving chase to the enemy. *Ibid*.

26. Stick, *Outer Banks*, p. 134.

27. R. Tomes, *The War with the South: A History of the Late Rebellion with Biographical Sketches of Leading Statesmen and Distinguished Naval and Military Commanders, etc. By Robert Tomes, M.D. Continued from the Beginning of Year 1864 to the End of the War by Benjamin G. Smith* (New York: Virtue and Yorston, 1862-67), I, 547.

28. W. L. Brown to R. C. Hawkins, Oct. 6, 1861, R. C. Hawkins Papers, BU; Tomes, *War with the South*, I, 547; Stick, *Outer Banks*, p. 155.

29. E. C. Yellowly to Nephew, Oct. 10, 1861, E. C. Yellowly Papers, SHC.

30. Tomes, *War with the South*, I, 547.

31. J. L. Reid to Wife, Oct. 7, 1861, J. L. Reid Papers, DU.

32. C. H. Andrews to Mother, Oct. 9, 1861, C. H. Andrews Papers, SHC.

33. Stick, *Outer Banks*, p. 136.

34. *OR*, VI, Ser. I, 623-24.

35. Hawkins, "Coast Operations," pp. 636-37.

36. *Ibid.*, p. 636.

37. "Citizens of Hatteras" to "Commander of Federal Forces at Hatteras Inlet," n.d., R. C. Hawkins Papers, BU; "Citizens of Hyde County" to R. C. Hawkins, n.d., R. C. Hawkins Papers, BU; H. T. Clark to J. P. Benjamin, Sept. 24, 1861, H. T. Clark Papers, NCDAH; *OR*, IV, Ser. I, 608-9.

38. W. S. Pettigrew to H. T. Clark, Nov. 3, 7, 1861, Pettigrew Family Papers, SHC; "Caroline" to "My Dear Mama," Nov. 12, 1861, Pettigrew Family Papers, SHC.

39. B. F. Havens to H. T. Clark, Sept. 17, 1861, H. T. Clark Papers, NCDAH.

40. R. H. Riddick to H. T. Clark, Sept. 28, 1861, H. T. Clark Papers, NCDAH.

41. H. T. Clark to C. Gatlin, Sept. 13, 1861, H. T. Clark Papers, NCDAH; "Deposition of Edward J. Willis, December, 1859—May, 1861, State ·of Massachusetts, Worcester County," S. R. Barton Papers, DU; J. G. deR. Hamilton, *Reconstruction in North Carolina* (New York: Columbia Univ. Press, 1914), pp. 81-82.

42. B. D. McNeill, "Two Fiddlers Played for the Funeral," Raleigh *N and O*, Feb. 22, 1959; N. C. Delaney, "Charles Henry Foster and the Unionists of Eastern North Carolina," *NCHR*, XXXVII, 352.

43. W. E. Dodge to R. C. Hawkins, Dec. 21, 1861, R. C. Hawkins Papers, BU; Delaney, "Foster and the Unionists," pp. 349-57; "Aid to Loyal North Carolinians," Broadside, R. C. Hawkins Papers, BU; Delaney, "Foster and the Unionists," p. 356.

44. *OR*, I, Ser. III, 630; N.Y. *Times*, Nov. 19, 1861; McNeill, "Two Fiddlers," Raleigh *N and O*, Feb. 22, 1959; Delaney, "Foster and the Unionists," pp. 357-58.

45. Hamilton, *Reconstruction*, pp. 85-86.

46. *OR*, IV, Ser. I, 608-9.

47. *Ibid.*, p. 610; M. Weber to R. C. Hawkins, Sept. 3, 1861, R. C. Hawkins Papers, BU; J. E. Wool to R. C. Hawkins, Sept. 10, 18, 1861, R. C. Hawkins Papers, BU.

48. *OR*, IV, Ser. I, 658-59.

49. H. T. Clark to J. P. Benjamin, Sept. 24. 1861, H. T. Clark Papers, NCDAH.

50. *OR*, IV, Ser. I, 613.

51. Delaney, "Foster and the Unionists," p. 354.

52. W. S. Boyce, *Economic and Social History of Chowan County, North Carolina, 1880-1915* ("Studies in History, Economics, and Public Law," LXXVI [New York: Columbia Univ. Press, 1917]), pp. 244-45. For more on the activities of the "Buffaloes" see below pp. 174-79.

53. *NR*, VI, Ser. I, 160, 173. See also below pp. 68-69.

54. Hawkins, "Coast Operations," pp. 635-36; *OR*, IV, Ser. I, 607-9.

55. Hawkins, "Coast Operations," p. 636; *OR*, IV, Ser. I, 609-10.

56. Margaret B. Stillwell, "General Hawkins as He Revealed Himself to His Librarian," *Papers of the Bibliographical Society of America*, XVI (1923), 86-89; *OR*, IV, Ser. I, 627-28; Margaret B. Stillwell, "Hawkins of the Hawkins' Zouaves," *Bookmen's Holiday Notes and Studies Written and Gathered in Tribute to Harry Miller Lydenberg*, ed., Margaret B. Stillwell (New York: New York Public Library, 1943), pp. 88-89; Hawkins, "Coast Operations," pp. 641-42. While in Washington, Hawkins became convinced of General McClellan's incompetency and set to work to bring about his removal. He urged the necessity of such a move upon the President and members of Congress. Stillwell, "General Hawkins as He Revealed Himself," pp. 69-97.

57. H. T. Clark to R. C. Gatlin, Sept. 13, 1861, H. T. Clark Papers NCDAH; E. L. Perkins to H. T. Clark, Sept. 30, 1861, H. T. Clark Papers, *NCDAH;* T. Jones to H. T. Clark, Sept. 1, 1861, H. T. Clark Papers, NCDAH; C. P. Jones to H. T. Clark, Sept. 16, 1861, H. T. Clark Papers, NCDAH; [?] to Wife, Sept. 1, 1861, Starke-Marchant-Martin Papers, SHC; M. B. Hale to K. B. Haigh, Oct. 3, 1861, Badger Family Papers, SHC; Joseph W. Graham to Father, Sept. 5, 1861, W. A. Graham Papers, SHC; John W. Graham to Father, Sept. 22, 1861, W. A. Graham Papers, SHC.

58. J. P. Benjamin to H. T. Clark, Sept. 29, 1861, H. T. Clark Papers, NCDAH; L. O'B. Branch to H. T. Clark, Sept. 17, 1861, H. T. Clark Papers, NCDAH; H. T. Clark to R. C. Gatlin, Sept. 13, 1861, H. T. Clark Papers, NCDAH.

59. L. O'B. Branch to H. T. Clark, Sept. 17, 1861, H. T. Clark Papers, NCDAH.

60. H. T. Clark to L. P. Walker, Sept. 8, 1861, H. T. Clark Papers, NCDAH; Hill, *Bethel to Sharpsburg*, I, 185.

61. H. T. Clark to J. P. Benjamin, Oct. 25, 1861, H. T. Clark Papers, NCDAH.

62. S. R. Mallory to J. P. Benjamin, Oct. 25, 1861, H. T. Clark Papers, NCDAH.

63. General Gatlin was a native of Perquimans County and an 1832 graduate of West Point.

64. *OR*, IV, Ser. I, 574; R. C. Gatlin to S. Cooper, Sept. 4, 1861, Rec. Gr. 109, NA.

65. Hill, *Bethel to Sharpsburg*, I, 186. See also "Copy of agreement signed by Gilbert Elliott, agent for J. G. Martin and Flag Officer W. F. Lynch, Oct. 22, 1861," W. F. Martin Papers, SHC; Gilbert Elliott to H. I. Hines, Nov. 3, 1861, W. F. Martin Papers, SHC; N. S. Perkins to Gilbert Elliott, Jan. 20, 1862, W. F. Martin Papers, SHC; S. R. Mallory to Gilbert Elliott, Jan. 4, 1862, W. F. Martin Papers, SHC.

66. Hill, *Bethel to Sharpsburg*, I, 188.

67. *Ibid.*, pp. 187-88.

68. *OR*, IV, Ser. I, 682.

69. *Ibid.*, p. 693. Two days earlier Hill had written from Fort Macon that there were only seven shells for the thirty-two pounder, making it "almost wholly useless." D. H. Hill to J. D. Whitford, Oct. 25, 1861, D. H. Hill Papers, NCDAH. The men of the Third Georgia Regiment worked tirelessly on the Roanoke Island fortifications, hoping that once they were completed General Huger would order the regiment back to Virginia. J. L. Reid to Wife, Sept. 8, 1861, J. L. Reid Papers, DU.

70. R. C. Gatlin to D. H. Hill, Oct. 28, 1861, Rec. Gr. 109, NA.

71. *OR*, IV, Ser. I, 693-94; Hill, *Bethel to Sharpsburg*, I, 191-92.

72. H. T. Clark to J. Davis, Dec. 16, 1861, H. T. Clark Papers, NCDAH.

73. H. T. Clark to H. A. Wise, Jan. 21, 1862, H. T. Clark Papers, NCDAH; B. Estván, *War Pictures from the South* (New York: D. Appleton and Co., 1863), pp. 235-45; J. S. Wise, *End of an Era* (New York: Houghton, Mifflin and Co., 1899), p. 177.
74. H. T. Clark to J. P. Benjamin, Jan. 31, 1862, H. T. Clark Papers, NCDAH; H. T. Clark to J. Davis, Dec. 16, 1861, H. T. Clark Papers, NCDAH; Hill, *Bethel to Sharpsburg,* I, 193.
75. *OR,* IX, Ser. I, 172, 177, 179; Hill, *Bethel to Sharpsburg,* I, 195.
76. *OR,* IX, Ser. I, 129.

CHAPTER V

1. R. W. Daly, "Burnside's Amphibious Division," *MCG,* XXXV (Dec., 1951), 30.
2. A. E. Burnside, "The Burnside Expedition," *B and L,* eds. R. U. Johnson and C. C. Buel (New York: Century Co., 1887), I, 660-61.
3. Daly, "Burnside's Amphibious Division," pp. 30-31.
4. *Ibid.,* p. 31; W. A. Willoughby to Wife [?], Dec. 1, 1861, W. H. Noble Papers, DU.
5. D. R. Larned to "Dear Henry," Dec. 21, 1861, D. R. Larned Papers, LC.
6. Burnside, "Expedition," pp. 660-61.
7. Daly, "Burnside's Amphibious Division," p. 32.
8. Burnside, "Expedition," p. 661. Bands played "Dixie" as the troops embarked and a large number of ladies came down to see the expedition off. D. R. Larned to "Dear Sister," Jan. 4, 1862, D. R. Larned Papers, LC.
9. G. B. McClellan, *McClellan's Own Story. The War for the Union. The Soldiers Who Fought It. The Civilians Who Directed It and His Relations to It and to Them* (New York: Charles L. Webster and Co., 1887), pp. 206-7.
10. Burnside, "Expedition," p. 661. Daniel R. Larned, Burnside's private secretary, noted in a letter that his chief preferred the "quiet undress uniform" whereas Foster was very particular about his dress. Larned failed to comment on how the other two officers attired themselves. D. R. Larned to "Dear Henry," Dec. 21, 1861, D. R. Larned Papers, LC.
11. T. L. Livermore, "McClellan, 1861-1862," *PMHS,* L, Pt. I (May, 1917), 328; A. Woodbury, *Burnside and the Ninth Army Corps* (Providence: Sidney S. Rider, 1867), p. 31; W. W. Hassler, *General George B. McClellan: Shield of the Union* (Baton Rouge: Louisiana State Univ. Press, 1957), p. 40.
12. *OR,* IX, Ser. I, 354-55; D. R. Larned to Sister, Jan. 4, 11, 1862, D. R. Larned Papers, LC; Burnside, "Expedition," p. 602.
13. D. R. Larned to Sister, Jan. 4, 1862, D. R. Larned Papers, LC; Burnside, "Expedition," p. 602.
14. M. Emmons to Brother, Jan. 13, 1862, E. C. Southworth Papers, DU; D. R. Larned to Sister, D. R. Larned Papers, LC; W. H. Chenery, "Reminiscences of the Burnside Expedition," *Personal Narratives of Events in the War of the Rebellion. Being Papers Read Before the Rhode Island Soldiers and Sailors Historical Society* (Providence: Published by the Society, 1905), Ser. 2, No. 2, p. 18.
15. David Stick, *The Outer Banks of North Carolina* (Chapel Hill, Univ. of N.C. Press, 1958), p. 139.
16. P. H. Niles Diary, Jan. 23, 1862, MS Div., LC; D. R. Larned to "Dear Henry," Jan. 18, 1862, D. R. Larned Papers, LC.
17. C. A. Barker Journal, Jan. 23, 1862, EI; H. C. Pardee to Father, Jan. 15, 1862, H. C. Pardee Papers, DU.
18. H. C. Pardee to Mother, Jan. 25, 1862, H. C. Pardee Papers, DU.
19. *OR,* IX, Ser. I, 354-57; *NR,* VI, Ser. I, 526; J. S. C. Abbott, "Heroic Deeds of Heroic Men—The Navy in the North Carolina Sounds," *HNMM,* XXXII (Apr., 1866), 567-83; Stick, *Outer Banks,* p. 139; Burnside, "Expedition," p. 665.

20. D. L. Day, *My Diary of Rambles with the Twenty-fifth Volunteer Infantry with Burnside's Coast Division* (Milford: King and Billings, 1884), p. 23.

21. J. W. Denny, *Wearing the Blue in the Twenty-fifth Massachusetts Volunteer Infantry* (Worcester: Putnam and Davis, 1879), p. 59; C. A. Barker to "Folks at Home," Feb. 14, 1862, C. A. Barker Papers, EI; Stick, *Outer Banks,* p. 139.

22. C. A. Barker to "Folks at Home," Feb. 14, 1862, C. A. Barker Papers, EI.

23. M. Emmons to Brother, Jan. 13, 1862, C. E. Southworth Papers, DU; Stick, *Outer Banks,* p. 140.

24. H. C. Pardee to Father, Jan. 26, 1862, H. C. Pardee Papers, DU; Chenery, "Reminiscences," p. 20; A. Woodbury, "Ambrose Everett Burnside," *Personal Narratives of the Events in the War of the Rebellion. Being Papers Read Before the Rhode Island Soldiers and Sailors Historical Society* (Providence: N. Bangs Williams and Co., 1882), Ser. 2, No. 17, pp. 24-28.

25. L. M. Goldsborough to Wife, Jan. 30, 1862, L. M. Goldsborough Papers, LC.

26. *OR,* IX, Ser. I, 75. R. A. Ward, "An Amphibious Primer: Battle for New Bern," *MCG,* XXXVI (Aug., 1952), 37.

27. *Harper's Weekly* quoting Richmond *Examiner,* Feb. 4, 1862, Extracts from *Harper's Weekly,* Folder on Burnside Expedition, NCC.

28. David Schenck Journal, Feb. 1, 1862, SHC.

29. W. A. Graham to Wife, Feb. 10, 1862, W. A. Graham Papers, SHC.

30. B. Estvàn, *War Pictures from the South* (New York: D. Appleton and Co., 1863), p. 243.

31. H. M. Shaw to H. T. Clark, Jan. 10, 1862, H. T. Clark Papers, NCDAH.

32. H. C. Pardee to Father, Feb. 22, 1862, H. C. Pardee Papers, DU.

33. *OR,* IX, Ser. I, 166, 170-73; O. Taft to Father [?], Feb. 12, 1862, Edwin and Orison Taft Papers, DU.

34. H. MacRae to Brother, Dec. 22, 1861, Hugh MacRae Papers, DU; W. H. Battle to H. P. Battle, Jan. 8, 1862, Battle Family Papers, SHC; A. S. Roe, *The Twenty-fourth Regiment Massachusetts Volunteers, 1861-1866* (Worcester: Twenty-fourth Veteran's Association, 1907), pp. 63-64; W. F. Draper, *Recollections of a Varied Career* (Boston: Little, Brown and Co., 1908), p. 58; Daly, "Burnside's Amphibious Expedition," p. 35; Stick, *Outer Banks,* p. 141.

35. Henry MacRae to Brother, Dec. 22, 1861, Hugh MacRae Papers, DU; Margaret D. Owens, "The Confederate Flag (8th Regiment Flag)," *Year Book—Pasquotank Historical Society,* ed., J. E. Wood (Elizabeth City: Historical Society, 1956), II, 116.

36. *OR,* IX, Ser. I, 75; Daly, "Burnside's Amphibious Division," p. 35. Aboard the *New Brunswick* the chaplain held a service before the ship got underway and "took the thread of his discourse," said one of those present, "from the text 'prepare to meet thy God.'" H. C. Pardee to Father, Feb. 2, 1862, H. C. Pardee Papers, DU.

37. D. R. Larned to [?], Feb. 5, 1862, D. R. Larned Papers, LC.

38. D. L. Craft to Sister, Feb. 9, 1862, D. L. Craft Papers, DU.

39. D. R. Larned to [?], Feb. 5, 1862, D. R. Larned Papers, LC.

40. *Ibid.,* Feb. 6, 1862; C. B. Springer Diary, Feb. 6, 1862, SHC.

41. W. H. Parker, *Recollections of a Naval Officer, 1841-1865* (New York: Charles Scribner's Sons, 1883), pp. 112-14.

42. J. W. Wright Diary, Feb. 6, 7, 1862, Murdock-Wright Papers, SHC.

43. D. L. Craft to Sister, Feb. 9, 1862, D. L. Craft Papers, DU; J. M. Drake, *The History of the Ninth New Jersey Veteran Volunteers* (Elizabeth: Journal Printing House, 1889), p. 40.

44. L. Traver, *Soldiers and Sailors Historical Society of Rhode Island. Personal Narrative of the Events in the War of the Rebellion. The Battles of Roanoke Island and Elizabeth City* (Providence: N. Bangs and Co., 1880), Ser. 2, No. 5, p. 18.

45. Drake, *9 N.J.,* p. 40.

46. W. E. Vaughn to "Dear Sir," Feb. 7, 1862. Extract from *Harper's Weekly*, Folder on Burnside Expedition, NCC; *OR*, IX, Ser. I, 76.

47. J. W. Wright Diary, Feb. 7, 1862, Murdock-Wright Papers, SHC; D. R. Larned to [?], Feb. 8, 1862, D. R. Larned Papers, LC. General Burnside said the first shot was at 9:05 A.M. Still the firing did not become general until around 10:30 A.M. *OR*, IX, Ser. I, 15.

48. J. W. Wright Diary, Feb. 7, 1862, Murdock-Wright Papers, SHC; Mrs. J. H. Anderson, *North Carolina Women of the Confederacy* (Fayetteville: Privately printed, 1926), p. 66; *OR*, IX, Ser. I, 181.

49. Parker, *Recollections*, p. 230.

50. *NR*, VI, Ser. I, 594-97.

51. *OR*, IX, Ser. I, 76; Stick, *Outer Banks*, p. 144; H. C. Pardee to Father, Feb. 11, 1862, H. C. Pardee Papers, DU; Burnside, "Expedition," p. 667.

52. D. R. Larned to [?], Feb. 8, 1862, D. R. Larned Papers, LC; Daly, "Burnside's Amphibious Division," pp. 36-37; D. L. Craft to Sister, Feb. 9, 1862, D. L. Craft Papers, DU.

53. *OR*, IX, Ser. I, 76. At least one of the steamers ran "her nose up on the shore. . . ." Unidentified diary, Feb. 7, 1862, C. A. Barker Papers, EI. Both the Twenty-third and the Twenty-fifth Massachusetts claimed the honor of first planting the United States flag on Roanoke Island. J. A. Emmerton, *A Record of the Twenty-third Regiment Massachusetts Volunteer Infantry* (Boston: William Ware and Co., 1886), p. 45; O. Taft to Parents, Feb. 13, 1862, Edwin and Orison Taft Papers, DU.

54. H. C. Pardee to Father, Feb. 11, 1862, H. C. Pardee Papers, DU.

55. J. S. C. Abbott, "Heroic Deeds of Heroic Men: True Chivalry—Benjamin H. Porter," *HNMM*, XXXIV (Apr., 1867), 559; *OR*, IX, Ser. I, 76; Daly, "Burnside's Amphibious Division," p. 37.

56. O. Taft to Parents, Feb. 13, 1862, Edwin and Orison Taft Papers, DU.

57. *OR*, IX, Ser. I, 77.

58. D. H. Hill, *North Carolina in the War Between the States—Bethel to Sharpsburg* (Raleigh: Edwards and Broughton, 1926), I, 204-5.

59. *OR*, IX, Ser. I, 86; Hill, *Bethel to Sharpsburg*, I, 204-5; Stick, *Outer Banks*, pp. 145-46.

60. H. C. Pardee to Father, Feb. 15, 1862, H. C. Pardee Papers, DU.

61. *OR*, IX, Ser. I, 86.

62. C. A. Barker to "Dear Folks," Feb. 14, 1862, C. A. Barker Papers, EI.

63. H. C. Pardee to Father, Feb. 15, 1862, H. C. Pardee Papers, DU; *OR*, IX, Ser. I, 87; Abbott, "Heroic Deeds—B. H. Porter," p. 559.

64. *OR*, IX, Ser. I, 78.

65. M. Emmons to Brother, Feb. 14, 1862, C. E. Southworth Papers, DU.

66. *OR*, IX, Ser. I, 87; H. C. Pardee to Father, Feb. 15, 1862, H. C. Pardee Papers, DU.

67. *OR*, IX, Ser. I, 87.

68. M. Emmons to Brother, Feb. 14, 1862, C. E. Southworth Papers, DU.

69. C. F. Walcott, *History of the Twenty-first Regiment Massachusetts Volunteers* (Boston: Houghton, Mifflin and Co., 1882), pp. 34-35.

70. *Report of Roanoke Island Investigating Committee*, pp. 5-8.

71. J. W. Wright Diary, Feb. 8, 1862, Murdock-Wright Papers, SHC.

72. *OR*, IX, Ser. I, 87; [Anon.], *Memorial of Thomas Greely Stevenson* (Cambridge: Welch, Bigelow and Co., n.d.) pp. 11-15.

73. W. A. Willoughby to Wife, Feb. 9, 1862, W. H. Noble Papers, DU.

74. *OR*, IX, Ser. I, 156.

75. *Ibid.*, p. 79. Before departing General Wise had the hotel at Nags Head burned. M. J. Graham, *The Ninth Regiment New York Volunteers* (New York: E. P. Corby and Co., 1900), p. 159.

76. *OR*, IX, Ser. I, p. 85.
77. *Ibid.*, p. 173.
78. Daly, "Burnside's Amphibious Division," pp. 33-37.
79. *NR*, VI, Ser. I, 595-96; C. H. Andrews to Wife, Feb. 18, 1862, C. H. Andrews Papers, SHC; G. P. Dixon, "The Battle of Elizabeth City," *Year Book—Pasquotank Historical Society*, ed., J. E. Wood (Elizabeth City: Historical Society, 1955), I, 77-78; J. M. Merrill, "Battle of Elizabeth City, 1862," *USNIP*, LXXXIII (March, 1957), 321-23.
80. *NR*, VI, Ser. I, 607.
81. *Ibid.*, p. 596; Parker, *Recollections*, p. 237.
82. Dixon, "Battle of Elizabeth City," pp. 77-78; Merrill, "Battle of Elizabeth City," pp. 321-23; Parker, *Recollections*, pp. 240-45; *NR*, VI, Ser. I, 596-607; S. A. Ashe, "End of the North Carolina Navy" (Unpublished article), NCC.
83. R. B. Creecy to Daughter, Feb. 13, 23, 29, 1862, R. B. Creecy Papers, SHC; "Old Times In Betsy," Elizabeth City *Economist*, Aug. 10, 1900; *RR*, IV, 125.
84. *NR*, VI, Ser. I, 608.
85. *Ibid.*
86. *Ibid.*, p. 637.
87. J. Norcum, "The Eastern Shore of North Carolina in 1861 and 1862: A Statement of James Norcum to General F. Sigel," *HM*, VIII (Nov., 1870), 301-6.
88. R. Dillard, *The Civil War in Chowan County, North Carolina* (Edenton: Privately printed, 1916), pp. 27-28.
89. Norcum, "Eastern Shore—Statement of J. Norcum," pp. 301-6.
90. *NR*, VI, Ser. I, 637; R. R. Heath to H. T. Clark, Feb. 19, 1862, H. T. Clark Papers, NCDAH. The Federals captured two schooners in the sound, one of the vessels having four thousand bushels of corn on board. *NR*, VI, Ser. I, 637; R. Tomes, *The War with the South: A History of the Late Rebellion with Biographical Sketches of Leading Statesmen and Distinguished Naval and Military Commanders, etc. By Robert Tomes, M.D. Continued from the Beginning of Year 1864 to the End of the War by Benjamin G. Smith* (New York: Virtue and Yorston, 1862-67), II, 67-68.
91. *NR*, VI, Ser. I, 608, 638-39.
92. Merrill, "Battle of Elizabeth City," p. 323.
93. H. T. Clark to J. P. Benjamin, Feb. 17, 1862, H. T. Clark Papers, NCDAH. Major Thomas Rowland, a Virginian, thought the Roanoke Island disaster would "have the effect of causing our soldiers to re-enlist for the war more promptly than they would have done had our prospects been more bright in the future." Kate M. Rowland, "Letters of Major Thomas Rowland, C.S.A. from North Carolina, 1861 and 1862," *WMCQ*, XXV (Oct., 1916), 228.
94. W. L. Saunders to Mother, Feb. 12, 1862, W. L. Saunders Papers, SHC.
95. Caroline Pettigrew to "Dearest Mama," Feb. 13, 1862, Pettigrew Family Papers, SHC.
96. T. J. Wilson to J. F. Poindexter, Feb. 12, 1862, J. F. Poindexter Papers, DU.
97. Margaret McK. Jones, ed., *The Journal of Catherine Devereux Edmondston, 1860-1866* (Mebane: Privately printed, 1954), p. 38.
98. F. M. Martin to "My dear friends," Feb. 11, 1862, J. M. Culbertson Papers, DU.
99. J. H. Saunders to Mother, Feb. 11, 1862, J. H. Saunders Papers, SHC. James L. Reid, in camp near Portsmouth, Virginia, expressed similar sentiments. J. L. Reid to Wife, Feb. 10, 1862, J. L. Reid Papers, DU.
100. L. F. Emilio, *Roanoke Island, Its Occupation, Defence, and Fall* (New York: Roanoke Associates, 1891), p. 16.
101. C. F. Walcott, *History of the Twenty-first Regiment Massachusetts Volunteers* (Boston: Houghton, Mifflin and Co., 1882), p. 55.
102. Caroline Pettigrew to "My dear Mama," Mar. [?], March 3, 1862, Pettigrew Family Papers, SHC; Caroline Pettigrew to [?], March 3, 1862, Pettigrew Family Papers,

SHC. James L. Reid, an officer in a Georgia regiment, charged that the "officers of the regiments on the Island were badly deficient in courage and judgment." J. L. Reid to Wife, Feb. 9, 1862, J. L. Reid Papers, DU.

103. David Schenck Journal, Feb. [?], 1862, SHC. When the members of the Convention heard about the Roanoke Island defeat "there was a mild panic for a few minutes." Some delegates advocated immediate adjournment as if there was imminent danger of Burnside making a dash on Raleigh. K. P. Battle, "The Secession Convention of 1861," *NCB*, XV (Apr., 1916), 197-98.

104. See *Report of the Roanoke Island Investigating Committee* (Richmond: Enquirer Book and Job Press, 1862).

105. Woodbury, *Burnside*, pp. 49-50; B. F. Underwood, *Burnside Expedition*, Pamphlet, NCC.

106. H. C. Pardee to Father, Feb. 20, 1862, H. C. Pardee Papers, DU; W. A. Willoughby to Wife, Feb. 22, 1862, W. H. Noble Papers, DU.

107. J. H. Saunders to Mother, Jan. 10, 1862, J. H. Saunders Papers, SHC. When a planter moved inland, he usually took his slaves with him. However, many of the slaves either fled to the safety of the Union lines or took refuge in the swamps to avoid the move to the interior of the state. Some of those hiding out formed themselves into marauding bands of robbers. W. Pettigrew to R. Smith, Feb. 12, 1862, Pettigrew Family Papers, SHC; J. W. Hinton to Z. B. Vance, Feb. 10, 1863, Z. B. Vance Papers, DU; Schenck Journal, Feb. 22, 1862, SHC; Emily R. B. Haywood, "A Little Ancedote" (Unpublished anecdote), Benbury-Haywood Papers, SHC; W. C. Campbell to "Mrs. Miller," Mar. 18, 1862, Pettigrew Family Papers, SHC.

108. Benjamin Quarles, *The Negro in the Civil War* (Boston: Little, Brown and Co., 1953), p. 95; see also V. Colyer, *Report of the Services Rendered by the Freed People to the United States Army, in North Carolina, in the Spring of 1862, After the Battle of New Bern* (New York: Vincent Colyer, 1864).

109. Stick, *Outer Banks*, 161; see also Colyer, *Report of Services Rendered Freed People.*

110. Burnside, "Expedition," p. 668; Woodbury, *Burnside*, pp. 51-52.

111. Hill, *Bethel to Sharpsburg*, I, 214.

112. J. L. Reid to Wife, Mar. 9, 1862, J. L. Reid Papers, DU.

113. For a very good and full account of the burning of Winton see T. C. Parramore, "The Roanoke-Chowan Story—Chapter 7.—The Burning of Winton," Ahoskie *Daily Roanoke-Chowan News*, Civil War supplement, 1960.

114. *OR*, IX, Ser. I, 195; *NR*, VI, Ser. I, 654; R. C. Hawkins, "Early Coast Operations in North Carolina," *B and L*, eds., R. U. Johnson and C. C. Buel (New York: Century Co., 1887), I, 646.

115. *OR*, IX, Ser. I, 195; *NR*, VI, Ser. I, 654; Hawkins, "Coast Operations," p. 646; Parramore, "Burning of Winton," pp. 73-74.

116. G. H. Allen, *Forty-six Months with the Fourth Rhode Island Volunteers* (Providence: J. A. and R. A. Reid, 1887), pp. 84-86.

117. Parramore, "Burning of Winton," p. 74.

118. *NR*, VI, Ser. I, 654.

119. Parramore, "Burning of Winton," p. 76.

120. *OR*, IX, Ser. I, 195.

121. B. B. Winbourne, *The Colonial and State Pictorial History of Hertford County, N. C.* (Raleigh: Edwards and Broughton, 1906), p. 224; Parramore, "Burning of Winton," p. 77.

122. *Ibid.*

123. *OR*, IX, Ser. I, 196. Hawkins also stated in his report: "This, I believe, is the first instance during the war on our side where fire accompanied the sword." *Ibid.*

124. N.Y. *Herald*, Feb. 25, 1862.

125. Raleigh *N.C. Standard,* Mar. 12, 1862. A story circulated among the Federal troops on Roanoke Island that Winton was found "entirely deserted" and therefore burned. However, not all the soldiers believed this to be true. D. L. Craft to Sister, Feb. 23, 1862, D. L. Craft Papers, MS Div., Duke Univ. Lib.

126. *NR,* VI, Ser. I, 639.

127. L. Jackman and A. Hadley, *History of the Sixth New Hampshire Regiment* (Concord: Republican Press Association, 1891), p. 35.

128. J. M. Hough to W. Pettigrew, Mar. 18, 1862, Pettigrew Family Papers, SHC.

129. Woodbury, *Burnside,* p. 79.

130. J. M. Hough to W. Pettigrew, Mar. 18, 1862, Pettigrew Family Papers, SHC.

131. Hawkins, "Coast Operations," p. 647.

132. *OR,* IX, Ser. I, 242.

133. *Ibid.,* p. 241; J. F. Speight to Mother, Feb. 1, 1862, R. V. Howell Papers, NCDAH.

134. L. O'B. Branch to H. T. Clark, Feb. 23, 1862, H. T. Clark Papers, NCDAH.

135. *OR,* IX, Ser. I, 241-42.

136. Hill, *Bethel to Sharpsburg,* I, 219.

137. W. G. Lewis to "Cousin William," Mar. 20, 1862, Battle Family Papers, SHC.

138. *OR,* IX, Ser. I, 242; Hill, *Bethel to Sharpsburg,* I, 221.

139. *OR,* IV, Ser. I, 518. See also Estvàn, *War Pictures,* pp. 251-54.

140. R. A. Ward, "Battle for New Bern," *MCG,* XXXVI (Aug., 1952), 38.

141. Woodbury, *Burnside,* pp. 51-52.

142. L. M. Goldsborough to Wife, Mar. 14, 1862, L. M. Goldsborough Papers, MS Div., LC; Woodbury, *Burnside,* pp. 51-52. A ship was sent to Hatteras to contact Admiral Goldsborough.

143. N.Y. *Times,* Mar. 19, 1862.

144. D. L. Craft to Sister, Mar. 18, 1862, D. L. Craft Papers, MS Div., Duke Univ. Lib.

145. C. H. Barney, "A Country Boy's First Three Months in the Army," *Personal Narratives of Events in the War of the Rebellion. Being Papers Read Before the Rhode Island Soldiers and Sailors Historical Society* (Providence: N. Bangs Williams and Co., 1880), Ser. 2, No. 2, p. 33.

146. H. C. Pardee to Father, Mar. 12, 1862, H. C. Pardee Papers, DU.

147. H. C. Pardee to Father, Mar. 12, 1862, (later in the day), H. C. Pardee Papers, DU.

148. D. R. Larned to Sister, Mar. 18, 1862, D. R. Larned Papers, LC.

149. J. H. Saunders to "My Dear Dick," Feb. 20, 1862, J. H. Saunders Papers, SHC.

150. J. W. Williams to Father, Jan. 22, 1862, J. W. Williams Papers, DU.

151. J. H. Saunders to Mother, Jan. 23, 1862, J. H. Saunders Papers, SHC.

152. W. T. Loftin to Mother, Jan. 22, 1862, W. T. Loftin Papers, DU.

153. J. H. Saunders to "My Dear Ann," Mar. 2, 1862, J. H. Saunders Papers, SHC.

154. *NR,* VII, Ser. I, 117; *OR,* IX, Ser. I, 197.

155. D. R. Larned to Sister, Mar. 18, 1862, D. R. Larned Papers, MS Div., LC; H. C. Pardee to Father, Mar. 18, 1862, H. C. Pardee Papres, DU; *RR,* IV, 312-13.

156. *NR,* VII, Ser. I, 116; *RR,* IV, 308.

157. Roe, *24 Mass.,* p. 80. Before leaving Roanoke Island, Burnside received from spies a report on the fortification at New Bern.

158. H. C. Pardee to Father, Mar. 19, 1862, H. C. Pardee Papers, DU.

159. Ward, "Battle for New Bern," p. 40.

160. *OR,* IX, Ser. I, 242-43; Hill, *Bethel to Sharpsburg,* I, 222-23.

161. L. O'B. Branch to H. T. Clark, Mar. 23, 1862, L. O'B. Branch Papers, NCDAH.

162. *RR,* IV, 314.

163. R. P. Campbell to L. O'B. Branch, Mar. 25, 1862, L. O'B. Branch Papers, NCDAH.

164. J. M. Drennan Diary, Mar. 14, 1862, SHC.

165. *OR*, IX, Ser. I, 212.

166. *Ibid.*

167. D. R. Larned to Sister, Mar. 18, 1862, D. R. Larned Papers, LC.

168. *NR*, VII, Ser. I, 117.

169. H. C. Pardee to Father, Mar. 19, 1862, H. C. Pardee Papers, DU.

170. Heavy fog made visibility poor.

171. *OR*, IX, Ser. I, 221.

172. *Ibid.*, p. 267; R. D. Graham to Mrs. J. Graham, Mar. 14, 1862, W. A. Graham Papers, SHC.

173. R. P. Campbell to L. O'B. Branch, Mar. 25, 1862, L. O'B. Branch Papers, NCDAH; J. W. Graham to Father, Mar. 17, 1862, W. A. Graham Papers, SHC.

174. *OR*, IX, Ser. I, 255.

175. *Ibid.*, pp. 244-45. As Colonel Avery entered the breastworks with Carmichael, two companies from the Thirty-third North Carolina under Lieutenant Colonel R. F. Hoke joined Vance's right center.

176. R. F. Hoke to L. O'B. Branch, Mar. 18, 1862, L. O'B. Branch Papers, NCDAH; W. G. Lewis to Cousin, Mar. 20, 1862, Battle Family Papers, SHC; W. G. Lewis to K. P. Battle, April 1, 1862, Battle Family Papers, SHC.

177. *OR*, IX, Ser. I, 226.

178. R. P. Campbell to L. O'B. Branch, Mar. 25, 1862, L. O'B., Branch Papers, NCDAH; E. G. Haywood to L. O'B. Branch, Mar. 25, 1862, L. O'B Branch Papers, NCDAH.

179. Hill, *Bethel to Sharpsburg*, I, 229.

180. E. G. Haywood to L. O'B. Branch, Mar. 25, 1862, L. O'B. Branch Papers, NCDAH.

181. *OR*, IX, Ser. I, 213.

182. *Ibid.*, p. 245. The Twenty-eighth North Carolina arrived "too late to reach the battlefield." *Ibid.* See also D. R. Larned to "Henry," Mar. 28, 1862, D. R. Larned Papers, LC.

183. R. F. Hoke to L. O'B. Branch, Mar. 18, 1862, L. O'B. Branch Papers, NCDAH; W. G. Lewis to "Cousin William," Mar. 20, 1862, Battle Family Papers, SHC; D. R. Larned to "Henry," Mar. 28, 1862, D. R. Larned Papers, LC; *OR*, IX, Ser. I, 204-56.

184. G. Cochran, "Eye-Witness Tells How Zeb Vance Bolstered Men's Courage with Brandy," Raleigh *N and O*, June 21, 1936.

185. *OR*, IX, Ser. I, 213, 245; Day, *My Diary*, pp. 44-47; D. R. Larned to "Dear Uncle," Mar. 14, 1862, D. R. Larned Papers, LC.

186. S. C. Rowan to L. M. Goldsborough, Mar. 20, 1862, L. M. Goldsborough Papers, LC; *NR*, VII, Ser. I, 112. A man named Westervelt, who had commanded a vessel plying between New York and New Bern, piloted Rowan up the river. Hill, *Bethel to Sharpsburg*, I, 232.

187. *OR*, IX, Ser. I, 245-46.

188. *Ibid.*, p. 245. New Bern resident, James G. Bryan, said Branch gave the orders to burn the town. *Ibid.*, XXIX, Ser. I, Pt. II, 289.

189. H. M. Wagstaff, ed., *The James A. Graham Papers, 1861-1884* (Chapel Hill: Univ. of N.C. Press, 1928), p. 117.

190. *OR*, IX, Ser. I, 246; L. O'B. Branch to H. T. Clark, Mar. 23, 1862, L. O'B. Branch Papers, NCDAH.

191. Cochran, "Eyewitness," Raleigh *N and O*, June 21, 1936.

192. J. A. Hedrick to B. S. Hedrick, June 10, 1862, B. S. Hedrick Papers, DU; J. W. Page [?] to B. S. Hedrick, Apr. 10, 1862, B. S. Hedrick Papers, DU; D. L. Craft to Sister, Mar. 18, 1862, D. L. Craft Papers, DU; H. C. Pardee to Father, Mar. 28, 1862, H. C. Pardee Papers, DU; D. R. Larned to Mrs. A. E. Burnside, Mar. 23, 1862, D. R.

Larned Papers, LC; D. R. Larned to "Dear Uncle," Mar. 14, 1862, D. R. Larned Papers, LC; D. R. Larned to [?] Mar. 25, 1862, D. R. Larned Papers, LC; D. R. Larned to Sister, Mar. 18, 1862, D. R. Larned Papers, LC; Caroline Pettigrew to C. Pettigrew, Mar. 24, 1862, Pettigrew Family Papers, SHC; Day, *My Diary*, pp. 44-47; N.Y. *Times*, Mar. 19, 20, 26, 1862.

193. H. T. Clark to J. P. Benjamin, Mar. 25, 1862, H. T. Clark Papers, NCDAH.

194. Mary B. Pettigrew to J. Pettigrew, Mar. 28, 1862, Pettigrew Family Papers, SHC.

195. J. W. Graham to Father, Mar. 17, 20, 1862, W. A. Graham Papers, SHC.

196. OR, IV, Ser. I, 578-79.

197. *Ibid.*, LI, Ser. I, Pt. II, 512.

198. Hill, *Bethel to Sharpsburg*, I, 301.

199. *NR*, VI, Ser. I, 664.

200. OR, IX, Ser. I, 455.

201. Hill, *Bethel to Sharpsburg*, I, 302.

202. R. C. Gatlin to L. O'B. Branch, Mar. 20, 1862, L. O'B. Branch Papers, NCDAH.

203. J. W. Graham to Father, Mar. 20, 1862, W. A. Graham Papers, SHC.

204. OR, LI, Ser. I, Pt. II, 512.

205. *Ibid.*, IX, Ser. I, 250-51. General J. R. Anderson, commanding at Wilmington, held the post between the time of Gatlin's removal and Holmes's appointment.

206. T. Branson to Emily Branson, May 7, 1862, Emily Branson Papers, SHC; R. B. MacRae to J. W. Collins, Apr. 19, 1862, Hugh MacRae Papers, DU; Hill, *Bethel to Sharpsburg*, I, 305.

207. B. E. Stiles to Mother, Apr. 4, 1862, MacKay-Stiles Papers, SHC; W. W. Lenoir to "Dear Joe," Apr. 19, 1862, Lenoir-Norwood Papers, SHC.

208. C. L. Price, "North Carolina Railroads" (M.A. thesis, Univ. of North Carolina, 1951), pp. 168-69.

209. Woodbury, *Burnside*, p. 69.

210. OR, IX, Ser. I, 281.

211. Woodbury, *Burnside*, p. 69.

212. Allen, *4 R.I.*, p. 99. Morehead City was the terminus of the railroad. Also, it was situated on the west shore of Beaufort harbor at the north end of Bogue Sound.

213. OR, IX, Ser. I, 280.

214. Allen, *4 R.I.*, pp. 98-99.

215. Shackleford Banks extended from Barden Inlet at Cape Lookout on the east to Beaufort Inlet on the west.

216. OR, IX, Ser. I, 271.

217. *Ibid.*, p. 317; Hill, *Bethel to Sharpsburg*, I, 240.

218. Hawkins, "Coast Operations," p. 655. "This guide was taken to a woods out of sight of the troops and shot," said Hawkins. *Ibid.*

219. E. A. Kimball to R. C. Hawkins, Apr. 21, 1862, R. C. Hawkins Papers, BU; H. S. Fairchild to R. C. Hawkins, Apr. 21, 1862, R. C. Hawkins Papers, BU; Jackman, *6 N.H.*, pp. 43-44.

220. OR, IX, Ser. I, 327-28; Hill, *Bethel to Sharpsburg*, I, 241; J. L. Reid to Wife, Apr. 20, 22, 1862, J. L. Reid Papers, DU; C. H. Andrews to Wife, Apr. 23, 1862, C. H. Andrews Papers, SHC.

221. OR, IX, Ser. I, 318; Hill *Bethel to Sharpsburg*, I, 242.

222. H. S. Fairchild to R. C. Hawkins, Apr. 21, 1862, R. C. Hawkins Papers, BU; C. H. Andrews to Wife, Apr. 23, 1862, C. H. Andrews Papers, SHC; W. P. Avery, "The Maine Artillery with the Burnside Expedition and the Battle of Camden, N.C.," *Personal Narrative of Events in the War of the Rebellion. Being Papers Read Before the Rhode Island Soldiers and Sailors Historical Society* (Providence: N. Bangs Williams and Co., 1880), Ser. 2, No. 2, p. 20; Hawkins, "Coast Operations," p. 656.

223. OR, IX, Ser. I, 328; C. H. Andrews to Mother and Wife, Apr. 20, 1862, C. H.

Andrews Papers, SHC; J. L. Reid to Wife, Apr. 24, 1862, J. L. Reid Papers, DU; S. G. Griffin to R. C. Hawkins, Apr. 21, 1862, R. C. Hawkins Papers, BU.

224. *OR*, IX, Ser. I, 306; J. L. Reid to Wife, Apr. 22, 1862, J. L. Reid Papers, DU.

225. E. A. Kimball to R. C. Hawkins, Apr. 21, 1862, R. C. Hawkins Papers, BU; Hill, *Bethel to Sharpsburg*, I, 244; Hawkins, "Coast Operations," p. 657. The rumor of Confederate reinforcements was false.

226. T. W. Conway to R. C. Hawkins, Apr. 20, 1862, R. C. Hawkins Papers, BU; *OR*, IX, Ser. I, 322.

227. R. B. Creecy to Daughter, Apr. 28, 1862, Creecy Papers, SHC.

228. *OR*, IX, Ser. I, 322; R. B. Creecy to Daughter, Apr. 28, 1862, Creecy Papers, SHC.

229. H. Biggs to Wife, Apr. 27, 1862, H. Biggs Papers, SHC.

230. See above p. 10.

231. *OR*, IX, Ser. I, 277-78.

232. R. S. Barry, "Fort Macon: Its History," *NCHR*, XXVII(Apr., 1950), 171-72; Hill, *Bethel to Sharpsburg*, I, 247-48; H. Biggs to Wife, Apr. 27, 1862, H. Biggs Papers, SHC; L. O'B. Branch to H. T. Clark, Feb. 24, 1862, H. T. Clark Papers, NCDAH; *OR*, LI, Ser. I, Pt. II, 120.

233. *Ibid.*, IV, Ser. I, 693; Hill, *Bethel to Sharpsburg*, I, 248.

234. Barry, "Fort Macon," p. 172; *OR*, IX, Ser. I, 278-83.

235. *OR*, IX, Ser. I, 283.

236. J. W. Sanders, "Additional Sketch Tenth Regiment," *Histories of the Several Regiments and Battalions from North Carolina in the Great War 1861-'65. Written by Members of the Respective Commands*, ed., W. Clark (Raleigh: E. M. Uzzell, 1901), I, 505; Hill, *Bethel to Sharpsburg*, I, 250; Wagstaff, *J. A. Graham Papers*, p. 107; E. Wadsworth to Cousin, Sept. 5, 1861, Confederate States Arch., Soldiers Letters, DU.

237. Sanders, "Tenth Regiment," p. 505.

238. *OR*, IX, Ser. I, 283.

239. *Ibid.*, 283, 286, 288.

240. Barry, "Fort Macon," pp. 172-73.

241. *OR*, IX, Ser. I, 291.

242. *Ibid.*, p. 293.

243. A. C. Evans to Mother, Apr. 9, 1862, A. C. Evans Papers, SHC; Sanders, "Tenth Regiment," p. 507. The men stood in mortal fear of Colonel White. D. R. Larned to "Henry," Apr. 26, 1862, D. R. Larned Papers, LC.

244. D. R. Larned to Mrs. A. E. Burnside, Apr. 25, 1862, D. R. Larned Papers, LC; Sanders, "Tenth Regiment," p. 504; Barry, "Fort Macon," p. 173; J. A. Sloan, *Reminiscences of the Guilford Grays, Co. B, Twenty-seventh North Carolina Regiment* (Washington: R. O. Polkinborn, 1883), p. 28.

245. D. R. Larned to Mrs. A. E. Burnside, Apr. 25, 1862, D. R. Larned Papers, LC.

246. *Ibid.;* Barry, "Fort Macon," p. 173; *OR*, IX, Ser. I, 284.

247. Tomes, *War with the South*, II, 166-67; *OR*, IX, Ser. I, 294.

248. *OR*, IX, Ser. I, 284.

249. *NR*, VII, Ser. I, 279; D. R. Larned to Mrs. A. E. Burnside, Apr. 25, 1862, LC.

250. W. S. Andrews to A. J. Myer, May 1, 1862, N. C. Confederate Papers, SHC; *OR*, IX, Ser. I, 288; Barry, "Fort Macon," p. 173; H. Biggs to Wife, Apr. 27, 1862, H. Biggs Papers, SHC.

251. W. S. Andrews to A. J. Myer, May 1, 1862, N. C. Confederate Papers, SHC; H. Biggs to Wife, Apr. 27, 1862, H. Biggs Papers, SHC.

252. *OR*, IX, Ser. I, 284. Colonel White puts the time at 6:30 P.M. *Ibid.*, p. 294.

253. Sanders, "Tenth Regiment," pp. 509-10; *OR*, IX, Ser. I, 294; H. Biggs to Wife, Apr. 27, 1862, H. Biggs Papers, SHC.

254. D. R. Larned to "Henry," Apr. 26, 1862, D. R. Larned Papers, LC; H. Biggs to Wife, Apr. 27, 1862, H. Biggs Papers, SHC; *OR*, IX, Ser. I, 276.

255. D. R. Larned to "Henry," Apr. 26, 1862, D. R. Larned Papers, LC.

256. *Ibid.;* D. R. Larned to Mrs. A. E. Burnside, Apr. 27, 1862, D. R. Larned Papers, LC; J. K. Burlingame, *History of the Fifth Regiment of Rhode Island Heavy Artillery During Three Years and a Half of Service in North Carolina* (Providence: Snow and Farnham, 1892), pp. 64-65; D. R. Larned to Sister, Apr. 26, 1862, D. R. Larned Papers, LC.

257. D. R. Larned to Sister, Apr. 26, 1862, D. R. Larned Papers, LC. The Confederate soldiers no longer sang: "If Lincoln wants to save his bacon, Had better keep away from old Fort Macon, Look Away." Drake, *9 N.J.,* p. 73.

258. *OR,* IX, Ser. I, 294; H. Biggs to Wife, Apr. 27, 1862, H. Biggs Papers, SHC. Colonel White was so disliked by his men, said Burnside's secretary, that after going aboard ship he had to lock himself in his room every night "for fear of violence from his own men." D. L. Larned to "Henry," Apr. 26, 1862, D. R. Larned Papers, LC.

259. D. R. Larned to Mrs. A. E. Burnside, May 1, 1862, D. R. Larned Papers, LC; D. R. Larned to Sister, Apr. 28, 1862, D. R. Larned Papers, LC.

260. See above pp. 68-69.

261. D. R. Larned to Sister, Apr. 28, 1862, D. R. Larned Papers, LC; D. R. Larned to "Henry," Apr. 26, 1862, D. R. Larned Papers, LC.

262. *OR,* IX, Ser. I, 390; G. T. Walton to Wife, May 2, 1862, G. T. Walton Papers, SHC; A. MacRae to Brother, Apr. 15, 1862, H. MacRae Papers, DU.

263. Woodbury, *Burnside,* pp. 84-85.

264. *OR,* IX, Ser. I, 375, 379-80; D. L. Craft to Sister, Apr. 6, 1862, D. L. Craft Papers, DU; J. E. Bartlett to Cousin, May 7, 1862, Federal Soldiers Letters, SHC.

265. D. R. Larned to "Henry," Mar. 31, 1862, D. R. Larned Papers, LC.

266. *OR,* IX, Ser. I, 389.

267. D. R. Larned to "Henry," Apr. 26, 1862, D. R. Larned Papers, LC.

268. *OR,* IX, Ser. I, 374.

269. M. W. Boatner, *The Civil War Dictionary* (New York: David McKay Co., 1959), p. 632.

270. Woodbury, *Burnside,* pp. 86-88.

271. McClellan, *Own Story,* p. 245.

272. *OR,* IX, Ser. I, 392.

273. *Ibid.,* p. 441; H. R. Paschal, Jr., "The Story of Washington," Washington *Daily News,* Apr. 24-28, 1952.

274. *OR,* IX, Ser. I, 269; NR, VII, Ser. I, 151-53; L. C. Warren, *Beaufort County's Contribution to a Notable Era of North Carolina History* (Washington: GPO, 1930), p. 7.

275. Woodbury, *Burnside,* p. 78.

276. *OR,* IX, Ser. I, 269. Some accounts say the banner was stretched across the street. Warren, *Beaufort County,* p. 11.

277. D. R. Larned to Sister, Mar. 24, 1862, D. R. Larned Papers, LC.

278. *OR,* IX, Ser. I, 269; D. R. Larned to "Henry," Mar. 28, 1862, D. R. Larned Papers, LC.

279. W. J. Walker to L. O'B. Branch, Apr. 17, 1862, H. T. Clark Papers, NCDAH.

280. Hill, *Bethel to Sharpsburg,* I, 317. There was an abundance of Negro labor available for work on the fortifications. Roe, *24 Mass.,* p. 128.

281. R. D. W. Connor, *North Carolina, Rebuilding an Ancient Commonwealth* (New York: American Historical Society, 1929), II, 241-42.

282. See above, p. 95; H. G. Spruill, "Memorandum on Interviews with Officers of Federal Fleet" (Unpublished interviews), Pettigrew Family Papers, SHC.

283. *Ibid.,* pp. 2-3; NR, VII, Ser. I, 383.

284. *Ibid.,* pp. 283-84.

285. *Ibid.,* p. 372; Spruill, "Memorandum on Interviews with Officers of Federal Fleet," Pettigrew Family Papers, SHC.

286. M. J. Graham, *The Ninth Regiment New York Volunteers* (New York: E. P. Corby and Co., 1900), p. 217.

287. *OR*, IX, Ser. I, 295.

288. *Ibid.*, pp. 296-97.

289. *Ibid.*, pp. 298-303; Hill, *Bethel to Sharpsburg*, I, 320.

290. D. L. Craft to Sister, May 15, 1862, D. L. Craft Papers, DU; M. Emmons to Brother, May 30, 1862, C. E. Southworth Papers, DU; J. M. Drennon Diary, May 16, 1862, SHC; R. C. Osborne to Sister, May 18, 1862, Mary Gash and Family Papers, NCDAH; Hill, *Bethel to Sharpsburg*, I, 332-39.

291. *OR*, IX, Ser. I, 340-43; Roe, *24 Mass.*, pp. 118-21; Paschal "Washington," Washington *Daily News*, Apr. 25, 1952; Hill, *Bethel to Sharpsburg*, I, 323-24.

292. Connor, *N.C.*, II, 242. In the North a genuine feeling prevailed that Union sentiment was so strong in North Carolina that the state under a capable leader could be returned to the Union. J. G. deR. Hamilton, *Reconstruction in North Carolina* (New York: Columbia Univ. Press, 1914), p. 88; D. R. Larned to Sister, May 5, 1862, D. R. Larned Papers, LC; J. H. Smith to W. Pettigrew, June 26, 1862, Pettigrew Family Papers, SHC; H. Hardison to W. Pettigrew, Feb. 25, 1862, Pettigrew Family Papers, SHC.

293. Connor, *N.C.*, II, 242.

294. *OR*, IX, Ser. I, 396, 397, 401.

295. *Ibid.*, p. 394; Hill, *Bethel to Sharpsburg*, I, 272; Woodbury, *Burnside*, p. 89.

296. H. C. Pardee to Father, Mar. 28, 1862, H. C. Pardee Papers, DU; H. T. Clark to J. G. Martin June 12, 1862, H. T. Clark Papers, NCDAH.

297. Hill, *Bethel to Sharpsburg*, I, 278.

298. D. L. Craft to Sister, Apr. 6, 1862, D. L. Craft Papers, DU; J. Graham to Mother, Apr. 15, 1862, W. A. Graham Papers, SHC; Roe, *24 Mass.*, p. 128; Quarles, *Negro in the Civil War*, p. 96.

299. *OR*, IX, Ser. I, 400; D. L. Larned to Mrs. S. E. Burnside, Mar. 30, 1862, D. L. Larned Papers, LC.

300. *OR*, IX, Ser. I, 400.

301. Hamilton, *Reconstruction*, p. 90.

302. *Ibid.*, pp. 91-92.

303. *Ibid.*, p. 91.

304. *OR*, IX, Ser. I, 405.

305. *Ibid.*, p. 404.

306. *Ibid.*

307. Hill, *Bethel to Sharpsburg*, I, 300.

308. *OR*, IX, Ser. I, 73, 406, 410, 414.

309. A. Gordon, "Organization of Troops," *Histories of the Several Regiments and Battalions from North Carolina in the Great War 1861-'65. Written by Members of the Respective Commands,* ed. W. Clark (Raleigh: E. M. Uzzell, 1901), I, 12; W. Clark, *Memorial Address Upon the Life of General James Green Martin* (Raleigh: n.p., 1916), p. 11; H. T. Clark to J. Gorgas, May 5, 1862, H. T. Clark Papers, NCDAH. The Confederate soldiers remaining in eastern North Carolina were not too concerned about developments because they knew the Federals were concentrating everything in Virginia. J. A. Benbury to Wife, May 16, 1862, Benbury-Haywood Papers, SHC.

310. Gordon, "Organization of Troops," p. 12.

311. Hill, *Bethel to Sharpsburg*, I, 259-60.

CHAPTER VI

1. C. C. Howard to H. Stanly, Aug. 21, 1862, E. R. Beckwith Papers, SHC; Statement of W. Wilson, July 2, 1862, H. Briggs Papers, SHC; N. C. Delaney, "Letters of a Maine Soldier Boy," *CWH*, V (March, 1959), 49; J. L. Stackpole, "The Department of

North Carolina under General Foster, July, 1862—July, 1863," *MHSM* (Boston: Military Historical Society of Massachusetts, 1912), IX, 88.

2. *NR*, VII, Ser. I, 556-57; W. H. Cheek, "Additional Sketch Ninth Regiment," *Histories of the Several Regiments and Battalions from North Carolina in the Great War 1861-'65. Written by Members of the Respective Commands*, ed. W. Clark (Raleigh: E. M. Uzzell, 1901) I, 446-47; D. H. Hill, Jr., *North Carolina*, ed., C. A. Evans, *Confederate Military History* (Atlanta: Confederate Publishing Co., 1899), IV, 140; D. D. Porter, *Naval History of the Civil War* (New York: Sherman Publishing Co., 1886), p. 117; *RR*, V, 550-51.

3. *OR*, IX, Ser. I, 344-51; Stackpole, "Dept. of N.C.," p. 88; H. T. King, *Sketches of Pitt County: A Brief History of the County, 1704-1910* (Raleigh: Edwards and Broughton, 1911), pp. 132-33; W. G. MacRae to J. W. K. Dix, Aug. 7, 1862, Hugh MacRae Papers, DU; S. F. Harrison to Wife, Aug. 1, 1862, Jesse Harrison Papers, DU.

4. Stackpole, "Dept. of N.C.," p. 88; *RR*, V, 578-79; A. S. Roe, *The Twenty-fourth Regiment Massachusetts Volunteers, 1861-1866* (Worcester: Twenty-fourth Veteran's Association, 1907), pp. 143-45.

5. D. L. Craft to Sister, Aug. 29, 1862, D. L. Craft Papers, DU.

6. Union Soldier to "My Dear Nate and George," Dec. 6, 1862, New Bern Occupation Papers, SHC; E. T. Hale to Mother, Nov. 15, 1862, E. T. Hale Papers, SHC; Delaney, "Letters of a Maine Soldier," pp. 49-53.

7. H. T. Clark to R. E. Lee, Aug. 3, 1862, H. T. Clark Papers, NCDAH.

8. R. E. Lee to H. T. Clark, Aug. 8, 1862, H. T. Clark Papers, NCDAH. See above p. 129n.

9. *OR*, XVIII, Ser. I, 4-10; Hugh MacRae to J. W. K. Dix, Sept. 12, 1862, Hugh MacRae Papers, DU; Henry MacRae to Brother, Sept. 22, 1862, Hugh MacRae Papers, DU; Roe, *24 Mass.*, p. 148; S. F. Blanding, *Recollection of a Sailor Boy or the Cruise of the Gunboat Louisiana* (Providence: E. A. Johnson and Co., 1886), pp. 144-54: Hill, *Confederate Military History*, pp. 141-42. Henry MacRae of the Eighth North Carolina thought the attack on Washington "foolish." He complained that "some of our men and officers . . . behaved very badly down there." Henry MacRae to Brother, Sept. 22, 1862, Hugh MacRae Papers, DU.

10. *OR*, XVIII, Ser. I, 5; Hill, *Confederate Military History*, p. 142; Hugh MacRae to J. W. K. Dix, Sept. 12, 1862, Hugh MacRae Papers, DU.

11. *OR*, XVIII, Ser. I, 10; W. P. Jacocks, "Federal Operations in Eastern North Carolina During the Civil War" (M.A. thesis, Univ. of North Carolina, 1905), p. 8.

12. *NR*, VIII, Ser. I, 230-33.

13. S. G. French to Z. B. Vance, Oct. 22, 1862, Battle Family Papers, SHC.

14. Hill, *Confederate Military History*, pp. 142-43.

15. *OR*, XVIII, Ser. I, 45-49; J. B. Gardner, *Massachusetts Memorial to Her Soldiers and Sailors Who Died in the Department of North Carolina, 1861-1865* (Boston: Gardner and Toplin, 1909), p. 33. The captain of the *Southfield* said he was afraid to fire because the "shore was all lined with people flying from the enemy. . . ." *Message of the President of the United States and Accompanying Documents, to the Two Houses of Congress, at the Commencement of the First Session of the Thirty-Eighth Congress* (Washington: GPO, 1863), pp. 33-35.

16. Stackpole, "Dept. of N.C.," pp. 89-90.

17. *OR*, XVIII, Ser. I, 21. On October 30, Foster had written Major General H. S. Halleck: "These counties [Washington and Hyde] form a bag, the mouth of which is between Washington and Plymouth. . . . I hope to engage and capture this force." Gardner, *Mass. Memorial to Her Soldiers*, p. 30.

18. *OR*, XVIII, Ser. I, 21.

19. *RR*, VI, 192.

20. *OR*, XVIII, Ser. I, 21-23; Newton Wallace Diary, Nov. 2, 1862, NCC; A. S. Roe,

The *Fifth Regiment Volunteer Infantry* (Boston: Fifth Regiment Veteran's Association, 1911), p. 142.

21. *OR*, XVIII, Ser. I, 21-23; "Corporal" (Z. T. Haines), *Letters from the Forty-fourth M.V.M. in the Department of North Carolina in 1862-3* (Boston: Herald Job Office, 1863), p. 42.

22. D. L. Day, *My Diary of Rambles with the Twenty-fifth Volunteer Infantry with Burnside's Coast Division* (Milford: King and Billings, 1884) pp. 70-72.

23. J. K. Burlingame, *History of the Fifth Regiment of Rhode Island Heavy Artillery During Three Years and a Half of Service in North Carolina* (Providence: Snow and Farnham, 1892), p. 92; C. A. Barker to Father, Nov. 19, 1862, C. A. Barker Papers, EI; Wallace Diary, Nov. 3, 1862, NCC.

24. *Ibid.*, Nov. 4, 1862; *RR*, VI, 193; C. A. Barker to Father, Nov. 19, 1862, C. A. Barker Papers, EI; Day, *My Diary*, pp. 70-72; J. M. Drake, *The History of the Ninth New Jersey Veteran Volunteers* (Elizabeth: Journal Printing House, 1889), p. 91; "Corporal," *Letters from the Forty-Fourth Regement*, p. 43.

25. *RR*, VI, 193.

26. *OR*, XVIII, Ser. I, 21; *RR*, VI, 193.

27. P. S. Chase, *Battery F, First Regiment Rhode Island Light Artillery in the Civil War* (Providence: Snow and Farnham, 1892), p. 56.

28. *OR*, XVIII, Ser. I, 21; Gardner, *Mass. Memorial to Her Soldiers*, pp. 32-33.

29. C. A. Barker to "Helen," Dec. 6, 1862, C. A. Barker Papers, EI.

30. *OR*, XVIII, Ser. I, 477.

31. *Ibid.*, p. 54. A Federal soldier commented that the entire population of New Bern, especially the Negroes, "seemed to be abroad in the streets" on the morning the army departed. T. Kirwan, *Soldiering in North Carolina . . . By One of the Seventeenth* (Boston: Thomas Kirwan, 1864), p. 72.

32. *OR*, XVIII, Ser. I, 55; C. A. Barker to Father, Dec. 23, 1862, C. A. Barker Papers, EI; E. J. Cleveland, "Early Campaigns in N.C.," *NJHS*, LXVIII (April, 1950), 136-37.

33. J. S. C. Abbott, "Heroic Deeds of Heroic Men: A Military Adventure," *Harper's New Monthly Magazine*, XXX (Dec., 1864), 14.

34. *OR*, XVIII, Ser. I, 54-55, 67-75.

35. *Ibid.*, pp. 55, 91-92, 112-13; Cleveland, "Early Campaigns in N.C.," pp. 138-39; W. F. Loftin to Mother, Jan. 22, 1863, W. F. Loftin Papers, DU.

36. *OR*, XVIII, Ser. I, 55.

37. *Ibid.*, p. 113.

38. *Ibid.*, pp. 55, 92; W. I. Budington, *A Memorial of Giles F. Ward, Jr.* (New York: Anson D. F. Randolph, 1866), pp. 54-56; Wallace Diary, Dec. 14, 1862, NCC.

39. Cleveland, "Early Campaigns in N.C.," p. 143.

40. Abbott, "Heroic Deeds—A Military Adventure," p. 14.

41. W. W. Sullivan to "My dear Friend," Dec. 27, 1862, Lalla Pelot Papers, DU.

42. *OR*, XVIII, Ser. I, 55.

43. A. W. Mann, *History of the Forty-fifth Regiment Massachusetts Volunteer Militia* (Boston: Wallace Spooner, 1908), p. 386.

44. Cleveland, "Early Campaigns in N.C.," p. 144.

45. E. T. Hall to "Dear Cousin Anna," Dec. 24, 1862, E. T. Hall Papers, SHC.

46. W. W. Sullivan to "My dear Friend," Dec. 27, 1862, Lalla Pelot Papers, DU.

47. P. Mallett to S. Cooper, Feb. 13, 1863, P. Mallett Papers, SHC.

48. W. W. Sullivan to "My dear Friend," Dec. 27, 1862, Lalla Pelot Papers, DU.

49. *OR*, XVIII, Ser. I, 56, 113; J. J. Wyeth, *Leaves from a Diary Written While Serving in the Department of North Carolina from September, 1862, to June, 1863* (Boston: L. F. Lawrence and Co., 1878), p. 25; Roe, *24 Mass.*, p. 169.

50. W. W. Sullivan to "My dear Friend," Dec. 27, 1862, Lalla Pelot Papers, DU.

51. Stackpole, "Dept. of N.C.," p. 93; L. Leon, *Diary of a Tar Heel Confederate Soldier* (Charlotte: Stone Publishing Co., 1913), pp. 13-14.

52. Kirwan, *Soldiering in N.C.,* pp. 84-89; C. F. Pierce, *History and Camp Life of Company C, Fifty-first Regiment, Massachusetts Volunteer Militia, 1862-1863* (Worcester: Charles Hamilton, 1886), 81-82; DeF. Safford, *The Bay State Forty-fourth: A Regimental Record* (Boston: W. F. Brown and Co., 1863), p. 8.

53. *OR,* XVIII, Ser. I, 56-57, 69, 121; Abbott, "Heroic Deeds—A Military Adventure," p. 19; G. P. Erwin to Mother, Dec. 21, 1862, G. P. Erwin Papers, SHC; F. W. Bird to Sister, Dec. 23, 1862, R. W. Winston Papers, SHC.

54. *OR,* XVIII, Ser. I, 57; S. D. Pool, "Battle of White Hall," *Histories of the Several Regiments and Battalions from North Carolina in the Great War 1861-'65. Written by Members of the Respective Commands,* ed. W. Clark (Goldsboro: Nash Brothers, 1901), V, 87.

55. C. A. Barker [?] "Goldsboro Raid" (Unpublished account), C. A. Barker Papers, EI; C. A. Barker Diary, Dec. 16, 1862, EI.

56. Hill, *Confederate Military History,* p. 144; *OR,* XVIII, Ser. I, 121.

57. Pool, "White Hall," pp. 87-91; *OR,* XVIII, Ser. I, 121-22.

58. L. Warlick to Cornelia McGimsey, Dec. 18, 1862, Cornelia McGimsey Papers, SHC.

59. G. P. Erwin to Sister, Dec. 26, 1862, G. P. Erwin Papers, SHC. The presence of these logs along the banks was explained by the fact that a gunboat was under construction near by.

60. Abbott, "Heroic Deeds—A Military Adventure," p. 19.

61. C. A. Barker [?], "Goldsboro Raid," C. A. Barker Papers, EI.

62. *OR,* XVIII, Ser. I, 57; "Corporal," *Letters from the Forty-fourth Regiment,* p. 58.

63. *OR,* XVIII, Ser. I, 57-58.

64. *Ibid.,* pp. 106-22.

65. Hill, *Confederate Military History,* p. 146; *OR,* XVIII, Ser. I, 117-18; Wallace Diary, Dec. 17, 1862, NCC.

66. *OR,* XVIII, Ser. I, 58.

67. *Ibid.,* pp. 58, 86-87, 118-19.

68. *Ibid.,* p. 489.

69. W. A. Willoughby to Wife, Dec. 14, 1862, W. H. Noble Papers, DU.

70. Burlingame, *5 R.I.,* p. 113.

71. D. L. Craft to Sister, Dec. 24, 1862, D. L. Craft Papers, DU.

72. C. L. Price, "The Railroads of North Carolina During the Civil War" (M.A. thesis, Univ. of North Carolina, 1951), p. 176; L. Warlick to Cornelia McGimsey, Dec. 22, 1862, Cornelia McGimsey Papers, SHC; G. Lewis to Mother, Dec. 22, 1862, Battle Family Papers, SHC.

73. G. P. Erwin to Sister, Dec. 31, 1862, G. P. Erwin Papers, SHC. He expressed similar sentiments to his mother in another letter written on this same date. G. P. Erwin to Mother, Dec. 31, 1862, G. P. Erwin Papers, SHC.

74. W. Badham to [?], Feb. 1, 1863, W. Badham Papers, DU. See also D. G. Coward to W. Pettigrew, Dec. 19, 1862, Pettigrew Family Papers, SHC.

CHAPTER VII

1. *OR,* XVIII, Ser. I, 893.

2. *Ibid.,* p. 903.

3. *Ibid.,* p. 907.

4. *Ibid.,* p. 951. J. Longstreet, *From Manassas to Appomattox* (Philadelphia: J. B. Lippincott, Co., 1896), p. 324.

5. *OR,* XVIII, Ser. I, 2. Hill had been assigned "to the command of the troops in the State of North Carolina" on February 7, 1863. *Ibid.,* p. 872.

6. Address to Soldiers by Major General D. H. Hill, Feb. 25, 1863, D. H. Hill Papers, SLR.

7. G. W. Wills to Sister, Mar. 5, 1863, G. W. Wills Papers, SHC. Many other youths in gray shared Wills's sentiments. L. Warlick to Cornelia McGimsey, Mar. 8, 1863, Cornelia McGimsey Papers, SHC; J. L. Stuart to Mother, May 5, 1863, J. L. Stuart Papers, DU.

8. Raleigh *Progress*, Mar. 1, 1863, quoted in P. S. Chase, *Battery F, First Regiment Rhode Island Light Artillery in the Civil War* (Providence: Snow and Farnham, 1892), pp. 75-76.

9. J. C. Haskell, "Reminiscence" (Unpublished reminiscence), SHC.

10. D. H. Hill to J. Longstreet, Feb. 25, 1863, D. H. Hill Papers, SLR.

11. *OR*, VIII, Ser. I, 902-3.

12. *Ibid.*

13. *Ibid.*, pp. 950-51.

14. D. H. Hill to J. Longstreet, Mar. 16, 1863, D. H. Hill Papers, SLR; B. H. Robertson to A. Anderson, Mar. 21, 1863, D. H. Hill Papers, SLR; J. J. Pettigrew to D. H. Hill, Mar. 17, 1863, D. H. Hill Papers, SLR; J. Daniel to D. H. Hill, Mar. 11, 1863, D. H. Hill Papers, SLR.

15. J. J. Iredell to "Dear Sam," Mar. 17, 1863, Hayes Collection, SHC.

16. D. H. Hill to J. Longstreet, Mar. 16, 1863, D. H. Hill Papers, SLR.

17. S. R. Bunting to "Friend Elliot," Mar. 22, 1863, Bunting Papers, SHC.

18. *OR*, XVIII, Ser. I, 184; H. A. Cooley to Father, Apr. 8, 1863, H. A. Cooley Papers, SHC.

19. D. H. Hill to J. Longstreet, Mar. 16, 1863, D. H. Hill Papers, SLR.

20. *Ibid.; OR*, XVIII, Ser. I, 184; L. Leon, *Diary of a Tar Heel Confederate Soldier* (Charlotte: Stone Publishing Co., 1913), p. 19. "Yanks" burned the bridge behind them. W. McLeod to J. M. Harrington, Mar. 25, 1863, J. M. Harrington Papers, DU.

21. J. J. Pettigrew to D. H. Hill, Mar. 17, 1863, D. H. Hill Papers, SLR; G. E. Govan and J. W. Livingood, *Haskell Memoirs* (New York: G. P. Putnam's Sons, 1960), pp. 41-42.

22. J. J. Pettigrew to D. H. Hill, Mar. 17, 1863, D. H. Hill Papers, SLR; J. C. Haskell to N. C. Hughes, Mar. 16, 1863, D. H. Hill Papers, SLR.

23. J. J. Pettigrew to D. H. Hill, Mar. 17, 1863, D. H. Hill Papers, SLR; *RR*, VI, 450; Govan and Livingood, *Haskell Memoirs*, p. 42; J. C. Haskell to N. C. Hughes, Mar. 16, 1863, D. H. Hill Papers, SLR; W. I. Budington, *A Memorial of Giles F. Ward, Jr.* (New York: Anson D. F. Randolph, 1886), pp. 57-58; J. K. Burlingame, *History of the Fifth Regiment of Rhode Island Heavy Artillery During Three Years and a Half of Service in North Carolina* (Providence: Snow and Farnham, 1892), p. 135. More than one hundred shots marked the small building occupied as the Colonel's quarters. Trees were cut and splintered by the fire.

24. *OR*, XVIII, Ser. I, 184.

25. J. J. Pettigrew to D. H. Hill, Mar. 17, 1863, D. H. Hill Papers, SLR.

26. B. H. Robertson to A. Anderson, Mar. 21, 1863, D. H. Hill Papers, SLR.

27. D. H. Hill to J. Longstreet, Mar. 16, 1863, D. H. Hill Papers, SLR.

28. D. H. Hill to J. A. Seddon, Feb. 23, 1863, D. H. Hill Papers, SLR.

29. B. R. Hood to Father, Mar. 23, 1863, J. C. Hood Papers, DU.

30. W. MacRae to D. MacRae, Mar. 26, 1863, Hugh MacRae Papers, DU. A soldier, not as literate as young MacRae, summarized the expedition as follows: "I have bin down about newborn—within eight miles of the sitty-went down to fight but didn't git into hit but a little. . . ." W. M. Hedgecock to Father, Mar. 17, 1863, W. M. Hedgecock Papers, SHC.

31. *OR*, XVIII, Ser. I, 966.

32. *Ibid.*, p. 959.

33. *Ibid.*, p. 1007. P. G. T. Beauregard to D. H. Hill, Apr. 23, 1863, D. H. Hill Papers, SLR.

34. *OR*, XVIII, Ser. I, 970; *NR*, VIII, Ser. I, 674; G. P. Erwin to Father, Apr. 3, 1863, G. P. Erwin Papers, SHC; Burlingame, *5 R.I.*, pp. 148-49; C. F. Warren, "Washington During the Civil War," *The Confederate Reveille* (Raleigh: Edwards and Broughton, 1898), pp. 14-15; H. R. Paschal, Jr., "The Story of Washington," Washington *Daily News*, Apr. 24-28, 1952.

35. *OR*, XVIII, Ser. I, 211-16; John to "My dear Sallie," Aug. 30, 1862, Letter from Washington, N.C., 1862, NCC; J. B. Gardner, *Record of the Service of the Forty-fourth Massachusetts Volunteer Militia in North Carolina, August 1862 to May 1863* (Boston: Privately printed, 1887), p. 163. Warren, "Washington During the War," pp. 14-15; Paschal, "Washington," Washington *Daily News*, Apr. 26, 1952; S. F. Blanding, "Siege of Washington," Washington *Daily News*, Aug. 17, 1951; R. B. Garnett to D. H. Hill, Apr. 6, 1863, D. H. Hill Papers, SLR.

36. *OR*, XVIII, Ser. I, 212-16; Leon, *Diary of a Tar Heel*, pp. 21-23; Newton Wallace Diary, Apr. 1-14, 1863, NCC.

37. Extracts from letters of Robert Ware in *Harvard Memorial Biographies* (Cambridge: Sener and Francis, 1867), I, 238-51, Pamphlet, NCC.

38. Gardner, *44 Mass.*, p. 193. A few shells fell in the town, causing some citizens to construct "bombproofs upon their lots." Warren, "Washington During the War," p. 15.

39. R. B. Garnett to D. H. Hill, Apr. 11, 1863, D. H. Hill Papers, SLR.

40. Govan and Livingood, *Haskell Memoirs*, p. 43. G. P. Erwin to Father, Apr. 3, 1863, G. P. Erwin Papers, SHC; *OR*, XVIII, Ser. I, 212-16.

41. Extracts from letters of Ware in *Harvard Memorial Biographies*, I, 238-51, NCC; J. J. Iredell to "My dear Cousin," May 30, 1863, Hayes Collection, SHC. A Confederate soldier remarked: "We were shelled uncomfortably several times." *Ibid.*

42. Blanding, "Siege of Washington," Washington *Daily News*, Aug. 17, 1951; Govan and Livingood, *Haskell Memoirs*, p. 43; *NR*, VIII, Ser. I, 649-98; *Message of the President of the United States and Accompanying Documents, to the Two Houses of Congress, at the Commencement of the First Session of the Thirty-Eighth Congress* (Washington: GPO, 1863), pp. 33-35.

43. W. M. Hedgecock to Father, Apr. 8, 1863, W. M. Hedgecock Papers, SHC.

44. Govan and Livingood, *Haskell Memoirs*, p. 46. Haskell also said Hill "was a good fighter and had much merit, though some extra ordinary queer notions." *Ibid.*

45. R. B. Garnett to D. H. Hill, Apr. 6, 11, 15, 1863, D. H. Hill Papers, SLR.

46. J. Longstreet to H. L. Benning, Apr. 13 [?], 1863, H. L. Benning Papers, SHC; M. Sorrell to H. L. Benning, Apr. 13, 1863, H. L. Benning Papers, SHC; D. W. Grantham, Jr., ed., "Letters from H. J. Hightower, A Confederate Soldier, 1862-1864," *GHQ*, XL (June, 1956), 184. This new duty, said Thomas Kennon of the Twenty-third Georgia, was quite different from service in Virginia, in particular after serving under Generals Lee and Jackson. T. Kennon to Rachel Crawford, June 9, 1863, T. Kennon Papers, NCDAH.

47. J. J. Wyeth, *Leaves from a Diary Written While Serving in the Department of North Carolina from September, 1862, to June, 1863* (Boston: L. F. Lawrence and Co., 1878), p. 46.

48. D. L. Craft to Sister, Apr. 15, 1863, D. L. Craft Papers, DU.

49. J. L. Stackpole, "The Department of North Carolina under General Foster, July, 1862—July, 1863," *MHSM* (Boston: Military Historical Society of Massachusetts, 1912), IX, 104-7; *OR*, XVIII, Ser. I, 211-55; L. T. Rightsell, "Siege of Washington, N.C. Unique in Civil Annals," n.d., Newspaper clipping, NCC.

50. H. K. Burgwyn to N. C. Hughes, Apr. 26, 1863, Z. B. Vance Papers, NCDAH; G. P. Erwin to Father, Apr. 12, 1863, G. P. Erwin Papers, SHC; Mrs. Archbell, "Battle

of Blount's Mill" (Unpublished account), U.D.C. Essays Relating to Slavery and Civil War Incidents, NCDAH.

51. Stackpole, "Dept. of N.C.," p. 106.

52. *OR,* XVIII, Ser. I, 215; W. W. Douglas, "Relief of Washington, North Carolina, by the Fifth Rhode Island Volunteers," *Personal Narratives of Events in the War of the Rebellion. Being Papers Read Before the Rhode Island Soldiers and Saliors Historical Society* (Providence: Published by the Society, 1886), Ser. 3, No. 17, pp. 16-26; Wallace Diary, Apr. 15, 1863, NCC. The idea for this bold move on the part of the Fifth Rhode Island belonged to Colonel H. T. Sisson, who had recently joined the regiment "and who was anxious to distinguish himself and his command by some daring exploit." *Ibid.*

53. J. B. Gardner, *Massachusetts Memorial to Her Soldiers and Sailors Who Died in the Department of North Carolina, 1861-1865* (Boston: Gardner and Toplin, 1909), p. 45; *OR,* XVIII, Ser. I, 215; Wallace Diary, Apr. 15, 1863, NCC.

54. L. Warlick to Cornelia McGimsey, Apr. 26, 1863, Cornelia McGimsey Papers, SHC.

55. J. T. Ellis to "Dear Charles," Apr. 25, 1863, G. W. Mumford Papers, DU.

56. Gardner, *Mass. Memorial to Her Soldiers,* p. 45.

57. Leon, *Diary of a Tar Heel,* p. 23.

58. D. H. Hill to Z. B. Vance, May 11, 1863, D. H. Hill Papers, SLR.

59. R. E. Lee to D. H. Hill, May 25, 1863, D. H. Hill Papers, SLR.

60. In General Orders, No. 20. Hill announced to his troops the death of his brother-in-law, General "Stonewall" Jackson:

"The department commander announces the well-known fact of the death of the great and good Jackson, not merely in order to pay a tribute to the illustrious dead, but also to incite the troops to imitate his example. His name has been identified with almost all the great battles of the war, and his genius and courage have been the chief elements in Southern success and Yankee discomfiture. The eagle glance and iron will of the great commander were happily united in him with the patient, uncomplaining endurance of the common soldier.

"His wonderful battles have contributed largely to our independence, and his great fame has shed a halo of glory over his beloved South. But his virtues as a man will be as fondly remembered by his countrymen as the brilliant deeds of his military career. He has taught us that he who most fears God the least fears man; that the most exalted courage may be associated with the modesty of the shrinking girl; that the lips which were never defiled with ribaldry and profanity could cheer on most loudly amidst the roar of cannon and clash of arms. His whole life was a rebuke to the intriguing, the selfish, the cowardly, the vulgar, and the profane.

"The pure man will be loved as much as the heroic soldier will be admired in the future ages of the republic.

"Let us drop our laurel upon his bier, but remember that we may best honor him by striving day and night, and with his unwavering trust in God, to secure the independence for which he gave his life." General Orders, No. 20, Goldsboro, May 26, 1863, D. H. Hill Papers, SLR. North Carolina troops were charged with firing the volley that wounded Jackson.

61. A. W. Mangum to Sister, May 1, 1863, A. W. Mangum Papers, SHC; R. E. Lee to D. H. Hill, May 16, 25, 1863, D. H. Hill Papers, SLR; D. H. Hill to J. A. Seddon, May 7, 1863, D. H. Hill Papers, SLR; S. Cooper to D. H. Hill, Apr. 29, 1863, D. H. Hill Papers, SLR.

62. *OR,* XVIII, Ser. I., 362-72.

63. *Ibid.;* R. D. Graham, "Fifty-sixth Regiment," *Histories of the Several Regiments and Battalions from North Carolina in the Great War 1861-'65. Written by Members of the Respective Commands,* ed. W. Clark (Goldsboro: Nash Brothers, 1901), III, 324-28; R. D. Graham to Father, May 25, 1863, W. A. Graham Papers, SHC; B. R. Hood to

Father, May ·27, 1863, J. C. Hood Papers, DU; J. W. Denny, *Wearing the Blue in the Twenty-fifth Massachusetts Volunteer Infantry* (Worcester: Putnam and Davis, 1879), pp. 204-5.

64. R. D. Graham to Father, May 25, 1863, W. A. Graham Papers, SHC; *OR*, XVIII, Ser. I, 363. The Twenty-fifth North Carolina, in a less exposed position, escaped with very few losses.

65. S. H. Putnam, *The Story of Company A, Twenty-fifth Regiment, Massachusetts Volunteers in the War of the Rebellion* (Worcester: Putnam, Davis and Co., 1886), p. 182; *OR*, XVIII, Ser. I, 363; H. M. Wagstaff, ed., *The James A. Graham Papers, 1861-1884* (Chapel Hill, Univ. of N.C. Press, 1928), pp. 145-46. Part of the Federal command took cars back to New Bern. *OR*, XVIII, Ser. I, 368; A. S. Roe, *The Fifth Regiment Volunteer Infantry* (Boston: Fifth Regiment Veteran's Association, 1911), pp. 234-35.

66. R. D. Graham to Father, May 25, 1863, W. A. Graham Papers, SHC; J. L. Stuart to Mary A. Harper, May 27, 1863, J. L. Stuart Papers, DU.

67. R. D. Graham to Mother, May 28, 1863, W. A. Graham Papers, SHC. Robert Ransom's brother, Brigadier General Matt W. Ransom, fully redeemed this distinguished North Carolina name a few weeks later in a small but important skirmish at Boone's Mill. See below pp. 166-70.

68. *OR*, XXVII, Ser. I, Pt. II, 964-65; H. A. Cooley to Father, July 26, 1863, H. A. Cooley Papers, SHC; Mrs. P. Atkinson to Z. B. Vance, July 28, 1863, Z. B. Vance Papers, NCDAH; H. T. King, *Sketches of Pitt County; a Brief History of the County, 1704-1910* (Raleigh: Edwards and Broughton, 1911), pp. 138-41.

69. *OR*, XXVII, Ser. I, Pt. II, 965; Mrs. P. Atkinson to Z. B. Vance, July 28, 1863, Z. B. Vance Papers, NCDAH.

70. *OR*, XXVII, Ser. I, Pt. II, 965.

71. *Ibid.*, p. 968; H. T. Clark to Z. B. Vance, Dec. 20, 1863, Z. B. Vance Papers, NCDAH.

72. Mrs. P. Atkinson to Z. B. Vance, July 28, 1863, Z. B. Vance Papers, NCDAH; H. T. Clark to Z. B. Vance, Dec. 5, 1863, Z. B. Vance Papers, NCDAH.

73. *OR*, XXVII, Ser. I, Pt. II, 965-74; H. A. Cooley to Father, July 26, 1863, H. A. Cooley Papers, SHC; King, *Pitt County*, pp. 138-41; C. Elliott to J. N. Whitford, July 25, 1863, Rec. Gr. 109, NA.

74. *NR*, IX, Ser. I, 135-36, 790; *OR*, XXVII, Ser. I, Pt. II, 981-85.

75. T. C. Parramore, "The Roanoke-Chowan Story—Chapter 8. Five Days in July 1863," Ahoskie *Daily Roanoke-Chowan News*, Civil War Supplement, 1960, pp. 85-89; *OR*, XXVII, Ser. I, Pt. II, 979-81; E. J. Cleveland, "Early Campaigns in North Carolina," *HJHS*, LXIX (July, 1951), 249-50.

76. Cleveland, "Early Campaigns in N.C.," pp. 257-58.

77. *OR*, XXVII, Ser. I, Pt. II, 981-85; *NR*, IX, Ser. I, 790. The Federal cavalry included the First New York Mounted Rifles, Eleventh Pennsylvania, and a mounted battery of artillery.

78. *OR*, XVII, Pt. III, 1043.

79. W. H. S. Burgwyn, "Thirty-fifth Regiment," *Histories of the Several Regiments and Battalions from North Carolina in the Great War 1861-'65. Written by Members of the Respective Commands,* ed. W. Clark (Goldsboro: Nash Brothers, 1901), II, 613-14. In June, 1863, Matt Ransom succeeded his brother, Robert, as commander of Ransom's Brigade.

80. Henry A. Chambers Diary, July 28, 1863, NCDAH; Burgwyn, "Thirty-fifth Regiment," pp. 613-14; W. H. S. Burgwyn, *General Matt W. Ransom* (Raleigh: Ladies Memorial Association and Citizens, 1906), pp. 17-21; Parramore, "Five Days in July, 1863," pp. 92-93; *OR*, XXVII, Ser. I, Pt. II, 981-85.

81. Parramore, "Five Days in July, 1863," p. 93.

82. Burgwyn, *General Matt. W. Ransom,* p. 20.

83. Hugh T. Lefler and A. R. Newsome, *North Carolina: The History of a Southern State* (Chapel Hill: Univ. of N.C. Press, 1954), p. 431.

CHAPTER VIII

1. A. MacRae to D. MacRae, July 15, 1863, Hugh MacRae Papers, DU.
2. David Schenck Journal, July [n.d.], 1863, SHC.
3. David T. Merritt Diary, July 10, 1863, Roxboro *Courier*, Aug. 5, 1941.
4. J. A. Forsyth to Sister, July 30, 1863, J. A. Forsyth Papers, DU.
5. R. D. W. Connor, *North Carolina, Rebuilding an Ancient Commonwealth* (New York: American Historical Society, 1929), II, 25. For good accounts of the peace movement in North Carolina, see H. W. Raper, "William W. Holden and the Peace Movement in North Carolina," *NCHR*, XXXI (Oct., 1954), 493-517; R. E. Yates, "Governor Vance and the Peace Movement," *NCHR*, XVII (Jan., Apr., 1940), 1-26, 89-114; A. S. Roberts, "The Peace Movement in North Carolina," *MVHR*, XI (Sept., 1924), 190-99.
6. J. G. deR. Hamilton, *History of North Carolina Since 1860* (Chicago: Lewis Publishing Co., 1919), p. 23.
7. *OR*, XXIX, Ser. I, Pt. I, 1-6; *NR*, IX, Ser. I, pp. v-vii; J. A. Emmerton, *A Record of the Twenty-third Regiment Massachusetts Volunteer Infantry* (Boston: William Ware and Co., 1886), p. 150; H. T. King, *Sketches of Pitt County: A Brief History of the County, 1704-1910* (Raleigh: Edwards and Broughton, 1911), pp. 143-44; J. C. Johnston to W. Pettigrew, June 22, 1863, Pettigrew Family Papers, SHC. A Federal soldier at Plymouth wrote: "Some expedition is out nearly all the time." N. Lanpheur to L. C. Newton, Aug. 9, 1863, N. Lanpheur Papers, DU.
8. J. C. Johnston to H. G. Spruill, Feb. 2, 1863, Pettigrew Family Papers, SHC. H. B. Shert [?] to W. Pettigrew, May 17, 1863, Pettigrew Family Papers, SHC.
9. G. D. Pool and other "J.P.s" of Pasquotank County to Z. B. Vance, Nov. 17, 1863, Z. B. Vance Papers, NCDAH.
10. W. G. MacRae to "Dear Don," Aug. 2, 1862, Hugh MacRae Papers, DU. Even though young MacRae scouted the Trenton-Pollocksville area in the summer of 1862, the devastation was still very much in evidence a year later.
11. W. A. Willoughby to Wife, Jan. 22, 1863, W. H. Noble Papers, DU.
12. Ladies of Jones County to Z. B. Vance, Aug. 11, 1863, Z. B. Vance Papers, NCDAH; "Anonymous" to Z. B. Vance, Apr. 24, 1863, Z. B. Vance Papers, NCDAH; Sophia Bowen and other Ladies of Washington County to Z. B. Vance, May 27, 1863, Z. B. Vance Papers, NCDAH; W. J. Clarke to Z. B. Vance, Nov. 28, 1863, Z. B. Vance Papers, NCDAH; Mrs. V. Atkinson to Z. B. Vance, Aug. 25, 1863, Z. B. Vance Papers, NCDAH.
13. Governor Stanly's resignation was accepted in March, 1863. He then returned to California.
14. J. G. deR. Hamilton, *Reconstruction in North Carolina* (New York: Columbia Univ. Press, 1914), p. 94. See also Broadside, Sept. 24, 1862, in B. Tyson Papers, DU.
15. Hamilton, *Reconstruction*, p. 94. See also E. Stanly to J. C. Johnston, Jan. 20, 1863, Hayes Collection, SHC; E. Stanly to J. Goodling, May 31, 1871, E. R. Beckwith Papers, SHC; C. C. Howard to Cousin, Aug. 21, 1862, E. R. Beckwith Papers, SHC.
16. G. D. Pool and other "J.P.s" of Pasquotank County to Z. B. Vance, Nov. 17, 1863, Z. B. Vance Papers, NCDAH.
17. J. W. Hinton to Z. B. Vance, Feb. 10, 1863, Z. B. Vance Papers, NCDAH. For an account of the activities of armed bands of Negroes in the Elizabeth City area see "Old Times In Betsy," Elizabeth City *Economist*, Sept. 14, 21, Oct. 19, 1900.
18. See above p. 59; W. S. Boyce, *Economic and Social History of Chowan County, North Carolina, 1880-1915* ("Studies in History, Economics, and Public Law," LXXVI [New York: Columbia Univ. Press, 1917]), pp. 244-45.

19. W. Pettigrew to Sister, Oct. 13, Nov. 27, 1862, Pettigrew Papers, SHC; Mrs. E. P. Fearing, "Buffalo Brutality," *Year Book—Pasquotank Historical Society,* ed. J. E. Wood (Elizabeth City: Historical Society, 1956), II, 114; "Elizabeth City and Lurid Civil War Days," Newspaper clipping, NCC. A correspondent of the Savannah *Republican,* writing from a camp near Gatesville on April 7, 1863, observed: "The Buffaloes, as the Tories are called, infest the swamps and depredate upon peaceful citizens. Those who sympathize with the South have been special objects as prey and have greatly suffered from these desperadoes." T. C. Parramore, "Roanoke-Chowan Plays Rare Role in War," Ahoskie *Daily Roanoke-Chowan News,* Civil War Supplement, 1960, p. 99.

20. R. Dillard, *The Civil War in Chowan County, North Carolina* (Edenton: Privately printed, 1916), pp. 11-13; Boyce, *Chowan County,* pp. 244-45; W. Pettigrew to Sister, Nov. 26, 1862, Pettigrew Family Papers, SHC; T. C. Parramore, "The Roanoke-Chowan Story—Chapter 10. Jack Fairless and the Wingfield Buffaloes," Ahoskie, *Daily Roanoke-Chowan News,* Civil War Supplement, 1960, pp. 109-12; *NR,* VIII, Ser. I, 139-40.

21. *NR,* VIII, Ser. I, 95.

22. Parramore, "Jack Fairless and the Wingfield Buffaloes," p. 113.

23. "These guerillas, styled Partisan Rangers, were recruited within Federal lines to defend the homes of civilian families from Federal depredations and to harrass Yankee lines of supply and communication." *Ibid.* See also below pp. 180-81.

24. *NR,* VIII, Ser. I, 217-18; Dillard, *Civil War in Chowan County,* p. 5.

25. Parramore, "Jack Fairless and Wingfield Buffaloes," pp. 113, 116; Dillard, *Civil War in Chowan County,* pp. 15-16.

26. *OR,* XVIII, Ser. I, 201-3; Dillard, *Civil War in Chowan County,* p. 17.

27. For an account of the difficulties experienced by Colonel Brown during his retreat see T. J. Brown, "Forty-second Regiment," *Histories of the Several Regiments and Battalions from North Carolina in the Great War 1861-'65. Written by Members of the Respective Commands,* ed. W. Clark (Goldsboro, Nash Brothers, 1901), II, 794-95.

28. Parramore, "Jack Fairless and the Wingfield Buffaloes," p. 117.

29. *OR,* XXIX, Ser. I, Pt. I, 5.

30. D. L. Craft to Sister, Nov. 25, 1863, D. L. Craft Papers, DU.

31. *Ibid.,* Dec. 15, 1863.

32. *OR,* XXIX, Ser. I. Pt. II, 595-96.

33. *RR,* VIII, 299-300.

34. *OR,* XXIX, Ser. I, Pt. I, 910-11.

35. *Ibid.,* p. 911.

36. *OR,* XXIX, Ser. I, Pt. I, 911; "Old Times In Betsy," Elizabeth City *Economist,* Aug. 24, 1900.

37. *Ibid.*

38. *Ibid.; OR,* XXIX, Ser. I, Pt. I, 911.

39. *Ibid.,* p. 912; *RR,* VIII, 300.

40. *OR,* XXIX, Ser. I, Pt. I, 912. Bright was executed at Hinton's Cross-Roads on the day General Wild evacuated Elizabeth City. *RR,* VIII, 300-1; "Recent Expedition to Elizabeth City," Milledgeville *Southern Recorder,* Jan. 19, 1864, Newspaper clipping, NCC. For a full description of the execution of Daniel Bright see *RR,* VIII, 300-1.

41. *OR,* XXIX, Ser. I, Pt. I, 912.

42. *Ibid.,* pp. 910-12. General Wild also sent part of his command back to Norfolk at this time.

43. *Ibid.,* pp. 912-13.

44. *Ibid.,* pp. 913-14.

45. *RR,* VIII, 304.

46. "Recent Expedition to Elizabeth City," Milledgeville, *Southern Recorder.* Jan. 19, 1864, Newspaper clipping, NCC.

47. *OR,* XXIX, Ser. I, Pt. I, 917.

48. *Ibid.,* p. 916.

49. *Ibid.,* Pt. II, 597-98.

50. *OR,* LII, Pt. II, 209.

51. W. D. Cotton, "Appalachian North Carolina" (Ph.D. dissertation, Univ. of North Carolina, 1954), p. 96.

52. R. J. Davis, "Cleveland Men Respond," Shelby *Daily Star,* Cleveland Centennial Edition, Aug., 1940; D. J. Whitener, *History of Watauga County* (Boone: Watauga Centennial Commission, 1949), p. 7; Schenck Journal, Sept. 13, 1861, SHC.

53. A. H. Jones, *Knocking at the Door. Member-Elect to Congress: His Career Before the War, During the War, and After the War* (Washington: McGill and Withrow, 1866), pp. 4-5; Cotton, "Appalachian North Carolina," p. 86.

54. *Ibid.*

55. Muriel Early Sheppard, *Cabins in the Laurel* (Chapel Hill: Univ. of N.C. Press, 1935), p. 65.

56. Raleigh *Weekly N.C. Standard,* July 3, 1861.

57. *Ibid.,* Nov. 13, 1861; Cotton, "Appalachian North Carolina," p. 90; G. W. F. Harper Diary, May 18, 1861, SHC.

58. Cotton, "Appalachian North Carolina," p. 92.

59. *Ibid.,* p. 94.

60. Georgia Lee Tatum, *Disloyalty in the Confederacy* (Chapel Hill: Univ. of N.C. Press, 1934), p. 109.

61. *Ibid.,* p. 113; Raper, "Holden and the Peace Movement," pp. 493-516. William J. Johnston was a railroad official and an original secessionist. He was from Charlotte.

62. P. Mallett to G. W. Randolph, Aug. 14, 1862, P. Mallett Papers, SHC; P. Mallett to T. S. Robards, n.d., P. Mallett Papers, SHC; Hamilton, *Reconstruction,* p. 45.

63. B. Craven to H. T. Clark, Mar. 13, 1862, Trinity College Papers, DU; Jane McIntosh to A. S. Caddell, Mar. 12, July 26, Sept. 7, 1862, A. S. Caddell Papers, DU; H. T. Clark to S. Whitaker, Mar. 6, 1862, H. T. Clark Papers, NCDAH; I. Wright to H. T. Clark, Mar. 10, 1862, Trinity College Papers, DU.

64. Tatum, *Disloyalty in Confederacy,* p. 113.

65. P. Mallett to D. H. Hill, Aug. 22, 1862, P. Mallett Papers, SHC; Hamilton, *Reconstruction,* p. 45.

66. *OR,* X, Ser. I, Pt. I, 628-29.

67. Fayetteville *Observer,* June 16, 1862.

68. C. D. Douglas, "Conscription and Writ of Habeas Corpus in North Carolina During the Civil War," *TCHSP,* XIV (1922), 19-20. See also "Mat" to "My Dear Aunt," July 1, 1862, Jones Family Papers, SHC; J. Blanton to Z. B. Vance, Feb. 13, 1863, Z. B. Vance Papers, NCDAH.

69. T. W. Atkin and other citizens of western North Carolina to J. A. Seddon, July 29, 1863, Z. B. Vance Papers, NCDAH.

70. Cotton, "Appalachian North Carolina," p. 103; Douglas, "Conscription and Writ of Habeas Corpus," p. 12; *Journal of the Congress of the Confederate States of America, 1861-1865. Senate Document No. 234,* 2 Sess., 58 Cong. (Washington: GPO, 1904-5), V, 228.

71. A. J. White to Wife, Jan. 29, 1863, A. J. White Papers, DU.

72. Raleigh *N.C. Standard,* May 7, 1862.

73. R. E. Yates, *The Confederacy and Zeb Vance,* ed., W. S. Hoole, *Confederate Centennial Studies* (Tuscaloosa: Confederate Publishing Co., 1958), p. 39.

74. R. G. Armfield to Z. B. Vance, Feb. 19, 1863, Z. B. Vance Papers, NCDAH; W. W. Stafford to Z. B. Vance, Feb. 15, 1863, Z. B. Vance Papers, NCDAH; Mary E. Frazer to S. Frazer, Sept. 16, 1862, J. A. Foster Papers, DU.

75. J. S. Brooks to Sister, Apr. 26, 1862, J. S. Brooks Papers, SHC.

76. "Observer," "Devices Practised to Avoid Going in the Army," *HM,* IX (June,

1871), 400-1. Some of those attempting to avoid conscription would build false partitions and secret trap doors in their homes. *Ibid.*

77. T. N. Grant to Z. B. Vance, Feb. 26, 1863, Z. B. Vance Papers, NCDAH; Z. B. Vance to J. A. Seddon, Mar. 21, 1863, Z. B. Vance Papers, NCDAH.

78. W. A. Joyce to Z. B. Vance, Feb. 16, 1863, Z. B. Vance Papers, NCDAH; R. G. Armfield to Z. B. Vance, Feb. 19, 1863, Z. B. Vance Papers, NCDAH; "Confederate friends" to Z. B. Vance, Feb. 17, 1863, Z. B. Vance Papers, NCDAH.

79. Cotton, "Appalachian North Carolina," pp. 97-98; Raleigh *N.C. Standard,* Apr. 15, 1863; J. P. Arthur, *Western North Carolina: A History from 1730-1913* (Raleigh: Edwards and Broughton, 1914), pp. 615-16; *OR,* II, Ser. IV, 732; F. W. [?] Johnstone to Z. B. Vance, Aug. 14, 1863, Z. B. Vance Papers, NCDAH; S. J. Buchanan to Z. B. Vance, June 20, 1863, Z. B. Vance Papers, NCDAH; J. W. McElroy to Z. B. Vance, July 13, 1863, Z. B. Vance Papers, NCDAH.

80. T. W. Atkin and other citizens of western North Carolina to J. A. Seddon, July 29, 1863, Z. B. Vance Papers, NCDAH; Sarah Jones to Z. B. Vance, Oct. 15, 1863, Z. B. Vance Papers, NCDAH; N. C. Hughes, *Hendersonville in Civil War Times, 1860-1865* (Hendersonville: Blue Ridge Specialty Printers, 1936), pp. 25-26.

81. *OR,* II, Ser. IV, 783-85.

82. J. T. Mitchell to W. A. Graham, May 4, 1864, W. A. Graham Papers, SHC.

83. Officers of the First and Third North Carolina Regiments to R. E. Colston, May 29, 1863, R. E. Colston Papers, SHC; R. E. Lee to R. E. Colston, Sept. 16, 1863, R. E. Colston Papers, SHC.

84. Yates, *Confederacy and Zeb Vance,* pp. 40-41; *OR,* II, Ser. IV, 114-15; Cotton, "Appalachian North Carolina" p. 115.

85. Raper, "Holden and the Peace Movement," pp. 493-517; J. L. Reid to Wife, Mar. 7, 1862, J. L. Reid Papers, DU; "Females of Rutherfordton" to Z. B. Vance, June 15, 1863, Z. B. Vance Papers, NCDAH.

86. P. Black to Z. B. Vance, Mar. 9, 1863, Z. B. Vance Papers, NCDAH.

87. "David" to "Miss Kate," Apr. 15, 1863, Catherine (McG) Buie Papers, DU.

88. M. Bollinger to Z. B. Vance, Mar. 4, 1863, Z. B. Vance Papers, NCDAH; Raleigh *N.C. Standard,* Aug. 14, Dec. 29, 1863.

89. M. Brown to Z. B. Vance, Mar. 18, 1863, Z. B. Vance Papers, NCDAH. The demoralization of the populace was increased by the irresponsible searches of private homes at night for deserters. Also, the impressing of property and the terrorizing of women, thought to be concealing husbands or sons, helped to increase the spirit of rebellion. J. A. Parks to Z. B. Vance, Nov. 16, 1863, Z. B. Vance Papers, NCDAH; M. Nelson to Z. B. Vance, June 11, 1863, Z. B. Vance Papers, NCDAH; J. Buchanan to Z. B. Vance, May 8, 1863, Z. B. Vance Papers, NCDAH; J. H. Forest to Z. B. Vance, Mar. 17, 1863, Z. B. Vance Papers, NCDAH.

90. R. L. Abernathy to Z. B. Vance, Feb. 20, 1863, Z. B. Vance Papers, NCDAH; C. Cowly to Z. B. Vance, Dec. 10, 1863, Z. B. Vance Papers, NCDAH; C. Dowd, *Life of Zebulon B. Vance* (Charlotte: Observer Publishing and Printing House, 1897), p. 87; Cotton, "Appalachian North Carolina," pp. 117-18.

91. Peter Mallett was commandant of conscripts in North Carolina. His correspondence for the war years is very revealing on matters of conscription and desertion. See P. Mallett Papers, SHC.

92. Ella Lonn, *Desertion During the Civil War* (New York: Century Co., 1928), pp. 24-26, 32, 65; Tatum, *Disloyalty in Confederacy,* pp. 107-35; Cotton, "Appalachian North Carolina," pp. 130-131; J. K. Connally to E. White, Aug. 20, 1862, T. L. Clingman Papers, SHC.

93. *OR,* XVIII, Ser. I, 860-61; Tatum, *Disloyalty in Confederacy,* p. 115; S. O. Deavers to Z. B. Vance, Mar. 24, 1863, Z. B. Vance Papers, NCDAH; L. Hanes to Z. B. Vance, Mar. 14, 1863, Z. B. Vance Papers, NCDAH; A. W. Zachery to Z. B. Vance, Mar. 23, 1863, Z. B. Vance Papers, NCDAH.

94. *OR*, XVIII, Ser. I, 998.

95. R. E. Lee to J. A. Seddon, May 21, 1863, Z. B. Vance Papers, NCDAH.

96. *Ibid.;* Captain Henry McCoy to W. S. [?] Winder May 25. 1863, Z. B. Vance Papers, NCDAH.

97. J. L. Stuart to Mother, Feb. 28, Aug. 30, 1863, J. L. Stuart Papers, DU; Mary A. Harper to J. L. Stuart, Mar. 22, 1863, J. L. Stuart Papers, DU; J. Harper to J. L. Stuart, Feb. 20, 1863, J. L. Stuart Papers, DU; Schenck Journal, June 11, 1863, SHC.

98. *OR*, XXIII, Ser. I, Pt. II, 950-52.

99. D. H. Hill, "The Women of the Confederacy," *Addresses at the Unveiling of the Memorial to the North Carolina Women of the Confederacy* (Raleigh: Edwards and Broughton, 1914), pp. 12-13.

100. *OR*, II, Ser. IV, 674; Cotton, "Appalachian North Carolina," pp. 135-36.

101. *OR*, III, Ser. IV, 732-34.

102. *Ibid.*, p. 786.

103. *Ibid.*, XXIX, Ser. I, Pt. II, 676.

104. *Ibid.;* Schenck Journal, Sept. 11, 1863, SHC.

105. J. W. Graham to Father, Nov. 21, 1863, W. A. Graham Papers, SHC; J. W. Graham to Z. B. Vance, Dec. 6, 1863, Z. B. Vance Papers, NCDAH; J. W. Hunt to Z. B. Vance, Mar. 6, 1863, Z. B. Vance Papers, NCDAH; J. W. Tomlinson to B. Tyson, Nov. 2, 1863, B. Tyson Papers, DU; W. H. Powell to Z. B. Vance, Apr. 29, 1863, Z. B. Vance Papers, NCDAH; T. Munroe to Z. B. Vance, Apr. 17, 1863, Z. B. Vance Papers, NCDAH; W. R. Stred to Z. B. Vance, Apr. 10, 1863, Z. B. Vance Papers, NCDAH; Mary A. Harper to J. L. Stuart, Jan. 12, Mar. 22, 1863, J. L. Stuart Papers, DU; J. Harper to J. L. Stuart, Feb. 20, 1863, J. L. Stuart Papers, DU; D. McIntosh to A. S. Caddell, Sept. 7, 1863, A. S. Caddell Papers, DU; Dowd, "Reminiscences from Moore County," Raleigh *Morning Post,* Aug. 17, 1905; H. Berrier to Z. B. Vance, Feb. 3, 1963, Z. B. Vance Papers, NCDAH; A. K. Pearce to B. Tyson, Nov. 25, 1863, B. Tyson Papers, DU; S. G. Worth to Z. B. Vance, Nov. 17, 1863, Z. B. Vance Papers, NCDAH; Citizens of Randolph County to "Capt. Branson," July 28, 1863, Z. B. Vance Papers, NCDAH. In early September "200 deserters and traitors" in Iredell County had a "fight" with a small group of Confederate soldiers. But David Schenck of Lincolnton thought that Wilkes, Yadkin, and Forsyth counties were "more disloyal than others." Schenck Journal, Sept. 11, 1863, SHC.

106. W. A. Pugh to A. Anderson, July 1, 1863, Z. B. Vance Papers, NCDAH; Z. B. Vance to D. H. Hill, Apr. 22, 1863, Z. B. Vance Papers, NCDAH; S. L. Holt to Z. B. Vance, May 24, 1863, Z. B. Vance Papers, NCDAH; H. W. Ayers to Z. B. Vance, Mar. 10, 1863, Z. B. Vance Papers, NCDAH. Lieutenant Pugh's command operated in Moore as well as Randolph County.

107. Nancy Royal to Z. B. Vance, Aug. 9, 1863, Z. B. Vance Papers, NCDAH. Similar conditions existed in Davidson and Moore counties. L. S. Wright to Parents, Nov. 27, 1863, L. S. Wright Papers, DU; O. S. Hanner to Z. B. Vance, Aug. 3, 1863, Z. B. Vance Papers, NCDAH.

108. S. G. Worth to Z. B. Vance, Sept. 3, 1863, Z. B. Vance Papers, NCDAH.

109. Lonn, *Desertion,* pp. 73-74. For a fuller account see D. Dodge, "The Cave-Dwellers of the Confederacy," *Atlantic Monthly,* LXVIII (Oct., 1891), 516-20.

110. J. W. Graham to Father, Nov. 21, 1863, W. A. Graham Papers, SHC.

111. J. W. Graham to Z. B. Vance, Dec. 6, 1863, Z. B. Vance Papers, NCDAH.

112. J. Kinley to Z. B. Vance, Oct. 17, 1863, Z. B. Vance Papers, NCDAH; Jane Bryan to Z. B. Vance, Dec. 23, 1863, Z. B. Vance Papers, NCDAH; R. F. Hoke to R. F. Hackett, Dec. 8, 1863, Gordon-Hackett Papers, SHC.

113. M. Nelson to Z. B. Vance, June 11, 1863, Z. B. Vance Papers, NCDAH.

114. J. W. Graham to Father, Nov. 21, 1863, W. A. Graham Papers, SHC.

115. Peter W. Hairston Diary, Nov. 23, 1863, SHC.

116. *Ibid.*, Nov. 24, 1863.

117. *Ibid.*

118. S. Cooper to H. L. Benning, Sept. 18, 1863, H. L. Benning Papers SHC; W. S. Shepherd to H. L. Benning, Oct. 8, 1863, H. L. Benning Papers, SHC; Z. B. Vance to J. A. Seddon, Oct. 15, 1863, H. L. Benning Papers, SHC; [?] Whitford to Z. B. Vance, Oct. 31, 1863, H. L. Benning Papers, SHC; Z. B. Vance to [?] Whitford, Nov. 10, 1863, H. L. Benning Papers, SHC; W. S. Shepherd to S. Cooper, Oct. 6, 1863, H. L. Benning Papers, SHC; L. P. [?] Walker to "Mrs. P.," Sept. 14, 1863, Lindsay Patterson Papers, SHC; W. W. Holden to T. Settle, Dec. 22, 1863, T. Settle Papers, SHC; D. S. Burwell to "Dear Ed.," Sept. 11, 1863, Burwell Papers, SHC; Yates, *Confederacy and Zeb Vance*, pp. 92-93; Hairston Dairy, Nov. 24, 1863, SHC; "Sis" to "My Dear Brother," Sept. 14, 1863, R. V. Howell Papers, NCDAH; Schneck Journal, Sept. 11, 1863, SHC; G. L. Tatum, *Disloyalty in the Confederacy* (Chapel Hill: Univ. of N.C. Press, 1934), p. 122.

119. W. W. Stringfield, "Sixty-Ninth Regiment," *Histories of the Several Regiments and Battalions from North Carolina in the Great War 1861-'65. Written by Members of the Respective Commands,* ed. W. Clark (Goldsboro: Nash Brothers, 1901), III, 736.

120. In January, 1862, Colonel Thomas began raising troops for local defense in the mountains. From this beginning came the Sixty-ninth North Carolina (or Thomas' Legion.) On July 19, 1862, Colonel Thomas' command was increased to battalion size and became the Sixty-ninth North Carolina. In September of the same year the regiment's organization was completed with the election of staff and field officers. Stringfield, "Sixty-ninth North Carolina," pp. 729-32. Mattie Russell, "William Holland Thomas" (Ph.D. dissertation, Duke Univ., 1956), p. 365.

121. *OR*, XX, Ser. I, Pt. II, 466; W. H. Thomas to Wife, Jan. 28, 1863, W. H. Thomas Papers, DU; W. G. M. Davis to Z. B. Vance, Jan. [n.d.], 1863, Z. B. Vance Papers, NCDAH; H. Heth to Z. B. Vance, Jan. 17. 1863, Z. B. Vance Papers, NCDAH.

122. *OR*, XVIII, Ser. I, 854.

123. M. Erwin to H. T. Clark, Apr. 17, 1862, H. T. Clark Papers, NCDAH; N. W. Woodfin to H. T. Clark, Apr. 17, 1862, H. T. Clark Papers, NCDAH; Cotton, "Appalachian North Carolina," pp. 147-48; Raleigh *N.C. Standard*, Apr. 22, 1863.

124. *OR*, XVIII, Ser. I, 810-11, 853-54, 881, 893, 909; G. W. F. Harper to Wife, Jan. 15, 1863, G. W. F. Harper Papers, SHC.

125. *OR*, XVIII, Ser. I, 853-54. "From that point on the story is confusing and reports highly contradictory." Cotton, "Appalachian North Carolina," pp. 148-49.

126. See above p. 197.

127. *OR*, XVIII, Ser. I, 853-54.

128. A. S. Merrimon to Z. B. Vance, Feb. 16, 1863, Z. B. Vance Papers, NCDAH; W. H. Bailey to Z. B. Vance, Feb. 18, 1863, Z. B. Vance Papers, NCDAH; B. T. Morris, "Sixty-fourth Regiment," *Histories of the Several Regiments and Battalions from North Carolina in the Great War 1861-'65. Written by Members of the Respective Commands,* ed. W. Clark (Goldsboro: Nash Brothers, 1901), III, 661; *OR*, XVIII, Ser. I, 893-97.

129. A. S. Merrimon to Z. B. Vance, Sept. 18, 1863, Z. B. Vance Papers, NCDAH; *OR*, XVIII, Ser. I, 909; J. W. Woodfin to Z. B. Vance, Feb. 1, 1863, Z. B. Vance Papers, NCDAH; Cotton, "Appalachian North Carolina," pp. 119-20, 148-49.

130. Wilma Dykeman, *The French Broad* (New York: Rhinehart and Co., 1955), p. 98.

131. J. W. McElroy to Z. B. Vance, Oct. 28, 1863, Z. B. Vance Papers, NCDAH; S. F. Patterson to Z. B. Vance, Sept. 1863, Z. B. Vance Papers, NCDAH.

132. W. W. Stringfield, "Reminiscences" (Unpublished reminiscence), W. W. Stringfield Papers, NCDAH.

133. Schenck Journal, Dec. 12, 1863, SHC.

134. A. S. Merrimon to Z. B. Vance, Sept. 16, 1863, Z. B. Vance Papers, NCDAH. See also W. Murdock and others to Z. B. Vance, Sept. 16, 1863, Z. B. Vance Papers, NCDAH. Within a few days after this disaster Vance was asking Secretary Seddon to

assist in the defenses of the western border. The Governor especially wanted the mountain region made into a separate district and put under a competent commander. Russell, "William Holland Thomas," p. 378. Governor Vance got his wish. See below p. 363.

135. Stringfield, "Sixty-ninth Regiment," p. 739; *OR,* XXX, Ser. I, Pt. III, 501.

136. M. L. Brittain to Z. B. Vance, Nov. 1, 1863, Z. B. Vance Papers, NCDAH.

137. *OR,* XXVIII, Ser. I, Pt. II, 449-50, 457-59; R. B. Vance to Z. B. Vance, Sept. 23, 1863, Z. B. Vance Papers, NCDAH.

138. *OR,* XXIX, Ser. I, Pt. II, 836-37.

139. *Ibid.,* p. 836.

140. For a full account of Longstreet's operations in east Tennessee, see J. Longstreet, *Manassas to Appomattox* (Philadelphia: J. B. Lippincott Co., 1896), pp. 497-550.

141. Dykeman, *French Broad,* p. 103.

142. *OR,* XXXI, Ser. I, Pt. III, 759, 770, 777-78, 782, 786.

143. *Ibid.,* XXXII, Ser. I, Pt. II, 518.

144. *Ibid.,* Pt. I, 73-76; Stringfield, "Reminiscences," W. W. Stringfield Papers, NCDAH; *RR,* VIII, 337; Arthur, *Western North Carolina,* p. 610; W. H. Humly [?] to Z. B. Vance, Jan. 24, 1864, Z. B. Vance Papers, NCDAH.

145. *OR,* XXXII, Ser. I, Pt. I, 76.

146. Hill, *Confederate Military History,* IV, 218; Jacocks, "Federal Operations in Eastern North Carolina," (M.A. thesis, Univ. of North Carolina, 1905), p. 10.

147. L. S. Gash to Z. B. Vance, Dec. 25, 1863, Z. B. Vance Papers, NCDAH.

CHAPTER IX

1. R. E. Lee to J. Davis, Jan. 2, 1864, R. E. Lee Papers, DU.

2. *OR,* XXXIII, Ser. I, 1101.

3. *Ibid.,* pp. 1099-1104; J. G. deR. Hamilton, "General R. F. Hoke and His Military Career," (Unpublished article in possession of J. G. deR. Hamilton estate, Chapel Hill, N.C.).

4. *OR,* XXXIII, Ser. I, 1201; G. W. Gift to Ellen A. Shackelford, Feb. 2, 1864, Ellen A. Shackelford Papers, SHC. The boats did not arrive until the thirty-first. See below p. 208.

5. *OR,* XXXIII, Ser. I, 92-97, 1102; Hamilton, "General R. F. Hoke and His Military Career."

6. *OR,* XXXIII, Ser. I, 93, 95-96; W. Hoyle to Sarah Cornell, Feb. 10, 1864, Sarah Cornell Papers, DU.

7. *OR,* XXXIII, Ser. I, 97-98. In Kinston there was great excitement as the Confederate troops departed. "Isn't it exciting," wrote the Reverend A. W. Mangum. "We are all in terrible suspense but feel confident that the attack will succeed." A. W. Mangum to Sister, Feb. 1, 1864, A. W. Mangum Papers, SHC.

8. Henry A. Chambers Diary, Jan. 31, 1864, NCDAH; J. L. Stuart to Mrs. M. A. Harper, Feb. 5, 1864, J. L. Stuart Papers, DU.

9. E. Phifer to Mother, Feb. 4, 1864, Phifer Papers, SHC.

10. Chambers Diary, Feb. 1, 1864, NCDAH.

11. *Ibid.;* *OR,* XXXIII, Ser. I, 98-99.

12. T. R. Roulhac, "Forty-ninth Regiment," *Histories of the Several Regiments and Battalions from North Carolina in the Great War 1861-'65. Written by Members of the Respective Commands,* ed. W. Clark (Goldsboro: Nash Brothers, 1901), III, 133. The cavalry was wasted on the first as the horsemen did little more than give the Federal pickets a "lively chase." Chambers Diary, Feb. 1, 1864, NCDAH.

13. *OR,* XXXIII, Ser. I, 98.

14. *Ibid.,* pp. 98-99.

15. *Ibid.,* p. 99. J. L. Stuart to Mother, Feb. 7, 1864, J. L. Stuart Papers, DU.

16. Chambers Diary, Feb. 1, 1864, NCDAH.

17. *OR*, XXXIII, Ser. I, 93-94, 99.

18. *Ibid.*, p. 94.

19. J. L. Stuart to Mary A. Harper, Feb. 5, 1864, DU.

20. Chambers Diary, Feb. 3, 1864, NCDAH. The march described above was actually made on the night of the second when General Barton withdrew from Brice's Creek to Pollocksville.

21. General Butler thought that Lee, by sending Pickett into North Carolina, had weakened his forces in Virginia to such an extent that "now is the time to strike" for Richmond. He also concluded that Pickett's failure at New Bern had "relieved" that place "permanently." This latter conclusion was not accepted, understandably, by General Peck, commanding at New Bern. He had new fortifications built and asked for reinforcements. B. F. Butler to E. Stanton, Feb. 5, 1864, B. F. Butler Papers, LC; B. F. Butler to H. W. Halleck, Mar. 3, 1864, B. F. Butler Papers, LC; B. F. Butler to J. J. Peck, Mar. 9, 1864, B. F. Butler Papers, LC; H. J. H. Thompson to Wife, Mar. 2, 1864, DU.

22. *OR*, XXXIII, Ser. I, 93.

23. Hamilton, "General R. F. Hoke and His Military Career"; W. R. Burwell to Brother, Mar. 10, 1864, Burwell Papers, SHC.

24. Clara B. Boyd to "Mrs. Carter," Feb. 23, 1864, D. M. Carter Papers, SHC.

25. Hamilton, "General R. F. Hoke and His Military Career."

26. *OR*, XXXIII, Ser. I, 94.

27. Commander Wood also carried the rank of Colonel in the army. G. W. Gift to Ellen Shackelford, Feb. 10, 1864, Ellen S. Gift Papers, SHC.

28. *NR*, IX, Ser. I, 451.

29. G. W. Gift to Ellen Shackelford, Feb. 7, 1864, Ellen S. Gift Papers, SHC.

30. *Ibid.*, Jan. 29, 1864; *NR*, IX, Ser. I, 451-52.

31. G. W. Gift to Ellen Shackelford, Feb. 7, 1864, Ellen S. Gift Papers, SHC; A Confederate, "Capture of the Underwriter," *The Grayjackets: And How They Lived, Fought and Died for Dixie* (Richmond: Jones Brothers & Co., 1867), pp. 464-69; *NR*, IX, Ser. I, 451-53; T. J. Scharf, *History of the Confederate States Navy from its Organization to the Surrender of its Last Vessel* (New York: Rogers and Sherwood, 1887), p. 396.

32. G. W. Gift to Ellen Shackelford, Feb. 7, 1864, Ellen S. Gift Papers, SHC; *NR*, IX, Ser. I, 452.

33. Scharf, *Confederate Navy*, pp. 396-97.

34. G. W. Gift to Ellen Shackelford, Feb. 7, 1864, Ellen S. Gift Papers, SHC.

35. A Confederate, "Capture of the Underwriter," pp. 464-69.

36. *Ibid.*; Scharf, *Confederate Navy*, p. 398.

37. G. W. Gift to Ellen Shackelford, Feb. 2, 7, 1864, Ellen S. Gift Papers, SHC.

38. *Ibid.*, Feb. 7, 1864.

39. *NR*, IX, Ser. I, 452. For quite some time after the raid, bodies from the *Underwriter* kept floating ashore. H. J. H. Thompson to wife, Mar. 2, 1864, H. J. Thompson Papers, DU. The wheelhouse of the gunboat also washed up on the banks. The Federal soldiers used the wood to make fires and the long "copper or galvanized" nails for various purposes. One trooper said he got enough nails "to make a man rich." H. J. H. Thompson to Wife, Mar. 1, 1864, H. J. H. Thompson Papers, DU.

40. *OR*, XXXIII, Ser. I, 1103; see also above p. 204.

41. *Ibid.*, pp. 80, 85-88.

42. Newport Barracks was near a village called Shepperdsville (Shepherdsville), now known as Newport. D. H. Hill, Jr., *North Carolina*, ed., C. A. Evans, *Confederate Military History* (Atlanta: Confederate Publishing Co., 1899), IV, 221; C. G. Elliott, "Martin's Brigade—Hoke's Division, 1863-64," *SHSP*, XXIII (Jan.-Dec., 1895), 221.

43. *OR*, XXXIII, 81-82, 85-86, 88; J. S. Dancy to K. P. Battle, Feb. 12, 1864, Battle Family Papers, SHC.

44. J. A. Hedrick to B. S. Hedrick, Feb. 6, 1864, B. S. Hedrick Papers, DU.

45. *OR*, XXXIII, Ser. I, 85; J. A. Hedrick to B. J. Hedrick, Feb. 4, 1864, B. S. Hedrick Papers, DU.

46. W. A. James to Wife, Feb. 9, 1864, W. A. James Papers, DU.

47. *OR*, XXXIII, Ser. I, 86.

48. *Ibid.*, p. 88.

49. *Ibid.*, pp. 86, 89.

50. Hill, *Confederate Military History*, IV, 222.

51. J. S. Dancy to K. P. Battle, Feb. 12, 1864, Battle Family Papers, SHC.

CHAPTER X

1. *NR*, IX, Ser. I, 625-53; D. H. Hill, Jr., *North Carolina*, ed., C. A. Evans, *Confederate Military History* (Atlanta: Confederate Publishing Co., 1899), IV, 222; A. Cooper, *In and Out of Rebel Prison* (Oswego: R. J. Olephant, 1888), pp. 9-10; G. Tilghman, "Men Who Fought Ram's Battle Were Tougher Than Her Sons," Norfolk *Virginian-Pilot*, Apr. 22, 1951; W. M. Smith, "The Siege and Capture of Plymouth," *Personal Recollections of the War of the Rebellion. Addresses Delivered before the New York Commandery of the Loyal Legion of the United States* (New York: Published by the Commandery, 1891), I, 326-27; J. C. Long to Sarah MacKay, May 30, 1864, MacKay-Stiles Papers, SHC.

2. G. Elliott, "The Career of the Confederate Ram 'Albemarle,'" *CM*, XXXVI (May-Oct., 1888), 420.

3. *Ibid.*, pp. 420-21; P. E. Smith, Untitled article on the *Albemarle*, P. E. Smith Papers, SHC; [Anon.], "Building of the *Albemarle*" (Unpublished article, P. E. Smith Papers, SHC; B. D. McNeill, "The Albemarle," Raleigh *N and O*, Mar. 22, 1925.

4. *NR*, IX, Ser. I, 799; R. J. Roske and C. Van Doren, *Lincoln's Commando: The Biography of Commander W. B. Cushing, U.S.N.* (New York: Harper and Brothers, 1957), p. 194.

5. Hill, *Confederate Military History*, IV, 223.

6. Elliott, "Career of the *Albemarle*," pp. 420-21; Smith, Untitled article on the *Albemarle*, P. E. Smith Papers, SHC.

7. Elliott, "Career of the Albemarle," pp. 421-22; Hill, *Confederate Military History*, IV, 222-23; J. G. deR. Hamilton, "General R. F. Hoke and His Military Career" (Unpublished article in possession of J. G. deR. Hamilton estate, Chapel Hill, N.C.).

8. J. W. Graham to Father, Apr. 24, 1864, W. A. Graham Papers, SHC; N. Lanpheur, "Fall of Plymouth" (Unpublished reminiscence), N. Lanpheur Papers, DU; S. D. Newsum [?] to B. Jones, June 27, 1864, Jones Family Papers, SHC; A. S. Billingsley, *From the Flag to the Cross; or Scenes and Incidents of Christianity in the War* (Philadelphia: New-World Publishing Co., 1872), p. 63.

9. J. W. Graham, "Capture of Plymouth," *Histories of the Several Regiments and Battalions from North Carolina in the Great War 1861-'65. Written by Members of the Respective Commands*, ed. W. Clark (Goldsboro: Nash Brothers, 1901), V, 178; Lanpheur, "Fall of Plymouth," N. Lanpheur Papers, DU; *NR*, IX, Ser. I, 653.

10. Graham, "Capture of Plymouth," p. 178; *NR*, IX, Ser. I, 653.

11. J. W. Graham to Father, Apr. 24, 1864, W. A. Graham Papers, SHC; Graham, "Capture of Plymouth," p. 179.

12. Smith, "Siege and Capture of Plymouth," p. 330; *NR*, IX, Ser. I, 654; Graham, "Capture of Plymouth," p. 180; Lanpheur, "Fall of Plymouth," N. Lanpheur Papers, DU. The Federal gunboats were dropping shells into the fort. The defenders, therefore, were afraid that the magazine might blow up at any minute. *Ibid.*

13. J. W. Graham to Father, Apr. 24, 1864, W. A. Graham Papers, SHC.

14. *NR*, IX, Ser. I, 637.

15. *Ibid.*, p. 636. Gilbert Elliott in an article for *Century Magazine* states that the

Albemarle got underway "on the morning of April 18, 1864." Elliott, "Career of the Albemarle," p. 422.

16. *Ibid.*, pp. 422-23; *NR*, IX, Ser. I, 637.

17. Elliott, "Career of the Albemarle," p. 423.

18. *Ibid.*, pp. 423-25; *NR*, IX, Ser. I, 641-42; F. W. Hackett, "Flusser and the Albemarle," *Papers Read Before the Military Order of the Loyal Legion of the United States, Commandery of the District of Columbia* (Washington: Published by the Commandery, 1899), No. 31, pp. 12-16; W. I. Budington, *A Memorial of Giles F. Ward, Jr.* (New York, Anson D. F. Randolph, 1886), p. 68. Cooke and Flusser had engaged each other before. See above p. 87.

19. *NR*, IX, Ser. I, 657.

20. J. W. Graham to Father, Apr. 24, 1864, W. A. Graham Papers, SHC; Graham, "Capture of Plymouth," pp. 181-83.

21. J. W. Graham to Father, Apr. 24, 1864, W. A. Graham Papers, SHC; Graham, "Capture of Plymouth," pp. 183-90; Henry A. Chambers Diary, Apr. 22, 1864, NCDAH.

22. *NR*, IX, Ser. I, 655.

23. Graham, "Capture of Plymouth," p. 192; J. C. Long to Sarah MacKay, May 30, 1864, MacKay-Stiles Papers, SHC.

24. *NR*, IX, Ser. I, 655.

25. Graham, "Capture of Plymouth," p. 193.

26. *Ibid.*, p. 192. Hoke was a native of Lincolnton and Cook was from Beaufort. A. Tredwell, "North Carolina Navy," *Histories of the Several Regiments and Battalions from North Carolina in the Great War 1861-'65. Written by Members of the Respective Commands*, ed. W. Clark (Goldsboro: Nash Brothers, 1901), V, 312.

27. *OR*, XXXIII, Ser. I, 312.

28. *Ibid.*, pp. 311-12; D. M. Carter to Z. B. Vance, Oct. 5, 1864, D. M. Carter Papers, SHC; W. Hoyle to Sarah Cornell, May 5, 1864, Sarah Cornell Papers, DU; Henry J. H. Thompson Diary, Apr. 30, 1864, DU; L. C. Warren, *Beaufort County's Contribution to a Notable Era of North Carolina History* (Washington: GPO, 1930), p. 19.

29. *OR*, XXXIII, Ser. I, 310.

30. James Evans to Father, May 10, 1864, James Evans Papers, SHC.

31. C. F. Warren, "Washington During the Civil War," *The Confederate Reveille* (Raleigh: Edwards and Broughton, 1898), pp. 16-20.

32. A. Roman, *The Military Operations of General Beauregard in the War Between the States 1861-1865. Including a Brief Sketch and Narrative of Service in the War with Mexico* (New York: Harper and Brothers, 1884), II, 544-45. General Beauregard's department included "Virginia south of the James and Appomatox, and all that portion of North Carolina east of the mountains." On his own initiative the General designated his command as the "Department of North Carolina and Southern Virginia." This was more of a paper command than anything else. The department was "large, the boundries of it vaguely defined, and the command responsibility in it confused." *Ibid.*, p. 195. See also T. H. Williams, *P. G. T. Beauregard: Napoleon in Gray* (Baton Rouge: Louisiana State Univ. Press, 1954), p. 208.

33. Roman, *Beauregard*, II, 545.

34. J. C. Long to Sarah MacKay, May 30, 1864, MacKay-Stiles Papers, SHC; *NR*, IX, Ser. I, 768-811.

35. See above p. 216n.

36. *NR*, IX, Ser. I, 735-36; E. Holden, "The 'Albemarle' and the 'Sassacus,' " *CM*, XXXVI (May-Oct., 1888), 427-28.

37. *NR*, IX, Ser. I, 737-40; Holden, "Albemarle and the Sassacus," pp. 428-31; Elliott, "Career of the Albemarle," p. 426.

38. *Ibid.*, p. 739; [Anon.], *The Union Army*, VIII (The Navy) *A History of the Military Affairs in the Loyal States, 1861-65* (Madison: Federal Publishing Co., 1908), 274-75.

39. *NR*, IX, Ser. I, 771; J. G. Sills to "My dear," May 6, [1864], R. V. Howell Papers, NCDAH; J. G. Martin to Wife, May 6, 1864, Starke-Marchant-Martin Papers, SHC. The *Albemarle* was soon repaired and in good working order. J. C. Long to Sarah MacKay, May 30, 1864, MacKay-Stiles Papers, SHC.

40. *OR*, XXXVI, Ser. I, Pt. II, 3-6; Budington, *Memoiral of G. F. Ward*, pp. 69-71; R. D. Graham, "Fifty-sixth Regiment," *Histories of the Several Regiments and Battalions from North Carolina in the Great War 1861-'65. Written by Members of the Respective Commands,* ed. W. Clark (Goldsboro: Nash Brothers, 1901), III, 349; R. W. Wharton, "Sixty-seventh Regiment," *Histories of the Several Regiments and Battalions from North Carolina in the great War 1861-'65. Written by Members of the Respective Commands,* ed. W. Clark (Goldsboro: Nash Brothers, 1901), III, 705; W. Hoyle to Sarah Cornell, May 5, 1864, Sarah Cornell Papers, DU; Thompson Diary, May 4-6, 1864, DU.

41. Graham, "Fifty-sixth Regiment," p. 350.

42. Roman, *Beauregard*, II, 199.

43. Williams, *Napoleon in Gray*, p. 210.

44. Graham, "Fifty-sixth Regiment," p. 350.

45. J. C. Gray and J. C. Ropes, *War Letters, 1862-1865, of John Chipman Gray and John Codman Ropes* (New York: Houghton Mifflin Co., 1927), p. 465.

46. John G. Barrett, *Sherman's March Through the Carolinas* (Chapel Hill: Univ. of N.C. Press, 1956), pp. 17-26. At Goldsboro a Confederate soldier wrote: "Glorius news from Atlanta. . . . Yanks driven from their works. "E. D. E." to J. N. Whitford, July 23, 1864, J. N. Whitford Papers, DU.

47. H. J. H. Thompson to wife, Mar. 27, 1864, H. J. H. Thompson Papers, DU.

48. *Ibid.*, Nov. 27, 1864.

49. Commander Stephen C. Rowan was first asked to do the job but he refused. For the earlier exploits of Cushing see above pp. 134-35 and below pp. 256-57, 270n, 276n, 279n.

50. W. B. Cushing, "The Destruction of the 'Albemarle,'" *CM*, XXXVI (May-Oct., 1888), 432-33.

51. *Ibid.*, p. 433.

52. *Ibid.*, pp. 433-34; Roske and Van Doren, *Lincoln's Commando,* pp. 211-13.

53. *NR*, X, Ser. I, 611-24; Cushing, "Destruction of the Albemarle," pp. 434-38; T. W. Haight, *Three Wisconsin Cushings,* Original Papers No. 3 (Madison: Wisconsin History Commission, 1910), pp. 67-81; Roske and Van Doren, *Lincoln's Commando,* p. 230.

CHAPTER XI

1. W. D. Cotton, "Appalachian North Carolina" (Ph.D. dissertation, Univ. of North Carolina, 1954), pp. 147, 149-50.

2. C. D. Smith to Z. B. Vance, Feb. 15, 1864, Z. B. Vance Papers, NCDAH. One officer "remarked . . . scarcely half of them [home guard] will do to trust." *Ibid.* See also *OR*, LIII, Ser. I, 313-14, 335; *Ibid.*, XXXIII, Ser. I, Pt. III, 741-42; Raleigh *N.C. Standard,* Feb. 16, 1864.

3. C. D. Smith to Z. B. Vance, Feb. 15, 1864, Z. B. Vance Papers, NCDAH.

4. *OR*, XXXII, Ser. I, Pt. I, 137-38; L. F. Siler to Z. B. Vance, Feb. 8, 1864, Z. B. Vance Papers, NCDAH; C. D. Smith to Z. B. Vance, Feb. 15, 1864, Z. B. Vance Papers, NCDAH; Mattie Russell, "William Holland Thomas" (Ph.D. dissertation, Duke Univ., 1956), p. 384-85.

5. C. D. Smith to Z. B. Vance, Feb. 15, 1864, Z. B. Vance Papers, NCDAH.

6. L. F. Siler to Z. B. Vance, Feb. 19, 1864, Z. B. Vance, Papers, *NCDAH.*

7. *Ibid.*; *OR*, XXVII, Ser. I., Pt. I. 404-6.

8. *OR*, XXXIX, Ser. I, Pt. I, 234.

9. *Ibid.*, pp. 232-37; J. P. Arthur, *Western North Carolina: A History from 1730-1913* (Raleigh: Edwards and Broughton, 1914), pp. 605-6; J. P. Arthur, *A History of Watauga County, North Carolina, with Sketches of Prominent Families* (Richmond: Everett Waddey

Co., 1915), pp. 164-65. Franklin described the raid in a letter to J. P. Arthur, dated March 2, 1912. Arthur relied heavily upon this letter in covering Kirk's raid in the above volumes.

10. *OR,* XXXIX, Ser. I, Pt. I, 237.

11. *Ibid.,* pp. 236-37. The fires also consumed large quantities of commissary stores and unissued ordnance supplies. *Ibid.*

12. *Ibid.;* Arthur, *Western North Carolina,* p. 606; C. L. Price, "The Railroads of North Carolina During the Civil War" (M.A. thesis, Univ. of North Carolina, 1951), pp. 179-80; Arthur, *Watauga County,* pp. 164-65; Peter Mallett to T. H. Holmes, June 28, 29, 1864, Peter Mallett Papers, SHC; Peter Mallett to J. Prior, June 29, 1864, Peter Mallett Papers, SHC; Peter Mallett to C. B. Duffield, June 29, 1864, Peter Mallett Papers, SHC. At Salisbury there was a large Confederate prison. See below p. 356.

13. *OR,* XXXIX, Ser. I, Pt. I, 233-37. Kirk captured practically everyone at Camp Vance, but it was impossible for him to take all of his prisoners back to Tennessee.

14. G. W. F. Harper to W. W. Lenoir, July 11, 1864, G. W. F. Harper Papers, SHC; Arthur, *Watauga County,* pp. 164-65. Harper was at home on sick leave from the army when he learned of Kirk's raid.

15. Arthur, *Western North Carolina,* pp. 606-7. This skirmish is not mentioned in the *Official Records.* Arthur based his account of the fight on a statement made to him by Colonel George A. Loven "at Cold Spring Tavern, near Jonas's Ridge post office, N.C., June, 1910." Colonel Loven lived only a mile from where the skirmish occurred and was a member of the attacking party. *Ibid.,* pp. 606, 626.

16. *OR,* XXXIX, Ser. I, Pt. I, 236; A. C. Avery, "Seventeenth Battalion," *Histories of the Several Regiments and Battalions from North Carolina in the Great War 1861-'65. Written by Members of the Respective Commands,* ed., W. Clark (Goldsboro: Nash Brothers, 1901), IV, 372. Peter Mallett to T. H. Holmes, June 30, 1864, Peter Mallett Papers, SHC; Arthur, *Western North Carolina,* pp. 607-8.

17. *OR,* XXXIX, Ser. I, Pt. I, 234.

18. *Ibid.,* p. 235. "That Colonel Kirk's command was made up of regular enlisted men, although they were from the mountains, their Southern neighbors would never concede." Wilma Dykeman, *The French Broad* (New York: Rhinehart and Co., 1955), p. 118.

19. D. J. Whitener, *History of Watauga County* (Boone: Watauga Centennial Commission, 1949), p. 47; Arthur, *Watauga County,* p. 162.

20. Arthur, *Watauga County,* pp. 165-66.

21. *Ibid.,* pp. 160-61.

22. *Ibid.;* Nancy Alexander, *Here Will I Dwell: The Story of Caldwell County* (Salisbury: Rowan Printing Co., 1956), pp. 136-37.

23. Hendersonville *Times-News,* July 29, 1938; Forest City *Courier,* Aug. 12, 1943; Cotton, "Appalachian North Carolina," p. 127; A. H. Jones, *Knocking at the Door. Member-Elect to Congress: His Career Before the War, During the War, and After the War.* (Washington: McGill and Witherow, 1866), pp. 24-32; [Anon.], *Seven Months a Prisoner* (Indianapolis: J. M. and E. J. Meikel and Co., 1868), pp. 169, 137-40; G. W. Cable and others, *Famous Adventures and Prison Escapes* (London: T. Fisher Unwin, 1894), pp. 262-64; J. H. Browne, *Four Years in Secessia . . .* (Hartford: O. D. Cass and Co., 1865), pp. 377-93; A. D. Richardson, *The Secret Service, the Field, the Dungeon, and the Escape* (Hartford: American Publishing Co., 1865), pp. 450-56.

24. F. L. Klement, ed., "Edwin B. Bigelow: A Michigan Sergeant in the Civil War," *Mich. Hist.,* XXXVIII (1954), 249-52; Cotton, "Appalachian North Carolina," p. 127.

25. Arthur, *Western North Carolina,* p. 614; Muriel Earley Sheppard, *Cabins in the Laurel* (Chapel Hill: Univ. of N.C. Press, 1935), pp. 66-67; Cotton, "Appalachian North Carolina," p. 128.

26. S. M. Hughes to Z. B. Vance, Nov. 18, 1864, Z. B. Vance Papers, NCDAH; C. D. Smith to Z. B. Vance, Feb. 15, 1864, NCDAH; Peter Mallett to C. B. Duffield, June 28,

1864, Peter Mallett Papers, SHC; A. C. Cowles to Z. B. Vance, Sept. 19, 1864, Z. B. Vance Papers, NCDAH; Cotton, "Appalachian North Carolina," pp. 128-29; Cable, *Famous Adventures and Prison Escapes*, pp. 267-68; A. Cooper, *In and Out of Rebel Prisons* (Oswego: R. J. Olephant, 1888), pp. 178-83; Richardson, *Secret Service*, pp. 451-52.

27. Cotton, "Appalachian North Carolina," p. 128; Georgia L. Tatum, *Disloyalty in the Confederacy* (Chapel Hill: Univ. of N.C. Press, 1934), p. 135.

28. *OR*, XLII, Ser. I, Pt. III, 1253-54.

29. C. D. Smith to Z. B. Vance, Nov. 20, 1864, Z. B. Vance Papers, NCDAH.

30. *OR*, XLII, Ser. I, Pt. III, 1253-54.

31. L. F. Siler to Z. B. Vance, Feb. 19, 1864, Z. B. Vance Papers, NCDAH.

32. "Rufus" to "Dear Brother," Nov. 7, 1864, Lenoir-Norwood Papers, SHC. See also R. L. Patterson to Father, Dec. 3, 1864, Lindsay Patterson Papers, SHC.

33. R. V. Blackstock to Z. B. Vance, Apr. 29, 1864, Z. B. Vance Papers, NCDAH; Arthur, *Western North Carolina*, p. 604; *OR*, LIII, Ser. I, 326-27; Sheppard, *Cabins in the Laurel*, p. 62. The day previous to the raid a band of women took sixty bushels of wheat from a government storehouse. Arthur, *Western North Carolina*, p. 604.

34. Cotton, "Appalachian North Carolina," p. 138.

35. *Ibid.*; W. H. McNeil to Z. B. Vance, Nov. 19, 1864, Z. B. Vance Papers, NCDAH.

36. A. C. Cowles to Z. B. Vance, Sept. 19, 1864, Z. B. Vance Papers, NCDAH.

37. J. Taylor to W. H. Thomas, Aug. 10, 1864, J. W. Terrell Papers, DU.

38. I. Lowdermilk to B. Tyson, Nov. 22, 1864, B. Tyson Papers, DU. See also J. L. Henry to Z. B. Vance, Sept. 30, 1864, Z. B. Vance Papers, NCDAH.

39. *OR*, XLII, Ser. I, Pt. III, 1251.

40. Cotton, "Appalachian North Carolina," p. 118. Longstreet was ordered back to Virginia from east Tennessee in April, 1864.

41. W. W. Avery to Z. B. Vance, Mar. 24, 1864, Z. B. Vance Papers, NCDAH.

42. T. R. Caldwell to Z. B. Vance, March 18, 1864, Z. B. Vance Papers, NCDAH.

43. J. C. Wills to Z. B. Vance, Apr. 29, 1864, Z. B. Vance Papers, NCDAH. See also T. York to Z. B. Vance, May 5, 1864, Z. B. Vance Papers, NCDAH; W. G. De Journet to Z. B. Vance, May 4, 1864, Z. B. Vance Papers, NCDAH.

44. J. C. Vaughn to D. M. Key, Sept. 28, 1864, D. M. Key Papers, SHC. Since several months elapsed between the time (Apr., 1864) J. C. Wills observed Vaughn's cavalry and the date (Sept., 1864) of the above letter, it is possible General Vaughn was referring to another occasion when his troops were in North Carolina. Regardless of the circumstances of the Wills and Vaughn letters, these bits of correspondence show that Vaughn's cavalry was not very well disciplined.

45. Mother [?] to J. B. Jones, June 3, 1864, Jones Family Papers, SHC; P. Taylor and other to Z. B. Vance, Sept. [?], 1864, Z. B. Vance Papers, NCDAH; Tatum, *Disloyalty in Confederacy*, p. 127.

46. R. E. Yates, *The Confederacy and Zeb Vance*, ed., W. S. Hoole, *Confederate Centennial Studies* (Tuscaloosa: Confederate Publishing Co., 1958), No. 8, p. 44.

47. *Ibid.*, p. 106; Tatum, *Disloyalty in the Confederacy*, pp. 127-32; H. W. Raper, "William W. Holden and the Peace Movement in North Carolina," *NCHR, XXXI* (Oct., 1954), 493-517; James B. Jones Diary, Aug. 4, 1864, SHC; C. H. Stephenson to W. H. Pope, Mar. 21, 1864, J. Haywood Papers, SHC; D. A. Buie to "Miss Kate," May 1, 1864, Catherine (McG) Buie Papers, DU; C. J. Iredell to "Mattie," Aug. 3, 1864, C. J. Iredell Papers, SHC; N. A. Boyden to Z. B. Vance, Apr. 2, 1864, Z. B. Vance Papers, NCDAH.

48. C. D. Smith to Z. B. Vance, Nov. 20, 1864, Z. B. Vance Papers, NCDAH.

49. Elizabeth [?] Abernathy to C. P. Abernathy, Dec. 26, 1864, C. P. Abernathy Papers, SHC.

50. For ample evidence of dissaffection in the central counties see Z. B. Vance Papers, NCDAH; A. S. Caddell Papers, DU.

CHAPTER XII

1. J. Johns, "Wilmington During the Blockade," *HNMM*, XXXII (Sept., 1866), 407.

2. F. B. C. Bradlee, *Blockade Running During the Civil War* (Salem: Essex Institute, 1925), p. 261.

3. S. R. Mallory to J. N. Maffitt, Feb. 24, 1865, J. N. Maffitt Papers, SHC; H. Cochran, *Blockade Runners of the Confederacy* (New York: Bobbs-Merrill, 1958), p. 299.

4. J. Sprunt, *Chronicles of the Cape Fear: Being Some Account of Historic Events on the Cape Fear River* (Raleigh: Edwards and Broughton, 1914), p. 390.

5. J. M. Merrill, "Notes on the Yankee Blockade of the South Atlantic Seaboard, 1861-1865," *CWH*, IV (Dec., 1958), 388.

6. Sprunt, *Chronicles of the Cape Fear*, p. 390.

7. *Ibid.*, pp. 390-91; *NR*, VIII, Ser. I, 313-14; T. E. Taylor, *Running the Blockade: A Personal Narrative of Adventure, Risks, and Escapes During the American Civil War* (New York: Charles Scribner's Sons, 1896), p. 46; R. S. West, Jr., *Mr. Lincoln's Navy* (New York: Longmans, Green and Co., 1957), p. 290. See also below p. 255.

8. See below p. 265.

9. See above p. 6.

10. "Old Brunswick" was the site of the town of Brunswick laid out by Maurice Moore about 1727. Long before the Civil War, the town had disappeared. About all that remained was the ruins of St. Philips Church.

11. J. R. Randall to "Kate," Feb. 26, 1864. J. R. Randall Papers, SHC.

12. J. Wilkinson, *The Narrative of a Blockade Runner* (New York: Sheldon and Co., 1877), pp. 130-35, 149-56, 202; Taylor, *Running the Blockade*, pp. 46-56; A. Roberts [A. C. Hobart-Hampden], *Never Caught: Personal Adventures Connected with Twelve Successful Trips in Blockade-Running During the American Civil War, 1863-64* (London: John Camden Hotten, 1867), pp. 18-26; H. Pasha, *Sketches from My Life* (London: Longmans, Green and Co., 1886), pp. 89-101; J. Sprunt, *Tales and Traditions of the Lower Cape Fear, 1661-1896* (Wilmington: Le Gwin Brothers, 1896), p. 114; J. S. Reilly, *Wilmington, Past, Present, and Future* (Wilmington: J. S. Reilly, 1884), pp. 17-22; J. D. Hill, *Sea Dogs of the Sixties: Farragut and Seven Contemporaries* (Minneapolis: Univ. of Minnesota Press, 1935), pp. 128-61; J. R. Soley, *The Blockade and the Cruisers* (New York: Charles Scribner's Sons, 1883), pp. 151-67; Sprunt, *Chronicles of the Cape Fear*, pp. 379-459; T. J. Scharf, *History of the Confederate States Navy from its Organization to the Surrender of its Last Vessel* (New York; Rogers and Sherwood, 1887), pp. 462-65; D. H. Hill, *North Carolina in The War Between the States—Bethel to Sharpsburg* (Raleigh: Edwards and Broughton, 1926), I, 367-68; Cochran, *Blockade Runners*, pp. 155-81; Merrill, "Yankee Blockade," pp. 387-97; R. Stevenson, "Wilmington and the Blockade-Runners of the Civil War," *N.C. Univ. Mag.*, XXXII (March, 1902), 154; C. Hallock, "Bermuda in Blockade Times," *New Eng. Mag.*, VI (May, 1892), 339-39; J. Sprunt, "What Ship Is That?" *Southport Leader*, Nov., 1893-Nov., 1895; M. de Wolf Stevenson to W. Stevenson, Apr. 17, 1907, M. de Wolf Stevenson Papers, SHC; J. R. Randall to "Kate," Feb. 26, 1864, J. R. Randall Papers, SHC; L. H. de Rosset to Sister, Oct. 25, 1863, De Rosset Family Papers, SHC; "Orders for Blockaders, 1864," Broadside, NCC. Every blockade-runner carried both a pilot and signal officer.

13. D. A. Buie to "Kate," July 8, 1862, Catherine (McG.) Buie Papers, DU; L. Warlick to Cornelia McGimsey, July 15, 1862, Cornelia McGimsey Papers, SHC; G. P. Erwin to Sister, July 10, 1862, G. P. Erwin Papers, SHC; "David" to "Kate," Oct. 18, 1862, Catherine (McG.) Buie Papers, DU; "Husband" to "Dear Wife," Nov. 18, 1862, Confederate States Archives, DU; Eliza de Rosset to [one of her children], Nov. 9, 1863, De Rosset Family Papers, SHC; A. J. White to Wife, Jan. 19, 1862, A. J. White Papers, DU; Oliver Mercer to Father, Jan. 11, 1862, Mercer Family Papers, SHC; J. W. F. Dix to D. MacRae, Sept. 29, 1862, H. MacRae Papers, DU; [D. A. Buie] to "Kate," June 6, 1862, Catherine (McG.) Buie Papers, DU; L. Warlick to Cornelia McGimsey, June 3,

1862, Cornelia McGimsey Papers, SHC; T. W. Higginson to "Dear Ropes," Sept. 12, 1895, T. W. Higginson Papers, DU; Taylor, *Running the Blockade*, p. 56; Kate M. Rowland, "Letters of Major Thomas Rowland, C.S.A. from North Carolina, 1861 and 1862," *WMCQ*, XXV (Oct., 1916), 76-82, 225-35; E. F. Shaw to Wife, Sept. 27, 1862, Fayetteville *Observer*, Apr. 12, 1954; A. MacRae to D. MacRae, Aug. 24, 1863, H. MacRae Papers, DU; David Stick, *Graveyard of the Atlantic* (Chapel Hill: Univ. of N.C. Press, 1952), pp. 6-63; W. Lamb, "Fight with Blockaders," *Histories of the Several Regiments and Battalions from North Carolina in the Great War 1861-'65. Written by Members of the Respective Commands*, ed. W. Clark (Goldsboro: Nash Brothers, 1901), V, 351-52. The Federals lost only one blockader off Wilmington. Stick, *Graveyard of the Atlantic*, p. 63; W. Wheeler to J. H. Wheeler, Jan. 16, 1863, J. H. Wheeler Papers, SHC.

14. W. R. Hooper, "Blockade Running," *HNMM*, XLII (Dec., 1870), 108.

15. Sprunt, *Chronicles of the Cape Fear*, pp. 387-88; A. S. Roberts, "High Prices and the Blockade in the Confederacy," *SAQ*, XXIV (Apr., 1925), 155-62; W. K. Boyd, "Fiscal and Economic Conditions in North Carolina During the Civil War," *NCB*, XIV (Apr., 1915), 195-208; J. W. F. Dix to D. MacRae, Aug. 19, 1862, H. MacRae Papers, DU; R. MacRae to Brother, Sept. 2, 1863, H. MacRae Papers, DU. Professor H. T. Lefler says that 4c to 8c cotton sold in Europe for 50c to 70c. Hugh T. Lefler and A. R. Newsome, *North Carolina: The History of a Southern State* (Chapel Hill: Univ. of N.C. Press, 1954), p. 435.

16. J. R. Randall to "Kate," Oct. 6, 1863, J. R. Randall Papers, SHC.

17. W. H. Battle to K. P. Battle, Feb. 15, 1864, Battle Family Papers, SHC.

18. J. R. Randall to "Katie," Oct. 15, 1863, J. R. Randall Papers, SHC.

19. J. R. Randall to "Katie," Mar. 10, 1864, J. R. Randall Papers, SHC; W. A. Burgess to E. Burgess, Mar. 13, 1864, Confederate States Archives, DU; W. H. C. Whiting to J. A. Seddon, Mar. 11, 1864, W. H. C. Whiting Papers, NCDAH; Sprunt, *Chronicles of the Cape Fear*, p. 487.

20. W. F. Lynch to Z. B. Vance, Nov. 15, 1863, Z. B. Vance Papers, NCDAH; W. Calder to Mother, June 7, 1864, W. Calder Papers, SHC; J. R. Randall to "Katie," Mar. 10, 1864, J. R. Randall Papers, SHC; Sprunt, *Chronicles of the Cape Fear*, pp. 486-87.

21. Jim Chaney, "South's Grey Ghosts," Raleigh *N and O*, May 26, 1957.

22. A. MacRae to D. MacRae June 8, 1864, H. MacRae Papers, DU; *Ibid.*, Oct. 17, 1863; W. H. Brawley [?] to "My dear friend," May 17, 1864, T. M. Logan Papers, SHC; Mother to W. Calder, Feb. 6, 22, 27, April 23, 1863, W. Calder Papers, SHC; E. C. Yellowly to Nephew, Feb. 18, 1863, E. C. Yellowly Papers, SHC.

23. J. R. Randall to "Katie," June 10, 1864, J. R. Randall Papers, SHC; Sprunt, *Chronicles of the Cape Fear*, p. 387.

24. The State of North Carolina also had interest in several steamers.

25. A. Gordon, "Organization of Troops," *Histories of the Several Regiments and Battalions from North Carolina in the Great War 1861-'65. Written by Members of the Respective Commands*, ed. W. Clark (Goldsboro: E. M. Uzzell, 1901), I, 28-30; Hill, *Bethel to Sharpsburg*, 329-97; *NR*, X, Ser. I, 56; Z. B. Vance to J. J. Guthrie, Oct. 18, 1863, J. J. Guthrie Papers, NCDAH; T. Boykin to Z. B. Vance, Feb. 29, 1864, Z. B. Vance Papers, NCDAH; "Tom" to "Harriet," Mar. 7, 1864, Confederate Papers, SHC; Mary B. Van Wyck to Brother, Nov. 1, 1863, Battle Family Papers, SHC; W. A. Graham, Jr. to Mother, Jan. 20, 1864, W. A. Graham Papers, SHC; J. G. Martin to Wife, Oct. 23, 1863, Starke-Marchant-Martin Papers, SHC; E. Warren to Z. B. Vance Nov. [?] 22, 1863, Telegram, Z. B. Vance Papers, NCDAH. One reason the *Advance* was overtaken at sea was because she had given her good coal to the *Tallahassee*. S. R. Mallory to Z. B. Vance, Jan. 28, 1865, Z. B. Vance Papers, NCDAH.

26. C. A. Post "A Diary on the Blockade in 1863," *USNIP*, XXXIV (Oct.-Nov., 1918), 2343-2574; H. B. Rommel to Father, April, n.d., 1863, H. B. Rommel Papers, DU; S. P. Lee to B. F. Sands, Sept. 20, 1864, Confederate Papers, SHC; H. L. Sturgis to Friend, Feb. 20, 1862, Confederate Papers, SHC; J. J. Almy, "Incidents of the Blockade,

1861-65," *War Papers Read Before the Military Order of the Loyal Legion of the United States, Commandery of the District of Columbia* (Washington: Published by the Commandery, 1892), No. 9, pp. 3-4; (Anon.), "Life on a Blockader," *Continental Monthly,* VI (July, 1864), 49-50; Merrill, "Yankee Blockade," p. 389; W. H. Anderson, "Blockade Life," *War Papers Read Before the Commandery of the State of Maine, Military Order of the Loyal Legion of the United States* (Portland: Lefavor-Tower Co., 1902), II, 2-10.

27. W. Calder to Mother, May 22, 1864, W. Calder Papers, SHC; W. Lamb to Z. B. Vance, June 11, 1863, Z. B. Vance Papers, NCDAH; W. M. Hedgecock to Father, Jan. 1, 1862, W. M. Hedgecock Papers, SHC; "Friend" to Catherine Buie, Jan. 18, 1862, Catherine (McG) Buie Papers, DU; D. A. Buie [?] to "Miss Kate," Feb. 2, 1862, Catherine (McG) Buie Papers, DU.

28. A. Congleton to Mother and Sister, Dec. 6, 1864, Confederate States Archives, DU.

29. *NR,* IX, Ser. I, 511; "D. A. B." to "Kate," Mar. 1, 1864, Catherine (McG) Buie Papers, DU; W. Calder to Mother, Mar. 24, 1864, W. Calder Papers, SHC; J. R. Randall to "Kate," Mar. 1, 1864, J. R. Randall Papers, SHC.

30. "D. A." to "Miss Kate," June 6, 1864, Catherine (McG) Buie Papers, DU; (Anon.) *Union Army,* VII (The Navy) (Madison: Federal Publishing Co., 1908), 270-71; *NR,* X, Ser. I, 202-4; J. R. Randall to "Kate," June 29, 1864, J. R. Randall Papers, SHC. Cushing cut the telegraph wires connecting Wilmington with Fort Fisher.

31. Wilkinson, *Narrative of a Blockade Runner,* p. 199.

32. Johns, "Wilmington During the Blockade," p. 497. There was still an active social life in Wilmington. In fact one soldier complained that the "Wilmington ladies . . . [had] become entirely too fashionable and worldly" for him. A favorite type of entertainment for the ladies was to take a steamer down the river and visit the soldiers stationed at the mouth of the Cape Fear. W. Calder to Mother, Jan. 28, Mar. 8, 10, 1864, W. Calder Papers, SHC; W. Calder to Brother, Apr. 18, 1864, W. Calder Papers, SHC; Oliver Mercer to Sister, Dec. 29, 1861, Mercer Family Papers, SHC; J. W. Graham to W. A. Graham, Apr. 18, 1863, W. A. Graham Papers, SHC.

33. J. R. Randall to "Kate," Nov. 2, 1863, J. R. Randall Papers, SHC; D. A. Buie [?] to "Miss Kate," Mar. 31, 1863, Catherine (McG) Buie Papers, DU.

34. Wilkinson, *Narrative of a Blockade Runner,* p. 199.

35. *Ibid.* One soldier complained that he never saw so many police in a small town. J. W. Albright Diary, Jan. 20, 1864, SHC.

36. Wilmington *Journal,* May 4, 1864.

37. J. R. Randall to "Kate," June 26, 1864, J. R. Randall Papers, SHC.

38. Johns, "Wilmington During the Blockade," p. 499; Cochran, *Blockade Runners,* p. 178.

39. J. R. Randall to "Kate," Nov. 12, 1863, J. R. Randall Papers, SHC; G. W. Gift to Ellen Shackelford, Jan. 27, Oct. 18, 1864, Ellen S. Gift Papers, SHC; A. MacRae to D. MacRae, Sept. 4, 1864, H. MacRae Papers, DU; J. W. K. Dix to D. MacRae, July 9, 1862, H. MacRae Papers, DU; Johns, "Wilmington During the Blockade," p. 498.

40. W. T. Loftin to Mother, Oct. 2, 1862, W. T. Loftin Papers, DU; L. Warlick to Cornelia McGimsey, Sept. 16, 1862, Cornelia McGimsey Papers, SHC; [?] to "Dear Cousin," Nov. 12, 1862, De Rosset Family Papers, SHC; A. J. White to Wife, Dec. 21, 1862, A. J. White Papers, DU; A. MacRae to D. MacRae, Sept. 22, 1862, H. MacRae Papers, DU; J. W. K. Dix to D. MacRae, Sept. 23, 24, 29, 1862, H. MacRae Papers, DU; A. MacRae to Brother, Sept. 24, 1862, H. MacRae Papers, DU.

41. Mother to W. Calder, May 28, 1863, W. Calder Papers, SHC; J. R. Randall to "Kate," Nov. 2, 1863, J. R. Randall Papers, SHC; J. R. Randall to "Kate," Feb. 10, 1864, J. R. Randall Papers, SHC. See also the Wilmington *Journal,* 1863, 1864.

42. Albright Diary, Feb. 24, 1864, SHC.

43. W. H. C. Whiting to Z. B. Vance, Apr. 29, 1864, Z. B. Vance Papers, NCDAH; J. C. Hackett to Parents, May 22, 1864, J. C. Hackett Papers, DU; W. Calder to Mother, Apr. 25, 1864, W. Calder Papers, SHC; F. P. B. Sands, "A Volunteer's Reminiscence of

Life in the North Atlantic Blockading Squadron, 1862-65," *War Papers Read Before the Military Order of the Loyal Legion of the United States, Commandery of the District of Columbia* (Washington: Published by the Commandery, 1894), No. 20, p. 10.

44. J. T. Watts to J. Brown, July 27, 1864, C. B. Mallett Papers, SHC; J. R. Randall to "Kate," Jan. 16, Mar. 16, 1864, J. R. Randall Papers, SHC; Taylor, *Running the Blockade,* pp. 64-65.

45. J. Dawson to R. H. Cowan, Feb. 10, 1864, Z. B. Vance Papers, NCDAH.

46. Wilkinson, *Narrative of Blockade Runner,* p. 200-1; Sprunt, *Chronicles of the Cape Fear,* p. 25.

47. J. R. Randall to "Kate," Oct. 21, 1863, J. R. Randall Papers, SHC; J. R. Randall to "Kate," May 20, June 6, 18, July 3, 10, 1864, J. R. Randall Papers, SHC; F. B. Simkins and J. W. Patton, *The Women of the Confederacy* (Richmond: Garrett and Massie, 1936), p. 20; Mary A. Buie to "Editor," June 27, 1864, Newspaper clipping, J. R. Randall Papers, SHC.

48. J. R. Randall to "Kate," Oct. 21, 1863, J. R. Randall Papers, SHC.

49. Lefler and Newsome, *N.C.,* p. 436; A. D. Osborne, *The Capture of Fort Fisher by Major General Alfred H. Terry* (New Haven: The Tuttle, Morehouse and Taylor Press, 1911), p. 4.

50. R. E. Lee to Z. B. Vance, Aug. 29, 1864, Z. B. Vance Papers, NCDAH.

51. *NR,* XI, Ser. I, 620.

52. Osborne, *Capture of Fort Fisher,* p. 4.

CHAPTER XIII

1. G. Welles, *Diary of Gideon Welles, Secretary of the Navy under Lincoln and Johnson* (New York: Houghton-Mifflin Co., 1911), II, 127.

2. E. H. Simmons, "The Federals and Fort Fisher," Part I, *MCG,* XXXV (Jan., 1951), 52-54; J. Parker, "The Navy in the Battles and Capture of Fort Fisher," *Personal Recollections of the War of the United States* (New York: G. P. Putnam's Sons, 1897), II, 106-7; D. D. Porter, *Naval History of the Civil War* (New York: Sherman Publishing Co., 1886), 683-85; *NR,* X, Ser. I, 473, 554-57; Welles, *Diary,* II, 127-55. Admiral Dahlgren invented the Dahlgren gun, a rifled cannon, and boat howitzers with iron carriages. M. W. Boatner, *The Civil War Dictionary* (New York: David McKay Co., 1959), p. 218.

3. *OR,* XLII, Ser. I, Pt., 964-70; Parker, "Navy at Fort Fisher," p. 107; Simmons, "Fort Fisher," Pt. I, 53; Porter, *Naval History,* pp. 683-85.

4. (Anon.) "Story of the Powder Boat," *Galaxy,* IX (Jan., 1870), 78-79; J. R. Soley, *Admiral Porter* (New York: D. Appleton and Co., 1903), p. 414; D. D. Porter, *Incidents and Anecdotes of the Civil War* (New York: D. Appleton and Co., 1885), p. 269.

5. (Anon.), "Story of Powder Boat," p. 79.

6. *Ibid.*

7. *Ibid.,* pp. 82-87; *NR,* XI, Ser. I, 228-32.

8. *OR,* XLII, Ser. I, Pt. I, 964-70; Simmons, "Fort Fisher," Pt. I, 56; J. B. Foote to Father, Dec. 11, 1864, J. B. Foote Papers, DU.

9. J. Davis to B. Bragg, Oct. 15, 1864, B. Bragg Papers, WRHS; D. A. Buie to "Kate," Oct. 24, 1864, Catherine (McG) Buie Papers, DU; W. Calder to Mother, Oct. 18, 1864, W. Calder Papers, SHC.

10. D. C. Seitz, *Braxton Bragg: General of the Confederacy* (Columbia: The State Co., 1924), p. 463.

11. W. Lamb, "Fort Fisher," *SHSP,* XXI (Jan.-Dec., 1893), 226; *OR,* XVIII, Ser. I, 770; J. Hagood, *Memoirs of the War of Secession* (Columbia: The State Co., 1910), p. 328; "Kate" to "My Dear Friend," Dec. 12, 1862, J. Gwyn Papers, SHC.

12. See above p. 246.

13. W. Lamb, "Defence of Fort Fisher," *Histories of the Several Regiments and Battalions from North Carolina in the Great War 1861-'65. Written by Members of the*

Respective Commands, ed. W. Clark (Goldsboro: Nash Brothers, 1901), V, 218: W. Calder to Mother, Feb. 9, 1864, W. Calder Papers, SHC; A. D. McEwen to Uncle, Mar. 26, 1864, Ann Kelly Papers, DU; F. W. Bird to Sister, June 16, 1862, R. W. Winston Papers, SHC; L. Warlick to Cornelia McGimsey, June 17, 1862, Cornelia McGimsey Papers, SHC; "David" to "Kate," Dec. 4, 1862, Catherine (McG) Buie Papers, DU.

14. See above p. 249.

15. Lamb, "Fort Fisher," 257-63; Lamb, "Defence of Fort Fisher," pp. 217-20.

16. *NR,* XI, Ser. I, 444-45.

17. *Ibid.,* pp. 254-55; *OR,* XLII, Ser. I, Pt. I, 966-67; W. Calder to Brother, Dec. 24, 1864, W. Calder Papers, SHC; F. E. Smith to Daughter, Dec. 23, 1864, F. E. Smith Papers, DU.

18. *NR,* XI, Ser. I, 225; (Anon.), "Story of Powder Boat," p. 87.

19. *NR,* XI, Ser. I, 226-30, 255; (Anon.), "Story of Powder Boat," p. 87.

20. *NR,* XI, Ser. I, 222, 226.

21. *Ibid.,* pp. 226-55; (Anon.), "Story of Powder Boat," p. 87; Parker, "Navy at Fort Fisher," p. 108; Lamb, "Fort Fisher," 269; G. Dewey, "The Autobiography of Admiral Dewey," *Hearst's Mag.* (Oct., 1910), p. 50.

22. *NR,* XI, Ser. I, 255; *OR,* XLII, Ser. I, Pt. I, 993; Simmons, "Fort Fisher," Pt. I, 56-57.

23. Parker, "Navy at Fort Fisher," p. 108; *NR,* XI, Ser. I, 255-256; Simmons, "Fort Fisher," p. 56.

24. A Confederate, "Under Fire," *The Grayjackets: And How They Lived, Fought and Died for Dixie* (Richmond: Jones Brothers & Co., 1867), pp. 223-29; Lamb, "Fort Fisher," p. 271.

25. *NR,* XI, Ser. I, 255.

26. A Confederate, "Under Fire," pp. 223-29; J. L. Quince to Mother, Jan. 3, 1865, Quince-Walters Papers, SHC.

27. W. Calder to Mother, Dec. 27, 1864, W. Calder Papers, SHC.

28. "David" to "Kate," Jan., n.d., 1865, Catherine (McG) Buie Papers, DU.

29. W. Calder to Mother, Jan. 2, 1865, W. Calder Papers, SHC.

30. *OR,* XLII, Ser. I, Pt. I, 967.

31. H. M. Rogers, *Memories of Ninety Years* (Boston: Houghton-Mifflin Co., 1928), p. 88.

32. Lamb, "Fort Fisher," p. 272; W. Calder to Mother, Dec. 27, 1864, W. Calder Papers, SHC.

33. Lamb, "Fort Fisher," p. 212.

34. *NR,* XI, Ser. I, 256.

35. C. Steedman to Wife, Dec. 27, 1864, C. Steedman Papers, DU; C. Steedman to D. Porter, Dec. 30, 1864, C. Steedman Papers, DU.

36. *NR,* XI, Ser. I, 256.

37. W. H. C. Whiting to "Col. Anderson," Dec. 31, 1864, W. H. C. Whiting Papers, NCDAH.

38. A Confederate, "Under Fire," pp. 223-29.

39. *NR,* XI, Ser. I, 257.

40. *OR,* XLII, Ser. I, Pt. I, 967-68; W. Calder to Mother, Dec. 27, 1864, W. Calder Papers, SHC; A. MacRae to D. MacRae, Dec. 21, 1864, H. MacRae Papers, DU; R. E. Lee to Z. B. Vance, Dec. 21, 1864, Z. B. Vance Papers, NCDAH; *OR,* XLII, Ser. I, Pt. I, 1020-21.

41. *Ibid.,* pp. 967-68; *NR,* XI, Ser. I, 251-57; E. H. Hall, "Reminiscences of the War: The Wilmington Expedition," *U.S. Service Mag.,* (Oct., 1865), p. 316.

42. *OR,* XLII, Ser. I, Pt. I, 968; A. Ames, "The Capture of Fort Fisher," *Civil War Papers Read before the Commandery of the State of Massachusetts, Military Order of the Loyal Legion of the United States* (Boston: Published by the Commandery, 1900), I,

275-78; H. C. Lockwood, "The Capture of Fort Fisher," *AM*, XXVII (May-June, 1871), 633-36.

43. *NR*, XI, Ser. I, 318.

44. *OR*, XLII, Ser. I, Pt. I, 1021.

45. F. E. Smith to Daughter, Dec. 25, 1864, Smith Papers, DU.

46. H. Cochran, *Blockade Runners of the Confederacy* (New York: Bobbs-Merrill, 1958), p. 311.

47. C. Steedman to "Sally," Jan. 6, 1865, C. Steedman Papers, DU.

48. F. E. Smith to Daughter, Dec. 25, 1864, F. E. Smith Papers, DU.

49. *OR*, XLII, Ser. I, Pt. I, 999.

50. W. H. C. Whiting to B. Bragg, Jan. 12, 1865, Rec. Gr. 109, NA; W. H. C. Whiting to J. A. Seddon, Jan. 1, 1865, Rec. Gr. 109, NA; W. H. C. Whiting to Z. B. Vance, Jan. 4, 1865, Rec. Gr. 109, NA; Lamb, "Defence of Fort Fisher," p. 222.

51. W. Calder to Mother, Jan. 2, 1865, W. Calder Papers, SHC; W. Calder to Brother, Dec. 31, 1864, W. Calder Papers, SHC.

52. M. W. Wellman, "Last Battle for Fort Fisher," Raleigh *N and O*, Jan. 10, 1960.

53. *NR*, XI, Ser. I, 436; Lamb, "Defence of Fort Fisher," p. 222; Lamb, "Fort Fisher," p. 276.

54. Lamb, "Defence of Fort Fisher," p. 223; Rogers, *Memories of Ninety Years*, pp. 105-8; *NR*, XI, Ser. I, 438; Cochran, *Blockade Runners*, p. 314.

55. Lamb, "Defence of Fort Fisher," p. 223.

56. *NR*, XI, Ser. I, 438; B. F. Butler to B. F. Wade, Jan. 9, 1865, B. F. Butler Papers, LC. General Butler gave up his command very reluctantly, defending his actions in the first expedition. Nevertheless, "this . . . affair . . . brought down Butler's stock amazingly." B. F. Butler, *Speech of Maj.-Gen. Benj. F. Butler upon the Campaign before Richmond, 1864. Delivered at Lowell, Mass., January 29, 1865. With an Appendix* (Boston: Wright and Potter, 1865), pp. 15-79; J. R. Hamilton to J. Swinton, Jan. 5, 1865, J. Swinton Papers, SHC.

57. *OR*, XLVI, Ser. I, Pt. I, 396; (Anon.) "A Yankee Account of the Battle at Fort Fisher," *Our Living and Our Dead*, I (Dec., 1874), 317-18; J. R. Hamilton to J. Swinton, Jan. 17, 1865, J. R. Swinton Papers, SHC.

58. *OR*, XLVI, Ser. I, Pt. I, 396-97; *NR*, XI, Ser. I, 438-39.

59. A. J. Palmer, *History of the Forty-eighth Regiment New York State Volunteers in the War for Union, 1861-1865* (New York: Charles T. Dillingham, 1885), p. 185; D. Ammen, "A Sketch of Our Second Bombardment of Fort Fisher," *War Papers Read before the Military Order of the Loyal Legion of the United States. Commandery of the District of Columbia, November 2, 1887* (Washington: Judd and Detweiler, 1887), No. 4, pp. 1-8; W. Calder to Mother, Jan. 15, 1865, W. Calder Papers, SHC; J. A. Montgomery, "A Fort Fisher Defender" (Unpublished article), Mary B. Heyer Notebooks, SHC; Cochran, *Blockade Runners*, p. 319.

60. *OR*, XLVI, Ser. I, Pt. I, 433; Lamb, "Defence of Fort Fisher," pp. 226-27; Hagood, *Memoirs of the War*, pp. 324-25.

61. Lamb, "Defence of Fort Fisher," p. 226.

62. *NR*, XI, Ser. I, 439; Simmons, "Fort Fisher," Pt. I, pp. 50-51; Parker, "Navy at Fort Fisher," p. 112.

63. *OR*, XLVI, Ser. I, Pt. I, 398.

64. Lamb, "Defence of Fort Fisher," p. 227; Lamb, "Fort Fisher," p. 280.

65. *NR*, XI, Ser. I, 446-48; Parker, "Navy at Fort Fisher," pp. 112-14; F. P. B. Sands, "The Last of the Blockade and the Fall of Fort Fisher," *War Papers, Read before the Military Order of the Loyal Legion of the United States, Commandery of the District of Columbia* (Washington: Published by the Commandery, 1902), No. 40, pp. 20-25; J. Becker, "Fort Fisher and Wilmington," *Frank Leslie's Popular Monthly*, XXXVIII (Aug., 1894), 234-35; J. S. C. Abbott, "Heroic Deeds of Heroic Men: True Chivalry—Benjamin

H. Porter," *HNMM*, XXXIV (April, 1867), pp. 568-69; Lamb, "Defence of Fort Fisher," p. 228; Wellman, "Last Battle of Fort Fisher," Raleigh *N and O*, Jan. 10, 1960.

66. *OR*, XLVI, Ser. I, Pt. I, 394-447; *NR*, XI, Ser. I, 433-57; Lamb, "Defence of Fort Fisher," pp. 228-34; D. Porter to G. V. Fox, Jan. 21, 1865, G. V. Fox Papers, NYHS; J. B. Foote to Sister, Jan. 16, 1865, J. B. Foote Papers, DU; J. B. Foote to Mother, Jan. 21, 1865, J. B. Foote Papers, DU; H. F. W. Little, *The Seventh Regiment New Hampshire Volunteers* (Concord: Ira C. Evans, 1896), pp. 391-92; D. Eldredge, *The Third New Hampshire and All About It* (Boston: E. B. Stillings and Co., 1893), pp. 615-16; I. Price, *History of the Ninety-seventh Regiment Pennsylvania Volunteer Infantry* (Philadelphia: Privately published, 1875), p. 354; A. Ames, "Capture of Fort Fisher," pp. 290-95; N. M. Curtis, "The Capture of Fort Fisher," *Civil War Papers Read before the Commandery of the State of Massachusetts, Military Order of the Loyal Legion of the United States* (Boston: Published by the Commandery, 1900), I, 299-327; (Anon.) "Terry's Fort Fisher Expedition," *Old and New*, XI, 290-304; C. C. Craven, "If These Rebels Should Succeed . . . ," Raleigh *N and O*, Dec. 28, 1958.

67. J. Reilly, "Report on the Battle of Fort Fisher," Battle report, W. L. de Rosset Papers, NCDAH; R. S. Johnson, "The Charge at Fort Fisher," *Wake Forest Student*, XLVI (Oct., 1928), 171.

68. E. S. Martin, "Defense of Fort Anderson, 1865," *Historical Addresses Delivered at the Ruins of Saint Philips Church under the Auspices of the North Carolina Society of Colonial Dames* (n.p.: Colonial Dames, 1901), p. 39; E. S. Martin, "Services of E. S. Martin during the War" (Unpublished account), NCC; William Calder Diary, Jan. 15, 1865, DU.

69. H. M. Rogers, *Memories of Ninety Years* (Boston: Houghton Mifflin Co., 1928), pp. 105-8.

70. W. H. C. Whiting to D. Blanton, Mar. 2, 1865, Newspaper clipping, W. H. C. Whiting Papers, NCDAH.

71. D. A. Buie to "Kate," Jan. 21, 1865, Catherine (McG) Buie Papers, DU.

72. W. Calder to Mother, Feb. 10, 1865, W. Calder Papers, SHC.

73. John Paris, "Campaign of 1865" (Unpublished account), Rev. John Paris Papers, SHC. See also Z. Ellis to Sister, Feb. 12, 1865, Z. Ellis Papers, SHC.

74. *OR*, XLVI, Ser. I, Pt. I, 399.

75. *Ibid.*, p. 405.

76. *NR*, XI, Ser. I, 444.

77. *Ibid.*, p. 441; Simmons, "Fort Fisher," Pt. II, 52.

78. *OR*, XLVI, Ser. I, Pt. I, 399, 434, 442; *Ibid.*, XLVII, 909-10; Calder Diary, Jan. 12-19, 1865, DU; W. Calder to Mother, Jan. 18, 23, 1865, W. Calder Papers, SHC; W. Badham to Wife, Jan. 20, 1865, W. Badham Papers, DU; J. D. McGeachy to "Kate," Jan. 17, 1865, Catherine (McG) Buie Papers, DU; M. Baxter to Brother, Feb. 6, 1865, Confederate States Archives, DU.

79. *OR*, XLVII, Ser. I, Pt. I, 910-11; J. M. Schofield to D. Porter, Feb. 9, 1865, Confederate Papers, SHC; J. B. Foote to Mother, Feb. 17, 1865, J. B. Foote Papers, DU; D. A. Buie to "Kate," Feb. 13, 1865, Catherine (McG) Buie Papers, DU; Calder Diary, Feb. 11, 12, 1865, DU; J. D. Cox, *The March to the Sea: Franklin and Nashville* (New York: Charles Scribner's Sons, 1882), p. 148.

80. *OR*, XLVII, Ser. I, Pt. I, 910-11, 929-30, 959-61, 1077; *NR*, XII, Ser. I, 33-34; Calder Diary, Jan. 19-Feb. 18, 1865, DU; Z. Ellis to Mother, Mar. 1, 1865, Z. Ellis Papers, SHC; W. Calder to Mother, Jan. 23, 28, Feb. 2, 12, 15, 1865, W. Calder Papers, SHC; Hagood, *Memoirs of the War*, pp. 333-40; W. Badham to Wife, Feb. 28, 1865, W. Badham Papers, DU.

81. *OR*, XLVII, Ser. I, Pt. I, 911, 929-30, 961-62, 1077; *NR*, XII, Ser. I, 34-35; Hagood, *Memoirs of the War*, pp. 340-48; Calder Diary, Feb. 19-20, 1865, DU; J. J. Wescoat Diary, Feb. 20, 1865, DU; W. Calder to Mother, Feb. 26, 1865, W. Calder,

Papers, SHC; Z. Ellis to Mother, Mar. 1, 1865, Z. Ellis Papers, SHC; W. Badham to Wife, Feb. 28, 1865, W. Badham Papers, DU.

82. W. Pettigrew to Susan Hines, Jan. n.d., 1865, Pettigrew Family Papers, SHC; D. MacRae to "Julia," Feb. 7, 1865, H. MacRae Papers, DU; Son to Father, Jan. 20, 1865, De Rosset Family Papers, SHC; E. D. Bellamy, *Back With the Tide* (Wilmington: Privately printed, 1941), pp. 4-5.

83. Kate Fulton to "Friend," Jan. 16, 1865, J. Gwyn Papers, SHC.

84. Calder Diary, Feb. 21, 1865, DU.

85. W. Calder to Mother, Mar. 1, 1865, W. Calder Papers, SHC.

86. Z. Ellis to Mother, Mar. 1, 1865, Z. Ellis Papers, SHC.

87. *OR*, XLVII, Ser. I, Pt. I, 1077; R. E. Lee to B. Bragg, Feb. 22, 1865, B. Bragg Papers, WRHS; Calder Diary, Feb. 22, 1865, DU.

88. Hagood, *Memoirs of the War*, pp. 348-49.

89. L. S. Burkhead, "History of the Difficulties of the Pastorate of the Front Street Methodist Church, Wilmington, N. C., For the Year 1865," *TCHSP*, VIII-XI, Ser. 8 (1908-9), 37-38; *OR*, XLVII, Ser. I, Pt. I, 911.

90. *OR*, XLVII, Ser. I, Pt. I, 930.

91. J. B. Foote to Father, Feb. 22, 1865, J. B. Foote Papers, DU.

CHAPTER XIV

1. *OR*, XLVII, Ser. I, Pt. I, 909-10.

2. See below p. 295.

3. *OR*, XLVII, Ser. I, Pt. I, 911. Cox assumed command of the District of Beaufort on March 1, 1865. *Ibid.*, p. 4.

4. *Ibid.*, pp. 973-74.

5. *Ibid.*, p. 1078; J. G. Sills to Father, Mar. 7, 1865, NCDAH.

6. J. D. Cox, *Military Reminiscences of the Civil War* (New York: Charles Scribner's Sons, 1900), II, 429.

7. *OR*, XLVII, Ser. I, Pt. I, 910-11; J. D. Cox, *The March to the Sea: Franklin and Nashville* (New York: Charles Scribner's Sons, 1882), pp. 156-58; J. W. Griffith Diary, Mar. 7, 1865, OHS.

8. D. H. Hill to "Colonel," Mar. 29, 1865, D. H. Hill Papers, NCDAH; W. Calder Diary, Mar. 8, 1865, DU.

9. *Ibid.; OR*, XLVII, Ser. I, Pt. I, 1078, 1086-87.

10. *Ibid.*, pp. 997-98; H. J. H. Thompson to Wife, Mar. 11, 1865, H. J. H. Thompson Papers, DU; Cox, *Reminiscences*, II, 436.

11. D. H. Hill to "Colonel," Mar. 29, 1865, D. H. Hill Papers, NCDAH; E. Wills to Mother, Mar. 14, 1865, W. H. Wills Papers, SHC; Calder Diary, Mar. 8, 1865, DU; J. Hagood, *Memoirs of the War of Secession* (Columbia: The State Co., 1910), p. 354.

12. *OR*, XLVII, Ser. I, Pt. I, 62, 979; W. Calder to Mother, Mar. 9, 1865, W. Calder Papers, SHC; J. D. Whitford to Z. B. Vance, Mar. 8, 1865, Telegram, Z. B. Vance Papers, NCDAH.

13. The quote in the text is taken from two letters. H. J. H. Thompson to Wife, Mar. 11, 1865, Mar., n.d., 1865, H. J. H. Thompson Papers, DU.

14. *OR*, XLVII, Ser. I, Pt. I, 932; Cox, *March to the Sea*, p. 159; W. C. Benson, "Civil War Diary of William C. Benson," *IMH*, XXIII (Sept., 1927), pp. 360-64.

15. D. H. Hill to "Colonel," Mar. 29, 1865, D. H. Hill Papers, NCDAH; E. Wills to Mother, Mar. 14, 1865, W. H. Wills Papers, SHC.

16. D. H. Hill to "Colonel," Mar. 29, 1865, D. H. Hill Papers, NCDAH; Calder Diary, Mar. 9, 1865, DU; E. S. Martin, "Services of E. S. Martin During the War" (Unpublished account) NCC.

17. D. H. Hill to "Colonel," Mar. 29, 1865, D. H. Hill Papers, NCDAH.

18. Calder Diary, Mar. 10, 1865, DU; J. M. Drake, *The History of the Ninth New Jersey Veteran Volunteers* (Elizabeth: Journal Printing House, 1889), pp. 275-79; H. J. H. Thompson Diary, Mar. 10, 1865, DU; H. J. H. Thompson to Wife, Mar. 11, 15, 1865, H. J. H. Thompson Papers, DU.

19. D. H. Hill to "Colonel," Mar. 29, 1865, D. H. Hill Papers, NCDAH; Calder Diary, Mar. 10, 1865, DU; C. G. Elliott, "Kirkland's Brigade, Hoke's Division, 1864-65," *SHSP*, XXIII (Jan.-Dec., 1895), 170-72; Griffith Diary, Mar. 10, 1865, OHS; J. Davis, *Rise and Fall of the Confederate Government* (New York: D. Appleton and Co., 1881), p. 635.

20. *OR*, XLVII, Ser. I, Pt. II, 1274, 1334.

21. J. E. Johnston, *Narrative of Military Operations, Directed, During the Late War Between the States, by Joseph E. Johnston, General, C.S.A.* (New York: D. Appleton and Co., 1874), pp. 227, 378.

22. *OR*, XVII, Ser. I, Pt. II, 260.

23. W. T. Sherman, *Memoirs of General W. T. Sherman* (New York: D. Appleton and Co., 1875), I, 267. Guerrilla activity and unorganized civilian resistance in the region around Memphis helped bring Sherman to this conclusion.

24. An excellent study of Sherman's philosophy of total war may be found in J. B. Walters, "General W. T. Sherman and Total War" (Ph.D. dissertation, Vanderbilt Univ., 1947).

25. *Ibid.*, p. 138; *OR*, XXXVIII, Ser. I, Pt. V, 794.

26. Sherman, *Memoirs*, II, 126.

27. B. H. Liddell Hart, *Sherman: Soldier, Realist, American* (New York: Dodd, Mead, and Co., 1929), p. 426.

28. C. R. Ballard, *The Military Genius of Abraham Lincoln* (New York: World Publishing Co., 1952), p. 223.

29. Sherman, *Memoirs*, II, 206.

30. *Ibid.*, p. 209.

31. *Ibid.*, pp. 213-24.

32. See above pp. 286-87n.

33. Sherman, *Memoirs*, II, 223-24.

34. *OR*, XLVII, Ser. I, Pt. II, 154.

35. Sherman, *Memoirs*, II, 175-76.

36. M. H. Force, "Marching Across Carolina," *Sketches of War History, 1861-65. Papers Read before the Ohio Commandery of the Loyal Legion of the United States* (Cincinnati: R. Clark and Co., 1888-1908), I, 15; T. S. Gray, Jr., "The March to the Sea," *GHQ*, XIV (June, 1930), 118-24.

37. G. S. Bradley, *The Star Corps: or, Notes of an Army Campaign During Sherman's March to the Sea* (Milwaukee: Jermain and Brightman, 1865), pp. 474-75.

38. Force, "Marching Across Carolina," pp. 1-2.

39. W. W. Calkins, *The History of the One Hundred and Fourth Regiment of Illinois Volunteer Infantry. War of Great Rebellion 1862-1865* (Chicago: Donahue and Henneberry, 1895), p. 284.

40. Sherman, *Memoirs*, II, 269.

41. D. P. Conyngham, *Sherman's March Through the South with Sketches and Incidents of the Campaign* (New York: Sheldon and Co., 1865), p. 316.

42. Sherman, *Memoirs*, II, 269.

43. J. G. Barrett, "General William T. Sherman's Military Operations in North Carolina, March 4, 1865—March 25, 1865" (M.A. thesis, Univ. of North Carolina, 1949), pp. 1-2.

44. *OR*, XLVIII, Ser. I, Pt. I, 683.

45. *Ibid.*, p. 20.

46. Sherman, *Memoirs*, II, 175-76.

47. Mary E. Massey, "Southern Refugee Life," *NCHR*, XX, 15-16; Emma Le Conte Diary, Feb. 15, 1865, SHC; J. T. Trowbridge, *The South: A Tour of Its Battlefields and Ruined Cities. A Journey Through the Desolated States, and Talks with the People* (Hartford: L. Stebbins, 1866), p. 554; Mrs. T. Taylor, ed., *South Carolina Women of the Confederacy* (Columbia: The State Co., 1903), p. 219; D. E. H. Smith and others, eds., *Mason Smith Family Letters, 1860-1865* (Columbia: Univ. of S.C. Press, 1950), p. 168.

48. *OR*, XLVII, Ser. I, Pt. I, 1 ff.

49. Testimony of General William Tecumseh Sherman, March 26, 1872, in a lawsuit regarding the fire. Penciled copy of this testimony in W. T. Sherman Papers, LC; W. W. Black, ed., "Marching Through South Carolina: Another Civil War Letter of Lieutenant George M. Wise," *OHQ*, LXVI (Apr., 1957), 193.

50. *OR*, XLVII, Ser. I, Pt. I, 22.

51. J. C. Arbuckle, *Civil War Experiences of a Foot-Soldier Who Marched with Sherman* (Columbus: Privately printed, 1930), p. 135.

52. *OR*, XLVII, Ser. I, Pt. II, 1247. Johnston had been Sherman's opponent in Georgia until President Davis replaced him with Hood.

53. J. G. Barrett, *Sherman's March Through the Carolinas* (Chapel Hill: Univ. of N.C. Press, 1956) p. 113. In describing Sherman's campaign in North Carolina, the author relied heavily upon the sources he used and the conclusions he reached in the above volume.

54. *OR*, XLVII, Ser. I, Pt. I, 885.

55. J. Pike, *The Scout and Ranger: Being the Personal Adventures of Corporal Pike of the Fourth Cavalry* (Cincinnati: J. R. Hawley and Co., 1865), p. 382.

56. T. Atkinson to Cornelia P. Spencer, Jan. 30, 1866, D. L. Swain Papers, SHC.

57. Raleigh *Conservative*, Mar. 21, 1865, quoting the Charlotte *Democrat*, Mar. 7, 1865; James E. Green Diary, Feb. 23, 1865, SHC.

58. J. W. DuBose, "Fayetteville (N.C.) Road Fight," *Confed. Vet.*, XX (Feb., 1912), 84; *OR*, XLVII, Ser. I, Pt. I, 690, 1130; C. W. Hutson Diary, Mar. 5, 1865, SHC; J. D. Inskeep Diary, Mar. 7, 1865, OHS.

59. *OR*, XLVII, Ser. I, Pt. II, 704.

60. L. Lewis, *Sherman, Fighting Prophet* (New York: Harcourt, Brace and Co., 1932), p. 499, quoting Raleigh *Daily Progress*, Jan. 21, 1865; Raleigh *Conservative*, Mar. 10, 1865; Fayetteville *Observer*, Feb. 20, 1865.

61. R. Burnwell to "Edmund," Feb. 16, 1865, Burnwell Papers, SHC; Mrs. Pauline H. Brooks, "Extracts from School Girl's Journal During the Sixties" (Unpublished reminiscences of Confederate Veterans), NCC; C. B. Tompkins to Wife, Mar. 13, 1865, C. B. Tompkins Papers, DU; Cornelia P. Spencer Journal, Mar. 10, 1865, SHC.

62. R. E. Lee to Z. B. Vance, Feb. 24, 1865, Z. B. Vance Papers, NCDAH.

63. C. J. Iredell to "Mattie," Mar. 16, 18, 1865, C. J. Iredell Papers, SHC; Officers of North Carolina troops to W. A. Graham, Feb. 27, 1865, W. A. Graham Papers, SHC.

64. S. H. Walkup Diary, Feb. 21, 1865, SHC.

65. *Ibid.*, Mar. 6, 1865.

66. G. W. Nichols, *The Story of the Great March From the Diary of a Staff Officer* (New York: Harper and Brothers, 1865), p. 222.

67. *OR*, XLVII, Ser. I, Pt. II, 719.

68. *Ibid.*, p. 714.

69. *Ibid.*, pp. 714-17.

70. *Ibid.*, p. 728.

71. *Ibid.*, pp. 760-61.

72. *Ibid.*, p. 783.

73. Inskeep Diary, Mar. 9, 1865, OHS; J. R. Kinnear, *History of the Eighty-sixth Regiment Illinois Volunteer Infantry During Its Term of Service* (Chicago: Tribune Co., 1866), p. 101; W. D. Hamilton, *Recollections of a Cavalryman of the Civil War after Fifty Years*

(Columbia: F. P. Heer Printing Co., 1915), pp. 195-96. The Confederate soldiers also fired these great pine forests. W. A. Fletcher, *Rebel Private, Front and Rear* (Austin: Univ. of Texas Press, 1954), p. 140.

74. *OR*, XLVII, Ser. I, Pt. I, 690.

75. *Ibid.*, Pt. II, 704.

76. *OR*, XLVII, Ser. I, Pt. II, 1345, 1352.

77. *Ibid.*, 713.

78. N. H. Fitch Diary, Mar. 8, 1865, HSW; Inskeep Diary, Mar. 8, 1865, OHS.

79. Private in Sherman's army to Uncle, Mar. 28, 1865, W. T. Sherman Papers, UM.

CHAPTER XV

1. C. W. Wills, *Army Life of the Illinois Soldier: Letters and Diary of the Late Charles W. Wills* (Washington: Globe Printing Co., 1906), p. 357.

2. E. P. Burton, *Diary of E. P. Burton, Surgeon Seventh Regiment Illinois, Third Brigade, Second Division Sixteenth Army Corps* (Des Moines: Historical Records Survey, 1939), II, 68.

3. O. L. Jackson, *The Colonel's Diary: Journals Kept Before and During the Civil War by the Late Colonel Oscar L. Jackson Sometime Commander of the Sixty-third Regiment Ohio Volunteer Infantry* (Sherron: Privately printed, 1922), p. 194; W. C. Meffert Diary, Mar. 9, 1865, HSW; N. H. Fitch Diary, Mar. 8, 1865, HSW.

4. W. W. Calkins, *The History of the One Hundred and Fourth Regiment of Illinois Volunteer Infantry. War of Great Rebellion 1862-1865* (Chicago: Donahue and Henneberry, 1895), p. 294.

5. Wilbur F. Hinman, *The Story of the Sherman Brigade* (Privately printed, 1897), p. 918.

6. D. Oakey, "Marching Through Georgia and the Carolinas," *B and L*, eds. R. U. Johnson and C. C. Buel (New York: Century Co., 1888), IV, 677.

7. Hinman, *Sherman Brigade*, p. 918.

8. W. T. Sherman, *Memoirs of General W. T. Sherman* (New York: D. Appleton and Co., 1875), II, 293-94.

9. S. H. M. Byers, *With Fire and Sword* (New York: Neal Publishing Co., 1911), p. 181.

10. E. J. Sherlock, *Memorabilia of the Marches and Battles in Which the One Hundredth Regiment of Indiana Infantry Volunteers Took an Active Part* (Kansas City: Gerard-Wood Printing Co., 1896), p. 206.

11. J. A. Oates, *The Story of Fayetteville and the Upper Cape Fear* (Charlotte: Dowd Press, 1950), p. 719.

12. "Minutes of the Richmond Temperence and Literary Society, Apr. 22, 1865," quoted in Laurinburg *Exchange*, Feb. 13, 1959.

13. W. S. Chaffin Diary, Feb. 25, 1865, DU.

14. *Ibid.*, Mar. 9, 1865.

15. *OR*, XLVII, Ser. I, Pt. I, 382.

16. Chaffin Diary, Mar. 9, 1865, DU.

17. *OR*, XLVII, Ser. I, Pt. I, 861; See above p. 297.

18. *Ibid.*, Pt. II, 786; J. D. Cox, *The March to the Sea: Franklin and Nashville* (New York: Charles Scribner's Son, 1882), p. 179.

19. J. W. DuBose, "Fayetteville (N.C.) Road Fight," *Confed. Vet.*, XX (Feb., 1912), 84-86.

20. M. C. Butler, "General Kilpatrick's Narrow Escape," *Butler and His Cavalry in the War of Secession, 1861-1865*, ed., U. R. Brooks (Columbia: The State Co., 1909), p. 444.

21. *OR*, XLVII, Ser. I, Pt. II, 786.

22. Butler, "Kilpatrick's Escape," p. 444; Oates, *Fayetteville,* p. 405.

23. *OR,* XLVII, Ser. I, Pt. II, 786.

24. E. W. Watkins, "Another Account," *Confed. Vet.,* XX (Feb., 1912), 84.

25. E. L. Wells, *Hampton and Reconstruction* (Columbia: The State Co., 1907), p. 63.

26. E. L. Wells, *Hampton and His Cavalry in '64* (Richmond: Johnson Publishing Co., 1899), p. 461.

27. P. Hamilton, "The Effort to Capture Kilpatrick," *Confed. Vet.,* XXIX (Sept., 1921), 329; Fitch Diary, Mar. 10, 1865, HSW.

28. *OR,* XLVII, Ser. I, Pt. II, 786.

29. New Bern *N.C. Times,* Mar. 28, 1865, quoting the *N.Y. Tribune,* n.d.

30. C. J. Iredell to "Mattie," Mar. 25, 1865, C. J. Iredell Papers, SHC; Butler, "Kilpatrick's Escape," pp. 446-47.

31. E. L. Wells, "A Morning Call on General Kilpatrick," *SHSP,* XII (Mar., 1884), 128; J. W. DuBose, *General Joseph Wheeler and the Army of Tennessee* (New York: Neale Publishing Co., 1912), p. 499.

32. *OR,* XLVII, Ser. I, Pt. II, 787.

33. M. C. Butler, "The Curtain Falls—Butler Surrenders His Cavalry," *Butler and His Cavalry in the War of Secession, 1861-65,* ed., U. R. Brooks (Columbia: The State Co., 1909), p. 475.

34. Butler, "Kilpatrick's Escape," p. 445.

35. *OR,* XLVII, Ser. I, Pt. II, 787; *Ibid.,* Pt. I, 862.

36. *Ibid.,* p. 1130.

37. J. E. Johnston, *Narrative of Military Operations, Directed, During the Late War Between the States, by Joseph E. Johnston, General, C.S.A.* (New York: D. Appleton and Co., 1874), p. 381.

38. Butler, "Kilpatrick's Escape," pp. 446-47.

39. J. W. DuBose to M. C. Butler, Feb. 12, 1908, U. R. Brooks Papers, DU.

40. T. F. Northrup, "Other Side of the Fayetteville Road Fight," *Confed. Vet.,* XX (Sept., 1912), 423.

41. DuBose, "Road Fight," p. 85.

42. *OR,* XLVII, Ser. I, Pt. II, 787.

43. W. A. Law, "The War" (Unpublished reminiscence), W. A. Law Papers, DU; DuBose, "Road Fight," p. 85.

44. W. D. Hamilton, *Recollections of a Cavalryman of the Civil War after Fifty Years* (Columbia: F. P. Hear Printing Co., 1915), p. 199.

45. *OR,* XLVII, Ser. I, Pt. I, 203.

46. W. Hampton to "Lieutenant Harleston," Mar. 19, 1865, in U. R. Brooks, ed., *Butler and His Cavalry* (Columbia: The State Co., 1909), pp. 30-35.

47. Wells, *Hampton and His Cavalry,* pp. 30-35.

48. L. McLaws Order Book, 1865, SHC, p. 2.

49. D. E. H. Smith and others, eds., *Mason Smith Family Letters, 1860-1865* (Columbia: Univ. of S.C. Press, 1950), p. 201.

50. Wells, *Hampton and His Cavalry,* p. 35.

51. J. W. DuBose to U. R. Brooks, Aug. 19, 1911, U. R. Brooks Papers, DU.

52. *OR,* XLVII, Ser. I, Pt. I, 413.

53. *Ibid.,* pp. 203-4; Oates, *Fayetteville,* p. 408.

54. F. Y. Hedley, *Marching Through Georgia: Pen-Pictures of Every-Day Life in General Sherman's Army from the Beginning of the Atlanta Campaign Until the Close of the War* (Chicago: M. A. Donahue and Co., 1884), pp. 399-400.

55. J. F. Waring Diary, Mar. 11, 1865, SHC; J. Evans Diary, Mar. 11, 1865, SHC; M. H. Fitch Diary, Mar. 11, 1865, HSW.

56. D. P. Conyngham, *Sherman's March Through the South with Sketches and Incidents of the Campaign* (New York: Sheldon and Co., 1865), p. 357.

57. Mrs. J. H. Anderson, "Sherman's Army Entered Fayetteville" (Undated newspaper clipping), NCC; Eliza T. Stinson, "How the Arsenal Was Taken," *Our Women in the War: The Lives They Lived; the Deaths They Died*, ed., F. W. Dawson (Charleston: News and Courier Book Presses, 1885), p. 22.

58. *OR*, XLVII, Ser. I, Pt. II, 803; *U.S. Sanitary Commission Report, March, 1865*, p. 11.

59. *OR*, XLVII, Ser. I, Pt. II, 817.

60. *Ibid.*, p. 795.

61. *Ibid.*, p. 807. As many of the refugees as possible went down the Cape Fear by steamboat. McMillan Diary, Mar. 13, 1865, HSW.

62. Hedley, *Marching Through Georgia*, pp. 402-5.

63. H. W. Slocum, "Sherman's March from Savannah to Bentonville," *B and L*, eds., R. U. Johnson and C. C. Buel (New York: Century Co., 1888), IV, 689-90.

64. See above p. 12.

65. *OR*, XLVII, Ser. I, Pt. II, 794.

66. *Ibid.*, Pt. I, 23.

67. Mrs. J. H. Anderson, "Confederate Arsenal at Fayetteville, N. C.," *Confed. Vet.*, XXXVI (June, 1928), 223.

68. A. P. Ford and M. J. Ford, *Life in the Confederate Army* (New York: Neale Publishing Co., 1905), p. 47.

69. *OR*, XLVII, Ser. I, Pt. II, 779.

70. B. T. Johnson, *A Memoir of the Life and Public Service of Joseph E. Johnston, Once Quartermaster General of the United States and a General in the Army of the Confederate States of America* (Baltimore: R. H. Woodward and Co., 1891), p. 188; Wilmington *Herald of the Union*, Mar. 16, 1865; C. P. Spencer, *The Last Ninety Days of the War in North Carolina* (New York: Watchman Publishing Co., 1866), p. 246; C. Spencer Journal, Mar. 20, 1865, SHC.

71. E. J. Hale, Jr., "Sherman's Bummers and Some of Their Work—Letter from E. J. Hale, Jr., to J. H. Lane, July 31, 1865," *SHSP*, XII (July-Aug.-Sept., 1884), 427-28.

72. *OR*, XLVII, Ser. I, Pt. I, 551; Spencer, *Ninety Days*, p. 68; J. B. Worth, "Sherman's Raid," *War Days in Fayetteville North Carolina* (Fayetteville: Judge Printing Co., 1910), p. 51.

73. *OR*, XLVII, Ser. I, Pt. I, 551.

74. C. P. Mallett to C. P. Spencer, Mar. 22, 1865, C. P. Spencer Papers, SHC.

75. C. W. Wills, *Army Life of an Illinois Soldier: Letters and Diary of the Late Charles W. Wills* (Washington: Globe Printing Co., 1906), p. 360; J. Chormley Diary, Mar. 11, 1865, HSW; J. D. Inskeep Diary, Mar. 10, 1865, OHS.

76. C. S. Brown to "Etta," Apr. 26, 1865, C. S. Brown Papers, DU; Inskeep Diary, Mar. 10, 1865, OHS.

77. C. P. Mallett to C. P. Spencer, Mar. 22, 1865, C. P. Spencer Papers, SHC.

78. C. W. Hutson to Sister, Mar. 11, 1865, C. W. Hutson Papers, SHC; Spencer, *Ninety Days*, p. 54.

79. J. Evans Diary, Mar. 12-15, 1865, SHC.

80. J. Evans, "My Losses by the Infernal Yanks, March 13-15, 1865" (Unpublished statement) J. Evans Papers, SHC.

81. D. MacRae to Brother, Mar. 17, 1865, H. MacRae Papers, DU; C. B. Mallett to Son, Aug. 3, 1865, C. B. Mallett Papers, SHC; Spencer, *Ninety Days*, p. 50.

82. Hillsborough *Recorder*, Mar. 22, 1865.

83. C. Eaton, ed., "Diary of an Officer in Sherman's Army Marching through the Carolinas," *JSH*, IX (May, 1943), 248.

84. Worth, "Sherman's Raid," pp. 53-54.

85. *OR*, XLVII, Ser. I, Pt. II, 779.

86. G. W. Nichols, *The Story of the Great March From the Diary of a Staff Officer* (New York: Harper and Brothers, 1865), pp. 252-53.

87. O. O. Winther, ed., *With Sherman to the Sea: The Civil War Letters, Diaries, and Reminiscences of Theodora F. Upson* (Baton Rouge: Louisiana State Univ. Press, 1934), p. 156.

88. Eaton, "Diary of an Officer," pp. 248-49.

89. *OR*, XLVII, Ser. I, Pt. I, 23-24; C. Reynolds Order Book, Mar. 12, 1865, LC.

CHAPTER XVI

1. *OR*, XLVII, Ser. I, Pt. II, 803.

2. *Ibid.*, Pt. I, 24.

3. *Ibid.*, Pt. II, 1375; H. D. Bulkley to W. M. Tunno, Mar. 11, 1865, W. M. Tunno Papers, EU.

4. *OR*, XLVII, Ser. I, Pt. I, 1130.

5. *Ibid.*, Pt. II, 1361; J. E. Johnston, *Narrative of Military Operations, Directed, During the Late War Between the States, by Joseph E. Johnston, General, C.S.A.* (New York: D. Appleton and Co., 1874), p. 582.

6. *OR*, XLVII, Ser. I, Pt. I, 1089.

7. *Ibid.*, p. 880.

8. *Ibid.*, p. 637.

9. W. T. Sherman, *Memoirs of General W. T. Sherman* (New York: D. Appleton and Co., 1875), II, 301; C. W. Hutson to Sister, Mar. n.d., 1865, C. W. Hutson Papers, SHC.

10. *OR*, XLVII, Ser. I, Pt. I, 422, 586, 789, 871, 1084-85; S. Merrill, *The Seventieth Indiana Volunteer Infantry in the War of the Rebellion* (Indianapolis: Bobbs-Merrill, 1900), p. 257.

11. *OR*, XLVII, Ser. I, Pt. I, 24-25.

12. *Ibid.*, pp. 889-90.

13. *Ibid.*, pp. 1085-86.

14. *Ibid.*, Pt. II, 1400-1; B. S. Williams to Mother, Mar. 23, 1865, B. S. Williams Papers, DU.

15. *OR*, XLVII, Ser. I, Pt. I, 66.

16. Sherman, *Memoirs*, II, 302.

17. M. A. deW. Howe, ed., *Marching with Sherman: Passages from Letters and Campaign Diaries of Henry Hitchcock, Major and Assistant Adjutant General of the Volunteers, November 1864-May 1865* (New Haven: Yale Univ. Press, 1927), p. 283.

18. J. S. Smith, "On the Battlefield of Averasboro, N.C.," *Confed. Vet.*, XXXIV (Feb., 1926), 48-49; J. A. Oates, *The Story of Fayetteville and the Upper Cape Fear* (Charlotte: Dowd Press, 1950), 391-96; Mrs. J. H. Anderson, *North Carolina Women of the Confederacy* (Fayetteville: Privately printed, 1926), pp. 46-47; Rose S. Best, "Beginnings of Battle of Averasboro" (Unpublished article, U.D.C. Essays on Civil War Battles), NCDAH.

19. J. Smith to J. Robeson, Apr. 12, 1865, Raleigh *N and O*, May 10, 1953; W. Fowler, *They Passed This Way* (n.p.: Harnett Co. Centennial Commission. 1955), pp. 97-98.

20. W. Currell [?] to "My dear Major," Mar. 28, 1865, C. W. Hutson Papers, SHC; A. B. Underwood, *The Three Years Service of the Thirty-third Massachusetts Infantry Regiment, 1862-1865* (Boston: A. Williams and Co., 1881), p. 49; Sherman, *Memoirs*, II, 302; J. Smith to J. Robeson, Apr. 12, 1865, Raleigh *N and O*, May 10, 1953.

21. R. Mead to "Folks at Home," Mar. 30, 1865, R. Mead Papers, LC.

22. H. J. Aten, *History of the Eighty-fifth Regiment, Illinois Volunteer Infantry* (Hiawatha, Kan.: Regimental Association, 1901), p. 297.

23. *OR*, XLVII, Ser. I, Pt. I, 586.

24. *Ibid.*, p. 234.

25. *Ibid.*, Ser. I, Pt. II, 1429.

26. *Ibid.*, pp. 1427-28, 1435; W. Calder Diary, Mar. 18, 1865, DU.

27. A. P. Ford and M. J. Ford, *Life in the Confederate Army* (New York: Neale Publishing Co., 1905), p. 53.

28. *OR*, XLVII, Ser. I, Pt. II, 1427.

29. General Sherman's maps were also incorrect. *Ibid.*, p. 885.

30. Johnston, *Narrative*, p. 385.

31. *OR*, XLVII, Ser. I, Pt. II, 1428.

32. *Ibid.*, p. 1426.

33. *Ibid.*, p. 1430; *Ibid.*, Pt. I, 434, 484-85, 568; W. Hampton, "Battle of Bentonville," *B and L*, eds., R. U. Johnson and C. C. Buel (New York: Century Co., 1888), IV, 701-2.

34. Johnston, *Narrative*, pp. 385-86.

35. Hampton, "Bentonville," pp. 702-3.

36. J. Luvaas, "Bentonville—Johnston's Last Stand," *NCHR*, XXXIII (July, 1956), 337; A. H. Dougall, "Bentonville," *War Papers Read before the Indiana Commandery, Military Order of the Loyal Legion of the United States* (Indianapolis: Published by the Commandery, 1898), I, 214.

37. A. C. McClurg, "The Last Chance of the Confederacy," *AM*, L (Sept., 1882), 390.

38. E. C. Belknap, "Bentonville: What A Bummer Knows About It," *War Papers Read before the Military Order of the Loyal Legion of the United States, Commandery of the District of Columbia* (Washington: Published by the Commandery, 1893), No. 12, p. 7.

39. W. P. Carlin, "The Battle of Bentonville," *Sketches of War History of 1861-1865. Papers Read before the Ohio Commandery of the Military Order of the Loyal Legion of the United States* (Cincinnati: Robert Clarke and Co., 1888-1908), III, 236-37.

40. *OR*, XLVII, Ser. I, Pt. I, 423.

41. *Ibid.*, 25.

42. Johnston, *Narrative*, p. 386.

43. A. L. Brooks and H. T. Lefler, *The Papers of Walter Clark* (Chapel Hill: Univ. of N.C. Press, 1948-50), I, 136; F. A. Olds, "The Last Big Battle," *Confed. Mag.*, XXXVII (Feb., 1929), 51.

44. *OR*, XLVII, Ser. I, Pt. I, 178, 449. The left of Fitch's line rested on the road. *Ibid.*, p. 463.

45. *Ibid.*, pp. 449, 453, 467-68, 473, 476.

46. Johnston, *Narrative*, p. 386; Calder Diary, Mar. 19, 1865, DU.

47. L. McLaws Order Book, 1865, SHC, p. 39.

48. *OR*, XLVII, Ser. I, Pt. I, 453, 468.

49. C. S. Brown to Family, Apr. 18, 26, 1865, C. S. Brown Papers, DU; Luvaas, "Bentonville," p. 340.

50. Carlin, "Bentonville," pp. 239-40; H. W. Slocum, "Sherman's March from Savannah to Bentonville," *B and L*, eds., R. U. Johnson and C. C. Buel (New York: Century Co., 1888), IV, 692-93; *OR*, XLVII, Ser. I, Pt. I, 423, 449.

51. These three officers carried the rank of brigadier general.

52. *OR*, XLVII, Ser. I, Pt. I, 485. The encumbered division of the Fourteenth Corps did not engage in the fighting on the nineteenth, but the next morning two of its brigades arrived on the scene of battle.

53. Carlin, "Bentonville," p. 27.

54. *OR*, XLVII, Ser. I, Pt. I, 666.

55. *Ibid.*, pp. 637, 671.

56. *Ibid.*, p. 1106.

57. *Ibid.*, p. 1094; D. H. Hill to W. D. Gale, Mar. 31, 1865, D. H. Hill Papers, NCDAH.

58. E. Eisenchiml and R. Newman, eds., *The American Iliad: The Epic Story of the Civil War as Narrated by Eyewitnesses* (Indianapolis: Bobbs-Merrill, 1947), p. 664; Calder Diary, Mar. 19, 1865, DU.

59. W. A. Clark, *Under the Stars and Bars or Memories of Four Years Service with the Ogelthorpes of Augusta, Georgia* (Augusta: Chronicle Printing Co., 1900), p. 192.

60. Hampton, "Bentonville," p. 704; C. W. Broadfoot, "Seventieth Regiment," *Histories of the Several Regiments and Battalions from North Carolina in the Great War 1861-'65. Written by Members of the Respective Commands,* ed. W. Clark (Goldsboro: Nash Brothers, 1901), IV, 21.

61. Clark, *Stars and Bars,* p. 194.

62. *OR,* XLVII, Ser. I, Pt. I, 449, 468; Carlin, "Bentonville," p. 245; J. S. Robinson to L. T. Hunt, Apr. 20, 1865, J. S. Robinson Papers, OHS; W. C. Meffert Diary, Mar. 19, 1865, HSW; H. Reid Diary, Mar. 19, 1865, HSW; N. H. Fitch Diary, Mar. 19, 1865, HSW.

63. C. S. Brown to Family, Apr. 26, 1865, C. S. Brown Papers, DU.

64. McClurg, "Last Chance," p. 393.

65. J. S. Robinson to L. T. Hunt, Apr. 20, 1865, J. S. Robinson Papers, OHS; *OR,* XLVII, Ser. I, Pt. I, 435.

66. N. C. Hughes, "Battle of Bentonville" (Unpublished article in possession of the author).

67. *OR,* XLVII, Ser. I, Pt. I, 1094, 1102.

68. *Ibid.,* p. 535; McClurg, "Last Chance," pp. 293-94; Luvaas, "Bentonville," p. 244.

69. Calder Diary, Mar. 19, 1865, DU.

70. B. J. Lossing, *Pictorial History of the Civil War in the United States of America* (Hartford: Thomas Belknap, 1877), III, 501.

71. W. Lamb, "Thirty-sixth Regiment," *Histories of the Several Regiments and Battalions from North Carolina in the Great War 1861-'65. Written by Members of the Respective Commands,* ed. W. Clark (Goldsboro: Nash Brothers, 1901), II, 651.

72. McLaws Order Book, 1865, SHC; C. S. Brown to Family, Apr. 18, 1865, C. S. Brown Papers, DU.

73. McClurg, "Last Chance," p. 395; G. W. Nichols, *The Story of the Great March From the Diary of a Staff Officer* (New York: Harper and Brothers, 1865), p. 272.

74. General Cogswell commanded the Third Brigade, Third Division, Twentieth Corps.

75. *OR,* XLVII, Ser. I, Pt. I, 424, 1091, 1095, 1102, 1109-10; S. H. Hurst, *Journal-History of the Seventy-third Ohio Volunteer Infantry* (Chillicothe: n.p., 1866), 174-76; H. Osborn and others, *Trials and Triumphs: The Record of the Fifty-fifth Ohio Volunteer Infantry* (Chicago: A. C. McClurg, 1904), 201-2; Luvaas, "Bentonville," p. 346.

76. T. A. McNeill, "Ninth Battalion," *Histories of the Several Regiments and Battalions from North Carolina in the Great War 1861-'65. Written by Members of the Respective Commands,* ed. W. Clark (Goldsboro: Nash Brothers, 1901), IV, 312.

77. See above p. 329n.

78. J. S. Robinson to L. T. Hunt, Apr. 20, 1865, J. S. Robinson Papers, OHS; *OR,* XLVII, Ser. I, Pt. I, 637, 666. Robinson's right ultimately connected with Fearing's left. *Ibid.* p. 666.

79. *Ibid.,* 587. The Second Division, Twentieth Corps, was not engaged in the fighting on the nineteenth. It arrived at Bentonville on the twentieth.

80. *Ibid.,* pp. 587-88, 601, 612, 666-67; J. S. Robinson to L. T. Hunt, Apr. 20, 1865, J. S. Robinson Papers, OHS.

81. S. W. Ravenel, "Ask the Survivors of Bentonville," *Confed. Vet.,* XVIII (Mar., 1910), 124.

82. Luvaas, "Bentonville," p. 348.

83. *OR,* XLVII, Ser. I, Pt. I, 1091.

84. Hughes, "Battle of Bentonville" (Unpublished article in possession of author).

85. McClurg, "Last Chance," p. 399: F. K. Dunn, ed., "Major James Connolly's Letters to His Wife, 1862-1865," *TISHS* (Springfield: Illinois State Historical Society, 1928), No. 35, pp. 380-83; C. B. Tompkins to Wife, Mar. 22, 1865, C. B. Tompkins Papers, DU; *OR*, XLVII, Ser. I, Pt. I, 1056; Johnston, *Narrative*, pp. 389-90; Sherman, *Memoirs*, II, 304; J. K. Mahon, "The Civil War Letters of Samuel Mahon, Seventh Iowa Infantry," *IJH*, L (July, 1953), 260-61. Hoke's new position was parallel to the Goldsboro road and near enough to command it.

86. *OR*, XLVII, Ser. I, Pt. II, 912-13, 922.

87. *Ibid.*, p. 919.

88. Johnston, *Narrative*, p. 389.

89. *OR*, XLVII, Ser. I, Pt. II, 1444.

90. *Ibid.*, p. 919.

91. D. H. Hill to W. D. Gale, Mar. 31, 1865, D. H. Hill Papers, NCDAH; Calder Diary, Mar. 20, 1865, DU; B. S. Williams to Mother, Mar. 23, 1865, B. S. Williams Papers, DU.

92. Brooks and Lefler, *Clark Papers*, I, 53.

93. *Ibid.*, p. 136.

94. *OR*, XLVII, Ser. I, Pt. I, 1057.

95. *Ibid.*, p. 1092.

96. *Ibid.*, p. 391; R. C. Hackett, ed., "Civil War Diary of Sergeant James Louis Matthews," *IMH*, XXIV (Sept., 1928), 308-16.

97. *OR*, XLVII, Ser. I, Pt. I, 1057; Johnston, *Narrative*, p. 391; J. P. K. Blackburn, "Reminiscences," *SHQ*, XXII (July, Oct., 1918), 169; D. H. Hill to W. D. Gale, Mar. 31, 1865, D. H. Hill Papers, NCDAH; Calder Diary, Mar. 21, 1865, DU.

98. *OR*, XLVII, Ser. I, Pt. I, 27.

99. C. E. Macartney, *Grant and His Generals* (New York: McBride Co., 1953), p. 295.

100. For comments on the size of Mower's force and the Confederates opposing him, see Luvaas, "Bentonville," pp. 352-353.

101. O. O. Howard, *Autobiography of Oliver Otis Howard, Major General United States Army* (New York: Baker and Taylor Co., 1907), II, 151; C. W. Hutson to "Dear Em," Mar. 21, 1865, C. W. Hutson Papers, SHC.

102. *OR*, XLVII, Ser. I, Pt. I, 1057; Calder Diary, Mar. 24, 1865, DU; C. W. Hutson to "Dear Em," Mar. 21, 1865, C. W. Hutson Papers, SHC.

103. Hackett, "Diary of J. L. Matthews," pp. 308-16; *OR*, XLVII, Ser. II, Pt. I, 1131.

104. *Ibid.*, p. 259.

105. *Ibid.*, Ser. I, Pt. I, 1132.

106. *Ibid.*, p. 236.

107. *Ibid.*, p. 1057; Johnston, *Narrative*, p. 389; C. W. Hutson to "Dear Em," Mar. 21, 1865, C. W. Hutson Papers, SHC; D. H. Hill to W. D. Gale, Mar. 31, 1865, D. H. Hill Papers, NCDAH. W. M. Kelly, "A History of the Thirteenth Alabama Volunteer Confederate States Army," *AHQ*, IX (Spring, 1947), 166-68.

108. D. E. H. Smith and others, eds., *Mason Smith Family Letters, 1860-1865* (Columbia: Univ. of S.C. Press, 1950), p. 172.

109. *OR*, XLVII, Ser. I, Pt. II, 1373-74.

110. *Ibid.*, pp. 1453-54.

111. Ford and Ford, *Life in the Confederate Army*, p. 59.

112. *OR*, XLVII, Ser. I, Pt. III, 14.

113. *Ibid.*, Pt. I, 27.

114. T. C. Fletcher, ed., *Life and Reminiscences of General William T. Sherman by Distinguished Men of His Time* (Baltimore: R. H. Woodward Co., 1891), p. 292.

115. *OR*, XLVII, Ser. I, Pt. II, 803.

116. See above p. 318n.

117. *OR*, XLVII, Ser. I, Pt. II, 160-61.

118. Sherman, *Memoirs*, II, 304.

119. J. M. Schofield, *Forty-six Years in the Army* (New York: Century Co., 1897), p. 341.

120. *OR*, XLVII, Ser. I, Pt. I, 950.

121. *Ibid.*, Pt. II, 950, 970.

122. A. H. Burne, *Lee, Grant and Sherman: A Study in Leadership in the 1864-65 Campaign* (New York: Charles Scribner's Sons, 1939), p. 179.

123. L. McLaws to Wife, Mar. 23, 1865, L. McLaws Papers, SHC.

124. *OR*, XLVII, Ser. I, Pt. I, 76.

125. *Ibid.*, p. 1060.

126. *Ibid.*, p. 27.

127. *Ibid.*, p. 1060.

128. W. D. Hamilton, *Recollections of a Cavalryman of the Civil War after Fifty Years* (Columbia: F. P. Heer Printing Co., 1915), p. 194.

129. *OR*, XLVII, Ser. I, Pt. I, 28.

130. *Ibid.*, Pt. II, 941, 1453.

131. Howell, "Memoirs" (Unpublished memoirs), R. P. Howell Papers, SHC; New Bern *N.C. Times*, Mar. 24, 1865.

132. Goldsboro *News-Argus*, Oct. 4, 1947.

133. E. N. Hatcher, *The Last Four Weeks of the War* (Columbus: Edmund N. Hatcher Publisher, 1891), pp. 21-22; D. P. Conyngham, *Sherman's March Through the South with Sketches and Incidents of the Campaign* (New York: Sheldon and Co., 1865), p. 314.

134. S. Merrill, *The Seventieth Indiana Volunteer Infantry in the War of Rebellion* (Indianapolis: Bobbs-Merrill Co., 1900), 260-61; L. Lewis, *Sherman, Fighting Prophet* (New York: Harcourt, Brace and Co., 1932), p. 516; J. W. Griffith Diary, Mar. 23, 1865, OHS: C. B. Tompkins to Wife, Mar. 27, 1865, C. B. Tompkins Papers, DU; B. A. Dunbar to Cousin, Apr. 10, 1865, A. G. Beardsley Papers, DU.

135. M. H. Force, "Marching Across Carolina," *Sketches of War History, 1861-65. Papers Read before the Ohio Commandery of the Loyal Legion of the United States* (Cincinnati: R. Clark and Co., 1888-1908), I, 10; J. S. Robinson to L. T. Hunt, Apr. 3, 1865, J. S. Robinson Papers, OHS.

136. Merrill, *70 Ind.*, p. 261; J. D. Cox, *Military Reminiscences of the Civil War* (Charles Scribner's Sons, 1900), I, 447; "Oscar" to "Dear Parents," Mar. 30, 1865, E. O. Kimberly Papers, HSW; Griffith Diary, Mar. 23, 1865, OHS.

137. New Bern *N.C. Times*, Mar. 4, 1865.

138. Elizabeth Collier Diary, Mar. 11, 1865, SHC.

139. A. J. Boies, *Record of the Thirty-third Massachusetts Volunteer Infantry from August 1862 to August 1865* (Fitchburg: Sentinel Printing Co., 1880), p. 118.

140. New Bern *N.C. Times*, Mar. 28, 1865.

141. *OR*, XLVII, Ser. I, Pt. II, 970.

142. *Ibid.*, Pt. I, 424, 972; H. Reid to Sister, April 7, 1865, HSW; Hatcher, *Four Weeks*, pp. 67-68.

143. J. D. Inskeep Diary, Mar. 25, 1865, OHS; Hatcher, *Four Weeks*, pp. 67-68.

144. *OR*, XLVII, Ser. I, Pt. I, 487.

145. C. P. Spencer, *The Last Ninety Days of the War in North Carolina* (New York: Watchman Publishing Co., 1866), p. 94; Mrs. Harriet C. Lane, "For My Children" (Unpublished reminiscence), NCC.

146. Collier Diary, Apr. 20, 1865, SHC.

147. Spencer, *Ninety Days*, p. 94.

148. Goldsboro *News-Argus*, Oct. 4, 1947.

149. Raleigh *Conservative*, Mar. 27, 1865.

150. O. O. Winther, *With Sherman to the Sea: The Civil War Letters, Diaries, and Reminiscences of Theodora F. Upson* (Baton Rouge: Louisiana State Univ. Press, 1934), p. 162.

151. H. M. Dewey, to C. P. Spencer, Mar. 5, 1865, D. L. Swain Papers, SHC.

152. *OR*, XLVII, Ser. I, Pt. I, 28.

153. Rachel S. Thorndike, ed., *The Sherman Letters, Correspondence Between General and Senator Sherman from 1837 to 1891* (New York: Charles Scribner's Sons, 1894), p. 260.

154. *Ibid.*; "Mrs. Smyth" to O. O. Howard, Mar. 21, 1865, O. O. Howard Papers, BC.

155. C. B. Tompkins to Wife, Apr. 7, 1865, C. B. Tompkins Papers, DU; T. H. Capron, "War Diary of Thaddeus H. Capron, 1861-1865," *JISHS*, XII (Oct., 1919), 402; A. Ames to "My Dear General," Mar. 28, 1865, W. H. Noble Papers, DU; D. Oakey, "Marching Through Georgia and the Carolinas," *B and L*, eds. R. U. Johnson and C. C. Buel (New York: Century Co., 1888), IV, 671.

156. *OR*, XLVII, Ser. I, Pt. I, 28; N. G. Dye Diary, Mar. 27, 1865, DU.

157. J. C. Gray and J. C. Ropes, *War Letters 1862-1865 of John Chipman Gray and John Codman Ropes* (New York: Houghton-Mifflin Co., 1927), p. 465.

CHAPTER XVII

1. For a detailed and well-written account of Stoneman's raid see Ina W. Van Noppen, "The Significance of Stoneman's Last Raid," *NCHR*, XXXVIII (Jan.-Oct., 1961), Nos. 1-4. Coinciding with Stoneman's operations was Major General James H. Wilson's raid into Alabama and Georgia. *OR*, XLIX, Ser. I, Pt. I, 339-587.

2. *Ibid.*, 325.

3. F. H. Mason, "General Stoneman's Last Campaign and the Pursuit of Jefferson Davis," *Sketches of War History of 1861-1865. Papers Read before the Ohio Commandery of the Military Order of the Loyal Legion of the United States* (Cincinnati: Robert Clarke and Co., 1888-1908), II, 23; C. S. Davis, "Stoneman's Raid into Northwest North Carolina," Winston-Salem *Journal and Sentinel*, Oct. 4, 1953.

4. *OR*, XLIX, Ser. I, Pt. II, 112.

5. *Ibid.*; R. L. Beall to C. P. Spencer, n.d. 1866, C. P. Spencer Papers, SHC.

6. R. L. Beall to C. P. Spencer, n.d., 1866, C. P. Spencer Papers, SHC; J. P. Arthur, *A History of Watauga County North Carolina, with Sketches of Prominent Families* (Richmond: Everett Waddey Co., 1915), p. 177.

7. *OR*, XLIX, Ser. I, Pt. I, 331.

8. Wife to G. W. F. Harper, Mar. 25, 1865, G. W. F. Harper Papers, SHC; Mrs. G. W. F. Harper Diary, Mar. 30, 1865, SHC.

9. J. C. Norwood to "Dear Walter," Apr. 2, 1865, Lenoir-Norwood Papers, SHC. For some time the people around Patterson had been "under constant apprehension about tory or robber raids. . . ." *Ibid.*

10. *OR*, XLIX, Ser. I, Pt. I, 331.

11. J. C. Norwood to "Dear Walter," Apr. 2, 1865, Lenoir-Norwood Papers, SHC; Harper Diary, Mar. 30, 1865, SHC.

12. *OR*, XLIX, Ser. I, Pt. I, 331; J. Crouch, *Historical Sketches of Wilkes County* (Wilkesboro: Chronicle Job Office, 1902), pp. 93-94.

13. C. P. Spencer, *The Last Ninety Days of the War in North Carolina* (New York: Watchman Publishing Co., 1866), p. 196; Van Noppen, "Stoneman's Last Raid," p. 154; R. L. Beall to C. P. Spencer, n.d., 1866, C. P. Spencer Papers, SHC.

14. *OR*, XLIX, Ser. I, Pt. I, 327-28; H. K. Weand, "Our Last Campaign and Pursuit of Jeff Davis," *History of the Fifteenth Pennsylvania Volunteer Cavalry*, ed. C. H. Kirk (Philadelphia: Society of the Fifteenth Pennsylvania Cavalry, 1906), p. 494.

15. *OR,* XLIX, Ser. I, Pt. I, 331.

16. R. L. Beall to C. P. Spencer, n.d., 1866, C. P. Spencer Papers, SHC.

17. *OR,* XLIX, Ser. I, Pt. I, 324, 328, 331-32. Palmer had a skirmish at Martinsville, Virginia. *Ibid.,* 332.

18. *Ibid.*

19. *Ibid.*

20. D. leT. Rights, "Salem in the War between the States," *NCHR,* XXVII (July, 1950), 286-87.

21. A. L. Fries, *Forsyth County* (Winston: Stewart's Printing House, 1898), pp. 96-97; A. L. Fries and others, *Forsyth: A County on the March* (Chapel Hill: Univ. of N.C. Press, 1949), pp. 67-68.

22. "Memorabilia of the Congregation at Salem, 1865" (Unpublished memorabilia), Moravian Archives, Winston-Salem; Fries, *Forsyth County,* pp. 96-97.

23. "Memorabilia of the Congregation at Salem, 1865," Moravian Archives, Winston-Salem.

24. Salem *People's Press,* May 27, 1865, quoted in D. leT. Rights, "Salem in the War," *NCHR,* XXVII (July, 1950), p. 287.

25. J. H. Clewell, *History of Wachovia in North Carolina* (New York: Doubleday, Page and Co., 1902), pp. 249-50; Davis, "Stoneman's Raid," Winston-Salem *Journal-Sentinel,* Oct. 4, 1953; Rights, "Salem in the War," p. 287. Guards placed around Salem Academy undoubtedly had much to do with the protection of the valuables hidden there. Winston-Salem *Journal-Sentinel,* Apr. 24, 1938.

26. Weand, "Our Last Campaign," pp. 501-2; Spencer, *Ninety Days,* pp. 197-98; J. T. Wood Diary, Apr. 10, 1865, SHC; S. R. Mallory, "Reminiscences" (Unpublished reminiscence), S. R. Mallory Papers, SHC.

27. Van Noppen, "Stoneman's Last Raid," p. 170.

28. *Ibid.,* pp. 167-68; R. L. Beall to C. P. Spencer, n.d., 1866, C. P. Spencer Papers, SHC; Spencer, *Ninety Days,* pp. 197-98; R. S. Patterson to Father, Apr. 14, 1865, Lindsay Patterson Papers, SHC; J. Robertson, *Michigan in the War* (Lansing: W. S. George and Co., 1880), p. 567; G. Jenkins, "From Harper's Ferry to the Surrender" (Unpublished article), Gertrude Jenkins Papers, DU; Mrs. J. S. Welborn to E. B. Bowie, Mar. 20, 1930, Mrs. J. S. Welborn Papers, SHC; J. S. Welborn, "High Point During the Confederacy" (Unpublished article), J. S. Welborn Papers, SHC.

29. Robertson, *Michigan in the War,* p. 567; R. L. Beall to C. P. Spencer, n.d. 1866, C. P. Spencer Papers, SHC; Spencer, *Ninety Days,* pp. 197-98; Van Noppen, "Stoneman's Last Raid," pp. 167-71; *OR,* XLIX, Ser. I, Pt. I, 324.

30. *OR,* XLIX, Ser. I, Pt. I, 333; Fries, *Forsyth County,* p. 96; R. S. Patterson to Father, Apr. 14, 1865, Lindsay Patterson Papers, SHC.

31. *OR,* XLIX, Ser. I, Pt. II, 333.

32. *Ibid.;* R. L. Beall to C. P. Spencer, n.d., 1866, C. P. Spencer Papers, SHC.

33. Von Noppen, "Stoneman's Last Raid," pp. 341-61; *OR,* XLIX, Ser. I, Pt. I, 324-34; Spencer, *Ninety Days,* p. 204; Z. B. Vance to C. P. Spencer, Feb. 17, 1866, D. L. Swain Papers, SHC; A. W. Mangum to Sister, Feb. 24, 1865, A. W. Mangum Papers, SHC.

34. W. B. Hesseltine, *Civil War Prisons: A Study in War Psychology* (Columbus: Ohio State Univ. Press, 1930), p. 170; J. S. Brawley, *The Rowan Story, 1753-1953: A Narrative History of Rowan County, North Carolina* (Salisbury: Rowan Printing Co., 1953), pp. 196-97; Theresa Thomas, "National Cemetery Is Only Trace of Salisbury Prison," Charlotte *Observer,* July 2, 1961; R. L. Drummond, "Reminiscences" (Unpublished reminiscence), A. W. Mangum Papers, SHC; A. W. Mangum to Sister, Feb. 20, 1865, A. W. Mangum Papers, SHC; A. W. Mangum, "History of Salisbury Prison" (typed copy of article which appeared in the Charlotte *Observer,* n.d.), A. W. Mangum Papers, SHC; A. W. Mangum, "History of the Salisbury N. C. Confederate Prison," *Pub. of So.*

Hist. Assoc., III (Oct., 1899), 334: G. W. Booth to Z. B. Vance, Feb. 3, 1865, Z. B. Vance Papers, NCDAH.

35. Spencer, *Ninety Days,* p. 199.

36. E. H. M. Summerell, to C. P. Spencer, Sept. 4, 1866, C. P. Spencer Papers, SHC; Spencer, *Ninety Days,* p. 199. Both Gillem and Stoneman put the Confederate force at near three thousand. This figure is obviously too high since General B. T. Johnson had been ordered to Greensboro with most of the Salisbury garrison.

37. J. C. Pemberton, *Pemberton: Defender of Vicksburg* (Chapel Hill: Univ. of N.C. Press, 1942), pp. 265-66; D. Rowland, ed., *Jefferson Davis, Constitutionalist, His Letters, Papers and Speeches* (Jackson: Mississippi Department of Archives and History, 1923), VII, 74-75; J. C. Pemberton, "Sketch of General Pemberton" (Unpublished article), J. C. Pemberton Papers, SHC; Z. Walker [?] to "Dear Welford," Dec. 30, 1864, I. H. Carrington Papers, DU; Spencer, *Ninety Days,* p. 199; Davis, "Stoneman's Raid," Winston-Salem *Journal-Sentinel,* Oct. 4, 1953.

38. *OR,* XLIX, Ser. I, Pt. I, 324, 333-34; E. H. M. Summerell to C. P. Spencer, Sept. 4, 1866, C. P. Spencer Papers, SHC; Mason, "Stoneman's Last Campaign," p. 26; Brawley, *Rowan County,* pp. 197-99.

39. A. W. Mangum to Sister, Mar. 23, 1865, A. W. Mangum Papers, SHC; Harriet E. Bradshaw, "Stoneman's Raid" (Unpublished reminiscence), Harriet E. Bradshaw Papers, SHC; Spencer, *Ninety Days,* p. 202.

40. *OR,* XLIX, Ser. I, Pt. I, 323; Bradshaw, "Stoneman's Raid," Harriet E. Bradshaw Papers, SHC; R. L. Beall to C. P. Spencer, n.d., 1866, C. P. Spencer Papers, SHC; Brawley, *Rowan County,* pp. 197-99. There are various estimates as to the number of Confederate troops at the bridge. Also, there is no agreement on who commanded the defenses. One source says it was Brigadier General Zebulon York. This is possible because during the latter stages of the war he was recruiting "among the foreign-born prisoners of war held in Confederate prison camps." Spencer, *Ninety Days,* p. 204; E. J. Warner, *Generals in Gray* (Baton Rouge: Louisiana State Univ. Press, 1959), p. 347.

41. Bradshaw, "Stoneman's Raid," Harriet E. Bradshaw Papers, SHC.

42. *Ibid.;* T. White to Z. B. Vance, Apr. 17, 1865, Z. B. Vance Papers, NCDAH; H. S. Chamberlain, *This Was Home* (Chapel Hill: Univ. of N.C. Press, 1938), p. 119.

43. *OR,* XLIX, Ser. I, Pt. I, 324, 334; R. L. Beall to C. P. Spencer, n.d. 1866, C. P. Spencer Papers, SHC.

44. *OR,* XLIX, Ser. I, Pt. I, 334.

45. *Ibid.*

46. Van Noppen, "Stoneman's Last Raid," p. 358. See also Chamberlain, *This Was Home,* p. 120.

47. R. L. Beall to C. P. Spencer, n.d., 1866, C. P. Spencer Papers, SHC; Spencer, *Ninety Days,* pp. 213-16. R. L. Beall to C. P. Spencer, n.d., 1866, C. P. Spencer Papers, SHC.

48. *OR,* XLIX, Ser. I, Pt. I, 334.

49. R. L. Beall to C. P. Spencer, n.d., 1866, C. P. Spencer Papers, SHC; Mrs. Laura P. Cochran, "Stoneman's Raid Described in the Diary of Mrs. Laura Pruett Cochran," *Uplift,* XXXV (Aug., 1947), 18-19.

50. David Schenck Journal, Apr. 16, 1865; W. L. Sherrill, *Annals of Lincoln Conuty, North Carolina* (Charlotte: Observer Printing House, 1937), pp. 181-82.

51. Mason, "Stoneman's Last Campaign," p. 30; *OR,* XLIX, Ser. I, Pt. II, 446.

52. Harper Diary, Apr. 15, 1865, SHC.

53. *Ibid.,* Apr. 16, 1865.

54. R. L. Beall to C. P. Spencer, Sept. 20, 1866, C. P. Spencer Papers, SHC; Louisa Norwood to W. Lenoir, Apr. 24, 1865, Lenoir *News-Topic,* Sept. 12, 1941; R. L. Beall to C. P. Spencer, n.d. 1866, C. P. Spencer Papers, SHC; Nancy Alexander, *Here Will I Dwell: The Story of Caldwell County* (Salisbury: Rowan Printing Co., 1956), 141-42; Spencer, *Ninety Days,* 22, 213-23.

55. *OR,* XLIX, Ser. I, Pt. II, 446.

56. Spencer, *Ninety Days,* p. 223; Louisa Norwood to W. Lenoir, Apr. 24, 1865, Lenoir *News-Topic,* Sept. 12, 1941. Colonel Walton said he had seventy soldiers from the western counties supported by the home guard. T. G. Walton, "Home Guards Face Stoneman," *Histories of the Several Regiments and Battalions from North Carolina in the Great War 1861-'65. Written by Members of the Respective Commands,* ed. W. Clark (Goldsboro: Nash Brothers, 1901), V, 635.

57. R. L. Beall to C. P. Spencer, Sept. 20, 1866, C. P. Spencer Papers, SHC; Walton, "Home Guards Face Stoneman," pp. 635-36. Gillem said Major General John Porter McCown was in command of the Confederate forces.

58. R. L. Beall to C. P. Spencer, Sept. 20, 1866, C. P. Spencer Papers, SHC; Louisa Norwood to W. Lenoir, Apr. 24, 1865, Lenoir *News-Topic,* Sept. 12, 1941; *OR,* XLIX, Ser. I, Pt. I, 334-35; Walton, "Home Guards Face Stoneman," pp. 635-36.

59. R. L. Beall to C. P. Spencer, Sept. 20, 1866, C. P. Spencer Papers, SHC.

60. "Ellen S" to C. P. Spencer, Apr. 19, 1866, C. P. Spencer Papers, SHC; Spencer, *Ninety Days,* p. 224.

61. *OR,* XLIX, Ser. I, Pt. I, 329; Emma L. Rankin, "Women's Experience in the War between the States as Described in Stoneman's Raid" (Unpublished reminiscence), NCC; R. L. Beall to C. P. Spencer, n.d., 1866, C. P. Spencer Papers, SHC.

62. *OR,* XLIX, Ser. I, Pt. I, 335.

63. General Martin, in the summer of 1864, was conspicuous by his bravery in the fighting around Petersburg. However, his health failed and he was sent to command the District of Western North Carolina.

64. J. G. Martin to C. P. Spencer, June 11, 1866, C. P. Spencer Papers, SHC.

65. *OR,* XLIX, Ser. I, Pt. I, 335. General Gillem said he met "with but slight resistance" at Howard's Gap. *Ibid.* The official records list this as a skirmish. *Ibid.,* p. 323. See also S. S. Patton, *Sketches of Polk County History* (Asheville: Tryon Kiwanis Club and others, 1950), p. 45.

66. J. G. Martin to C. P. Spencer, June 11, 1866, C. P. Spencer Papers, SHC.

67. See below pp. 383-85.

68. J. G. Martin to C. P. Spencer, June 11, 1866, C. P. Spencer Papers, SHC.

69. *Ibid.;* Verina M. Chapman to C. P. Spencer, May 8, 1866, C. P. Spencer Papers, SHC; F. L. P., "Historical Sketch," Asheville *Daily Citizen,* Nov. 28, 1895; W. Clark, *Memorial Address Upon the Life of General James Green Martin* (Raleigh: n.p., 1916), pp. 15-17. On the twenty-third, Palmer had been ordered to Rutherfordton. Two days later Gillem ordered him to Asheville and the Tennessee passes. *OR,* XLIX, Ser. I, Pt. I, 335-36; Weand, "Our Last Campaign," p. 508.

70. J. G. Martin to C. P. Spencer, June 11, 1866, C. P. Spencer Papers, SHC; *OR,* XLIX, Ser. I, Pt. I, 336.

71. J. G. Martin to C. P. Spencer, June 11, 1866, C. P. Spencer Paper, SHC; Verina M. Chapman to C. P. Spencer, May 8, 1866, C. P. Spencer Paper, SHC; Clark, *Memorial Address on General Martin,* pp. 15-17; Mrs. J. H. Anderson, *North Carolina Women in the Confederacy* (Fayetteville: Privately printed, 1926), 71-72; Spencer, *Ninety Days,* pp. 229-34.

72. J. G. Martin to C. P. Spencer, June 27, 1866, C. P. Spencer Papers, SHC; Van Noppen, "Stoneman's Last Raid," pp. 522-23.

73. Davis, "Stoneman's Raid," Winston-Salem *Journal-Sentinel,* Oct. 4, 1953.

CHAPTER XVIII

1. See above p. 349.

2. U. S. Grant, *Personal Memoirs of U. S. Grant* (New York: Charles L. Webster, 1886), II, 434.

3. J. Myers to "Mr. Van Dyne," Mar. 29, 1865, J. F. Boyd Papers, DU; A. S. Flagg to J. F. Boyd, Apr. 2, 1865, J. F. Boyd Papers, DU; C. B. Tompkins to Wife, Apr. 2, 1865, C. B. Tompkins Papers, DU. In drawing new supplies it was like "throwing off our old dirt and filth," said a Wisconsin soldier. "Oscar" to "Dear Parents," Mar. 30, 1865, E. O. Kimberly Papers, HSW.

4. J. E. Johnston, *Narrative of Military Operations, Directed, During the Late War Between the States, by Joseph E. Johnston, General, C.S.A.* (New York: D. Appleton and Co., 1874), p. 394.

5. *Ibid.*, pp. 394-95; *OR*, XLVII, Ser. I, Pt. III, 770; C. W. Hutson to "Dear Em," Apr. 1, 1865, C. W. Hutson Papers, SHC.

6. Johnston, *Narrative*, p. 395.

7. *OR*, XLVII, Ser. I, Pt. I, 1061; W. Calder to Mother, Mar. 31, 1865, W. Calder Papers, SHC; C. W. Hutson to Sister, Mar. 31, 1865, C. W. Hutson Papers, SHC.

8. W. Calder Diary, Apr. 8, 1865, DU; B. L. Ridley, *Battles and Sketches of the Army of Tennessee* (Mexico: Missouri Printing and Publishing Co., 1906), p. 456; L. P. Thomas, "Their Last Battle," *SHSP*, XXIX (Jan.-Dec., 1901), 215-22. A young soldier of the Army of Tennessee thought the review "the saddest spectacle of his life." Ridley, *Army of Tennessee*, p. 456.

9. D. A. Deckert, *History of Kershaw's Brigade, with Complete Roll of Companies, Biographical Sketches, Incidents, Anecdotes, etc.* (Newberry: Elbert H. Aull Co., 1899), p. 526.

10. Ridley, *Army of Tennessee*, p. 456; J. L. Swain to "Dear Julius," Apr. 10, 1865, J. L. Swain Papers, SHC.

11. C. W. Hutson to [?], Apr. 8, 1865, C. W. Hutson Papers, SHC; C. W. Hutson, "Reminiscences" (Unpublished reminiscence), C. W. Hutson Papers, SHC.

12. L. McLaws Order Book, 1865, SHC, p. 35. A large number of the Senior Reserves at Raleigh deserted. H. J. Wright to "B & E & M & H Wright," Mar. 26, 1865, L. S. Wright Papers, DU.

13. A. L. Brooks and H. T. Lefler, *The Papers of Walter Clark* (Chapel Hill: Univ. of N.C. Press, 1948-50), II, 139-40.

14. Johnston, *Narrative*, pp. 395-96; *OR*, XLVII, Ser. I, Pt. III, 755-67.

15. *OR*, XLVII, Ser. I, Pt. III, 129. See also W. T. Sherman to O. O. Howard, Apr. 7, 1865, W. T. Sherman Papers, UM.

16. Calder Diary, Apr. 10, 1865, DU; Johnston, *Narrative*, p. 396.

17. *OR*, XLVII, Ser. I, Pt. I, 249.

18. *Ibid.*, p. 30; G. W. Nichols, *The Story of the Great March From the Diary of a Staff Officer* (New York: Harper and Brothers, 1865), p. 291; A. B. Underwood, *The Three Years of Service of the Thirty-third Massachusetts Infantry Regiment, 1862-1865* (Boston: A. Williams and Co., 1881), p. 289.

19. M. A. deW. Howe, ed., *Marching with Sherman; Passages from the Letters and Campaign Diaries of Henry Hitchcock, Major and Assistant Adjutant General of the Volunteers, November, 1864-May, 1865* (New Haven: Yale Univ. Press, 1927), p. 296; G. R. Stormont, ed., *History of the Fifty-eighth Regiment of Indiana Volunteer Infantry. Its Organization Campaigns and Battles from 1861-1865. From the Manuscript Prepared by the Late Chaplain John J. Hight During His Service with the Regiment in the Field* (Princeton: Press of the Clarion, 1895), p. 514.

20. *OR*, XLVII, Ser. I, Pt. III, 177.

21. *Ibid.*, p. 180.

22. H. J. Aten, *History of the Eighty-fifth Regiment, Illinois Volunteer Infantry* (Hiawatha, Kan.: Regimental Association, 1901), p. 303.

23. J. S. Johnson to L. T. Hunt, Apr. 15, 1865, J. S. Robinson Papers, OHS. There were a few skeptics in the Federal army who did not believe the news at first. H. H. Orendorff and others, eds., *Reminiscences of the Civil War from Diaries of the One Hun-*

dred and Third Illinois Volunteer Infantry (Chicago: J. F. Learning and Co., 1905), p. 205.

24. O. O. Winther, ed., *With Sherman to the Sea: The Civil War Letters, Diaries, and Reminiscences of Theodora F. Upson* (Baton Rouge: Louisiana State Univ. Press, 1934), pp. 164-66.

25. J. F. Woods to "My Dear Friends," Apr. 14, 1865, J. F. Woods Papers, DU.

26. R. S. Henry, *The Story of the Confederacy* (New York: New Home Library, 1931), p. 467.

27. M. W. Wellman, *Giant in Gray: A Biography of Wade Hampton of South Carolina* (New York: Charles Scribner's Sons, 1949), p. 180.

28. J. M. Mullen, "Last Days of Johnston's Army," *SHSP*, XVIII (Jan., 1890), 105.

29. J. M. Hough, "Last Days of the Confederacy," *Stories of the Confederacy*, ed., U. R. Brooks (Columbia: The State Co., 1912), p. 306.

30. Ridley, *Army of Tennessee*, p. 457.

31. Stormont, *High Diary*, p. 510.

32. C. P. Spencer, *The Last Ninety Days of the War in North Carolina* (New York: Watchman Publishing Co., 1866), p. 136.

33. *Ibid.*, p. 140.

34. *Ibid.*, p. 142.

35. Z. B. Vance to C. P. Spencer, Feb. 17, 1866, D. L. Swain Papers, SHC; C. Dowd, *Life of Zebulon B. Vance* (Charlotte: Observer Publishing and Printing House, 1897), p. 483.

36. Z. B. Vance to W. A. Graham, Apr. 11, 1865, W. A. Graham Papers, SHC.

37. *OR*, XLVII, Ser. I, Pt. III, 178.

38. L. Lewis, *Sherman, Fighting Prophet* (New York: Harcourt, Brace and Co., 1932), p. 530.

39. J. Devereux to D. L. Swain, July 7, 1866, W. Clark Papers, NCDAH; *OR*, XLVII, Ser. I, Pt. III, 791.

40. J. G. Burr to D. L. Swain, June 18, 1866, W. Clark Papers, NCDAH; E. Warren, *A Doctor's Experience in Three Continents* (Baltimore: Cushing and Bailey, 1885), pp. 335-39; J. D. Inskeep Diary, Apr. 12, 1865, OHS.

41. W. T. Sherman, *Memoirs of General W. T. Sherman* (New York: D. Appleton and Co., 1875), II, 345.

42. Spencer, *Ninety Days*, p. 151.

43. W. T. Sherman to D. L. Swain, Apr. 12, 1865, D. L. Swain Papers, SHC; *OR*, XLVII, Ser. I, Pt. III, 178.

44. Dowd, *Vance*, p. 484.

45. Z. B. Vance to W. T. Sherman, Apr. 12, 1865, quoted in J. G. Barrett, *Sherman's March Through the Carolinas* (Chapel Hill: Univ. of N.C. Press, 1956), p. 216.

46. Z. B. Vance to C. P. Spencer, Feb. 17, 1866, D. L. Swain Papers, SHC; Dowd, *Vance*, p. 485.

47. Z. B. Vance to C. P. Spencer, Apr. 7, 1866, C. P. Spencer Papers, SHC.

48. Z. B. Vance to C. P. Spencer, Feb. 17, 1866, D. L. Swain Papers, SHC.

49. Spencer, *Ninety Days*, p. 157; R. E. Yates, "Governor Vance and the End of the War in North Carolina," *NCHR*, XVIII (Oct., 1941), 330.

50. D. T. Ward, *The Last Flag of Truce* (Franklinton: Privately printed, 1914), p. 15.

51. R. H. Battle to C. P. Spencer, Feb. 26, 1866, D. L. Swain Papers, SHC; *OR*, XLVII, Ser. I, Pt. I, 1132; Spencer, *Ninety Days*, p. 157; Inskeep Diary, Apr. 13, 1865, OHS.

52. Spencer, *Ninety Days*, pp. 157-60.

53. R. H. Battle to C. P. Spencer, Feb. 6, 1866, D. L. Swain Papers, SHC; Calder Diary, Apr. 11, 1865, DU.

54. Raleigh *N and O*, Apr. 7, 1935.

55. R. H. Battle to C. P. Spencer, Feb. 26, 1866, D. L. Swain Papers, SHC; Spencer, *Ninety Days*, p. 145.

56. A. J. Boies, *Record of the Thirty-third Massachusetts Volunteer Infantry from August 1862 to August 1865* (Fitchburg: Sentinel Printing Co., 1880), p. 126.

57. C. Manly to D. L. Swain, Apr. 8, 1865, D. L. Swain Papers, SHC.

58. Z. B. Vance to C. P. Spencer, Feb. 17, 1866, D. L. Swain Papers, SHC.

59. R. H. Battle to C. P. Spencer, Feb. 26, 1866, D. L. Swain Papers, SHC.

60. B. F. Moore to D. L. Swain, Apr. 9, 1865, D. L. Swain Papers, SHC. See also R. S. Patterson to Father, Apr. 16, 1865, Lindsay Patterson Papers, SHC.

61. C. Manly to D. L. Swain, Mar. 29, 1865, D. L. Swain Papers, SHC.

62. *Ibid.*, Apr. 8, 1865.

63. R. H. Battle to C. P. Spencer, Feb. 26, 1866, D. L. Swain Papers, SHC.

64. Margaret Devereux, *Plantation Sketches* (Cambridge: Riverside Press, 1906), p. 150.

65. K. Rayner to B. F. Moore, May 13, 1867, Moore-Gatling Papers, SHC; Unidentified newspaper clipping, NCC.

66. Spencer, *Ninety Days*, pp. 160-62; S. A. Ashe, *History of North Carolina* (Raleigh: Edwards and Broughton, 1925), II, 999-1000; F. A. Olds, "Story of the Surrender of Raleigh to the Federal Army," *Orphan's Friend and Masonic Jour.*, L (Dec., 1925), 8; *OR*, XLVII, Ser. I, Pt. III, 197; Raleigh *N and O*, July 3, 1927.

67. G. W. Pepper, *Personal Recollections of Sherman's Campaign in Georgia and the Carolinas* (Zanesville: Hugh Dunne, 1866), p. 386; Raleigh *N and O*, Feb. 25, 1934.

68. Nichols, *Great March*, pp. 296-97; *OR*, XLVII, Ser. I, Pt. III, 191.

69. H. Hitchcock, "General W. T. Sherman," *War Papers and Personal Reminiscences, 1861-1865. Read before the Commandery of the State Missouri Military Order of the Loyal Legion of the United States* (St. Louis: Becktold and Co., 1892), I, 425; Raleigh *N and O*, July 7, 1940.

70. Hitchcock, "Sherman," p. 425.

71. Sherman, *Memoirs*, II, 346-47.

72. Johnston, *Narrative*, p. 397.

73. Ridley, *Army of Tennessee*, pp. 458-59. See also L. H. Webb Diary, Apr. 15, 18, 1865, SHC.

74. *OR*, XVII, Ser. I, Pt. III, 872.

75. Johnston, *Narrative*, pp. 397-98.

76. See above p. 378.

77. *OR*, XLVII, Ser. I, Pt. III, 207.

78. *Ibid.*, p. 234; Johnston, *Narrative*, p. 401.

79. *OR*, XLVII, Ser. I, Pt. III, 220-24.

80. Sherman, *Memoirs*, II, 347-48.

81. Pepper, *Recollections*, p. 408.

82. U. R. Brooks, *Butler and His Cavalry* (Columbia: The State Co., 1909), p. 288.

83. Sherman, *Memoirs*, II, 348; M. W. Wellman, "Bennett Home Took Place in History," Raleigh *N and O*, Apr. 26, 1953; E. N. Hatcher, *The Last Four Weeks of the War* (Columbus: Edmund N. Hatcher Publisher, 1891), p. 330; R. O. Everett, "War Between the States Ended a Few Miles West of Durham," *Uplift*, XXVII (June, 1939), 11.

84. Sherman, *Memoirs*, II, 351.

85. W. C. Meffert Diary, Apr. 18, 1865, HSW; H. Reid to Sister, Apr. 20, 1865, H. Reid Papers, HSW.

86. J. D. Cox, *Military Reminiscences of the Civil War* (New York: Charles Scribner's Sons, 1900), II, 465.

87. Sherman, *Memoirs*, II, 351. General Carl Schurz voiced objection to the terms on the grounds that the military could not decide civil policy. C. Schurz, *The Reminiscences of Carl Schurz with a Sketch of His Life and Public Services from 1869 to 1906 by Frederick Bancroft and William A. Dunning* (New York: McClure Co., 1908), III, 754.

88. Breckinridge was a major general.
89. J. E. Johnston, "My Negotiations with Sherman," *North American Review*, CXLIII (Aug., 1886), 188-89; H. Van Ness Boynton, *Sherman's Historical Raid: The Memoirs in the Light of the Record* (Cincinnati: Wilshach, Baldwin and Co., 1875), pp. 244-58; OR, XLVII, Ser. I, Pt. III, 806; Everett, "War Ended West of Durham," p. 10.
90. Pepper, *Recollections*, p. 414.
91. Sherman, *Memoirs*, II, 352.
92. Pepper, *Recollections*, p. 416; J. S. Wise, *End of an Era* (New York: Houghton, Mifflin and Co., 1899), pp. 449-53; S. F. Horn, *The Army of Tennessee: A Military History* (New York: Bobbs-Merrill Co., 1941), p. 427; (Anon.) "A Little Whiskey," Newspaper clipping, 1926, NCC.
93. Pepper, *Recollections*, p. 419; Sherman, *Memoirs*, II, 326-27, 353.
94. OR, XLVII, Ser. I, Pt. III, 806-7; Sherman, *Memoirs*, II, 353; Wise, *End of an Era*, p. 453.
95. OR, XLVII, Ser. I, Pt. III, 243-44.
96. See below pp. 390-91.
97. R. S. Naroll, "Lincoln and the Sherman Peace Fiasco—Another Fable?" *JSH*, XX (Nov., 1954), 478.
98. OR, XLVII, Ser. I, Pt. III, 243-44.
99. *Ibid.*, 293-94, 298; Sherman, *Memoirs*, II, 358; "Oscar" to "Dear Parents," Apr. 25, 1865, E. O. Kimberly Papers, HSW.
100. OR, Ser. I, Pt. III, XLVIII, 821-34.
101. Johnston, *Narrative*, pp. 441-42; OR, XLVII, Ser. I, Pt. III, 303.
102. OR, XLVII, Ser. I, Pt. III, 304.
103. Wood Diary, Apr. 21, 1865, SHC.
104. Johnston, *Narrative*, p. 410.
105. New Bern *N. C. Times*, Apr. 25, 1865.
106. S. R. Mallory, "Reminiscences" (Unpublished reminiscence), S. R. Mallory Papers, SHC.
107. A. Baird to W. T. Sherman, Apr. 24, 1865, W. T. Sherman Papers, LC.
108. Waring Diary, Apr. 19, 21, 22, 26, 1865, SHC.
109. OR, XLVII, Ser. I, Pt. III, 304; J. M. Schofield, *Forty-six Years in the Army* (New York: Century Co., 1897), 351-52; Johnston, *Narrative*, pp. 412; Sherman, *Memoirs*, II, 362.
110. OR, XLVII, Ser. I, Pt. III, 320, 482; Schofield, *Forty-six Years*, p. 352; Johnston, *Narrative*, pp. 415-18.
111. Howe, *Marching With Sherman*, p. 316; Sherman, *Memoirs*, II, 363.
112. Underwood, *33 Mass.*, p. 293.
113. Aten, *85 Ill.*, p. 307.
114. Underwood, *33 Mass.*, p. 293.
115. Raleigh *Daily Standard*, Apr. 28, 1865.
116. N. Y. *Times*, Apr. 24, 1865.
117. Sherman, *Memoirs*, II, 365.
118. OR, XLVII, Ser. I, Pt. III, 277.
119. *Ibid.*, p. 249.
120. OR, XLVII, Ser. I, Pt. III, 277.
121. *Ibid.*, p. 411.
122. M. A. deW. Howe, ed., *Home Letters of General Sherman* (New York: Charles Scribner's Sons, 1909), p. 350.
123. J. R. Daniels, "In 60's Town Missed Being Burned to Ground by Margin of One Day," Franklin *Press and the Highlands Maconian*, June 16, 1955; L. B. Porter, "Macon's Sole Civil War Battle Told," Franklin *Press and the Highlands Maconian*, June 16, 1955; W. W. Stringfield, "Memoirs" (Unpublished memoirs), W. W. Stringfield Papers, DU. See above p. 364n.

Critical Essay on Selected Sources

MANUSCRIPTS

The voluminous manuscript collections at the University of North Carolina, Duke University, and the State (N.C.) Department of Archives and History are the most valuable primary sources available for a study of the Civil War in North Carolina. These unpublished papers provide the core of documentation for this work. However, numerous other collections deposited throughout the country were examined. A few of the more important ones are: R. C. Hawkins Papers, Brown University; O. O. Howard Papers, Bowdoin College; C. A. Barker Papers, Essex Institute; G. V. Fox Papers, New York Historical Society; D. H. Hill Papers, State Library, Richmond, Virginia; B. Bragg Papers, Western Reserve Historical Society; W. T. Sherman Papers, University of Michigan; B. F. Butler, L. M. Goldsborough, D. R. Larned, and W. T. Sherman Papers, Library of Congress.

Of considerable help also was the War Department Collection of Confederate Records in the National Archives. For an insight into the life of soldiers in Sherman's army various diaries and letters in the possession of the state historical societies of Ohio and Wisconsin proved useful.

OFFICIAL DOCUMENTS

The standard works on military affairs are: *The War of Rebellion: A Compilation of the Official Records of the Union and Confederate Armies* (Washington: 1880-1901), 128 vols.; *Atlas to Accompany the Official Records of the Union and Confederate Armies* (Washington: 1891-95), 2 vols.; and the *Official Records of the Union and Confederate Navies in the War of Rebellion* (Washington: 1880-1927), 30 vols. The *Report of the Joint Committee on the Conduct of War* (Washington, 1863), 3 vols., is a verbatim account of the testimony of high-ranking officers and serves to correct some of the extravagant statements made by these men in their official reports. For information on how the soldiers fared both in camp and on the march *The Medical and Surgical History of the War of the Rebellion* (Washington, 1875-88), 6 vols., can be of use.

Newspapers are unreliable for details of the fighting but are of great help in gauging public opinion. Northern papers examined were the New York *Herald* (1860-65) and the New York *Times* (1860-65). Far more valuable for the local story were the following state papers: Fayetteville *Observer* (1860-65); Hillsborough *Recorder* (1860-65); New Bern *North Carolina Times* (1865); Raleigh *Conservative* (1865); Raleigh *Weekly North Carolina Standard* (1860-65), and the Wilmington *Daily Herald* (1860-65).

During the war *Harper's Weekly*, which was illustrated, and *Harper's New Monthly Magazine*, along with *The Atlantic Monthly*, were the primary periodicals. The South had no publication to match these. But once the war was over, magazines such as the following presented the Southern view of the war: *The Land We Love* (Charlotte, 1866-69); *Our Living and Our Dead* (New Bern and Raleigh, 1873-76); *The Southern Bivouac* (Louisville, 1882-87); *Southern Historical Society Papers* (Richmond, 1876——), and *The Confederate Veteran* (Nashville, 1893-1932). These periodicals were depositories for official reports, reminiscences, and anecdotes. In the meantime (1884-87) the New York *Century Magazine* had run a series of articles on the major battles of the war written by surviving officers on both sides. These turned out to be so popular that the editors, R. U. Johnson and C. C. Buel, decided to reprint the entire series in four volumes under the title *Battles and Leaders of the Civil War* (New York, 1887-88). This set provides the student of the period with much useful material, but it should be used with caution because the accounts are probably the principal monuments of self-justification for officers, both North and South.

Among the most interesting and important sources on the war in North Carolina are the published diaries, correspondence, and memoirs of those who visited the state. Many of these letters and diaries can be found in the various historical journals. To name a few: W. W. Black (ed.), "Civil War Letters of E. N. Boots from New Bern and Plymouth," *North Carolina Historical Review*, XXXVI (April, 1959); F. and D. E. Bruce (eds.), "Daniel Bruce: Civil War Teamster," *Indiana Magazine of History*, XXXIII (June, 1937); F. K. Dunn (ed.), "Major James Austin Connally's Letters to His Wife, 1862-1865," *Transactions of the Illinois State Historical Society*, No. 35; N. C. Delaney (ed.), "Letters of a Maine Soldier Boy," *Civil War History*, V (March, 1959); C. Eaton (ed.), "Diary of an Officer in Sherman's Army Marching Through the Carolinas," *The Journal of Southern History*, IX (May, 1943); J. D. Hayes and Lillian O'Brien (eds.), "The Early Blockade and Capture of the Hatteras Forts—from the Journal of John Sanford Barnes . . . 1861," *The New York Historical Quarterly*, XLVI (January, 1962); J. M. Merrill (ed.), "The Fort Fisher and Wilmington

Campaign: Letters from Admiral David D. Porter," *North Carolina Historical Review,* XXXV (October, 1958).

Most high-ranking officers and a great number of lesser personalities wrote their memoirs: W. T. Sherman, *Memoirs* . . . (New York, 1875), 2 vols.; J. E. Johnston, *Narrative of Military Operations.* . . . (New York, 1874), and J. D. Cox, *Military Reminiscences* . . . (New York, 1900), 2 vols., are very good for the last year of the war.

Blockade-running is the subject of A. C. Hobart-Hampden, *Never Caught* . . . (London, 1867); T. E. Taylor, *Running the Blockade* . . . (New York, 1896), and J. Wilkinson, *The Narrative of a Blockade Runner* (New York, 1877). Fighting on the inland waters is covered in W. H. Parker, *Recollections of a Naval Officer 1841-1865* (New York, 1883).

REGIMENTAL HISTORIES

A great many regimental histories are of considerable value either because they were written soon after the war, before memories had a chance to dim, or they were based on the soldiers diaries and correspondence. Federal histories, though, far outnumber Confederate accounts. The regimental records of the New England troops that served in eastern North Carolina throughout the war are surprisingly complete. And the same can be said for the western regiments in Sherman's army.

Especially good for Stoneman's raid is C. H. Kirk (ed.), *History of the Fifteenth Pennsylvania Volunteer Cavalry* (Philadelphia, 1906).

Even though Confederate regimental histories are scarce, the story of all the North Carolina commands has been recorded in W. Clark (ed.), *Histories of the Several Regiments and Battalions from North Carolina in the Great War 1861-'65. Written by Members of the Respective Commands* (Goldsboro, 1901), 5 vols. At a meeting of the State Confederate Veteran's Association in Raleigh, October, 1894, it was resolved: "That a history of each regiment from North Carolina which served in the Confederate Army shall be prepared by a member thereof, and that Judge Walter Clark be requested to select the historians from each command and to supervise and edit the work, and further, that the General Assembly be memorialized to have these sketches printed at the expense of the State." When completed the work contained material not only on the individual regiments but also on a variety of other subjects. This five volume work is indispensable. No other Southern state has a publication to compare with it.

LOCAL AND GENERAL HISTORIES

There are a number of excellent general histories of North Carolina: S. A. Ashe, *History of North Carolina* (vol. I, Greensboro, 1908; vol. II, Raleigh, 1925); R. D. W. Conner, *North Carolina: Rebuilding an Ancient Commonwealth* (New York, 1929), 4 vols.; J. G. deR. Hamilton, *History of North Carolina Since 1860* (Chicago, 1919); A. Henderson, *North Carolina: The*

Old North State and the New (New York, 1941), 5 vols.; and H. T. Lefler, *History of North Carolina* (New York, 1956), 2 vols.

Local histories vary greatly in worth. J. P. Arthur's two books, *A History of Watauga County* (Richmond, 1915) and *Western North Carolina: A History from 1730-1913* (Raleigh, 1914) are informative on affairs in the mountain region, as are F. A. Sondley, *A History of Buncombe County North Carolina* (Asheville, 1930), 2 vols., and D. J. Whitener, *A History of Watauga County* (Boone, 1949). Adelaide L. Fries, *Forsyth County* (Winston, 1898) has an interesting coverage of Stoneman's visit to Salem. The activities of the "Buffaloes" in eastern North Carolina are discussed in R. Dillard, *The Civil War in Chowan County . . .* (Edenton, 1916) and J. F. Pugh, *Three Hundred Years Along the Pasquotank* (Durham, 1957).

MILITARY HISTORIES

D. H. Hill, *North Carolina in the War Between the States—Bethel to Sharpsburg* (Raleigh, 1926), 2 vols., and D. H. Hill, Jr., *North Carolina,* C. A. Evans, (ed.), *Confederate Military History* (Atlanta, 1899), Vol. IV, are volumes that should be examined by everyone working on North Carolina Civil War history. Both works deal not only with what happened in the state but also with North Carolina's contributions on the Virginia battlefields and elsewhere. *Bethel to Sharpsburg,* which takes the story only up through September, 1862, is very good on North Carolina's early efforts to construct defenses. Hill's *North Carolina,* a volume in a cooperative set, is helpful for some of the campaigns in eastern North Carolina but of little value either for the fighting in the mountains or the last stages of the war. Nevertheless, in the back of the volume there are sketches of all the generals credited to North Carolina and these are of value.

A great deal of interesting military history can be found in the war papers read before the various state commanderies of the "Military Order of the Loyal Legion of the United States," and before the "Military Historical Society of Massachusetts." Also, F. Moore (ed.), *Rebellion Record . . .* (New York, 1864-68), 12 vols., is a useful compilation of newspaper reports, military records, official papers, and even poetry. Cornelia P. Spencer, *The Last Ninety Days of the War in North Carolina* (New York, 1866) is good for the work of Sherman's "bummers" and Stoneman's raiders. J. G. Barrett, *Sherman's March Through the Carolinas* (Chapel Hill, 1956) is a detailed study of this Federal march from Savannah to Raleigh. David Stick in *The Outer Banks of North Carolina* (Chapel Hill, 1958) has an excellent chapter on the Civil War. Over one-third of James Sprunt's large volume *Chronicles of the Cape Fear River, 1660-1916* (Raleigh, 1916) is devoted to the war in the Wilmington area and blockade-running. The best work on privateering is W. M. Robinson, Jr., *The Confederate Privateers* (New Haven, 1928). The standard volume on the Southern navy is still J. T. Scharf, *History of the Confederate States Navy from Its Organization to the*

Surrender of its Last Vessel (*New York,* 1887). This cumbersome work contains a mine of information.

Articles on the different campaigns, expeditions, and battles are, quite naturally, of considerable value. Some of the best of these are to be found in scholarly and military journals: R. S. Barry, "Fort Macon: Its History," *North Carolina Historical Review,* XXVII (April, 1950); R. W. Daly, "Burnside's Amphibious Division," *Marine Corps Gazette,* XXXV (December, 1951); J. Luvaas, "Johnston's Last Stand—Bentonville," *North Carolina Historical Review,* XXXIII (July, 1956); J. M. Merrill, "Battle for Elizabeth City, 1862," *United States Naval Institute Proceedings,* LXXIII (March, 1957); J. M. Merrill, "The Hatteras Expedition, August, 1861," *North Carolina Historical Review,* XXIX (April, 1952); T. C. Parramore, "The Burning of Winton in 1862," *North Carolina Historical Review,* XXXIX (Winter, 1962); E. H. Simmons, "The Federals and Fort Fisher," *Marine Corps Gazette,* XXXV (nos. 1-2, January-February, 1951); Ina W. Van Noppen, "The Significance of Stoneman's Last Raid," *North Carolina Historical Review,* XXXVIII (January-October, 1861); R. A. Ward, "An Amphibious Primer: Battle for New Bern," *Marine Corps Gazette,* XXXVI (August, 1962).

The story of the war in the northeastern part of the state is covered in an extremely interesting and complete manner by T. C. Parramore in "The Roanoke-Chowan Story—Chapters 7-10," Ahoskie *Daily Roanoke-Chowan News,* Civil War Supplement, 1960. This source is very good for the details of several relatively minor engagements and the activities of the "Buffaloes." Affairs in eastern North Carolina are also recorded in J. E. Wood (ed.), *Year Book—Pasquotank Historical Society* (Elizabeth City, 1955-56), 2 vols.; A. Woodbury, *Burnside and the Ninth Army Corps* (Providence, 1867): and C. F. Warren, "Washington During the War," *The Confederate Reveille* (Raleigh, 1898).

Total war as related to General W. T. Sherman is the subject of: J. G. Barrett, "Sherman and Total War in the Carolinas," *North Carolina Historical Review,* XXXVIII (July, 1960) and J. B. Walters, "General William T. Sherman and Total War," *The Journal of Southern History,* XIV (November, 1948). Barrett is more tolerant of the General than Walters is.

MONOGRAPHS AND SPECIAL STUDIES

Ella Lonn, *Desertion During the Civil War* (New York, 1928) and Georgia L. Tatum, *Disloyalty in the Confederacy* (Chapel Hill, 1934) are the best studies on disaffection and disloyalty in the South. D. Dodge, "The Cave-Dwellers of the Confederacy," *Atlantic Monthly,* LXVIII (October, 1891) is an interesting account of how the deserters lived. The effect of conscription in lowering Confederate morale is examined in A. B. Moore, *Conscription and Conflict in the Confederacy* (New York, 1924). The peace movement in North Carolina is well treated in H. W. Raper, "William W.

Holden and the Peace Movement in North Carolina," *North Carolina Historical Review,* XXXI (October, 1954); A. S. Roberts, "The Peace Movement in North Carolina," *Mississippi Valley Historical Review,* XI (September, 1924) and R. E. Yates, *The Confederacy and Zeb Vance,* W. S. Hoole (ed.), *Confederate Centennial Studies* (Tuscaloosa, 1958), No. 8. Efforts to establish a Union government in eastern North Carolina are described in J. G. deR. Hamilton, *Reconstruction in North Carolina* (New York, 1914) and N. C. Delaney, "Charles Henry Foster and the Unionists of Eastern North Carolina," *North Carolina Historical Review,* XXXVII (July, 1960).

There are a number of very useful monographs on the home front. The women's role in the war is handled in Mrs. J. H. Anderson, *North Carolina Women of the Confederacy* (Fayetteville, 1926); M. P. Andrews, *The Women of the South in War Times* (Baltimore, 1927); and F. B. Simkins and J. W. Patton, *The Women of the Confederacy* (Richmond, 1936). This latter volume is the best of the three. Mary E. Massey's studies, *Ersatz in the Confederacy* (Columbia, 1952) and "Southern Refugee Life during the Civil War," *North Carolina Historical Review,* XX (January-April, 1943), are well-written, highly informative treatments of wartime shortages in the South and displaced persons of the Confederacy, respectively. J. C. Sitterson, *The Secession Movement in North Carolina, (The James Sprunt Studies,* eds. F. M. Green and others, Vol. XXIII [Chapel Hill, 1939]) is the authoritative source on North Carolina's withdrawal from the Union. Other works relating to secession are: W. K. Boyd, "North Carolina on the Eve of Secession," *American Historical Association Report* (1910); K. P. Battle, "The Secession Convention of 1861," *North Carolina Booklet,* XV (April, 1916); J. G. deR. Hamilton, "Secession in North Carolina," *North Carolina in the War Between the States,* ed. D. H. Hill (Raleigh, 1926), Vol. I, and H. M. Wagstaff, *States Rights and Political Parties in North Carolina, 1776-1861* (Ser. XXIV) (*Johns Hopkins Studies in History and Political Science,* Ser. XXIV [Baltimore, 1906]). A good work in the neglected field of agricultural history is C. O. Cathy, "The Impact of the Civil War on Agriculture in North Carolina," *Studies in Southern History in Memory of Albert Ray Newsome,* ed. J. C. Sitterson (Chapel Hill, 1957). The economic conditions in the state are examined in W. K. Boyd, "Fiscal and Economic Conditions in North Carolina During the War," *North Carolina Booklet,* XIV (April, 1915). For the story of the Negro see: B. H. Nelson, "Some Aspects of Negro Life in North Carolina During the Civil War," *North Carolina Historical Review,* XXV (April, 1948); B. Quarles, *The Negro in the Civil War* (Boston, 1953); T. L. Spraggins, "Moblization of Negro Labor for the Department of Virginia and North Carolina, 1861-1865," *North Carolina Historical Review,* XXIV (April, 1947).

The last stages of the conflict are exceedingly well done in R. E. Yates, "Governor Vance and the End of the War in North Carolina," *North Carolina Historical Review,* XVIII (October, 1941). The peace negotiations ending the four-year struggle are given a provocative consideration by R. S. Naroll in his article entitled "Lincoln and the Sherman Peace Fiasco—Another Fable," *Journal of Southern History*, XX (November, 1954). Stoneman's raid, which also occurred in 1865, is given coverage in D. LeT. Rights, "Salem in the War between the States," *North Carolina Historical Review*, XXVII (July, 1950).

Two articles reveal much on the little-known Charlotte Navy Yard: V. G. Alexander, "The Confederate States Navy Yard at Charlotte, N. C., 1862-1865," *North Carolina Booklet*, XXIII (January-October, 1926) and R. W. Donnelly, "The Charlotte, North Carolina, Navy Yard, C.S.N.," *Civil War History*, V (March, 1959).

By far the best work on North Carolina railroads is C. L. Price, "North Carolina Railroads during the Civil War," *Civil War History*, VII (September, 1961). R. C. Black, *The Railroads of the Confederacy* (Chapel Hill, 1952) covers the entire South and the result is a richly rewarding study.

BIOGRAPHIES

Some of the most important information on the Civil War is contained in biographies of its participants: C. Dowd, *Life of Zebulon B. Vance* (Charlotte, 1897); J. P. Dyer, *"Fightin Joe" Wheeler* (Baton Rouge, 1941); G. E. Govan and J. W. Livingood, *A Different Valor: The Story of General Joseph E. Johnston, C.S.A.* (New York, 1956); T. W. Haight, *Three Wisconsin Cushings (Wisconsin History Commission*, Original Papers No. 3 [Madison, 1910]); W. W. Hassler, *General George B. McClellan: Shield of the Union* (Baton Rouge, 1957); L. Lewis, *Sherman, Fighting Prophet* (New York, 1932); B. H. Liddell Hart, *Sherman: The Genius of the Civil War* (London, 1930); B. P. Poore, *The Life and Services of Ambrose E. Burnside, Soldier—Citizen—Statesman* (Providence, 1882); R. J. Roske and C. Van Doren, *Lincoln's Commando: The Biography of Commander W. B. Cushing, U.S.N.* (New York, 1957); D. C. Seitz, *Braxton Bragg: General of the Confederacy* (Columbia, 1924); C. E. Slocum, *Life and Services of Major-General Henry Warner Slocum, Officer in the United States Army* (Toledo, 1913); J. R. Soley, *Admiral Porter* (New York, 1903); T. H. Williams, *P. G. T. Beauregard: Napoleon in Gray* (Baton Rouge, 1954); E. L. Wells, *Hampton and His Cavalry in '64* (Richmond, 1899).

M.A. THESES AND PH.D. DISSERTATIONS

R. S. Barry, "The History of Fort Macon" (M.A. thesis, Duke University, 1950) covers the entire story of this old fort. H. J. Becker, "Wilmington During the Civil War" (M.A. thesis, Duke University, 1941) is good for life on the home-front. J. S. Brawley, "The Public and Military Career of Lawrence O'Bryon Branch" (M.A. thesis, University of North Carolina, 1951) has a chapter on the Battle of New Bern. W. D. Cotton, "Appalachian North Carolina: A Political Study, 1860-1889" (Ph.D. dissertation, University of North Carolina, 1954) contains much valuable information on disaffection and military activities in the mountains. Annie W. Garrard, "John W. Ellis: Governor of North Carolina" (M.A. thesis, Duke University, 1930) is helpful on the seizure of the coastal forts at the outbreak of the war. N. C. Hughes, "William Joseph Hardee, C.S.A., 1861-1865" (Ph.D. dissertation, University of North Carolina, 1959) is excellent for the Battles of Averasboro and Bentonville. C. L. Price, "The Railroads of North Carolina During the Civil War" (M.A. thesis, University of North Carolina, 1951) thoroughly covers the problems of rail transportation. Mattie Russell, "William Holland Thomas: White Chief of the Cherokees" (Ph.D. dissertation, Duke University, 1956) provides invaluable information on the Indian in the Confederate army. J. B. Walters, "General W. T. Sherman and Total War" (Ph.D. dissertation, Vanderbilt University, 1947) deals with evolution of modern war as applied by this union commander.

MISCELLANEOUS

Anyone working in North Carolina history will find the large pamphlet and clipping collections at the University of North Carolina well worth examining.

Reference works that should be used: W. W. Boatner, *The Civil War Dictionary* (New York, 1959); T. L. Livermore, *Numbers and Losses in the Civil War in America, 1861-1865* (Boston, 1900); J. W. Moore, *Roster of North Carolina Troops in the War Between the States* (Raleigh, 1882), 4 vols.; F. Phisterer, *Statistical Record of the Armies of the United States* (New York, 1883); and E. J. Warner, *Generals in Gray* (Baton Rouge, 1959).

Index